A Journey Through

North America

TEACHER'S EDITION
VOLUME 2

Gibbs Smith, Publisher
Salt Lake City

NC STATE UNIVERSITY

D1247390

This series is dedicated to Burt and Pauline Beers
for their dedication to history and social studies education
but most importantly for their dedication to North Carolina's students.

Published by
Gibbs Smith, Publisher
P.O. Box 667
Layton, UT 84041
800-748-5439
www.NCJourneys.com

Cover Design: Jeremy C. Munns, John Vehar

Printed and bound in China
ISBN 978-1-4236-0322-1

13 12 11 10 09 08   10 9 8 7 6 5 4 3 2

Gibbs Smith, Publisher wishes to thank all the contributors to the second and third editions of this series.

Gibbs Smith, Publisher

Julie Dumont Rabinowitz
Managing Editor

Christopher Harlos, Ph.D.
Editor

John Vehar
Lead Designer

Michelle Brown, Alan Connell, Robert Jones, Jeremy C. Munns
Designers

Carrie Gibson
Production Editor

Janis J. Hansen
Photo Editor

Lynn P. Roundtree, Wendy Knight
Photo Researchers

Content Specialists

Writers

Alvis Dunn, Ph.D.
Latin America
Guilford College

Stephen Middleton, Ph.D.
United States History
North Carolina State University

Linda Scher
Raleigh, North Carolina

Area Specialists

Joel Cline
Meteorology, National Weather Service
Raleigh, North Carolina

Charles R. Ewen, Ph.D.
Anthropology
East Carolina University

Clifford E. Griffin, Ph.D.
Latin America and the Caribbean
North Carolina State University

Steve Martinez
Chicano Studies
University of New Mexico

Douglas C. Wilms, Ph.D.
Geography
East Carolina University

Tom Parker
Consultant
Bard College

James A Wood, Ph.D.
Latin American History
NC A&T State University

Curriculum Specialists

Mary Vann Eslinger
Social Studies Consultant
Morehead City, North Carolina

Jacqueline Boykin
Social Studies Consultant
Williamston, North Carolina

Candy Beal, Ph.D.
Middle Grades Social Studies Education
North Carolina State University

Consulting Teachers

Gloria E. Arriagada
Wiley Elementary School
Raleigh, North Carolina

Judy Craig
Claremont, North Carolina

Pat Brooks Ellington
New Hanover County Public Schools

Rose H. Cooper
Carthage, North Carolina

Ann Hamzé
C. M. Eppes Middle School
Greenville, North Carolina

Wanda Dale Henries
Hardin Park Elementary School
Boone, North Carolina

Patsy Hill
High Point, North Carolina

Pamela S. Myrick
Greensboro, North Carolina

Rhonda V. O'Janpa
South Topsail Elementary School
Hampstead, North Carolina

Sharon S. Pearson
High Point, North Carolina

Linda Weeks Peterson
Raleigh, North Carolina

Constance Schwarz
Hampstead, North Carolina

Sue Trent
Charlotte, North Carolina

Laurie Walsh
Bend, Oregon

Cathleen T. Wilson
Bradley Creek Elementary School
Wilmington, North Carolina

Michele Lynn Woodson
Southern Middle School
Burlington, North Carolina

Susan D. Zárate
Wake County Public Schools
Raleigh, North Carolina

Cathie A. McIntyre
Durham Public Schools
Durham, North Carolina

NC State University

Humanities Extension/Publications

James W. Clark, Ph.D.
Director & Professor of English

Burton F. Beers, Ph.D.
Editor Emeritus
Humanities Publications & Professor of History

Regina Higgins, Ph.D.
Editor
Humanities Publications

James Alchediak
Chief Videographer & Lecturer in Communications

Pamela H. Ellis
Administrative Assistant

Lisa Morgan
Bookkeeper

Zachary H. Jackson
Editorial Assistant

Pallavi Talwar
Editorial Assistant

Frances Higgins
Editorial Assistant

Editorial Support

Bryan Smithey
Copy Editor
Warrenton, North Carolina

Contents

Volume 2

Contents

Unit 4 Our Nation Today

The unit opens with a photograph of a group of fifth graders saluting the flag of the United States. Their observance of the flag-raising ceremony and recitation of the Pledge of Allegiance expresses our identity as one nation. Your students will learn about the land upon which our country is built. They will trace changes in industry, from early farming to today's high-technology businesses. The unit also explores the regions of our nation. Finally, this unit introduces students to the structure of our national, state, and local governments.

UNIT LESSON PLAN

	LESSON 1	LESSON 2	LESSON 3
CHAPTER 13 Our Nation Today	All of the world's climates can be found in the United States. The land is rich in vegetation and resources. **Essential Question:** What effect does the range of climates have on the United States? **Suggested Time:** 1 day	The United States economy is based on free enterprise. American industries trade with partners throughout the world. **Essential Question:** What does free enterprise mean, and how does it impact the United States? **Suggested Time:** 2 days	Americans have good health care, education, and quality of life. But Americans face many challenges, too **Essential Question:** What quality of life do Americans have? **Suggested Time:** 2 days
CHAPTER 14 Eastern Regions of the United States	The states of Maine, New Hampshire, Vermont, Massachusetts, Rhode Island, and Connecticut make up New England. **Essential Question:** Where is New England, and what states make up the region? **Suggested Time:** 1 day	The Mid-Atlantic region includes New York, New Jersey, Pennsylvania, Delaware, Maryland, and the District of Columbia. **Essential Question:** Where is the Mid-Atlantic, and what states make up the region? **Suggested Time:** 1 day	Virginia, West Virginia, Kentucky, Tennessee, North Carolina, South Carolina, Georgia, Florida, Alabama, Mississippi, Louisiana, and Arkansas are the states of the Southeast. **Essential Question:** Where is the Southeast, and what states make up the region? **Suggested Time:** 2 days
CHAPTER 15 Western Regions of the United States	The Midwest includes Ohio, Illinois, Indiana, Michigan, Wisconsin, Missouris, Iowa, Kansas, Minnesota, Nebraska, North Dakota, and South Dakota. **Essential Question:** Where is the Midwest, and what states make up the region? **Suggested Time:** 1 day	Arizona, New Mexico, Oklahoma, and Texas make up the Southwest. **Essential Question:** Where is the Southwest, and what states make up the region? **Suggested Time:** 1 day	Colorado, Wyoming, Montana, Idaho, Utah, and Nevada are states of the Rocky Mountain region. **Essential Question:** Where is the Rocky Mountain region, and what states make up the region? **Suggested Time:** 1 day
CHAPTER 16 The Pacific Region of the United States	The Pacific Coast states are California, Oregon, and Washington. **Essential Question:** Where is the Pacific Coast region, and what states make up the region? **Suggested Time:** 1 day	The Land of the Midnight Sun is our nation's largest state. **Essential Question:** What is special about Alaska? **Suggested Time:** 1 day	The fiftieth state is a chain of tropical islands formed by volcanic action. **Essential Question:** How can we describe the state of Hawaii? **Suggested Time:** 1 day
CHAPTER 17 Government of the People	The United States government is divided into three branches. The president is the head of the executive branch. **Essential Question:** What is the role of the executive branch in our government? **Suggested Time:** 2 days	The legislative branch creates laws, and the judicial branch interprets laws. **Essential Question:** What are the roles and responsibilities of the legislative and judicial branches in our government? **Suggested Time:** 2 days	The federal government shares powers with state and local governments. State and local governments provide many needed services. **Essential Question:** How is our state government organized, and what is its role in our state? **Suggested Time:** 2 days

Preparing the Unit

- Display posters, artifacts, pictures, and maps in your room to give students images of the regions being studied in this unit.
- Share the suggested ideas for art and music with your cultural arts teachers so that they may help integrate the curriculum.
- Set up a resource center in your classroom using the suggested titles in the unit for students to use for research or reading time.

Unit Teaching Strategies

- If you want to focus more on geography in the beginning of the year, this unit could easily be combined with Unit One.
- If you are pressed for time, you might consider teaching Chapter 13 and then assigning Chapters 14, 15, and 16 to the students for group presentations. Each group could present a different region of the United States. Students could become the experts on a region and use their presentations to teach their classmates.

- Review the suggested activities and select the ones that are most appropriate for your classroom.
- For each region, bring in regional foods for students to sample.
- Pace yourself through this unit so that students learn about each of the regions of the United States.
- Create a large blank map of the United States to post on a wall in your classroom. As you study each region, students should add pictures that represent the region. At the end of Chapter 16, you will have created a visual depiction of the United States.
- There are many opportunities for guest speakers in this unit. Arrange for representatives of federal, state, county, and municipal government offices to speak to your class about services their agency or office provides. Also bankers, lawyers, farmers, agricultural officials, and environmental resource managers are good resources. Students' parents or others in your community who grew up or lived in other regions are other possible resources.
- Check **NCJourneys.com** for updates and materials.

Unit Projects

Students will have ten days to complete their project. They have the option of choosing from five different projects, and should only choose one. The five projects offer a lot of variety so students can pick an area that interests them. Suggested report format: one page in length, typed, and double-spaced.

PROJECT CHOICES

 OBJECTIVES: 1.03, 3.02, 3.03, 5.01, 5.07

Cultural Differences

Have students research one important cultural tradition from each region. They should illustrate the traditions on a poster, and then write one descriptive paragraph for each tradition. Finally, students should write a paragraph describing which one they think is the most interesting and that they would like to participate in.

The Economy of the Regions

Have students make charts comparing the economies of each region of the United States. They should then classify these activities according to the descriptions (manufacturing, service, agriculture, and so on) found in Chapter 13. Students should then write a paragraph identifying the three most important economic activities across the entire United States and support their choices.

Graphic Organizer of Regions

Have students research each region, determining who settled it, its absolute and relative location, the states that make up the region, its major cities, and the economic

basis of the region. After completing their research, they should compile the data on a graphic organizer.

Government Compare and Contrast

Have students use a graphic organizer to compare the United States government and North Carolina's government. Students should identify which offices are elected and which are appointed and what the responsibilities of each major branch and department are.

Government and Economy

Have students collect newspaper articles about the relationship between the government and economy in North Carolina. The student should write a report describing what types of industries are located in North Carolina and what North Carolina does to attract and keep businesses.

Bulletin Board Ideas

Regional Mural

Divide the class into nine groups. Assign each a region of the United States to research and create a regional mural. Display all the murals as one continuous mural. Illustrations are to be hand-drawn and may also include phrases or short sentences about the subject.

Extension Novice ELL students should learn state names one region at a time and practice good pronunciation.

Region Features

On a large blank map of the United States, color each region a different color. Have students, working in groups, make symbols representing the important resources, crops, products, and places of interest in each region. Post them accordingly.

State Scramble

Put up a large outline map of the United States without state borders. Using push pins, put cut-out shapes of the states on the board in the wrong places. As each region is studied, have student reorder that region's states in the appropriate place.

Introductory Activity

A Calendar of North America

OBJECTIVES: .01, 1.03, 4.02

Students will create a calendar that depicts major landforms, cities, climates, vegetation, bodies of water, and minerals/fossil fuels in North America. Share with the class a variety of calendars as examples of the expected product. Divide the class into pairs. Assign each set of pairs a specific month and a topic from the examples above to illustrate for the class calendars. Hand-drawn illustrations are preferred over professional pictures.

After the illustrations are made, use a computer program that prints a monthly calendar. Attach the illustrations to calendar months. Bind the calendar. Depending on class size, it may be necessary for some students to produce additional months to complete an extra calendar.

Options: Make copies for each student; donate a calendar to the office, cafeteria, or media center; give as a gift to parents on a special occasion.

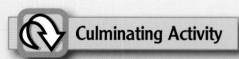 **Culminating Activity**

Class Magazine

OBJECTIVES: 3.04, 4.02, 4.07

Have students publish an issue of their class magazine. Refer to the Unit Culminating Activity from Unit 1 for suggestions about how to organize the work. After studying Unit 3, discuss as a class what articles should be included. Use some of the story ideas suggested below or create your own. Prompt students by asking what other features could be included in this issue besides stories, maps, illustrations, or charts and graphs.

Students should add this issue to a folder with their copies of the previous issues so that they will have a complete set of magazines on North America at the end of the year.

Story ideas: New England, the Mid-Atlantic region, the Southeastern region, the Midwest, the Rockies, the Southwest, the Pacific Coast, Alaska, Hawaii, the modern United States economy, things we import, things we export, agriculture in North Carolina, NAFTA, the president, Congress, the Supreme Court, our governor, the General Assembly, the North Carolina court system, law enforcement agencies at the federal, state, and local levels, our county government, how our local government works, things our local government does, how North Carolina's public schools are managed, voting, elections, or the electoral college.

 Math Activity

Human-Environmental Interaction

OBJECTIVES: 1.03, 1.06

The changes in climate in the United States can be dramatic from west to east or from north to south. One conclusion drawn from this is that the United States is, as the chapter states, vast and varied. The variety within the land reflects upon the variety of ways individuals in this country live. Have students list all of the various climate data, for example: temperature, rainfall, and humidity.

The students should next record the data and create a variety of graphs indicating each item. These graphs should be varied (pie, line, pictograph). In class discussion students should share the graphs, indicate trends, and explain how things are the same as well as how things are different in each region. This should again help build the foundation of understanding how people live differently based on where they live.

Extension ELL students should use the worksheet in the Teacher's Resource Guide.

 Technology Activity

Travel Across America

OBJECTIVES: 1.01, 1.03, 4.07

Have students use a map or atlas computer program to map Interstate 40 from North Carolina to California. Each student should record at least ten cities or towns along the route to California. Students will use the Internet to connect with each of the selected town's Chamber of Commerce Web sites. The students will either print the information or just record important and interesting information about the town. After they have compiled a list of information about cities between North Carolina and California they will put this into a Powerpoint or hyperstudio presentation, for example, "Come with me to see the United States." This presentation should have at least 12 slides with great information about the entire United States, reflecting on what an individual might find traveling along I-40. This is a wonderful item to display at an open house, and just let it run. Students can add pictures, sound effects, animation, or other illustrations. Use a grading rubric when evaluating the presentation.

 Science Activity

Rich Land

OBJECTIVES: 1.01, 5.01, 5.02

Have the students, as a group, research the natural resources of each region. Afterward, have them compare the regions. On a class map the students should see which regions are the "most" rich in each of the different natural resources. The same exercise can be done for vegetation.

Unit Resources

Print Resources

Geography

Arnold, Caroline. *The Geography Book: Activities for Exploring, Mapping, and Enjoying Your World.* John Wiley & Sons, 2001. ISBN 0471412368.

Bell, Neill. *The Book of Where.* Scholastic, 1982.

Davis, Kenneth C. *Don't Know Much About Geography.* William Morrow & Co., 1993. ISBN 0380713799.

Exploring Your World. National Geographic Society, 1995.

Literature Based Map Skills. Sniffen Court Books, 1994.

Singleton, Laurel. *G is for Geography.* Boulder: Social Science Consortium, 1993. ISBN 0899943705.

VanCleave, Janice. *Geography for Every Kid.* John Wiley & Sons, 1993. ISBN 0471598429.

Northeast

Aylesworth, Jim. *The Folks in the Valley: A Pennsylvania Dutch ABC.* Harper-Collins, 1998. ISBN 0694009814.

Egan, Joseph. *Lost on a Mountain in Maine.* Beech Tree Books, 1992. ISBN 068811573.

Field, Rachel. *Hitty—Her First Hundred Years.* Aladdin Paperbacks, 1998. ISBN 0689822847.

Fritz, Jean. *The Cabin Faced West.* Viking Press 1997. ISBN 0140322566.

George, Jean Craighead. *My Side of the Mountain.* Scott Foresman, 2000. ISBN 0140348107.

Krull, Kathleen. *City Within a City: How Kids Live in New York's Chinatown.* Lodestar Books, 1994. ISBN 0525674373.

Krupinski, Loretta. *A New England Scrapbook.* HarperCollins, 1994. ISBN 0060229519.

Speare, Elizabeth George. *The Witch of Blackbird Pond.* Laurel Leaf, 1978. ISBN 0440995779.

Southeast

Cleaver, Vera and Bill. *Where the Lillies Bloom.* HarperTrophy, 1989. ISBN 0064470059.

Douglas, Marjory Stoneman. *Friend of the Everglades.* Millbrook Press, 1994. ISBN 1562943847.

Houston, Gloria. *Mountain Valor.* Paper Star, 1996. ISBN 0698113837.

Johnson, Delores. *Seminole Diary: Remembrances of a Slave.* Atheneum, 1994. ISBN 0027478483.

Krull, Kathleen. *Bridges to Change: How Kids Live On a South Carolina Sea Island.* E .P. Dutton, 1995. ISBN 052567441.

West

Ancona, George. *Powwow.* Harcourt, 1993. ISBN 0152632697.

Arnold, Carolina. *The Ancient Cliff Dwellers of Mesa Verde.* Clarion Books, 1992. ISBN 0395562414.

Brin, Carol Ryrie. *Caddie Woodlawn.* Aladdin Paperbacks, 1990. ISBN 0689713703.

Burns, Diane L. *Rocky Mountain Seasons: From Valley to Mountaintop.* Atheneum, 1993. ISBN 0027161420.

Byers, Betsy. *Trouble River.* Viking Press, 1989. ISBN 0140342435.

Creech, Sharon. *Walk Two Moons.* HarperCollins, 1994. ISBN 0060233346.

George, Jean Craighead. *One Day in the Alpine Tundra.* HarperTrophy, 1996. ISBN 6064420272.

Gregory, Kristianna. *Jimmy Spoon and the Pony Express.* Apple, 1997. ISBN 0590465783.

Levine, Ellen. *If You Traveled West in a Covered Wagon.* Scholastic Trade, 1992. ISBN 0590451588.

Love, Anne D. *Dakota Spring.* Holiday House, 1995. ISBN 082341189.

Morrow, Honore. *Seven Alone.* Scholastic Paperbacks, 1977. ISBN 0590102915.

Rawls, Wilson. *Where the Red Fern Grows.* Prentice Hall, 1984. ISBN 0553274295.

Staub, Frank. *Yellowstone's Circle of Fire.* Carolrhoda Books, 1994. ISBN 0876147783.

Wilder, Laura Ingalls. *On the Way Home.* HarperTrophy, 1994. ISBN 0064400808.

Southwest

Cherry, Lynne. *Armadillo from Amarillo.* Harcourt Brace & Company, 1994. ISBN 0152003592.

Gipson, Fred. *Savage Sam.* Harper-Collins, 1986. ISBN 0060803770.

Henry, Marguerite. *Brighty of the Grand Canyon 1991.* Aladdin Paperbacks, 1991. ISBN 0689714858.

continued on page 317

Paideia Seminar

We the People

OBJECTIVES: 3.01, 3.04, 4.03

Pre-seminar Give students a copy of the Preamble of the Constitution. Students should read it and identify the central issues. They will need a dictionary to look up the words. (Note: The Preamble of the Constitution can be found in the appendix of the textbook.)

Opening Questions

• What word or phrase would you use to summarize this text?

Core Questions

• Based on the text, what is meant by perfect union?
• Did the people of the United States need to form a more perfect union?
• How do the other ideas mentioned support this idea of a perfect union?
• Which of these ideas do you think are most important to the people of the United States?

Closing Questions

• What does the text teach us about the United States of America?

Post-seminar The class will write a preamble for their class, supporting classroom rules as the body of the constitution of the class. They will include what the (class) citizens determine must be placed in the document.

Map Activity

Our Nation Today

NATIONAL GEOGRAPHY STANDARDS: 1, 2

GEOGRAPHIC THEMES: Place

OBJECTIVES: 1.01

Have the students look at the map on page 317. Ask them the following questions:

- Which hemispheres is the United States within? *Northern and Western Hemispheres*
- What is the relative location of the United States? *Northern and Western Hemispheres, north of Mexico, south of Canada, bordered by the Pacific Ocean on the west and the Atlantic Ocean on the east*
- What two states are not touching the others? *Alaska and Hawaii*

Have students close their books and sketch the United States in 10 minutes. When they have completed their maps, analyze the reasons the maps look like they do. How many states were they able to draw?

Unit 4

One flag, one land,
one heart, one hand,
One nation, evermore!

Oliver Wendell Holmes wrote this to describe the unity of our nation. These fifth graders are raising the flag on a beautiful spring morning. They are saying the Pledge of Allegiance. When they do actions like these, they are joining Oliver Wendell Holmes. They are showing their loyalty to our country.

Fifth graders raise the flag at a Raleigh public school.

316

Social Studies at Work

Public Official

A public official is someone who works for the government.

Meet G. K. Butterfield, Jr.

Representative, North Carolina's First Congressional District

When G. K. Butterfield, Jr., decided to become an attorney he had some big shoes to fill. His father, G. K. Butterfield, Sr., was a doctor and the first African American elected official in eastern North Carolina. His mother was a school teacher in Wilson for 48 years. Both of them were well regarded in the community and respected for jobs well done.

Apparently, the good example set by Butterfield's parents paid off. Butterfield has devoted his life to serving North Carolina and its people first as an attorney, then as resident superior court judge for Wilson and Edgecombe Counties. He then served as associate justice on North Carolina's Supreme Court. He was elected to the United States House of Representatives in 2004.

A judge is someone with experience as an attorney who has been appointed or elected to serve in a local, state, or federal court system.

As a superior court judge, Butterfield presided over court cases in 46 North Carolina counties. As a supreme court justice,

Our Nation Today

Unit Preview

CHAPTER 13
A Rich Land
The United States is a country of varied climates, vegetation, and resources. It has many industries. People now work together to preserve America's environment.

CHAPTER 14
Eastern Regions of the United States
New England, the Mid-Atlantic, and the Southeast form the eastern regions of the United States.

CHAPTER 15
Western Regions of the United States
The Midwest, Southwest, and Rocky Mountains make up the western United States.

CHAPTER 16
The Pacific Region of the United States
The Pacific Coast, Alaska, and Hawaii make up the Pacific region of the United States.

CHAPTER 17
Government of the People
The Constitution gives the United States a plan of government. It protects the rights of Americans.

317

continued from page 316D

Hobbler, Dorothy. *The Trail on Which They Wept: The Story of a Cherokee Girl.* Scott Foresman, 1992. ISBN 0382243536.

O' Dell, Scott. *Sing Down the Moon.* Laurel Leaf, 1997. ISBN 0440979757.

Pitts, Paul. *Racing the Sun.* Camelot, 1988. ISBN 0380754967.

Pacific Region

Bruchac, Joseph. *Sacajawea.* Silver Whistle, 2000. ISBN 0152022341.

Craven, Margaret. *I Heard the Owl Call My Name.* Laurel Leaf, 1994. ISBN 0440343690.

Fitch, Ken. *Call of the Wild.* Acclaim Books, 1997. ISBN 1578400422.

George, Jean Craighead. *Julie of the Wolves.* HarperTrophy, 1999. ISBN 0064493504.

Hobbs, Will. *Far North.* Camelot, 1997. ISBN 0380725363.

Hoobler, Dorothy. *Treasure in the Stream: The Story of a Gold Rush Girl.* Silver Burdett Press, 1991. ISBN 0382241444.

Kroll, Virginia. *The Seasons and Someone.* Harcourt, 1994. ISBN 015271233X.

Morey, Walt. *Kavik, the Wolf Dog.* Puffin, 1997. ISBN 0140384235.

Salisbury, Graham. *Under the Blood Red Sun.* Yearling Books, 1995. ISBN 0440411394.

Sharpe, Susan. *Spirit Quest.* Puffin, 1993. ISBN 0140362827.

Smith, Roland. *Sea Otter Rescue: The Aftermath of an Oil Spill.* Puffin, 1999. ISBN 014056621X.

Stone, Lynn. *Grizzlies.* Children's Press, 1997. ISBN 0516261002.

Butterfield sits on the most powerful court in North Carolina and makes decisions about important cases that often affect every citizen in the state.

Butterfield did not preside over jury trials to find out if someone is guilty or innocent of various crimes. He sat on a panel in Raleigh with five other associates justices and the chief justice. Their job is to catch and correct mistakes that other judges make in interpreting the law and to catch errors in legal procedures. The supreme court is North Carolina's highest court. Once the justices make a decision, it stands as law. The only people with authority to change these rulings are the justices who sit on the United States Supreme Court.

Today, Butterfield represents North Carolina in the United States House of Representatives.

Judge for a Day
Conduct a simplified mock trial in your classroom to give your students a birds-eye view of what it's like when court is in session. Hold class elections to appoint a judge, choose an issue from current newspaper headlines, and allow teams of students to debate the pros and cons of the issue.

CHAPTER 13

A Rich Land

Social Studies Strands

Geographic Relationships
United States climate and vegetation

Economics and Development
United States economy and agriculture
The environment and pollution

Technological Influences and Society

Global Connections

North Carolina Standard Course of Study

Goal 1 The learner will apply key geographic concepts to the United States and other countries of North America.

Goal 5 The learner will evaluate ways the United States and other countries of North America make decisions about the allocation and use of economic resources.

Goal 6 The learner will recognize how technology has influenced change within the United States and other countries in North America.

Teaching & Assessment

• English Language Learner Modified Lesson Plans for this chapter are found in the Teacher's Resource Guide.

• *ExamView® Assessment Suite* is provided at **NCJourneys.com.** It includes customizable assessments for all chapters. Paper tests are also available in the Teacher's Resource Guide. See pages T16–T17 for information about how to use the assessments and the Scoring Guide.

Worksheets

Worksheets and answer keys are found both in the Teacher's Resource Guide and at **NCJourneys.com,** including Reading Guides, Reading Strategies, Chapter Reviews, English Language Learner and others.

Activities and Integrations

SOCIAL STUDIES

▲ ■ Paper People States, p. 318B
Problem Based Learning: The Business of America, p. 318B
Activator: Environmental Detectives, p. 318
United States, Physical Map, p. 319
▲ ■ Introduction to Regions of the United States, p. 320
▲ ■ United States Vegetation and Resources, p. 322
■ Trading/Bartering, p. 326
● Concentration, p. 327
Global Marketplace, p. 333
Population Connection, p. 330
Skill Lesson: Build a Factory, p. 341
▲ ■ Scrambled Eggs Arizona Style, p. 323

READING/LANGUAGE ARTS	READING/LANGUAGE ARTS OBJECTIVES
▲ ■ Recycle Fair, p. 318B	4.03
Writing Prompt: Wilderness, p. 318	4.09
● Reading Strategy: Making a Sharing Board, p. 320	2.05, 3.05
★ Fossil Fuels Debate, p. 324	1.03, 3.06
Reading Strategy: Main Idea Mapping, p. 326	2.06
★ Service Industries, p. 329	4.09
River Timeline, p. 331	2.08, 2.09
Types of Resource Material, p. 332	1.04
Reading Strategy: Story Mapping, p. 334	2.01
National Parks, p. 336	3.06
■ Conservation and National Parks, p. 337	3.06
★ Clean Water Act, p. 340	4.09
Becoming Better Readers, p. 342	2.01

MATHEMATICS	MATHEMATICS OBJECTIVES
Climagraph, p. 321	4.01
▲ ■ The Geography Cube, p. 322	3.01

SCIENCE	SCIENCE OBJECTIVES
Climate, p. 320	3.05, 3.06
Climagraph, p. 221	3.05, 3.06
Collage, p. 321	3.06
River Time Line, p. 331	2.01, 2.02, 2.04
Acid Rain, p. 339	3.01
Global Warming, p.339	3.04, 3.05

TECHNOLOGY	TECHNOLOGY OBJECTIVES
★ Carolina Connection—Land Grant Universities, p. 319	2.13

VISUAL ARTS	VISUAL ARTS OBJECTIVES
● Recyclable Trash Cans, p. 318B	2.01
Collage, p. 321	3.02
Understanding Culture Through Art, p. 343B	4.01, 5.01, 5.06

CHARACTER AND VALUES EDUCATION	TRAITS
What Would You Do?, p. 338	good judgment
What Would You Do?, p. 329	perseverance
Literature Seminar, p. 338	good citizenship

● Basic Activities ★ Challenging Activities ▲ English Language Learner Novice ■ English Language Learner Intermediate

Introductory Activity

Paper People States

OBJECTIVES: 1.01, 1.02, 1.06

Fold a long sheet of butcher paper fan-style. You will need 50 layers of folded paper. Or you can use several square sheets of paper, but you will need to connect them at the end. Draw a paper doll on the top sheet with its arms going out to the edges of the folds. Cut the doll out, being sure to leave the ends of the arms connected. Write the name of a different United States state on each doll.

Have the students research major landforms and geographical features of each state using physical maps and encyclopedias. Write the characteristics on the appropriate doll. Hang up the chain and discuss how the United States is physically diverse yet unified or connected.

Variations You could use the dolls to discuss cultural diversity instead of geographical and physical diversity.

Extension ELL students should work with a partner.

Culminating Activity

Recycle Fair Activity

OBJECTIVES: 1.05, 1.06, 1.07

Ask students to search their homes for things that are now considered "junk" or trash by their families. Direct the students to get their parents' permission to use the items for a classroom project. Have them "recycle" the items by creating new uses for them. The items might now be used for another purpose (for instance, an old shoe as a planter) or the items might be used as art (for instance old bolts and screws arranged as a modern collage). Have students write about their thinking as they redesigned uses for the "junk" and how they came upon their new creations. Display the students' items and their writing in a classroom "Recycle Fair."

Art Activity

Recyclable Trash Cans

OBJECTIVES: 3.04, 3.07, 4.07

To promote recycling at your school, have students decorate plastic trash cans to be placed around the school or donated to a community agency.

Materials plastic trash cans—medium to large size (purchase at dollar store, or have parents donate), paints

Divide the class into pairs. Assign a type of recyclable trash can for each pair to decorate, for example, aluminum, bottles/glass, paper, and so on. Encourage the students to use various forms of art for decorating, such as leaf printing, gluing objects to the trash can, painting. Distribute the finished recycling containers.

Activity

The Business of America

OBJECTIVES: 5.01, 5.04, 5.05

Situation
The United States economy has changed dramatically over the years with inventions and new developments. Today the United States is an economic giant, although many other countries also have advanced economic systems.

Task Have students consider the most exciting technologies and products that Americans make today (or consider what types of products are made specifically in North Carolina). To get an idea of these items, students should research these topics on the Internet, and cut out advertising of these products from newspapers, brochures, or magazines. Create a class collage. As a class or in small groups discuss how these products help the economy of the United States. Why are they important to the economy, and how might they improve so that the economy will grow? How might these companies advertise their products to Americans (and even people around the world), in order to keep the United States in the forefront of the world's economy?

As a group, discuss the following questions:
- Are all the elements of many United States-"made" products produced in the United States?
- Does this help trade? How does it affect trade surpluses or trade deficits?
- How does foreign trade help and/or hurt United States companies?
- What would American economies be like if there were no free enterprise? If the government owned all of the companies, how would things be different?

Reflection How do American products help our economy make money? Are there people in your community that rely on these products in order to feed their families? How can the United States keep growing? What have you learned about making buying decisions? How does the free enterprise system make your life easier? How would your life be different if we did not have free enterprise in the United States today?

Teaching Strategies

Involve students in a variety of hands-on activities to help them better understand the geographic and economic concepts introduced in this chapter. Focus on the role natural resources have played in the development of the United States economy. Emphasize the concept of the free market system, but also discuss the increasing importance of economic cooperation around the world—especially in North America. This chapter offers opportunities for guest speakers from agriculture, business, and conservation organizations, as well as ideas for field trips so that students may view these aspects of our economy firsthand.

Activator

 OBJECTIVES: 1.01, 1.02, 1.03, 1.06

Pair students together and take the class outside. Give each pair a clipboard, paper, and pencil. Students should walk around the school grounds and find evidences of man's impact on the environment. List evidences observed. Come back to class and have students share findings. Record their findings on a chart divided in two parts labeled "Positive Effects on the Environment" and "Negative Effects on the Environment." Assign each pair one negative effect on the environment. Write a possible solution to the problem and discuss.

Writing Prompt

OBJECTIVES: 1.01, 1.06, 3.05

Narrative Think of a time you have visited a place that you would consider a "wilderness"—in other words, a place that has been left in its natural condition, with no buildings or construction. Write about visiting this place. Be sure to tell whom you were with, where the place was, when you were there, and what activities you enjoyed while you were there.

Essay As a fifth grade student, what steps can you take to help preserve our environment? Write an essay explaining three ways you can help.

CHAPTER 13

PLURIBUS UNUM

President Eisenhower initiates the national highway system.

A Rich Land

Dwight D. Eisenhower was commander of Allied forces in World War II. He later became president of the United States. Eisenhower learned from the war the importance of a good transportation system. He asked Congress to build the Interstate Highway System. This cost billions of dollars. Today, the highways have paid for themselves. They have helped our economy grow.

These highways connect the resources and businesses of the United States. On the highway you can see trucks carrying goods—like the one belonging to Jim in Chapter 1. You can see the varied landforms and vegetation of our nation. You can also see the ways in which Americans have changed the land.

Chapter Preview

LESSON 1
A Vast and Varied Land
All of the types of climates can be found in the United States. The land is rich in vegetation and resources.

LESSON 2
Modern Economy and Agriculture
The United States economy is based on free enterprise. American industries trade with partners throughout the world.

LESSON 3
Promises and Problems
Americans have good health care, education, and quality of life. But Americans face many challenges, too.

318

Chapter Resources

Print Resources
Nonfiction
Cherry, Lynne. *A River Ran Wild: An Environmental History*. Harcourt Brace. 1992. ISBN 0152005420.
Kudlinski, Kathleen V. *Rachel Carson: Pioneer of Ecology* (Women of Our Time series). Scott Foresman, 1997. ISBN 0140322426.
Seattle, Chief. *Brother Eagle, Sister Sky*. Penguin Putnam, 1991. ISBN 0803709692.

Maps
Millennium Map Series (double-sided, laminated, write-on/wipe-off surfaces). National Geographic Society catalog, (800) 368-2728. Cost is $23.95 per map.
February 1999—Biodiversity
August 1999—Cultures
February 1998—Exploration
May 1998—Physical earth
October 1998—Population

United States—Physical

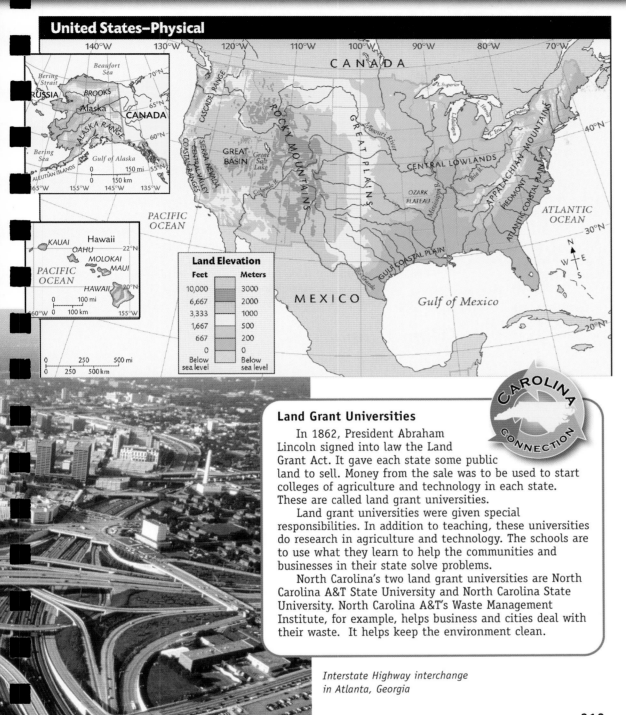

Land Elevation

Feet	Meters
10,000	3000
6,667	2000
3,333	1000
1,667	500
667	200
0	0
Below sea level	Below sea level

Land Grant Universities

In 1862, President Abraham Lincoln signed into law the Land Grant Act. It gave each state some public land to sell. Money from the sale was to be used to start colleges of agriculture and technology in each state. These are called land grant universities.

Land grant universities were given special responsibilities. In addition to teaching, these universities do research in agriculture and technology. The schools are to use what they learn to help the communities and businesses in their state solve problems.

North Carolina's two land grant universities are North Carolina A&T State University and North Carolina State University. North Carolina A&T's Waste Management Institute, for example, helps business and cities deal with their waste. It helps keep the environment clean.

Interstate Highway interchange in Atlanta, Georgia

319

Web Sites

Visit **NCJourneys.com** for links:
- National Council on Economic Education
- Federal Reserve Bank Economic Education
- EcEdWeb
- Energy Page, Energy Information Administration
- Exxon Valdez Oil Spill Trustee Council
- Junior Achievement
- Minerals Management Service, U.S. Department of the Interior Kid's Pages
- North Carolina Department of Agriculture Kid's Section
- U.S. Census Bureau
- U.S. Department of Agriculture, Agriculture in the Classroom
- U.S. Environmental Protection Agency, Environmental Kids Club
- Yes I Can
- Union of Concerned Scientists

Map Activity

United States—Physical

NATIONAL GEOGRAPHY STANDARDS: 14

GEOGRAPHIC THEMES: Region, Place, Human-Environmental Interaction, Movement, Location

OBJECTIVES: 1.02, 1.03, 4.02

Place students in groups and have them study the map with the idea that they must choose a place to live using this map only. Students will have an opportunity to revise their decisions after they complete this chapter and all of the lessons and activities within.

- Possible land use (what do landforms encourage/prohibit)
- Possible climate (latitude, proximity to large bodies of water)
- Proximity to waterways (transportation, industry)
- Relative location of existing cities
- Possible job availability and type

Students should discuss all of the possible regions where they would choose to live and then state their case as to where they would like to live and why. After studying the chapter or unit have the students amend their choices and present their revised choices to the class.

Activity

Carolina Connection: Land Grant Universities

OBJECTIVES: 2.06, 5.05

Go to **NCJourneys.com** for a link to a website with the text of the 1862 Land Grant Act. In the opening portions of the act, it states the acts purpose: "Donating public lands to the several States and Territories which may provide colleges for the benefit of agriculture and the mechanic arts." Ask students to look through the document for more examples of how the land should be used. You could also ask them what role land grant universities played in helping farmers and ranchers.

319

LESSON 1 A Vast and Varied Land

OBJECTIVES: 1.01, 1.02, 1.03

Caption Answer

Florida experiences a humid, subtropical climate. Continental and Highland climates are two climates that allow snowboarding.

Reading Strategy Activity

Making a Sharing Board

OBJECTIVES: 3.01, 3.03, 4.06

Divide the class into seven groups and assign each group one of the topics below. Each event is described in this lesson. The groups may use the worksheet titled "Sharing Board" in the Teacher's Resource Guide, or a large sheet of paper may be folded into eight sections. Tell the students they will share the boards with the class.

- A Rich Land (p. 318)
- Land Grant Universities (p. 319)
- Locating the United States (p. 320)
- Climate (p. 320–321)
- Vegetation (p. 322)
- George Washington Carver (p. 323)
- Natural Resources (p. 323)

Activity

Climate

OBJECTIVES: 1.03

Students will need a blank map of the United States, colored pencils or crayons, and a copy of *USA Today* or some other newspaper that shows the weather of the United States in color. Have students identify the different climate types in the United States. Using the blank map, have students set up a key. They should color code the key to illustrate each type of climate found in the United States. After students have their key set up, have them color their maps of the United States to identify the climate regions of the country.

KEY IDEAS

- Most of the states of the United States are contiguous. Alaska and Hawaii are not contiguous with the other 48 states.
- All of the world's climate types—from desert to tundra—can be found in the United States.
- The varied climates in the United States allow many kinds of vegetation to grow.
- Minerals and other resources make the United States a rich land.

KEY TERMS

contiguous
erosion
fossil fuels
petroleum

PEOPLE TO KNOW

George Washington Carver

Summers in Florida are hot and humid (right). This snowboarder shows off his skill (far right). **What kind of climate does Florida have? What kind of climate allows snowboarding?**

You know that the United States has 50 states. Forty-eight of these states are contiguous. That means that each state touches at least one other state.

Locating the United States

The *contiguous* states are located on the North American continent. They are south of Canada and north of Mexico. They are bordered by the Atlantic Ocean to the east and the Pacific Ocean to the west.

Two states, Alaska and Hawaii, are not contiguous. The state of Alaska is north of the contiguous states. It borders Canada on the east and the Pacific Ocean on the south. To the west is the Bering Sea, and the Arctic Ocean is to the north. Alaskans call the contiguous states "the lower forty-eight."

The island group that makes up the state of Hawaii is found in the Pacific Ocean. The islands are more than 2,000 miles (3,220 km) west of California. Hawaiians often call rest of the United States "the mainland."

Many Climates

As you read in Chapter 1, Brendan and his dad took a trip around the United States. They saw some of North America's many landforms. There are many climates, too.

Climate, you remember, means all the weather conditions in an area over a long period of time. The average temperatures for various seasons are part of a place's climate. So is average rainfall, snowfall, and humidity.

All the world's climate types are found in the United States. No other nation has so many.

Chapter 13

Activity

Introduction to Regions of the United States

OBJECTIVES: 1.01, 1.03

Materials large map of the United States and shower curtain liner

As the class begins its regional study of the United States, have a large map of the United States in the classroom. A large outline map can be drawn on a shower curtain liner and

displayed in the classroom for the entire time the United States is being studied. As they "travel" across the United States, students, in their cooperative learning groups, will cut out or draw pictures or bring in photographs or postcards that represent each region and glue them in their proper place on the map. Pictures could represent climate, industries, recreation, agriculture, tourist attractions, ethnic groups, historical characters, and occupations. Students will explain to the class why they are placing each picture on the map. This activity will allow students to note the similarities and differences of each region as the United States is studied.

What Affects Climate?

Look at the map on page 45. It shows the different climates of the United States. As you learned in Chapter 3, there are three major things that influence a place's climate. One is its nearness to the Equator. Another is landforms, like mountains. The third is its nearness to large bodies of water, like oceans.

In general, the part of a country that is farthest from the oceans has colder winters and hotter summers. Large bodies of water, such as oceans, can make climates milder.

San Francisco, California, and Kansas City, Missouri, are about the same distance from the Equator. But San Francisco is much warmer in winter and cooler in summer. That is because San Francisco is on the shore of the Pacific Ocean.

The climate becomes warmer as you move closer to the Equator. So Arkansas is usually warmer than Montana. Elevation is height above the earth's surface. It affects climate, too. It is colder and snowier at higher elevations, like mountain tops, than at lower ones.

Where is Which Climate?

Florida has the hot, humid summers and rainy winters of the humid subtropical climate. So does most of the south. In the North, from the Rockies to the Atlantic, people live in a continental climate. Winters are cold and snowy there. Summers are warm.

In the West, the climate is drier. Many areas receive only a little rainfall in the steppe climate. This dry desert climate is found in the southwestern United States.

Along the southern California coast the climate is Mediterranean. Winters are mild and rainy, and summers are hot and dry. The northern Pacific Coast enjoys a Marine West Coast climate. It is mild and rainy all year.

Most of Alaska has a subarctic climate. Summers are short and winters are long, cold, and snowy. Northern Alaska has a cold tundra climate. There it is cold and dry all year with short, cool summers. At the tip of Florida and in much of Hawaii, it is hot all year with wet and dry seasons. Here you will find tropical rain forest and tropical savanna climates.

Discussion Questions

1 The text states that the interior of our nation has colder winters and hotter summers than the coastal area. Why is this true? How does nearness to an ocean affect the climate of a region?

Research Activity

Collage

OBJECTIVES: 1.01, 1.02, 1.06

Using the climate map of the United States on page 45, have a discussion of the various climates found in the United States. Divide the class into cooperative groups. Assign each group a climate region. Each group should research the climate in its given area and then list those climatic characteristics on a piece of chart paper. The information should include: a) the area's location, b) what the weather is like for each season of the year, c) the annual precipitation and the form(s) it takes, and d) the average temperature for each month of the year (this information could be graphed). Then have the students share this information with the rest of the class. Create a collage using the information you have gathered. The collage should show how the climate of a given area affects the way people live there. Include seasonal recreational activities, housing, types of clothing, types of industry, and sports popular the region. When collages are complete, each climate region should be represented.

A Rich Land

321

Math Activity

Climagraph

OBJECTIVES: 1.03, 1.06, 1.07

After a discussion of various types of climate regions in the United States, have students create a climagraph for different cities across the United States. Give students the information in the table (left) on temperatures and precipitation. Have them work in pairs to plot the information on a climagraph.

	Raleigh, NC		Portland, OR		Honolulu, HI	
	Temp.	Prec.	Temp.	Prec.	Temp.	Prec.
January	39	3.6	39.6	5.7	73	3.2
February	42	3.4	43.6	4.7	73	2.2
March	50	3.7	47.3	4.3	74	2.2
April	59	2.9	51.0	3.2	76	1.5
May	67	3.7	57.0	2.4	78	1.1
June	74	3.7	63.0	1.5	79	0.5
July	78	4.4	68.0	0.9	81	0.6
August	77	4.4	68.6	1.0	81	0.4
September	71	3.3	63.3	1.7	81	0.8
October	60	2.7	54.5	3.0	80	2.3
November	51	2.9	46.1	5.6	77	3.0
December	43	3.1	40.2	6.4	74	3.8

Temperature is in degrees Farenheit. Precipitation is in inches.

Caption Answer

The Mediterranean climate produces Mediterranean types of vegetation. Deciduous and evergreen forests grow in the humid subtropical climate region. Forest resources are found in the Northwest, oil resources are found in Texas, copper is found in the Southwest, and coal and mining are important in the Rocky Mountains and the Appalachian Mountains.

Map Activity

United States Vegetation and Resources

NATIONAL GEOGRAPHY STANDARDS: 1, 3, 4, 5, 8, 15

GEOGRAPHIC THEMES: Region, Human-Environmental Interaction

OBJECTIVES: 1.04, 1.06, 5.02

Divide the class in half. Using the map and text information (you may want to provide additional resources for the students to use, such as *National Geographic* magazines or other pictures), the students will sketch different vegetation or resources. Provide students with large pieces of construction paper. Have them fold the paper into eighths (as the map legend shows, vegetation has only seven types and resources has nineteen).

One half of the class will work on vegetation types; the other will work on the resources. In each square the students will draw and label the vegetation types and/or landscape of each vegetation type shown on the map *or* eight of the resources shown on the map. Display and discuss the students' work. Compare their work to photos of actual vegetation and resources. Have students deduce the types of jobs people have in each of these regions.

Vegetation

Climate and soil affect the kinds of trees and plants that can grow in an area. The soils and climates of the United States help create the richest land in the world. Many different types of vegetation grow here.

Trees

Two types of trees grow in the forests of the eastern United States. Deciduous trees, such as maples and oaks, lose their leaves every year. They are amazing in the autumn. Their leaves change from green to gold, red, and orange before falling.

Evergreens stay green all year. The Douglas fir and the spruce thrive in eastern mountains. Other kinds of evergreen trees, especially pine trees, grow well in the Coastal Plain.

Grasses

The natural plant of the Central Plains is grass. If humans did not farm, grasses would cover the area from Iowa all the way westward to Wyoming. They would also cover from Montana and North Dakota southward all the way to Texas.

Prairie grass was a challenge for the first farmers on the plains. But the grass protected the rich soil from erosion. *Erosion* is when the top soil blows away or runs off with the rain. This rich soil provided the rich farmland of the plains states.

Sage and short grass are found in the western desert regions. Cactus plants love the

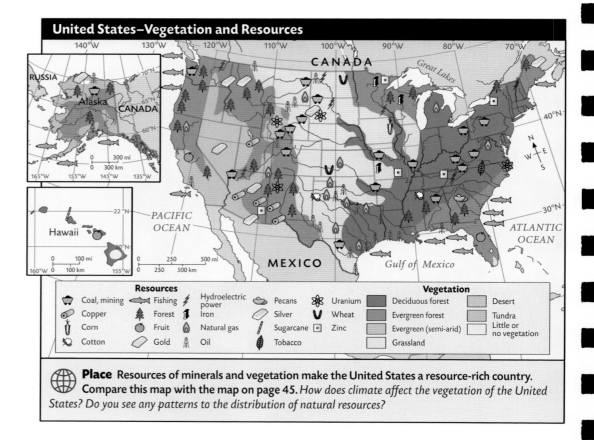

Place Resources of minerals and vegetation make the United States a resource-rich country. Compare this map with the map on page 45. *How does climate affect the vegetation of the United States? Do you see any patterns to the distribution of natural resources?*

Math Activity

The Geography Cube

OBJECTIVES: 1.01, 1.02, 1.06

Materials: 18-inch by 24-inch sheet of construction paper, ruler, glue or tape, scissors, a marker, and a sketch to show them where to draw the flaps for gluing the cube

The United States is a land of great diversity. Students can illustrate this diversity by decorating the six sides of a cube. Use the cube pattern in the Teacher's Resource Guide. This activity will have an additional math benefit if students measure and construct their cube rather than trace a pattern.

Direct students to measure and draw six squares. Each square is to be 6 by 6 inches. Students will use their spatial visualization skills to remember which direction is going to be "up" as they draw their illustrations on each side of the cube. Scenes may include various

George Washington Carver
1864–1943

Science Helps Farmers

During the 1900s, scientists and inventors solved problems and invented new products that made life easier. One of these scientists was from Missouri.

George Washington Carver was born at the end of the Civil War. His parents had been slaves. He never knew his father. When Carver was a baby, Confederates kidnapped him and his mother. Moses Carver, his owner, went searching for them. He found only little George.

The Carver family raised George. As he grew, he was often sick. He did not have the strength to work in the fields. Instead, he helped Mrs. Carver in the house and in the garden. He spent his free time outdoors.

Going to School

Mrs. Carver taught George to read and write because there was no school in Diamond for black children. When he got a little older, George left the Carvers and walked to Neosho to go to school. George was very smart and did well in schools.

George spent his teenage years traveling all over the Midwest. He worked and went to school when he could. It was a hard life. Finally, George ended up in Iowa. He became the first African American to graduate from Iowa State University. He was the first African American to teach there, too. Later, he taught at Tuskegee Institute in Alabama. It was a famous school for former slaves and their children.

A Famous Professor

Carver taught at Tuskegee for almost 50 years. He became one of the most famous scientists in the world. He found better ways to grow plants such as peanuts. He found hundreds of uses for peanuts, pecans, soybeans, and sweet potatoes.

Carver also helped people be better farmers. For decades, southern farmers had grown only cotton. This was bad for the soil. It left the soil with few minerals. Carver said farmers should plant cotton one year and peanuts, peas, or soybeans the next year. These crops put minerals back into the soil. His advice saved many farms.

After he became famous, Carver spoke all across the nation. He told young people that all races could get along.

dry conditions of the desert. Arizona chose the bloom of the Saguaro Cactus as its state flower.

Much of Alaska is tundra, a treeless plain. Only a few low-growing plants, such as grasses, lichens, and mosses, are able to survive.

Flowers, vines, and other plants grow in Hawaii. Many are found nowhere else. Some plants once thought to be native to Hawaii, such as coconuts and pineapples, were imported.

Natural Resources

The United States has become an industrial giant. This is partly because its land contains so many different raw materials.

Look at the map. Very few other countries have so many different kinds of resources or as large amounts of them.

A Rich Land

323

landforms, vegetation, seasonal variations in climate, climate regions, or other characteristics. Once scenes are drawn and colored, students are to assemble their cubes. Cubes could be shared with the class and then placed on display in the Media Center. The title could be "The United States: A Vast and Varied Land."

Extension ELL students should work with a partner.

Discussion Questions

1 Why do you think Arizona chose the Saguaro cactus bloom as its state flower?

2 What are some ways that George Washington Carver helped farmers?

Activity

Scrambled Eggs Arizona Style

OBJECTIVES: 1.06, 3.04

1 or 2 cactus leaves
8 eggs
¼ pound cheese
Salt and pepper to taste

Scrub cactus leaves and remove spines. Use a potato peeler to cut around spiney nodules and remove. Slice cactus leaves into bite-size pieces. Sauté cactus leaves in a small amount of butter for 5 minutes. Remove. Beat eggs in a mixing bowl and add shredded cheese and cooked cactus leaves. Pour in heated skillet and scramble. Serve warm.

323

Activity

Fossil Fuels Debate

 OBJECTIVES: 1.03, 5.01, 5.02

See the Guide to Student Debates on page T39 in the Teacher's Edition. Divide the class into two groups to research information in preparation for a debate. Have materials available for students to use. You may want to ask the public library to reserve materials on the topic.

Topic: Should offshore drilling for fossil fuels be allowed?

Make sure students can identify the source of each reason they have, whether pro or con. Have students use the worksheet to outline their arguments.

Discuss debate etiquette and rules. Stage a debate in the classroom or for another fifth grade class. Before the debate, poll the class as to which way they would vote. After the debate, let the class vote again. Note the differences in opinions if there are any. Ask why some of the students changed their minds. Which particular facts convinced them?

Teacher Notes

Energy Statistics

- United States production of crude oil has declined from 9.6 million barrels per day to 5.8 million barrels per day since 1970.
- Petroleum consumption is projected to grow at an average annual rate of 1.5 percent through 2020.
- Natural gas consumption has increased by roughly 13 percent over the last decade, and is projected to increase nearly 50 percent by 2020.
- Total coal consumption is expected to increase from 1,081 to 1,365 million tons between 2000 and 2020.
- In 1999, 104 nuclear power plants produced about 727.9 billion kilowatt-hours of electricity, a record high.
- Renewable energy options are diverse and may be converted into electricity, heat, or mechanical power. Renewable energy resources include solar radiation, running water, wind, bio-mass, and geothermal heat. Total renewable electric generation is projected to increase by 1.3 percent per year by 2020.
- Electricity demand (retail sales plus industrial generation for own use) is projected to grow by 1.8 percent per year from 2000 through 2020.

How Do We Get Petroleum?

Petroleum is another word for crude oil. People build large machines to pump oil out of the grown. After drilling to get to the oil, the machines pump the oil to the surface.

1. Workers remove the derrick and set up a pump like this one. Can you see why this is called a "grasshopper pump?"

2. A motor makes the gear box move a lever. This gives the pump power to draw up the oil.

3. The oil is pumped into a pipe at the surface. The pipe moves the oil to tanker trunks. Trucks and barges carry oil to the refinery.

324

Fossil Fuels

For example, there are three types of *fossil fuels* in the United States. *Petroleum* (the oil you read about in Chapter 12), natural gas, and coal are found in many states. They come from decayed plants and animals from thousands of years ago.

Petroleum is found mainly in Alaska, Texas, Oklahoma, and Louisiana. The country's need for oil is greater than the amount those wells can produce. So America must import oil from other countries.

Minerals

When our nation was young, many raw materials were found in the East. This gave new industries the resources to grow.

As the nation expanded westward, cities were built near places where raw materials could be found. For example, boomtowns sprung up where copper or silver mines were built in places like Arizona. When the metal was gone, people sometimes left. Other towns found new industries upon which to build.

The largest deposits of iron are in Minnesota. Most copper is mined in western states. Both of these minerals can also be found in other parts of the country.

An offshore oil rig pumps crude oil from beneath the Gulf of Mexico. **What is an alternative to fossil fuel for generating power?**

Energy

During the 1900s, electricity became more and more important as an energy source. Much electric power has been generated with fossil fuels.

As the demand for electricity has grown, the nation has turned to its many waterways to make electric power. The water is used to turn electric generators.

If you have visited Fontana Dam in western North Carolina, you have seen how water from a river can generate an endless supply of electricity. Hundreds of dams like Fontana are found throughout the United States.

Discussion Questions

1 How can citizens of the United States help to preserve our nation's natural resources?

2 Industrial growth has been beneficial to our country in many ways. However, it has also caused some concerns for citizens. What are some problems involved with industrial growth?

3 What does "native to" an area mean? Can you name some plants, trees, or crops that are native to our area?

 **Caption Answer**

Hydroelectric power is mentioned in the text. Wind and solar power are other possible answers.

LESSON **1** REVIEW

Fact Follow-Up

1. Define climate and give examples of differences between climate and weather.
2. What influences determine the climate of an area?
3. Name two types of deciduous trees that grow in the eastern United States.
4. Where are grasslands areas in the United States?
5. Name four minerals or three fossil fuels that have been important to the nation.

Talk About It

1. What can a farmer in Hawaii raise that a farmer in Minnesota cannot?
2. What sports do Minnesota children play that Florida children don't? Why?
3. Why are minerals and fuels important to a nation?
4. How would our resources be different if the nation still had only 13 colonies?
5. What did George Washington Carver do?

A Rich Land

LESSON **1** REVIEW

Fact Follow-Up Answers

1. Climate refers to all the weather conditions in an area over a period of time and includes such things as average temperature for various seasons and average rainfall, snowfall, and relative humidity.
2. Nearness to the Equator, landforms, and nearness to large bodies of water influence climate.
3. Maples and oaks are two types of deciduous trees that grow in the eastern United States.
4. If humans did not farm, grasses would cover the area from Iowa westward to Wyoming and from Montana and North Dakota southward to Texas.
5. Among the minerals are iron, copper, silver, and gold. Fossil fuels include petroleum, natural gas, and coal.

Talk About It Answers

1. A farmer in Hawaii can raise more than one crop a year because of the climate. Differences in the length of the growing season are key.
2. Minnesota children can enjoy such winter sports as skiing and outdoor ice skating and ice hockey because the winter climate.
3. Important points: Among reasons are these: Minerals and fuels supply basic needs for manufacturing industries; it is difficult, at least in the beginning, for a nation to build its own industries if it has to import all its basic minerals and fuels.
4. Important points: Students should use the United States—Vegetation and Resources map on page 322 and the original 13 colonies map on page 115 to answer this question.
5. He found better ways to grow plants and helped farmers know how to better use the land.

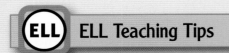 **ELL Teaching Tips**

Learning Styles

Most new ELL students learn best kinesthetically. Don't expect them to sit and listen to lectures. Use lots of gestures, drawings, or other visual aids. Give students hands-on activities to complete.

 **Reading Strategy Activity**

Main Idea Mapping

Students remember facts and details much better when they write about what they read. It seems to cement the information into their brain. Main Idea-Mapping is a way to see the main idea and the details of the material in the text. It helps with any content subject: social studies, science, health, and so on.

Students should first read Lesson 2, Modern Economy and Agriculture. This could be read in groups, with a buddy, or silently, depending on your class. Use the Main Idea-Mapping worksheet in the Teacher Resource Guide.

Ask students to make a web with the word "Contigueous" as the center. Have students work in pairs to think of things that are contiguous. Examples include desks that touch, holding hand, pictures on the board that rouch, North and South Carolina, etc. Share the findings with the entire class. See if the examples follow the meaning of the word.

 **Activity**

Trading/Bartering

Break the class into groups of four students to form "villages." Each student should choose a farm product to sell as a value-added product (bananas could be sold as banana pudding or corn could be sold as muffins). Each student will

KEY IDEAS

- The United States' economy is a system of free enterprise.

- The economy of the United States includes manufacturing, high-technology, agricultural, and service industries.

- Many industries can produce more goods and services with fewer people.

- American businesses trade with countries all over the world.

KEY TERMS

capital resources
competition
consumers
entreprenuer
export
foreign trade
free enterprise
gross domestic product
human resources
import
mechanized farming
monopoly
scientific farming
service industry

A fter Julie, a new doctor, graduated from medical school in North Carolina, she needed a job. Julie, her husband Biff, and their son moved to Utah so Julie could work in a hospital there. Their family made choices about where to live and how to work. These are economic choices.

America's Economy

Economics is the study of how people get the goods and services they need and want. There are different kinds of economic systems. A traditional economy is one where people grow or make what they need. There is very little trading. Many of the Native American societies in Chapter 4 had traditional economies.

The Soviet Union, as described in Chapter 12, had a Communist government and economy. In that system, the government decided what people needed and what factories should make. That is a command economy. The United States has a capitalist economy. Capitalism is a *free enterprise* system. Private citizens, not the government, make the decisions. They can make or buy what they want. People are free to choose how to spend their money and what type of work to do.

Our system also has *competition.* This means that more than one company may make the same item or provide the same service. *Consumers,* people who buy the item or service, have a choice. They can buy the product or service they like best. Companies compete to make the best products. They improve the products they sell to make them better. This helps our economy grow.

Our free enterprise system does have some limits. As you discussed in Chapter 9, the government passed laws to protect people and the environment. For example, the government limits things like the number of hours a person can work in a day. It also makes sure that places to work are safe, and that the food and drugs we have are safe, too.

The government also wants to make sure that the competition is fair. If one company gets too big and does not allow competition, this is called a *monopoly.* The government makes rules to prevent monopolies.

WORD ORIGINS

Scottish economist Adam Smith wrote in 1776 about a new system of economics. In "An Inquiry into the Nature and Causes of the Wealth of Nations," Smith wrote that wealth is created through **free enterprise**. This would be fair competition among people in the marketplace. He argued for an economy free from government controls.

"harvest" the product (likely from a grocery store) and prepare the product for sale (like a manufacturer might turn a natural resource into a finished product). On "Market Day," each village should present their products to be bartered with the products from the other villages. Each student will start the class with only his or her product. After bartering with others, students should end up with a wide variety of products. Students can then eat the products produced from the farm resources.

Discuss how farming and bartering can expand the lives of farmers. How does farming more than what a family needs help the farmer? How does this same system work today as we import and export food?

Extension Intermediate ELL students should look up selected vocabulary words in bilingual dictionaries.

Using Our Resources

An economy's resources can be placed into three groups: natural, human, and capital. As you read in Lesson 1, the United States is rich in natural resources.

Human Resources

Human resources are the people who do the work, or our workforce. Human resources include truck drivers, teachers, doctors, farmers, and sales clerks.

An educated workforce is an important resource. Today, businesses need educated people to work with computers or complicated machines. To do some jobs, like doctors, nurses, lawyers, or engineers, people need to go to college.

Many people try to learn new skills. That way, they can find a new job if they have to.

Capital Resources

Capital resources are the things people use to make, grow, or deliver goods or services. These include tools, equipment, and buildings. Capital resources may be used over and over during a long period of time without being used up. Trucks, ovens, computers, and desks are capital resources.

Things that are used up in making a product to sell are not capital resources. The nails used to build a bookcase would not be a capital resource. But the hammer used to hit the nails would be a capital resource.

Henry Heinz
1844–1919

Do you like ketchup on your hamburgers? Henry Heinz started in the food business when he was eight years old. He sold extra vegetables from his mother's garden near Pittsburgh, Pennsylvania.

Heinz grew up and formed the the the H. J. Heinz Company. Starting it made him an *entreprenuer.* Heinz made ketchup, pickles, sauerkraut, and vinegar. Business soared. By the time he started advertising "57 Varieties," the company already sold more than 60 products.

To make sure its foods were top quality, the company owned its own farms. It also owned the factories for processing and packing foods. Heinz packed whatever he could in clear glass bottles, not cans. He wanted people to see the quality of his products.

To make more money, other food manufacturers added fillers. They added chalk to milk and sawdust to bread and hot dogs. Heinz believed this was unsafe and dishonest. He urged Congress to pass the Pure Food and Drug Act, which made this kind of dishonesty against the law.

Heinz also ran his factories differently. He treated workers fairly and paid them well. They got free medical care. They got manicures to keep hands clean for handling food. The factories had special lunchrooms with music and art. Washrooms had hot and cold showers, which most homes did not have at the time.

Henry Heinz started his family's tradition of giving back to the community. He founded the Sarah Heinz House in Pittsburgh. It was a place for immigrant children to go after school to learn English and have fun. It was named for Henry's wife.

AMERICAN PORTRAIT

Activity

Concentration

OBJECTIVES: 5.01, 5.06

Each group will need the text, two dozen 3-inch by 3-inch squares, and a clasp envelope.

Preparing the game: After students have studied the chapter, pairs of students will write 10 to 12 questions and answers (or words and meanings) on 3-inch by 3-inch squares of construction paper. Write one question or answer per card. Shuffle the cards and number them on the reverse side. A "Q" or an "A" could also be written on the numbered side to designate questions and answers.

Playing the game: Each player pulls one card from the envelope. The person with the higher number will start the game. Arrange the cards in rows of four or five cards each in numerical order with the numbers facing up. The first player calls a number, turns that card over, and reads the card aloud. That same player chooses another card. If the cards match, that player picks up the two cards, scores a point, and takes another turn. If the cards do not match, the cards are returned to their original position, and it is the other player's turn. The game is over when all matches have been made. The player with the most matches is the winner. After students have played their own game, they can exchange games with other pairs of students.

Discussion Questions

1 Why do you think United States farmers are the most productive in the world?

2 What advantages do United States farmers have that farmers in many smaller, poorer countries do not have?

1 What types of "old" occupations do you think are disappearing? Why?

2 Name some changes that have occurred in the last 50 years of our country that involve technology.

1 Why do you think so many people work in the service industries?

2 Why are service industry jobs so important to the growth of the United States?

3 Which service industry do you think is most important? Why?

Caption Answer

75 percent

Caption Answer

Employers want to hire people who have specific knowledge and skills.

Teaching is part of the service industry. **What percentage of workers in the United States are in service jobs?**

The New Economy

Biff's and Julie's jobs are part of big changes taking place in the economy of the United States. Julie's work as a doctor reflects another new trend. She works with patients, helping them get well. In doing this, she is not producing a product. Products come from farms, factories, or mines. Instead, she is providing a service to other people.

Service Industries

The many different kind of jobs that help people are part of the *service industry.* These jobs now make up the largest part of the nation's economy. Schools, law firms, insurance companies, restaurants, real estate firms, and repair shops are a few examples of service industries.

Manufacturing

One of the first industries created during the Industrial Revolution was manufacturing. It is still an important part of our economy. United States factories make products others want to buy, especially automobiles, food products, and chemicals. Sometimes the parts of products are made in other countries, but the final product is assembled in America. This section of our economy is shrinking as more and more things are made overseas.

The construction industry builds all our new buildings: houses, factories, offices, and schools.

High-Technology Industries

The United States is now a world leader in high-technology (high-tech) industries. High-tech industries are businesses that require special systems, such as computers, to make something.

For example, Boeing Aircraft continues to be one of the world's largest makers of large airplanes. IBM, Microsoft, and other companies lead in making computer hardware and software. Companies that research and produce medicines are also part of the high-tech industry.

Agricultural Industries

As you read in Chapter 9, new machines were invented to help farmers grow more crops. Farms grew in size. Machines were needed to run them. *Mechanized farming* is farming that needs machines to do the work.

Scientific farming uses science to improve farming. This has brought great changes. Scientists help farmers get more from their crops. When our nation was young, a farm family could feed itself and three other people. Most people farmed for a living. Today, the number of farms and farmers continues to decrease. But the size of farms is getting larger.

Most jobs require basic computer skills. **Why is education important to finding a job?**

Chapter 13

United States Industries and Workforce*

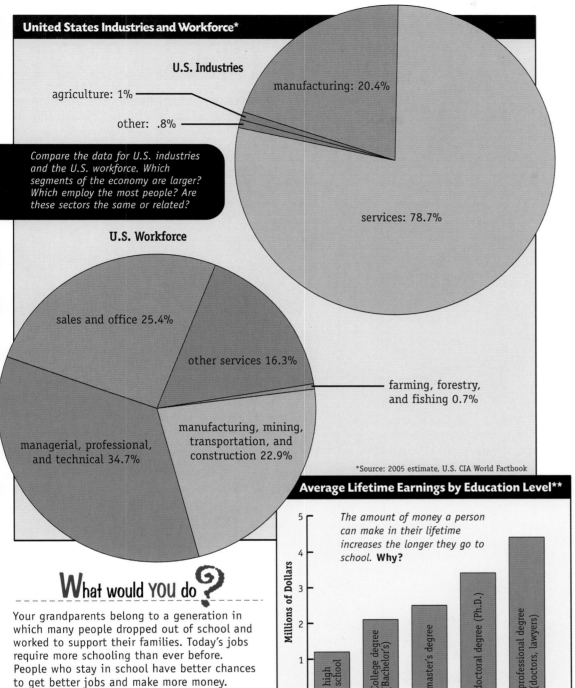

U.S. Industries

agriculture: 1%

other: .8%

manufacturing: 20.4%

services: 78.7%

Compare the data for U.S. industries and the U.S. workforce. Which segments of the economy are larger? Which employ the most people? Are these sectors the same or related?

U.S. Workforce

sales and office 25.4%

other services 16.3%

farming, forestry, and fishing 0.7%

managerial, professional, and technical 34.7%

manufacturing, mining, transportation, and construction 22.9%

*Source: 2005 estimate, U.S. CIA World Factbook

What would YOU do?

Your grandparents belong to a generation in which many people dropped out of school and worked to support their families. Today's jobs require more schooling than ever before. People who stay in school have better chances to get better jobs and make more money.

The decision to stay in school is partly yours right now. What will you do?

Average Lifetime Earnings by Education Level**

The amount of money a person can make in their lifetime increases the longer they go to school. **Why?**

Millions of Dollars

- high school
- College degree (Bachelor's)
- master's degree
- doctoral degree (Ph.D.)
- professional degree (doctors, lawyers)

**2002 U.S. Dept. of Commerce

A Rich Land

329

Activity

Service Industries

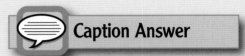 **OBJECTIVES:** 5.01, 5.04, 5.05

Divide the class into small cooperative groups. Each group will need chart paper to make a list of all the types of service jobs they can think of. Each group will present their list to the class to create one master list. After the master list has been compiled, each student will take one or two of the jobs to research. (What is required to enter this position? What kind of education and training is involved?) They will also need to determine any age requirements for this job. After learning about the job, they will need to write a want ad for the newspaper, advertising it in a pleasing way so that someone would want to apply for it. When finished, the classroom will have an entire newspaper's worth of service job want ads.

Caption Answer

Services are the largest industry. The largest number of people work in managerial, professional, and technical jobs. These jobs are services too.

Caption Answer

People with higher levels of education usually qualify for higher-paying jobs.

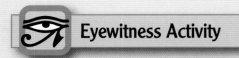

Eyewitness Activity

Population Connection

OBJECTIVES: 1.05, 5.06, 5.07

Go to **NCJourneys.com** for a link to a Web site for Population Connection. This resource has many resources and activities for teaching about population. Some of the activities include:

- **300 Million Reasons:** So many of today's headlines are connected to population pressures. Students collect and analyze newspaper articles on local and national issues for their population connection, challenges and solutions.
- **Connecting the Dots:** Students map the changing size and density of the country's population over the past 200 years in this timely geography activity.
- **A Family Perspective:** Students chart family-size trends over several generations and discuss factors that influence family-size decision-making.
- **Global Warming Begins at Home USA:** How much CO2 to do you spew? Students collect data and compute word problems to calculate their household's contribution of atmospheric greenhouse gases.
- **The Good Old Days:** In this lively simulation, U.S. presidents from 1800, 1850, 1900, 1950 and 2006 compare resource use, wealth, health, education and more with some interesting facts and symbols of quality of life.
- **A Hill of Beans:** A powerful visual and auditory demonstration helps students compare the lifetime use of resources of an average American with an average citizen of one of the world's poorest nations.
- **Looking to the Future:** In creating a futuristic news telecast and a letter to a friend 50 years from now, students think about what their future might look like, given current realities, hopes and dreams.
- **Population Clock in the USA:** How many people do we add to our population every year? Day? Minute? Students multiply ratios, divide units of time, and subtract death rates from birth rates to calculate population growth rates.
- **Watch Your Step:** Students compare their "ecological footprints" with those of teens around the world using an eye-opening online quiz and engaging in thoughtful discussion about individual impacts and sustainability.

EYEWITNESS TO HISTORY

Passing 300 million

The U.S. Census Bureau estimated that the population of the United States reached the historic milestone of 300 million on October 17, 2006. This happened almost 39 years after the 200 million mark was reached on November 20, 1967.

Immigrants arrive at Ellis Island, New York, 1907

The United States averages one birth every 7 seconds and one death every 13 seconds. Immigrants arriving and Americans leaving to live overseas were also included as part of the estimate. This movement adds one person every 31 seconds. Together, these numbers mean that one person is added to America's population every 11 seconds.

In 1915, America's population reached 100 million. In 1967 it reached 200 million. Let's compare some figures from these years to 2006.

There are only two other countries with populations larger than the United States. India and China (left) both have more than 1 billion people.

U.S. Population and Emigration

1915	1967	2006
100 Million	200 Million	300 Million
15%	5%	12%

- Total U.S. Population
- Percentage of Immigrants

330

In 2006 there were 34.3 million immigrants living in the United States. They made up 12 percent of the total population. Most of the immigrants came from Mexico. In 1967 there were 9.7 million immigrants living here. They made up 5 percent of the total population. The most immigrants had come from Italy. In 1915, there were 13.5 million immigrants living here. They made up 15 percent of the total population. The most immigrants had come from Germany.

In 1915, only 13.5 percent of Americans had graduated from high school. By 1967, that number had grown to 51. 1 percent. In 2006, more than 85 percent of Americans graduated from high school.

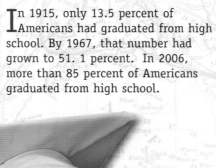

In 1915, the average life span of an American was 54.5 years. In 1967, it grew to 70.5. In 2006, it was 77.8. Americans are living much longer than they were almost 100 years ago. This affects the number of people who live past 65. In 2006, 36.8 million people were age sixty-five and older. In 1967, 19.1 million people were age sixty-five and older. In 1915, there were only 4.5 million people age sixty-five and older.

A Rich Land

331

Activity

River Time Line

OBJECTIVES: 1.01, 1.02, 4.07

Read the picture book *The River Ran Wild* by Lynne Cherry aloud to the students. Ask them if they were surprised to hear this level of pollution was going on such a short time ago. Review the book and have the students record important points in the history of the Nashua River. Be sure to include the dates mentioned in the text and the author's note. Provide copies of the author's note to the class.

Either in groups or individually, have students create a time line of the Nashua River. (Hint: There's a key in the front of the book . . . don't tell the kids). Discuss the time lines.

Activity

Types of Resource Materials

 OBJECTIVES: 1.01

Use the following example:

What if your best friend told you he was moving to Hyde County. Do you know how far away he or she will be from you? If you don't know the location of Hyde County, what book would you look in to find it?

There are several different types of research materials that can be found in the library. If readers know what these materials contain and how to use them, they can find the answers to many of the questions you may have.

Bring in examples of references in the table below as they are taught. Use the Types of Resource Materials worksheet in the Teacher's Resource Guide to practice this skill.

Textbook References

The **table of contents** is located at the beginning of textbooks. It is a list of the units, chapters, and page numbers of the book.

Textbooks, along with other books, have a section at the back of the book called the **Appendix**. It contains a small atlas, a dictionary of geographic terms, a gazetteer (an alphabetical list of geographical names), and other items.

Most texts have a **glossary** located at the back. The glossary listed alphabetically is a small dictionary giving meanings of words used in the text.

An **index** is another list located at the back of the book. It has topics found in the book and the page numbers where they are located.

Moving Goods, People, and Ideas

Do you remember reading about the importance of ports early in our history? Or how canals and trains moved goods to market? Today, moving people, goods, and ideas is still important to our economy.

America's transportation network is huge. Airplanes, trains, trucks, and ships move people and goods across the country. They also connect us with other countries.

Another way we move things today is with computers. We do not send a package over a computer network or the Internet. But we do send information and ideas.

Some companies use and sell information. Newspapers, magazines, radio, and TV are all businesses that provide information.

The Interstate System

President Eisenhower is credited with creating the interstate highway system. This idea was talked about for a long time. Eisenhower had traveled across the country as a young Army officer. He went from Washington, D.C., to San Francisco on a series of dirt roads. It took him two months to make the trip.

The United States needed a national interstate system in case the mainland was ever attacked. An uninterrupted system of roads would allow the military to move troops and equipment quickly.

After Eisenhower became president, he convinced Congress to fund the project. The government paid for most of the work. Interstates had to be at least two lanes in each direction. The roads had to handle speeds of 50 to 70 miles (80 to 112 km) per hour. The national system of roads that Eisenhower and others imagined is called the Dwight D. Eisenhower National System of Interstate and Defense Highways.

Scientists share ideas over the Internet. Sometimes this leads to new products or faster ways of doing things. Sharing infomation has made our economy grow.

People also move. Just like Julie and Biff, people move to where there are jobs. They also move to go to special schools. As people move, they bring new ideas with them.

Our Future

Throughout its history, America's economy has had times of growth and depression. Over the long run, however, the economy has grown.

By 2004, the United States' GDP, or *gross domestic product,* had reached about $10,756 trillion. The GDP is the value of all the goods and services in a nation. America's GDP was the largest in the world. It means that the United States is still a giant in agriculture, manufacturing, the production of natural resources, and newer industries such as services and high-tech.

What will our economy look like in the future? Economists, people who study the economy, tell us that the service industry will be very strong. High-tech businesses will be important.

The United States economy has changed with the times. Once, farms and factories made the economy grow. Today, the service and high-tech industries help make the economy strong. The United States' economy is the world's strongest.

Million, Billion, Trillion

What does a trillion look like? The United States' economy is measured in trillions of dollars.

A trillion looks like this:
1,000,000,000,000

The U.S. Gross Domstic Product in 2004 was $10,756,000,000,000!!

A container ship unloads in Los Angeles harbor. **What are some of our imports?**

Trading with the World

Foreign trade is the buying and selling of items between the United States and other countries. Look around your house. You will probably find many things made overseas.

What you may not see so easily are the products Americans sell, or *export.* For example, North Carolina exports medicines.

Our nation's biggest exports are transportation equipment, computers, chemicals, plastics, metals, and paper. We also export many agricultural products.

We also *import,* or buy from other countries. America imports many everyday items such as clothing, shoes, and toys. We buy TVs, DVD players, and many of our cars from other nations. We also import oil, iron,

steel, other metals, and chemical products. In the winter, much of our fruit and vegetables come from countries with warmer climates.

World Trade

Many large United States buinesses have locations in other countries. General Electric and IBM have offices and factories worldwide. In turn, foreign-owned companies have opened offices and factories here.

As you read in Chapter 12, the United States is linked with the economies of other nations. Trade policies such as NAFTA link us to our neighbors Canada and Mexico. More and more, the United States' economy is tied to the economies of the nations in North America and the world.

LESSON 2 REVIEW

Fact Follow-Up

1. What are high-technology industries?
2. What is the difference between a command economy and a free-enterprise system?
3. What are service industries?
4. What are our nation's most important exports?

Talk About It

1. Why is education more important today than ever before in our history?
2. Why do you think United States corporations open offices in other countries?
3. Should the United States import as much as it does? Explain your answer.

A Rich Land

 Caption Answer

Clothing, shoes, toys, and electronics

 Activity

Global Marketplace

OBJECTIVES: 5.01, 5.04, 5.07

Have students determine which country made each of the following items they have at home. If they cannot find a "Made in (country)" label on the item they should ask their family for help.

When students have compiled all of the data, they will plot the source countries of the different items on a world map. Each item will have a different colored sticky dot. (For example, car = red; a red dot will be placed on Germany if a student's car was made in Germany.)

Item	Prediction	Actual
television		
stereo		
camera		
watches		
car		
bicycle		
VCR		
computer		
clothes you're wearing		

LESSON 2 REVIEW

Fact Follow-Up Answers

1. High-technology industries are businesses that require specialized systems, such as computers, to make something.
2. In a command system, the government decides what should be made and said. In a free enterprise system, private people and businesses can decide what to make and sell.
3. Service industries are those employing workers who do things, or perform services, for other people (teachers, lawyers, doctors, nurses, salespersons, day-care and healthcare workers) or who provide special expertise that others do not have (researchers, computer programmers, consultants).
4. Our nation's biggest exports are transportation equipment, computers, measuring devices, chemicals, plastics, metals, and paper. We also export many agricultural products.

Talk About It Answers

1. High-technology industries need well-educated workers. Even jobs that are not considered to be high-tech now require that people know how to use computers and understand technical and sometimes complicated systems. As the economy changes in the future, Americans must be prepared to change jobs as old occupations disappear and new types of work are created.
2. These offices make it easier to deliver goods and services to people all over the world.
3. Important points: Students should take a position and explain it. Lead students to understand that products would not be imported if they could be produced as cheaply and efficiently in this country and that businesses choose to export products that may not be produced in other parts of the world (for example, the United States exports transportation equipment and computers).

OBJECTIVES: 1.06, 1.07, 4.07

Discussion Questions

1 What conflicts do you think arose between Native Americans and Europeans from these different ways of thinking about resources?

 Reading Strategy Activity

Story Mapping

OBJECTIVES: 1.01

Story Maps are used to extract main ideas under organized categories, framing topics in a visual, comprehensive way. Nonfiction writing, such as social studies or science, can be framed as well as fictional writing. When teaching a history lesson, the parts of the "map" could include the following:

• Historical event
• People or groups involved
• Setting (time and place)
• Problem
• Key events
• Resolution or outcome

After reading Lesson 3, Promises and Problems, the worksheet called "History Map" can be completed by filling in the graphic organizer. Student History Maps do not have to be identical. Some students may choose to focus on American Achievements, while others may write more about preserving wilderness and fighting pollution. If a more hands-on method is desired, have students fold a piece of construction paper into 6 parts. Label each section with the "map" parts listed above. Students may illustrate and display completed History Maps. Students may also want to compare maps in small groups, using peer review to check that main ideas have been identified.

LESSON ③ Promises and Problems

KEY IDEAS

• Changes in the uses of land changed air and water too, especially as cities and industries grew.

• Since the late nineteenth century, Americans have shown concern for protecting resources of air, land, and water.

• Cleaning up pollution and living with the changes to the environment are important issues.

KEY TERMS

Earth Day
ecology
Environmental Protection Agency (EPA)
global warming
National Park System
smog
spawn
recycling

Early Europeans discovered in North America a land of Native American villages. The Native Americans and Europeans had different ideas about land.

Native Americans lived by using resources on the land around them. They killed game and caught fish. They cleared land for farming. Native Americans lived lightly on the land. Most believed that they must not take too much from nature.

European settlers brought with them different ideas. They had crossed the ocean searching for new opportunities. They wanted to own the land. They wanted to build communities by using the many resources they found.

American Achievements

As you have read, the United States is a resource-rich nation. These resources have been used to support a growing population. They also have been used to improve our quality of life.

Most families in the United States make more money than families in other nations of North America. This is because of America's strong economy. Most Americans can afford healthy food and a place to live.

Healthcare

America's resources also have created a good health care system. In many Middle American countries, 22 to 72 babies out of every 1,000 die soon after birth. The infant death rate in the United States is 12 out of every 1,000. Our young people also may expect to live for a long

Chapter 13

Appalachian State University is one of the many universities in North Carolina. **Why is college education important?**

1 What advances have been made in the medical field that have helped to increase life expectancy? Has increasing life expectancy caused any problems? If so, how?

 Caption Answer

It opens the door to better jobs and opportunities. Students should provide other ideas as well.

time. People born in these times generally live until they are almost eighty years old. Among our neighbors, only Canadians live as long.

Educating Everyone

When America was founded, only the very wealthy sent their children to school. Often they had private tutors. Usually only boys were educated.

Public Schools The first American public school was created in 1643 by the town of Dedham in the Massachusetts Bay Colony. Later, Virginia's constitution required the legislature to "provide for a system of free public elementary and secondary schools for all children of school age."

Americans believed that being able to read, write, and do math was important. Freed slaves and immigrants valued their education. Many times education included learning a trade.

By the twentieth century most children went to elementary school. But by the time World War II ended, most children completed high school. As you read in Chapter 12,

desegregation brought better education to African Americans.

Colleges and Universties The colonies also saw a need for higher education. Colleges trained ministers and lawyers. Harvard College (now Harvard Univeristy) was founded in 1636.

The University of North Carolina was the first public, state-run university. It was created by the state assembly in 1789. Building it in Chapel Hill began in 1793.

In the 1800s, colleges in the West gave more opportunities to women and African Americans. Many Eastern schools would not allow them to attend.

Congress passed the G.I. Bill of Rights in 1944. This let World War II veterans go to college and graduate school. Most of these people could not have afforded college before the war. This opened the door for many to better jobs in business, law, and medicine. Desegregation of colleges and universities in the 1960s again opened doors to African Americans.

A Rich Land

335

Yellowstone National Park is home to different types of wildlife. **Why does the government create national parks?**

 Caption Answer

To protect special areas of land

 Activity

National Parks

 **OBJECTIVES:** 1.06, 1.07, 4.03

Divide the students into groups to research three men who are associated with National Parks: Teddy Roosevelt, John Muir, and Ansel Adams. Why would we remember each of these men when thinking about national parks? Ask students to decide with which man they are more closely aligned, and why?

Search for names of national parks from each of the five regions of the United States. Create a wall chart that tells facts about each park: where it is located (state and region), when it was founded, why it was founded (as a preservation, recreation, or historic site), how large it is, numbers of visitors each year, and other interesting facts. Interested students could add their original art to decorate the wall chart.

Extension Have students survey classes in the school (some or all) to see the percentage of people in your school who have actually visited each park included on your wall chart.

336

Chapter 13

Future Challenges

Our nation used its vast resources to achieve health, educate its people, and grow the economy. To support the growing population, sometimes people or businesses damaged the land. Sometimes they wasted resources. Now we try to take better care of nature's gifts while improving the quality of life for all.

Preserving Wilderness

John Muir loved America's wilderness. In 1892, he founded the Sierra Club to "do something for wildness." During a camping trip he asked President Theodore Roosevelt to set protect forests from being destroyed.

Roosevelt loved the outdoors. But he also knew that the United States needed to use its resources wisely. He preserved a number of forests. Yet he also believed lumber companies and farmers should be able to use the forests to cut timber or grow crops.

National Parks

Other government lands began to be set aside for protection. These were soon called national parks.

Yellowstone became the world's first national park in 1872. Congress set aside more than 2 million acres in Idaho, Wyoming, and Montana to protect the geysers, waterfalls, canyons, and wildlife of the region.

Congress created the *National Park System* in 1916. There are now 390 places protected by the National Park Service. Eighty million acres of wilderness and historic sites are protected.

Other Protected Land

Millions of acres, mainly in the West, are controlled by other parts of the national government. The Fish and Wildlife Service's 96 million acres protect animals' habitats and migration routes. The Bureau of Land Management oversees 261 million acres. The Forest Service runs 155 national forests. These agencies allow some logging and mining companies, ranchers, and others to use the land.

Customs

Earth Day is celebrated annually in April. It is one way Americans show their concern about the environment. Schools and local governments plan events to show the importance of caring for the environment. We are learning to reduce the amount of waste thrown away. Schools teach us to reuse things instead of throwing them away, and to recycle plastic, glass, paper, and metal.

John Muir (right) convinced President Theodore Roosevelt (left) to preserve "wildness" by protecting forest land. **How does the government preserve wilderness today?**

A Rich Land

337

Discussion Questions

1 Why is it important to preserve natural forests? What can we do to help protect the natural environment?

 Caption Answer

The National Park System preserves about 80 million acres of wilderness. The Fish and Wildlife Service protects animals' habitats and migration routes. The Bureau of Land Management administers 261 million acres. The United States Forest Service runs 195 national forests.

 Research Activity

Conservation and National Parks

OBJECTIVES: 1.06, 1.07, 4.03

Students will research the following topics and share their findings with the class.
1. Theodore Roosevelt—the conservation president. Find out what Roosevelt did to ensure that the landscape of America would be preserved for future generations. What is a national park? What was the first national park? What national park is nearest to where you live? What activity did President Roosevelt enjoy, which led to his creating the national park system?
2. John Muir—Muir Woods. Who was John Muir? What did he do to support the national park program? What is Muir Woods? Where is it?
3. National Parks—A Gift to the Future of America. What is the definition of a national park? What restrictions are placed on the use of its land and resources? How many national parks are there? When was each park set aside? What state has the most national parks? How many states share national parks? Where are those parks that cross state lines?

Discussion Questions

1 What types of pollution problems still exist? What can the citizens of our country do to help solve these problems?

2 What types of places are most likely to have a problem with smog? Why?

 Caption Answer

Answers will vary. Recycling and conserving energy and water are possible answers.

 Teacher Notes

A Book that Made A Difference

In the history of environmentalism, Rachel Carson's *Silent Spring* played roughly the same role that Harriet Beecher Stowe's *Uncle Tom's Cabin* played in the history of the abolitionist movement. One important manifestation of the book's impact was the 1970 passage of the National Environmental Policy Act (NEPA).

Immediately following passage of the NEPA, on April 22, 1970, the first Earth Day celebration brought 20 million Americans out into the spring sunshine for peaceful demonstrations in favor of environmental reform. The phenomenal success of Earth Day gave greater priority than ever to environmental issues. That prioritization eventually led to the creation of the Environmental Protection Agency in December of 1970.

 Activity

Literature Seminar

OBJECTIVES: 3.02, 3.05, 6.04

Brother Eagle, Sister Sky, paintings by Susan Jeffers (Penguin Putnam, 1991. ISBN 0803709692.)

Brother Eagle, Sister Sky is a book that translates Chief Seattle's famous message into a beautiful picture book. After reading the book, conduct a seminar with students using the following questions:

1. Chief Seattle said, "We are part of the

Pollution

The United States had begun to be polluted long before the government began to protect our land, water, and air. Cities were choked with the smoke of factories. Streets were filled with horse and cow manure. People heated their homes and cooked their food with wood and coal stoves.

As industry grew, pollution grew. One famous river, the Cuyahoga in Cleveland, Ohio, was so full of oil and chemicals that it often caught fire. The shores of the Great Lakes were full of dead fish. They were killed by pollution dumped into the lakes. The air in many cities was so dirty that laundry hung outside in the morning was dark with gritty dirt by evening. Farmers used chemicals to kill diseases and insects that hurt their crops.

Finally, Americans began to see what was happening. The author Rachel Carson sounded an alarm with her book *Silent Spring* in 1962. *Silent Spring* showed that some chemicals used to kill bugs and insects on crops were doing more harm than good. The chemicals got into the water and killed fish, birds, and other wildlife. Because of Carson's book and other studies, the government banned the use of the dangerous chemical DDT.

Over the next two decades, Americans learned with horror that poisons in the air and in the water were causing serious illnesses. The poisons came from the trash from factories or from the chemicals sprayed on crops.

Rachel Carson's Silent Spring *helped awaken citizens to the effects of chemicals on the environment.* **What are ways that you daily protect the environment?**

What would YOU do?

In parts of the Northwest, dams have been built to harness electricity and provide water for irrigation and drinking. Some dams prevent salmon from swimming upstream to **spawn,** or lay their eggs. Experts have found that the numbers of salmon have dropped since the dams were built. Imagine you are in charge of figuring out a way to modify the dams to get the salmon past them to their spawning grounds. What would you do?

Americans also began to worry about the waste from nuclear power plants. Such waste, if not handled correctly, can cause terrible problems for many, many years.

Ecology

All over the country, Americans began to think about the environment. People began to learn about **ecology.** That is the study of the way plants and animals relate to one another and to the environment.

In 1970, the government created the **Environmental Protection Agency (EPA).** Its job is to protect the environment and help clean up pollution.

People began to look for ways to fix some of the damage from pollution. Although we have made great progress in cleaning up, there is still plenty of work to do.

Smog

One of the most difficult pollution problems is **smog.** The word smog is a combination of two words: smoke and fog. Smog is like smoky fog.

Smog is made when warm, dry air high above the ground traps cooler air underneath it. The cooler air collects polluted air, like factory smoke or the exhaust, or air, from a car's engine. Until automobile exhaust is clean, pollution will remain a problem.

Earth and it is part of us." What does this mean to you?

2. How can eagles be our brothers and "perfumed flowers" be our sisters?

3. Seattle said, "The shining water that moves in the streams and rivers is not simply water, but the blood of your grandfather's grandfather." How can that be?

4. How can we "keep the land and air apart and sacred"?

5. Explain what Chief Seattle means: "The Earth does not belong to us. We belong to the Earth."

6. Chief Seattle said "What befalls the Earth befalls the sons and daughters of the Earth." What is "befalling" us today?

7. "It will be the end of living, and the beginning of survival." What is the difference between living and survival?

8. "This we know: All things are connected like the blood that unites us. We did not weave the web of life, we are merely a strand in it. Whatever we do to the web, we do to ourselves." How can we help the "web" endure in a healthy way? What kind of strand are you? A weak one or a strong one

 Caption Answer

Acid Rain

OBJECTIVES: 1.05, 1.06, 1.07

Have the students research acid rain by using encyclopedias, books, and the Internet. Have them compile a class report or chart of their findings about harmful effects, the causes, and what can be done to combat the effects.

Ask students to design a rain catcher for this activity. It should have a container of clear plastic that is unused and has been rinsed with distilled water. Remind students that the rainwater does not have to be measured or collected in great quantities.

Over a period of a month, have students collect rain samples from your schoolyard, their neighborhoods, and parents' place of work. Use ph (litmus) paper and accompanying scales to determine acidity of rain in each area. Numbers of 5 and lower are considered acidic.

Students should attempt to determine the causes of acidity in different parts of the city. Local power plants might be able to provide information about the source of electrical power (Was use of coal a factor?).

Chart and/or graph the data to compare the areas where samples were taken. Write letters to legislators explaining the class's findings and asking for their help in solving this problem.

Pollution choked the air of Pittsburgh and other cities during the nineteenth and early twentieth centuries. Pollution is still a problem, as shown above (inset) by the Exxon Valdez oil spill in Alaska. **What forms of pollution are found today?**

A Rich Land

339

 Science Activity

Global Warming

OBJECTIVES: 1.05, 1.06, 1.07

Have the students research Global Warming. A good place to start is the Union of Concerned Scientists educator resources Web page (link found at **NCJourneys.com**). Have students research the changes in the earth's temperature over the past century. They can use this data to make a spreadsheet and sort it by year and by temperature.

Students should note any trends they see in the data and write a short paragraph interpreting what they believe the data means.

Also, have students research the causes of global warming and related terms, such as renewable energy and energy footprint. Divide the class into six cooperative groups. Have each group research a different energy form: coal, oil, solar, nuclear, wind, and biofuels. Each group should identify ways in which this energy source contributes to or can help address global warming. Each group should present their findings to the class.

Caption Answer

Answers will vary. Look into local celebrations.

Research Activity

Clean Water Act

OBJECTIVES: 1.06, 1.07, 3.03

Have students research the Clean Water Act of 1965 and the formation of the Environmental Protection Agency. Ask students if they feel that water pollution of this magnitude is still an issue (examples: recent hog waste spills in North Carolina; raw sewage leaks in North Carolina, sewage being dumped into the Pacific; "un-surfable" water in Southern California; oil spills in Alaska and Scotland; Chernobyl; and Three Mile Island). Discuss the difference between point-source pollution (like the examples listed above) and nonpoint-source pollution (caused by difficult to pin-point sources, such as fertilizer and insecticide runoff).

Have students write to the EPA and/or other organizations for current information regarding our streams, rivers, and coastal waters. Research can be done on the river keepers of the United States as well.

Schoolchildren observe Earth Day at Blue Jay Point in Wake County, North Carolina. They examine water for insect life to test its quality. **What do you do on Earth Day?**

Global Warming

The earth has warmed by about 1°F over the past century. Many of the worlds scientists think that things people do are making the earth warmer.

Greenhouse Effect Scientists know that the greenhouse effect is happening. Gases in the air, like carbon dioxide, are increasing. Burning fossil fuels, for example, puts carbon dioxide into the air. Carbon dioxide is one kind of greenhouse gas. Greenhouse gases make the earth warmer by trapping the sun's warmth and energy.

Global Warming is the average increase in the earth's temperature. The warmer temperature causes changes in climate. A warmer earth may lead to other changes, too. Things like more rain in certain places, a rise in sea level, and other changes to plants, wildlife, and humans might happen. When scientists talk about the issue of climate change, their concern is about global warming caused by human activities.

Reduce, Reuse, Recycle

Young people all across the United States share the chore of taking out the trash. Many experts worry that soon we will run out of places to put it all. The average American throws away about 1,000 pounds of trash each year. That is close to 4 pounds (1.8 kilograms) of trash every day.

Recycling is one way to reduce this huge trash pile. Glass, steel, iron, tin, aluminum, paper, and plastic can be reused.

Many Americans are working hard to find ways to make a cleaner environment. Many of our rivers are cleaner. The air over many of our cities is clearer. No one, however, thinks the job is done.

LESSON 3 REVIEW

Fact Follow-Up
1. What is ecology?
2. What age do Americans generally live to be?
3. What is global warming?
4. Why did Americans establish public schools and colleges?

Talk About It
1. Why do we need the National Park System? Explain.
2. Describe the effects of Rachel Carson's book *Silent Spring*.
3. Why is recycling important?

340

LESSON 3 REVIEW

Fact Follow-Up Answers
1. Ecology is the study of the way plants and animals relate to one another and to the environment.
2. Americans generally live to be almost eighty years old.
3. Global warming is the average increase in the earth's temperature. Scientists think it is caused by the rise of greenhouse gasses, like carbon dioxide.
4. Since colonial times, Americans believed that being able to read, write, and do math was important. Schools also helped people learn trades.

Talk About It Answers
1. We need the National Park System to protect lands that are important because they are home to wildlife or resources important to the United States.
2. The book made many more Americans aware of the effects of poisons used to kill insects. As a result of the book, the government banned the use of the chemical DDT.
3. It keeps landfills from growing too large. It also conserves important resources.

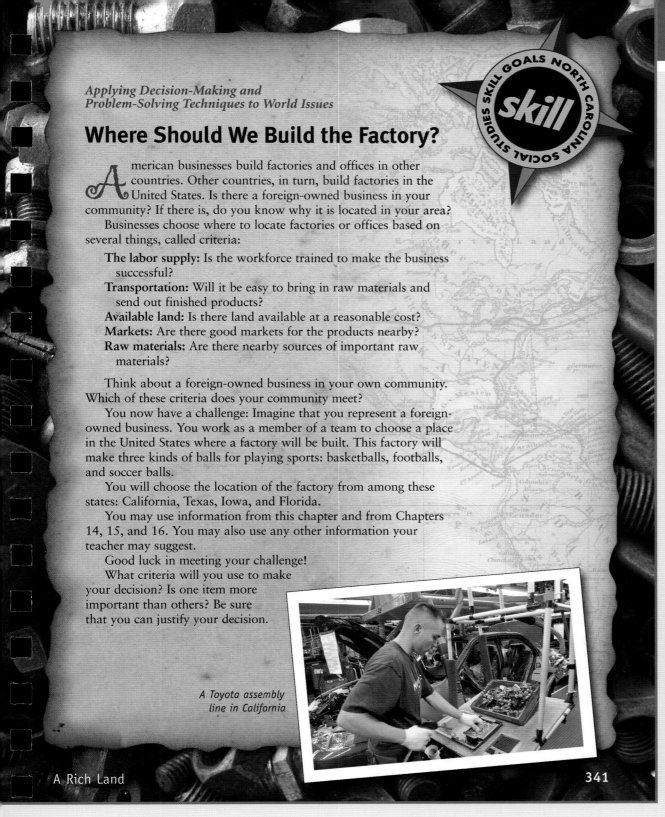

Applying Decision-Making and Problem-Solving Techniques to World Issues

Where Should We Build the Factory?

American businesses build factories and offices in other countries. Other countries, in turn, build factories in the United States. Is there a foreign-owned business in your community? If there is, do you know why it is located in your area?

Businesses choose where to locate factories or offices based on several things, called criteria:

The labor supply: Is the workforce trained to make the business successful?

Transportation: Will it be easy to bring in raw materials and send out finished products?

Available land: Is there land available at a reasonable cost?

Markets: Are there good markets for the products nearby?

Raw materials: Are there nearby sources of important raw materials?

Think about a foreign-owned business in your own community. Which of these criteria does your community meet?

You now have a challenge: Imagine that you represent a foreign-owned business. You work as a member of a team to choose a place in the United States where a factory will be built. This factory will make three kinds of balls for playing sports: basketballs, footballs, and soccer balls.

You will choose the location of the factory from among these states: California, Texas, Iowa, and Florida.

You may use information from this chapter and from Chapters 14, 15, and 16. You may also use any other information your teacher may suggest.

Good luck in meeting your challenge!

What criteria will you use to make your decision? Is one item more important than others? Be sure that you can justify your decision.

A Toyota assembly line in California

A Rich Land

341

Skill Lesson Review

1. Was it equally easy to work with all five criteria? Explain. *Encourage students to discuss their use of the criteria, focusing on any difficulties and the reasons behind them.*

2. Was one criterion more important than others in making your decision? Explain. *Encourage student responses and explanations.*

3. Would more information have been helpful in making your decision? If so, what kinds of information would have helped? *Encourage student discussion.*

Teaching This Skill Lesson

Materials Needed textbooks, paper, pencils; reference materials such as almanacs, atlases, encyclopedias; information about Texas, Iowa, California, and Florida from Internet sites for those states; overhead projector with markers

Classroom Organization whole class, small groups

Beginning the Lesson Ask students if they know of any foreign-owned businesses in their community. (Most communities in North Carolina have at least one foreign-owned business!) Ask students why businesses from other countries might locate a factory in North Carolina. Accept responses, listing them on the chalkboard. Tell students they will be choosing the location for a foreign-owned business in the United States.

Lesson Development Refer to the list on the chalkboard as you discuss the five criteria on page 341 with students. Students will be choosing a location to manufacture sports balls and they will be looking at California, Florida, Iowa, and Texas.

Divide class into four or eight committees, one or two for each state. These committees are to look for information about the criteria using the reference works. (If you use eight committees, you will need to allow time for the one or two state committees to meet and finalize their reports.) *It is very important that the committees focus on the five criteria.*

Conclusion Once the committees have done their work, have each committee report to the class. Take notes on the presentations using the overhead projector and a simple data retrieval chart. Once all student groups have presented their reports, discuss their findings using the five criteria. If desired, have students choose one of the four states, giving reasons for their choice.

Extension If there is an "industry hunter" at your local chamber of commerce (in smaller towns, the industry hunter is usually the chamber of commerce executive), invite this person to the students' reporting session and have him or her comment on the work students have done.

CHAPTER 13 REVIEW

Talk About It

1. Important points: Encourage students to suggest as many differences as they can. Among the differences are these: more travel by automobile and truck, less use of railroads for transportation, the creation of new transportation hubs as interstate highways connect.
2. Important points: Encourage students' responses, leading them to focus on changes to the physical environment over time.
3. High-technology machines allow fewer workers to produce more goods. Workers of the future will need to be well educated to use new machines and to adapt to changing jobs from time to time.
4. Important points: Students' responses should mention cutting down forests, damming rivers and steams, using mechanized equipment in agriculture, building transportation systems (e.g., railroads, roads and highways, airports, and the service facilities to support them), mining, industrialization, and pollution.

Mastering Mapwork

1. The Great Plains lie in the midsection of the United States and stretch from Canada in the north to Mexico in the south. They lie between the Rocky Mountains to the west and the Central Lowlands to the east.
2. The Appalachian Mountains, the Piedmont, and the Atlantic Coastal Plain lie in North Carolina.
3. The Great Basin lies in the western United States between the Sierra Nevada to the west and the Rocky Mountains to the east.
4. The Coastal Range, the Central Valley, and the Sierra Nevada lie in California.
5. The Ozark Plateau
6. The Brooks Range stretches across northern Alaska.
7. The Coastal Range and the Sierra Nevada lie south of the Cascade Range.
8. The Gulf Coastal Plain lies along the Gulf of Mexico.

Lessons Learned

LESSON 1
A Vast and Varied Land
Most of the states of the United States are contiguous. Alaska and Hawaii are not. All of the world's climate types can be found in the United States. The varied climates in the United States allow all kinds of vegetation to grow here. Minerals and other resources make the United States a rich land.

LESSON 2
Modern Economy and Agriculture
The United States' economy is a system of free enterprise. It includes the manufacturing, high-technology, agricultural, and service industries. Today, many industries can produce more goods and services with fewer people. American businesses trade with countries all over the world.

LESSON 3
Promises and Problems
The United States has good health care and educational systems. Protecting wilderness is a challenge. Americans now work harder to protect the environment.

Becoming Better Readers

Students should note that the three main features are: climate, vegetation, and natural resources.

Talk About It

1. How do you think the United States might be different without the interstate highway system?
2. How is the story of the United States a story of environmental change?
3. How is it possible to produce more goods with fewer workers? What does this mean for the workers of the future?
4. Native Americans lived lightly on the land. European settlers wanted to build communities by using the plentiful resources they found. How did they change our environment?

Mastering Mapwork

LOCATIONS
Use the map on page 319 and the map on page 682 in the atlas to answer the following questions.

1. Describe the relative location of the Great Plains.
2. Which three physical features noted on this map lie in North Carolina?
3. Describe the relative location of the Great Basin.
4. Which three physical features noted on this map lie in California?
5. What plateau is located between the Central Lowlands and the Gulf Coastal Plain?
6. Describe the relative location of the Brooks Range in Alaska.
7. Which two mountain ranges lie roughly south of the Cascade Range?
8. Which landform identified on the map lies along the Gulf of Mexico?

Becoming Better Readers

More on Main Idea
Good readers are continually looking for ways to remember what they read. One way to do this is by mapping out the information. You make a graphic organizer by writing the main idea in the center and then writing the details around the main idea. In Lesson 1, the main idea is "A Vast and Varied Land." What are the three main features that make the United States vast and varied?

Go to the Source

Understanding Culture Through Art

Study and compare the two paintings below. Answer the questions based on what you see in the artwork.

Christina's World by *Andrew Wyeth*

100 Cans by *Andy Warhol*

Go to the Source

Questions

1. What is happening in Andrew Wyeth's painting?
2. What effect is created by Warhol's painting?
3. Andy Warhol's painting *100 Cans* turns advertising into art. Where else can we see art in everyday things?
4. Both of these paintings were done in the twentieth century. What do they say about modern American life?
5. List the differences you notice about the two styles of the paintings.

A Rich Land

343

Go to the Source

Understanding Culture Through Art

OBJECTIVES: 3.07

SOCIAL STUDIES SKILLS: 3.05, 4.02

Wyeth has said that he "happen[s] to paint things that reflect the basic truths of life: sky, earth, friends, the intimate things." *Christina's World* (1948) is Wyeth's most famous work and one of the best-known twentieth-century American paintings.

Warhol defined the pop art genre. His repetition of images, such as *100 Cans* (1967), represents modern commercialization and manufactured "sameness". He shows objects in simple form where the concept behind the image is more important than the image itself.

Answers

1. The young woman is sitting in a field looking at her house in the country.
2. Possible answers: The viewer will remember the product because of the image; it represents how advertising influences the consumer. The wall of cans remind us that we live in a world of advertising.
3. Important points: Today all commercial products, from cars to toothpaste tubes, are designed, and thus can all be considered art. Students may also point out that there is beauty in all things.
4. Possible answers: Wyeth's painting could remind us that we are part of nature or that we long to go back to a time when we were closer to nature; we like the wide open spaces of the country. Warhol's painting may remind us of the busy, modern world we live in, where we are surrounded by information, advertising, and technology.
5. Possible answers: landscape and people versus objects/things, imagination versus real things, traditional art versus pop art

---

How to Use the Chapter Review

There are four sections in the Chapter Review: Talk About It, Mastering Mapwork, Becoming Better Readers, and Go to the Source. Use the Vocabulary Worksheets and the Chapter Review Worksheet in the Teacher's Resource Guide for additional reinforcement and preparation for the Chapter Assessments. The Chapter and Lesson Reviews and the Chapter Review Worksheets are the basis of the assessment for each chapter.

Talk About It questions encourage students to speculate about the content of the chapter and are suitable for class or small-group discussion. They are not intended to be assigned for homework.

Mastering Mapwork has students apply one or more of the Five Themes of Geography to maps within the chapter.

Becoming Better Readers focuses on building reading strategy skills necessary for reading comprehension in the content areas.

Go to the Source activities allow students to analyze a primary source that relates to the content of the chapter. The questions and activities familiarize students with different types of primary sources and also build content-reading skills.

Eastern Regions of the United States

Social Studies Strands

Geographic Relationships

Economics and Development

Culture and Diversity

Historical Perspectives

Technological Influences and Society

North Carolina Standard Course of Study

Goal 3 The learner will apply key geographic concepts to the United States and other countries of North America.

Goal 3 The learner will examine the roles various ethnic groups have played in the development of the United States and its neighboring countries.

Goal 5 The learner will evaluate ways the United States and other countries of North America make decisions about the allocation and use of economic resources.

Goal 6 The learner will recognize how technology has influenced change within the United States and other countries in North America.

Teaching & Assessment

• English Language Learner Modified Lesson Plans for this chapter are found in the Teacher's Resource Guide.

• *ExamView® Assessment Suite* is provided at **NCJourneys.com.** It includes customizable assessments for all chapters. Paper tests are also available in the Teacher's Resource Guide. See pages T16–T17 for information about how to use the assessments and the Scoring Guide.

Worksheets

Worksheets and answer keys are found both in the Teacher's Resource Guide and at **NCJourneys.com**, including Reading Guides, Reading Strategies, Chapter Reviews, English Language Learner and others.

Activities and Integrations

SOCIAL STUDIES

▲ ■ Activator: Suitcase, p. 344
Major Regions Book Fairs, p. 345
● ▲ ■ Lobsters, p. 350
● ▲ Maple Syrup, p. 350
Regional Experts, p. 353
Quartering a State, p. 354
Skill Lesson: Region, p. 363
Photo-Journaling Before and After, p. 360

READING/LANGUAGE ARTS

	READING/LANGUAGE ARTS OBJECTIVES
★ Urban vs. Rural, p. 344B	1.02, 3.02
▲ ■ Regional Recipes, p. 344B	2.03
▲ ■ Problem Based Learning: City Issues, p. 345B	3.01
Writing Prompt: Four Seasons, p. 344	3.01
Reading Strategy: Using Headers to Find Details, p. 346	1.03, 1.05
★ Northeastern History, p. 348	3.02, 3.06
Reading Strategy: Finding Details, p. 352	4.02
● Haiku Poetry, p. 355	4.03, 4.07
Reading Strategy: Two Column Notes, p. 357	2.01, 2.02
● A North Carolina Diamante, p. 358	4.07
Becoming Better Readers, p. 364	2.01
Reading a Recipe, p. 365	2.02

TECHNOLOGY

	TECHNOLOGY OBJECTIVES
★ ■ City Issues, p. 345B	2.13
Carolina Connection: The Appalachian Trail, p. 345	2.13
Virtual New England, p. 348	213
Washington, D.C., p. 354	2.13
Hurricane Stories, p. 361	2.13

VISUAL ARTS

	VISUAL ARTS OBJECTIVES
● ▲ ■ Symbolic Flags, p. 345B	2.01, 3.02
Regions of the United States Micro Skit, p. 351	1.06 2.05 2.07 (theatre)
Song of the South, p. 357	9.03, 9.04, 9.05 (music)
Music of the Southeast, p. 359	9.03, 9.04 (music)
Southeastern Products, p. 362	2.01, 3.02

CHARACTER AND VALUES EDUCATION

	TRAITS
What Would You Do?, p. 359	kindness

● Basic Activities   ★ Challenging Activities   ▲ English Language Learner Novice   ■ English Language Learner Intermediate

Introductory Activity

Urban vs. Rural

OBJECTIVES: 1.06, 4.02, 4.07

To introduce the concepts of urban and rural living, read the picture book *City Mouse, Country Mouse* by Isabelle Chantellard (Abbeville Press, 1999. ISBN 0789205130.).

Divide the class into cooperative groups and have them use a graphic organizer such as a Venn diagram or T-chart to compare urban and rural living. Each group will share their graphic organizer with the rest of the class. Make a large class diagram displaying all the information as it is shared. Assign each group an urban or rural environment. Each group is to design or create the "perfect" urban or rural community. Assign a region in the United States where this community will be located. Their final products need to include a map and model or poster of the community. An oral presentation explaining the choices they have made will be required. Students need to base choices on location, resources, climate, and other factors.

Culminating Activity

Regional Recipes

OBJECTIVES: 1.02, 1.03, 1.06

After studying the Northeast and Southeast regions, ask your students to work in small groups to research recipes from different areas: New England, the Mid-Atlantic, or Southeast. Each group can then produce its own regional cookbook,

complete with illustrations for the recipes showing scenes from that particular area.

Extension Choose recipes from each region and set aside time to sample them. Novice ELL students can learn or review food vocabulary by making a mini-book. A few terms for quantities can be included.

Art Activity

Symbolic Flags

OBJECTIVES: 3.03, 4.02, 4.07

Driving through neighborhoods in America, one may see decorative flags displayed on porches of homes. Students will create a decorative flag symbolic of a given state in the eastern regions. This project can be a group, a pair, or an individual assignment. Assign each student or group a state of the eastern regions of the United States. After researching the state, the students will design a flag that is the best representation of that state.

Suggested materials for a flag include paper, felt, muslin, or any other fabric. Ask parents to donate fabric, fabric paints, or thread. Connect flag to a long dowel stick. Display around the room or hang in halls.

Extension ELL students can work with a partner or in a small group

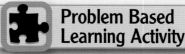

Problem Based Learning Activity

City Issues

OBJECTIVES: 1.05, 4.02, 4.07

Situation There are many busy cities and towns up and down the East coast. As time goes on these cities continue to grow and prosper.

Task The class should name seven major cities located in the eastern regions. Divide the class into groups to research these cities using the Internet. Students might also look up articles in the cities' newspapers. Next, the group should categorize and discuss the current issues of their city, answering the questions below. Finally, groups should propose growth plans in a poster format for their cities.
- What is the name of your city? In which region is this city located?
- What interesting facts have you found about your city? What kinds of assets/benefits does your city have to offer? Why would you like to visit the city, or why might a family want to live there?
- What problems might your city have (traffic, crime, politics, water/natural resources and so on). Based on your research, has growth had a negative or positive impact upon the city? How might you, as a city manager, plan ahead for future growth? What kinds of things would you need to consider?

Reflection How does the growth of cities impact the education of students there? Is this a good thing or a bad thing? How does continual growth help you as a student in the Southeast? What might the impact be for you as a student or individual?

Extension Provide novice ELL students with a copy of a simple map showing the states and big cities of the regions. You or a classmate can use gestures, point clearly to a city and state, and say slowly, "Charlotte is a big city in North Carolina." The sentence is to be written on the board as a sample for students to copy later. A second example may be necessary for a student to understand what he or she needs to do. Once this is done orally a few times, have students write the sentences and color the map.

Teaching Strategies

Set up a resource center for your classroom that includes books, pictures, posters, artifacts, and so on. This will help students gain a better understanding of the regions found in this chapter.

Use graphic organizers to help student compare and contrast the eastern regions of the United States. Invite speakers from different states to give presentations on what it is like in their region.

Discussion Questions

1 Do you have relatives from other regions of the United States who call everyday items by different names? Does this cause confusion, puzzlement, or maybe even laughter?

2 In which region is North Carolina located?

3 Which two states are not contiguous?

4 Have you visited any other region in the United States? If so, which one?

Activator

 OBJECTIVES: 1.02, 3.03, 4.02

Bring in a suitcase with items from the eastern regions of the United States. Prepare name cards for all of the items. Prepare a chart divided into three sections with the following headings: New England, Mid-Atlantic, and Southeast. Take out one item at a time from the suitcase. Students are to guess which region the item is from and come to a consensus. Place the item card under the correct region on the chart. Once you have taken every item out of the suitcase and have placed the cards under the headings, share the correct answers with the students.

Writing Prompt

OBJECTIVES: 1.02, 1.03

Clarification
Using the four seasons, describe New England in four different ways. Create a spreadsheet or chart and present it to the class.

Extension ELL students should use the worksheet in the Teacher's Resource Guide.

CHAPTER 14

Enjoying ice cream in Pennsylvania

Chapter Preview

LESSON 1
The Northeast Region: New England
The states of Maine, New Hampshire, Vermont, Massachusetts, Rhode Island, and Connecticut make up New England.

LESSON 2
The Northeast Region: The Mid-Atlantic
The region is made up of New York, New Jersey, Pennsylvania, Delaware, Maryland, and the District of Columbia.

LESSON 3
The Southeast Region
Virginia, West Virginia, Kentucky, Tennessee, North Carolina, South Carolina, Georgia, Florida, Alabama, Mississippi, Louisiana, and Arkansas are the states of the Southeast.

344

Eastern Regions of the United States

What do you call the small candies sprinkled on ice cream cones? In different places of the United States, they are called jimmies, ants, sprinkles, dots, or nonpareils. What do you call a carbonated drink? Soda? Pop? Soft drink? Tonic?

Different regions of the United States use different words to describe everyday things. Regions are places on the earth that share common features. Language and words like soda or tonic are one of those features.

In the next three chapters, you will discover other features each of our nation's regions have in common.

The Appalachian Trail

Chapter Resources

Print Resources
Northeast
Carrick, Carol. *Whaling Days.* Clarion Books, 1993. ISBN 0395509483

Fendler, Donn. *Lost on a Mountain in Maine.* Beech Tree Books, 1992. ISBN 068811573X.

Martin, Jacqueline Briggs. *Snowflake Bentley.* Houghton Mifflin, Boston. 1998. ISBN 0395861624.

St. Antoine, Sara, ed. *The North Atlantic Coast.* Milkweed Editions, 2000. ISBN 1571316272.

Mid-Atlantic
Bial, Raymond. *Amish Home.* Houghton Mifflin Co., 1993. ISBN 0395720214.

Cheripko, Jan. *Voices of the River: Adventures on the Delaware.* Boyds Mills Press, 1996. ISBN 1563976226.

Jakobsen, Kathy. *My New York.* Little Brown & Co, 1993. ISBN 0316456535.

Lourie, Peter. *Hudson River: An Adventure*

United States—Major Regions

Legend:
- Northeast: New England
- Northeast: The Mid–Atlantic
- Southeast
- Midwest
- Southwest
- Rocky Mountains
- Pacific Coast
- Alaska
- Hawaii

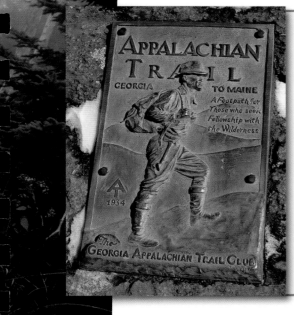

The Appalachian Trail

What is a valley road, a mountain footpath, a field, and a city street all at the same time? The Appalachian Trail!

The trail runs more than 2,000 miles (3,220 km) through the eastern United States. It starts at Spring Mountain in Georgia. It runs through the North Carolina mountains to the peak of Mount Katahdin in Maine.

Parts of the trail are hiked by nearly 40,000 people a year. A few hikers start out from Georgia in early March, intending to hike all the way to Maine before winter. Most of them reach the North Carolina mountains in time to see the mountain laurels bloom in April.

345

Map Activity

Major Regions Book Fair

NATIONAL GEOGRAPHY STANDARDS: 3, 4, 5, 6, 7, 8

GEOGRAPHIC THEMES: Region

OBJECTIVES: 1.03, 1.07

Ask the students if they have ever been to a fair where livestock was shown. The animals are judged and a winner is chosen in different animal groups. Students will pretend that they are from different regions in the country and are going to "show" a book. Divide students into nine groups (one for each region). Have students individually research to find an outstanding book with the same setting as their region. The setting needs to be a very strong part of the story—not just a backdrop. Students can "show" their book however they choose, but the setting should be related to how they show their book. Have the students make their presentations regionally and then review the like characteristics of those books' settings.

Activity

Carolina Connection: The Appalachian Trail

OBJECTIVES: 1.06, 3.03, 4.02

The Appalachian Trail home page is a great site to jump off into an Appalachian Trail simulation. For a link to this site go to **NCJourneys.com** Show students the online maps of the trail and how to access information regarding the 14 states the trail passes through. Share the hikers' journals that can be accessed from the Appalachian Trail home page.

Divide the class into 14 groups. Each group will take a virtual tour of one state from the information posted at the clickable links. Students will then write interesting journal entries about their trek.

From the Mountains to the Sea. Syracuse University Press, 1999. ISBN 0815603169.

Southeast

Burch, Robert. *Ida Early Comes Over the Mountain.* Puffin. ISBN 0140345345.

Craighead, Jean. *Everglades.* Scott Foresman, 1997. ISBN 0064461947.

Sterling, Dorothy. *Freedom Train: The Story of Harriet Tubman.* Econo-Clad Books, 1998. ISBN 0808580345.

Audiovisual

The Northeast: People and Places. Humanities Extension/Publications, North Carolina State University. 27 minutes.

New Orleans. International Video Network (IVN.com).

The Southeast: People and Places. Humanities Extension/Publications, North Carolina State University. 33 minutes.

Washington, D.C. International Video Network.

LESSON 1 The Northeast Region: New England

 **OBJECTIVES:** 1.02,1.03, 3.03, 5.07

Discussion Questions

1 What are some possible reasons that this area is called "New England"?

2 What is the main crop farmed in this region?

 **Caption Answer**

The land is mountainous and the soil is thin and rocky, which makes it unsuitable for farming.

Reading Strategy Activity

Using Headers to Find Details

 **OBJECTIVES:** 1.02, 1.03, 3.03, 5.07

Details are the facts that help readers understand the main idea of each lesson. They are the parts that give meaning. The author of the text wants students to understand and learn as much as they can about the topic, so many details are given.

When reading a lesson, students should search for the main idea. Detail questions are the easiest questions to answer. They should simply read the subheadings until the section the question is about is found. Then they should skim the section. Explain that skimming is reading quickly, searching for the answer.

The trick to skimming for answers is to look for the main words in the question. Ask students to consider the question "What is the climate of New England?" What words are most important in this question? New England and climate are the main words to search for so students should glance over the section until they locate one of the words. Then they should reread the sentence to find the answer. If it is not in this sentence, they are to keep skimming until another main word is found and then read again for the answer.

KEY IDEAS

- New England is part of the Northeast. Maine, New Hampshire, Vermont, Massachusetts, Connecticut, and Rhode Island make up this region.

- Farming is difficult because of the rocky soil.

- New England had an economy based on the sea and factories.

KEY TERMS

New England

Every morning, the first rays of morning sun in America shine on West Quoddy Head. That is an island off the coast of Maine. This is the easternmost point in the United States.

Then the sun hits the mainland at the top of Mount Katahdin (ka·TAH·din), one peak of the Appalachian Mountains.

The northeastern states of Maine, New Hampshire, Vermont, Massachusetts, Rhode Island, and Connecticut make up the region called ***New England.*** When people picture New England, they may think of rocky beaches or colorful fall foliage. Some may think of farmland bordered by stone walls and maple trees.

Location and Landforms

As beautiful as New England is, the land poses some challenges. The soil is rocky. Stone walls dot the fields and woods of New England. They were built by farmers who took the rocks from the fields. They placed them along the borders with neighboring farm fields.

The mountains and rocks make much of New England a poor place to grow crops such as wheat. The land is better for other types of agriculture, such as dairy farming—raising cows for milk.

This is a view of the White Mountains in New Hampshire. **What are some of New England's challenges?**

346

Chapter 14

Teacher Notes

The Great Molasses Flood

New England's legacy as one leg of the triangle trade is evidenced by the Great Molasses Flood of 1919. Prior to Prohibition, New England was home to several rum distillaries. On January 15, 1919, in the North End of Boston, a large tank holding molasses at the Purity Distilling Company burst. A wave of molasses ran through the streets at about 35 miles per hour (56 km/h). The flowing molasses killed 21 people and injured 150. Several blocks were flooded with about 2 to 3 feet of the sweet stuff. Buildings were knocked of their foundations and a train was derailed. Some local residents still claim that they can smell the molasses on hot days.

New England

Land Elevation

Feet	Meters
3,333	1000
1,667	500
667	200
0	0

▲ Mountain peak
★ State capital

0 75 150 mi.
0 75 150 km

CANADA

St. Lawrence R.

L. Champlain

Mooseheaad Lakes

Mt. Katahdin (5,267 ft.) ▲

A P P A L A C H I A N   M O U N T A I N S

Maine

Vermont
•Burlington

WHITE MTS.

Mt. Washington (6,288 ft.) ▲

New Hampshire

Montpelier ★

New York

GREEN MTS.

Connecticut R.

Merrimack R.

★ Augusta

•Portland

West Quoddy Head

Gulf of Maine

ATLANTIC OCEAN

Concord ★

Cape Ann
Salem

Massachusetts
•Springfield   Boston ★

Massachusetts Bay

42°30'N

N W E S

Connecticut
Hartford ★   •Providence

Cape Cod

New Haven•

Rhode Island

Hudson R.

Long Island Sound

NANTUCKET

72°30'W   70°W   67°30'W

🌐 **Region** The Northeast region is split into two parts. *What characteristics of New England set it apart from the other region of the Northeast, the Mid-Atlantic?*

Maine is famous for its lobsters.
Where is the most eastern point in the United States?

Climate

New England has a humid continental climate. The winters are cold and snowy. Summers can be warm and humid. The cities and towns in northern Vermont, New Hampshire, and Maine, and those along the coast enjoy milder summers. The mountains also have cooler summers because of their elevation. New Englanders enjoy the variety of weather that the four seasons bring.

New England's long coastline, huge forests, and strong rivers helped industries grow.

Economy

From colonial times through the 1800s, many New Englanders made a living from the sea. Shipbuilding, trade, and fishing were the center of the economy.

WORD ORIGINS

The word **Appalachian** came from the name of a Native American group called the *Apalateans.* They lived in part of these mountains. The Appalachians run from Maine south to Georgia.

Eastern Regions of the United States

347

1 The state of Vermont is named for the French words vert (green) and mont (mountain). What landform do you see on the map that runs through Vermont?

2 How do the mountains shown on the map compare to North Carolina's Mount Mitchell (elevation 6,684 feet)?

💬 **Caption Answer**

West Quoddy Head, Maine

🌳 **Name Origin**

Connecticut "long river place." Nicknames: Nutmeg State, Constitution State. Motto: He who transplanted still sustains. Admitted: 5th ; ratified Constitution in 1788.

Maine Named for a former province in France. Nickname: Pine Tree State. Motto: I direct. Admitted: 23rd, 1820.

Massachusetts "great hill place." Nicknames: Bay State, Old Colony. Motto: By the sword we seek peace, but peace only under liberty. Admitted: 6th, 1788.

New Hampshire Named for county of Hampshire, England. Nickname: Granite State. Motto: Live free, or die. Admitted: 9th, 1788.

Rhode Island There are two theories regarding its name: Dutch explorer named it "red island" because of the red clay; or an Italian explorer named it for the Isle of Rhodes in the Mediterranean. Nickname: Little Rhody, Ocean State. Motto: Hope. Admitted: 13th, 1790.

Vermont French for "green mountain." Nickname: Green Mountain State. Motto: Freedom and unity. Admitted: 14th, 1791.

Discussion Questions

1 What were the other ways New Englanders had of making a living from the colonial time until the 1800s?

2 Why are so many United States cities named after cities in England?

3 Why do you think the demand for new ships has declined in recent decades?

Caption Answer

New England's natural resources, like lumber for ship masts, and its location and deep water harbors made it a center for trade.

Caption Answer

Shipbuilding was the foundation of the region's economy, and good harbors encouraged the growth of trade and whaling.

Research Activity

Virtual New England

OBJECTIVES: 1.01, 1.06, 3.03

Ask the students to imagine that they are in one of the states in New England. They rise this morning and set about planning their day. Have the students do an Internet activity to arrange plans for the day. They may want to be online first before they determine where they want to visit. After this research is complete the students will then write a description of their day in New England as though they were actually there. What would they have seen, what would the land and environment have been like? What would the weather have been like?

Shipbuilding

There are many tall trees in New England's forests. These gave shipbuilders wood for masts and decks. The pitch and tar from pine trees made the ships watertight. They used turpentine made from the pines as a cleaner and paint thinner.

Fewer ships are needed today. Large ships are no longer made from wood. But ships are still built in Bath, Maine, and New London and Groton, Connecticut. New London is also the home of the United States Coast Guard Academy.

Trade and Whaling

Boston and Salem, Massachusetts, were the home ports of sea captains who sailed worldwide. New England's coastline has many good harbors. Several towns on the water grew into important trading centers.

New England's merchants became wealthy. They exported New England's timber and ship stores (materials for ship construction). Then they imported English products. They sailed to China. Then the traders sold China's tea and porcelain in world markets.

Some coastal New England towns were centers of the whaling industry. Whales were used to provide many household goods in the 1700s and 1800s.

Scrimshaw on this whale's tooth shows scenes from the whaling industry. **Why was the sea important?**

Whaling was an important industry in New England. **What made New England a center for international trade?**

Chapter 14

Research Activity

Northeastern History

OBJECTIVES: 3.03, 3.05, 4.07

The Northeast region is rich in historic culture. The Puritans, the Quakers, the Dutch, and the French influence from the St. Lawrence area added a great deal to the culture of the Northeast. Divide your class into four or five groups representing the various early European settlers. Have the students research that particular culture: how they dressed, their religion, their food, their customs. Allow the students to dress up. You can even have an early Northeastern day with food samples, dances, and music. Finally, after the research is completed, have the students compare those early colonial heritages with the diversity of the Northeastern people today. Do those customs still show themselves in restaurants, home styles, and food?

Henry David Thoreau
1809–1865

A Young Boy in Concord

Henry David Thoreau was born in Boston, Massachusetts. When he was a young boy, his family moved to Concord. Thoreau loved Concord. He explored the woods and took long walks. As he walked, he looked and listened. He liked to think while he was in the woods.

Thoreau went to Harvard and was the only one of the four children in his family to go to college. He became a teacher but soon quit. Thoreau did not want to whip his students when they did not behave. Later, he tried teaching again with his brother John. They started a school together, but John died. Theoreau was too sad to go on with the school alone.

In Good Company

Thoreau had a group of friends who liked to think and write. One of his friends was named Ralph Waldo Emerson. Emerson taught Thoreau many things, including how to keep a journal. Thoreau wrote his thoughts in his journal for the rest of his life. He wrote about nature and people.

"In warm evenings I . . . sat in the boat playing the flute, and saw the perch [fish], which I seemed to have charmed, hovering around me, and the moon traveling over the ribbed bottom, which was strewed with the wrecks of the forest."

"I Went to the Woods . . ."

To live out his ideas, Thoreau built a small cabin next to Walden Pond. He lived there for two years. He worked in his garden and read books. He fished and wrote in his journal. Every day he spent time enjoying nature. He studied plants, animals, and the weather.

Although he liked to be alone, every few days he went to the village. He visited friends and heard the latest news. Sometimes he had friends over.

Some of Thoreau's best writings came from the time he spent at Walden Pond. His most famous book is called *Walden*. Thoreau had a good sense of humor. He wrote about changing the week to six days of rest and one day of work. It wasn't all a joke—he wanted people to see that they did not need to rush around busy all the time. They could make or grow what they needed to live. They could do things for themselves.

One Can Make a Difference

After living at the pond, Thoreau kept writing and doing important things. He hated slavery, so he and his family helped runaway slaves escape to freedom. He wrote about a time when he spent a night in jail for standing up to a law he thought was wrong. He tried to show that one person can make a difference.

Thoreau died in Concord when he was only 44 years old. He was buried near many of his friends on Author's Ridge in Sleepy Hollow Cemetery.

Eastern Regions of the United States

349

Teacher Notes

The Wreck of the Whaleship *Essex*

On November 20, 1820, The whaleship *Essex,* which had left Nantucket, Massachusetts, in August of the previous year, was rammed by a 80-foot sperm whale. It was the first reported case of a whale ramming a ship in more than 100 years of American whaling. After salvaging what they could from the ship, the crew of 21 escaped on the whale boats and set out for the closest land. By late December, the crew found a small island, but they soon discovered that there was too little freshwater and food to sustain them. Three men opted to stay on the island, and having set out once again, the remaining crew were divided among the three boats. One boat was lost in a storm, but the survivors in the other two boats were eventually rescued, as were the men who stayed on the island. During the ordeal however, 13 of the original crew perished.

ELL ELL Teaching Tips

Utilize Peer Helpers

If possible, have more advanced students who speak the newcomers' languages take your new students on a tour of the important places in your school, such as the bathroom, office, cafeteria, and so on. Make sure they also explain to the student what the expectations are for the classroom.

 Background Information

New England: Economic Survivor

One geographer has described New England as an "economic survivor." Early English settlers found a land with a cold climate, a short growing season, and thin, rocky soil with few coal and other mineral resources. New Englanders turned to fishing, shipping and shipbuilding, and forest products. Even before the Civil War, New England became a center of industry, specializing in textiles, shoes, and high-skill products like clocks and small arms. When most textiles mills moved south, the region reinvented itself, producing computers, machine tools, aircraft engines, and precision instruments. In the late 1900s, New Englanders found renewed prosperity in developing high-tech and service-based businesses.

Discussion Questions

1 Where is the United States Coast Guard Academy located?

2 Are some of the jobs found in New England also found in North Carolina? If so, which ones?

 Caption Answer

Whaling and trade used to be two of New England's ocean-related industries. Today, shipbuilding is still important.

 Activity

Maple Syrup

OBJECTIVES: 3.03, 3.04, 3.07

Maple syrup is a staple in the Northeastern states, especially in Vermont. In the spring of the year the sap begins to flow. Many communities will get together and have huge sap parties, cooking down the sap and preparing it to make wonderful foods with maple flavors.

Maple Syrup

3 tablespoons maple extract
1 teaspoon vanilla
2 1/2 cups sugar
1 cup corn syrup

Combine the ingredients and cook down. Use cornstarch to thicken. Once the syrup is made, you can serve it over pancakes, biscuits, and so on. Many children in the Northeast have syrup on snow for snow cream. You can also make maple sugar, maple honey, and maple candy.

Have a tasting party or turn the tasting party into a maple festival with research about the maple tree on display and fun games and activities.

There are four different grades of pure maple syrup. The grades relate to color and flavor. You may order small amounts of each and have students taste to determine the differences.

Fishing always has strengthened New England's ties to the sea.
What other industries closely connect the region to the ocean?

Fishing

Fishing also brought wealth to the region. Many kinds of fish filled the ocean near New England. Ships from around the world caught cod and lobster.

Fishing has declined in recent years. Too many fish have been caught. Strict rules now limit fishing so the population can grow again. But there are very few fishermen left. Many can no longer make a living like their fathers and grandfathers did.

Rivers and Mills

New England's rivers are shallow. Loggers used the rivers to float logs to the coast. There they were used to make ships or were exported.

Rivers were an important source of power for factories. Textile mills were built on rivers like the Merrimack. The region became an important center of the Industrial Revolution.

350

 Activity

Lobsters

OBJECTIVES: 3.03, 3.04, 5.05

Maine is famous for its lobsters. Lobsters are a mainstay in the fishing industry and a backbone of Maine's economy. Have the students determine how much of Maine's economy comes from the sale of lobsters. Discuss how lobsters are caught, the type of boats used, and how they get to market.

- Have the students research the habits of lobsters.
- Bring in some lobster shells (get them from a restaurant). You can do lobster prints with paint.
- Have lobster-tasting parties with imitation seafood and make lobster bisque, seafood dip with lobster, and so on. Check to make sure students have no seafood allergies.

Extension Debate possibilities are pollution and its effects on the fishing industry, and disagreements over fishing rights off the New England and New Brunswick coasts.

Novice ELL students can make a mini-book with the most common fish and shellfish.

Today's Economy

After World War II, New England, like many other parts of the United States, became a center for service industries. Service industries help other people and businesses.

High Tech and Higher Education

New England has become an electronics and engineering center. These companies work with experts from the almost 270 colleges and universities in the region. Harvard and Yale are two of the nation's oldest and most respected universities. The Massachusetts Institute of Technology (M.I.T.) is known worldwide for research in science and technology. These schools provide many jobs.

Resources

A profitable product in New England is maple syrup. In March, pipes are tapped into trees to create a spout. The pipe catches the running sap, which is caught in a pail. The sap is collected from the pails. It is cooked in boilers until the sap turns into maple syrup. Vermonters made 460 thousand gallons of syrup in 2000.

The largest granite quarry in the world is located in Vermont near its capital, Montpelier. Granite from this quarry is used for buildings all over the country.

Tourism is an important industry in New England.
What other industries are important there?

Tourism

New England's beautiful scenery has helped build a strong tourism industry. They come to see its historic sites, to ski, and to play on the beaches. Autumn is the peak tourist season. During the crisp fall days, the deciduous trees, especially the maples, turn to brilliant yellows, reds, and oranges.

Culture

The area is also famous for its many libraries and museums. Theaters and orchestras enrich the region's culture. Many famous writers come from New England, too. Louisa May Alcott, Nathaniel Hawthorne, Robert Frost, and Emily Dickenson are just a few of the region's authors. Norman Rockwell, a famous painter, was also inspired by New England.

 **OBJECTIVES: 2.01, 3.01, 5.01**

Discussion Questions

1 Why do you think maple trees are tapped in March rather than in other months?

2 Judging from the fact that trees are tapped in March, what conditions do you think are necessary for producing maple syrup?

Caption Answer

Other important industries are service industries, including education, electronics, and engineering; agriculture, including dairy and maple syrup production; and granite quarrying.

Activity

Regions of the United States Micro Skit
 **OBJECTIVES: 1.06, 1.07, 5.07**

Divide the class into groups of four or five students each. The group(s) will select one of the nine regions of the United States shown on the map on page 345. Students in each group will research the region chosen. Present a micro-skit sharing the information and facts learned. They should be creative and include hats, costumes, and props.

LESSON 1 REVIEW

Fact Follow-Up
1. What states are included in New England?
2. What are some physical features of New England?
3. What were important parts of the New England economy in its early history?
4. How did shipbuilding develop as an industry?

Talk About It
1. How might New England be different if the soil were fertile?
2. How has New England's economy changed over time?
3. How is a service industry different from a manufacturing industry?

Eastern Regions of the United States

351

LESSON 1 REVIEW

Fact Follow-Up Answers
1. Maine, New Hampshire, Vermont, Massachusetts, Rhode Island, and Connecticut.
2. It's mountainous with a long coastline. There is little good soil, and the soil's quality as well as many large rocks prevent farming from being a major economic activity.
3. Fishing, trading, whaling, and shipbuilding were important to the economy.
4. From colonial times through the 1800s, New Englanders turned to the sea for their living. Ships were needed to support the fishing and whaling industry. New England's huge forests provided the raw materials for the shipbuilding industry.

Talk About It Answers
1. Important points: People might farm more, and the economy might have less dependence on fishing.
2. Fishing is still a major industry, but it is going through a hard time because of strict regulations imposed by overfishing. Shipbuilding is still a major activity. Service industries and high-tech industries are becoming more and more important.
3. Manufacturing uses such raw materials as iron or rubber to make a finished product such as an automobile. A service industry uses the talents and skills of people to provide a service such as a haircut or a medical examination rather than providing a product such as an automobile or a TV set. A service industry might be a school, a library, a hospital, even a beauty salon.

OBJECTIVES: 1.02,1.03, 3.03, 5.07

Discussion Questions

1 Why do you think the Northeast region is such a highly populated area?

Caption Answer

The Ohio River

Teacher Notes

The Northeast Corridor

Some people call the Northeastern megalopolis "Boshwash." This includes the cities of Boston, Massachusetts; Providence, Rhode Island; Hartford, Connecticut; New Haven, Connecticut; New York, New York; Trenton, New Jersey; Philadelphia, Pennsylvania; Baltimore, Maryland; and Washington, D.C.

Reading Strategy Activity

Finding Details

OBJECTIVES: 1.02,1.03, 3.03, 5.07

Detail questions are the easiest ones to answer because the answer is in the passage. It may be a lower-level comprehension skill, but it is a skill that all students need to master. This game using the information in Lesson 2 will help students practice finding details.

Read the lesson in the text. Have students choose an important sentence from the text and write it on the unlined side of an index card. (You could make the cards ahead of time if that is preferred.) On the lined side of the card, have the student write a question that could be asked from the sentence he or she wrote on the other side. Then the student writes the answer after the question. Collect the cards.

Hand the stack of cards to a student to choose one card to read aloud to the class. The question is then read and the student next to the reader must answer it. If the answer is correct the student

keeps the card; if not, the card goes back into the pile. Pass the stack of cards around the room so everyone has a turn. See the example to the left.

This activity reinforces finding details in a text, but it also strengthens listening skills.

KEY IDEAS

- The Mid-Atlantic states are New York, New Jersey, Pennsylvania, Delaware, and Maryland.

- The Mid-Atlantic has varied landforms and many economic activities.

KEY TERMS

megalopolis
Mid-Atlantic
St. Lawrence Seaway
Tidewater
truck farms

There is a chain of cities along the coast of the Northeastern United States. This area runs from Washington, D.C., north to Boston, Massachusetts. This chain of cities is called a *megalopolis,* which means a huge urban area where cities sprawl into one another. The area's population was about 53 million in 2004.

About one sixth of the nation's population is squeezed into the small but diverse *Mid-Atlantic* part of the Northeast. It is very diverse. Both the Asian and Hispanic populations here grew by more than 50 percent in the last decade.

Location and Landforms

The Mid-Atlantic region lies southwest of New England. It is bounded on the east by the Atlantic Ocean and on the west by the Appalachians.

The Mid-Atlantic contains more varied landforms than New England. The Coastal Plain widens in the Mid-Atlantic states of New York, New Jersey, Pennsylvania, Delaware, and Maryland.

In southern New Jersey and Delaware the shoreline is sandy and marshy. Farther north, in Pennsylvania, there are wooded hills and lakes as well as miles of rolling farmland.

The Appalachian Mountains run through the northwest corner of New Jersey and through much of Pennsylvania.

Pittsburgh, Pennsylvania, grew where the Monongahela and the Allegheny Rivers meet. **What river is formed as those two rivers flow together?**

352

Chapter 14

Teacher Notes

St Lawrence Seaway

The St. Lawrence Seaway is covered in Chapter 20, pages 494–497.

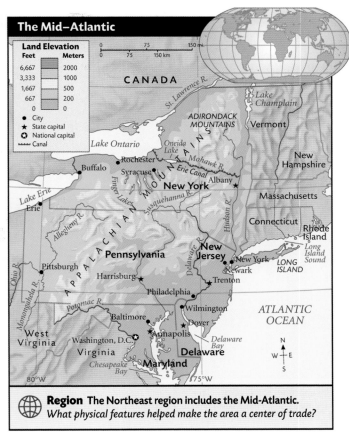

The Mid–Atlantic

Land Elevation

Feet	Meters
6,667	2000
3,333	1000
1,667	500
667	200
0	0

● City
★ State capital
◉ National capital
〰 Canal

🌐 **Region** The Northeast region includes the Mid-Atlantic. *What physical features helped make the area a center of trade?*

The Empire State Building in New York City is a symbol of New York state. **What is New York City's relative location?**

Bodies of Water

Many important rivers flow through the Mid-Atlantic. Several carried early settlers away from the coast. They still carry goods today. In the east there are the St. Lawrence, the Hudson, and the Delaware Rivers.

The Ohio River is in the west. It begins where the Allegheny River and the Mon-ongahela River flow together. Pittsburgh, Pennsylvania, is located at that point.

The eastern Great Lakes, Ontario and Erie, have connected the Mid-Atlantic states with the Midwest since the early 1800s. The Erie Canal and Hudson River linked the Great Lakes with New York City.

The **St. Lawrence Seaway** is a series of canals and locks built by Canada and the United States in the 1950s. It lets ocean-going ships sail directly from the Atlantic to the ports of the Great Lakes.

To the south, the Chesapeake Bay almost divides Maryland into two parts. The **Tidewater** is the area of rivers and inlets affected by the changing tides. It is a sporting paradise. Boaters can sail and explore, catch crabs, fish, or watch ducks and shore birds. In a good year, about 60 million pounds of blue crabs are harvested from the Tidewater.

Eastern Regions of the United States

353

Discussion Questions

1 Why was the area where the Allegheny and Monongahela Rivers flow together a favorable place for growth?

2 What are the two largest states in the Mid-Atlantic region?

3 What are the names of the mountains in the Mid-Atlantic region? What other major landforms are in the Mid-Atlantic?

4 Why was the water link of Lake Erie and Lake Ontario so important to the United States' economy in the early 1800s?

💬 **Caption Answer**

Natural harbors and rivers provided ports and transportation to inland cities.

💬 **Caption Answer**

It is surrounded by the Hudson River, Long Island Sound, and Atlantic Ocean.

💡 **Activity**

 **OBJECTIVES:** 1.02, 1.05, 3.01, 3.02

Regional Experts

Divide students into five or six groups. Each group's task is to become experts on an assigned topic related to the Northeast or Southeast states, such as:

- Group A—historical events
- Group B—places to visit
- Group C—landforms, bodies of water
- Group D—climate and resources
- Group E—ways of making a living

Each student is to record the information gathered by the group. When the research is completed, form new groups consisting of one student from each of the previous groups. Now each group has one "expert" on each topic, and they can share their information with one another.

 ## Name Origin

Delaware Named for Baron De La Warr, early governor of Virginia. Nicknames: First State, Diamond State. Motto: Liberty and Independence. Admitted: 1st, 1787.

Maryland Named for Queen Henrietta Maria, wife of Charles I of England. Nicknames: Old Line State, Free State. Motto: Manly deeds, womanly words. Admitted: 7th, 1788.

New Jersey "Named for England's Isle of Jersey. Nickname: Garden State. Motto: Liberty and prosperity. Admitted: 3rd, 1788.

New York Named for the Duke of York and Albany, brother of Charles II of England. Nickname: Empire State. Motto: Ever upward. Admitted: 11th, 1788.

Pennsylvania "Penn's sylvania or woodlands," land grant to Admiral William Penn from Charles II, as a partial debt payment. Penn's son, also named William, led the Quakers to settle in Pennsylvania. Nick-name: Keystone State. Motto: Virtue, liberty and independence. Admitted: 2nd, 1788.

Discussion Questions

1 Why are the port cities important to the United States?

 **Caption Answer**

Agriculture is an important industry in the Mid-Atlantic because the soil is very fertile.

 **Activity**

Quartering a State

OBJECTIVES: 1.02, 1.06, 4.03

Assign each student a state in the Northeast region. Explain that students will be responsible for gathering information on four topics about their assigned state: **Industry, Agriculture, Economics,** and **Resources.** Give each student a 12-inch by 18-inch piece of drawing paper and instruct him or her to divide the paper into four equal quadrants. In the center of the paper the student will draw an outline of the given state, then write the name of the state within the outline. Have students label the top left quadrant **Resources** and draw symbols that represent the natural resources of that state; label the top right quadrant **Agriculture.** Again draw symbols to represent the agriculture of the state. Label the left lower quadrant **Industries** and continue same procedure as described above. Label lower right quadrant **Economics** and draw symbols representative of the economic activities of the state. After the poster is completed students will give an oral presentation about the information on the poster.

In the Catskills *(1836)* by Thomas Doughty captures the beauty of the rural Mid-Atlantic state of New York. **Despite its high population, why does the Mid-Atlantic still have many rural areas?**

The Economy

The Mid-Atlantic region has many industries. It is a center of world trade.

Ports

Many ports connect the Mid-Atlantic states to the world. Bays, coves, and islands create many harbors along the Atlantic coast. Deepwater ports have been major points of entry to the United States since colonial times.

The nation's busiest port is New York City. Other important ports are Philadelphia and Baltimore. Philadelphia is the nation's largest freshwater port. It is located on the Delaware River, about 90 miles (145 km) from the Atlantic. Baltimore has direct access to the Atlantic Ocean through the Chesapeake Bay.

Agriculture

The fertile soil of the Mid-Atlantic has always helped farmers. Today, about one third of New Jersey is farmed. Its nickname is the Garden State. New Jersey's farms are called *truck farms.* Farmers once brought their produce into Philadelphia and New York City in their trucks. They sold it from the backs of their trucks. Some still do.

New York State has about 38,000 working farms. They produce several kinds of fruit. Grapes for its famous wines are grown in vineyards around Lake Ontario, Lake Erie, and in the Finger Lakes regions.

Pennsylvania and Delaware produce corn, hay, and poultry. Pennsylvania also is known for its beautiful dairy farms.

354

 Activity

Washington, D.C.

OBJECTIVES: 1.02, 1.06, 3.03

Have students create a product to demonstrate the positive aspects of moving to Washington, D.C., to present to their families.

Each student will use at least five of the subject areas listed below in his or her presentation. Possible products include mobiles, brochures, tagboard displays, Web pages, or PowerPoint or other digital story presentations.

Topics

- arts and recreation
- museum and parks
- dining
- transportation
- housing
- news and weather
- other local information
- sports
- White House
- Congress
- Supreme Court
- government servers
- universities and colleges
- libraries

The Mid-Atlantic, like New England, has varied landform, from the Atlantic Coast to the Appalachian Mountains. **What are some important bodies of water in this region?**

New Jersey

Fenwick Island Lighthouse in Delaware

Antietam Bridge in Maryland

Eastern Regions of the United States

355

Writing Activity

Haiku Poetry

OBJECTIVES: 1.06, 3.03, 3.04

Discuss with students a form of Japanese poetry called Haiku. It usually focuses on nature, natural resources, and so on. It has three lines and follows a specific pattern:

Line 1 has 5 syllables
Line 2 has 7 syllables
Line 3 has 5 syllables

Show the Humanities Extension/ Publications video *The Northeast: People and Places.* Ask students to think about particular scenes of beauty and vast resources they saw in the video. After the discussion, model a haiku.

Example:

Fall in New England
Crisp days, cold nights, maple trees
Bright shades of color.

Have students write and illustrate their own haiku about the Northeast region. Share poems aloud, then bind them in a booklet to be shared with other students and classes. Or read the chapter and discuss the region's physical features.

Caption Answer

The Atlantic Ocean, Chesapeake Bay, Long Island Sound, Hudson River, the Delaware River, the Potomac River, Lake Erie, and Lake Ontario.

Background Information

Mid-Atlantic Region

The Mid-Atlantic region, especially along the Atlantic coast, is a densely populated, highly urban area. It is the most densely populated part of the eastern megalopolis that stretches from Boston to Washington, D.C. Three of the nation's largest metropolitan areas are in this region: New York-northern New Jersey; Baltimore-Washington, and the Philadelphia, Wilmington, Delaware-Atlantic City, New Jersey metroplex. Geographers point to the mid-Atlantic's good harbors, good routes to the interior, a location between New England and the South, and its access to both Europe and the interior of North America as reasons for its rapid early growth.

Before steel is produced, the iron ore is smelted. **What industries are important in the Mid-Atlantic states?**

Discussion Questions

1 Have you visited any of the tourist sites mentioned here? If not, which ones would you like to visit one day?

2 Why do you think New York City is the home of the fashion industry and TV networks?

Caption Answer

Business, finance, communications, tourism, agriculture, and fishing

Industry

The key to the Mid-Atlantic economy today is business, finance, and communications. New York City's Wall Street is the headquarters of finance. The New York and American stock exchanges are located there. New York is also the home of the fashion industry, TV networks, and other communication businesses.

Coal from the mountains of Pennsylvania was, and still is, an important power source. The nation's petroleum industry also began here. Iron ore is the basic raw material for the steel industry. It was taken by ships on the Great Lakes from Minnesota to Pittsburgh and other steel manufacturing cities.

The area around Philadelphia and northeastern New Jersey became an industrial powerhouse. In Delaware, a gun powder plant was started in the early 1800s by the Dupont family. It has become the world's largest chemical producer.

Changing Times

Industry is still important here. But most of the steel plants are gone now. They were either forced to close by competition from other countries or they moved to other parts of the United States.

New Jersey is still one of the most heavily industrialized states. Buffalo, New York, is on the Great Lakes. It still has a few small steel mills and some auto assembly plants, chemical plants, and flour mills. Nearby, Rochester, New York, is known for plants that make optical (lenses), photographic, and office equipment.

Tourism is an important industry in the Mid-Atlantic. Tourists flock to New York City to see plays on Broadway. They visit the Liberty Bell at Independence Hall in Philadelphia, the Naval Academy at Annapolis, Maryland, and Niagara Falls in upstate New York.

LESSON 2 REVIEW

Fact Follow-Up
1. What states are in the Mid-Atlantic region?
2. What are some physical features of the Mid-Atlantic region?
3. What are the important parts of the Mid-Atlantic economy?

Talk About It
1. How did the physical characteristics of place encourage trade in the Mid-Atlantic region?
2. Why has the economy of the Mid-Atlantic region changed in this century?

Chapter 14

LESSON 2 REVIEW

Fact Follow-Up Answers
1. New York, New Jersey, Pennsylvania, Delaware, and Maryland
2. Sandy, marshy shorelines in some areas, with rolling hills and lakes and a mountainous interior. The area is laced with rivers.
3. Keys to the Mid-Atlantic economy are business, finance, and communications. Tourism is also important.

Talk About It Answers
1. Many important rivers flow through the region, and excellent ports such as New York, Philadelphia, and Baltimore connect the region with the world.
2. The steel industry and the petroleum industry both began in the region. Many of the steel mills have closed because of foreign competition or movement of the industry to other parts of the United States. Manufacturing remains, but the key to the economy today is business, finance, and communications.

LESSON 3 The Southeast Region

T he rapidly changing Southeast was once mostly a rural region. It is now the home of a growing population. Many people live in such cities as Charlotte, North Carolina; Miami, Florida; and Atlanta, Georgia. The Southeast is growing more urban.

Location and Landforms

The *Southeast* extends from the Ohio River to the Gulf of Mexico. In the east it stretches from the southern Chesapeake Bay to the southernmost tip of Florida. In the west the region reaches from Kentucky south to Arkansas and Louisiana.

The Southeast covers about 460,000 square miles (1,196,000 sq km). It includes 12 states: Virginia, North Carolina, South Carolina, Georgia, Florida, Alabama, Mississippi, Louisiana, Arkansas, Tennessee, Kentucky, and West Virginia.

KEY IDEAS

- The Southeast states are Virginia, West Virginia, Kentucky, Tennessee, North Carolina, South Carolina, Georgia, Florida, Alabama, Mississippi, Louisiana, and Arkansas.

- The Southeast is an agricultural region.

- Other important economic activities are oil production, mining, fishing, and high-tech industries.

KEY TERMS

fall line
Southeast
strip mine

This southern Arkansas farm field is part of the wide Coastal Plain of the Gulf Coast.
Why do you think the Gulf Coastal Plain is wider than the Atlantic Coastal Plain?

Eastern Regions of the United States

357

OBJECTIVES: 1.02, 1.03, 3.03, 5.07

Discussion Questions

1 What is meant by a rural area?

2 As you have traveled along the highways of North Carolina, have you seen both rural and manufacturing areas? Where?

 **Caption Answer**

The Atlantic Coastal Plain is shortened by the Appalachian Mountains.

 **Reading Strategy Activity**

Two Column Notes

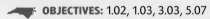 **OBJECTIVES: 1.02, 1.03, 3.03, 5.07**

Two-column notes are a good way of organizing details as students read. For this lesson, have them write the title "Southeast Region" across the top of their note page. The have them make two columns labeled "Location and Landforms" and "Climate." They should then add in details as they read the chapter.

Advanced learners could make out a practice test instead of note-taking. Reiterate the importance of asking main idea questions instead of trick details. Let the class take the test, then have a critiquing session of their questions. Discuss how hard it is to make a test that everyone thinks is fair.

 Activity

Song of the South

OBJECTIVES: 3.03, 3.07, 4.03

After studying the Southeastern states, divide the students into groups of two or three. Their task is to write descriptive sentences or phrases about the region that could be sung to a familiar tune, such as "Row, Row, Row Your Boat." Collect the verses. Compile, duplicate, and distribute the copies to your class. Sing the completed "Song of the South" as a large group.

Background Information

Southeast Region

Beginning in the 1970s, the Southeast began to experience rapid population growth as both industries and retirees moved south to take advantage of a warmer climate, lower fuel costs, cheaper land, and lower wages for workers. The Southeast has changed from a largely agricultural region with such labor-intensive industries as textiles to the development of many service-based industries.

Today, Charlotte is a leading center of banking and finance, and the Research Triangle Park is a high-tech complex encompassing a variety of areas from telecommunications to information technology. Atlanta, Georgia, provides headquarters for many United States companies and has one of the world's busiest airports.

Discussion Questions

1 Why do you think most of the Southeast's industry is located along the fall line?

2 What cities have you visited that are located in the Southeast?

3 What major landform covers most of the Southeast?

4 What is the fall line?

 **Caption Answer**

The climate is warmer and wetter than in the Northeast. Crops have a longer growing season. Hurricanes can threaten the Southeast coast in July, August, September, and October. They can cause millions of dollars of damage.

Writing Activity

A North Carolina Diamante

 OBJECTIVES: 1.02, 1.06, 3.05

Create a diamante (a diamond-shaped poem) about a Southeastern state.
Line 1—Write the name of your South-eastern state.
Line 2—Write the names of two animals native to the state.
Line 3—Write the names of three of the state's important cities.
Line 4—Write the names of four of the state's important industrial or agricul-tural products.
Line 5—Write the names of the state bird, state flower, and state tree.
Line 6—Write the names of two of the state's geographical features.
Line 7—Write the state's nickname.

Example:
North Carolina
Grey squirrel, Black bear
Charlotte, Greensboro, Wilmington
Textiles, Tobacco, Chickens, Engines
Cardinal, Dogwood, Longleaf Pine
Mount Mitchell, Cape Hatteras
Old North State
Use any and all resources available to gather the information needed to complete the activity.

Region The Atlantic and Gulf Coastal Plains cover most of the Southeast region, but the Appalachian Mountains and the Piedmont are also distinctive landforms of the region. *What are the region's characteristics of climate? How does climate affect the Southeast?*

Landforms

The Coastal Plain widens from about 100 miles (161 km) along the Atlantic Coast to 200 miles (322 km) along the Gulf Coast. The Mississippi River flows through the Gulf Coastal Plain on its way to the Gulf of Mexico.

Inland from the Coastal Plain, the Piedmont begins to rise. The plain meets the Piedmont at the *fall line.* The Potomac and other rivers flow through the Piedmont. They often flow over waterfalls at the fall line. Most of the Southeast's industry is located along the fall line.

West of the Piedmont are the Appalachians. Fertile lowland is good for raising corn, soybeans, peanuts, and tobacco. It is found west of the Appalachians in Kentucky, Tennessee, and Alabama. Dairy cattle and the famous race horses of Kentucky thrive there.

Chapter 14

Name Origin

Alabama "thicket clearers," Choctaw for the Creek Native American farmers. Nicknames: Heart of Dixie, Camellia State. Motto: We dare defend our rights. Admitted: 22nd, 1819.

Arkansas "south wind." Nicknames: Natural State, Razorback State. Motto: The people rule. Admitted: 25th, 1836.

Florida "flowery Easter." Nickname: The Sunshine State. Motto: In God we trust. Admitted: 27th, 1845.

Georgia Named for George II of England. Nicknames: Empire State of the South, Peach State. Motto: Wisdom, justice and moderation. Admitted: 4th, 1788.

Kentucky several translations depending on native language: "dark and bloody ground," "land of tomorrow," or "meadowlands." Nickname: Bluegrass State. Motto: United we stand, divided we fall. Admitted: 15th, 1792.

Louisiana Named for King Louis XIV of France. Nickname: Pelican State. Motto: Union, justice and confidence. Admitted: 18th, 1812.

Strip mining, such as shown above in Kentucky, is an efficient method of extracting coal.
Why are some opposed to this way of mining?

Discussion Questions

1 How does the climate of the Southeast compare to the Northeast's?

2 What are some of the resources found in the Southeast?

3 Do you have relatives who work in a job related to these resources?

 **Caption Answer**

Strip mining causes damage by erosion.

 **Activity**

Music of the Southeast

⬥ **OBJECTIVES:** 3.03, 3.07, 4.03

This lesson can be spread out over one to three days.

Day 1: View and discuss the clip on music of the Southeast from the video *People and Places of the Southeast.*

Day 2: Talk about other types of music not on the video, such as gospel and beach music. Bring in examples of all the various styles of music of the Southeast or have students bring in samples. Listen to the music. Discuss the lyrics, instruments (have various pictures of the instruments to show the class), and rhythm of the music. You may want to make a chart as the class discusses the music.

Day 3: Give each student a set of cards (made by you prior to the lesson) printed on both sides. Each card will be one type of music from the Southeast, on one side, and the other side will have the place the music originated. Play a sample of music from the Southeast. Students will hold up the appropriate card and name either the type of music or the place of origin.

Climate

The climate of most of the Southeast is warmer than the Northeast. Crops have a longer growing season. In the southernmost states and along the coast, temperatures are mild. Parts of the Southeast enjoy a humid subtropical climate.

Hurricanes often threaten the Southeast coast. They can cause millions of dollars of damage. In 2004, four hurricanes hit Florida. They caused great damage. In 2005, however, Hurricane Katrina hit Louisiana and Mississippi. It was the costliest natural disaster in American history (see Eyewitness to History, page 360).

Resources

The Southeast benefits from many natural resources. Coal deposits are found in West Virginia, Kentucky, Virginia, Alabama, and Tennessee. Alabama contains large deposits of iron ore. Tennessee produces zinc and pyrites. Pyrites are used to refine copper and make chemicals. Florida and North Carolina produce phosphate rock that is used for fertilizer.

Louisiana, Mississippi, and Kentucky have petroleum deposits. There are great oil deposits in the waters of the Gulf of Mexico.

Forestry is an important industry in the Southeast. Trees grow quickly in the warm, moist climate. North Carolina is famous for its fine wood furniture.

Fishing is important to the Southeast. Shellfish from the Chesapeake Tidewater and the Gulf Coast are shipped throughout the country. Mississippi catfish farmers produce most of the catfish eaten in the United States.

What would YOU do?

One kind of coal mine found in the Southeast is called a ***strip mine.*** In strip mining, huge earth movers, bulldozers, and shovels strip soil to find the coal. Strip mining is used to mine a great deal of coal cheaply.

People who are against strip mining say it hurts the environment. They believe it causes erosion. Yet coal fuels many industries. It provides heat and electricity for many homes. How would you try to mine the coal without damaging the environment? Explain why.

Eastern Regions of the United States

359

Mississippi "gathering of all the waters." Nickname: Magnolia State. Motto: By valor and arms. Admitted: 20th, 1817.

North Carolina Carolus, Latin for Charles I. Nickname: Tar Heel State, Old North State. Motto: To be rather than to seem. Admitted: 12th, 1789.

South Carolina same as North Carolina (they became two separate colonies in 1710). Nickname: Palmetto State. Motto: While I breathe, I hope. Admitted: 8th, 1788.

Tennessee Cherokee for "chief village." Nickname: Volunteer State. Motto: Agriculture and commerce. Admitted: 16th, 1796.

Virginia Named for Queen Elizabeth I, virgin queen of England. Nickname: Old Dominion. Motto: Thus always to tyrants. Admitted: 10th, 1788.

West Virginia same as Virginia. Separated in 1861 after refusing to secede. Nickname: The Mountain State. Motto: Mountaineers are always free. Admitted: 35th, 1863.

Type of Music	Place of Origin
Blues	Mississippi Delta
Jazz	Louisiana (New Orleans)
Bluegrass	Appalachian Mountains
Country/Western	Tennessee (Nashville)
Cajun	Louisiana
Gospel	Southeast
Beach Music	Atlantic Coastline

Eyewitness Activity

Photo-Journaling Before and After

 **OBJECTIVES:** 1.02, 1.06

Tell students to imagine they have been given the job of reporting on Hurricane Katrina to someone who has never been to Louisiana. Discuss how Louisiana's present-day geography was impacted by the destruction of Hurricane Katrina. Students should label the first page of their report "Before" and include maps, photographs, or drawings of Louisiana before Hurricane Katrina. They should label the second page "After" and fill the page with items that portray Louisiana after the storm.

This is a good chance for students to engage in historical research, looking critically for reliable resources and evaluating appropriateness and effect. If needed, students can draw their own maps and pictures. When students have completed the activity, have them share their reports with the class. This provides an opportunity for serious discussion on preparedness and response at individual, local, state, and national levels. Discuss how Louisiana is rebuilding. Ask how the economy has been affected and how life has changed on many levels.

EYEWITNESS TO HISTORY

Hurricane Katrina

Katrina was so large, it destroyed much of the Gulf Coast for 100 miles (161 km) from the storm's center. It was the sixth-strongest Atlantic hurricane ever recorded. It was also the third-strongest hurricane to hit the United States on record.

In New Orleans, there were levees, or barriers, that separated Lake Pontchartrain from New Orleans. These were damaged by the massive amounts of water coming in from the storm. Then they broke. Water rushed in. Eighty percent of the city was flooded (below). Many neighborhoods were flooded for months after the storm.

On August 29, 2005, Hurricane Katrina made landfall in southeast Louisiana and along the Louisiana-Mississippi state line. It left a trail of unbelievable destruction behind it.

The storm surge wiped out much of the Gulf Coast. The cities of Mobile, Alabama, Waveland, Biloxi, and Gulfport in Mississippi, and New Orleans and other towns in Louisiana were crippled.

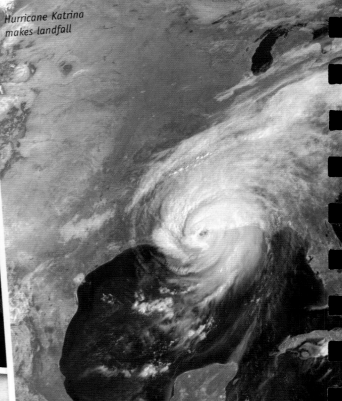

Hurricane Katrina makes landfall

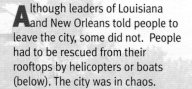

Although leaders of Louisiana and New Orleans told people to leave the city, some did not. People had to be rescued from their rooftops by helicopters or boats (below). The city was in chaos.

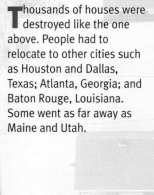

Thousands of houses were destroyed like the one above. People had to relocate to other cities such as Houston and Dallas, Texas; Atlanta, Georgia; and Baton Rouge, Louisiana. Some went as far away as Maine and Utah.

Sadly, the governments at the federal, state, and local levels were not prepared for a storm that size and its great damage. It took several days to get all the people out of New Orleans. At least 1,836 people lost their lives in Hurricane Katrina and the floods. The storm is estimated to have caused $81.2 billion in damage. It will take years to rebuild the region.

361

Activity

Hurricane Stories

OBJECTIVES: 1.02, 1.06, 4.01

Go to **NCJourneys.com** for a link to a Web site that provides primary source stories about personal experiences living through Hurrican Katrina and its aftermath. This site includes stories about youth and children. It also includes lesson plan and activity suggestions for teachers.

Discussion Questions

1 Why do you think land is cheaper in the Southeast than the Northeast? What types of things determine the value of property?

2 How does tourism affect the economy of an area?

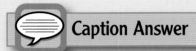 **Caption Answer**

Norfolk, Virginia; Wilmington, North Carolina; Charleston, South Carolina; and Savannah, Georgia, are all ports. Raleigh-Durham-Chapel Hill has the Research Triangle Park. Orlando, Florida, includes entertainment businesses. Memphis, Tennessee, is home to the nation's largest cotton market.

 Writing Activity

Southeastern Products

OBJECTIVES: 3.03, 4.07, 5.01

Have students brainstorm a list of products of the Southeast and where each product is manufactured. List these products on a piece of chart paper. Have the students choose from one to three products and create an advertisement for their product(s).

Extension Use a blank map of the Southeast region to make a product map using the list of products.

Atlanta, Georgia, is one of the key cities of the Southeast region. It is a financial and transportation center. What are other important cities in the region?

Economy

For much of its early history, the Southeast was an agricultural region. As you read in Chapter 8, cotton was the most important crop before the Civil War. After the war, planters still produced cotton. Then the cotton-eating insect called the boll weevil forced farmers to grow a wider variety of crops.

Alabama produces cattle, peanuts, and poultry. Large poultry farms also can be found in Arkansas and North Carolina. North Carolina is now a leading hog producer. It still grows more sweet potatoes and tobacco than any other state.

Florida, has a long growing season. It produces more than half of the nation's oranges and grapefruit. Even cotton has returned to the region. Memphis, Tennessee, is home to the nation's largest cotton market.

In recent years, the economy of the Southeast has changed in many exciting ways. New industries have started or moved into the region because of lower wages and less costly land. The fastest growing state economies are those of Arkansas, Georgia, North Carolina, and Florida.

Tourism

Many people visit the sunny south. Atlanta, Georgia, drew huge crowds for the 1996 Summer Olympics. Golfers enjoy playing in Florida and the Carolinas. The Kentucky Derby horse race is watched around the world on television each May.

Florida's warmth attracts people year-round. People enjoy boating in the Florida Keys. The Keys are a string of small islands off the tip of Florida. Families relax on sunny beaches and visit Disney World.

LESSON ③ REVIEW

Fact Follow-Up
1. Describe the landforms of the Southeast.
2. What are the resources of the Southeast?
3. What was Hurricane Katrina? What did it do?

Talk About It
1. How has the economy of the Southeast region changed over time?
2. What are some of the challenges facing the Southeast after Hurricane Katrina.

LESSON ③ REVIEW

Fact Follow-Up Answers
1. The Coastal Plain stretches across the entire region. In the interior, low mountains rise from the Piedmont. To the south of the mountains are fertile lowlands that are good for raising a variety of crops.
2. Coal deposits, iron ore, zinc, phosphate, and oil deposits are just some of the Southeast's mineral wealth. Other resources include fertile farmland, timber, and fishing.
3. Hurricane Katrina was the third largest hurricane to hit the United States. It devestated and destroyed many places along the Gulf Coast and caused the levees to break in New Orleans.

Talk About It Answers
1. The Southeast has been an agricultural region until recently. Small and large industries have boomed, and many areas are growing quickly.
2. Students could express several ideas, including many homes and businesses need to rebuild.

Accessing a Variety of Sources; Gathering, Synthesizing, and Reporting Information

Using Geography's Themes: Region

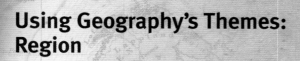

This skill lesson focuses on the fifth theme of the Five Themes of Geography: Region. You practiced using the first four themes in earlier chapters. Now you are studying the regions of the United States.

A region is an area on the surface of the earth that contains many similar features. One feature might be political. A city, county, state, or nation may be a political region.

Another feature might be physical. What landforms or climates are shared? For example, why is the Coastal Plain thought of as a physical region?

You have been reading about the three eastern regions of the United States. In the next two chapters you will learn about six other regions of our nation.

Below is a graphic organizer that will help you organize information about the eastern regions. Review Chapter 14 to complete the chart.

Why is the Northeast divided into New England and the Mid-Atlantic regions? What similar features make the Southeast all one region?

After you have completed this chart, look again at the chart you made earlier of the three cities. Can you tell which political regions each city occupies? What economic regions do they occupy? How are they alike or different?

Comparing Regions	Northeast Region	Southeast Region
1. Political Units (states)		
2. Landforms		
3. Climate		
4. Natural Resources		
5. Size		
6. Economic Activities		

Teaching This Skill Lesson

Materials Needed textbooks, paper, pencils

Classroom Organization whole class, individual, small groups

Beginning the Lesson Ask: "What is a region?" Accept students' responses, recording them on the chalkboard. Remind students of the various regions in which they live: city or county, state, nation. Tell them they will be using Chapter 14 to gather information about two regions in the eastern United States, the Northeast and Southeast regions.

Lesson Development Have students sketch the graphic organizer "Comparing Regions," reminding them to leave plenty of space for recording information. Circulate as students begin their work, making sure that all understand the assignment. The graphic organizers may be completed as a homework assignment.

Conclusion When students have completed their charts, allow them to meet in small groups to compare and polish their work. Conclude the lesson, focusing on the questions posed in the last paragraph of the Skill Lesson. If desired, display students' charts in the classroom.

 Skill Lesson Review

1. How many different regions do you live in?
   People may live in language, religious, political, physical (landform and climate), and economic regions—and perhaps others.
2. Is the theme of region easier or harder to use than the other four themes of geography?
   Encourage student responses.

Talk About It

1. Industries have been attracted to the Southeast because of lower wages, less costly land, mild climate, and resources.
2. The Southeast region stretches from the Ohio River in the north to the Gulf of Mexico. On the east it stretches from the southern Chesapeake Bay to the southern-most tip of Florida. On the west, the region extends from Kentucky south to Arkansas and Louisiana.
3. Tourism is important to New England's economy. It is also important in the Mid-Atlantic states, with popular destinations being New York and Washington, D.C.
4. Important points: Students should choose one state other than their own and explain their choice. Encourage students to be specific in explaining their choices.
5. Important points: Encourage students to take a position and support it with reasons. Because many of the oldest and best-known schools and universities are in the Northeast, we tend to associate education strongly with the region. But all regions of the nation are concerned with quality education, and excellence is not the product of a single state or region.
6. Climate, resources, lower wages, and cheaper land are some of the reasons businesses are moving to the Southeast. Although answers will vary, encourage students to think about which factors contribute most strongly to business success.
7. At the time, it was where much of the nation's food was grown. However, with refrigerated shipping, food may come from all over the country and all over the world.

 Mastering Mapwork

1. The tallest peak is Mount Washington in New Hampshire. Mount Washington is a part of the Appalachian chain.
2. The Susquehanna flows through New York, Pennsylvania, and Maryland.
3. The tallest peak is Mount Mitchell, located in western North Carolina.
4. Yes. A region is an area that contains many similar features.

CHAPTER 14 REVIEW

Lessons Learned

LESSON 1
The Northeast Region: New England
New Englanders made their living from shipbuilding, trade, and fishing. Today, New England is an important region for education and service industries.

LESSON 2
The Northeast Region: The Mid-Atlantic
The land and resources made the Mid-Atlantic states an early center for industry and trade in the United States. Manufacturing, finance, communications, and tourism are important parts of the economy.

LESSON 3
The Southeast Region
The Southeast has changed from a rural and agricultural region to one that is more industrialized and urban. Agriculture is still important. Its resources and mild climate attract new residents.

364

 Becoming Better Readers

Students should provide a list of details that could include:
• There are almost 270 colleges and universities in the region, including Harvard, Yale, and MIT.
• maple syrup is a profitable product
• largest granite quarry in the world is in Vermont
• beautiful scenery supports strong tourism industry
• Many famous authors come from the region and are part of its culture.

Talk About It

1. What are some reasons for the recent rapid growth of industry in the Southeast region?
2. Describe the boundaries of the Southeast region.
3. Explain the importance of tourism in New England and the Mid-Atlantic region.
4. Imagine that you and your family could live for a year in any state in New England, the Mid-Atlantic, or the Southeast. In which state would you choose to live? Give reasons for your answer.
5. Why is education said to be a New England product? Is education more a product of New England than of the Mid-Atlantic or the Southeast? Explain your answer.
6. What are some reasons why businesses are moving to the Southeast? Which do you think is the most important reason?
7. The Mid-Atlantic in the early years of our nation's history was called the "breadbasket" of the United States. Why do you think it was given this name?

Mastering Mapwork

REGIONS
Use the maps on page 347, 353, and 358 to answer these questions:

1. Use the map on page 347 to describe the relative location of the tallest peak in New England.
2. Through what states of the Mid-Atlantic region (see map, page 353) does the Susquehanna River flow?
3. Use the map on page 358 to describe the location of the tallest peak in the Appalachian chain, found in the Southeast region.
4. New England is a region as are the Mid-Atlantic states and the Southeast. Are the Appalachian Mountains also a region?

Becoming Better Readers

Finding Details
Good readers know how to read to find detail. Details provide more information and support for the main ideas. If books only had main ideas, readers would be left with lots of questions. When reading a textbook or a nonfiction book, heads and subheads give clues to where to find the details. Go back to page 351 and reread the section titled, *Today's Economy*. Find three details that support how technology, resources, and tourism affect today's economy in the New England states.

Chapter 14

Go to the Source

Reading a Recipe

This recipe features two important products of the northeastern United States. People use maple sugar or syrup to sweeten and flavor food. They get it from maple trees that grow well in the region. Dairy farming is a key part of the region's agriculture. Read the recipe below and answer the questions using information from the recipe.

Maple Walnut Ice Cream

1 cup maple syrup
2 cups heavy cream
1 cup whole milk
1/4 teaspoon salt
2 large eggs
1/3 cup walnuts,
   toasted and chopped

DIRECTIONS:

Boil syrup in a 2-quart pot over medium high heat until it has reduced to 3/4 cup (about 5 to 10 minutes). Stir in cream, milk, and salt. Bring to a boil.

Whisk eggs in a large bowl. Add the hot cream mixture in a slow stream, whisking all the time.

Transfer this mixture, now a custard, to the pot. Cook over medium low heat, stirring constantly, until slightly thickened and a thermometer registers 170 degrees, about 1 to 2 minutes. Do not let it boil!

Pour and strain custard into a clean metal bowl. Cover and chill until cold, at least 3 hours. Freeze custard in an ice-cream maker until soft-frozen. Then with the motor running, add the nuts. Continue churning until frozen. Transfer to an airtight container and put in freezer to harden.

1. What are the two important products of the northeastern United States featured in the recipe?

  a. Eggs and maple syrup
  b. Milk, cream, and maple syrup
  c. Walnuts and maple syrup
  d. Eggs and dairy

2. What is the first step in making maple walnut ice cream?

  a. Wisk eggs in a bowl
  b. Mix cream, milk & salt
  c. Boil syrup in a 2—quart heavy saucepan
  d. Add hot cream into a bowl

3. What do you do to the ice cream after it is soft–frozen?

  a. Put it in the freezer to harden
  b. Keep churning until frozen
  c. Cover and chill for three hours
  d. With the motor running, add nuts

4. What does the mixture become when you whisk the eggs and add hot cream in a slow stream?

  a. Pudding   **b.** Ice cream   **c.** Yogurt   **d.** Custard

Go to the Source

 Go to the Source

Reading a Recipe

OBJECTIVES: 1.06

SOCIAL STUDIES SKILLS: 3.05

Maple Walnut Ice Cream

The cuisine of New England reflects the region's agriculture. Other important foods in addition to maple syrup and milk include cranberries, clams, lobster, cod, haddock, mussels, potatoes, blueberries, and other dairy products such as cheese.

Ice cream also relates to New England because, in the 1800s and early 1900s, ice harvesting was a key agricultural industry. Ice was harvested in the winter and stored in huge ice houses so it could be distributed year-round. Ice from New England was sent to places including China, India, New Orleans, and the West Indies. Even Queen Victoria bought ice from New England in the 1840s.

Answers
1. b
2. c
3. d
4. d

 **How to Use the Chapter Review**

There are four sections in the Chapter Review: Talk About It, Mastering Mapwork, Becoming Better Readers, and Go to the Source. Use the Vocabulary Worksheets and the Chapter Review Worksheet in the Teacher's Resource Guide for additional reinforcement and preparation for the Chapter Assessments. The Chapter and Lesson Reviews and the Chapter Review Worksheets are the basis of the assessment for each chapter.

Talk About It questions encourage students to speculate about the content of the chapter and are suitable for class or small-group discussion. They are not intended to be assigned for homework.

Mastering Mapwork has students apply one or more of the Five Themes of Geography to maps within the chapter.

Becoming Better Readers focuses on building reading strategy skills necessary for reading comprehension in the content areas.

Go to the Source activities allow students to analyze a primary source that relates to the content of the chapter. The questions and activities familiarize students with different types of primary sources and also build content-reading skills.

CHAPTER 15

Western Regions of the United States

Social Studies Strands

Geographic Relationships

Economics and Development

Culture and Diversity

Historical Perspectives

Technological Influences and Society

North Carolina Standard Course of Study

Goal 3 The learner will apply key geographic concepts to the United States and other countries of North America.

Goal 3 The learner will examine the roles various ethnic groups have played in the development of the United States and its neighboring countries.

Goal 5 The learner will evaluate ways the United States and other countries of North America make decisions about the allocation and use of economic resources.

Goal 6 The learner will recognize how technology has influenced change within the United States and other countries in North America.

Teaching & Assessment

• English Language Learner Modified Lesson Plans for this chapter are found in the Teacher's Resource Guide.

• *ExamView® Assessment Suite* is provided at **NCJourneys.com.** It includes customizable assessments for all chapters. Paper tests are also available in the Teacher's Resource Guide. See pages T16–T17 for information about how to use the assessments and the Scoring Guide.

Worksheets

Worksheets and answer keys are found both in the Teacher's Resource Guide and at **NCJourneys.com**, including Reading Guides, Reading Strategies, Chapter Reviews, English Language Learner and others.

Activities and Integrations

SOCIAL STUDIES	
Problem Based Learning: Progress, p. 366B	
★ The Cowboy, p. 366B	
States' Admittance to the Union, p. 367	
● ▲ Who Am I?, p. 372	
■ Oklahoma Land Rush, p. 376	
■ The Settlement of Oklahoma, p. 377	
Hot Potato Review, p. 382	
■ Rocky Mountain Minerals, p. 383	
■ Potato Battery, p. 383	
Rocky Mountain Music, p. 384	
Skill Lesson: Using Maps, p. 385	

READING/LANGUAGE ARTS	READING/LANGUAGE ARTS OBJECTIVES
Writing Prompt: Parks, p. 366	4.06
● Reading Strategy: Cause and Effect, p. 368	2.01, 2.02
● ▲ ■ Little House on the Prairie, p. 370	2.09, 4.07
If It Doesn't Make it in Peoria, It Won't Make It, p. 373	4.07
Reading Strategy: Making Inferences, p. 374	2.02
Reading Strategy: Sequencing, p. 380	3.05
★ National Parks, p. 381	1.04, 3.06
Becoming Better Readers, p. 385	2.01
Understanding Advertisements, p. 387	3.07

MATHEMATICS	MATHEMATICS OBJECTIVES
■ Oklahoma , p. 377	1.02

SCIENCE	SCIENCE OBJECTIVES
■ Biomes, p. 366B	1.01, 1.02,

TECHNOLOGY	TECHNOLOGY OBJECTIVES
★ Donner Party Research, p. 367	2.13
★ ■ A Study of Dams, p. 378	2.13

VISUAL ARTS	VISUAL ARTS OBJECTIVES
● ▲ ■ Corn Husk Dolls, p. 366B	3.02
Activator: Cowboy Song, p. 366	9.03, 9.04, 9.06
● ▲ ■ Southwestern Art, p. 375	3.02
★ National Parks, p. 381	3.02

CHARACTER AND VALUES EDUCATION	TRAITS
What Would You Do?, p. 383	good judgement, justice, responsibility

● Basic Activities   ★ Challenging Activities   ▲ English Language Learner Novice   ■ English Language Learner Intermediate

Introductory Activity

Biomes

 OBJECTIVES: 1.01, 1.02, 1.03

Introduce students (or review with students) the various biomes in the different regions of the United States. Begin with the Rocky Mountains (since this is where a lot of potatoes are grown) and continue discussion into the Northeast and make comparisons. Divide class into groups and assign each group a different biome, such as desert, grasslands, and so on. Discuss with students the various biomes and have students locate on a map where they can be found. Have students research their group's selected biome and plan an activity that illustrates what the biome looks like. Go to **NCJourneys.com** for links to Web sites to help in research. Share information in an oral presentation with the class.

 ## Culminating Activity

The Cowboy

 OBJECTIVES: 3.02, 3.03, 4.02

In the Western Hemisphere there are people who brand and herd cattle for a living. These men are known as the "cowboys" of the Americas. The American cowboy, the Mexican vaquero, the Venezuelan llanero, and the Argentine gaucho have adapted to the tough outdoor environment and their rigorous responsibilities.

Divide the class into cooperative groups. Assign each group one of the cowboys of the Americas to research. Within each group, individual students will become "experts" on one topic pertaining to the cowboy to be researched: location, dress/clothing, tools used by the cowboy, food, and tasks performed by the cowboy.

After students research a given topic, the group will come together and prepare a presentation to teach fellow classmates about the cowboy their group researched. Using a Venn Diagram compare the cowboys of the Americas.

 ## Art Activity

Corn Husk Dolls

OBJECTIVES: 3.02, 3.05, 5.01

Corn is one of the most important crops grown in the Western region of the United States. Settlers used corn husks to make dolls. Students will make a corn husk doll. Because corn husks may be difficult to obtain for this project, a paper twist can be used in place of the corn husk.

Untwist the paper twist. Cut strips of desired length (a 12-inch strip will make a doll about 5 to 6 inches long when folded).

Take the paper strip and fold in half. Place a cotton ball inside the fold to resemble a head. Tie below the cotton ball (head) with yarn or thread. Cut another strip 6 inches long. Insert the strip between the layers of paper twist. This will form the arms. Tie around the body below arm strips. Fluff out the bottom to resemble the dress of a doll. Glue wiggly eyes on head. Cut strips of yarn and glue for hair. For facial features, draw or attach various materials.

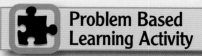 ## Problem Based Learning Activity

Progress

OBJECTIVES: 1.05, 4.02, 4.07

Situation The Western regions of the United States have beautiful landscapes. Some people want to develop this land because it contains valuable resources. Some areas, like national parks, are protected by the government. Yet land around the protected area could be developed.

Task Break students into groups. Each group should identify an area that could be developed, such as the grasslands of the Midwest, and research it. What types of animals and plants are found in these areas? What kinds of development are proposed? What is being done to protect this area? The Internet will be helpful.

Once the information is gathered, ask the group to consider what are the benefits of development? disadvantages? What could be done to prevent destruction while allowing progress to continue? How might individuals compromise between progress and preservation?

Reflection Ask students to write their answers to the following questions individually but reflect upon the group work.
- What is the area you researched?
- How is this landform or area important?
- Why is it important for Americans to appreciate this area of our country?
- Why might progress threaten this area?
- How could this be resolved? Has this exercise changed the way you view the ideas of developers or preservationists?

Teaching Strategies

Stress the similarities and differences between the Western regions and between the Western and European regions. Although we often refer to "The West" as one place, there is great diversity within it.

This chapter also lends itself to group projects and presentations if time is an issue. Refer to Chapters 7 and 9 for additional activities and resources.

Discussion Questions

1 Why did the definition of the "West" keep changing over the years?

2 Why is the date 1787 the earliest one in which states were admitted to the union?

3 According to the map, which state was admitted to the union 100 years after North Carolina?

4 Why do you think that people like the Donner family would leave their homes and join a caravan to settle in a new part of the country?

 Activator

🔺 **OBJECTIVES:** 1.06, 3.02, 3.03

Choose a "cowboy" song to play for the class (see suggested song list below). After students have listened to the song, they are to draw a picture of the images that came to mind as they listened to the song. Share pictures in cooperative groups or as a whole class, then discuss the song and the life of a cowboy.

Cowboy songs:
"Back in the Saddle Again"–Gene Autry
"Cowboy's Lament"–Sons of the Pioneers
"Home on the Range"–Gene Autry
"El Paso"–Marty Robbins
"Mama Don't Let Your Babies Grow Up to be Cowboys"–Willie Nelson, Waylon Jennings
"Streets of Laredo"–Rex Allen
"Whoppie Ti Yi Yo"–Jimmy C. Newman

   Ask the music teacher in your school for further suggestions. Search for songs that describe the life of the Mexican vaquero, Venezuelan llanero, or Argentine gaucho.

 Writing Prompt

🔺 **OBJECTIVES:** 1.02, 1.06, 3.03

Clarification Writing National Parks have millions of visitors each year, which creates environmental problems. Should tourism be limited? Why or why not?

CHAPTER 15

cowboy boots

Chapter Preview

LESSON 1
The Midwest Region
The Midwest includes Ohio, Illinois, Indiana, Michigan, Wisconsin, Missouri, Iowa, Kansas, Minnesota, Nebraska, North Dakota, and South Dakota.

LESSON 2
The Southwest Region
Arizona, New Mexico, Oklahoma, and Texas make up the Southwest.

LESSON 3
The Rocky Mountain Region
Colorado, Wyoming, Montana, Idaho, Utah, and Nevada are states of the Rocky Mountain region.

Western Regions of the United States

Where is the West?
Who shall fix its limits?
He who attempts will soon learn that
it is not a fixed but a floating line.
—Eleuthoros Cook, 1858

   In colonial days, "the West" meant the land along the Appalachian Mountains. In the early days of the new nation, the West was the Ohio territory. Later the West was California and Oregon, then New Mexico and Arizona. Today, the West includes the Midwest, the Southwest, the Rocky Mountains, and the Pacific Coast. Today's West is still a vast, varied, rich, and promising region.

Spring Turning (1936) by Grant Wood

Chapter Resources

Audiovisual
The Midwest and Southwest: People and Places. Humanities Extension/Publications, North Carolina State University.

Print Resources
Southwest
Cherry, Lynne. *Armadillo from Amarillo.* Harcourt, 1994. ISBN 0152003592.
Gipson, Fred. *Savage Sam.* HarperCollins, 1986. ISBN 0060803770.
Henry, Marguerite. *Brighty of the Grand Canyon.* Aladdin Paperbacks, 1991. ISBN 0689714858.
Hobbler, Dorothy. *The Trail on Which They Wept: The Story of a Cherokee Girl.* Scott Foresman, 1992. ISBN 0382243536.
O' Dell, Scott. *Sing Down the Moon.* Laurel Leaf, 1997. ISBN 0440979757.
Pitts, Paul. *Racing the Sun.* Camelot, 1988. ISBN 0380754967.

Midwest
Bial, Raymond. *County Fair.* Houghton Mifflin, 1997. ISBN 039557644X.

States' Admission to the Union

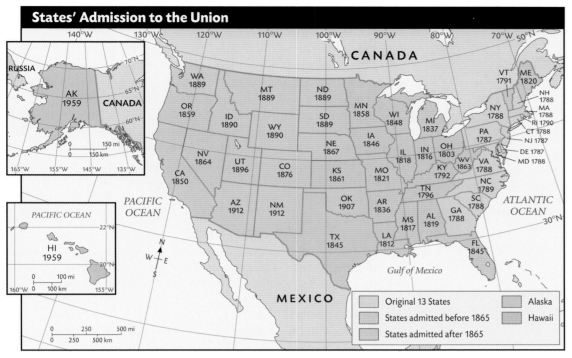

As people settled in western territories, additional states were added to the Union.

Donner Pass

The Donner family of Rowan County, North Carolina, decided to move west. They met many hardships on their journey.

George Donner first settled west of the Appalachians in Kentucky in 1818. A decade later he moved to Indiana, then Illinois. George married his third wife, Tamsen Eustis Donner. She was a teacher from Elizabeth City, North Carolina. They sold their farm and joined a wagon train headed to California in 1846.

The Donner party was trapped by early snows in a high pass of the Sierra Nevada mountains. George and Tamsen did not survive. Their children were rescued. The Donner's descendants live today in California. The site of the Donners' deaths is now named Donner Pass (above).

Western Regions of the United States

367

Freedman, Russell. *An Indian Winter.* Holiday House, 1995. ISBN 0823411583.

Ingoglia, Gina. *Johnny Appleseed and the Planting of the West.* Disney Press, 1994. ISBN 1562822586.

King, Sandra. *Shannon: An Ojibway Dancer.* First Avenue Editions, 1993. ISBN 0822596431.

McGovern, Ann. *If You Grew Up with Abraham Lincoln.* Scholastic Trade, 1976. ISBN 0590451545.

Waters, Kate. *The Mysterious Horseman: An Adventure in Prairietown, 1836.* Scholastic Trade, 1994. ISBN 0590455036.

Web Sites
Visit **NCJourneys.com** for links to:
• Great Plains Nature Center
• Hoover Dam
• John Wesley Powell Museum
• Illinois State Museum
• National Parks Service—The Grand Canyon
• Oklahoma Land Rush Resources
• Southwest Information Gateway

Map Activity

States' Admittance to the Union

NATIONAL GEOGRAPHY STANDARDS: 1, 3, 5, 9, 12, 17

GEOGRAPHIC THEMES: Movement

OBJECTIVES: 1.07, 4.07

Have the students study the map on page 367 and bookmark the page so they can refer to it quickly. They are going to put the states in chronological order by their admittance date. Instruct them to list the state by abbreviation and date (OR–1859). Ask: Where on the map should you start looking for the earliest admitted states? (*East*) Why? (*Those states were populated first.*) How many total states should be listed? (*50*)

After students finish, have students draw a line between states admitted before 1800 and those admitted after 1900. Ask: Which states were the first to be admitted? (*PA, DE, NJ in 1787*) Which states were admitted last? (*AK, HI in 1959*) What patterns did you notice while doing this activity? (*States admitted from east to west for the most part*). Which states did not fit that pattern? (*FL, OK, NM, AZ, OR, NV, CA*) Discuss why these states do not fit the pattern.

Activity

Carolina Connection: Donner Party Research

OBJECTIVES: 1.06, 3.03, 4.02

Go to **NCJourneys.com** for a link to PBS's *American Experience* about the Donner Party. The site includes many primary sources and an interactive map. Patrick Breen, the patriarch of the Breen family, started keeping a journal when they were stranded at Donner Lake (formerly Truckee Lake) in November of 1846. Excerpts from his journal are part of this site.

367

OBJECTIVES: 1.06, 3.02, 3.03

Discussion Questions

1 Why do you think the Midwest region has such fertile farmland?

Caption Answer

Many more people from the Northeast have moved to the South, West, and Southwest in recent years.

Reading Strategy Activity

Cause and Effect

OBJECTIVES: 4.05, 4.06, 4.08

Problems usually have a reason or cause behind them. For example, "We can't go outside and play today because it is raining." What caused us not to go outside? (*It's raining.*) The effect of rain is that we can't go outside. Learning to find the causes will help students become better readers. A way to find a cause of a specific problem is to look for the "cause" words in the lesson: because, cause, so, thus, therefore, led to, due to, as a result, a result of, and resulted in.

An example from another section of the textbook: "Climate and changes in technology and industry affect patterns of movement. Plant closings, like the one in Michigan, and the warm Florida climate are two of the many factors that cause people to move within the United States." What are two things that cause people to move within the United States? (*plant closings and warm climate*)

Caution students to be careful when reading some lessons. Sometimes authors do not use cause words, for example: "It is hard for some students to stay after school for basketball practice. Their parents may work late and cannot pick them up, or they may be needed at home to do chores." What causes some students not to stay after school? (*parents work late or chores to be done*)

Have students re-read the last paragraph of the farming section on

page 372. They should use cause and effect to determine what is/are the cause/s of this effect: Today's Midwesterns farms are large. (*fewer people are needed to grow crops; farm machinery and science have increased the amount of food a farmer can raise*)

Extension Intermediate ELL students should learn the "cause" words so that they can find answers to "why" and "what" questions.

KEY IDEAS

- The Midwest is the nation's heartland because of its location. It is also the center of rich farmland.

- The fertile soil of the Midwest has made it the nation's breadbasket. Dairy, corn, and hogs are also important farm products.

- Its great rivers and lakes are key transportation links.

- Resources include iron ore, lead, limestone, and soft coal.

- Making automobiles is still an important industry here.

KEY TERMS

loess
prairie
tributaries

Wallace Stegner called the West "Hope's native home." This means that people look to the west with hope for the future. The Donners of North Carolina headed west with hopes for a better life. Millions of other settlers moved west, too. They shared the same dreams.

The 12 states of the Midwest make up a huge territory. Ohio, Illinois, Indiana, Michigan, Wisconsin, Missouri, Iowa, Kansas, Minnesota, Nebraska, North Dakota, and South Dakota are often called the nation's heartland. That means they are the center of the nation.

Location and Landforms

The Midwest is best known for miles of rolling plains. The plains are also called the *prairie.* There we can find "amber waves of grain." We sing about these fields in the song "America the Beautiful."

The Central Lowlands

Much of the Midwest is part of the Central Lowlands (see map, 369). It includes central Ohio, Indiana, Illinois, northern Missouri, eastern Kansas, Iowa, most of Minnesota, southern Wisconsin, and the eastern edges of Nebraska and the Dakotas. This is some of the most fertile farmland in the world.

The Mississippi River and its tributaries flow through this region. *Tributaries* are rivers that flow into a larger river. The Ohio and Missouri Rivers are two tributaries of the Mississippi.

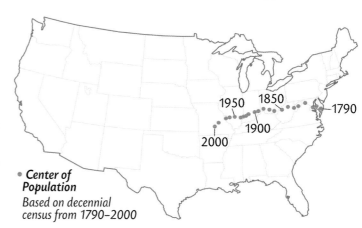

As people moved westward, the population center moved westward. Today it is in southwest Missouri. **Why do you think the center moved toward the Southwest from 1950 to 2000?**

• *Center of Population*
Based on decennial census from 1790–2000

The Midwest Region

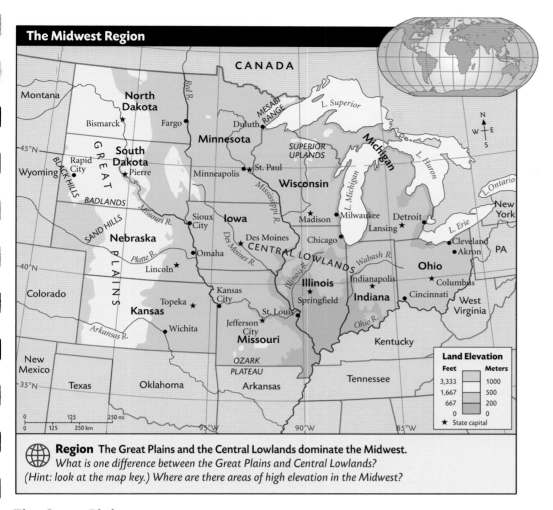

🌐 **Region** The Great Plains and the Central Lowlands dominate the Midwest. *What is one difference between the Great Plains and Central Lowlands? (Hint: look at the map key.) Where are there areas of high elevation in the Midwest?*

The Great Plains

West of the Central Lowlands are the Great Plains. These plains are dry. There are few trees. As you have read, the first European explorers called the plains the "Great American Desert."

Farming the Plains The pioneers moving west did not think anything useful would grow on land that did not have trees. All they could see were the thick prairie grasses. Sometimes the grass grew as tall as a person on horseback.

New inventions and new farming methods helped them grow wheat and other crops on the dry land. John Deere invented a steel plow that could tear through the toughest prairie grass. Farmers also learned ways to save water as they worked the land.

But the plowed soil of the Midwest rewarded the farmers' hard work. The thick, rich soil was formed by glaciers millions of years ago. In some areas, the soil is powdery, with no rocks at all. This deep soil is called *loess* (LOH·ehs). In some parts of Iowa the soil reaches down 600 feet (180 m) into the earth.

Western Regions of the United States

369

Discussion Questions

1 What invention finally made farming possible on the Great Plains?
2 Why was it impossible before this invention?

 Caption Answer

The elevation of the Central Lowlands is about 667 feet (200 meters), and the Great Plains rise to 1,667 feet (500 meters). Areas of high elevation are in the far west of the region, in the Black Hills and Sand Hills.

ℹ️ **Background Information**

The Industrial Midwest

The vacuum cleaner, Ferris wheel, and steel skyscraper were all invented in the Midwest. It is an area known both for its industrial might and its inventors. In the last quarter of the twentieth century, this region, particularly the area around the Great Lakes, experienced some difficult economic challenges. Sometimes known as the "Rust Belt," the region saw massive job losses as foreign competition in such areas as steel and automobile production led to closings or downsizing of many factories. Such major Midwest cities as Detroit, Cleveland, Toledo, Milwaukee, and Cincinnati saw population growth slow and in some cases decline.

369

Discussion Questions

1 How is the soil different in the Midwest compared to other areas of the United States?

Activity

Little House on the Prairie

 OBJECTIVES: 1.05, 1.06, 4.02

Read *Little House on the Prairie* by Laura Ingalls Wilder (HarperCollins, 1976. ISBN 0060264454.) or excerpts from it to your class. Then have students write stories or diary entries with a prairie life setting. Make dioramas of old farmhouse scenes or prairie settler scenes.

Name Origin

Illinois "land of Illini (warriors)." Nickname: Prairie State. Motto: Sovereignty, national unity. Admitted: 21st, 1818.

Indiana "land of the Indians." Nickname: Hoosier State. Motto: Crossroads of America. Admitted: 19th, 1816.

Iowa "Here I rest, or beautiful land." Nickname: Hawkeye State. Motto: Our liberties we prize, and our rights we will maintain. Admitted: 29th, 1846.

Kansas "south wind people." Nickname: Sunflower State. Motto: To the stars through difficulties. Admitted: 34th, 1861.

Michigan "great water." Nicknames: Great Lakes State, Wolverine State. Motto: If you seek a pleasant peninsula, look about you. Admitted: 26th, 1837.

Minnesota "Cloudy water, or sky-tinted water," referring to the river. Nicknames: North Star State, Gopher State. Motto: Star of the North. Admitted: 32nd, 1858.

Missouri "river of big canoes." Nickname: The Show Me State. Motto: The welfare of the people shall be the

Hills of the Midwest

The Midwest does have other landforms. Some parts are not flat. The Black Hills of the Dakotas are hilly and rugged. The hills of the Ozark Plateau of southern Missouri are forested.

There are forests in the hilly areas around the Great Lakes. They are what is left of the miles of "big woods," as settlers called them. The "big woods" once covered the upper Midwest.

 # A Journey to THE MIDWEST

Living on the Plains in a Sod House

Pioneers settled the vast plains of the American Midwest. They found fertile soil, broad, grassy pastures there. But there was little wood.

Building a home without wood was a challenge. A lot of settlers had to use sod. Sod is the thick, grassy, top layer of prairie soil. They used it to build the floors, ceilings, and walls of their new homes.

Glen Rounds wrote in his book *The Treeless Plains* about the settlers and their sod houses:

But for folk who for months had been living in a dugout canoe, a sod house was a luxury simply to be able to look out of the doorway or through the tiny window hole and see the horizon instead of the face of another cutback [riverbank]. Even when divided into rooms by hanging canvas or blankets, the tiny building seemed almost spacious [roomy]....

But in spite of the improved view, the increased living space, and the added ventilation [air flow]—due to having a window as well as a door—the sod houses did have certain drawbacks [problems]. The interiors were dark even on the sunniest days. And after the grass underfoot had worn away, the floors, even when carefully smoothed and packed, were dusty in dry weather and muddy in wet.... Bits of earth

fell from the rough surfaces of the walls at the slightest touch, making housekeeping difficult. Mice, gophers, and a dozen kinds of beetles quickly took advantage of the ease with which burrows and nests could be made.... Somehow the discovery of a mouse swimming in the water bucket, or a huge beetle dropping into the flapjack batter did little to improve [one's] temper.

Home with a sod roof

supreme law. Admitted: 24th, 1821.

Nebraska "broad or flat river" (Platte). Nickname: Cornhusker State. Motto: Equality before the law. Admitted: 37th, 1867.

North Dakota "friend or ally." Nickname: Peace Garden State. Motto: Liberty and union, now and forever, one and inseparable. Admitted: 39th, 1889.

Ohio "fine or good river." Nickname: Buckeye State. Motto: With God, all things are possible. Admitted: 17th, 1803.

South Dakota same as North Dakota. Nicknames: Coyote State, Mount Rushmore State. Motto: Under God, the people rule. Admitted: 40th, 1889.

Wisconsin "grassy place." Nickname: Badger State. Motto: Forward. Admitted: 30th, 1948.

The Gateway Arch, symbolic of the city's position as the Gateway to the West, rises above downtown St. Louis, Missouri. **What major rivers join each other at St. Louis?**

Climate

The Midwest usually enjoys hot summers and long, cold winters. These are features of a continental climate. In the eastern part of the region, the average precipitation (rain and snow) is about 36 inches (91 centimeters) per year. The climate is excellent for farming. There is a long growing season and, usually, plenty of rain.

In the western part, there is much less rainfall. Some parts of western Nebraska, for example, receive only about 16 inches (41 cm) of precipitation in an average year.

Natural Resources

The Midwest has more to offer than just rich farmland. Waterways also are an important resource.

Transportation

As you have read, the Great Lakes and the Midwest's long rivers have played a key role in the region's growth. Four of the five Great Lakes form the Midwest's northern boundary. The Mississippi River runs through its center. Other rivers include the Missouri, the Ohio, the Platte, and the Arkansas.

Easy and cheap water transportation helped Midwestern cities grow. For example, St. Louis, Missouri, is located where the Missouri River flows into the Mississippi. It is known as the Gateway to the West. Many pioneers left St. Louis on wagon trains to follow the western trails to Oregon, California, and Utah.

Chicago and other Midwest cities developed as trading posts for travelers. Chicago became a railroad hub, as you read in Chapter 9. Today, its airports are also transportation hubs, too.

Western Regions of the United States

371

1 What is the meaning of the phrase "Gateway to the West" ? Why is St. Louis, Missouri, called this?

 Caption Answer

The Missouri and the Mississippi

 Activity

A Journey to: Technology

"A Journey to the Midwest" calls to mind Laura Ingalls Wilder's books. Wilder's papers are located at the Herbert Hoover Presidential Library, part of the National Archives and Records Administration. For a link to this site, go to **NCJourneys.com** You will find the following resources at this site:

1. **Rose Wilder Lane Collection** An explanation of what is in the collection and why it is housed at the Hoover Presidential Library

2. **Dear Laura** The Hoover Library's online resource person, June Silliman, a retired teacher from Mount Vernon, Iowa, will answer by e-mail all of your questions about Laura and her family.

3. **Laura Ingalls Wilder teaching unit** Pioneer Life With Laura, a social studies and language arts teaching unit

4. **Bibliographies** The Little House Books, The Pioneer Experience

5. **Activities** time line activity; mapping the journeys of the Ingalls family; patterns for constructing a pioneer town; map of De Smet, South Dakota; making a nine-patch quilt; cousin Ed's straw hat; Grandma Minnie's sunbonnet; wildflower seed packet

Discussion Questions

1 How have the farms changed over the years in the Midwest?

Caption Answer

Corn and grain production requires plowing, seeding, irrigation, and fertilization. The flat land helps farmers plow and plant seed efficiently. The rivers provide water sources for irrigation. The soil is not rocky, and the climate is appropriate for those types of crops.

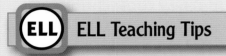

ELL Teaching Tips

Use the Cultures in Your Classroom

Tie the cultures of your ELL students to your lesson. These children with diverse backgrounds have stories and experiences that are unique. You should build on the background knowledge and cultures the students bring from their home countries.

Activity

Who Am I

OBJECTIVES: 1.02, 3.03, 4.02

Materials: laminated map of United States, research materials about states in the Midwest and Southwest

Assign a Midwestern or Southwestern state to each pair of students. They are to use their textbook and other resource materials to list ten facts about their assigned state. Have students arrange their facts in order from little known to commonly known, such as the state's capital city. Number the state facts from 1 to 10, putting 1 beside the most commonly known fact and 10 beside the least known fact. Have students turn in the fact sheets. They will be used as clues for a game.

The game is played as follows: Divide the class into two teams. Flip a coin to see which team gets the first clue. The teacher reads a 10-point clue to that team. If they name the correct state, they score ten points. If they do not name the correct state, the other team gets a chance to name the state. If the second team does not correctly identify the state, they get to hear the 9-point clue. Continue in this manner until one team names the correct state. A laminated map or transparency of the United States could be used to cross off the states as they are correctly identified. Play continues until all states of these regions have been named. The team with the higher score wins. The clue cards can also be used for competition

between two students instead of the entire class.

Sample clue card: **Missouri**
10 Mississippi River to the east
9 the 24th state to join the United States
8 ranks first in lead production
7 has Lake of the Ozarks
6 "Show Me State"
5 Capital is Jefferson City
4 south of Iowa
3 St. Louis is a large city
2 Kansas City is here
1 abbreviation is MO

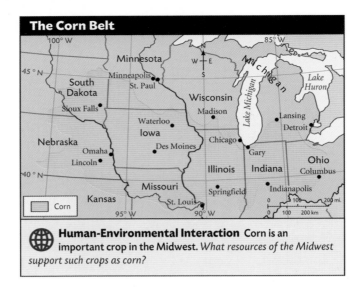

The Corn Belt

Human-Environmental Interaction Corn is an important crop in the Midwest. *What resources of the Midwest support such crops as corn?*

Raw Materials

The region's location and natural resources helped industries grow. The area around the Great Lakes is rich in iron ore, copper, and limestone. In the Mesabi Range of Minnesota, there are rich deposits of iron ore. This provided much of the nation's iron. Some of the richest deposits have been used up.

There are other important minerals in the Midwest. There is lead in Missouri, limestone in Indiana, and soft coal in Illinois. South Dakota has gold. Kansas produces salt and petroleum.

Customs

Corn Toys Many settlers farming the Midwest found some things in short supply. Materials used to make toys—like cloth or wood—were usually scarce. But the settlers knew how to make do.

Settlers on the plains used corn husks and cobs to make toys for their children. They carved whistles and miniature pipes out of cobs. They used the husks to make dolls. Today, many of these old corn toys are valuable. People like to collect them.

Farming

The farmers of the Midwest grow much of America's food. So the region is often called the nation's "breadbasket." The Midwest also exports food to other countries. The dairy farms of Wisconsin have a total of about 1.25 million cows. They produce more dairy products, such as milk, butter, cheese, and ice cream, than any other state.

Eighty-nine percent of Iowa is farmed. Iowa leads the nation in the production of pork, corn, soybeans, and eggs. Iowa also is putting in place programs that protect the soil and water. The land and water are important resources.

The Midwest once was home to many small family farms. Today, most farms in the region are large. Fewer people are needed to grow the enormous amounts of food produced each year. As you read in Chapter 13, improved farm machinery and science have increased the amount of food a farmer can raise.

Industry

Most Midwesterners today do not live on the farm. They live in the region's many cities. The urban areas around Minneapolis and St. Paul, Minnesota; Chicago, Illinois; St. Louis, Missouri; Detroit, Michigan; Milwaukee, Wisconsin; and Columbus, Ohio, have more than a million people each.

Food Processing

Since the Midwest produces so much food, food processing became a key industry. Food processing plants turn the raw foods into products we buy in grocery stores. For example, pork from hogs is made into sausage. Milk is bottled or made into cheese.

The region's transportation system carries farm products to cities where they are processed. Then they are shipped to markets around the country and around the world.

Factories

Good transportation is important for other Midwestern industries. Gary, Indiana, became a major steel manufacturing center. Iron ore could be shipped cheaply from Minnesota on the Great Lakes.

Being close to the production of steel helped make Detroit, Michigan, the home of the automobile industry. Auto production, in turn, helped grow related industries in neighboring cities.

As you read in Chapter 13, these manufacturing industries have undergone significant changes. Some steel plants closed in the 1970s and 1980s. Since then, auto factories have modernized and today produce more cars with fewer workers.

Culture

Even though many people now live in cites, the rural heritage of the Midwest influences its culture. Midwesterners are viewed as open, friendly, and plain-speaking people.

Food processing plants are built close to regions of food production. This meatpacking plant in Chicago is near the hog-producing state of Iowa. **What kinds of food processing are done near your home?**

As you read in Chapter 10, Many African Americans moved north to work in Midwestern factories. In Detroit, African Americans created the "Motown Sound" of rock and roll.

The area has many professional sports teams. College football is important in Nebraska, Indiana, and Michigan. Many teams have won national championships. Auto racing is popular. The Indianapolis 500 is run each spring in Indiana. Music fans visit the Rock and Roll Hall of Fame in Cleveland, Ohio.

LESSON ① REVIEW

Fact Follow-Up
1. What are the Midwestern states?
2. What landforms are in the Midwest?
3. Describe the climate and natural resources of the Midwest.

Talk About It
1. Why did the farming and food processing industries develop in the Midwest?
2. Explain why good transportation has been so important to the Midwest's economy.

Discussion Questions

1 If you could give the Midwest region a nickname, what would it be? Why?

Caption Answer

Answers will vary. Check the local chamber of commerce or a business directory. North Carolina processes pork, pickles, wine, fruit and vegetables, and poultry as well as other food products.

Activity

If it Doesnt Make it in Peoria, It Won't Make it

OBJECTIVES: 3.02, 5.04, 5.06

Peoria, Illinois, is the test-market capital of the United States. When companies want to come out with a new product, they will often test the response from Peoria. Peoria is found in America's Midwest. The residents of this city are supposedly good examples of average Americans.

Ask the students: Why do you think that companies have chosen the Midwest of the United States to represent or stand in for the entire country?

Have students think of a product to be tested in Peoria. It can be food, a tool, or a toy. Ask: How would you write an advertisement for your new product so that the people in Peoria would like it? Have students write such an advertisement.

LESSON ① REVIEW

Fact Follow-Up Answers
1. Ohio, Illinois, Indiana, Michigan, Wisconsin, Missouri, Iowa, Kansas, Minnesota, Nebraska, North Dakota, and South Dakota.
2. Much of the Midwest is part of the Central Lowlands. Land there is fertile and flat. Before settlement, it was covered in grasslands. West of the Central Lowlands are the Great Plains. The land there is dry and flat, with few trees. Settlers passing through the Great Plains referred to it as "the Great American Desert."
3. The Midwest usually has hot summers and long, cold winters characteristic of a continental climate. In the eastern portion of the region, the climate is excellent for farming, with a long growing season and (usually) plenty of rain. The western part of the region is much drier. Natural resources include rich soil for farming, iron ore, copper, limestone, soft coal, lead, gold, salt, and petroleum.

Talk About It Answers
1. The Midwest's rich soil and good climate made the region well suited for farming. The Great Lakes and the Midwest's great rivers provided a transportation system for carrying farm products to cities where they could be processed and shipped to markets.
2. Rivers were important to the settlement and growth of the Midwest. Cities such as St. Louis, Missouri, grew up at the intersections of rivers. The Great Lakes, the Mississippi River, the Ohio River, railways, and good highways provide the Midwest with a good system for transporting heavy goods.

OBJECTIVES: 1.02, 1.06, 3.03

 Caption Answer

Answers will vary. Encourage students to imagine stories set in the past and future as well as the present.

 Reading Strategy Activity

Making Inferences

 OBJECTIVES: 1.02, 1.06, 3.03

Give students the following information:

Words beginning with the same prefixes have similar meanings. Bicycle means a cycle with two wheels. Biweekly means twice a month. What does biannual mean? (*twice a year*)

Tell students they have just made an inference. An inference is a guess based on facts. Everyone makes inferences every day, but to make good ones students must look at the information they have and draw conclusions about what is meant.

Let students try this one:

Long ago, people often took their name from what they did for a living. A man with the name Baker worked in a bakery, or a man with the name Carpenter was probably a man who made furniture or houses. What do you think a man with the name of Weaver did? (*made cloth*)

Students can use the same method to make inferences in social studies and science. Remind students that the answers to inference questions are not in the book. They should use the information in the textbook to make good guesses.

KEY IDEAS

- The Southwest states are Arizona, New Mexico, Oklahoma, and Texas. They have a warm and often dry climate.

- The Southwest contains mineral resources of oil, gas, copper, and gold.

- Agriculture is dependent on water, which is often scarce.

KEY TERMS

Four Corners
plateau

As far as we know, the oldest continuously settled community in the United States is located in the Southwest. Native Americans have lived at the Acoma Pueblo in New Mexico for more than 1,000 years. The Southwest is the home of many Native Americans.

The Spanish heritage is also still strong in the Southwest. Families descended from Spanish explorers have lived in the region for hundreds of years. Newcomers from Mexico are attracted by its familiar culture and wider economic opportunities.

The Southwest attracts people from other places, too. It is one of the fastest-growing regions of the country.

Location and Landforms

The Southwest is a place where people want to live because of its beauty. Some of the most thrilling natural wonders in the United States are in Arizona, New Mexico, Oklahoma, and Texas.

Visitors to the Grand Canyon are awed by its size and beauty. It has inspired artists and storytellers. **What kind of story would you write using the Grand Canyon as your setting?**

374

Chapter 15

The Southwest Region

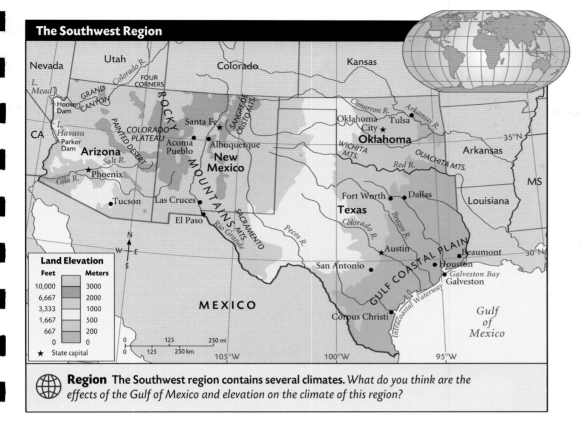

Land Elevation

Feet	Meters
10,000	3000
6,667	2000
3,333	1000
1,667	500
667	200
0	0

★ State capital

Region The Southwest region contains several climates. *What do you think are the effects of the Gulf of Mexico and elevation on the climate of this region?*

Texas

Many think of flat desert when they think of the Southwest. Yet the eastern part of the region has rolling woodlands. Fields of wildflowers bloom in the Hill Country of Texas, between Austin and San Antonio.

Along Texas' Gulf Coast, the Coastal Plain is sandy. There are many swamps and offshore islands. The Gulf Coastal Plain also has wide stretches of fertile farmland. Here farmers grow cotton, rice, fruit, and vegetables.

The Ozark Plateau borders the region to the east. The Great Plains extend into eastern Texas and Oklahoma. Cattle country, home to hardy beef cattle and the tough cowboys who herd them, is in northwest Texas and in eastern New Mexico. This is high plains country—dry, and mostly treeless.

Plateau

Southwest Texas, western New Mexico, and Arizona lie in the *plateau* (plah·TOE) country. Plateaus are flat highlands. Rivers have flowed across the plateaus for millions of years. They have cut deep canyons into the land. The most spectacular is the Grand Canyon of Arizona. It was carved 6 to 10 million years ago by the Colorado River.

The borders of Arizona, New Mexico, Colorado, and Utah meet at a point called the *Four Corners*. Novelist Willa Cather described its beauty: "Elsewhere the sky is the roof of the world; but here the earth was the floor of the sky."

Western Regions of the United States

375

Caption Answer

New Mexico and Arizona have a desert climate and a higher elevation. They receive less rainfall because of the mountains. Southeast Texas is humid subtropical because the Gulf of Mexico moderates the climate, making it milder and rainier than the rest of the region.

Activity

Southwestern Art

OBJECTIVES: 3.03, 3.05, 3.07

Have students research Southwestern art forms and designs, noting the influence of Native Americans. Have them consider as well the influence of the area's natural resources, such as silver, turquoise, and clay. Then have students create their own Southwestern designs.

Ideas for crafts:

- Make mats. Use either cloth strips or paper strips. Define the geometrical shapes used in such designs.
- Make jewelry. Use fake silver wire and turquoise stones from a crafts store to make necklaces and earrings, bracelets, and belt buckles.
- Make pottery. Use clay and let the students create their own pots. Paint the finished pots with Southwestern designs. Pots can air dry, but firing is better.
- Make sand art. Using sand or salt, color with food coloring or tempura paint and use to draw pictures on paper over a light layer of glue or layer designs in baby food jars.

Name Origin

Arizona "little spring water/silver bearing." Nickname: Grand Canyon State. Motto: God enriches. Admitted: 48th, 1912.

New Mexico once a province of Mexico, "place of the war god." Nickname: Land of Enchantment. Motto: It grows as it goes. Admitted: 47th, 1912.

Oklahoma "red man." Nickname: Sooner State. Motto: Labor conquers all things. Admitted: 46th, 1907.

Texas "friends or allies." Nickname: Lone Star State. Motto: Friendship. Admitted: 28th, 1845.

Activity

Oklahoma Land Rush

OBJECTIVES: 1.07, 4.07

To introduce the Oklahoma Land Rush, rent the movie Far and Away starring Nicole Kidman and Tom Cruise. The film in its entirety is not appropriate to show to students, but the foundation of the story is. Kidman and Cruise are Irish immigrants who come to America and end up in the Oklahoma land rush. The images of the wagons lining up and the chaos that follows will be very illustrative for students.

Before sharing the movie clip with students, share a primary source document about the land rush. You can find a link to this source at **NCJourneys.com** The site provides an article from Harper's Weekly (May 18, 1889; pages 393–94). The reporter of the article was present on the day the Oklahoma territory was opened up.

The Settlement of Oklahoma

By the end of the 1880s, almost all of the western frontier had been settled. The only unsettled area left was the Oklahoma Territory. This had been controlled by Native Americans. But on March 23, 1889, President Benjamin Harrison declared that the Oklahoma Territory would be opened to settlement. Land would be given away in "runs" and lotteries.

Before each run, thousands of people gathered at the line, ready to stake their claims to farmland. "At last the revolvers barked, and along the line pandemonium broke loose. Men whipped up their horses, wagons careened wildly forward—all was hurrah and excitement. Noise and confusion reigned."

Many of them met people who had already staked claims in the Oklahoma Territory several hours or days before. These people were called "sooners." They arrived in the territory sooner than they were allowed to.

Racing to stake a claim in Oklahoma during the Cherokee Outlet run, 1893

376

Teacher Notes

Boley

The most famous of Oklahoma's all African American towns was founded in 1903 in the Creek Nation of "Indian Territory." Located on the Fort Smith & Western Railroad, the town was at first a camp for African American railroad workers and was officially incorporated on May 11, 1905. The population soon grew to 4,000 residents. The town was often visited by Booker T. Washington. The annual Boley Rodeo, which began in 1905 and continues to be held each summer, was advertised throughout the South. The purpose of this event was to attract African Americans to the area with hope that they would purchase land and join the community (which, in many cases, did occur).

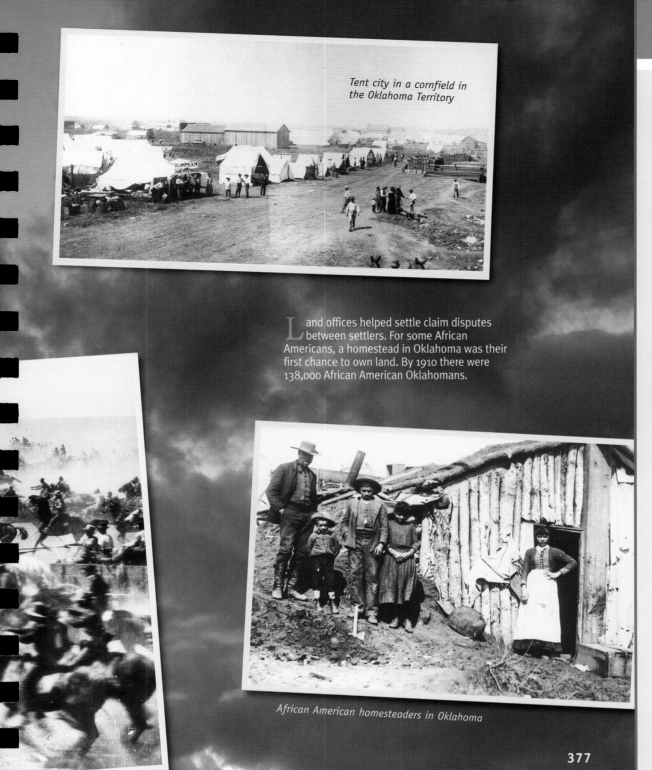

Tent city in a cornfield in the Oklahoma Territory

L and offices helped settle claim disputes between settlers. For some African Americans, a homestead in Oklahoma was their first chance to own land. By 1910 there were 138,000 African American Oklahomans.

African American homesteaders in Oklahoma

377

 Eyewitness Activity

The Settlement of Oklahoma

OBJECTIVES: 3.02, 4.02, 4.03

Move the desks in order to run a relay race in your classroom, or take the class outside or to the gym for this activity. Go over the rules for the relay: Each runner is to stay in his or her lane, tag the next runner's hand gently, and go to the end of the line and squat down so the winning team may be determined.

In one part of the room or on the field, have an outline map of Oklahoma that has been divided into about 20 sections. (Possibly a group of students could prepare a map for you from the overhead or opaque projector.) This will represent parcels of land the pioneers claimed in Oklahoma.

Divide the class into teams and run several relays. Use the following ways of moving for each race:

- "Prairie fires are behind you, flap your arms to put them out as you run."
- "Clouds of locusts are after your crops. Stomp your feet as you run."
- "High winds are blowing. Whirl around while you run."
- "Searing summer temperatures are making you hot. Fan yourself as you run."
- "It has not rained for months. Pant for water as you run."

The winning team for each race may choose a section of the state as their winning prize. The team that has the most pieces of Oklahoma becomes the "Sooners," or winners!

 Math Activity

Oklahoma!

OBJECTIVES: 3.03, 3.07

The Broadway musical *Oklahoma!* opened in New York in 1943 and served as the model for modern musical theater. Its initial run was comprised of 2,212 performances, the top ticket price being $4.80. It then moved to London where another 1,548 were performed.

If the average ticket price was $4.00 (in both the United States and London), and the average audience size was 1,750 people, how many people saw it during its first two runs? Based on these averages, what was the total in ticket sales? *total number of performances = 3,760; total attendance = 6,580,000; total ticket sales = $22,320,000*

1. Why was oil referred to as "black gold"?
2. What other minerals are abundant in the Southwest?

Caption Answer

Cities need plenty of water to support the population. Only a certain number of people and cities can get sufficient water from one river.

Research Activity

A Study of Dams

▶ OBJECTIVES: 1.06, 4.02, 5.01

Materials: copies of a political map of the western United States, atlas with individual state maps, wall map of the United States, and colored markers

Divide students into pairs. Give students colored markers/pencils and a copy of a map showing the western United States. Have students locate the Colorado River on the large wall map and atlas, then use markers to locate dams and cities along the Colorado River on their group map. They will use blue to trace the Colorado River, and another color to trace the tributaries along the Colorado River. A different color will mark the spot for dams located along the river (see list below). Another color will mark cities located along the river. As students locate and mark the dams and cities, ask students to discuss the relationship between the dams and cities and discuss ways people depend on the Colorado River. Write a paper (one per pair) on the "Effects of Dams on the Colorado River." Have students as a group research the Central Arizona Project and report their findings by making a Central Arizona Project Fact Sheet.

Major dams along the Colorado River: Davis Dam, Glen Canyon Dam, Parker Dam, Laguna Dam, Blue Mesa Dam, Dixon Canyon Dam, Granby Dam, Olympus Dam, Hoover Dam, Navajo Dam, Deer Creek Dam, Moon Lake Dam, Fontenelle Dam.

The Central Arizona Project is a water-control system that supplies Arizona's cities with water. **How do limited water resources impact the growth of cities in the Southwest?**

Deserts and Mountains

This part of the Southwest is very dry. Deserts reach toward the Rocky Mountains. The Rio Grande (rio means river in Spanish) begins in the Rockies and flows southeast. It forms the border between the United States and Mexico.

The Southwest is called the "land of open sky." It has thousands of acres of unspoiled land, national parks, and forests. As one resident says, "The land is so full of silence that there is no room for sound."

Climate

The Southwest makes up a large part of the nation's Sun Belt. The Southeastern region and southern California are also part of the Sun Belt.

The region's climates change with elevation and nearness to water. The Texas Gulf Coast is humid subtropical. People in the higher mountain areas have the highlands climate.

The mostly dry parts of the Southwest are in the steppe and desert climates. This dry part of the Southwest receives fewer than ten inches (25 cm) of precipitation a year. Because of the scarcity of rain, farms depend on irrigation. Irrigation brings water to the plants, like using a sprinkler on your lawn.

Natural Resources

Great reserves of oil and natural gas lie below the surface of Texas and Oklahoma. The oil industry began in both states in 1901. They soon replaced western Pennsylvania as the center of the nation's oil industry.

Oil

The discovery of oil was like a gold strike. Oil wells were called gushers. Wells gushed, or exploded, in great fountains of "black gold."

People from everywhere rushed to the oil fields of Texas and Oklahoma. They hoped to strike it rich. Boom towns, such as Beaumont and Houston, Texas, and Tulsa, Oklahoma, grew with the oil industry.

Other Resources

The Southwest contains many other minerals. More than half of the nation's copper supply is found in Arizona. The region also is mined for gold, silver, lead, uranium, and zinc.

Other natural resources are found here, too. The almost constant sunshine is ideal for solar power. Flat land and clear air make the Arizona deserts perfect for United States air bases and military sites.

Water

One resource has created major problems and challenges in the dry Southwest. Its future depends on water.

Hundreds of years ago, Native Americans living in this region watered their crops using irrigation ditches. Today, farmers also irrigate the land to grow crops.

The Southwest's growing population has greatly increased demand for water. The Central Arizona Project is a system of 336 miles (541 km) of pipes and canals. It brings water to Phoenix and Tucson from Lake Havasu on the Colorado River.

The Colorado River provides much of the water in the Southwest. Much of the river is used for irrigation, hydroelectric power, and

378

Background Information

Southwest Water Wars

For people in the Southwest, water and how it should be shared is a topic of heated debate. In this region most agriculture relies on irrigation. In Texas that water comes from an underground water supply, the Ogallala aquifer. The water in this aquifer, which stretches from the Texas Panhandle to South Dakota, accumulated over several thousand years. It cannot be replaced naturally for many centuries. Growing cities and industries do not want to share this water with farmers, making water wars a real possibility in the future.

drinking water. These uses have reduced the river to a trickle before it empties into the Gulf of California.

As the Southwest continues to grow, making sure people, animals, and crops have enough water will be a serious problem.

Industry

Petroleum and its related industries are the biggest industries in the Southwest. Oil is used to make gasoline and many other products, such as nylon and plastic. Houston is the capital of the oil industry. Houston is connected to Galveston Bay and the Intercoastal Waterway by the Houston Ship Canal.

Major crops are grown in the Southwest. They include cotton, wheat, fruit, and vegetables.

The Southwest is famous as cowboy country. Texas leads the nation in cattle production. The cattle now are processed for market right in Texas.

Mining was the center of the Southwest's economy for many years. Copper mining is still important in Arizona. Uranium, is used to make nuclear power. It is mined in New Mexico. Electronics has grown into a major industry in Texas.

Houston is a "space" city. The space shuttle and other spacecraft are guided on their journeys from "Mission Control." Mission Control is located at the Lyndon B. Johnson Space Center in Houston.

Agriculture in the Southwest depends on irrigation. Mobile irrigation pipes used on this New Mexico farm keep the soil fertile. **How would population patterns change if water supplies ran out in the Southwest?**

Culture

The Southwest has a diverse culture. Native Americans, Spanish, European, and African American settlers have all influenced each other.

Many tourists visit the area to see the amazing landscapes. They buy lovely crafts like silver jewelry from Native American artists. They enjoy delicious foods.

Texans are famous for beef barbeque. Corn and peppers are used in many Southwestern dishes. These flavors show the region's Spanish and Mexican heritage.

Discussion Questions

1 What is the major problem that will continue as the Southwest grows?

2 What modern inventions have helped the economy of the Southwest?

3 Why do you think that the Southwest is one of the fastest-growing regions of the United States?

4 What modern inventions have made life easier in the Southwest region?1800s?

 **Caption Answer**

The population would decline as there would not be enough water to support all human activities.

LESSON 2 REVIEW

Fact Follow-Up
1. Describe the landforms, soil, and vegetation of the Southwest.
2. Describe the changing economy of the Southwest.
3. Why is irrigation important here?

Talk About It
1. Which natural resource is most important to the Southwest?
2. How did settlement change the Southwest's landscape?
3. Which groups influence culture here?

LESSON 2 REVIEW

Fact Follow-Up Answers
1. The Southwest landforms include the sandy coastlines of the Coastal Plain, the rolling woodlands and wildflowers of the hill country, the dry, treeless plains country near the southwestern corner of the region, the plateau and canyon country of Arizona and northern New Mexico, and the desert country near Utah.
2. Oil is the biggest industry in the Southwest, as are such crops as cotton, wheat, and other fruit and vegetables. Texas remains the capital of the cattle industry. Mining remains vital to the economy of several states in the region. Uranium is produced in New Mexico, and copper is mined in Arizona.
3. Irrigation is the way farmers can grow crops in this dry region,

Talk About It Answers
1. Important points: Encourage students to suggest various resources, choose one as being most important, and explain their choice. Different resources have been especially important at different times. Water is perhaps most important today.
2. Important points: Encourage students to suggest various ways the landscape has been changed. Among these are the building of roads, railroads, towns, cities; digging mines; clearing prairies for farming; and building dams for water control and irrigation.
3. Native Americans, Spanish, European, and African American settlers. The Southwest is also home to many artists.

LESSON 3 The Rocky Mountain Region

 OBJECTIVES: 1.06, 3.02, 3.03

Discussion Questions

1 Why do you think this area is not densely populated?

2 What made Salt Lake City an ideal place to hold the Winter Olympics?

 Caption Answer

Highlands

 Reading Strategy Activity

Sequencing

 OBJECTIVES: 1.06, 3.02, 3.03

Tell students that when following a recipe, it is important to do each step in the right order. Share the following example: Mix 2 eggs and 1 cup of milk with cake mix. Pour into a greased 9-inch pan. Bake at 350° F for 30 minutes. Would you pour the mix in the pan before you add the milk and eggs? No. The steps are written in the order that they should be done.

When reading, students must recall the order in which events occur. Clue words help order, or sequence, events in their reading.

first, last, after, before
finally, next, prior to, and then.

Read aloud the American portrait of John Wesley Powell on page 382. Have students notice the words and the order of events. Discuss that dates and references to major events, like the Civil War, also can be sequence clues. Students should make a list of the words that suggest a sequence (in 1869; in the Civil War; day after day; finally; later; then).

The clue words help us better see the order of events in Powell's life. Have students look for clue words and notice the sequence of events in their reading. Use the Sequencing worksheet in the Teacher's Resource Guide to practice the skill.

KEY IDEAS

- The Rocky Mountain states are Montana, Idaho, Wyoming, Colorado, Utah, and Nevada.

- The Rocky Mountains are the central landform of the region.

- Like the Southwest, the lack of water is a problem.

- Farming is important in Idaho, but elsewhere the economy is based on mineral production.

KEY TERMS

cardinal directions
Continental Divide
intermediate directions
map key
north arrow
scale
symbols

Do you remember reading about the Mormon Trail in Chapter 7? Brigham Young led members of the Mormon church to the site of present-day Salt Lake City, Utah. He was looking for "a place on this earth nobody else wants."

Today, Salt Lake City is a modern city. It hosted the 2002 Winter Olympic Games. The city is located in one of the most rapidly changing regions of the country—the Rocky Mountain region.

Location and Landforms

Colorado, Idaho, Montana, Nevada, Utah, and Wyoming are not densely populated. Less than 4 percent of the nation's population live here. Stretches of these states are undeveloped. The open landscape is dotted with tourist resorts or small mining towns. Most people live in the region's cities.

Rocky Mountain states are in a region named for its major landform. **What climate is common in mountain regions?**

380

Chapter 15

 Name Origin

Colorado "red," referring to the river. Nickname: Centennial State. Motto: Nothing without providence. Admitted: 38th, 1876.

Idaho Shoshone for "Look, the sun is coming down the mountain," or a coined phrase: "Gem of the Mountain." Nickname: Gem State. Motto: It is perpetual. Admitted: 43rd, 1890.

Montana "mountainous." Nickname: Treasure State. Motto: Oro y Plata (gold and silver). Admitted: 41st, 1889.

Nevada "snow clad." Nicknames: Sagebrush State, Battleborn State, and Silver State. Motto: All for our country. Admitted: 36th, 1864.

Utah "hill dwellers or upper people." Nickname: Beehive State. Motto: Industry. Admitted: 45th, 1896.

Wyoming "on the great plain." Nicknames: Equality State, Cowboy State. Motto: Equal Rights. Admitted: 44th, 1890.

The Rocky Mountain Region

(map)

PACIFIC OCEAN

Washington • Columbia R. • Willamette R. • Oregon • California • Carson City ★ • L. Tahoe • SIERRA NEVADA • Nevada • GREAT BASIN • Las Vegas • Hoover Dam • L. Mead • Colorado R. • Arizona

CANADA

Montana • ★Helena • Billings • Missouri R. • Yellowstone R. • Idaho • ★Boise • Pocatello • Snake R. • Grand Teton • Yellowstone National Park • ROCKY MOUNTAINS • Wyoming • Continental Divide • Casper • Cheyenne ★ • North Platte R. • Powder R. • South Platte R. • Colorado • ★Denver • Pikes Peak ▲ • Pueblo • Arkansas R. • Rio Grande • San Juan R. • Four Corners • New Mexico • Texas

North Dakota • South Dakota • Nebraska • Kansas • Oklahoma

Salt Lake City ★ • Great Salt Lake • Provo • Utah

Land Elevation

Feet	Meters
10,000	3000
6,667	2000
3,333	1000
1,667	500
667	200

★ State capital

125 W 120 W 115 W 110 W 105 W 45 N 40 N

0 125 250 mi
0 125 250 km

🌐 **Region** The Rocky Mountain region is an example of the dilemma of deciding which places should be included in a region. All of the states in the region include the Rocky Mountains, but the Rocky Mountains extend into other states. *Do you think other states should be included in this region? not included?*

The Rockies

The Rocky Mountain region, of course, takes its name from the mountains. They reach from Canada all the way south to Mexico.

The highest peaks are located in the southern part of the Rocky Mountains. The Rockies stretch from Canada down through Wyoming, Montana, Idaho, and Colorado.

The *Continental Divide* twists through the mountains. Water on the eastern side of the divide flows toward the Mississippi River. It makes its way into the Gulf of Mexico. Water on the western side of the divide flows toward the Pacific Ocean.

Other Features

Many other different features mark the Rocky Mountain region. One of the most beautiful is the Great Salt Lake. There

Brigham Young brought the Mormons to settle in peace.

The Great Salt Lake covers almost 1,500 square miles (3,900 square kilometers). It is located in the Great Basin, a huge area of desert. It has such a high salt content that swimmers cannot sink.

Climate

In most of the region, the highlands climate changes with elevation. In higher elevations, winters are colder and summers are shorter. Lower elevations have the cold winters of the continental climate. The amount of precipitation varies greatly within the Rocky Mountain region. The entire region is dry. Nevada is the driest state in America. It averages about 9 inches (23 cm) of rainfall a year.

Western Regions of the United States

381

Discussion Questions

1 Why do you think Nevada receives so little rainfall?

2 Which is the driest state in the United States?

3 Why do you suppose Brigham Young thought the Mormons would be left in peace if they settled in the Salt Lake region?

Caption Answer

Answers will vary. Region can be defined culturally as well as physically. In this definition, Arizona, New Mexico, and Texas might be categorized as a region with a strong Hispanic cultural influence.

Activity

National Parks

🔖 **OBJECTIVES:** 1.02, 1.06, 4.02

Have students make a list of National Parks in the Rocky Mountain region. A United States almanac is a useful source. Put students into cooperative groups to research a particular national park. You might want to help students focus on exactly what information they need. Some examples of the types of information found on national parks are listed below:

year established	where located
size	major attractions
history	wildlife
vegetation	purpose
how funded	how operated and by whom

Suggestions: Have students put the information on a data sheet, or put each topic on a large note card, or use chart paper. Have class share the information.

Extension Each group is to design a large postcard to attract visitors to the park. On the back of the postcard, students should give factual information as it is found on real postcards. Bring in some postcards to show them some examples.

Activity

Hot Potato Review

 OBJECTIVES: 1.06, 3.02, 5.01

Potatoes are an important crop in Idaho.

Have students form a circle. Pass a nerf ball (the hot potato) around the circle quickly. While the ball is being passed (if indoors) play the song "Rocky Mountain High" by John Denver. When the music stops or you say "Stop," the student holding the nerf ball must answer a review question about the Rocky Mountain region. If the answer is incorrect, the student sits down. The relay continues until the last student is declared the winner. Students who are sitting can write down notes on the questions or sit quietly until the game is over.

Review questions

1. True or False Is this area densely populated? *false*
2. The Rocky Mountain States are in a region named for a major landform. What is the name of the landform? *Rocky Mountains*
3. What root vegetable is grown more here than in any other state? *potato*
4. In what state is gambling legal? *Nevada*
5. Name two of the popular recreations of the Rocky Mountain region. *skiing, bicycling, hiking, rock climbing, and rafting*
6. Name of a religious leader who led members of his religion to the present-day site of Salt Lake City. *Brigham Young*
7. The lack of what natural resource is a problem in the Rocky Mountain region? *water*
8. Name of an important river that supplies water to California and Arizona. *Colorado*
9. What two minerals does Nevada lead in the production of? *gold and silver*
10. What unusual mineral is mined that is used to make glass, detergent, and baking soda? *trona*
11. In what state are the famous Idaho potatoes grown? *Idaho*
12. What has helped create new jobs in this region? *computers*

AMERICAN PORTRAIT

John Wesley Powell
1834–1902

In 1869, Major John Wesley Powell was thirty-five years old. He had lost an arm fighting in the Civil War. Despite this, he rode a train to Wyoming, bringing four wooden boats with him. He and nine men set out to explore the Green and Colorado Rivers, which until that time were largely unknown.

Powell and his crew bravely followed the Green River into a steep canyon, rowing through foaming rapids. To get samples of rocks and plants above the river, the men struggled to scale the red rock cliffs in sweltering heat. One boat crashed; supplies were lost. Food was running out. Only some rotting ham and damp sacks of rice, beans, and dried apples were left.

The Green River flowed into the Colorado. Day after day, the men floated through canyons so rough that the last of their scientific equipment broke. The men were starving. Finally, the crew emerged victorious from the Grand Canyon (in today's Arizona) and drifted to a pioneer settlement.

Later, Major Powell led two more expeditions down the rivers. He explored all over the West, and then argued for laws he felt were needed to best conserve the land and the waters flowing through it.

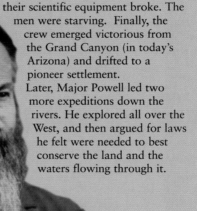

382

Natural Resources

Like the rest of the West, the Rocky Mountain states are also rich in resources.

Water

As in the Southwest, the supply of water is a problem in the Rockies. The Colorado River brings water from the Rockies to the growing populations of California and Arizona.

Drier Utah and Colorado must provide for their growing cities. The Central Utah Water Project should provide enough water for Salt Lake City until 2020. The Colorado Water Conservation Board has more than nine agreements with other states that regulate water usage.

Idaho, on the other hand, has a smaller population. It also has many rivers. So Idaho does not have major water problems.

Minerals

Miners have raced to the mountain states since the 1800s. They found gold, copper, uranium, and silver. Nevada leads the nation in the mining of gold and silver. Large reserves of oil are also located in the mountain states.

The region has some unusual minerals. Vermiculite is used in insulation. It and talc are found in Montana. Wyoming has the largest supply of trona in the world. Trona is a mineral used to make glass, detergent, and baking soda.

The soil and climate of the Snake Valley in Idaho are perfect for growing the famous Idaho potatoes. More potatoes are harvested in Idaho than any other state. Many of the "spuds" are turned into french fries and potato chips before they ever cross the state's borders.

Chapter 15

Teacher Notes

John Wesley Powell

John Wesley Powell grew up in the Midwest and taught himself geography, geology, and other natural sciences. Serving as a major in the Civil War, he lost the lower part of his right arm at the Battle of Shilo. After the war he led summer research trips to the Rocky Mountains in search of fossils. In 1869, he secured a small stipend for an ambitious survey of the Colorado River. Powell's party of ten men started out from the newly completed Union Pacific railroad at Green River, Wyoming, on May 24, 1869, in four boats. Three months, 900 miles, one mutiny, and many near-disasters later, Powell and party emerged at the mouth of the Grand Canyon, the first people to pass through the canyon by river. To this day, Powell's enthusiastic and accurate accounts of these canyons are the most readable descriptions of the region.

Powell's journey is an excellent opportunity to discuss the character traits of courage and perseverance.

Las Vegas, Nevada, is one of the fastest-growing cities in the United States, partly because of the tourists attracted to such places as the MGM Grand Hotel. **Where would you want to live in the Rocky Mountain region?**

The Economy

"It's spring in the Rockies!" declare business owners and employees in the mountain states. The economies of Colorado, Idaho, Montana, Nevada, Utah, and Wyoming are growing faster than the economy of the nation as a whole. Las Vegas is the fastest-growing city in the region.

Las Vegas, Nevada

In 1931, the state of Nevada made gambling legal. This brings many people to Nevada on vacation. About 27 percent of Nevada's population now work in tourism.

Each month, 2.5 million visitors and 6,000 new residents go to Las Vegas. Las Vegas has ranked first in the nation for employment growth since 1995. The current population is estimated at 1.6 million.

Other Changes

In other areas of the region, new technologies like computers help people live and work in more rural areas. Many people have wanted to live in the mountains. But it has been hard to earn a living there unless you were a miner or a rancher.

Today, small businesses or individuals can work where they like. A telecommuter is the name for a person who works at home and communicates with coworkers and customers by telephone and computer.

Of all the mountain states, Colorado has the most varied economy, with government facilities, mines, resorts, farms, ranches, and industry.

What would YOU do?

Imagine you are in charge of managing the water supply for a town in the dry western part of the United States. You know that your town needs more water for its people and businesses.

But more water used today will mean less water in the future. That will stop economic growth in your town. Some businesses might close. Jobs will be lost. How would you try to solve the problem?

Western Regions of the United States

383

Background Information

Public Lands in the Rocky Mountain Regions

In addition to Yellowstone, some of the best-known parks are Glacier in Montana, Grand Teton in Wyoming, and Bryce and Zion national parks in Utah. National parks make up only a small portion of the public lands in the region. Much of the public land is managed by the Bureau of Reclamation, in the Department of Interior, which oversees its use for cattle grazing and supervises construction of irrigation and hydroelectric dams. The National Forest Service, within the Department of Agriculture, is another government agency that regulates the region's public land, especially logging, grazing, and recreational uses in some forested

Discussion Questions

1 Describe the feelings John Wesley Powell and his men might have felt floating down the river on their trip.

 Caption Answer

Answers will vary. Encourage students to be specific in their reasons.

 Activity

Rocky Mountain Minerals

OBJECTIVES: 4.06, 4.07, 5.01

The Rocky Mountains are packed with a variety of minerals. Have students create a map showing where these minerals are located. A partial list of minerals to include:

Nevada   gold and silver, oil
Montana   vermiculite and talc
Wyoming   trona

Give each student a blank map of the Rocky Mountain region. Have the students design their own symbols for each mineral and then place the symbol on the map where the mineral is found. The students should then create a key for their maps to identify their symbols.

 Activity

Potato Battery

OBJECTIVES: 1.06, 3.02, 5.01

Materials needed: Idaho potato, two lengths of copper and zinc metal (no substitutes)

Directions: Stick the copper into one side of the potato and the zinc in the other side. The zinc and copper should not touch each other. Using ordinary electrical wire, you can use the potato battery to power a small bulb (really small because the potato battery will only put out about half a volt.) The power of the battery comes from the electro-chemical reaction of zinc with copper. The potato does not participate directly in the reaction. It is there as an electrolyte to facilitate the transport of the zinc and copper ions in the solution while keeping the copper and zinc fingers apart.

Discussion Questions

1 Tourism increases the economy of an area. It also, however, brings with it some problems. What are some of these problems?

2 Which do you agree with, the people controlling this land or the federal government? Why?

3 If you could choose any place mentioned in this chapter to live, where would it be? Why?

 Caption Answer

Many people put stress on resources, and that will change the wilderness environment.

 Activity

Rocky Mountain Music

OBJECTIVES: 1.03, 3.07

Play the ballad "My Home's in Montana" from Silver Burdett Ginn; the folk song "Sweet Betsy from Pike" from Silver Burdett Ginn, and "Rocky Mountain High" by John Denver. Discuss what is meant by a ballad. Let students listen to the songs and talk about the story that is told in each one.

Skiing, bicycling, hiking, rock climbing, and rafting are popular recreations in the Rocky Mountain region. **If many people visit wilderness areas, how will that affect the environment?**

Land Use

The future of large sections of this region depends on the decisions of its owner—the United States government. The government owns about 50 percent of the land in Wyoming and about 80 percent of the land in Nevada.

Some people in these states would like to control how this land is used. They might mine the rich minerals, pump the large oil reserves, or ranch. Others want the federal government to keep control of the land.

Culture

The population of Utah is about 62 percent Mormon. Some of them are descended from the followers of Brigham Young. When Young chose a site on the Great Salt Lake for settlement, his followers irrigated the desert and built an attractive city.

Despite the area's growth, there are still plenty of wide open spaces in the Rockies. Much of Idaho and northwestern Montana are wilderness, welcoming hikers, campers, and rafters. Wyoming, with the smallest population of any state, attracts skiers and tourists.

Yellowstone National Park is the largest and most famous national park. It was founded in 1872. Today, Yellowstone attracts more than 4 million visitors annually.

Many Native Americans also call the Rocky Mountain region their home. The Rockies provide a good quality of life for people who love the outdoors.

LESSON 3 REVIEW

Fact Follow-Up
1. How is the Rocky Mountain region changing?
2. Describe the climate and landforms of the Rocky Mountain region.
3. What are some of the activities taking place in the Rocky Mountains?

Talk About It
1. Why is the Rocky Mountain region growing in population? What problems does growth bring?
2. How did gambling change Nevada?
3. How does this region use its resources?

LESSON 3 REVIEW

Fact Follow-Up Answers
1. It is changing because it is booming. Many people from elsewhere in the country are flocking to the Rocky Mountain region. Some are spurred on by such technological changes as modems, faxes, and dependable Internet service, which allow them to work anywhere in the country.
2. The most important feature is the Rocky Mountains, which twist through the region. Found in the middle of the Rockies is the Continental Divide. Elsewhere in the region is the Great Salt Lake, which measures approximately 1,500 square miles in area. The climate of the area varies with elevation. Places of high elevation have shorter summers and colder winters. On the western side of the divide, the climate is moderate and humid year-round. On the eastern side the climate is continental, with cold winters and hot summers.
3. Mining, gambling, and such tourist activities as backpacking, rafting, skiing, and hiking are all taking place in the Rocky Mountains.

Talk About It Answers
1. It is growing in population because many people want to live in an area of such great natural beauty. The growth puts stress on resources, especially water.
2. It caused tourism to increase, and many jobs have been created.
3. Minerals are mined, the mountains support tourism, fertile land is farmed or used for ranches.

*Analyzing, Interpreting, Creating,
and Using Resources and Materials*

Using Maps

This lesson will help you read maps better. Maps provide a lot of information.

Finding Your Direction

On most maps you will find a *north arrow.* This is a small arrow that shows the direction to the North Pole.

Find the north arrow on the maps in this chapter. These maps have been drawn so the top of the map points north. East points toward the right. West points left. South points to the bottom.

Always find the north arrow on a map, and you can figure out how to look at it.

Cardinal Directions

North, south, east, and west are called *cardinal directions.* They are the major directions. Halfway between each of the cardinal directions are the *intermediate directions.* These are northeast, southeast, southwest, and northwest.

Using Scale

Every map in this book is much, much smaller than the area shown by the map. The *scale* shows what the distances are on the map. On some maps, 1 inch may equal 50 miles. On other maps, 1 inch might represent 500 or 1,000 miles.

Look at the maps on pages 369, 372, 375, and 381. Note that each has two scales. The top line tells you how many miles are represented by one inch. The bottom scale line tells you how many kilometers (km) are represented by two centimeters (cm).

Symbols

Mapmakers use different kinds of *symbols* to give us information. These keep the map from getting crowded with too many words. The *map key* tells us the meanings of the symbols.

Now look at the map on page 322. Look at the key called Resources. The symbols represent different natural resources. You can see where our nation's resources are by matching these symbols with those on the map.

What other symbols are used on maps you have used already this year?

a north arrow

a scale showing miles and kilometers

| 0 | 100 | 200 mi. |
| 0 | 100 | 200 km |

Teaching This Skill Lesson

Materials Needed A set of five to eight highway maps is highly desirable. Otherwise, the maps in the textbook Atlas may be used. Paper, pencils

Classroom Organization whole class, small groups, individuals

Beginning the Lesson Introduce concepts of direction, scale, and map symbols using maps in this chapter.

Lesson Development If you have highway maps available, divide the class into small groups and conduct a map quiz asking questions such as the following: "What cities lie north of Charlotte?" or "In what direction is Asheville from Manteo?" If such maps are not available, the map in the Atlas at the end of the textbook may be used. Each group is to give one answer on which members agree. Keeping score is optional. In the quiz, ask questions about direction, symbols, and scale. If you wish, ask questions about distance so students will make use of the scale of distance. As a homework assignment, have individual students construct ten questions (without answers!) about direction, scale, and symbols using a designated textbook map.

Conclusion Place students in pairs and have them exchange tests. Each is to answer the other's test.

Skill Lesson Review

1. Which was easiest and hardest to use: scale, direction, or symbols? Why? *Encourage student responses. Reteach if necessary.*
2. Would you use scale, distance, and symbols more with a physical or a political map? *Scale, distance, and symbols would be important with either map.*

REVIEW

Talk About It

1. The Midwest is facing the consequences of industrialization. The Southwest and Rocky Mountain states must balance tourism and mineral exploration with the requirements of a delicate environment.
2. Important points: Encourage students to choose one region as most important and state reasons for their choice. The Midwest contributes most to agricultural production. Energy resources of the Southwest and Rocky Mountain regions are important.
3. Important points: Students should choose one region and state reasons for their choice. Criteria might include climate, vegetation, landforms, economy. The Midwest and Southwest, like the Southeast, have important agricultural economies. The Rocky Mountain states are least like the Southeast in landform, climate, and resources.
4. The climate of the Midwest region is well suited for farming: long growing season and plenty of rain.
5. Important points: Encourage students to compare the big cities, industry, and recreation among the regions.

Mastering Mapwork

1. There are twelve states in the Midwest region.
2. The Midwest has elevation ranging from sea level to 3,333 feet above sea level. The lowest land lies in the area where the Ohio, Mississippi, and Missouri Rivers come together. The highest elevations lie in the western areas of Kansas, Nebraska, and South Dakota.
3. The elevation of the Midwest is not as high as in the Southwest.
4. The Rocky Mountain region has the highest overall elevation and the Midwest, the lowest.
5. The Rocky Mountain chain also extends into the Southwest and the Pacific Coast regions.

Lessons Learned

LESSON 1
The Midwest Region
The Midwest region is the nation's heartland because of its location, farming, and industrial activities.

LESSON 2
The Southwest Region
The Southwest region has a variety of landforms. The region is rich in mineral resources, but it lacks water.

LESSON 3
The Rocky Mountain Region
The Rocky Mountain region is dominated by the Rocky Mountains. The region attracts newcomers who are telecommuters.

Becoming Better Readers

Look for students to create a simple outline of how the unit is organized. Chapters 14, 15, and 16 cover the regions of the United States in order from east to west.

Talk About It

1. In each region discussed in this chapter, what problems are faced in protecting the environment? Are problems much the same in all four regions, or are they different? Explain.
2. Which of the regions described in the chapter do you think is the most important to the national economy? Give reasons for your answer.
3. Which of the regions described in the chapter is most like the Southeast region? least like the Southeast region? Give reasons for your answer.
4. What is the impact of climate on the economy of the Midwest region? Explain.
5. Which of the regions in this chapter are most like the Northeast region? Explain.

Mastering Mapwork

LOCATION
Use the maps on pages 369, 372, 375, and 381 to answer these questions:

1. How many states make up the Midwest region?
2. Describe the elevation of the Midwest region.
3. Compare the elevation of the Midwest and the Southwest.
4. Which regions have the highest and lowest overall elevations?
5. All of the states in the Rocky Mountain region include the Rockies. Into which other regions do the Rockies extend?

Becoming Better Readers

Understanding the Text
To help understand the text, good readers have to think outside of what is written on the page. A good reader will organize the information into a sequence, look for cause and effect relationships, and make inferences. Chapter 15 is part of a unit called, *Our Nation Today*. Read the Unit Preview on page 317. How has the author organized this unit? How does Chapter 15 fit in with rest of the unit?

Chapter 15

Understanding Advertisements

You have read about resources of the West. Chapter 9 talks about railroads advertising for people to move to the West. This poster is one of those advertisments. Study it and answer the questions using information from the advertisement.

Questions

1. Who is the poster trying to attract?
2. What clues show you who the poster is trying to attract?
3. What resources does the poster claim are available in southwestern Kansas?
4. What crops can be grown in Southwestern Kansas according to the poster?
5. If you wanted to move west in the 1870s, what in this poster would attract you, why or why not?
6. Using clues from the pictures on the poster, why is the prairie a better place to start a farm rather than the woodlands?

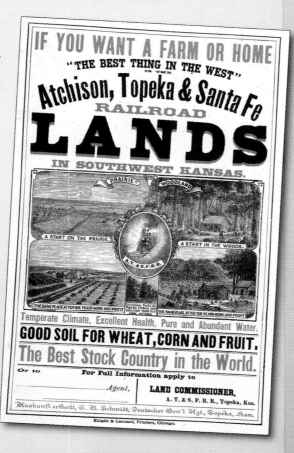

IF YOU WANT A FARM OR HOME
"THE BEST THING IN THE WEST"
Atchison, Topeka & Santa Fe
RAILROAD
LANDS
IN SOUTHWEST KANSAS.

PRAIRIE — WOODLAND

A START ON THE PRAIRIE. — A START IN THE WOODS.

A. T. & S. F. R. R.

THE SAME PLACE AFTER SIX YEARS WORK AND PROFIT — THE SAME PLACE AFTER TEN YEARS WORK AND PROFIT

Temperate Climate, Excellent Health, Pure and Abundant Water.
GOOD SOIL FOR WHEAT, CORN AND FRUIT.
The Best Stock Country in the World.

Or to   For Full Information apply to

Agent.   LAND COMMISSIONER,
A. T. & S. F. R. R., Topeka, Kas.

Knight & Leonard, Printers, Chicago.

Western Regions of the United States   387

Understanding Advertisements

🔖 **OBJECTIVES:** 1.02, 4.02
SOCIAL STUDIES SKILLS: 3.05, 4.06

Railroad Land Advertisement

Being able to understand advertisements and to distinguish between realistic images and images that are designed to attract customers are important skills. Use this advertisement to discuss truth in advertising.

During the late 1800s, the Federal Land Grant Program promoted immigration and western settlement, partly by granting land to railroad companies. The companies promised to build along proposed routes, and then in turn, sold some of the land to raise money for buiding the railroad. Almost every American frontier state had representatives in Europe promoting emigration. Many states even had offices in New York to help newly arrived immigrants make it to their state.

Answers

1. Farmers
2. Phrases on the poster such as: "If you want a farm or home," "good soil for wheat, corn and fruit," " best stock country in the world"
3. Temperate climate, pure and abundant water, good soil
4. Wheat, corn, and fruit
5. Accept any answers that use evidence. For example, climate: not too hot or cold; open land: for growing crops; and so on.
6. Possible answers: Easier because farmers don't have to clear land for crops because there aren't any trees to chop down; lots of sunny, open spaces for growing crops vs. the shady woods; farmers can have a large, prosperous farm (six years vs. ten years) faster.

How to Use the Chapter Review

There are four sections in the Chapter Review: Talk About It, Mastering Mapwork, Becoming Better Readers, and Go to the Source. Use the Vocabulary Worksheets and the Chapter Review Worksheet in the Teacher's Resource Guide for additional reinforcement and preparation for the Chapter Assessments. The Chapter and Lesson Reviews and the Chapter Review Worksheets are the basis of the assessment for each chapter.

Talk About It questions encourage students to speculate about the content of the chapter and are suitable for class or small-group discussion. They are not intended to be assigned for homework.

Mastering Mapwork has students apply one or more of the Five Themes of Geography to maps within the chapter.

Becoming Better Readers focuses on building reading strategy skills necessary for reading comprehension in the content areas

Go to the Source activities allow students to analyze a primary source that relates to the content of the chapter. The questions and activities familiarize students with different types of primary sources and also build content-reading skills.

The Pacific Region of the United States

Social Studies Strands

Geographic Relationships

Economics and Development

Culture and Diversity

Historical Perspectives

Technological Influences and Society

North Carolina Standard Course of Study

Goal 3 The learner will apply key geographic concepts to the United States and other countries of North America.

Goal 3 The learner will examine the roles various ethnic groups have played in the development of the United States and its neighboring countries.

Goal 5 The learner will evaluate ways the United States and other countries of North America make decisions about the allocation and use of economic resources.

Goal 6 The learner will recognize how technology has influenced change within the United States and other countries in North America.

Teaching & Assessment

- English Language Learner Modified Lesson Plans for this chapter are found in the Teacher's Resource Guide.

- *ExamView® Assessment Suite* is provided at **NCJourneys.com.** It includes customizable assessments for all chapters. Paper tests are also available in the Teacher's Resource Guide. See pages T16–T17 for information about how to use the assessments and the Scoring Guide.

Worksheets

Worksheets and answer keys are found both in the Teacher's Resource Guide and at **NCJourneys.com**, including Reading Guides, Reading Strategies, Chapter Reviews, English Language Learner and others.

Activities and Integrations

SOCIAL STUDIES

Problem Based Learning: Other Countries?, p. 389B
■ Comparing Alaska and Hawaii, p. 389
● ▲ ■ Flip Books, p. 394
California Kids, p. 395
★ Design a Tool, p. 399
Land of the Midnight Sun, p. 400
■ Hawaiian Mobiles, p. 404
American Imperialism Socratic Seminar, p. 406
■ Hawaiian Luau, p. 407
Skill Lesson: Asking Questions, p. 410
Hawaiian Islands, p. 405

SCIENCE

SCIENCE	SCIENCE OBJECTIVES
★ Carolina Connection: Triangle Orchid Society, p. 389	1.03, 1.06
Earthquakes, p. 391	2.01
★ Salmon, p. 392	1.02, 1.05, 1.06
Hawaii, p. 405	3.02, 3.03, 3.04, 3.06

TECHNOLOGY

TECHNOLOGY	TECHNOLOGY OBJECTIVES
★ Carolina Connection: Triangle Orchid Society, p. 389	2.13
Hawaii, p. 405	2.13

READING/LANGUAGE ARTS

READING/LANGUAGE ARTS	READING/LANGUAGE ARTS OBJECTIVES
Fire and Ice, p. 389B	3.02, 4.07
Writing Prompt: Alaska or Hawaii, p. 388	2.01
Reading Strategy: T Notes, p. 390	2.02, 2.08
★ Salmon, p. 392	3.06, 4.07
Tim-ber!, p. 393	2.02, 2.04
Reading Strategy: Venn Diagrams, p. 396	1.03, 3.02
Alaska's Rich Edible Resources, p. 398	4.07
● ▲ ■ Bumper Sticker, p. 399	3.01
Reading Strategy: Making Comparisons, p. 402	3.02
▲ ■ Hawaii Picture Dictionary, p.403	2.02, 2.04
Learn More About Princess Kaiulani, p. 407	3.06
Tourism in Hawaii, p. 408	4.07
Becoming Better Readers, p. 412	2.01
Analyzing Song Lyrics, p. 413	3.01

VISUAL ARTS

VISUAL ARTS	VISUAL ARTS OBJECTIVES
● ▲ ■ Fish Kites, p. 389B	3.02
Treasures of the Pacific, p. 389B	3.02
Activator, Songs of the West, p. 388	9.03, 9.04, 9.05 (music)
★ Salmon, p. 392	3.02
▲ ■ Moccasins, p. 397	3.02
▲ ■ Stand-Up Display, p. 398	3.02
▲ ■ Arctic Tundra Homes, p. 401	2.01, 3.02
● Hawaii Culture Party, p. 408	1.01, 2.04 (dance)

CHARACTER AND VALUES EDUCATION

CHARACTER AND VALUES EDUCATION	TRAITS
Tim-ber!, p. 393	good citizenship
Alaska's Rich Edible Resources, p. 398	good citizenship

MATHEMATICS

MATHEMATICS	MATHEMATICS OBJECTIVES
● Alaska's Size, p. 396	4.02

● Basic Activities   ★ Challenging Activities   ▲ English Language Learner Novice   ■ English Language Learner Intermediate

 **Introductory Activity**

Fire and Ice

🏴 **OBJECTIVES:** 1.01, 1.02, 1.03

Read aloud the poem *Fire and Ice* by Robert Frost (see **NCJourneys.com** for a link). Students will write a poem to illustrate the differences between Alaska and Hawaii. For example:

Some say the world will end in fire, Some say in ice.
From what I've seen of the land of the cold, I think I'd rather prefer to be warm than bold. *But if I had to perish twice,* the constant heat would get quite boring.
Maybe it'd be cool to see the ice flows warring, *And that alone would suffice.*
(Italicized portions are quotes from Frost's poem.)

Discuss the poem. The description of the differences in climate is the most obvious. There are also metaphors in the first two lines of this poem. The "world will end in fire" section can be associated with volcanic activity (Hawaii); the "some say ice" section can be related to glacial activity, "ending" land as it was known (Alaska). Fault lines and earthquakes can also be introduced at this time.

 **Culminating Activity**

Treasures of the Pacific

🏴 **OBJECTIVES:** 1.01, 1.02, 1.04

Have students use a box to create a treasure box to describe the Pacific region. The students can either paint the box brown or cover it with brown paper. They can also fashion straps of paper and a lock and key (to make the box look like a treasure box). The inside can also be decorated. Students should collect items while studying this region. Inside the box should be some "treasure" that represents natural resources, climate, landforms, economy, or other items of interest (a rock that looks like gold, pumice from a volcano in Hawaii, mittens, a bathing suit, seashells, mountain climbing equipment, tourist information, movies, or fishing equipment).

 **Art Activity**

Fish Kites

🏴 **OBJECTIVES:** 1.01, 1.03, 5.01

Materials brightly colored tissue paper, scissors, glue, pipe cleaners (10–12 inches long), sequins, glitter, smaller pieces of colored tissue paper, or stick-on dots

Student Directions Fold a piece of tissue paper in half lengthwise and make sure not to crease the paper. Trace a shape of a fish on the tissue paper. Cut through the layers of the tissue paper at one time.

Unfold the paper. Put glue along the short, straight edge of the paper. Lay a pipe cleaner next to the line of glue (on the side toward the body), then fold the glued paper over the pipe cleaner and press down. Turn the paper over. Decorate both sides of the fish by adding sequins, glitter, dots, other colored tissue paper.

Take the pipe cleaner end of the fish and bend the pipe cleaner into a circle. Twist the ends together. Place glue along the long edge of the fish and press the other edge of the paper to the glue, leaving the tail end open. Attach kite string to the mouth of the fish to form a bridle. Attach the bridle to a dowel stick, yard stick, or fishing pole to fly the kite.

 **Problem Based Learning Activity**

Other Countries

🏴 **OBJECTIVES:** 1.01, 1.02, 3.03

Situation
Suppose Alaska and/or Hawaii had never been annexed by the United States. These two areas might have become parts of other countries or established themselves as a territory or a new country.

Task Have students reflect upon the states of Alaska and Hawaii and determine how these areas have benefited by becoming a part of the United States. On the other hand, they should consider why these areas may not have appreciated annexation by the United States. Would these areas have enjoyed some special freedoms? Also consider the position of the existing United States. Why would it want additional territories to become states? How would this benefit the nation? How might adding states to the union be costly and difficult?

Now ask students to consider the idea of a new territory coming into the union. Divide the class into three groups. One group must be acting on behalf of the United States government, one group acting on behalf of the people of the territory to be annexed, and one group acting on behalf of the "people" of the United States. Have each group develop their point of view. Then have a classroom summit.

Reflection Ask students to discuss the pros and cons of state adoption. Ask students to write about their opinions in a persuasive paper.

Teaching Strategies

This chapter will certainly capture the interest of your students. Invite guests who have traveled to these states to make a presentation to your class.

Discussion Questions

 1 The name for the Sierra Nevada Mountains in Spanish translates to "snowy mountains." Why do you suppose the Spanish named them this?

 Activator

 OBJECTIVES: 3.03, 3.04, 3.07

Choose one of the following musical selections to use as an intro to Chapter 16 and as a listening skill activity. Play "North to Alaska" by Johnny Horton or "Tiny Bubbles" by Don Ho for the class. Instruct the class to listen carefully. Pass out a question sheet for students to answer after listening to the song. Once students have answered as many questions as they can, play the song again. Allow students to complete the question sheet after the second playing. Go over questions as a whole discussion. Give the history of the song. Visit **NCJourneys.com** for links to the lyrics.

 Writing Prompt

 OBJECTIVES: 1.02, 1.06, 4.02

Clarification

You are a fifth grade student, living in the beautiful state of Alaska or Hawaii. In a letter to a friend in North Carolina, describe all aspects of your life in both winter and summer. Detail how it is different from your friend's lifestyle in North Carolina.

CHAPTER 16

pineapple

Chapter Preview

LESSON 1
The Pacific Coast Region
The Pacific Coast states are California, Oregon, and Washington.

LESSON 2
Alaska
The Land of the Midnight Sun is our nation's largest state.

LESSON 3
Hawaii
The fiftieth state is a chain of tropical islands formed by volcanoes.

388

The Pacific Region of the United States

The Pacific Region is the largest and most diverse of all regions in the United States. Imagine you are drawing a giant triangle. You start from the beaches of Honolulu. Then go north to the summit of Alaska's Mount McKinley. After that, go south, down the coast of the Pacific Ocean, to southern California. The triangle is completed when you go back to Hawaii. In that triangle, you would find several active volcanoes, old growth forests, large cities, huge stretches of wilderness, rich farmland, and miles and miles of ocean.

Glacier Bay, Alaska

Chapter Resources

Print Resources
Fiction
Dabcovich, Lydia (illustrator). *The Polar Bear Son: An Inuit Tale.* Clarion Books, 1999. ISBN 0395975670.

Paulsen, Gary. *Dogteam.* Dragonfly, 1995. ISBN 0440411300.

Wardlaw, Lee. *Punia and the King of Sharks: A Hawaiian Folktale.* Dial Books, 1997. ISBN 0803716826.

Non-Fiction
Feeney, Stephanie. *"A" is for Aloha.* University of Hawaii Press, 1985. ISBN 0824807227.

Silver, Donald M. *Arctic Tundra* (One Small Square series). McGraw Hill, 1997. ISBN 007057927X.

Stanley, Fay. *The Last Princess: The Story of Princess Ka'iulani of Hawai'i.* Harpercollins, 2001. ISBN 0688180205.University Press, 1999. ISBN 0815603169.

Alaska

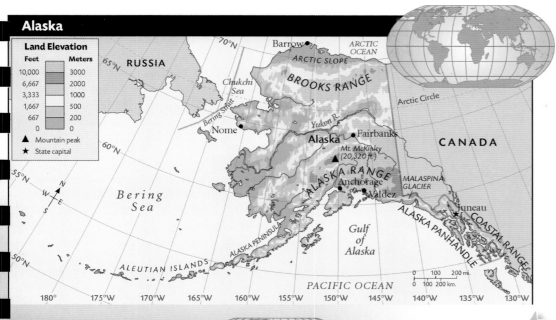

Land Elevation

Feet	Meters
10,000	3000
6,667	2000
3,333	1000
1,667	500
667	200
0	0

▲ Mountain peak
★ State capital

Hawaii

Land Elevation

Feet	Meters
10,000	3000
6,667	2000
3,333	1000
1,667	500
667	200
0	0

▲ Mountain peak
★ State capital

Orchid Societies

Hawaii has a tropical climate. it is a place where many varieties of orchids (below) grow naturally. In North Carolina, however, orchids must be grown in greenhouses or indoors. Our climate is cooler.

Many people from different backgrounds enjoy growing orchids as a hobby. Some orchid hobbyists belong to groups such as the Triangle Orchid Society. Society members share information and tips about growing lovely orchids. They have meetings and also chat over the Internet. Members compete to see who can grow the most beautiful orchids.

CAROLINA CONNECTION

389

Discussion Questions

1 What are the names of the cities in Alaska that are shown on the map?

2 What mountains are located on the Big Island of Hawaii?

3 What is the capital of Hawaii? What island is it on?

 Map Activity

Comparing Alaska and Hawaii

NATIONAL GEOGRAPHY STANDARDS: 1,4
GEOGRAPHIC THEMES: Place, Location
OBJECTIVES: 1.01, 1.02, 1.03

Have students locate Alaska and Hawaii on a globe. They should also note the absolute locations of the southernmost point and northernmost point of both states. Have students speculate how their locations may influence their climates.

Activity

Carolina Connection: Triangle Orchid Society

OBJECTIVES: 1.02, 1.06, 1.07

Go to **NCJourneys.com** for a link to the Triangle Orchid Society. There the user can find interesting information about the society, including upcoming events and tips for growing orchids. There are also interesting orchid links—many include pictures of beautiful orchids.

Using the Society's Web site and the links there, have students go on a scavenger hunt to answer the following questions:

- What is the ideal temperature for growing orchids?
- What type of mediums are orchids planted in?
- What is one type of orchid that does not have to be grown in a greenhouse?
- What is a hybrid?
- Where do orchids grow in the wild?

Audiovisual

Hawaii's Last Queen, The American Experience, PBS video.
Hawaii's Greatest Hits, Vol. 1. New Hawaiian Band (Audio CD).
National Geographic's Really Wild Animals: Polar Prowl. National Geographic, 1997.

Web Sites

Visit **NCJourneys.com** for links to:
- Alaska
- Alaska Climate Research Center
- Alaska State Museum
- California History Online
- Center for the Study of the Pacific Northwest
- Hawaii
- Hawaiian Sound Files and Pronunciation
- Hawaiian Pronunciation Guide
- History of Hawaii
- History of the Luau

Caption Answer

In the eastern part of the state

Reading Strategy Activity

T-Notes

OBJECTIVES: 1.02, 3.03, 4.02

Read the example below to the students. Share with students some of the words to notice when reading:

Different	Alike
unlike	both
but	like
however	just as
not the same as	similar to
instead of	too
different from	the same as

Note that other comparing words have -er or -est added to the end of words, as in "Farms have become larger in the Coastal Plain." Or words may have "more" or "most" added before the word, as in "the Piedmont has become more attractive to industries because of the Research Triangle Park." Have students look for compare/contrast words. If students do not find any, they should act like detectives and search the chapter lesson for similarities or differences.

The Compare and Contrast worksheet in the Teacher's Resource Guide practices this skill.

Sample

You live in North Carolina. Your family decides to fly to Los Angeles, California, in July for a vacation. You notice many buildings and large highways. As your family drives down the highway to a hotel, you see similar fast-food restaurants and shops in shopping centers.

LESSON ① The Pacific Coast Region

KEY IDEAS

- The Pacific Coast States are California, Oregon, and Washington.
- Three mountain ranges rise in the Pacific Coast: the Coast Range, the Sierra Nevada, and the Cascades.
- Many types of climate and natural resources are found in the Pacific Coast states.
- The Pacific Coast states are leaders in mineral production, timber, farming, fishing, and high technology.

KEY TERMS

Silicon Valley

When you walk on the shores of the Pacific Ocean in the contiguous United States, you might be in Washington, Oregon, or California. These states of the Pacific Coast region have a great diversity of landforms, climate, and resources.

Location and Landforms

These three states are found on the western edge of the United States. The Pacific Ocean breaks upon all of their coastlines. In the north, Washington state borders Canada. In the South, California borders Mexico.

Mono Pass, Sierra Nevada Mountains California *by William Keith, shows the stunning beauty of the Pacific Coast region.* **Where in California is this range?**

Looking at the similarities and differences in two places or things is called comparing. We were comparing California to North Carolina on the imaginary trip. Looking at just the ways California is different from North Carolina is called contrasting. Knowing how to compare and contrast things will help us in our study of North America. It will help you remember what you read.

Mountains

Three mountain ranges give the Pacific Coast states some of their incredible scenery. The ranges also affect climate.

You might think of these mountains as making the shape of the capital letter H. The Coast Range forms one long side of the H. It extends north to south along the Pacific Ocean. Farther east, higher mountains make the second long side. In the north, these are the Cascades. In the south, they are the higher Sierra Nevada. The Klamath Mountains form the cross line of the H.

Valleys and Deserts

Fertile river valleys stretch between the long lines of the H. North of the Klamath Mountains are rich lands along Puget Sound in Washington and the Willamette River in Oregon. South of the mountains lies California's great Central Valley.

Across southeastern California stretches a low-lying desert. It is part of the Great Basin. Death Valley is located here. It is the lowest point in the nation at 280 feet (84 m) below sea level.

Region The Pacific Coast region of the United States has grown quickly in population as barriers to movement were overcome. *What were some of the barriers, and how were they overcome?*

The Pacific Region of the United States

391

Discussion Questions

1 What rivers help bring water to the valleys used for agriculture in the Pacific Coast states?

 Caption Answer

Some barriers were desert and mountain ranges like the Sierra Nevada, the Cascades, and the Coastal Range. They were overcome by highways and air travel.

 Science Activity

Earthquakes

OBJECTIVES: 1.03, 1.06, 3.03

Put students in cooperative groups to research earthquakes. Help students focus on the following:

- causes of earthquakes
- locations of earthquakes in the United States
- location of the San Andreas fault

Then have students color a blank map of the United States to show where most earthquakes occur.

Extension Have students identify the pros or cons of living along fault lines of the San Andreas Fault.

Name Origin

California "imaginary treasure island"—the setting for a Spanish romance, or Latin for "hot furnace." Nickname: Golden State. Motto: Eureka—"I have found it." Admitted: 31st, 1850.

Oregon Shoshone for "place of plenty." Nickname: Beaver State. Motto: She flies with her own wings. Admitted: 33rd, 1859.

Washington named for George Washington. Nickname: Evergreen State. Motto: By and by. Admitted: 42nd, 1889.

Discussion Questions

1 What are the oldest, tallest, and largest trees in California? Why are they so important?

2 Many people live in the area of the San Andreas Fault. Why do you think they are willing to live here? Would you?

Science Activity

Salmon

OBJECTIVES: 1.01, 1.02, 5.01

To begin, ask students to help make a class list of fish that are favorites to eat. Ask them to identify what fish is especially important in the states of Oregon and Washington (salmon). Discuss what they know about the life of a salmon.

Ask students to think how much they depend on their parents. What are some things that students depend on their parents to do for them? At about what age can students start to have more independence from parents? List responses on a class chart to be used for comparing the dependency of a salmon on its parents.

Lead into a discussion of the life of a Pacific salmon and the ecosystem that supports salmon. Ask students to share what they know about the life cycle of a salmon. Following class discussion, invite students to do research on the Pacific salmon's life and habitat. Gather information on why the salmon is endangered. What is being done to restore salmon to the region?

Use the encyclopedia and the Web to find information about the salmon. Compile the information into reports to be shared orally in class.

Have students label on a map the Columbia River and Snake River and then check how many states the rivers pass through or touch.

Pretend to be the governors of the states of Washington and Oregon. Write a bill for Congress that would help keep the salmon from becoming extinct.

Some useful resources:

Cone, Joseph. *A Common Fate*. Henry Holt & Company, 1994. ISBN 0870713914.

Cone, Molly. *Come Back Salmon*. Sierra Club Books for Children, 1994. ISBN 0871564890.

House, Freeman. *Totem Salmon*. Beacon Press, 2000. ISBN 0807085499.

Lichatowich, Jim. *Salmon Without Rivers: A History of the Pacific Salmon Crisis*. Island Press, 2001. ISBN 1559633603.

Taylor, Joseph, III. *Making Salmon*. University of Washington Press, 2001. ISBN 0295978406.

Fault Lines and Volcanos

The Coastal Range mountains are young. They rise along the line where two huge plates of the earth's crust bump into each other. These two plates are the oceanic plate and the continental plate.

You can see the crack in the earth's surface where the plates meet. It is called the San Andreas Fault. Occasionally, the two plates shift. Great vibrations shake the land in the form of earthquakes.

Volcanic activity formed the Cascade mountains. Several volcanoes remain active there.

About 7,000 years ago, a volcano created Crater Lake. It is the deepest lake in the nation. Crater Lake attracts tourists to the eastern Cascade Mountains in Oregon. Volcanic ash also helped form the rich, loamy soils of the valleys of Washington, Oregon, and northern California.

Crater Lake in Oregon is now a national park.
How was the lake created?

Mount St. Helens Washington's Mount St. Helens erupted in 1980. It caused great damage and the loss of 57 lives. In 2004 it became active again. The volcano emits occasional steam and ash. Small earthquakes occur from time to time. Scientists say that an eruption similar to the one in 1980 is still possible, but the chances are very low. People can still camp and hike on the mountain.

Climate

The western parts of Washington, Oregon, and northern California have a cool and wet climate. This is a feature of the Marine West Coast climate. This is the result of warm, wet winds blowing off the Pacific Ocean.

Western Oregon can receive 130 inches (330 cm) of precipitation a year. Western Washington has about 140 inches (355 cm). East of the Coastal Range of the Cascades, the climate of both states is much drier. People there live in a continental climate.

Most of California has a rainy season and a dry season. In northern California, the rainy season lasts from October to April. Southern California's rainy season lasts from November to March or April. The southern part of the state's climate is warm and dry. They have a Mediterranean climate.

Natural Resources

Like the rest of the country, the Pacific Region has a varity of natural resources.

Forests

In California's great forests, you can find many amazing trees. The world's oldest living tree is the bristlecone pine. The world's tallest is the Douglas fir. The world's largest is the giant sequoia.

Oregon's forests cover about 28 million acres of land. Washington is close behind with about 21 million acres of forests. Together, these produce about 30 percent of the nation's timber.

Caption Answer

A volcano created Crater lake 7,000 years ago.

Today, people debate about how best to use the forests of the Pacific states. Some "old growth" forests have never been cut. The trees have been growing for hundreds of years. Some think these trees should never be cut.

But lumber companies prize the tall old-growth trees because they have a fine grain and few knots. Others are concerned that endangered species may be wiped out if forests are cut.

Fish

Fish are another resource here. California harvests anchovies, tuna, and mackerel. Salmon is important in Oregon and Washington.

Salmon was very important to Native Americans of the Northwest. A Kwakiutl (kwa·CUE·til) chant describes the respect and joy of a person eating a freshly caught fish:

When a man eats salmon by the river, he sings the salmon song. It is in the river in the roasting in the spearing in the sharing in the shoring in the shaking shining salmon. It is in the song too.

Logging is a source of income for many in the Pacific Coast region. Conservationists are concerned about the effects logging has on the land. **How would you balance logging and the environment?**

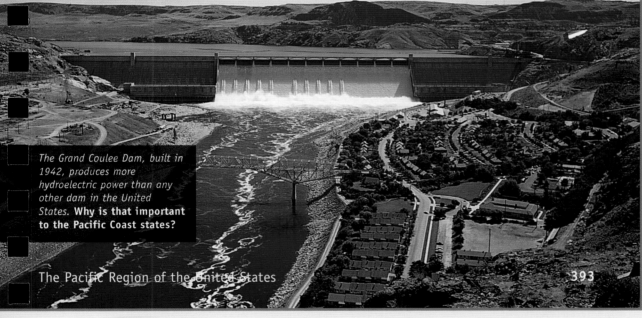

The Grand Coulee Dam, built in 1942, produces more hydroelectric power than any other dam in the United States. **Why is that important to the Pacific Coast states?**

The Pacific Region of the United States

393

Discussion Questions

1 Why did the Native American Aleuts call their state "Great Land"?

 Caption Answer

Answers will vary. Solutions include limiting logging and bringing in other industries.

 Caption Answer

Have students speculate why clean energy resources are important.

 Writing Activity

Tim-ber!

 OBJECTIVES: 1.02, 1.06, 3.03

During a reading period read the tall tale of Paul Bunyan. Use this time to reinforce reading skills and introduce the social studies lesson on the logging industry of the Pacific Coast states. Continue the lesson during social studies by having students write persuasive letters in favor of or against the cutting down of the forest in Oregon. Students should include possible solutions to the problem. Letters can be sent to logging or paper companies to see if the companies will respond.

 Background Information

Salmon

Mature Pacific salmon leave the Pacific Ocean as saltwater fish, never to eat again, as they travel their way up the Columbia River.

Those born in the uppermost part of the Snake River travel more than 1,000 miles inland to lay and fertilize their eggs. Without enough reserves in their bodies to get back to the ocean, the adult fish spawn and die. To spawn, a female will scoop a nest in the bottom of a stream by waving her tail and deposit her eggs in the hole. The male releases the sperm into the water that covers the eggs to fertilize them. The female brushes gravel over the eggs. Both parents lie exhausted in the stream until they die. Microorganisms in the water decompose their bodies during the winter.

Come spring the salmon eggs hatch tiny fish. The tiny fish never see their parents, of course, but are nourished by their decomposed bodies. When they grow large enough, they make the dangerous trip downstream, past dams and waterfalls to the ocean. There they grow into adults; the cycle starts anew.

Discussion Questions

1 There are opposing views as to whether the old-growth forests should be cut or preserved. What do you think, and why?

2 What crops and other products make the Pacific Coast states' economies strong?

3 What is the only state that produces nickel?

4 What other minerals are found in the Pacific Coast states?

5 What are some of the sights people enjoy seeing in California?

 **Caption Answer**

The Central Valley of California and the valleys of Washington and Oregon

 **Activity**

Flip Books

◆ **OBJECTIVES:** 1.01, 1.02, 1.06

Using 12-inch by 18-inch construction paper, fold the paper in half vertically, then fold horizontally. Open. Using scissors, cut each crease from the outside to the center, leaving the center intersection intact. Now you have four little pages (eight sides). Label the front side of each part as follows: Pacific Coast Region, Landforms, Natural Resources, and Industries. On the front and back sides of each page, have students write information and illustrations about the topic. For more pages, stack three or four sheets of paper and cut as explained above.

Minerals

These states are rich in minerals and oil. California is the fourth-largest state in oil production. Nickel comes from Oregon. It is the only state that produces that mineral. All three states contain gold, silver, copper, zinc, lead, sand, gravel, and coal.

Water

These states have rich soils and favorable climates. Water is either supplied by nature or by irrigation. These factors make the valleys of the Pacific Coast states productive farmland.

The dams spanning the great rivers of Washington State produce hydroelectric power. The Grand Coulee Dam on the Columbia River is the largest concrete dam in America.

Economy

The Pacific Coast states contribute a great deal to the nation's economy. California alone produces many different goods and services. If it were a separate country, it would be one of the top ten richest countries in the world.

The Pacific Coast states produce fruit and vegetables for the nation. **What parts of the states are agricultural regions?**

Farming

The Pacific Coast states rely on agriculture as part of their economies. Washington and Oregon grow fruit, especially apples, pears, and cherries. California produces most of the nation's canned and frozen fruit and vegetables. Crops can grow 300 days a year in the Imperial Valley in southern California.

In Oregon and Washington, logs and timber are the most important products. Oregon has led the nation in lumber production for 40 years.

Ships and Ports

Many activities involve the Pacific Ocean. Fishing, as you have read, is a key activity. In the ports of Washington, many people work in shipbuilding.

United States' trade with Asia depends on the ports of the Pacific Coast, especially San Francisco, California, and Portland, Oregon. Most of the cars imported to the United States from Japan arrive in Portland.

Manufacturing

The Pacific Coast states make different products. California's *Silicon Valley* is the headquarters for many companies that manufacture computer hardware and software. The region's nickname comes from silicon, the key component in computer chips.

Microsoft is a giant software developer. Its headquarters are in Seattle, Washington. It employs thousands of people.

The Boeing Company began building

 Background Information

California's Imperial Valley

Although California has more people than any other state and is home to Los Angeles, the nation's second-largest city, it leads many less urbanized states in agriculture. California earns more money from farming than any other state. Much of this farming depends on irrigation. The Imperial Valley, which borders Mexico, is today known for its production of winter farm crops. Before 1901, however, it was a desert wasteland. Its agricultural growth began in that year after the Imperial Canal brought water from the Colorado River into the valley. Today, the Imperial Valley has more than 3,000 miles of irrigation canals used to grow a variety of crops, including alfalfa, beets, cotton, and sugar.

airplanes in Washington in 1916. The industry really took off during World War II. Today, aviation and aerospace companies employ engineers and scientists in Seattle, Washington, and San Diego, California.

Urban Populations

Although agriculture and lumber are important, most people of the region live in cities. About 94 percent of all Californians are city dwellers. Los Angeles is second only to New York City in population.

Washington's largest city is Seattle. More than half of the state's residents live within 50 miles of Seattle. Oregon's largest city is Portland.

Culture

Tourism makes up a major part of California's income. People visit Hollywood and tour movie studios. They also want to see the California coast, the famous redwood trees, San Francisco's Golden Gate Bridge, the San Diego Zoo, and, of course, Disneyland.

California has a large Hispanic population. Many have lived in California since the first missions were founded by the Spanish hundreds of years ago. This heritage can be seen in the many Spanish names of cities and towns scross the state.

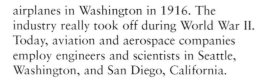

William E. Boeing
1881–1956

Bill Boeing was a young man when he took his first plane ride. It was 1909, just a few years after airplanes were invented, and people didn't know much about them yet. Boeing decided he could build a better one.

He and a friend began to work. They hired men to help make a plane and a pilot to fly it. The first one flew pretty well, but they knew they could do better. They kept on planning and testing new ideas.

The U.S. Navy bought the first 50 airplanes. Boeing, however, could see that planes had uses in peacetime as well as in war. Boeing made planes to carry the mail, then he made planes to carry people. Within 50 years, it was the biggest company in Washington state. Today, Boeing's planes are used all over the world.

LESSON 1 REVIEW

Fact Follow-Up
1. What landforms dominate this region?
2. What is Silicon Valley, and how did it get its name?
3. What are the most important economic activities in this region?

Talk About It
1. Which state in this region would you prefer to visit if you could? Explain why.
2. Why are there so many climates in the region?
3. Why do you think most people live in cities?
4. Describe California's Spanish heritage.

Research Activity

California Kids

OBJECTIVES: 1.02, 1.03, 1.06

The residents of northern California live differently than those of Southern California. What types of sports and clothing might a fifth grader in northern California have or wear? a fifth grader in southern California? Break the students into two groups and have them research climate, temperature, rainfall, recreational activities, sports, and so on. Have the groups present how kids their age in their region of California might live. Compare and contrast them.

Activity

Spanish Heritage

OBJECTIVES: 3.01, 3.03, 3.05, 3.06

Divide the class in teams of three or four students each. Give each team a map of California (a road map such as the California page from a national road atlas works well). Tell the teams that they have 5 mintues to study the map and write down as many cities with Spanish names as they can find, and also what they think the English translation is (for example, Los Angeles means the angels, or city of the angels; San means saint). When time is up, have each team read out their list and make a list on the board. The team with the most Spanish names wins, and the team with the most correct translations also wins. Discuss why these places may have gotten these names.

LESSON 1 REVIEW

Fact Follow-Up Answers
1. Three large mountain ranges with two volcanoes, the Central Valley, and the San Andreas Fault dominate the Pacific Coast region.
2. Silicon Valley in California is the headquarters for many companies that produce computers, software, and computer-related equipment; workers assemble the silicon chips for computers that gave the region its nickname.
3. Agriculture, timber, and fishing are all important. Ports make trade possible with Asia. California's Silicon Valley produces computers, software, and computer-related equipment. Aviation and aerospace industries are also an important part of the economy. Tourism is a major source of income.

Talk About It Answers
1. Important points: Students should choose one state and explain their choice. Criteria might include climate, landforms, recreational opportunities, cultural opportunities, or personal preference.
2. The region is affected by latitude and landforms including the coast and mountains.
3. Important points: Students should make the connection that cities are where jobs and educational opportunities are located. There is also more to do culturally in cities.
4. Important points: Students should describe the exploration and settlement of the region by the Spanish. Names of such cities as Los Angeles, San Fransisco, and San Diego reflect the Spanish heritage.

OBJECTIVES: 1.02, 1.03, 1.06, 3.03, 5.07

Caption Answer

Answers will vary. "Tallest" or "highest" are possible reasons for both sides.

Reading Strategy Activity

Venn Diagrams

OBJECTIVES: 1.02, 1.03, 1.06, 3.03, 5.07

A Venn diagram is a way to see similarities and differences between things and help students remember facts.

Use the Differences Between Hawaii and Alaska worksheet in the Teacher's Resource Guide as students read Lesson 2 and Lesson 3. The section that overlaps in the center is where students will write the information that is true of both Alaska and Hawaii. Write the facts that go with Hawaii on the right and the facts about Alaska on the left. These will be the differences between the two states.

The numbers in the Venn stand for the type of information that could be included. One stands for size, shape, and location of the state and so forth. Students may need help thinking of similarities for the two states. Share information and let students explain their answers.

After completing the worksheet, students may do research and write extra facts in the diagram. Ask students to write a paragraph generalizing what they learned about the two states.

Math Activity

Alaska's Size

OBJECTIVES: 1.01, 1.02, 1.06

How big is Alaska? Present students with maps of the United States, including Alaska and Hawaii (with the correct scale for all states). Have students cut apart the states to see how many they can fit inside Alaska. Which combinations should they choose to get the most states inside Alaska?

LESSON 2 Alaska

KEY IDEAS

- Alaska is the largest of the 50 states.
- It is a region of mainly tundra and subarctic climates.
- Its landforms make getting resources, such as oil and timber, expensive.

KEY TERMS

permafrost

In summer, the largest state, Alaska, is the land of the midnight sun. Wintertime means the dark of night almost all day for Alaskans living north of the Arctic Circle.

Alaska's 591,004 square miles (1,536,610 sq km) contain our 15 highest mountains, our largest glacier, and our longest chain of volcanoes. Alaska has more than 3 million lakes. It also has about 100,000 glaciers and about 1,800 islands.

Alaska's wildlife includes brown bears, caribou, bald eagles, puffins, seals, and whales. No wonder the Native American Aleuts of Alaska call their state "Great Land."

Location and Landforms

Alaska juts out from the landmass of Canada to form a huge peninsula. Bodies of water surround Alaska on three sides. The Arctic Ocean is on Alaska's north. The Chukchi Sea and the Bering Sea are to its west. The Gulf of Alaska and the Pacific Ocean lie to the south.

Look at the map on page 389. Do you see the "panhandle" of Alaska? The Alaska Panhandle points southeast. It is a narrow strip of land along the Gulf of Alaska. Juneau, the capital of Alaska, is located here. It sits at the edge of mountains that rise straight out of the water.

The Alaska Peninsula and the Aleutian Islands are also narrow. They extend from the southern coast toward the southwest. Volcanoes and glaciers dot the Alaska Peninsula and the Aleutian Islands.

Mount McKinley, the tallest mountain in North America at 20,320 feet (6,096 m), towers above mile-high mountains in front of it. Native Americans call the mountain Denali. **Would you want to climb this mountain? Why or why not?**

396   Chapter 16

To get an idea of just how big Alaska really is, consider the following:

State	Area: Millions of Acres	Area Square Miles
Alaska	365.04	571,951
Texas	167.63	261,797
California	99.82	155,959
North Carolina	31.18	48,718
Hawaii	4.10	6,423
Delaware	1.25	1,954
Rhode Island	.67	1,045

Note that Alaska is more than 11 times larger than North Carolina. How many times larger is Alaska than Rhode Island? *539 Rhode Islands could fit in Alaska.*

Extension Have students look up the populations of the states that they fit inside Alaska. Contrast that figure to Alaska's current population.

Mountains

Mountains ring Alaska. The Coastal Range runs from the United States through Canada and into southern Alaska (see map, page 389).

Mountains surround the interior. Land there has hills and wide valleys. The Brooks Range, part of the Rocky Mountains, forms the interior's northern boundary.

The Alaska Range marks the southern edge of the interior. Mount McKinley, the highest mountain in North America, dominates the Alaska Range.

Water and Glaciers

The Yukon River is the fourth-largest river in the United States. It flows from Canada through the interior of Alaska. It empties into the Bering Sea.

Most of Alaska's glaciers, including its largest and longest, are located in the south and southeastern part of the state. Malaspina Glacier covers 850 square miles (2,210 sq km). The Bering Glacier extends 100 miles (161 km).

The northernmost point in the United States is in Alaska at Point Barrow on the Arctic Ocean.

Summer cruise ships visit Juneau, the state capital. **Can you tell from this picture or the map on page 389 why visitors to Juneau can get there only by boat or plane?**

Climate and Vegetation

The climate of Alaska's southern coast gives it cold winters and warm summers. Heavy rain falls along the southeast coast and in the Aleutian Islands. The Alaska Panhandle also receives a great deal of precipitation. Most Alaskans live here along the southern coast.

Few people settle in the state's interior. Its subarctic climate features severely cold winters and short, cool summers. It has moderate rainfall.

The Arctic

The most northern region of Alaska is called the Arctic Slope. It stretches to the Arctic Ocean. This area has the Arctic tundra climate. Temperatures range from very cold to cool in the middle of the summer. Summer here lasts only about two months.

This cold region is north of the timberline. No trees grow here. The ground is *permafrost,* permanently frozen subsoil. It thaws only a bit at the surface during the arctic summer.

Glaciers flow throughout Alaska, even in southern Alaska. **What kind of climate keeps glaciers from melting and Alaskans cold most of the year?**

The Pacific Region of the United States

397

Discussion Questions

1 Where is Mount McKinley, North America's tallest mountain, located? How high is it?

Caption Answer

The mountains make overland travel difficult.

Caption Answer

Tundra

Art Activity

Moccasins

OBJECTIVES: 1.06, 3.03, 4.02

Native Americans' clothing had to be warm in this cold climate. Most clothing was made of reindeer skins and wool. The clothing was colorful in bright blues, reds, and yellows. The type of hat worn by the men and boys was called the "hat of the four winds." It had four corners that hung down in the back. Grass was placed inside the reindeer skin moccasins as insulation from the cold weather. It also absorbed moisture and was soft to walk on.

Make a pair of moccasins (skallers) by enlarging the pattern in the Teacher's Resource Guide. Make them from brown butcher paper or grocery bags. Staple them together and decorate with yarn and paint. Stuff them with dry grass or newspaper and use as a bulletin board border.

ELL Teaching Tips

Give Clear and Simple Directions

Give clear, simple directions to ELL students. Complex directions should be broken down into smaller steps. Ask students to explain in their own words what you are asking them to do before they do it.

Name Origin

Alaska "peninsula, land that is not an island." Nickname: The Last Frontier. Motto: North to the future. Admitted: 49th, 1959.

Discussion Questions

1 Why do some people consider the purchase of Alaska a great real-estate deal?

2 What are some of the natural resources found in Alaska?

 **Activity**

Alaska's Rich Edible Resources

 OBJECTIVES: 3.03, 3.04, 4.02

Bring in samples of crab, salmon, halibut, and herring recipes. Allow the students to taste these delicacies. Discuss the importance of this resource to Alaska's economy and the problem of overfishing. Divide the class into cooperative groups and have the groups give suggestions to a possible solution to overfishing. Chart the solutions and share with class.

Extension Write the fishing industry in Alaska and share best class solutions.

 Activity

Stand Up Display

 OBJECTIVES: 1.01, 1.06, 3.03

Have each student make an accordion-fold display about Alaska. Use three file folders or six pieces of 9-inch by 12-inch tagboard to make each stand-up display. Put the following information on the indicated folds; have students illustrate each fold appropriately.

Side 1—"Presenting the Great State of Alaska" (cover fold); Side 2—state symbols; Side 3—sights to see; Side 4—economy (industries, exports, agriculture, businesses); Side 5—interesting facts; Side 6—historical happenings; Side 7—(back of Side 6) famous people; Side 8—(back of Side 5) recreation areas and activities; Side 9—(back of Side 4) cultures; Side 10—(back of Side 3) major cities; Side 11—(back of Side 2) geographical map; Side 12—(back of Side 1) art forms. .

Natural Resources

Russia first claimed the land that is now Alaska. In 1867, the United States purchased Alaska from the Russians. The price was $7.2 million—or 2 cents per acre. Back then, some people thought that price was too high. Today, very few people would even try to put a price tag on Alaska's riches.

Fish are an important resource in Alaska. Valuable varieties include salmon, halibut, and herring. Alaskan king crab is important, too. Overfishing is a problem. To protect this resource, the Alaskan fishing industry operates under strict regulations. About 6 billion pounds of fish and seafood still are caught each year.

Logging is important in the Panhandle. Transportation costs are too high to make cutting lumber profitable in other parts of the state.

The climate of Alaska does not allow much farming. Garden vegetables grow in the Panhandle, in the Matanuska Valley around Anchorage, and in the Tanana Valley near Fairbanks. Alaskans must import almost 90 percent of their food.

Oil

In 1957, oil began being pumped in Alaska. In 1968, huge oil reserves were discovered at Prudhoe Bay on the Arctic Slope. However, tankers had to ship the oil all the way around the huge state.

A Journey to ALASKA

Building the Trans-Alaska Pipeline

The Trans-Alaska Pipeline cuts through the Alaskan wilderness. it stretches 800 miles (1,288 km) from Prudhoe Bay on the Arctic Slope to Valdez on the Gulf of Alaska.

Construction began on the pipeline in 1973. The cold climate affected pipeline construction in many ways. Engineers had to design the Trans-Alaska Pipeline carefully.

The biggest difficulty was permafrost, the permanently frozen ground. Engineers worried that the weight of the pipeline would melt the ice in the ground and cause the pipeline to sink. So engineers filled the pipeline's supports with liquid ammonia. The ammonia cools the ground beneath the pipeline. The permafrost stays frozen. The pipeline stays stable.

Another problem was keeping the oil in the pipeline warm enough to be pumped. So workers wrapped the pipeline in insulation. There is enough insulation to keep more than 21,000 homes warm.

Still another problem was how to inspect the inside of the pipeline after construction. Designers built a small, tube-shaped car called a "snoopy." Rolling down the pipeline inside the snoopy, workers checked welds. They made sure the pipeline was strong. It had to hold up to the pressure of thousands of gallons of oil being pumped through it every day.

In 2006, part of the pipeline was closed for repair. When the shutdown was announced, the price of oil went up briefly. The pipeline is very important to America's economy.

An 800-mile (1,288-km)-long pipeline was built to solve the problem. It carries oil from Prudhoe Bay to the port of Valdez. The pipeline is above the ground so it will not melt the permafrost.

Oil Spills When the pipeline was planned, people worried about the terrible damage that could be caused by even small leaks in the pipeline or a spill from an oil tanker.

A major oil spill did occur in Prince William Sound in 1989. The tanker Exxon Valdez spilled 11 million gallons of oil into the sound after hitting a reef. The loss of wildlife was huge. Birds, fish, otters, and seals died in large numbers.

Trans-Alaska Pipeline

The Athabascan people placed this fish wheel in the Tanana River. The water current turns the wheel that scoops up fish in a wire trap and deposits them in a holding pen. **Why is fishing an important industry in Alaska?**

Other Minerals

Alaska holds even more oil and many minerals that are not being pumped or mined. Some of these are gold, silver, nickel, tin, lead, zinc, and copper. It will be hard to mine these materials without harming the delicate environment. Transportation will also be costly.

Alaska's People

Alaska has the second-smallest population of all the states. Even in Alaska, most people make their homes in cities. About 70 percent of the population live in urban areas. More than 42 percent live in Anchorage, the state's largest city.

Native Americans make up about 19 percent of the population. This is the largest percentage of any state. The three groups of native peoples are Inuit, Aleuts, and other Native Americans.

The number of people who leave the state to find work elsewhere is on the rise. People move to the contiguous states for education and jobs.

The Pacific Region of the United States   **399**

Caption Answer

Alaska has a long coast and a plentiful supply of fish, and its climate does not allow for much farming.

Activity

Design a Tool

OBJECTIVES: 3.03, 6.01, 6.02

Today we often think of technology as referring to computers, cell phones, or MP3 players. Technology can be seen as the advancement of a tool that makes people's lives more productive or better. As seen in the picture, the Athabascan people developed this interesting fishing wheel in order to trap more and more fish. This tool was developed in order to make the fishing process more efficient and effective in the Alaskan waters. Alaskans also experienced technology when a pipeline was developed for pumping oil from the northern regions of Alaska all the way to the Gulf of Alaska. These forms of technology made life easier for Alaskans and changed the way in which they live, much like a computer has done.

Assign the students the job of developing a fishing tool. The students will pretend that they are residents of Alaska with no other means of income beside the trade of fishing. They could simply fish with a net or a pole; however, they will be limited to only a few fish per day. Ask students to use a limited supply list and develop a fishing tool that would make their fishing experience more efficient and beneficial. This tool should be practical and the supplies inexpensive and readily available. The students can present these inventions in an inventions fair to share with the class or the whole school.

Art Activity

Bumper Stickers

OBJECTIVES: 1.02, 1.06, 3.02

Give each student a strip of construction paper or tagboard on which to design a "bumper sticker" for Alaska, a city in Alaska, a landmark in Alaska, a region of Alaska, or something of special interest in Alaska.

Caption Answer

About 6 billion

Activity

Land of the Midnight Sun

 OBJECTIVES: 1.02, 1.06, 3.03

Ask your students why Alaska is called the "Land of the Midnight Sun." Demonstrate for your class how Alaska has months of sunshine and months of darkness. Using a globe, place a piece of clay the size of a quarter on Barrow, Alaska. Shine a filmstrip projector light on the globe. Turn the globe to show how the earth's tilt affects the months of the year the sun shines in Alaska. Guide students to the realization that Alaska is located so far north that during the summer the sun stays high late into the night. Then direct the students to observe the photograph on page 351. Discuss how the intense growing season allows more daily hours for the plants to grow. Next read about the world's biggest broccoli in the *Guinness World Records 2000* Millennium Edition (ISBN 1892051001). In 1993, John and Mary Evans of Palmer, Alaska, grew a head of broccoli that weighed 35 pounds. Then have students measure the weight of a normal head of broccoli for comparison.

Fishing is an important industry in Alaska. **How many pounds of fish and seafood are caught each year?**

400

Chapter 16

Background Information

Not-So-Foolish Alaska

Just like Texans, Alaskans enjoy bragging about the size of their state. They like to say that Alaska could be cut in half and Texas would still be the nation's third-largest state. In addition to Mount McKinley, the highest mountain in North America, Alaska has the nation's largest oil field at Prudhoe Bay. When Secretary of State William Seward bought Alaska from the Russians for the United States in 1867 for $7 million, many Americans criticized this purchase of snow-covered land, calling the deal Seward's Folly. As the treasure trove of natural resources Alaska held became clear, opponents of the agreement seemed the bigger fools.

The Economy

The high cost of transportation limits the economic activities of Alaskans. There are very few roads. This is due in part to natural barriers such as mountains and glaciers.

During World War II, the Al-Can Highway was built. This links Alaska with the states to the south. You can drive for hours on this 1,500-mile (2,415-km) highway without seeing another vehicle.

Economic activity also is limited because the federal government owns 47 percent of the land. About 48 million acres of Alaskan's land are in national parks. The U.S. Fish and Wildlife Service protects another 71 million acres. Alaskans disagree about how much land needs protection.

The government employs more people than any company in Alaska. More than 27 percent of Alaskan workers work for the federal, state, or local governments. This includes those who work on military bases.

Culture

Many tourists visit Alaska. Some watch the annual Iditarod sled race in March. Drivers mush dogs from Anchorage to Nome to win prizes. The tough trip takes from 10 to 15 days. Other tourists cruise on ships along the coast, seeing glaciers, whales, and other wildlife.

The Matanuska Valley near Anchorage is one of the few agricultural regions of Alaska. The short growing season is intense because of the long hours of sunlight. **What other areas of Alaska can grow garden vegetables?**

Alaska's native peoples are divided into eleven cultures. They speak twenty different languages. Many Alaska natives have kept their customs. Some natives still hunt and fish as they have done since "the creation times."

Discussion Questions

1 What are two factors that affect Alaska's economy?

 **Caption Answer**

The panhandle and the Tanana Valley near Fairbanks

 **Activity**

Arctic Tundra Homes

OBJECTIVES: 1.01, 1.02, 1.06

After reading the text on the climate of the Arctic tundra, students will design a home for that region. Students must justify their home designs through an oral presentation. Their design must be based on the knowledge they have about the climate, landforms, resources, and bodies of water.

LESSON 2 REVIEW

Fact Follow-Up

1. Describe the landforms and climate of Alaska.
2. What were some challenges faced by the people who built the Trans-Alaskan Pipeline?

Talk About It

1. What are some examples of human-environmental interaction in Alaska?
2. Who lives in Alaska? Where do they live? How do climate and landforms influence life?
3. What is Alaska's most valuable resource? Why?

The Pacific Region of the United States

401

LESSON 2 REVIEW

Fact Follow-Up Answers

1. The Coastal Range of the continental United States and Canada extends into Alaska. Islands and the Alaskan panhandle form two long, thin streamers of land in the surrounding waters of the Pacific Ocean.
2. The cold climate, permafrost, keeping oil warm enough to be pumped, and how to inspect the inside of the pipeline were challenges.

Talk About It Answers

1. Fishing is an important economic activity because so much of Alaska is surrounded by water. Logging is also important because there are many trees, but Alaska is so far away from everywhere else that trans-portation costs are too high to make logging profitable except in the panhandle.
2. Native Americans, including Inuit and Aleuts, make up about 16 percent of the population. About 70 percent of the population lives in cities, more than 42 percent in Anchorage. The climate and landforms make life difficult and expensive. Since nearly 90 percent of Alaska's food is imported, Alaskans must cope with a high cost of living.
3. Oil is Alaska's most valuable resource, because the Alaska pipeline ends at Alaska's shoreline. It is easier and more profitable to extract and move than other minerals and natural resources.

OBJECTIVES: 1.02, 1.03, 1.06, 3.03, 5.07

Discussion Questions

1 Have you or anyone you know traveled either to Alaska or Hawaii? If you have not been there, would you like to go someday? What would you like to see there?

Caption Answer

Hawaii has a tropical climate.

Reading Strategy Activity

Making Comparisons

OBJECTIVES: 1.02, 1.03, 1.06, 3.03, 5.07

Children need many opportunities to compare what they already know to new material. In this lesson students will read about Hawaii. Since this is the last lesson on the regions of the United States, students should be familiar with both its climate and landscape. Not only will this lesson provide the students an opportunity to use prior knowledge, but it will be a way for some students to also review previous material.

Make a chart like the one below. Explain the chart and show them that the first section is done for them. Divide the class into groups. Let each group read about the regions and fill out the chart with landforms' shape or size. Some of the landforms are not compared to places in the United States. Students must use the material they read and the maps in the textbook to choose a place in the United States that most compares in shape or size. Groups need to share their charts with the class and discuss their reasons for picking a place in the United States that they feel best compares to Hawaii. Many different answers will be found.

LESSON 3 Hawaii

KEY IDEAS

- Hawaii is made up of volcanic islands in the Pacific Ocean.
- Hawaii is in the Tropics. It receives a lot of rainfall and is usually hot.
- Tourism, the military, and government employment are the important parts of the economy.

KEY TERMS

leeward
Pacific Rim
taro
tsunamis
windward

Which state is not located in North America? Which state has both a former royal palace and a coffee plantation? Which state contains a volcano that erupts regularly? Which state is an island once ruled by kings and queens?

Hawaii (hah·WIGH·ee) is the answer to all of these questions. Hawaii became the fiftieth state in 1959. It is our most southern and most western state.

Hawaii is unique in many other ways. Its great beauty, resources, and location have made it an important part of the nation.

The Island State

The state of Hawaii is a chain of eight big islands and 124 smaller ones. A strong ruler, King Kamehameha, brought the islands together in 1810.

When the land of all the islands is measured and totalled up, we can see that Hawaii is the fourth smallest state. But the chain of islands stretches very far. The chain is about 1,500 miles (2,415 km) long!

The eight large islands are Niihau, Kauai, Oahu, Molokai, Lanai, Maui, Kahoolawe, and Hawaii. Because it is the largest, the island of Hawaii is often called the Big Island.

This volcanic beach gives a clue to how islands of Hawaii were formed. **What do the palm trees tell you about Hawaii?**

Chapter 16

Features of Hawaii	Details	Compares to What U.S. Place
Landforms	islands, volcanoes, mountains, coast	California
Climate		
Plant Life		
People		
Economy		
Culture		

WORD ORIGINS

The name for our fiftieth state comes from **"Hawaiki."** That is the Hawaiian word for homeland. British explorer James Cook wrote the word as "Owhyhee" on sea charts during his visit in 1778.

Cook named the islands the Sandwich Islands after Lord Sandwich, British First Lord of the Admiralty. But the native name for the islands, spelled Hawai'i, is the name we use today.

Location and Landforms

If you have a globe, you can see just how far Hawaii is from North America. The state is located in the North Pacific Ocean. It is 2,397 miles (3,859 km) southwest of San Francisco.

Volcanoes

The Hawaiian islands were formed when volcanoes pushed up from the floor of the Pacific Ocean. Two volcanoes on the Big Island are still active. The volcano Kilauea (kee·lou·WAY·ah) erupts regularly. Fortunately, the lava from this volcano flows slowly. Usually no one is hurt.

The islands in the north of the chain are the oldest. Scientists expect that another island will rise up from the ocean in the next 2,000 to 20,000 years.

A volcano can be dangerous when lava flows or hot ash erupts. **How did volcanoes form the islands of Hawaii?**

PRONOUNCING HAWAIIAN WORDS

Almost all Hawaiians speak English. But most place names and some other words are in the native Hawaiian language.

Hawaiian is different from English. The Hawaiian alphabet has only 12 letters: A E H I K L M N O P U W. Every Hawaiian word and syllable ends with a vowel. Two consonants never occur without a vowel between them.

Here are the vowel sounds: a—ah, e—ay, i—ee, o—o (as in cone), u—oo (as in moon). The letters "au" together sound like the "ou" in "house". Spoken words have an almost musical sound when pronounced correctly. It takes practice to learn how to say Hawaiian words.

Let's Practice!

Honolulu
(HOH·noh·LOO·loo)

Haleakala
(hah·lay·ah·kah·LAH)

Waikiki
(WIGH·kee·KEE)

Kamehameha
(kah·MAY·hah·MAY·hah)

Kalakaua
(kah·LAH·kah·ou·wah)

Nuuanu Pali
(noo·oo·ah·noo PAH·lee)

Caption Answer

The Hawaiian islands were formed when volcanoes pushed up from the floor of the Pacific Ocean.

Activity

Hawaii—Hawaiian Picture Dictionary

OBJECTIVES: 3.01, 3.04, 4.03

Vocabulary
haole   **how·lay** (a foreigner)
kai   **kah·ee** (the sea)
kane   **kah·neh** (man)
mahi mahi   MAH·**hee**·MAH·**hee** (fish)
manu   MAH·**noo** (bird)
mauna   MOW·**nah** (mountain)
nani   NAH·**nee** (beautiful)
oe   OH·**ee** (you)
moana   **moh**·AH·**nah** (ocean)
kokua   **koh**·KOO·**uh** (help [cooperation])
nui   **noo·ee** (large [great])
kei ki   KAY·**kee** (child)
lei   **lay** (garland [wreath])
mahalo   **mah**·HAH·**loh** (thanks)

Have each student staple several pieces of blank white paper together to form pages of a picture dictionary. On each page, students will write a word from the vocabulary list. They may wish to include other information about the word, for instance, its origin and meaning. Students should illustrate each page with either original artwork or pictures from magazines or other sources. Students should make a creative cover for their dictionary and share their picture dictionary with the class.

Extension Research to find more Hawaiian vocabulary. Encourage students to use a different way to present their findings. For instance, students may want to do a word mobile, a flip book, PowerPoint, or a "television" presentation of the vocabulary.

Background Information

Volcanic Hawaii

The Hawaiian Island group, 2,000 miles from the closest large landmass, is one of the world's most isolated archipelagoes. The islands are the tops of massive mountains rising from the Pacific floor. The volcanic eruptions that created the islands began on the ocean floor millions of years ago. The process began as molten rock, known as magma, slowly pushed up from the earth's core and spilled through cracks in the crust that forms the ocean floor. As these eruptions cooled, the magma piled up on the ocean floor. Over millions of years the piles grew taller and wider as more magma spilled from cracks in the Pacific floor. Over time these mountains rose above the surface of the sea to become the Aloha State.

Discussion Questions

1 Where did the people of the island come from?

2 Where did these immigrants come from?

3 The temperature in Hawaii does not have extremes since it is tropical. What extremes are there in precipitation?

Caption Answer

Their enthnicity or ancestry is Polynesian, and they are American because they are citizens of the United States. Hawaiians blend both cultures.

Activity

Hawaiian Mobiles

OBJECTIVES: 1.02, 1.06, 3.03

Make a fact-filled mobile about Hawaii. You will need wire coat hangers; string, twine, or thread; white or colored paper; crayons or markers; glue or stapler; hole punch or tape.

Students are to write their names on a strip of paper. Glue or staple the strip into a loop and slip it over the hook of the hanger. Write the name of the state and the capital city on a large triangle-shaped cloud. Attach it with string inside the hanger. Write State Symbols on a large cloud and hang it from the left side of the hanger. On smaller clouds, draw and label the state bird, the state flower, the state flag, and the state animal. Attach these smaller clouds to the State Symbols cloud.

Write the state nickname on a large cloud. Hang it from the center of the hanger. Write Places to See on a large cloud and hang it from the right side of the hanger. On additional clouds draw and label important places to see in the state. Hang these smaller clouds from the Places to See clouds. Write Natural Resources on a large cloud and hang it from the right side of the hanger. On additional clouds draw and label important state resources. Hang these smaller

clouds from the Resources cloud. Write Industries on a large cloud and hang it from the left side of the hanger. On additional clouds draw and label important state industries. Hang these smaller clouds from the Industries cloud.

Extension The mobile can revolve around the Five Themes of Geography. Use any ideas or themes that you find relevant.

Other Landforms

The major islands are cone-shaped. There are mountains near their centers. The eroding slopes of volcanoes gave Hawaii its soil.

Hawaiians have a unique way of giving directions. It comes from the slope of the land. Instead of north, south, east, and west, Hawaiians use two main directions. *Mauka* (MOW·kah) means toward the mountains *Makai* (mah·KIGH) means toward the sea.

There are few lakes and only two rivers in Hawaii. They are the Hanapepe (hah·nah·PAY·pay) and the Wailua (wigh·LOO·ah). Both are located on Kauai.

The People of Hawaii

The first Hawaiians came from Polynesia in the South Pacific. British Captain James Cook was the first European to visit Hawaii. He came in 1778. By then, native people had been in the islands for centuries.

This dancer performs the hula. Hula is a form of prayer and storytelling. **How are Hawaiians both American and Polynesian?**

Customs

The Lei

The custom of the lei (lay) was brought to Hawaii by Polynesian travelers. They journeyed from Tahiti to Hawaii in canoes. They used the stars as a guide.

A lei is a garland of flowers, leaves, shells, seeds, nuts, or feathers worn around the neck. Leis are symbols of friendship and welcome. You should never refuse a lei. Hawaiians believe that it is rude to take off a lei in the presence of the person who gave it to you.

Many other sailors, missionaries, and business people followed Cook. As in the Americas, Europeans carried new diseases to the islands. Many thousands of Hawaiians died.

Between 1852 and 1905, about 184,000 immigrants came to Hawaii. They came from Japan, China, the Philippines, Korea, Southeast Asia, Puerto Rico, Spain, and Portugal. These immigrants made Hawaii one of the most diverse states in our country.

Culture

Hawaii is a cultural crossroads. Hawaiians value their heritage. Children learn to speak Hawaiian in school. They learn about their Polynesian ancestors. People feel a connection to the ocean and the land.

But Hawaiians are citizens of the United States, too. Hawaii has modern cities with tall buildings. It even has federal interstate highways! And, like the culture of the mainland states, Hawaii has adopted traditions from the immigrants who have made the islands their home.

Have you ever been to a luau or done a hula dance? These are Hawaiian traditions. Hawaii's culture has influenced American culture, too.

The population of the state of Hawaii is about 1.3 million people. About 75 percent live on the island of Oahu (oh·AH·hoo). Most of them live in the capital city of Honolulu (HOH·noh·LOO·loo).

The Eight Big Islands

Oahu is the third largest of the islands (see map, page 389) but has 70 percent of the state's population. Oahu's nickname is "the Gathering Place." Legends say that Hawai'iloa, the Polynesian navigator who discovered the islands, named Oahu after a son.

Lush and beautiful **Kauai** (kah·WAH) contains many rare plants and animals.

Fertile fields form the center of **Molokai** (MOH·loh·KAH·ee). Mountains and canyons are on the eastern part of the island. Sandy beaches stretch along the western part.

Lanai (LAH·nigh) used to be the pineapple island. The Dole Corporation grew pineapples on a huge plantation that covered most of the island. Pineapple is no longer grown commercially on Lanai.

Maui (MOU·ee) has stunning landforms. Its mountains spread across the interior. Rugged sections cover western and eastern parts of the island also. Most people live along the shore. Maui's beaches are very popular.

The United States armed forces use **Kahoolawe** (koh·ho·o·LAH·vay), an uninhabited island, for military practice.

Niihau (nee·ee·HOU) is privately owned. Few people are allowed to visit. Naturally, it is called the Forbidden Island.

Farmers grow many products on the Big Island of **Hawaii.** They produce sugarcane, fruit, coffee, and macadamia nuts. Cattle are raised on one of the largest ranches in the United States.

Climate and Vegetation

The climate of Hawaii is tropical. It has almost no change in seasons. The

Mount Waialeale on Kauai is said to be the wettest spot in the world, receiving more than an inch of rain a day. **How does that amount of rainfall compare to North Carolina's?**

temperature generally stays between 70° and 85°F (21° and 29°C).

However, the temperature drops with elevation. The tops of Hawaii's highest mountains, Mauna Loa (MOU·nah LOH·ah) and Mauna Kea (MOU·nah KAY·ah), are sometimes covered with snow.

Rainfall

Most islands have a wet, windy *windward* side and a drier, calmer *leeward* side (away from the wind). The dry side receives as little as 8 inches (20 cm) of rain per year.

The wet sides can be very wet. Mount Waialeale (WIGH·ah·lay·AH·lay) on Kauai is the wettest place on earth. It receives an average of 460 inches (11.6 m) of rain per year.

Sometime hurricanes and tsunamis hit Hawaii. *Tsunamis* (soo·NAH·meez) are destructive ocean waves caused by earthquakes. When a hurricane in the Pacific Ocean crosses the International Date Line, it is called a typhoon.

The wind and birds brought the first seeds and insects to the islands. Today lush rain forests cover the land. Two mammals, the monk seal and the hoary bat, came to Hawaii on their own. Other animals were brought or came along with people.

Name Origin

Hawaii "homeland." Nickname: Aloha State. Motto: The life of the land is perpetuated in righteousness. Admitted: 50th, 1959.

Discussion Questions

1 What is unique about Hawaii?
2 How did the birds and animals come to inhabit Hawaii?

Caption Answer

It is much more. North Carolina has about 48 inches of rain a year.

Science Activity

Hawaii

OBJECTIVES: 1.01, 1.02, 1.06

Assign small groups of students to research typhoons and tsunamis using encyclopedias, media center books, and the Internet. Prepare written and oral reports for each. Encourage students to include the following information in their reports: causes of each, places most likely to occur, effects on people, recent occurrences, damage done or casualties, and other interesting findings.

Activity

Hawaiian Islands

OBJECTIVES: 1.02, 1.06, 3.03

Place students in groups of four and tell them that they will name and create an original island for more people to inhabit. They need to create a map, design an original flag, create a new language, develop a form of currency, create rules, devise sources of income, and explain the history of how the island was geographically created. Using posterboard, markers, and other materials, they will create a display and present it in an original way to the class.

Eyewitness Activity

American Imperialism Socratic Seminar

OBJECTIVES: 1.07, 3.02, 3.03, 3.06, 4.08

Use the Eyewitness as the text for a mini-Socratic Seminar about American Imperialism. Before the seminar, review the text as a group. You may also wish to assign additional research prior to the day of the seminar. See the Socratic Seminar Guidelines in the front of the Teacher's Edition for more information about Socratic Seminars.

Opening Question: Have business interests influenced the development of the United State as a world power? If so, is Hawaii an example of this?

Suggested Stem Questions:

Support
•   Can you give us an example of why American businessmen might not have wanted Hawaii to be an independent country?
•   Why do you think the ruling family accepted limited on their power?
•   Why did buesinessmen want the United States to take over Hawaii?
•   What is annexation?

Cause and Effect
•   Why do you think this happened?
•   How could it have been prevented?
•   Do you think that would happen that way again? Why?
•   What are some reasons people want to have control over governments?
•   Would that still happen if . . . ?
•   What might have made the difference in the way things turned out?

Compare / Contrast
•   How is the United States' takeover of Hawaii similar to the annexation of Texas and the Mexican-American War? Different?

Point of View / Perspective
•   How might the princess have felt to see her parents die and to lose her country?
•   What do you think she was thinking when she met with President Cleeveland?
•   Do you have a different interpretation?
•   How did you arrive at your view?

Structure / Function

PRINCESS KAIULANI

EYEWITNESS TO HISTORY

The last royal family to rule in what is now the United States was not King George III and Queen Charlotte of Great Britain. Hawaii was ruled by royalty until it became a territory of the United States in 1898.

Queen Liliuokalani

In 1877, powerful American owners of sugarcane plantations banded together. They forced King Kalakana to accept a constitution. This limited his authority. It also allowed non-natives to vote. Queen Liliuokalani succeeded King Kalakana. About that time, businessmen from America worked to get the United States to annex Hawaii. Princess Kaiulani, the heir to the throne, was in school in the United Kingdom. While she was there, U.S. Marines marched into Honolulu and forced Queen Liliuokalani to give up her throne.

Princess Kaiulani

Princess Kaiulani was only 17 years old. Yet she sailed to the United States to ask President Grover Cleveland to stop annexation.

Cleveland told the princess he would investigate what happened. He promised her the Hawaiian people would be treated fairly. But the Americans in Hawaii would not give up power. President Cleveland would not use force to make them give up power. All he could do was block annexation.

406

Chapter 16

•   What were her choices of how to keep Hawaii independent?
•   Why did she do what she did? What do you think of that approach?
•   What better choices could she have made?

Personal Experience
•   What are some things that you wonder about?
•   What would you like to know about?
•   What would you do in that situation?

Annexation ceremonies, Iolani Palace

A group of young Hawaiians tried to restore the throne, but Queen Liliuokalani was forced to give it up. Princess Kaiulani decided to sail home.

In 1898, After President Cleveland left office, Congress voted to annex Hawaii. Hawaiians did not celebrate. Princess Kaiulani stayed home alone, sitting under a banyan tree. Six months later, the last princess of Hawaii died at age twenty-three. Some said she died of respiratory [lung] illness. Others said she died of sadness about her land.

 Eyewitness Activity

Learn More About Princess Kalulani

OBJECTIVES: 1.07, 3.03, 3.05

There are some print resources on Princess Kaiulani for students to read. The first of these is *The Last Princess: The Story of Princess Ka'iulani of Hawai'i* by Fay Stanley (HarperCollins Juvenile Books, 2001; ISBN 0688180205). This picture book is beautifully illustrated with much historical detail. *Kaiulani: The People's Princess, Hawaii, 1889 (The Royal Diaries)* by Ellen Emerson White (Scholastic Trade, 2001; ISBN 0439129095) is a longer fictionalized account of the princess. Thanks in part to its length, there is more detail about the princess's life. Even though this is a fictionalized account of her life and the political climate of Hawaii, the author took great pains to remain historically accurate.

Sugar plantation mill

The Pacific Region of the United States

407

 Research Activity

Hawaiian Luau

OBJECTIVES: 3.03, 3.04, 3.05, 3.07

Divide your class into cooperative groups and ask them to research and report about the traditions and customs of the Hawaiian luau, including food, music, dance, and costumes. After each group has presented their information, hold a class luau. Have the class make paper leis. Assign each student or cooperative group certain Hawaiian dishes to bring to the luau. Bring in some traditional Hawaiian music. Learn the hula, and dance as a group. Make grass skirts out of brown or green bulletin board paper. Learn some Hawaiian songs

Discussion Questions

1 Why are Hawaiian-made goods so expensive in other parts of the world?

2 What do we call countries that lie within or border the Pacific Ocean?

 Caption Answer

Hawaii's environment attracts tourists.

 Activity

Tourism in Hawaii

OBJECTIVES: 3.03, 3.04, 4.07

Tourism is the most important industry in Hawaii. There can be problems when people depend too much on others being able to afford to visit.
Divide the class into two groups.
One group represents the tourist-based economy. The other group represents the self-supporting economy. Each group will list advantages and disadvantages of its economy on large chart paper. They will discuss and create three different role-play scenarios to convince the other group that their system is better. After each group presents, students will all write a short paper on the results. Economies that are very dependent on others can have problems.

Economy

Hawaii's climate is important to the islands' economy. It is a key influence on many of the island's industries.

Natural Resources

The climate and rich volcanic soil help orchids, ferns, and many rare plants grow. For example, the silversword plant grows only on Maui and Hawaii. After sprouting a stalk of purple flowers, the plant dies.

There are many edible plants and fruits that grow here. These include 50 different kinds of bananas, guavas, and, of course, pineapples. Taro also grows easily here.

Taro is a plant that produces a tuber, a swollen underground stem much like a potato. Hawaiians cook the tuber and pound it into poi (POH·ee). Poi is a sort of pasty pudding that many Hawaiians love.

Industry

Hawaii's environment contributes to the state's most important industry, tourism. In 2005, more than 7.5 million tourists visited Hawaii. That was the highest number ever. Tourists spend more than $11 billion a year.

Government and defense are important parts of the economy. More than 10 percent

Tourism is an important industry in Hawaii.
What "resource" attracts tourists?

of Hawaii's population is made up of military personnel and their families.

The high cost of shipping materials makes Hawaiian-made goods very expensive in other places. Manufacturers try to make small items that are not costly to ship but have high market value.

Today, agriculture makes up only about 1 percent of Hawaii's total income. Flowers and nursery plants, sugarcane, coffee, macadamea nuts, and pineapple are the leading crops. Sugarcane processing was an important industry but is now declining.

Cost of Living

Hawaii's cost of living is high. Life here costs 35 cents more for every dollar spent on the mainland. Much of this comes from the expense of shipping goods long distance. Even transportation among the islands is costly.

The Pacific Rim

Hawaii occupies what has been called "one of the world's most fortunate locations." Honolulu used to be known as the Crossroads of the Pacific. Today, people call the countries that lie within or border the Pacific Ocean the *Pacific Rim.*

These nations include Japan, Korea, Taiwan, and China. The Pacific Rim now produces more than half of the world's manufactured goods. Pacific Rim nations are already important markets. They will continue to be good customers for America.

With Hawaii's diverse population and close connections with Asia, its leaders believe their islands will serve as a link with the Pacific Rim for the United States.

408

Chapter 16

 Art Activity

Hawaiian Culture Party

OBJECTIVES: 1.02, 3.03, 3.07, 4.03

Have the girls make and wear grass skirts, the boys wear cut-offs or shorts with sleeveless shirts, and everyone wear leis. Have the students research the hula to learn hand motions and then sing and enact motions to the song. Ask students to bring tropical fruit to make a fruit salad. Serve pineapple juice or tropical punch to drink.

To make a grass skirt, use colored bulletin board paper cut in strips to the waist. Attach with tape at the waist. To make a lei, measure a length of string that will go over the students' heads. Alternate crepe paper shapes to represent flowers with 1-inch sections of straws.

The Shrinking Pineapple Industry

Once sugarcane and pineapple fields covered most of Hawaii's islands. Now you'll find houses, hotels, and fields with such other crops as coffee, macadamia nuts, and flowers.

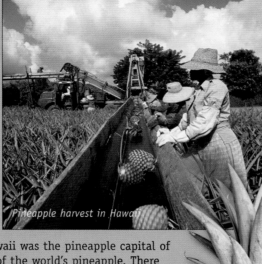
Pineapple harvest in Hawaii

The Pineapple Industry

In 1901, Harvard graduate James Dole moved to Hawaii. He created a company to grow and can pineapples. By 1922, Dole had bought the entire island of Lanai. It had been a cactus-covered island with 150 people. Lanai became the largest pineapple plantation in the world. It had 20,000 acres of pineapples. More than 1,000 pineapple workers and their families lived there.

By the middle of the last century, Hawaii was the pineapple capital of the world. It grew more than 80 percent of the world's pineapple. There were eight pineapple companies there. More than 3,000 people worked in the pineapple industry. Pineapple production was Hawaii's second largest industry (sugarcane was first).

Changing Times

Now it costs more to hire workers and raise pineapples in the United States. So companies have moved their plantations to countries where it is less costly. Fresh Del Monte, Produce Inc., announced in 2006 that they would stop growing pineapples in Hawaii in 2008.

Today, Hawaii is no longer among the top ten of the world's pineapple producers. Now Thailand, the Philippines, and Brazil together grow about a third of the world's pineapple. Hawaii produces only about 2 percent of the world's pineapple today.

Teacher Notes

Sliced, Chunked, or Crushed?

The pineapple is not native to Hawaii. Pineapples originated in South America and were transplanted throughout tropical areas by the Spanish and Portuguese in the early nineteenth century. James Drummond Dole moved to Hawaii in 1901, bought some land, and started to harvest and can pineapple and pineapple juice. In 1913, Henry Ginaca developed a machine that could peel and core a pineapple in less than 2 seconds, which, along with a larger cannery closer to the port in Honolulu, greatly increased production capacity. As the demand for canned pineapple products increased over the next decades, the advent of refrigeration and commercial aviation made it possible to ship fresh product as well. Fresh pineapple now reaches most major markets within 36 hours of their harvest. This is important since pineapples must be picked fully ripe.

LESSON 3 REVIEW

Fact Follow-Up
1. Describe the climate and vegetation of Hawaii.
2. How have Hawaii's location, resources, and climate influenced the state's economy?

Talk About It
1. Describe the different Hawaiian islands.
2. Why is climate Hawaii's most valuable resource?
3. What happened to the pineapple industry?

LESSON 3 REVIEW

Fact Follow-Up Answers
1. The climate of Hawaii is tropical, with almost no change in seasons. Temperature drops with elevation. Most islands have a wet, windy windward side and a drier, calmer leeward side. Because of the climate and the rich, volcanic soil, almost any vegetation will grow, including orchids, ferns, and many rare plants.
2. Because of Hawaii's strategic location in the Pacific Ocean, many military bases are there. The islands are also an important place for Americans to trade with people from the Pacific Rim countries. Hawaii's most important resource is its climate, which attracts tourists and brings the state about $11 billion a year. The climate and rich, volcanic soil contribute to farming. Hawaiian fruit, nuts, and sugarcane are shipped all over the world.

Talk About It Answers
1. Important points: Studenst should describe factors inclluding the sizes of the islands, their industries, and population.
2. The mild climate contributes much to the state's most important industry, tourism. Its temperate climate, together with its soil, also means that almost anything will grow in Hawaii. More than 50 kinds of bananas, guavas, and pineapples grow in Hawaii.
3. The costs of runnng a pineapple plantation in the United States became too high, so companies moved the industry to other countries where costs were lower.

Teaching This Skill Lesson

Materials Needed textbooks, paper, pencils, reference books

Classroom Organization whole class, individual

Beginning the Lesson Ask students if they would like to live in Alaska for a year and what they might expect life to be like during that time. Ask if they think life would be pretty much the same anywhere in Alaska or if location might make a difference. Accept all responses. Ask what they would need to find out about Alaska before moving there. Again, accept all responses, listing them on the chalkboard and suggesting that students make note of them.

Lesson Development Ask students to assume that they will, in fact, be moving to Alaska for a year and to write questions they have about the move and about life in Alaska. If desired, pair students to polish their questions. As a homework assignment, have students discuss the assignment with their parents to add other questions. Students can also ask parents how they might find out answers to questions. Students are to use their textbooks to answer as many of their questions about Alaska as possible.

Conclusion When students return with their homework assignments completed, ask how they can find the other answers they need. List these sources on the chalkboard.

Extension This is an opportunity to use online sources and media center materials once students have refined their questions.

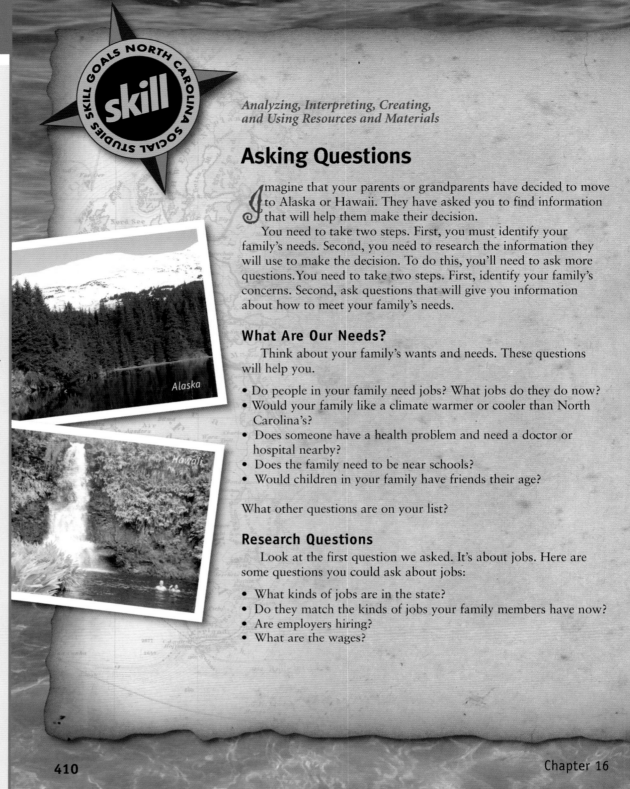

Analyzing, Interpreting, Creating, and Using Resources and Materials

Asking Questions

Imagine that your parents or grandparents have decided to move to Alaska or Hawaii. They have asked you to find information that will help them make their decision.

You need to take two steps. First, you must identify your family's needs. Second, you need to research the information they will use to make the decision. To do this, you'll need to ask more questions. You need to take two steps. First, identify your family's concerns. Second, ask questions that will give you information about how to meet your family's needs.

What Are Our Needs?

Think about your family's wants and needs. These questions will help you.

- Do people in your family need jobs? What jobs do they do now?
- Would your family like a climate warmer or cooler than North Carolina's?
- Does someone have a health problem and need a doctor or hospital nearby?
- Does the family need to be near schools?
- Would children in your family have friends their age?

What other questions are on your list?

Research Questions

Look at the first question we asked. It's about jobs. Here are some questions you could ask about jobs:

- What kinds of jobs are in the state?
- Do they match the kinds of jobs your family members have now?
- Are employers hiring?
- What are the wages?

Chapter 16

Skill Lesson Review

1. Was it harder to plan the questions or to find the answers? *Many students may find it difficult to ask precise questions and will need practice.*
2. Do you think there were some sources of information that were better than others? If so, why? *If students have precise questions, general sources of information may frustrate them since these sources may give few precise answers. Encourage students who were using online sources to go to secondary sites mentioned in the online sources.*

Finding Answers

Reading is one way of finding answers to questions. This chapter may have some answers. Your media center will have more answers. You can also do research on the Internet.

You may also interview someone who knows a lot about Alaska or Hawaii. An adult you know may have served on a military base in one of the states. You could interview other people through letters or e-mail. Could you send questions to other fifth-graders in Alaska or Hawaii using the Internet?

A Menu for Research

Let's make a graphic organizer. A menu will help us choose the types of research questions we need to ask.

Fold a piece of paper in half. On the front, come up with a name for your restaurant that relates to your state, for example, "Hawaii Haven" or "Alaska Trails." Be creative. You can decorate the menu with pictures and symbols of your state, too.

Make a list of your research subjects. We have discussed one subject you can use, Jobs. What other subjects do you need to research?

Open your menu. Divide the paper into the same number of boxes as the number of subjects you have. Make them big enough to fit your questions.

The Pacific Region of the United States

411

Chapter 16 Review

Talk About It

1. Important points: Students should choose one of the two and explain why. Volcanic activity has created lakes and fertile soils; earthquakes have destroyed property and lives.

2. Important points: The cities of the Pacific coast states are large. People move there for jobs and education.

3. Location on the Pacific Ocean encourages such economic activities as shipbuilding, fishing, and international trade.

4. Important points: Students should state whether or not the term could describe Hawaii and explain their statement. Hawaii is great in its variety of vegetation, its great beauty, and the diversity of its people.

5. Important points: Students should choose one state and explain their choice. Oil and mineral exploration threaten the delicate tundra environment of Alaska. Land use in Hawaii causes some concern.

6. Alaska was purchased from Russia for $7.2 million, about 2 cents per acre. Some people at the time thought the price was too high, but there was little comment other than that. Foreign owners of sugarcane plantations at first forced the king of Hawaii to accept a constitution, then forced the queen who succeeded him to give up her throne. Princess Kaiulani, heir to the throne, was in school in the United Kingdom at the time and went to Washington, D.C., to ask President Grover Cleveland to block annexation. After President Cleveland left office, the Congress of the United States voted to annex Hawaii.

Mastering Mapwork

1. Because Honolulu is the capital of Hawaii and its largest city, one would expect to see a busy urban environment. In Honolulu, humans have made great changes in the environment.

2. The northern location is on low-lying land near the Arctic Ocean. In this place it would be logical to expect to see little impact of humans on the environment and more impact of the environment on the few humans who might be there. Anchorage, farther south, is a city, and one would expect to see streets, large buildings, homes, and other evidence of people on the environment.

3. Hawaii is the largest of the Hawaiian

Islands. Farmers grow sugarcane, fruit, coffee, and macadamia nuts on the island, and one of the largest cattle ranches in the United States is located on the island. You would expect to see that humans have changed the environment in many ways in this location.

CHAPTER 16 REVIEW

Lessons Learned

LESSON 1
The Pacific Coast Region
The Pacific Coast region enjoys a varied climate. California, Washington, and Oregon have more resources for agriculture and industry than some countries.

LESSON 2
Alaska
Alaska is a mountainous state with a cold climate and few people, but it is rich in mineral, forest, and ocean resources. Most Alaskans live in cities. Forty-two percent live in its largest city, Anchorage.

LESSON 3
Hawaii
Hawaii is a state of many volcanic islands set in the Pacific Ocean. The eight large islands of Hawaii contain beautiful landforms. Tourism is Hawaii's main industry.

Talk About It

1. Which of these—volcanic activity or earthquakes—has been more important in the Pacific Coast states? Explain why.
2. Why do you think most people in the Pacific Coast states live in cities?
3. How does relative location affect the economy of the Pacific Coast region?
4. The Aleut people of Alaska call it Great Land. Could the same term describe Hawaii? Explain your answer.
5. Which state—Alaska or Hawaii—has the more endangered environment? Explain your answer.
6. Compare the means by which Alaska and Hawaii were acquired by the United States.

Mastering Mapwork

HUMAN-ENVIRONMENTAL INTERACTION
Use the maps on page 389 to answer the following questions.

1. Locate Honolulu on the island of Oahu in Hawaii. What patterns of human-environmental interaction would you expect to see?
2. Locate the intersection of 70°N and 150°W and Anchorage, Alaska, which lies farther south on 150°W. What differences in human-environmental interaction would you expect to see in these two places?
3. Locate Hilo at 155°W on the island of Hawaii. From what you have read in this chapter, what human-environmental interaction would you expect to see in this place?

Becoming Better Readers

More Strategies for Understanding the Text
Another strategy that good readers use to understand the text is to make comparisons. To understand the Pacific Coast Region, a good reader would think about how the land compares to the other regions in the United States. How does climate of the Pacific Coast Region (see page 392) compare to the climate of the Midwest Region (see page 371)?

Becoming Better Readers

Important points: Students should make comparisons and use examples from the text to support their answer. The climate of the northern Pacific Coast is cool and wet, while southern California is warm and dry. There is much variation in the the climates of the region. The Midwest has a different climate, mainly hot summers and long, cold winters.

Go to the Source

Analyzing Song Lyrics

Builders of the Grand Coulee Dam wanted to tell people how important making hydroelectric power was. They hired a famous folk singer for one month. His job was to write songs for a film about the dam.

Woody Guthrie wrote "Roll On, Columbia." In 1987, it became Washington's state folk song. Answer the questions using information from the lyrics below.

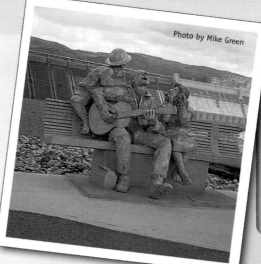
Photo by Mike Green

At the Grand Coulee Dam, this sculpture shows Woody Guthrie singing one of his Columbia River ballads.

Roll On, Columbia

Roll on, Columbia
Roll on, Columbia, roll on,
Roll on, Columbia, roll on.
Your power is turning the darkness to dawn,
Roll on, Columbia, roll on.
And far up the river is Grand Coulee Dam,
The mightiest thing ever built by man,
To run the great factories and water the land,
It's roll on, Columbia, roll on.

Questions

1. What is the Columbia?
2. Why is the Grand Coulee Dam important?
3. What is the effect of using the phrase: "Roll on, Roll on Columbia" over and over in the song?
4. Based on the context of the song, what does "Your power is turning the darkness to dawn" mean?
5. Who wrote "Roll on Columbia" and why?

Go to the Source

 ## Go to the Source

Analyzing Song Lyrics

OBJECTIVES: 5.01, 5.03, 3.07, 3.02
SOCIAL STUDIES SKILLS: 3.05, 4.06

"Roll On, Columbia"

Song lyrics are poems set to music. Often, songs are more popular than poems, so more people hear the message in a song than if they have to read a poem. The rhythm and melody also are a pneumonic device for remembering information, so a song becomes a powerful tool for spreading messages.

"Roll On, Columbia, Roll On" (1941) became a famous anthem about public works projects built by the New Deal programs during the Great Depression.

Visit **NCJourneys.com** for a link to the lyrics at the Woody Guthrie Foundation Web site.

Answers

1. A river
2. It generates hydroelectric power.
3. It creates a mental picture of a powerful, flowing, Columbia River.
4. The Columbia River, through the dam, is providing electricity to light up homes and factories.
5. Woody Guthrie wrote it to show the importance of the Columbia River and its roll in the production of electricity.

How to Use the Chapter Review

There are four sections in the Chapter Review: Talk About It, Mastering Mapwork, Becoming Better Readers, and Go to the Source. Use the Vocabulary Worksheets and the Chapter Review Worksheet in the Teacher's Resource Guide for additional reinforcement and preparation for the Chapter Assessments. The Chapter and Lesson Reviews and the Chapter Review Worksheets are the basis of the assessment for each chapter.

Talk About It questions encourage students to speculate about the content of the chapter and are suitable for class or small-group discussion. They are not intended to be assigned for homework.

Mastering Mapwork has students apply one or more of the Five Themes of Geography to maps within the chapter.

Becoming Better Readers focuses on building reading strategy skills necessary for reading comprehension in the content areas.

Go to the Source activities allow students to analyze a primary source that relates to the content of the chapter. The questions and activities familiarize students with different types of primary sources and also build content-reading skills.

CHAPTER 17

Government of the People

Social Studies Strands

Government and Active Citizenship

Historical Perspectives

North Carolina Standard Course of Study

Goal 2 The learner will analyze political and social institutions in North America and examine how these institutions respond to human needs, structure society, and influence behavior.

Teaching & Assessment

- English Language Learner Modified Lesson Plans for this chapter are found in the Teacher's Resource Guide.

- *ExamView® Assessment Suite* is provided at **NCJourneys.com.** It includes customizable assessments for all chapters. Paper tests are also available in the Teacher's Resource Guide. See pages T16–T17 for information about how to use the assessments and the Scoring Guide.

Worksheets

Worksheets and answer keys are found both in the Teacher's Resource Guide and at **NCJourneys.com**, including Reading Guides, Reading Strategies, Chapter Reviews, English Language Learner and others.

Activities and Integrations

SOCIAL STUDIES	
Setting Up a Student Council, p. 414B	
★ Problem Based Learning: Campaign Strategist, p. 414B	
Activator: Government of the People, p. 414	
■ States and Capital Tag, p. 415	
■ Elections, p. 422	
Graphic Organizer Mobiles, p.427	
● State Government, p. 428	
▲ ■ Municipal Government Day, p. 430	
● Skill Lesson: Reading a Chart, p. 431	

READING/LANGUAGE ARTS	READING/LANGUAGE ARTS OBJECTIVES
● ▲ President's Day, p. 414B	3.06, 4.03, 4.06
Writing Prompt: Rules, p. 414	4.09
Reading Strategy: Content Matrix, p. 416	1.03, 2.02
▲ ■ ★ Presidential Quotes, p. 417	3.06, 4.07
Writing to the President, p. 418	4.09
Voting Changes, p. 419	3.06
Radio Commercial, p. 420	2.01, 2.04
● Reading Strategy: Spider Map, Graphic Organizer, p. 425	4.03
★ Mock Trial, p. 424	2.10, 3.01, 4.06
Becoming Better Readers, p. 432	
Understanding an Inaugural Address, p. 433	

MATHEMATICS	MATHEMATICS OBJECTIVES
Elector Math, p. 423	1.02

TECHNOLOGY	TECHNOLOGY OBJECTIVES
★ Carolina Connection: James Iredell, p. 415	2.13
★ The Electoral College and the Elections of 1876 and 2000, p. 420	2.13
★ Supreme Court, p. 426	2.13

FINE ARTS	FINE ARTS OBJECTIVES
▲ ■ Campaign Art, p. 414B	2.01
● ▲ President's Day, p. 414B	3.06, 4.03
Political Logos, p. 421	

CHARACTER AND VALUES EDUCATION	TRAITS
E Pluribus Unum, p. 420	kindness, caring
What Would You Do?, p. 423	caring, citizenship

● Basic Activities ★ Challenging Activities ▲ English Language Learner Novice ■ English Language Learner Intermediate

Introductory Activity

Setting Up a Student Council

 OBJECTIVES: 2.02, 2.03, 3.03

Following a study of how government operates, plan to establish a student council in your class or school. Decide if your school would like a K–5 or 3–5 student council. Senior officers will be fifth-grade students (or 5–6). Candidates will be selected from each fifth-grade class. Each classroom should elect a representative to the council. Classroom representative guidelines can be written by teachers. Candidates will conduct a campaign for a week before elections. The day before elections, each candidate will present a speech in front of the student body (or make a video for lower grades to view). On election day announce the winners at the end of the day. The student council meets weekly, follows parliamentary procedures, and chooses projects to work on.

Culminating Activity

President's Day

OBJECTIVES: 2.03, 3.04, 4.03

Hold a Presidents Day in the classroom. This activity would require two class periods. Each student chooses a president to research. This research is done well in advance so students will be prepared to assume the character of their chosen president or first lady. Each student will have two roles. During one class period, half the class will dress as their researched character and be seated at various tables (desks) around the classroom. The other students will assume the roles of interviewers. Each interviewer will write at least five questions for five of the historical characters. Establish a rotation schedule for students to interview their chosen characters and suggest a time limit for each interview (possibly using a timer). When the time is up, students will then rotate and interview their next character. At the end of this activity, the reporters will choose one character and write the results of their interview. The written reports can be compiled in a class book. On the second day or in the second class period, have the students reverse roles and repeat the activity.

For another President's Day activity, assign each student a president. Have each students obtain a pumpkin and dress the pumpkin like the head of the president they are assigned. The students can use items found at home or ones they create to make hair, a hat, and so on. Once the pumpkins are finished, students can present a short report about each president and his contribution to America.

 Art Activity

Campaign Art

OBJECTIVES: 2.05

Share with students actual campaign signs, posters, bumper stickers, and buttons, or photos of them. Discuss the colors the candidates chose to use on the materials. Speculate about the reasons these might have been chosen. Find out if there are any restrictions on the size of or use of lawn signs in your community. Discuss how the designer might take into account the size restrictions. How big does the name have to be on the item? Have designers used the candidate's first name, last name, or full name?

Divide the class into groups of four. Have each group choose a candidate from a current or past election (for president, Congress, or state or local offices) and design a set of posters, signs, bumper stickers, and buttons. The group must chose their colors. Will they have a slogan? use photos or logos? Display the finished sets of campaign materials.

 Problem Based Learning Activity

Campaign Strategist

OBJECTIVES: 1.02, 1.06, 3.03

Situation You are working for the president of the United States. The president is getting ready to run for reelection. During the election process the president must become aware of and be in tune with all the various lands and regions throughout the United States.

Task What are the common and different land characteristics in our country? How do these land resources affect the people who live in that region? How does the land help the lives of the people? How do the affects of the land cause the people trouble?

Reflection In a cabinet/role play discussion have the students (after research) determine where in the country the president should spend his time. Should he focus his effort on everything or in certain areas more than others?

Teaching Strategies

Be sure to review checks and balances in the Skill Lesson.

Another option for teaching this chapter is to use it during Unit 2 after you teach the Revolutionary War and Lesson 1 of Chapter 7.

Call your local board of elections to inquire if they provide supplemental materials that will help teach the election process to your students.

Visit a local courthouse or invite local authorities to make presentations on the work of your local government. This chapter presents many opportunities for guest speakers.

Activator

Government of the People

➤ **OBJECTIVES:** 2.03, 2.04

Present to the class a hypothetical decision that ultimately affects them, such as school uniforms being required at their school, or a mandate that all lunches must be bought at school and cannot be brought from home.

Be convincing and keep a straight face when sharing this information with the class. Prompt the class with questions such as "Can you change this policy? How can you be a voice in government?"As students respond to questions, list possible solutions on board or chart. Guide class to give responses such as petitions, letters to board members, e-mail, protest, telephone calls, letter to newspaper, and speaking at a board meeting. Put students in groups and assign one solution per group and have them produce an example of that solution. Every member of the group is required to produce a sample of the assigned solution. Share and display.

Writing Prompt

➤ **OBJECTIVES:** 2.02, 2.03, 2.04

Clarification Civilized societies make rules for citizens to follow. Think of a rule that your family has that affects your life. Write about whether you think it is a good rule or not. Explain why it should be kept or done away with.

Imaginative Imagine you have an opportunity to have a conversation with one of our founding fathers, possibly George Washington, John Adams, Thomas Jefferson, Benjamin Franklin, or James Madison. What are three questions you would ask him? What three facts about modern American life would you tell him? What might his response be?

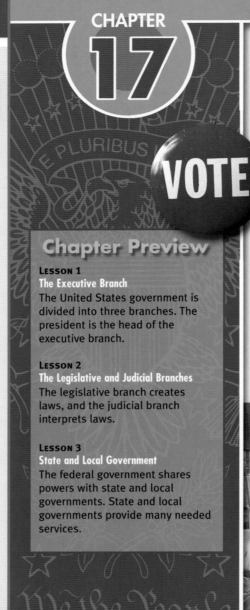

CHAPTER 17

Chapter Preview

LESSON 1
The Executive Branch
The United States government is divided into three branches. The president is the head of the executive branch.

LESSON 2
The Legislative and Judicial Branches
The legislative branch creates laws, and the judicial branch interprets laws.

LESSON 3
State and Local Government
The federal government shares powers with state and local governments. State and local governments provide many needed services.

414

Government of the People

History is a story. The history of voting in the United States is a story of struggle. It takes us from the Founding Fathers writing the Constitution to the amendment allowing eighteen-year-olds to vote.

At first, America only allowed white male property owners over twenty-one to vote. Then after the Civil War, the Thirteenth Amendment gave African American males the right to vote. But many states prevented them from voting.

In 1920, the Nineteenth Amendment gave all women the right to vote. The Civil Rights Act of 1964 and the Voting Rights Act of 1965 made it possible for African American men and women to vote in all states. Finally, in 1971, the Twenty-sixth Amendment gave eighteen-year-olds the right to vote.

Voters across the country, like these voters in Detroit, cast their ballots for the 2000 United States presidential election.

Chapter Resources

Print Resources

Kennedy, Edward M. *My Senator and Me: A Dog's-Eye View of Washington D.C.* Scholastic Inc., 2006. ISBN 0439650771.

Neufeld, John. *A Small Civil War.* Aladdin Paperbacks, 1996. ISBN 0689807716.

Magazines

Cobblestone Publishing.
Meaning of the Constitution. ISBN 0382403223.
Bill of Rights. ISBN 0382404300.

Elections in America. ISBN 0382407733.
Presidential Elections. ISBN 0382402995.
Supreme Court. ISBN 0382404009.
Two-Party System. ISBN 0382403967.

Web Sites

United States Government
• Ben's Guide, Federal Government for Kids
• Federal Resources for Educational Excellence
• The White House
• The Electoral College
• The Legislative Branch, Library of Congress

The United States—State Capitals and Number of Representatives*

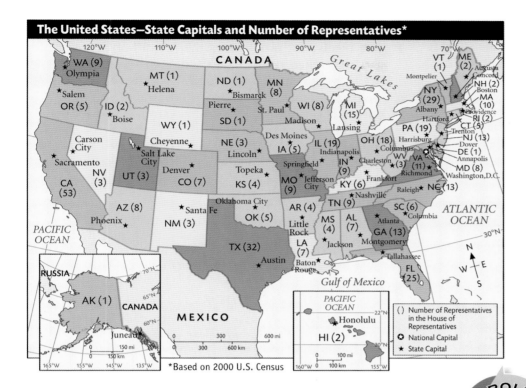

*Based on 2000 U.S. Census

James Iredell

James Iredell was a colonial leader of North Carolina. He had a great influence on both our state and national governments. Iredell was born in England in 1751 and moved to Edenton when he was seventeen. Iredell became a lawyer and was well respected. From the start of the Revolutionary War, he supported the Patriot cause. During the Revolution he served as attorney general of North Carolina.

Iredell was a delegate to the Constitutional Convention of 1788. As the leader of the Federalists of North Carolina, he argued in favor of the adoption of the new Constitution. President Washington appointed him to be a justice of the new United States Supreme Court. He gave speeches to juries that explained the meaning of the Constitution. They were published all over the country.

Iredell County is named after him.

James Iredell

415

• The House of Representatives
• House of Representatives: "Kids in the House"
• The Senate
• The Supreme Court

North Carolina Government
• North Carolina Government
• North Carolina Government for Kids
• North Carolina Court System for Kids
• Governor's Page
• General Assembly
• North Carolina Counties

Civics and Service
• C-SPAN
• Lawyers in the Schools, North Carolina Bar Association
• National Atlas, Department of the Interior
• National Peace Corps Association (returned volunteer outreach)
• North Carolina Civic Education Consortium
• Peace Corps' World Wise Schools
• Project Vote Smart
• The Preamble to the Constitution Lesson Plans, National Constitution Center
• Veterans Administration Kids Pages

Discussion Questions

1 Look at the map on page 415. Why do you think that states like New York have 31 representatives in the House and states like Montana have only three?

 Map Activity

States and Capitals Tag

NATIONAL GEOGRAPHY STANDARDS: 1, 4

GEOGRAPHIC THEMES: Place

OBJECTIVES: 1.01, 1.02, 1.03

This game can be played in small groups or as an entire class. Use cones or some other markers to set off a playing area suitable for the number of children playing. One student is "It" as the game begins. That student tries to tag a classmate, who will then name a state and its capital. If the student cannot name a state and its capital, that student becomes "It." List the states and capitals as they are named. If a tagged student repeats a state and its capital, that student becomes "It."

 Activity

Carolina Connection: James Iredell

OBJECTIVES: 2.03, 4.03

Links to Web sites with biographies of James Iredell can be found at **NCJourneys.com**.

Ask students to tell what they know about the duties of an attorney general. Remind the students that James Iredell was the attorney general of North Carolina during the American Revolution.

OBJECTIVES: 2 2.02, 2.03, 2.05

Discussion Questions

1 The executive branch of government holds the office of president and vice president. What are the requirements to become president? Should these requirements be updated?

 Caption Answer

The olive branch symbolizes peace, the arrows, war. The United States looks toward peace.

Reading Strategy Activity

Content Matrix

OBJECTIVES: 2.02, 2.03, 2.05

This lesson describes the Executive branch. Students can organize the information into a graphic organizer that will be easily read and remembered. They should add mores circes as the need. They should use this to help them learn about the other branches covered in Lesson 2. Let students share their graphic when they finish.

A worksheet like the one below accompanies this lesson.

Extension Novice ELL students can copy from an example and label the names of the plants and animals.

The United States Government

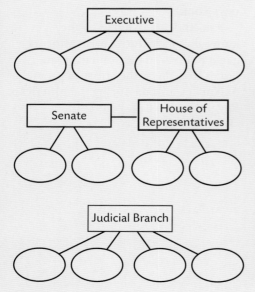

KEY IDEAS

- The federal government is divided into three parts: legislative, executive, and judicial.

- The executive branch is led by the president. It enforces laws.

KEY TERMS

Democratic Party
diplomats
electoral college
Executive
party
President
Republican Party
vice president

To solve the problems of the Articles of Confederation, the writers of the Constitution created a new government. It was a federal system. We call our national government the "federal" government.

The main offices of the federal government are located in Washington, D.C. The abbreviation D.C. stands for District of Columbia. The city of Washington, D.C., was built to be the headquarters of the national government.

Three Branches

The federal government has three branches. First is the legislative branch, called Congress. Second is the executive branch. The president is the head of the executive branch. The third branch is the judicial branch. The Supreme Court is the highest court in the judicial branch.

The Executive Branch

The *executive* branch is the branch of government that carries out the laws passed by Congress. The *president* is the head of the executive branch. The president enforces the laws passed by Congress. When we read about the history of the United States in this book, we are learning about many of the decisions our past presidents have made.

The eagle on the presidential seal represents the country. **What do you think the arrows and the olive branch represent? Why might the eagle be facing the olive branch?**

 Teacher Notes

Vice Presidents Take Office

Article II, Section 1, of the Constitution reads "In case of the removal of the president from office, or of his death, resignation, or inability to discharge the powers and duties of the said office, the same shall devolve on the vice president. . ." When William Henry Harrison died after only a few months in office in 1841, Vice President John Tyler took the presidential

oath. Some constitutional scholars challenged that move, arguing that it wasn't clear if the word "same" referred to "Powers and Duties" or "Office." If the former, then Tyler would have only been acting president until another had been chosen. If the latter, then he would have assumed the presidency just as if he had been elected. At the same time, it was not clear what would have happened if Harrison had remained incapacitated for an extended period, and then recovered—only to discover that Tyler, now having taken the oath, occupied his office. Would the presidency then

Vice President

The *vice president* is second-in-command to the president. The vice president replaces the president if the president dies while in office or if the president cannot do his or her duties. Often, the president asks the vice president to represent the United States at special events or meetings in other countries.

The vice president also serves as the president of the Senate in Congress. He or she can only vote to break a tie in the Senate.

The President's Responsibilities

The jobs of the president have grown over time. Today, the president has seven major responsibilities. Some of these jobs are listed in the Constitution. Some have been added in times of crisis, like wartime. These make up the president's five official responsibilities.

Head of State The first role of the president is *head of state*. In some nations, the head of state is a king or a queen. The president is the American head of state. He or she is a living symbol of the nation.

As head of state, the president stands for the highest values and ideals of our country. The president acts as head of state when he awards medals to war veterans.

Chief Executive The president is also the *chief executive*. As head of the executive branch, the president is the "boss." The president decides how the laws of the United States are to be enforced.

He or she oversees all government workers in the executive branch. The branch is divided into departments. Each department deals with a different government job.

The federal government is our nation's largest employer! There are many, many government workers—almost 2 million. The soldiers and sailors in the military are also government workers. There are another 1.4

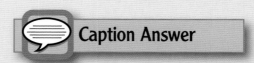
Federal Workers

Military Workers 1.4 million Civilian Workers 2 million

million active duty people in the military.

As chief executive, the president hires people to help run the executive branch. The heads of the departments make up the cabinet. The president meets with the cabinet to talk about what the government is doing. You read about the cabinet in chapter 7.

Chief Diplomat *Chief diplomat* is the third role of the president. The president makes the foreign policy of the United States. The advisors help him or her. The president decides what our **diplomats** should say to foreign governments. Diplomats are people who represent our country to other nations.

When the president travels to meet with the heads of other governments, such as the president of Mexico, he is acting as the chief diplomat.

The U.S. Fish and Wildlife Service is one of the many executive departments. **How many people work for the federal government?**

Government of the People

417

Discussion Questions

1 Before reading: What do you think the president does as a part of his job?

2 After reading: Are the president's responsibilities what you expected?

3 What types of tasks would you like to see the president do that he does not presently do?

Caption Answer

More than 2 million civilian and 1.4 million military workers

Activity

Presidential Quotes

OBJECTIVES: 2.03, 2.05, 4.03

Introduce the following quote by Abraham Lincoln: "Government of the people, by the people, for the people, shall not perish from the earth." Discuss why and how this quote reflects the life of Lincoln. Have students choose a president to research. After researching, the student will choose a quote from the chosen president. Based on the knowledge gained from their research, students will write how the quote highlights that president's life or term of office.

revert to Harrison? The question resurfaced twice when John Garfield, and later, Woodrow Wilson were unable to function in office—yet remained alive—with their vice-presidents reluctant to assume the presidency in case of just such a recovery. Finally, in 1963, the 25th Amendment to the Constitution was approved by Congress and ratified in February 1967. It surmounts the ambiguity in Article II, Section 1, declaring that if the president dies, resigns, or is removed from office, "the Vice President shall become President."

Discussion Questions

1 If you were to have a cabinet of advisors representing different areas of your life, in what areas would you want advice? Who would you choose?

2 The president is commander-in-chief. What kinds of advice does the president receive to help him or her make good decisions about using our armed forces? Who does that advice come from?

Caption Answer

He or she decides where and when the United States military will be used.

Activity

Writing to the President

OBJECTIVES: 2.01, 2.03, 4.03

Have students write letters to the president describing what they have learned about the presidency or what problems concern them. Begin letters with "Dear Mr./Ms. President." Glue student letters atop colorful pieces of construction paper. Draw pictures in open areas.

Send letters to: The President, The White House, 1600 Pennsylvania Ave. NW, Washington, D.C. 20500. Include your name and school address.

Extension Novice and intermediate ELL students should learn vocabulary terms related to the federal government. Intermediate students should use these words in sentences.

Teacher Notes

Washington's Cabinet

Refer students to Chapter 7, Lesson 2, in which they learned about President Washington selecting his first cabinet. Also refer students to the notes on Article II of the Constitution in the Appendix. Refer students to the list of U.S. presidents on pages 724–725 in the Appendix. See also pages 709–710.

AMERICAN PORTRAIT

Ronald Reagan
1911–2004

Ronald W. Reagan was born in Illinois. He worked his way through Eureka College. In addition to his studies, he played on the football team and acted in school plays. After graduation he became a radio sports announcer and then an actor in Hollywood, California.

Reagan had a long career in movies and on television before he became a politician. His wife, Nancy, was also an actress. He was elected the thirty-third governor of California and served two terms.

Reagan became the fortieth president of the United States. At age 69, he was the oldest person ever elected president. He was also the only president to be shot by an assassin (on March 30, 1981) while in office and live.

Reagan was nicknamed the "Great Communicator." He had excellent public speaking skills and a great sense of humor. He was one of our most popular presidents. In the last several years of his life, Reagan suffered from Alzheimer's disease. It is a disease that slowly destroys a person's memory and ability to talk or do daily tasks. When he died he was buried at the Ronald Reagan Presidential Library in Simi Valley, California.

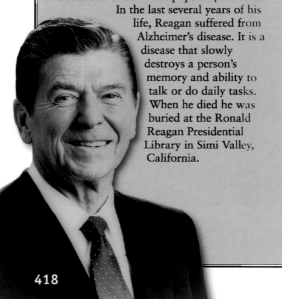

418

President George H. W. Bush visited American troops in Saudi Arabia in 1990. **What powers are granted the commander-in-chief?**

Commander-in-Chief In wartime, the president's job as *commander-in-chief* is easy to see. The president is in charge of the nation's armed forces: the army, navy, air force, marines, and Coast Guard. All military generals and admirals take their orders from the president. The president decides where troops, ships, and equipment should be sent and how weapons shall be used.

Chief Legislator Only Congress has the power to pass laws. But the Constitution does give the president power to advise Congress about what laws are needed. As *chief legislator* the president may propose legislation to members of Congress. He or she can ask Congress to pass new laws. The president can also veto bills that he or she does not like.

Unofficial Responsibilities

Head of Party One job of the president that is not an official one is *head of party*. As the leader of his or her political party, the president helps members of that party get elected. The president campaigns for party members who have supported his or her policies.

Chapter 17

Background Information

The Cabinet

When George Washington met with his first cabinet, it consisted of just four members. They were the Secretary of War, Secretary of the Treasury, Secretary of State, and Attorney General. Over time the cabinet has expanded as new departments have been added in response to foreign policy and domestic issues. Today, the cabinet consists of five department heads. While such presidents as James Monroe turned often to cabinets, Andrew Jackson convened his cabinet only 16 times in eight years. Instead he met often with a set of friends and loyal members of his political party. This group of unofficial advisors became known as the "Kitchen Cabinet" because they often met in the White House kitchen. In 1933, Franklin Roosevelt appointed the first woman to the cabinet when he made Frances Perkins Secretary of Labor.

Chief Guardian of the Economy The last role is also an unofficial role. The president does not control the economy. But citizens and businesses expect that the president will keep it running smoothly.

As *chief guardian of the economy*, the president thinks about such things as unemployment, high prices, taxes, business profits. He or she looks at the general well being of Americans.

The president meets with economists, people who study the economy, and business leaders. They discuss the country's needs and problems. The president makes decisions with their help.

The President's Cabinet

The Constitution says that the president "may require the opinion, in writing, of the principal officer in each of the executive departments, upon any subject relating to the duties of their . . . offices . . . " But the Constitution does not tell us how many executive departments should be created. It does not tell us which departments should be made.

This is an example of the flexibility of the Constitution. As the nation has grown, more departments have been added. We have not had to amend, or change, the Constitution to do this. Over time, some departments have been combined, broken apart, or renamed.

Cabinet Secretaries

The executive departments are led by people we call secretaries. The secretaries make up the president's cabinet. They are appointed by the president. But before they can start to work, they must be approved by a majority vote of the Senate. That is 51 votes.

The president is the "boss" of the department secretaries. Only the president can fire them. They are expected to resign, or quit, when a new president takes office.

Government of the People   419

President Bill Clinton spoke at the 2000 Democratic National Convention. **What is one of the unofficial duties of the president?**

There is no official schedule for cabinet meetings. Most presidents try to meet with their cabinets about once a week. Besides the president and department secretaries, cabinet meetings are usually attended by the vice president, the United States ambassador to the United Nations, and a few other top-level officials.

Executive Branch Departments in the Cabinet
Secretary of Agriculture
Secretary of Commerce
Secretary of Defense
Secretary of Education
Secretary of Energy
Secretary of Health and Human Services
Secretary of Homeland Security
Secretary of Housing and Urban Development
Secretary of Interior
Attorney General
Secretary of Labor
Secretary of State
Secretary of Transportation
Secretary of the Treasury
Secretary of Veteran Affairs

Cabinet members oversee specific areas of government and report to the president. **What does the Constitution say about the role of the cabinet?**

Discussion Questions

1 Are there other areas you would recommend for cabinet level officials? Why?

 Caption Answer

The United States had not had such strong African American or female candidates.

 Caption Answer

It says that the president may require (ask) the opinion of the heads of the executive departments on any subject relating to their duties.

 Activity

Voting Changes

OBJECTIVES: 2.02, 2.03, 2.05

Have students create a timeline of changes in voting in the United States. Draw a picture to go with each change (see below).

Have students research the struggles of key women's rights leaders of the time, such as Lucy Stone, Antoinette Brown, Harriet K. Hunt, Susan B. Anthony. What role did they play in earning women the right to vote?

Have students research the events at one of the women's rights conventions, such as the Seneca Falls Convention in 1848. What were some of the arguments for and against giving women the right to vote?

Read to the class the letters written by Abigail Adams to John Adams on March 31, 1776, and May 7, 1776, and John's letter to Abigail on April 14, 1776. Discuss John Adams' views on women's rights. You may want to tell the class that his views were similar to most American men at that time in our history. A good source is L. H. Butterfield (ed.), *Adams Family Correspondence, Vol. I.* (Cambridge, MA: The Belknap Press of Harvard University Press, 1963. ISBN 067400406X.).

Example:

Voting Changes in the United States: Who Can Vote?				
1791	1865	1919	1964–65	1971
White Males	African American Males 15th Amendment	Women 19th Amendment	African Americans	New voting age is eighteen

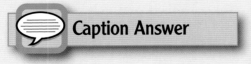 **Caption Answer**

Barack Obama and Hillary Clinton ran for the Democratic Party's nomination for the presidency. Why was this unusual?

Eyewitness Activity

The Electoral College and the Elections of 1876 and 2000

OBJECTIVES: 2.02, 2.03, 2.04

The United States Government Printing Office has a Web site for the election of the president and vice president. Go to **NCJourneys.com** for a link to the site. The site explains the primary election, general election, and electoral college.

Activity After reading the information on the Web site, divide students into two groups: one for the electoral college and the other against. Have students brainstorm in the groups and come up with an argument to support their stand.

Activity

Radio Commercial Activity

OBJECTIVES: 2.03, 2.05

Write a 1-minute radio commercial supporting the presidential campaign of a prominent political figure. Research the person and prepare your speech to be videotaped or taped on a cassette.

EYEWITNESS TO HISTORY

The Electoral College and the Elections of 1876 and 2000

The presidential election of 1876 has some similarities to the election of 2000. In 1876, Republican Rutherford B. Hayes ran against Democrat Samuel J. Tilden. In 2000, Republican George W. Bush ran against Democrat Albert Gore.

In both 1876 and 2000, politicians had to solve disagreements in the electoral college. In both elections, the electoral vote and the popular vote were won by different candidates. In each case, the Democrat won the popular vote and the Republican won the electoral college.

The 1876 election was undecided. There were problems with the voting in Florida. Congress appointed a special Electoral Commission to work things out. The commission made a backroom deal known as the Corrupt Bargain. It voted to make Hayes president. In return, Hayes promised to end Reconstruction and remove federal troops from Southern states. The election controversy's shadow never left Hayes. He was nicknamed "Rutherfraud."

Senate President Ferry announces the results of the close 1876 election.

Rutherford B. Hayes (left) and Samuel J. Tilden (right)

Activity

E Pluribus Unum Character Education

OBJECTIVES: 3.03, 4.03, 4.06

In 1776, when the United States was born, the founders of our country chose a Latin motto, "E Pluribus Unum." These words mean "one out of many." The leaders meant that 13 different colonies were joining hands to create one strong nation. We are many people, but we are one nation. As a country we are proud of all the people who make up the United States. Sometimes as individuals we do not do such a good job of accepting those who are different. Can we change that? Is it possible to accept others even if they speak a different language, dress differently, or have different ideas about how to do things?

Have a class discussion on what makes it easy to accept others. Make a list of those ideas. Make another note that shows why we don't accept others easily. On this list you might include: speaks a different language, shyness around new people, wears hair differently than

People rally for their candidate at the Supreme Court in December 2000.

The 2000 election had similar problems. The winner of Florida would get 21 electoral votes. On election day, news organizations first announced that they thought Gore would win Florida. Then early on election night, they called Bush the winner. They said that with Florida's 21 electoral votes, he had a total of 271 electoral votes. That was one more than Bush needed to win the presidency.

But Florida's votes were very close. Later in the night, the news organizations changed what they said again. They said the election was too close to call.

It looked like Gore had lost Florida by about 2,000 votes. Democrats argued that Gore had lost because of fraud, or cheating, and counting mistakes.

Democrats went to court. They asked judges to force Florida to recount thousands of votes. The Florida Supreme Court told the state to recount only ballots that had not been counted correctly the first time.

The election of 2000 was decided in the courts. The United States Supreme Court settled the dispute. It overturned the decision of the Florida Supreme Court. It told Florida that there would not be any more recounts. Florida then made Bush the official winner by 537 votes.

George W. Bush was then certified, or made official, as the winner of Florida's electors. Therefore he won a majority in the electoral college. He became our forty-third president.

George W. Bush (left) greets Albert Gore (right)

Government of the People

421

Teacher Notes

Article II

Refer students to Article II of the Constitution on pages 709 and 710 for a review of the presidency and the electoral college.

Art Activity

Political Logos

 **OBJECTIVES:** 2.03, 2.05, 4.06

Explain that logos are identifying symbols that are everpresent in today's society. Show examples of logos in the telephone directory, newspapers, and magazines. Place students in pairs or cooperative groups. The donkey is associated with the Democratic Party and the elephant is associated with the Republican Party. Challenge students to create a new political party. They are to name their new party, explain its platform, and then design a logo for their new party. Display on a bulletin board.

others. Compare the two lists. Have you ever had an opinion about someone, and after getting to know the person your opinion changed? Are the things on the unacceptable list really important? Should we accept everything about everyone? Evaluate these things and write a journal entry reflecting upon your opinions and your reasons for them.

Compliment card activity
Pass out an index card with a student's name on it to each student in the class room. Set your timer for 4 minutes. Ask students to write a compliment about the person they have written

on their card. After the timer rings pass the cards to the "right" and continue the process so that at the end of the activity each student can receive a card with many compliments written on it from their classmates.

1 Why do you think an electoral college was developed when the Constitution was written?

2 Why do political parties hold caucuses and primaries?

3 Why do you think electors in the electoral college will likely vote according to the popular vote of their state?

Activity

Election

OBJECTIVES: 2.02, 2.03, 2.05

In late October, begin discussing the upcoming November elections. Regardless of who is actually running, you can discuss with the class the importance of each race, both federal and local. At the time, you can discuss party relations, terms of office, and the positions for which the individuals are running. Most important, you can teach the children first hand about the electoral process.

After this process, the last week before election day, run a "mock election" for these same races. Have the students create election ballots and explain the voting process to young children. Also, they can create private voting booths and a system of counting the ballots. The children will be interested in the outcome of the election and how it compares to the real election.

Afterward, discuss the voting process, why it is so important to have a secret ballot, and how the forefathers protected this right.

Extension Graph results on large paper for the school, (by whole school, by grade, on both).

Presidential Elections

We elect a president and vice president every four years. Presidential elections are exciting and expensive events. They officially begin when political groups select candidates to run for president and vice president. An organized political group is a political party.

Political Parties

The United States has two major political parties, the *Democratic Party* and the *Republican Party.* . Most Americans consider themselves to be either a Democrat or Republican. Some people do not want to belong to a political party. They call themselves "independents."

There are other political parties (not the Democratic Party or the Republican Party) that sometimes offer candidates. They are called third-party candidates.

Primaries Parties choose the candidates for president. The political parties in each state have either an election, called a primary,

> **Democracy:** rule by the majority (more than half the voters)
>
> **Republic:** the people elect representatives to make the laws

or a special meeting, called a caucus. This is how the party decides who it will nominate to run for president. The person who wins the most primaries becomes the nominee.

The Democratic Party nominee and the Republican Party nominee, along with any third-party nominees, are the candidates for president.

The Election

The candidates campaign across the country. In a campaign, the candidates go out to meet people and ask for votes. They usually debate on television. Candidates spend millions of dollars campaigning. They buy many advertisements on television.

Finally, the citizens decide by voting on election day. Election day is always the Tuesday after the first Monday in November. This is when the Constitution says the vote should take place.

Electoral College The vote of the citizens is called the popular vote. But it is not the end of the election. In the popular vote, citizens are actually voting for members of the *electoral college.* The electors officially elect the president and vice president.

Each state has as many electors in the

*The new president takes the oath of office on Inauguration Day, January 20. **What is the electoral college?***

Caption Answer

The Electoral College is a group of people called electors who vote for the president, usually according to the popular vote in their state.

electoral college as it has senators and representatives in Congress. The District of Columbia has three electors. So with 100 senators, 435 representatives, and three electors from Washington, D.C., there are 538 electors.

The electors usually vote according to the popular vote in their state. For example, in most states, if a candidate wins 51 percent of the popular vote in a state, all of that state's electors will vote for that candidate.

To win the office of president, a candidate must win 270 electoral votes. If no candidate has a majority of electoral votes, the House of Representatives chooses the president. That has happened twice, in 1800 and 1824.

The person the electoral college chooses becomes the president-elect. Inauguration Day, when the new president and vice president take office, is January 20th.

What would YOU do?

Elections are exciting. They can stir up deep feelings. You want to have a discussion about an upcoming election in your class. You also want to avoid anger and hurt feelings among your classmates. What rules would you make to guide the discussion?

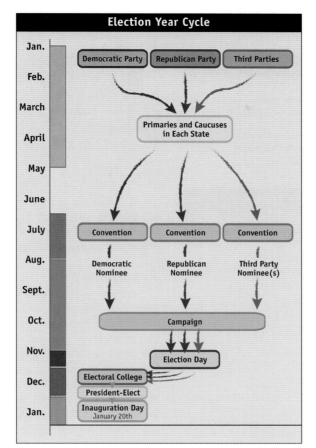

Election Year Cycle

It takes about a year for a president to run for office and be inaugurated. **What are primaries?**

Math Activity

Elector Math

 OBJECTIVES: 2.02

Have students use the map on page 415 to calculate the number of electors for the following states:
Texas—*34*
California—*55*
Florida—*27*
North Carolina—*15*
New York—*31*

Caption Answer

Primaries are the elections held by political parties in each state to choose a candidate for president.

LESSON 1 REVIEW

Fact Follow-Up
1. What are the official responsibilities of the president of the United States?
2. What are the unofficial responsibilities of the president?
3. What is the president's cabinet?
4. What is the electoral college?

Talk About It
1. The cabinet of the president is an example of the flexibility of the Constitution. Why?
2. What happens if no presidential candidate wins a majority of the electoral votes?
3. Why was the Election of 1876 called a "corrupt bargain"?

Government of the People

LESSON 1 REVIEW

Fact Follow-Up Answers
1. The president is head of state, chief executive, chief diplomat, commander-in-chief, and chief legislator.
2. The president is head of his political party and chief guardian of the economy.
3. The cabinet is composed of the heads of the federal agencies. Cabinet members are appointed by the president, answer only to him or her, and can be fired only by the president. They are expected to resign when a new president takes office.
4. The electoral college is the body that actually elects the president. Each state has as many electoral votes as it has senators and representatives in the United States Congress. There are 538 members; this number reflects the 100 senators, 435 members of the House of Representatives, and three electors for the District of Columbia.

Talk About It Answers
1. The cabinet is not mentioned in the Constitution, though the Constitution does say that the president "may require the opinion, in writing, of the principal officer in each of the executive departments, upon any subject relating to the duties of their respective offices. . . ." The Constitution does not specify what executive departments there will be nor how many there will be. As the nation has grown and changed, executive departments have been added, combined, separated, and renamed without changing the Constitution.
2. If there is not a majority of electoral votes, the House of Representatives chooses the president.
3. The 1876 election outcome depended on challenged votes, recounts, and legal questions in Florida. Congress appointed a special commission to work things out. In a backroom deal called a "corrupt bargain," the commissions gave the election to Rutherford Hayes.

OBJECTIVES: 2.01, 2.02, 2.03, 2.05

Caption Answer

Congress is the legislative branch. It is comprised of the House of Representatives and the Senate.

Activity

Mock Trial

OBJECTIVES: 2.04, 3.03, 3.04

Before the trial, divide students into cooperative groups of four or five. Have each group choose a familiar fairy tale. Let each group reread or retell the fairy tale to refresh their memories on the sequence of events. Then have each group rewrite the story from the villain's point of view, such as the Big Bad Wolf from "Little Red Riding Hood" or Goldilocks from "The Three Bears."

To prepare for court, discuss the roles of the judge, jury, prosecuting attorney, witnesses, court reporter, defense attorney, court clerk, bailiff, defendant, and plaintiff. Choose pupils to play each of the parts listed above, including six jurors. Choose which villain will be put on trial. Give copies of the new point-of-view story to the defendant and the defense attorney. They should read these and prepare their case based on the new point of view. Both attorneys should meet with their witnesses to plan their strategy.

Students are probably familiar with the physical arrangement needed for the court from watching television. You may still want or need to explain the reasons for the basic setup.

During the trial, have the clerk introduce the judge, plaintiff, and defendant, and swear in the jury. The prosecuting attorney will make an opening statement and tell the plaintiff's side of the story. The defense attorney then will make an opening statement. The prosecuting attorney will ask questions of each witness after the clerk swears in that witness.

The defense attorney will cross-examine each witness. The defense attor-

ney will call his or her witnesses. The prosecuting attorney will cross-examine the defense witnesses. During the closing arguments the attorneys will sum up their main points.

The judge will tell the jurors the law that relates to the case. You will need to help students understand which laws are involved. For the verdict, the jury will discuss the testimony of the witnesses and make a decision as to the guilt or innocence of the defendant.

Because this is a mock trial, the jury discussion can take place in front of the

class; explain to the students, however, that real jury discussions are private and known only to the members of the jury. When the jury has reached a decision, the judge will ask the jury foreman to announce the verdict.

Discuss with the class what took place during the trial. Do the students agree with the verdict? Did the jury use only the facts presented by the witnesses and attorneys to reach their verdict? Are there grounds for an appeal?

LESSON 2 The Legislative and Judicial Branches

KEY IDEAS

- The legislative branch of Congress passes laws.
- The judicial branch, led by the Supreme Court, interprets laws.

KEY TERMS

House of Representatives
judicial
legislative
override
Senate
Supreme Court

The Capitol is where Congress meets. **Which branch of government is Congress? What are its two houses?**

The Capitol Building is located in Washington, D.C. It is where Congress meets. Across the street from the Capitol is the Supreme Court Building.

When you visit Washington D.C., you can tour both buildings. If Congress or the Supreme Court are meeting that day, you can watch from the galleries.

The Legislative Branch

As you have read, Congress writes the laws for the nation. This lawmaking role makes Congress the *legislative* branch of government. There are two houses in Congress. They are the *Senate* and the *House of Representatives.*

Representation

Each state elects two senators. There are a total of 100 senators in the Senate. A senator's term is six years.

The number of representatives a state has in the House of Representatives is based on the state's population. States with larger populations elect more representatives. Representatives are elected to two-year terms.

In 1789, there were 65 members of the House. That number grew as more people and states were added to the country. It reached 435 members in 1913. Then Congress voted to make that number the limit.

States may gain or lose representatives as they gain or lose population. North Carolina has 13 representatives in Congress.

Making Laws

The main job of Congress is to make, change, or end the laws of the federal government. Congress decides what taxes American citizens must pay.

Before a law becomes a law, it is a bill. Members of Congress submit bills. Even if the president suggests an idea for a law, the bill for that law must be submitted by either a senator or a representative. All bills that propose to raise taxes must be submitted in the House.

Next, a bill is studied by a committee in the chamber of Congress where it was submitted. If the committee thinks the bill should be voted on, it gets sent out for a vote. The Senators or the House members vote on the bill. It must get a majority of votes to pass.

Say a bill passes in the Senate. Next, it gets sent to the House. A bill must pass both houses of Congress. After it has passed out of Congress, it is sent along to the president. If the president signs the bill, it becomes law.

Vetos

The president might not want the new law. If he rejects the bill, this is called a veto. The bill returns to Congress. It is voted on again. Both houses of Congress must pass the bill again with a two-thirds majority. Then the bill becomes law without the President's signature. This is called an *override.*

Sandra Day O'Connor
1930–

Sandra Day O'Connor grew up on the Lazy B Ranch in Greenlee County, Arizona. As a young girl, she was the first female to go on a cattle roundup on her father's ranch. O'Connor later became the first female to do some important things in the government.

She was the first female in the nation to serve as Senate majority leader. Later, President Ronald Reagan made her the first female to serve on the U.S. Supreme Court. She helped make important decisions for our country. She retired from the court in 2006 after serving 25 years.

Few cases are heard before the Supreme Court, but those that do often change the interpretation of the Constitution. **Why is it important to have a Supreme Court in our government?**

Government of the People

425

Discussion Questions

1 Do you know the process by which a law is made at the national level? What are those steps?

Caption Answer

The Supreme Court checks the power of the other two branches.

Reading Strategy Activity

Spider Map Graphic Organizer

◀ **OBJECTIVES:** 2.01, 2.03, 2.05

A spider map is one way to break down information into categories and describe the details so students will better understand what they read.

Make a graphic like the one below:

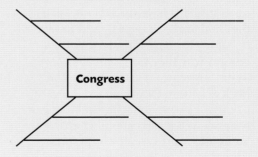

For the four spokes coming from the center, ask students to find the main subheads in the Legislative Branch section. Label each spoke with a head or sub head (Legislatiive Branch, Representation, Making Laws, Vetos). On the shorter lines, students are to add details. More lines may be added. Share webs when students finish.

Background Information

Speaker of the House

Under the Constitution, the Senate and House of Representatives are co-equal lawmaking branches. Unlike Senators, members of the House are elected from individual districts. They face the difficult task of looking out for the interests of both the voters in the district they represent and those of the state and nation as a whole. The leader of the House is called the Speaker of the House. This person is elected by the House members from the political party with the majority of members in the House.

The speaker has a great deal of power over the lawmaking process, assigning bills to certain committees and influencing the assignment of House members to committees. If the president dies in office or resigns, the Speaker is the first in line to succeed to the presidency after the vice president.

Discussion Questions

1 Why do you think some courts in the judicial system have a higher rule than others? For example, the Supreme Court can overrule a federal appeals court, which can overrule a federal district court.

2 Why do you think the framers of the Constitution developed the system of checks and balances?

3 Why is separating the powers of the different branches important?

Activity

Supreme Court

OBJECTIVES: 2.01, 2.03, 3.03

Explain that the appeals process is to try to ensure that laws are applied fairly to everyone. If someone feels that the law was not applied fairly or that a legal error was made, they have grounds for appeal. Review some court cases students have read about, such as the *Dred Scot* (Chapter 8) and *Brown* (Chapter 12) decisions. Discuss the reasons why they were sent all the way to the Supreme Court. Why did the justices believe they deserved appeals?

Invite an attorney or local judge in to speak to the class about a particular Supreme Court case, the Supreme Courts itself, or the appeals process.

The Judicial Branch

The *judicial* branch is the third branch of the federal government. The United States *Supreme Court* and federal courts make up the judicial branch.

The Supreme Court decides what the laws passed by Congress mean. It also makes sure that laws do not go against the Constitution. There are many Supreme Court decsions discussed in this book.

The president appoints the justices of the Supreme Court. The Senate must approve those choices. Justices may hold office for life or until they choose to retire.

Customs

Americans enjoy displaying the national flag, "the Stars and Stripes," on Independence Day, Memorial Day, and other holidays. A special day to honor the flag is Flag Day (June 14). It started as a class project in 1885. Teacher B. J. Cigrand and his class wanted to celebrate the anniversary of when America chose the stars and stripes as its flag. Now Flag Day is celebrated throughout the country.

Other federal courts include 13 federal courts of appeal and 95 federal district courts. The judges of these courts are also appointed by the president, with the approval of the Senate. They hold office for life.

A case may be heard in a federal court when it involves the Constitution, the laws of the federal government, or a conflict between states.

Checks and Balances

The writers of the Constitution created three branches of the federal government. Each branch "checks," or limits, the power of the others. One branch has the power to check the power of the other two branches.

An example of this is when the president appoints a new justice to the Supreme Court. The Court does not have the power to choose its own members. And the Senate has to approve of the person the president wants. So the president (executive branch) and the Senate (legislative branch) are checking the power of the Supreme Court (judicial branch).

This system of checks and balances prevents any one branch of government from becoming too strong. The Skill Lesson at the end of this chapter will help you learn how this system works.

LESSON 2 REVIEW

Fact Follow-Up
1. What two bodies make up the legislative branch of government?
2. What is the job of the legislative branch of government?
3. What is the job of the judicial branch of government?
4. What are checks and balances?

Talk About It
1. Why does our national government have a system of checks and balances?
2. Why do you think the number of members of the House of Representatives was set at 435?
3. When may a case be heard in a federal court?
4. Describe a veto.

LESSON 2 REVIEW

Fact Follow-Up Answers
1. The Senate and the House of Representatives make up the Congress, the legislative branch of government.
2. The main job of Congress is to make, change, or cancel laws of the federal government. Congress decides what federal taxes Americans must pay.
3. The judicial branch interprets laws passed by Congress.
4. Checks and balances are ways each of the three branches of the federal government can check the power of the other two branches. These checks keep the government balanced so that one branch does not become too strong.

Talk About It Answers
1. The writers of the Constitution wanted to keep any one branch of the government from becoming too strong and the powers of each branch balanced equally.
2. Important points: Encourage students' suggestions. Among reasons are these: If the House of Representatives had been allowed to grow larger, there would have been so many representatives a new capitol building would have had to be built; the important thing about the number of representatives is not how many there are but that each represents about the same number of people.
3. A case is heard in federal court when it involves the Constitution, the laws passed by the federal government, or a conflict between states.
4. The president has the power to veto a bill, or not let it become a law.

The last amendment in the Bill of Rights is important. It says that any powers in the Constitution that were not given to the national government belong to the states and to the people. This is called a federal system of government.

All states have their own constitutions. Each of these makes the rules for its state government. These state constitutions give certain rights to the state governments. They give other rights to local governments and to the citizens of the state.

The Federal System

In our federal system of government, the national government shares power with the states. Both can tax the people, make laws, enforce laws, and decide what laws mean. A state government makes state laws.

Sometimes state and national governments deal with different sides of the same problem. A state government, for example, may pass laws for companies that make medicine and sell the medicines in the state. The national government can make rules for the same companies, but only if they sell their medicines in more than one state.

Our Federal System		
Level	Place	Examples of Power
Local	Cities and counties	• city police and firefighters • county roads and bridges • water and sewer
State	North Carolina	• state lands and resources • state roads • drivers' licenses
National	United States	• national defense • printing money • relations with other countries

Government of the People

427

KEY IDEAS

- In our federal system of government, the national government shares power with the states.

- State governments are similar to the federal government.

- State governments deal with matters within state borders.

- County and local governments provide services.

KEY TERMS

appeal
General Assembly
governor
juries
municipal

OBJECTIVES: 2.01, 2.02, 2.03

Discussion Questions

1 Do you know why our country has both state and national governments?

2 Why would a federal system of government be better than another?

Activity

Graphic Organizer Mobiles

OBJECTIVES: 2.01, 2.02, 2.03

Graphic organizers are a great way to motivate active learning in students. They encourage active participation and discussion.

Making a concept map of a lesson in social studies is a helpful way to visually see the relationship of ideas. Ask students to read the lesson first and think about the topics included. Lead the class in a discussion about the lesson and let them suggest ways to organize the subject matter of state and local governments. An example could be Federalism, State Government, Local Government, and Taxes.

Divide the class into cooperative groups to make their mobile. Use a coat hanger to hold the mobile. Since the title is the concept of the lesson, write "State and Local Governments" on a large piece of paper and hang it over the main section of the hanger. Make a card for each of the topics of the lesson. Hang them from the bottom of the coat hanger. Make smaller cards for the details under each topic. Groups are to share their mobiles with the class and hang each around the room.

As a follow-up activity, have groups create a mobile on thefederal government and share them with the class. Add pictures for decoration.

Caption Answer

Homeless shelter, soup kitchen, job training center, recycling plant, police, school, library, health clinic, garbage truck, fire truck, town pool, paved roads, sidewalks, and others

Activity

State Government

 OBJECTIVES: 2.02, 2.03, 2.05

Invite your local state representative to the General Assembly to visit your classroom. Ask students to prepare questions ahead of time that they may ask the representative about his or her role in state government.

Alternative Take a field trip to Raleigh to the General Assembly.

ELL Teaching Tips

Be Positive

The more comfortable that new ELL students feel in your classroom, the faster they will learn. Find the positive things about your students' work and praise it. Put away the red pen for a little while and create frequent opportunities for their success in your class.

WORD ORIGINS

Columbia is a name for the United States. It honors Christopher Columbus. The name has been around since colonial times.

The British poet John Dyer called North America and the British colonies Columbia in a poem. Within several years, dictionaries listed Columbia with the meaning "the United States."

Artists sometimes draw Columbia as a woman. She is dressed in long, white robes.

National Government Powers

The Constitution gives the power to print money and declare war only to the national government. There would be problems if all the states printed their own money, or if one state wanted to go to war but the rest did not. For the same reason, only the national government can make relationships with the governments of other countries.

State Government Powers

Under the Constitution, powers that are not given to the national government are given to the states. State laws, however, cannot go against the laws passed by Congress.

State governments act on many things close to our everyday lives. For example, each state creates its own education system. The state government makes laws about how schools shall be run.

State Government

State governments must cooperate with the federal government. They are set up much like the national government. But each state government is slightly different from the other states.

Like the federal government, state governments have three branches. They have a legislature, an executive, and a judicial branch. These branches also have checks and balances, just like the national government.

In North Carolina, the three branches of state government have their headquarters in Raleigh. Raleigh is the capital of our state.

The General Assembly

The legislative branch in North Carolina is called the *General Assembly.* It has two branches, just like Congress. North Carolina's senate has 50 members. North Carolina's house of representatives has 120 members.

The job of the General Assembly is to make laws for the state. Adults vote to elect state senators and representatives every two years.

Local governments provide services. How many can you find in this town?

Chapter 17

Paying Taxes

Sales Tax

When you buy a toy at the store, you pay a sales tax. The sales tax in North Carolina is 4.5 percent. That means that for every dollar you spend, you must pay about four cents. The money from the taxes goes to state government.

Local governments also add on a sales tax of at least 2.5 percent.

Income Tax

People and businesses pay taxes on the money they make. This is called an income tax. Your parents have to pay income tax every year.

They pay federal income tax to the United States government. They also pay state income tax to North Carolina.

Property Tax

If you own land, a home, or a building, you have to pay property tax.

If you rent your home, the landlord uses part of your rent to pay property taxes.

The property taxes go to local governments.

Discussion Questions

1 What are the different state agencies that you know about?

2 What services do the state agencies provide?

3 How do these services or agencies help the people of your state?

4 What types of services are provided by your county and/or city government(s)?

5 What is tax money used for?

 Caption Answer

Water, libraries, roads, and support for schools

The Governor

The job of the executive branch of government is to carry out the laws passed by the General Assembly. The executive branch is led by the *governor.* In North Carolina, the governor is elected every four years. He or she can serve two consecutive, or back-to-back, terms.

The executive branch prepares the state budget. It must then be passed by the General Assembly. Like the president at the national level, the governor is the "boss" of state workers. The governor appoints the heads of state agencies.

State Agencies State agencies are the departments of state government. In North Carolina, these include the Division of Crime Control and Public Safety, the Department of Agriculture, the Department of Labor, the Department of Cultural Resources, and the Department of Public Instruction.

State agencies have offices across the state to help people. When you are helped by a State Highway Patrol Trooper, or visit a state historic site, or even open your textbook, you are using services provided by state agencies.

One role of county government is police protection. **What other services do citizens receive from county governments?**

Government of the People

429

 Background Information

Local Government

Citizens have the most contact with their local governments but often know the least about them. City governments provide a wide variety of services to their residents. Among these services are police and fire protection and maintenance of roads, traffic lights, parks, and other public facilities such as swimming pools and bike paths. Local governments are also responsible for garbage and snow removal. City

government makes sure that streets are swept and plants trees in parks or along roads. In some cities, public officials also oversee public housing, city-run docks or cemeteries, convention centers, and sports arenas.

Caption Answer

Possible answers: courthouses all over the state, when you meet a State Highway Patrol Trooper, and so on

Activity

Municipal Government Day

▰ **OBJECTIVES:** 2.02, 2.03, 4.03

How do all levels of government share in running schools? Invite a panel of local government officials to be guest speakers. Examples of the panel could be county commissioner, school board member, school superintendent, sheriff, judge, police chief, or fire chief. Have the class brainstorm possible questions before the guests come to visit.

Extension Have novice ELL students learn the names of different services provided by local governments and the job titles of people who work for your local government.

The Court System

The judicial branch of the state government of North Carolina has several levels. These levels make up the court system.

The Supreme Court The highest state court is the state supreme court. It is made up of seven justices. The head justice is called the Chief Justice. North Carolinians vote to elect the justices. They serve eight-year terms.

Other Courts Cases are first heard in superior and district courts. Superior courts hear serious criminal and civil cases. District courts hear less serious criminal and civil cases. The decisions in these courts are made by juries.

Juries are groups of ordinary people picked to make the decision. The Bill of Rights says that all Americans have the right to be tried by a jury. Serving on a jury is a responsibility of being a citizen.

Sometimes people believe that these courts did not follow the law in deciding their case. A person can ask, or *appeal,* to a higher court to review their case.

Appeals The main job of both the state supreme court and the court of appeals, like the U.S. Supreme Court, is to review cases. The court of appeals is the second-highest court in our state. Many people appeal, but not every case gets to be heard again. The judges and justices of these higher courts choose which cases should be heard again.

Local Government

Within each state there are also county and *municipal* (city or town) governments. These also are close to our daily lives. They provide law enforcement, help the state build roads, and assist with the support of schools.

Adults vote for the leaders of county and municipal governments, too. Voting is another responsibility of being a citizen.

The capitol building in Raleigh, North Carolina, is the seat of government for the state. **Where else can you find state government in action?**

LESSON 3 REVIEW

Fact Follow-Up
1. What things does the Constitution allow only the national government to do?
2. What are three levels of government in our state?
3. Describe the legislative branch of government in North Carolina.
4. What are the jobs of county and municipal governments in North Carolina?

Talk About It
1. Why is printing money one of the powers given only to the national government?
2. Why do we have both national and state court systems?
3. Even though powers not given to the national governments are given to the states, states cannot pass laws that go against laws passed by Congress. Why?

LESSON 3 REVIEW

Fact Follow-Up Answers
1. Only the national government can print money, declare war, or conduct relations with foreign governments.
2. The three levels are state government, county government, and municipal (town and city) government.
3. The legislative branch of government is called the General Assembly. There are two houses in the legislative branch: the Senate with 50 members and the House of Representatives with 120 members. The job of the General Assembly is to make laws for the state. Both senators and representatives are elected for two-year terms.
4. They provide law enforcement, help the state build roads, and assist with the support of schools.

Talk About It Answers
1. Important points: Encourage students to suggest reasons. One reason is the difficulty of doing business if there were as many as 50 different kinds of money.
2. Important points: Encourage students' suggestions. Among the reasons are these: Different states may have different laws and need their own court systems; having only federal courts might place too much power in the national government; the two court systems deal with different issues.
3. Important points: Encourage students' suggestions. If states could contradict laws passed by Congress, the national government would have little power.

Reading a Chart

The United States government has a system of checks and balances. Each of the three branches of government has certain powers. These powers "check," or limit, the powers of the other two. In this way, the authors of the Constitution hoped that one branch of government would not have more power than the other branches.

Look at the chart below. With your finger, trace the path of each arrow between each of the branches. What are the three branches of government? What powers do they have? What powers do they not have?

Now, answer the following questions.

1. Which branch of government passes laws?
2. Which branch can veto legislation, or bills?
3. Which branch can declare legislation unconstitutional, or against the Constitution?
4. Which branch can propose or suggest legislation?
5. Which branch can override a presidential veto?
6. Which branch can impeach, or remove, judges?
7. Which branch can appoint federal judges?

GOALS NORTH CAROLINA SOCIAL STUDIES SKILL
skill

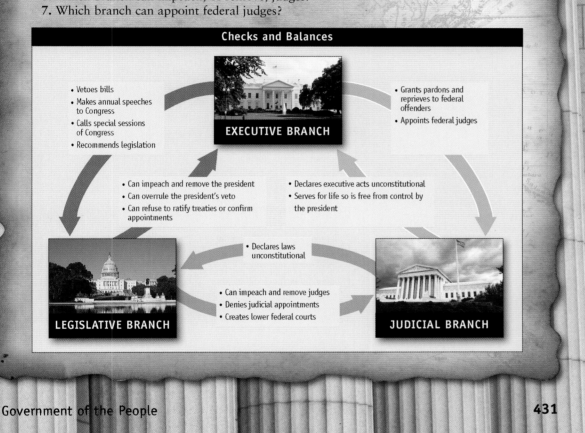

Checks and Balances

EXECUTIVE BRANCH
- Vetoes bills
- Makes annual speeches to Congress
- Calls special sessions of Congress
- Recommends legislation
- Grants pardons and reprieves to federal offenders
- Appoints federal judges

- Can impeach and remove the president
- Can overrule the president's veto
- Can refuse to ratify treaties or confirm appointments

- Declares executive acts unconstitutional
- Serves for life so is free from control by the president

- Declares laws unconstitutional

LEGISLATIVE BRANCH

- Can impeach and remove judges
- Denies judicial appointments
- Creates lower federal courts

JUDICIAL BRANCH

Government of the People

Teaching This Skill Lesson

Materials Needed textbooks, enough newspapers (not necessarily of the same date) for each student, marking pens for each student

Classroom Organization whole class

Beginning the Lesson Distribute newspapers and marking pens. Tell students they are to mark everything they see in the papers that has to do with a branch of the federal government. Circulate and coach as students mark the papers.

Lesson Development Place students in small groups to discuss what items they have marked. In the groups, students should be challenged to explain why they marked each item. Write the headings Legislative, Executive, and Judicial on the chalkboard or an overhead projector. Ask each group to report the newspaper items marked and identify the appropriate heading. Record as students respond and encourage and discuss challenges. Once the students have finished responding, have students copy the information under each heading. Ask students to turn to the Skill Lesson for Chapter 17 and answer the seven questions in order to determine whether they can read the graphic.

Conclusion As a homework assignment, each student is to choose one of the three headings, use the information from the graphic in the Skill Lesson, and tell which other branch of government can check the action/information in each item listed under the heading.

When students return to class with the completed work, place the class in three groups to compare work and answer any questions students might have.

---

skill **Skill Lesson Review**

1. How does the legislative branch "check" the power of the executive and judicial branches? *The legislative branch can override presidential vetoes. It can also vote down nominations to the Supreme Court and cabinet.*

2. How does the executive branch "check" the power of the judicial and legislative branches? *The executive branch checks the power of the legislative and judicial branches by vetoing legislation and appointing federal judges.*

3. How does the judicial branch "check" the power of the legislative and executive branches? *The judicial branch checks the power of the legislative and executive branches by declaring laws unconstitutional.*

CHAPTER 17 REVIEW

Talk About It

1. Important points: Students should suggest jobs, then choose the one they think most important and explain their choice. Formal jobs include chief executive, commander in chief, head of state, chief diplomat, and chief legislator. Informal jobs include head of the party and chief guardian of the economy.
2. Important points: Encourage students to suggest reasons. Among the reasons is the possibility that a candidate may lose the popular vote and still be elected president.
3. Important points: Students should take a position and explain it. Reasons for appointing judges include the fact that a judge should not have to depend on popularity but should be chosen because of knowledge and experience. Reasons for electing judges include the notion that most if not all government officials should be chosen by the people.
4. Important points: These governments affect the lives of people most directly; therefore their jobs have to do with the day-to-day lives of people—schools, law enforcement, health, and so forth.
5. Important points: The job chosen by a student is a matter of personal preference; the explanation of why the job was chosen is important.

Mastering Mapwork

1. North Carolina has 13 representatives, two senators, and 15 electors.
2. California has the largest number; it is located in the Pacific Coast region.
3. Texas has the second-largest number.
4. No, the total votes cast in New England would fall far short of being able to elect a president.

Lessons Learned

LESSON 1
The Executive Branch
The federal government has three branches: legislative, executive, and judicial. The executive branch, led by the president, enforces laws. The vice president becomes president if the president dies while in office. The president is advised by the cabinet, which is made up of the heads of government departments. The electoral college votes for the president.

LESSON 2
The Legislative and Judicial Branches
The legislative branch of Congress passes laws. The judicial branch, led by the Supreme Court, interprets laws.

LESSON 3
State and Local Government
The United States has a federal system of government. The national government shares power with the states. States have three branches of government. Local governments provide many services.

432

Talk About It

1. Which job of the president do you think is most important? Explain why.
2. Many people believe that the electoral college is no longer needed and that the president should be chosen by the direct vote of the people. Why might they feel this way?
3. Should federal judges be elected instead of appointed? Explain your answer.
4. Why do you think local governments have the responsibilities they have?
5. If you could hold any job in the United States or North Carolina government, which job would you choose? Explain why you would choose this job.

Mastering Mapwork

LOCATION
Use the map on page 415 to answer these questions:

1. How many representatives does North Carolina have in the House of Representatives? How many senators? How many electors in the Electoral College?
2. Which state has the largest number of electoral votes, and in which region is it located?
3. Which political region has the second-largest number of electoral votes?
4. A person needs 270 electoral votes to be elected president of the United States. Is it possible for New England to elect the president?

Becoming Better Readers

Using Graphic Organizers
Graphic organizers are good tools to build understanding. Good readers use graphic organizers to think about important ideas. Make a graphic organizer to show your understanding of the checks and balances system.

Becoming Better Readers

Students should have graphic organizer that shows the major points about each branch. It should not look exactly like the Check and Balances graphic on the Skill Lesson on page 431.

Go to the Source

Understanding an Inaugural Speech

This is an excerpt from President Ronald Reagan's Inaugural Address on January 20, 1980. It is the first speech he made as president. The inauguration is the ceremony in which the president-elect become the actual president. After presidents are sworn into the office, they make a speech to thank Americans and to tell them what they will do as their leader. Read the speech below and answer the following questions using information from the speech.

To a few of us here today, this is a solemn [serious] and most momentous [grand] occasion; and yet, in the history of our Nation, it is a commonplace occurrence. The orderly transfer of authority as called for in the Constitution routinely takes place....In the eyes of many in the world, this every-four-year ceremony we accept as normal is nothing less than a miracle.

Mr. President [Carter], I want our fellow citizens to know how much you did to carry on this tradition. By your gracious cooperation...you have shown a watching world that we are a united people pledged to maintaining a political system which guarantees individual liberty to a greater degree than any other, and I thank you...for all your help...

Those who say that we are in a time when there are no heroes just don't know where to look. You can see heroes every day going in and out of factory gates. Others...produce enough food to feed all of us and then the world beyond. You meet heroes across a counter—and they are on both sides of that counter...They are individuals and families whose taxes support the Government and whose voluntary gifts support church, charity, culture, art, and education. Their patriotism is quiet but deep. Their values sustain [support] our national life.

I have used the words "they" and "their" in speaking of these heroes. I could say "you" and "your" because I am addressing the heroes of whom I speak—you, the citizens of this blessed land. Your dreams, your hopes, your goals are going to be the dreams, the hopes, and the goals of this administration, so help me God.

Questions
1. Who was leaving the office of president during this ceremony?
2. Based on the information in this speech, why do many in the world consider this ceremony nothing less than a miracle?
3. Why did Reagan take the time to describe the everyday heroes in his speech?

Go to the Source (side tab)

 Go to the Source

Understanding Inaugural Addresses

OBJECTIVES: 2.01

SOCIAL STUDIES SKILLS: 3.05, 4.06

President Ronald Reagan's Inaugural Address

The inauguration of a president sets the tone for the administration. Each president puts his or her stamp on the events of the day, including the swearing in, the inaugural address, the parade, and the inaugural balls. Even though not everyone voted for the new president, it is a time to come together and celebrate what Reagan called in this address a "miracle" and Thomas Jefferson called an every-four-year revolution.

Answers
1. President Jimmy Carter
2. "The orderly transfer of authority as called for in the Constitution routinely takes place."
3. Those are the people Reagan considered the real heroes of the United States, the citizens.

 How to Use the Chapter Review

There are four sections in the Chapter Review: Talk About It, Mastering Mapwork, Becoming Better Readers, and Go to the Source. Use the Vocabulary Worksheets and the Chapter Review Worksheet in the Teacher's Resource Guide for additional reinforcement and preparation for the Chapter Assessments. The Chapter and Lesson Reviews and the Chapter Review Worksheets are the basis of the assessment for each chapter.

Talk About It questions encourage students to speculate about the content of the chapter and are suitable for class or small-group discussion. They are not intended to be assigned for homework.

Mastering Mapwork has students apply one or more of the Five Themes of Geography to maps within the chapter.

Becoming Better Readers focuses on building reading strategy skills necessary for reading comprehension in the content areas.

Go to the Source activities allow students to analyze a primary source that relates to the content of the chapter. The questions and activities familiarize students with different types of primary sources and also build content-reading skills.

Unit 5 Canada

The unit on Canada opens with *The Solemn Land,* a painting by Canadian artist J. E. H. MacDonald. Just like artists of the United States, Canadian artists sought to distinguish themselves from European traditions by celebrating the unique landscape of their homeland. This unit introduces the large, varied nation of Canada. In these chapters, your students will learn about Canada's land, people, environment, government, and economy. They will also explore the surprising diversity of Canada's cultures, which forms an intricate national mosaic.

UNIT LESSON PLAN

	LESSON 1	LESSON 2	LESSON 3
CHAPTER 18 **The Land and People**	Canada, the world's second-largest country, is north of the United States and shares many of our landforms. **Essential Question:** Where is Canada located? **Suggested Time:** 1–2 days	Canada's northern location and its cold climate affect the land, vegetation, animal life, and people. **Essential Question:** How does Canada's location affect the land, vegetation, animal life, and people? **Suggested Time:** 1 day	Canada faces environmental challenges in overfishing, logging, and energy development. **Essential Question:** What environmental challenges are facing Canada? **Suggested Time:** 1–2 days
CHAPTER 19 **Settling a Nation**	Canadians are descendents of Native American and Inuit settlers, British and French explorers, and new immigrants from Asia and Europe. **Essential Question:** Who are the Canadians? **Suggested Time:** 1–2 days	Native Americans, Inuit, and early European explorers were the first to settle permanently in Canada. **Essential Question:** Who were the first people to permanently settle Canada? **Suggested Time:** 1–2 days	Because of railroad construction and gold finds, the prairie provinces and the north attracted settlers. **Essential Question:** What attracted settlers to the north and prairie provinces? **Suggested Time:** 1 day
CHAPTER 20 **Economy and Government**	Canada has one of the world's strongest economies. **Essential Question:** Why is Canada's economy so strong? **Suggested Time:** 1 day	Canada's economic relationship with the United States is close. **Essential Question:** How can we describe the relationship between Canada and the United States? **Suggested Time:** 2 days	Canada is a parliamentary democracy with strong provincial governments. **Essential Question:** How can we describe Canada's government? **Suggested Time:** 2 days
CHAPTER 21 **Society and Culture**	Canada has changed as its major cities have grown. **Essential Question:** How has Canada changed? **Suggested Time:** 1 day	The British and French heritages still affect the lives of Canadians. **Essential Question:** How do the British and French heritages continue to affect the lives of the Canadians? **Suggested Time:** 1–2 days	The cultures of Canada are like the different pieces of a mosaic that are part of a whole. **Essential Question:** Why is the Canadian culture like a mosaic? **Suggested Time:** 1 day

Preparing the Unit

■ Worksheets, assessments, and reproducibles for this unit are found in the Teacher's Resource Guide and at **NCJourneys.com**

■ Decorate your room with pictures and posters that illustrate the geography, tourist attractions, people, and culture of Canada.

■ Set up a resource library of suggested resources in your classroom for students to use for research projects or during reading time.

■ Share some of the suggested resources and activities listed in the Teacher's Edition with your cultural arts teachers so they can incorporate some of the activities and topics in their classroom.

Unit Teaching Strategies

■ This unit, as well as Units 6 and 7, should be an adventure for students. There are many opportunities to compare and contrast these nations with what students have learned about the United States.

■ Use the ideas in the wrap-around as suggestions to help you meet the needs of your students and your teaching style. Please consider that there is a lot of material to be covered and that you must pace yourself in order to teach the curriculum. The variety of suggested activities are included to help you differentiate your instruction to meet the needs of your students. Use these activities to best enhance your instruction. Do not feel that you should implement them all.

■ If time is a factor, use this unit and Units 6 and 7 for student projects that culminate with a festival of nations. Assign topics from the list of suggested projects for students to complete. Students can teach each other by giving presentations. This type of instruction actively involves students and saves instructional time.

■ Check **NCJourneys.com** for updates and materials.

Students will have ten days to complete their project. They have the option of choosing from five different projects, and should choose only one. The projects offer variety so students can pick areas that interest them. Suggested report format: Reports should be one page in length, typed, and double-spaced.

PROJECT CHOICES

OBJECTIVES: 3.04, 3.06, 3.07

A Celebration of Canadian Culture

Have students select a major ethnic group of Canada: Scottish, Inuit, French, Vietnamese, Russian-Jewish, Chinese, Greek, Italian, Japanese, English, East Asian, or Pakistani. Students may then choose four of the following topics to research: religions, celebrations, traditions, customs, occupational preferences, music, dances, clothing/costumes, foods, and art works. Each student must make a map showing the location of their ethnic group in Canada, detailing the results of their research with illustrations.

Illustrated Timeline

Have students research the history of Canada. For the timeline, they should include the name and dates of important events and one or two important Canadian contributions to illustrate.

Trader's Journal

Students will research and create a travel journal of the *couriers de bois*. Have students imagine being a part of early trading expeditions. Have them write journal entries about a year-long journey. Entries can include descriptions and drawings of the landforms, the Native Americans they traded with, the animals, the weather, or other aspects of life in early Canada. Present the journals to the class.

The Great White North Diorama

Students will create a diorama of northern Canada using a big box. They should divide the box in half, one side illustrating tundra in summer and the other side illustrating tundra in winter. They should show the landforms, vegetation, and animals of the region.

Canadian Population Graph

Students will create two graphs showing the population of the provinces and territories of Canada. One graph will be a pictograph and the other will be a bar graph. Students should write a paragraph explaining why the population is distributed the way it is.

Bulletin Board Ideas

More Maps

Following the activity on Maps of Canada, students will display maps on the bulletin board. Turn the bulletin board into a learning center by having the students write five questions for each map on separate index cards. Assign each card a number. On a corresponding index card, students will write the answer to each question. They will then create separate pockets to hold both sets of index cards.

Government and Business

Following a discussion on how much government should be involved in business, create a bulletin board display that illustrates the web of low or high government involvement. (See debate activity for specific breakdown of the web.)

Train Vistas

Using mural paper, make a long train and place it on a bulletin board. The train is traveling along the Canadian Pacific Railway. Draw a conductor holding a sign announcing which province the train is going through at that time. Change the view from the train's "windows" as your class travels across Canada from the Atlantic to the Pacific. All aboard!

Introductory Activity

Canada and the United States—Compare and Contrast

OBJECTIVES: 2.04, 2.07, 2.08

Have students list all of the things they know about Canada, either individually or as a class. Draw a three-column chart on the board. Label the left column Canada, the middle column United States, and the third Same/Different. List all of the things that students have identified under the Canada heading. Go down the list, having students identify the same element in the United States. How are these elements similar? How are they different? Have students speculate why this might be the case.

Canada	United States	Same/Different
Capital is Ottowa	Capital is Washington, D.C.	Ottowa is in Canada's center; Washington is on the east coast.

Culminating Activity

Class Magazine

OBJECTIVES: 1.07, 3.06, 3.07

Tell the class that they are the publishers of a new magazine about North America. They must first come up with a title for their magazine, then decide how many pages each issue will have.

After studying each unit in their social studies textbook, students are to publish an issue of their magazine. As a class, discuss what articles should be included in the issue. Use some of the story ideas suggested below or create your own. What maps and illustrations will be needed? What types of charts and statistics will be necessary to help readers understand the important information students are writing about? Break the class into editorial teams of writers, cartographers, illustrators, statisticians, and designers. The writing team (this can be a larger group) will be responsible for writing the articles. The cartography team will be responsible for drawing the maps to go with the articles. The illustrators will be responsible for finding or drawing pictures to illustrate the articles. The design team will be responsible for putting the magazine together. Remind students that each group needs to coordinate with the others so that their final project will look professional and be easy for readers to understand.

Make several copies so that your students can share their magazine with the other classes in your school. Students should keep copies of the magazines from each unit so that they will have a complete set of magazines on North America at the end of the year.

Unit 5 story ideas: colonial Canada, the French in Canada, westward expansion in Canada, the Inuit, other Native Americans in Canada, Canada's climate and vegetation, Canada's government, or the British Commonwealth

Science Activity

Land of the Midnight Sun

OBJECTIVES: 1.02, 1.05, 1.06

Some areas near the earth's poles, such as in Canada, have almost 24 hours of sunlight or darkness at different points of the year. Due to Canada's location close to the Arctic Circle, the amount of daylight the region receives in the winter and summer differs from that in North Carolina. In groups or as individuals, have students investigate and report on this phenomenon. Resources include the Internet, local astronomers, planetariums, and the United States Naval Observatory. Have students collect data on sunrise and sunset times for three or more cities in Canada and North Carolina. Remind students to choose times at different points in the year. Students will use the data they collect to create charts comparing the cities. Have students present their findings. Discuss with students how the amount of daylight might affect agriculture, plant and animal life, and human behavior.

Technology Activity

A Trip Across Canada

OBJECTIVES: 1.02, 1.06, 1.07

Have students use a map/atlas program on the computer to map a route from Montreal to Vancouver. Each student should record at least ten cities or towns along the route. The students will use the Internet to connect with each of the selected town's Chamber of Commerce Web sites. The students will either print the information or just record important and interesting information about the town. After they have compiled information about cities between Montreal and Vancouver they will put this into a Power-Point or Hyperstudio presentation, for example, "Come with me to see Canada." This presentation should have at least 12 slides with information about Canada and what someone might find on a westward trip. Students can add pictures, sound effects, animation, or other illustrations.

Math Activity

United States–Canadian Currency Exchange Rate

OBJECTIVES: 4.08, 5.02, 5.06

Over the past several years, the rate of exchange between the U.S. dollar and the Canadian dollar has fluctuated between $.98 and $1.60 Canadian for $1.00 U.S. Have students calculate the value of Canadian dollars in exchange for U.S. dollars at the listed rates of exchange.

U.S. Currency	Rate of Exchange	Canadian Currency
$35.00	1.37	$47.95
$71.00	1.43	$101.53
$3.75	1.34	$5.03
$51.50	1.52	$78.28
$750.00	1.61	$1207.50
$1,205.43	1.58	$1904.58
$.33	1.40	$.46
$25.00	.98	$24.50

Unit Resources

Print Resources

Fiction

Durbin, William. *The Broken Blade.* Yearling Books, 1998. ISBN 044041184.

Gogo, Paul and Frank Ney. *A Canadian Legend.* Sunporch, 1995. ISBN 0969946805.

Higgins Andrew and Spaulding, Jesse. *World War II Adventures of Canada's Bluenose.* West Indies Trading Company, 1999. ISBN 0966307313.

Houston, James. *Frozen Fire.* Atheneum, 1997. ISBN 0689500831.

Montgomery, Lucy Maude. *Anne of Green Gables.* Bantam Doubleday Dell, 1991. ISBN 0553609416.

Paulsen, Gary. *Brian's Winter.* Laureleaf, 1998. ISBN 0440227194.

—. *Hatchet.* Aladdin Paperbacks, 1999. ISBN 0689826990.

Nonfiction

Brandenburg, Jim. *The Top of the World.* Walker and Company, 1995. ISBN 0802774628.

Corbett, William, R. *Adventures at Mitchell Lake: Retreating and Recharging in Canada's Wilderness.* Gordon Soules, 1997. ISBN 0919574920.

Joyce, William, et al. *Introducing Canada.* National Council for the Social Studies, 1997. ISBN 0879860758.

Landau, Elaine. *Canada (True Book).* Children's Press 2000. ISBN 0516270214.

Morse, Eric Wilton. *Fur Trade Routes, Then and Now.* Singing Shield Productions, 1985. ISBN 0802063845.

Tames, Richard. *A Journey Through Canada.* Troll Communications, 1991.

ISBN 0816721114.

Wilson, Ian and Sally Wilson. *Gold Rush: North to Alaska and the Klondike.* Gordon Soules, 1997. ISBN 0919574602.

—. *Wilderness Journey: Reliving the Adventures of Canada's Voyageurs.* Gordon Soules, 2001. ISBN 0919574742.

—. *Wilderness Seasons: Life and Adventure in Canada's North.* Gordon Soules, 1988. ISBN 0919574343.

Audiovisual

White Wolf. National Geographic, 1988.

British Columbia. International Video Network (IVN.com).

Canada. International Video Network (IVN.com). These videos are 30–60 minutes in length.

Web Sites

Visit **NCJourneys.com** for links to these Web sites:

- Census of Canada
- Conflict and War, CBC Archives
- People, CBC Archives
- Dictionary of Canadian Biography
- Online Resources for Canadian Heritage

Paideia Seminar

Wilderness Survival

OBJECTIVES: 1.02, 1.06, 1.07

Hatchet by Gary Paulson (ISBN 0689826990).

Theme Courage, life and death. In the book *Hatchet*, Brian Robeson is flying to visit his father. The plane crashes when the pilot dies of a heart attack. Brian is left to survive in the Canadian wilderness with only his clothing, a tattered windbreaker, and a hatchet—a present from his mother.

Pre-seminar Read the entire book to the class, type the excerpts from the book showing what Brian did to survive, then distribute them to students studying for the seminar. Pre-seminar assignment could be to have students list the ways that Brian was able to survive in the wilderness on his own.

Opening Questions
- If you were the author and you had to choose another title for the book, what would the title be?

Core Questions
- Based on the text, what acts of courage did you see from Brian?
- Is this theme consistent in the text?
- What do you think that Brian was feeling during this time period?
- What were some things Brian had to face in the wilderness?

Closing Questions
- If you were Brian, what would you have done?
- What does the text teach us about courage and life and death?
- If you were an artist, how would you represent courage? Explain.

Post-seminar Students will make a list of problems that Brian faced. Beside each they will explain how Brian was able to overcome it. They may add what they think the outcome would have been if they had been Brian.

Discussion Questions

1 Have you visited Canada? If so, where did you visit? What was it like?

2 What do you already know about Canada and its people?

Map Activity

Climate Regions

NATIONAL GEOGRAPHY STANDARDS: 1,2

GEOGRAPHIC THEMES: Location, Region, Place

 OBJECTIVES: 1.01, 1.05

Have the students look at the map on page 435. Ask:

Which hemispheres does Canada lie within? (*the Northern and Western Hemispheres*)

What is the relative location of Canada? (*in the Northern and Western Hemispheres, north of the contiguous United States, east of Alaska, south of the Arctic Ocean*)

Based on Canada's relative location, what do you think the climate is like? (*cold*) Where in Canada do you think it is coldest? (*far north*) Why? (*the area farthest from the Equator*)

Based on your last answer, where do you think most Canadians live? (*in the southern region, the warmest*)

Have students close their books and sketch Canada within ten minutes. When they complete their maps, analyze the reasons the maps look like they do. What did they remember most about Canada?

Unit 5

During the early 1900s, Canadian artists called the Group of Seven wanted to capture the spirit of Canada in their images of Canadian landscapes. Paintings like The Solemn Land *(right), by J. E. H. MacDonald, expressed the importance of Canada's wilderness to Canadians. MacDonald and the rest of the group showed the majesty, splendor, and power of Canada in their paintings of mountains, streams, and prairies. The Group of Seven helped Canadians appreciate their country. As you read about Canada's land and people, you also may come to appreciate our northern neighbors.*

The Solemn Land *by J. E. H. MacDonald*

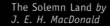 **Social Studies at Work**

Web Site Designer

A Web site designer is someone who creates interactive, multimedia Web sites for commercial, educational, governmental, or private use.

Meet Tim Songer
President, Interactive Knowledge

Students especially appreciate Tim Songer's work. That's because his job is to make learning fun. His company works with museums, publishers, libraries, and government agencies like the U.S. Department of Education to create learning experiences that capture the imagination of students both young and old.

For instance, Charlotte's Mint Museum of Art hired Songer's company to produce a multimedia Web site introducing a major new exhibit about the first team sport in human history, the Mesoamerican ball game. Perhaps the biggest challenge of the project was designing a product that would appeal to adults of all ages as well as to students in grades five through twelve.

The result? A Web site where people go back in time to explore the seven cultures known to play the game, examine the exhibit's 75 artifacts, and play an online version of the game itself. Songer has discovered that technology adds a

Canada

Unit Preview

CHAPTER 18
The Land and People
Canada's location, physical characteristics, resources, and environment are described.

CHAPTER 19
Settling a Nation
Canadians have made a nation that is a mosaic of many people.

CHAPTER 20
Economy and Government
Canada has one of the world's strongest economies and most stable governments.

CHAPTER 21
Society and Culture
Most Canadians live in cities. There, cultures inherited from the British and French mix with many other cultures. Canadians describe their cultures as a mosaic.

435

whole new dimension to the learning experience.

In fact, providing effective learning experiences is Songer's top priority. Unlike many designers who rely on technological "bells and whistles" to give their product pizzazz, Songer depends on the content itself to draw users in and keep them engaged. He is an educator first, having spent part of his early career working as a high school English teacher.

Long regarded as an expert in the area of adult literacy, Songer recognized early on the impact that technology could lend to reading and learning. This expertise not only fueled a new career for Songer but opened doors for him to speak before a Congressional subcommittee and at the United Nations.

Web Site Designer for a Day
If you have Internet access in your classroom, let students explore the case studies found at Songer's Web site (link available at **NCJourneys.com**). Ask them to come up with a plan for building a Web site using the content provided in this social studies unit.

Find Out More
For links to a variety of online educational portals visit **NCJourneys.com**.

CHAPTER 18

The Land and People

Social Studies Strands

Geographic Relationships

Historical Perspectives

Culture and Diversity

Global Connections

North Carolina Standard Course of Study

Goal 1 The learner will apply key geographic concepts to the United States and other countries of North America.

Goal 2 The learner will analyze political and social institutions in North America and examine how these institutions respond to human needs, structure society, and influence behavior.

Goal 3 The learner will examine the roles various ethnic groups have played in the development of the United States and its neighboring countries.

Goal 5 The learner will evaluate ways the United States and other countries of North America make decisions about the allocation and use of economic resources.

Teaching & Assessment

• English Language Learner Modified Lesson Plans for this chapter are found in the Teacher's Resource Guide.

• *ExamView® Assessment Suite* is provided at **NCJourneys.com.** It includes customizable assessments for all chapters. Paper tests are also available in the Teacher's Resource Guide. See pages T16–T17 for information about how to use the assessments and the Scoring Guide.

Worksheets

Worksheets and answer keys are found both in the Teacher's Resource Guide and at **NCJourneys.com**, including Reading Guides, Reading Strategies, Chapter Reviews, English Language Learner and others.

Activities and Integrations

SOCIAL STUDIES

● Canada Board Game, p. 436B
▲ ■ Problem Based Learning: Canadian Mining, p. 436B
Canada, p. 437
Carolina Connection: Snowbirds, p. 437
▲ Maps of Canada, p. 439
Canadian Shield/Great Lakes, p. 440
Region Journal, p. 441
■ Canada's Physical Regions, p. 442
▲ ■ The Land and Waters of Canada, p. 452
Renewable Energy Student Debate, p. 453
Skill Lesson: Acid Rain in Canada, p. 456

READING/LANGUAGE ARTS	READING/LANGUAGE ARTS OBJECTIVES
Activator: Poem for Canada, p. 436	4.09
▲ Writing Prompt: Advertisement, p. 436	3.06, 4.07
Reading Strategy: Vocabulay Comparisons, p. 384	2.02
★ ■ Regional Poem, p. 438	4.09
▲ ■ Travel Brochure, p. 440	4.03, 4.07, 4.09
▲ Jigsawing with a Twist, p. 439	3.06, 4.03
Land and People Canada, p. 442	4.09
Reading Strategy: Vocabulary: Read, Recite, Cover, Check p. 444	2.01, 2.02
▲ Endangered Canadian Animals, p. 451	4.09
Circle Graphic Organizer, p. 444	3.05
Reading Strategy: Vocabulary Mapping, p. 450	1.02, 1.03
Becoming Better Readers, p. 458	2.01
Understanding Rankings, p. 459	2.02

MATHEMATICS	MATHEMATICS OBJECTIVES
Graphing with Symbols, p. 451 Groups of Canada	4.01, 4.02

SCIENCE	SCIENCE OBJECTIVES
● Glacier Demonstration, p. 436B	2.01, 2.02
Endangered Canadian Animals, p. 451	1.01, 1.06
▲ ■ Botany Booklet, p. 449	1.01

TECHNOLOGY	TECHNOLOGY OBJECTIVES
★ Planning a Trip, p. 446	2.13

VISUAL ARTS	VISUAL ARTS OBJECTIVES
● ▲ ■ Leaf Printing, p. 436B	2.01, 2.02
▲ ■ Charting Routes Across Canada, p. 445	3.01, 5.02

CHARACTER AND VALUES EDUCATION	TRAITS
Meeting Challenge: Portrait Activity, p. 448	courage, perseverance
Endangered Canadian Animals, p. 451	good citizenship

● Basic Activities   ★ Challenging Activities   ▲ English Language Learner Novice   ■ English Language Learner Intermediate

Introductory Activity

Glacier Demonstration

 OBJECTIVES: 1.01, 1.02, 1.03

Put sand and small gravel in the bottom of a cake pan with at least 2-inch sides. Build a slight slope. Freeze water in a plastic or Styrofoam cup. Tear the cup away from the ice to create your own miniature glacier. In class, place your miniature glacier at the top of the slope and push it forward. This will demonstrate for your students how a glacier pushes the land as it advances. It will also show how the sand and gravel stick to the ice. Leave the ice overnight. The next day your class can see how the soil has moved and created landforms, and where the water has settled. Use this demonstration to introduce a discussion about how glaciers shaped and/or affected Canadian landforms.

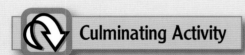 **Culminating Activity**

Canada Board Game

 OBJECTIVES: 1.02, 1.06, 3.04

Have students get into pairs and use their textbook as a guide. They will create a board game about Canada. They will use stiff posterboard as the background and will need to determine a name for the game and how to play it. The game will have information about the land of Canada. The students will need to design the game, the board, the rules, and so on. This activity will include all of the information studied in the unit. This works as an excellent review technique. When the games are completed, have pairs of students trade off—one student remaining the instructor of the game and the other playing another game. The groups of students will move around the room and get a chance to play each person's game. This is a great way to see all the other games and to study for a unit test.

 Art Activity

Leaf Printing

 OBJECTIVES: 1.02, 1.03, 1.06

Forests cover more than half of Canada. Maple forests make up a huge part of this land area. To help students appreciate the importance of the forests, they will create a design using leaf printing.

Materials paper, pencil, plate, fresh leaves and or flowers, paint brushes about an inch wide; poster or tempra paint, box of tissues

Directions Gather a variety of leaves and flowers and arrange them in a desired design on a piece of paper. Using a pencil, lightly draw an outline of your design. Brush paint on the back of a leaf and place it carefully on the design. Make sure not to move it or it will smudge.

Cover leaf with a tissue and smooth it lightly. After a few seconds, lift the tissue and peel off the leaf gently. Continue this process until the design is complete. When dry, laminate for protection, and display.

Problem Based Learning Activity

Canadian Mining

OBJECTIVES: 1.07, 3.06, 4.07

Situation
Suppose a mining company has a new means of excavating minerals in northern Canada. How will this company entice individuals to leave the Canadian southern areas so that they can build and develop cities and towns in the north? Workers will need to be paid well. They will require the kinds of services that a town provides for businesses. What kinds of services does your town provide to businesses that operate there? Break the students into groups and have them brainstorm things that would be needed for a successful community to be established.

Task After students make their list of services, have them work as a class to determine how this mining company will encourage people to begin a town in the northern regions of Canada. What kinds of things do people want from a community? If many things were offered, do you think that would encourage more people to move there? Has this kind of thing ever been done before (consider the Gold Rushes)?

Reflection Ask the students to answer the questions in writing:
- What kinds of things did you and your group think were very important to a town/city, and why were they so important?
- What would happen to people who might move to this northern region of Canada if there was no town to provide these resources? How much of a difference would this make in people's lives?
- What kinds of things do you think could be done to entice people to move and start again?
- Why do you think living in a community is so important to people?
- How is living in a community important to you? Why? What kinds of things does your community do for you?

Extension With the help of an English-speaking classmate, novice ELL students can make a booklet with pictures cut from magazines and the names of services needed in a community.

Teaching Strategies
Because the focus of the chapter is geography, make sure that you have a variety of maps and globes for students to use for hands-on activities. Use the suggested hands-on activities to keep students actively engaged in the instruction of the chapter. Plan ahead so that you can make the best use of your time and integrate where possible. If possible, find out if there is someone in your community who is Canadian or who has visited Canada and ask him or her to visit your classroom.

Discussion Questions

1 Where did the first settlers come from?

Activator

OBJECTIVES: 1.02, 1.03, 1.06

Poem for Canada Have students write a poem about Canada using one of the Five Themes of Geography for each line.
Line One: Location of Canada
Line Two: Description of Place (its human and physical characteristics)
Line Three: Human-Environmental Interaction (tell what people do in this area)
Line Four: Movement (describe movement of people, goods, or ideas)
Line Five: Region (describe the religions, a holiday, or special event in this area, common characteristics throughout the region)

Writing Prompt

OBJECTIVES: 01.07, 3.04, 4.07

Clarification Many places in Canada have a much colder climate than we do in North Carolina. Would you enjoy living in a colder climate? Explain why or why not.

Letter Writing After reading Lesson 3, Canada's Changing Environment, write a letter to the citizens of Canada offering advice to solve their environmental problems. Some problems to consider: the use of hydroelectric plants, overfishing, acid rain, and pollution.

Research and Writing Research an animal that lives in Canada. Write a report that includes the animal's characteristics and habitat and some interesting facts about the animal.

Extension Novice ELL students can draw an animal or cut out one from a magazine. They can describe the color and label the animal's body parts.

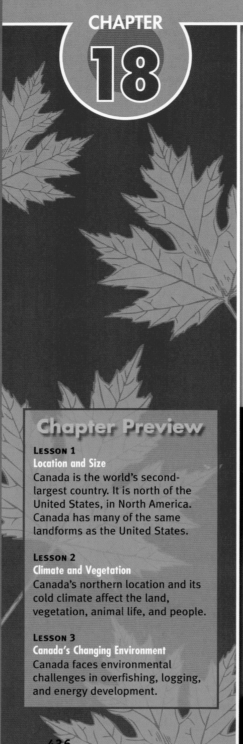

The Land and People

The night sky in Canada is often filled with colorful light. It is not starlight. It is the Northern Lights, also known as the Aurora Borealis. Green, pink, yellow, and blue lights arc and dance across the sky.

These are not special effects. The lights are actually collisions between electrically charged particles from the sun that enter the earth's atmosphere. The lights are seen above the poles of the Northern and Southern Hemispheres. They are known as Aurora Borealis in the north, meaning "dawn of the north."

The Northern Lights can be seen from anywhere in Canada, but the best places are the far northern territories of Yukon, Nunavut, and the Northwest Territories. The best time of year to see them is winter, when nights are long and often clear.

The Northern Lights are just one of the amazing sights to see in Canada. It is a land of wide-open spaces, high mountains, and modern cities. Canada's people have come from all over the world. They have created a country that honors their many backgrounds.

Chapter Preview

LESSON 1
Location and Size
Canada is the world's second-largest country. It is north of the United States, in North America. Canada has many of the same landforms as the United States.

LESSON 2
Climate and Vegetation
Canada's northern location and its cold climate affect the land, vegetation, animal life, and people.

LESSON 3
Canada's Changing Environment
Canada faces environmental challenges in overfishing, logging, and energy development.

436

Chapter 18

Chapter Resources

Print Resources
Nonfiction
Berton, Pierre. *Dr. Kane of the Arctic Seas: Exploring the Frozen North* (Adventures in Canadian History series). McClelland & Stewart, 1996. ISBN 0771014465.
—. *Trapped in the Arctic* (Adventures in Canadian History Series). McClelland & Stewart, 1995. ISBN 0771014473.
Gibbons, Gail. *The Great St. Lawrence Seaway.* William Morrow & Company, 1992. ISBN 0688069843.

Livesey, Robert. *The Loyal Refugees.* Stoddart Kids, 1999. ISBN 0773760431.
Lutz, Norma Jean, and George Sheppard. *Nunavat (Canada in the 21st Century).* Chelsea House, 2001. ISBN 079106073X.
Martin, Jacqueline Briggs. *The Lamp, the Ice, and the Boat Called Fish.* Houghton Mifflin, 2001. ISBN 061800341X.
Tames, Richard. *Journey Through Canada.* Troll Associates, 1991. ISBN 0816721114.
Waterman, Jonathan. *Arctic Crossing: A Journey Through the Northwest Passage*

Canada—Political/Physical

ARCTIC OCEAN

UNITED STATES

Beaufort Sea

Greenland (Den.)

ELLESMERE ISLAND

Baffin Bay

VICTORIA ISLAND

BAFFIN ISLAND

Dawson

Inuvik

Yukon Territory

Whitehorse

Great Bear Lake

Mackenzie R.

PACIFIC OCEAN

140°W

Northwest Territories

Nunavut

Great Slave Lake

Iqaluit

QUEEN CHARLOTTE ISLANDS

130°W

Peace R.

Athabasca R.

British Columbia

50°N

Victoria

Vancouver

Calgary

Edmonton

Alberta

Saskatchewan R.

Churchill R.

Manitoba

Hudson Bay

Newfoundland

50°W

St. John's

Regina

Saskatchewan

Lake Winnipeg

Lake Manitoba

Winnipeg

Ontario

James Bay

Quebec

Gulf of Saint Lawrence

Prince Edward Island

New Brunswick

Charlottetown

Nova Scotia

Fredericton

Halifax

Lake Superior

St. Lawrence R.

Quebec

Lake Huron

Montreal

Ottawa

Lake Ontario

ATLANTIC OCEAN

Toronto

Lake Erie

UNITED STATES

Lake Michigan

120°W   110°W   100°W   90°W   80°W   70°W   60°W

40°N

Land Elevations

Feet	Meters
13,333	4000
6,667	2000
3,333	1000
1,667	500
667	200
0	0

⊗ National capital
• City

0   250   500 mi.
0   250   500 km

CAROLINA CONNECTION

Canadian Snowbirds

If you and your family like to go to the beach during the fall or spring, you might see cars with Canadian license plates. Many Canadians take their vacations in the late fall or early spring. Favorite destinations are the North Carolina beaches.

There Canadians can fish, walk, and wade through surf instead of winter sports like skiing, snowshoeing, or ice skating. Year-round beach residents call the visitors "snowbirds." Canadians also have come to Carolina beaches in the fall to windsurf on the Outer Banks. The water off Avon is sometimes called the "Canadian hole" because so many Canadians visit there.

The Land and People

437

and *Inuit Culture.* Knopf, 2001. ISBN 0375404090.

Audiovisual

Canada. Rand McNally Video Traveller, 1992.
Canada: People and Places. North Carolina State University Humanities Extension/ Publications Program. 18 minutes.
Eyewitness Travel Guide to Canada. DK Publishing, 2000. ISBN 0789451697.
White Wolf. National Geographic video 1988.

Web Sites

Visit **NCJourneys.com** for links:
- The Atlas of Canada
- Canadian National Parks
- Confederation Bridge, Prince Edward Island
- James Bay Project Educational Site, CBC
- Meteorological Service of Canada
- Natural resources of Canada
- Northern Lights, Canada Space Agency
- Northern Lights article, *Washington Post*

Discussion Questions

1 What are the names of Canada's landform regions? What landforms of the United States are the same as Canada's?

2 Why do you think North Carolina beaches are so popular with Canadians? If you were a Canadian planning a vacation to North Carolina, where would you plan to visit? Why?

 Map Activity

Canada

NATIONAL GEOGRAPHY STANDARDS: 1,4
GEOGRAPHIC THEMES: Place
OBJECTIVES: 1.01

Discuss with students that most of Canada is north of the United States. Have them locate what parts of Canada are south of the majority of the United States–Canadian border. (*the areas east of Lake Superior and west of Maine*) How might this affect climate? (*The climate in this area is much like the climate of the bordering states.*)

Discuss the way Canada's landmass is broken up by large bodies of water. What are these bodies? (*Hudson Bay, James Bay, Baffin Bay, and the Arctic Ocean.*) How might this affect life in Canada? (*Larger bodies of water change the climate patterns and also affect movement. When some of these bodies freeze, they may limit the movement of people in the far north.*)

 Activity

Carolina Connection: Snowbirds

OBJECTIVES: 1.07, 6.02

Other Canadian Snowbirds are the Canadian Department of National Defence arial acrobatics team. Visit **NCJourneys.com** for a link to their Web site. Learn about the team and their crest. It symbolizes the location of the Snowbirds' home base in Moose Jaw, Saskatchewan. A prairie province, one of Saskatchewan's main crops is wheat. As a tribute to Saskatchewan, the Snowbird crest displays four planes, in formation, resembling an ear of wheat.

OBJECTIVES: 1.02, 1.03, 1.06

Discussion Questions

1 How does Canada rank in size compared to the other countries of the world?

2 What are provinces similar to in the United States?

3 How are territories different from provinces?

4 Why do you think the Canadian territories have not been formed into provinces?

Caption Answer

In the central and northern regions.

Reading Strategy Activity

Vocabulary Comparisons

 OBJECTIVES: 3.03. 3.04

Let students work in groups to compare the two terms listed. After reading the lesson, students should explain how the two terms are alike and how they are different.

Provinces / States
Landforms / Bodies of Water
Arctic / Interior Plains
St. Lawrence Lowlands / Mountains

Writing Activity

Regional Poem

 OBJECTIVES: 12.1

Have students write a poem about the different provinces and territories and illustrate it. Model different forms of poetry for the class, such as haiku, sonnet, acrostic, lyric, and free form.

Extension Model for intermediate ELL students. Haiku may be the best choice.

KEY IDEAS

- Canada is a large country north of the United States.
- Canada's six physical regions are varied.

KEY TERMS

muskeg
provinces
territories

Canada is a huge country. It runs almost 2,900 miles (4,669 km) from north to south. It is more than 3,200 miles (5,152 km) from east to west. Russia is the only country in the world with more territory than Canada.

Provinces and Territories

Canada's lands are divided into ten southern provinces and three northern territories. **Provinces** are political divisions similar to states in our country. **Territories** are also divisions. But they have less power than provinces. The national government has more control in territories.

The sizes of the provinces and territories go from very small to very large. The Canadian province of Manitoba is almost five times the size of North Carolina. But Canada's small eastern provinces of Prince Edward Island, Nova Scotia, and New Brunswick would fit inside North Carolina.

Canada's territories are huge. The Yukon, the Northwest Territories, and Nunavut together are three times larger than Alaska. Canadians call the territories "the North."

Location and Landforms

Canada covers most of the northern half of North America. Its coastlines touch the Atlantic, Pacific, and Arctic Oceans (see map, page 437). Alaska is on Canada's northwest border.

Canada shares many North American landforms, such as the Appalachian Mountains, the plains, and the Rocky Mountains. But much of Canada has a far northern coastline. Therefore, some Canadian landforms are different from any in the United States.

Canada's Size

Location Canada's larger area is contained within ten provinces and three territories. Some provinces are similar to the size of our states. *Where are those provinces?*

438

Chapter 18

Bodies of Water

Water is very important to Canada.

Canada has more lakes than any other nation. The Great Lakes of Ontario, Superior, Erie, and Huron make up part of Canada's southern border with the United States. The Great Lakes contain about 18 percent of the world's fresh water supply.

The Hudson Bay covers about a third of mainland Canada. The bay is usually frozen. During the short summer months, Hudson Bay is a waterway to the inside of Canada.

Rivers

Because of its location, the St. Lawrence River is key to Canada's economy. It links the Great Lakes with the Atlantic Ocean through the St. Lawrence Seaway. This seaway was built by the United States and Canada. It is Canada's most important waterway.

Canada's other great rivers are the Columbia, the Fraser, and the Yukon. These empty into the Pacific Ocean. The MacKenzie River is the second longest in North America. It moves away from cities, north into the Arctic Ocean. Its outlet is usually locked in ice.

Caption Answer

It links the Great Lakes with the Atlantic Ocean.

Montreal in Quebec was built along the St. Lawrence River. **What does the St. Lawrence connect?**

The Land and People

439

Activity

Jigsawing with a Twist

OBJECTIVES: 1.01, 1.02, 1.06

Divide the class into six cooperative groups. Each group's ability level should have a wide range from low to high. Be sure to explain to them that it is important for everyone to help one another. Assign each group a physical region of Canada. Each group is to research this region and write a set of six questions covering the important aspects of the region: landforms, bodies of water, climate, industry, natural resources, and population.

Redistribute the groups so that each new group has a member from each of the "regional" groups. Each member of these redistributed groups is responsible for teaching the remaining members. For instance, the person from the Canadian Shield group is responsible for teaching everyone else in the reformed group about the Canadian Shield.

Have students go back to their original group to review all materials. "The Twist" is used for assessment. Before testing, compose a new group of four students. Students should not be told that students have been grouped according to their abilities. All the AIG students should be in one group. The low ability is another group. Then give the test to all the students. Whoever scores the highest in each testing group receives four points, the next highest receives three, the next two, and the lowest receives one point. Students now go back to the original group to determine their group grade, which will be a culmination of the points the members scored during testing.

Extension Novice ELL students can learn to formulate questions using a map.

Activity

Maps of Canada

OBJECTIVES: 1.01, 1.02, 1.07

Brainstorm as a class about the different types of maps: political, physical, product, temperature, rainfall, land use, resources, population density, climate, road, ethnic group, and people. Divide the class into pairs. Hand out blank maps of Canada.

Assign a specific type of map to each pair. Students will fill in the information according to their assigned map type and identify the items by using a key. End the activity with oral presentations.

Extension Novice ELL students can work on a resources or climate map with the help of a bilingual dictionary.

Discussion Questions

 1 What is tundra? What animals live there?

2 Which provinces are located in Canada's Appalachian Highlands?

3 Besides the cold climate, what other factors do you think contribute to the low population numbers in the tundra? Would you want to live there? Why or why not?

 Caption Answer

The cold, dry climate supports only small plants.

Activity

Travel Brochure

OBJECTIVES: 1.02, 1.03, 1.06

Students will design a travel brochure promoting a given landform region in Canada. Brochures can include the following information:
1. Cover—name of region
2. Region profile (facts)
   a. provinces
   b. population
   c. landforms
   d. major cities
   e. ethnic groups
3. Interesting sights and historical sites
4. Economy
5. Vegetation and wildlife
   A map showing all physical features and major cities should be drawn on the inside of the brochure.
   Variations: Each brochure panel could cover one of the Five Themes of Geography.

Extension Novice or intermediate ELL students should pick two of the five areas listed above.

Canada's Regions

Geographers divide Canada into six regions. They are the Arctic Plains, the Appalachian Highlands, the Great Lakes-St. Lawrence Lowlands, the Canadian Shield, the Interior Plains, and the Western Mountains.

The Arctic Plains

Most arctic land is flat tundra plain. Tundra is so cold and dry that no trees can grow. But wildlife does live there. Canada's tundra is home to more polar bears, foxes, seals, and caribou than to people.

The Arctic Plains contains many minerals and energy resources. The costs of mining or drilling have limited their use. So have the fears of hurting the environment.

The Appalachian Highlands

The Appalachian Highlands run north from the United States into eastern Canada. These rolling hills are often covered with forests. Glaciers and ocean tides have carved the region's coast into bays and inlets. These are great natural harbors.

The four Atlantic provinces of Newfoundland, Prince Edward Island, Nova Scotia, and New Brunswick make up this region. Because these provinces are on the coast, they are also often called "the Maritimes."

The Appalachian Highlands includes such coastal areas as the Bay of Fundy in Newfoundland (below), where swift tides carve rocks. These tiny flowers (right) bloom on the tundra. **Why do only small plants grow on the Arctic Plains tundra?**

Chapter 18

Activity

Canadian Shield/Great Lakes

NATIONAL GEOGRAPHY STANDARDS: 1, 5, 9, 12
GEOGRAPHIC THEMES: Region
 **OBJECTIVES:** 1.03

Before students read the caption below the photos and map on page 441, ask the students which of the two regions (Canadian Shield or Great Lakes/St. Lawrence Lowlands) they think has the largest population. Students will probably say that the Canadian Shield is the more populated region because of its large size. Read the text with the students on page 441. Write the two regions as headings on the chalkboard. Ask the students to skim and scan the text again to look for strengths and attributes of each region. List these on the board under the proper heading. Go over the lists and ask the students if they can now see why the Great Lakes/St. Lawrence Lowlands region is the most densely populated.

ARCTIC OCEAN

UNITED STATES

CANADA

UNITED STATES

ATLANTIC OCEAN

Canadian Shield
Great Lakes–St. Lawrence Lowlands

The Great Lakes–St. Lawrence Lowlands

The Great Lakes–St. Lawrence Lowlands region is Canada's smallest. But more than half of all Canadians live here. It is Canada's most southern region.

Americans often think that all of Canada lies north of the United States. But this is not the case. Look at the map. The land in this region extends south into the Great Lakes. Parts of the region are south of at least 13 states of the United States, including all of New England.

The region's good farmland, central location, and transportation links have made it Canada's industrial center. The region is located in the provinces of Quebec and Ontario.

Kingston, Ontario, is a port city on Lake Ontario where the St. Lawrence River begins in the Great Lakes–St. Lawrence Lowlands. Glaciers scraped rock into layers in the Canadian Shield (above). **In which region do more people live? Why?**

The Canadian Shield

The Canadian Shield covers more than half of the nation. It touches parts of the Northwest Territories, Saskatchewan, Manitoba, Ontario, Nunavut, and Quebec.

More than 18,000 years ago, a huge glacier covered Canada. It moved south like a giant bulldozer. The ice sheet scraped away most of the soil. This left hard rock and thousands of holes. Over time, these holes filled with water and became rivers, bays, and lakes.

Parts of the shield that are not water or hard rock are flat and swampy lowland areas. These are called *muskeg*.

Under the ground in this region are many minerals. Iron, gold, lead, zinc, copper, and nickel can be found here. Do you remember what Brendan and his father picked up in Canada on their trip, way back in Chapter 1? Paper! Forests cover the surface of the Canadian Shield. Lumber, paper, and pulp from trees are important industries in Canada.

The Land and People   441

Discussion Questions

 1 In which region do most Canadians live? Why do you think this is true?

2 What is Canada's most important waterway?

3 The text says that more than half of all Canadians live in the Great Lakes–St. Lawrence Lowlands region, partly because of its location. What other reasons can you think of that make this area a desirable place to live?

4 Which region is Canada's largest physical region? What caused its formation?

5 What is muskeg?

6 Name some of the mineral wealth found under the Canadian Shield.

 ## Caption Answer

The Great Lakes–St. Lawrence Lowlands. It is the most southern region, with the most moderate climate and fertile farmland.

 ## Activity

Region Journals

OBJECTIVES: 1.03

After reading page 442, discuss with students which region (Interior Plains or Western Mountains) they would like to live in and why. Ask them to imagine themselves living in their chosen region and write a journal entry under the title: A Day in the Life on the Interior Plains or A Day in the Life in the Western Mountains. Have students share their writings and discuss.

Background Information

The Canadian Shield

The Canadian Shield contains North America's oldest rocks. All are at least 540 million years old. Some date back 2 billion to 3 billion years. The Canadian Shield was the first part of North America to be permanently lifted above sea level. It is one of the world's largest continental shields, extending some 3 million square miles across eastern, central and northwestern Canada. Although the Canadian Shield is among the best-known shields, every continent has one. In South America, the major shield area is called the Amazonian Shield. In Europe, the Baltic Shield covers much of Finland, Sweden, and eastern Norway.

Discussion Questions

 Which provinces are in the Interior Plains? How are they similar to the area of United States located south of them?

2 What is the name of Canada's highest mountain? How is the Western Mountain region geographically similar to the United State's West?

3 How do you think the physical environment of the Interior Plains affects population numbers?

Caption Answer

The mountainous landscape would make it difficult to build towns and cities.

Writing Activity

Land and People of Canada

OBJECTIVES: 1.01, 1.02, 1.03

Clarification Prompt Activity Using the map on page 437, emphasize to the students how some of the provinces are similar in size to our states. Discuss the locations of the provinces, and review the location of our states.

Canada's physical features are different from those of the United States. Give students this writing prompt: Canada is different from the United States. Give three reasons and explain why. Be sure to reference the text, and be specific.

Activity

Canada's Physical Regions

OBJECTIVES: 1.01, 1.02, 1.03

Have a map of Canada already showing (naming) the physical regions of the country and the political boundaries for the ten provinces and three territories. Students are to locate and name each province and then include one or two resources found in each physical region.

Extension Novice and intermediate ELL students can do this activity with a partner.

The Interior Plains

The southern parts of Alberta, Saskatchewan, and Manitoba make up the Interior Plains. The plains are west of the Canadian Shield.

The flat grasslands and low hills of the Interior Plains contain deep, fertile soil. The southern Interior Plains connects to the Great Plains of the United States. Evergreen forests cover the northern plains.

The Western Mountains

Huge mountains near the Pacific Coast run through North America. Look at the map of Canada on page 437. You can see the mountains between the Pacific Ocean and the plains. On the western side near the ocean are the Coast Ranges. On the eastern side, near the plains, are the Rocky Mountains.

The region covers almost all of British Columbia and the Yukon territories, and a small part of Alberta and the Northwest Territories.

Lake Louise in Alberta reflects the beauty of the Western Mountains region. **What might be some challenges that face people who live in this region?**

442

Chapter 18

"Fifty-four Forty or Fight!"

The western border between Canada and the United States was undecided for many years. The United Kingdom controlled Canada. It and the United States both claimed the Oregon Territory.

This area covered from the Pacific Ocean eastward to the Rocky Mountains, and between 42°N and 54°40'N (see the map, page 437). The parallel of latitude at 54°40'N marked Alaska's southern boundary (Russia claimed Alaska then).

The Americans wanted to divide Oregon along the 49th parallel. That was the border between the United States and Canada east of the Rocky Mountains to New England. The British wanted a border further south along the Columbia River. They could not agree, so the two countries decided in 1818 that they would share the region. This worked for several years.

By the 1840s, American settlers were moving to the region along the Oregon Trail. The land could no longer be shared. In 1844, James K. Polk a North Carolina native was elected president. Democrats told Polk that the United States position should be: "Fifty-four Forty or Fight!" This meant that they wanted to take control of all Oregon territory. They were willing to go to war for the land.

Polk compromised and the two countries came to an agreement. The Treaty of Oregon set the border at 49°N. Vancouver Island in Puget Sound went to Canada (see page 481 for more information about this part of the border). This border still exists today between the United States and Canada.

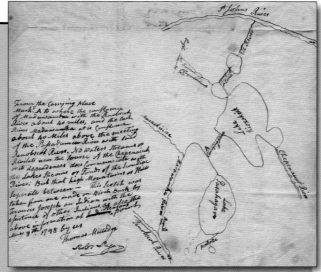

This sketch was made to determine the boundary between the United States and Canada.

Discussion Questions

1 What is a border? Why is it important to have borders between countries?

2 Who was willing to go to war for the land along the border with Canada?

3 Why do you think that the United Kingdom and the United States could no longer share the land in Oregon Territory?

Teacher Notes

This slogan, "Fifty-four Forty or Fight," is often believed to be President Polk's campaign slogan. However, the phrase did not arise until after the 1844 election.

After Polk took office, expansionists in the Democratic party shouted "Fifty-Four Forty or Fight!" They wanted Polk to hold firm in negotiations over the Oregon Territory border with the British. Polk compromised however, and agreed to the original American proposal. The Oregon Treaty of 1846 divided the Oregon Country along the 49th parallel.

LESSON 1 REVIEW

Fact Follow-Up
1. How large is Canada? How large is it in comparison to other world areas?
2. How many physical regions does Canada have? What are their names?
3. What is the most northerly physical region of Canada? The most southerly? The farthest west? The farthest east?

Talk About It
1. In what ways is the Mackenzie River different from the Mississippi River? How important are the differences?
2. Why do you think President Polk wanted all of the Oregon Territory for the United States?

LESSON 1 REVIEW

Fact Follow-Up Answers
1. Canada covers 3,849,672 square miles. It stretches almost 2,900 miles from north to south and more than 3,200 miles from east to west. Canada is the second-largest country in the world, second only to Russia.
2. Canada has six physical regions: Arctic Plains, Appalachian Highlands, Great Lakes-St. Lawrence Lowlands, Canadian Shield, Interior Plains, and Western Mountains.
3. The Arctic Plains make up most of the northerly region. The Great Lakes-St. Lawrence Lowlands is the most southerly region. The Western Mountains and the Appalachian Highlands are the regions farthest west and farthest east respectively.

Talk About It Answers
1. Important points: Encourage students to mention differences rather than similarities. The Mackenzie River flows north, and the Mississippi runs south. The Mackenzie's mouth is frozen most of the year. The Mackenzie also flows away from, not through, population centers, whereas the Mississippi passes large cities that have grown up in large part because of the river. The differences are important because the Mackenzie's characteristics make it unimportant for trade. The Mississippi is vital to the United States' trade and transportation.
2. Students will need to research this question, but they may be able to guess that Polk wanted to acquire Oregon Territory because the United States was interested in expanding its borders.

LESSON 2 Climate and Vegetation

OBJECTIVES: 1.02, 1.03, 5.07

Discussion Questions

1 Why does Canada have a harsher climate than North Carolina? What factors affect the climate of an area?

2 If the winters are so harsh in northern Canada, why do you think people continue to live there?

 Caption Answer

People must wear very warm clothing to protect themselves from frostbite. Transportation can be difficult in winter.

 Reading Strategy Activity

Vocabulary: Read, Recite, Cover, Check

OBJECTIVES: 3.02, 4.03, 4.05

This is a quick way for students to study their vocabulary words. First, they should read the word and examples with the picture. Next, they should cover the word and try to recite the meaning. Last, they should check to see if their statements were correct.

KEY IDEAS

- Canada's northern location and cold climate affect the land, vegetation, animal life, and people.

- Canada has three types of vegetation: tundra, forests, and grasslands.

KEY TERMS

lichens

Winter in Quebec City means snow and low temperatures. It also means cross-country skiing and ice skating. **How does the climate affect life there?**

O ne of Canada's best-known writers is Stephen Leacock. He once joked that life in Canada could be divided into three seasons. He called them, "preparing for winter, enduring [getting through] winter, and recovering from winter."

Many Canadians might agree with Leacock. In most of Canada, the winters are long and cold. The summers are warm but short.

The warmer parts of Canada have climates similar to the cooler parts of the United States.

Climate

In northern Canada, winter brings cold temperatures, fierce winds, and big snowstorms. Just how cold? North of the Arctic Circle temperatures can stay below –20°F (–29°C) for more than four months.

Winter turns the town of Churchill, located on the Hudson Bay, into an icebox. People bundle up. It can get so cold that parts of the body not covered by clothes, hats, gloves, or scarves can freeze quickly.

In the large southern cities it is not quite so cold. But it is much colder than North Carolina. The thermometer may not rise above 0°F (–17.8°C) for more than half the year.

 Activity

Circle Graphic Organizer

OBJECTIVES: 1.05, 1.06, 1.07, 3.04

The circle graphic organizer is another form of visual aid. The circle is chosen for a purpose. Canadians know their country is made up of diverse people. The circle graph helps demonstrate that although the people are different as in a mosaic art piece, as a nation, they are proud of their

diversity and believe that this diversity help the nation. Students should read Lesson 1 of Chapter 19. They will notice Canada is made up of people from different places other than Canada. As they read about each nationality, have them add details about the group to their graphic organizer, the People of Canada, in the Teacher's Resource Guide.

Tundra and Subarctic

Look at the climate map of North America on page 45 in Chapter 2. Northern Canada, including all of the Arctic Plains and much of the Canadian Shield, has short, cool summers. These regions have tundra and subarctic climates.

Steppe and Humid Continental

In southern Canada, summers are warm enough for raising crops. In the prairie provinces, farmers harvest large fields of grain, such as rye. They also grow a special type of wheat that does well in shorter growing seasons. Here, the southern Interior Plains region has steppe and humid continental climates.

The Appalachian Highlands, the southern part of the Canadian Shield, and the Great Lakes-St. Lawrence Lowlands regions also have a humid continental climate. All of these regions have cool, instead of warm, summers.

 A Journey to THE CANADIAN PRAIRIE

Life on a Large Farm

Life in the prairie provinces of Manitoba, Saskatchewan, and Alberta often means life on a large farm.

Read the following from William Kurelek's *A Prairie Boy's Summer*. How is your life is similar to or different from the life of William, the boy in the story?

Haying was an important early summer job on dairy farms. When his father went into dairying William had to learn many of the steps necessary to make a haystack out of a field of grass. His father planted grass, but his neighbors rented sections of the bog to the east and cut natural grass. William envied the neighbors' boys, for they sometimes stayed out on the bog for two whole weeks cooking out in the open and sleeping under the wagon just like gypsies.

The first machine that was used in haying was the mower, and it had to be oiled often. William liked the scent of fresh-mown hay.

William had to learn how to build the stack properly and at the same time catch bundles of hay thrown up by his father. Once, after they had begun building a stack of clover, an approaching thunderstorm during the night forced the family to get up at 2:00 A.M. to put a peak on the stack to shed the rain. They finished just before the downpour and returned to the house at dawn.

The Land and People

445

Teacher Notes

Refer students to the climate map of the Western Hemisphere on page 45 in Chapter 2.

Activity

Charting Routes Across Canada

 OBJECTIVES: 1.02, 1.03, 1.07

Students will pretend they are airline pilots. Using a large detailed map, they are to chart a route across Canada. On their route, have the "pilots" describe in detail to their passengers the landform regions of Canada. The pilots will point out particular places of interest—such as the Great Lakes, the St. Lawrence River and lowlands, salmon-producing rivers and streams, mountains, Hudson Bay, and so on.

Extension Give novice ELL students a physical map of Canada with landforms labeled. They can color the map and memorize the names of the landforms. As the class "pilots" describe the region, ELL students can follow their own maps by pointing at the mentioned landform.

Discussion Questions

1 What makes Canada's West Coast a more desirable place to live than other places in Canada?

2 Why did the writer Stephen Leacock call Canada's West Coast "an ideal home for the human race"?

3 What three types of plant life cover most of Canada?

 Caption Answer

Mild, warm winds blow into British Columbia from the Pacific Ocean.

 **Research Activity**

Planning a Trip

OBJECTIVES: 1.02, 1.03, 1.06

Students will plan a two-week trip to Canada using resources from travel agencies and Internet sites. They must research information about three or more provinces and study places to visit and things to see.

As they plan their trip, they should list the landforms they would see either while driving in Canada, taking the train, or flying in an airplane. They must calculate their mileage and the time, rate, and distance from place to place. They should plan to spend enough time visiting and enjoying a place as well as traveling. They must determine the cost of the trip. Students should review a time zone map to help plan time changes as they move from one province to another. Students should put this all together as a package with a folder including a schedule or itinerary, a cost guide, the travel times, locations, and so on.

For a list of Web sites useful to begin planning the trip, visit **NCJourneys.com** and check the Unit 5 resources and the resource lists for Chapters 18, 19, 20, and 21.

Butchart Gardens, on Vancouver Island in British Columbia, displays the lovely results of a mild climate. **Why is the climate here less harsh than in other parts of Canada?**

Marine West Coast and Highlands

Some Canadians took part in a survey. They were asked in which province they would most like to live. British Columbia ranked first.

Unlike the rest of Canada, the coast of British Columbia has mild winters and cool summers. Mild, warm winds blow into British Columbia from the Pacific Ocean. So it has the Marine West Coast climate.

This area also has the wettest climate in the country. Parts of British Columbia get more than 100 inches (254 cm) of precipitation a year. Very little of that is snow.

Mild winters and heavy rainfall have been good for the trees. This part of Canada has the tallest trees in the country. There are thick forests of fir and cedar. Stephen Leacock called the province "an ideal home for the human race, not too cold, not too hot, not too wet, not too dry."

The mountains of the Western Mountains region have the highlands climate. As you have learned, climate gets cooler the higher you go above sea level.

Plant Life and Animals

Three types of vegetation cover most of Canada. In each region, temperature and rainfall affect plant life.

In the Arctic Plains, most of the land is tundra. South of there, forests cover about half of Canada. Long and short grasses once covered the Interior Plains. Today, the Plains has Canada's most fertile farmlands.

Tundra

Winter temperatures can fall as low as −60°F (−51°C) in the Arctic Plains. It is too cold and dry for roots to take hold. Roots that reach down into the tundra soil freeze and die.

Most of the tundra is permafrost. That means the top layer of soil is frozen all the time, all year long. During the few weeks of arctic summer, the very top of the permafrost thaws to a soggy mud mixture.

Mosses, *lichens* (LIE·kens), and other small plants grow on the tundra. Lichen is a fungus. It grows together with algae and forms a kind of crust on rocks or tree trunks.

Arctic Animals Birds return for the short summer. Thousands of caribou cross the tundra. They grow fat by grazing on lichens and grasses.

By September, birds have flown south. Caribou have headed for the forests. By October, musk oxen, arctic foxes, and polar bears are the only large animals left on land. Walruses, seals, and whales can survive the cold, cold Arctic waters.

Caribou (below) live on the tundra, a frozen plain where only mosses, grasses, and flowers grow during a short summer. **Why do this Inuit mother and child wear such heavy clothing in the summer?**

The Land and People

447

Discussion Questions

1 What characteristics do the musk oxen, arctic foxes, and polar bears have that help them adapt to the cold climate? What other animals do you know of that are able to adapt to cold climates?

2 What is Canada's capital city?

3 What are some other large cities in Canada?

4 Why do you think so many people live within 200 miles of the United States border? What factors do you think influence this fact?

 Caption Answer

The tundra is cold even in summer.

 Background Information

Welcoming the Sun in the Far North

The Inuit village of Igloolik sits on the Arctic Circle some 1,200 miles from the North Pole. Residents there hold a special ceremony at the end of each winter honoring the sun's return. For seven weeks during the winter months, Igloolik remains dark for most of each day. In the past, light came mainly from soapstone lamps filled with seal blubber. Families lit the moss wicks of their lamps with sparks from flints. They marked with special celebrations the day the sun reappeared. The first person to see the sun rushed back to tell the others. Residents built a large igloo where they gathered, carrying their lamps. Villagers put out their lamps and the elders relit them from a single wick. After the village got electricity, the custom died out, but a decade ago, Igloolik elders revived it.

Discussion Questions

1 Who was Terry Fox? Why do Canadians honor him today?

2 What is the bravest thing you have ever done? Where did you find the courage to try it?

3 Why do you think Terry wanted to run across Canada?

4 Why do Canadians often play games on ice, like curling?

Activity

Meeting Challenges: Portrait Activity

OBJECTIVES: 4.03

Sometimes people are not famous because of what they set out to do, but because of what they had to do. Often, people are faced with challenges that they must overcome. Have students read the Portrait on this page. Divide the class into pairs. Let each pair choose an activity from this list or assign one or more of these activities to the class. In the activity, students should focus on how the person they are studying overcame the challenges he faced.

- Write a journal that recounts important events in the person's life.
- Write an interview with the person and role play it for the class.
- Draw or paint a portrait of the figure at work or meeting a challenge.
- Make a scrapbook of the person's life. Students should journal in the scrapbook to describe the elements they have placed in it.
- Design a Web page that tells a story about the person.
- Illustrate a timeline with eight to twelve important events in the person's life.

CANADIAN PORTRAIT

Terrence "Terry" Fox
1958–1981

Terry Fox was born in Manitoba and raised in British Columbia. He played many sports as a teen. When he was eighteen, doctors told him he had bone cancer. Terry had to have his right leg amputated (removed) 6 inches (15 cm) above his knee.

While in the hospital, Terry met other cancer patients. Many were young children. He decided that he would run across Canada to raise money for cancer research. He trained for 18 months to get ready. He called his run the "Marathon of Hope."

Terry began by dipping his artificial leg in the Atlantic Ocean in Newfoundland on April 12, 1980. His goal was to dip his leg in the Pacific Ocean at the end. He wanted to run about 26.2 miles (42 km) a day. No one had ever done anything like this before.

During his run Terry kept a journal. Early in the trip he wrote, "Today we got up at 4:00 A.M. As usual, it was tough. If I died, I would die happy because I was doing what I wanted to do. How many people could say that? . . . I want to set an example that will never be forgotten."

As he ran, people heard Terry's story. They gave him money and support. He made it through Newfoundland, Nova Scotia, Prince Edward Island, New Brunswick, Quebec, and Ontario.

But after 143 days and 3,339 miles (5,373 km), Terry had to stop running. He had cancer in his lungs. Everyone was shocked and sad. Terry died the following year.

Terry is an inspiration to many people. He did not let physical challenges get in his way. He did something with only one leg that many able-bodied people would not even try.

Canadians still honor Terry as a hero today.

Customs

Curling is a popular winter sport in Canada. It is played on ice, but is not like hockey. In curling two teams of four players each slide 42-pound granite rocks toward the center of a 12-foot diameter target.

Each player throws two rocks toward the target, alternating with the opponent. The team with the rock closest to the center scores points. A unique part of curling is the sweeping. Players brush the ice in front of the rock to keep it moving. The friction of the brooms melts a thin layer of ice in front of the rock allowing it to travel farther and straighter.

Canada's Women's Olympic Curling Team won the bronze medal in 2006.

Most of Canada's regions, such as the Appalachian Highlands, are heavily forested. **Which regions lack forests?**

Forests

South of the tundra, the subarctic climate is still too cold for farming. The soil is poor, too. But trees grow well here.

Forests cover almost half of Canada's land area. Mountain wilderness spreads over the Yukon and part of the Northwest Territories. Forests also stretch across southern Canada. They run from Queen Charlotte Island on the Pacific Coast to Newfoundland, a large island in the Atlantic.

The West Coast has heavy rainfall. It also has Canada's longest growing season. There you can find giant evergreen trees. Douglas fir, cedar, and hemlock grow well.

The St. Lawrence Lowlands and other parts of southern Canada have huge maple forests. Maple syrup is an important product. The maple leaf is the country's symbol. Canada's flag has one large maple leaf in the center.

Grasslands

Like the plains in the United States, the grasslands in Canada are good for farming. The prairie provinces of the Interior Plains are Canada's breadbasket. Farmers there grow wheat and barley for their nation and the world. Farmers also raise hay, corn, and grain for cattle ranches and dairy farms.

LESSON 2 REVIEW

Fact Follow-Up
1. Describe Canadian winters in detail.
2. What are the three types of vegetation of Canada? How do they differ?
3. Why are the prairie provinces called Canada's "breadbasket"?

Talk About It
1. Why is the West Coast climate unlike that of the rest of Canada? How is it different?
2. Do differences in the region's climates affect the lives of people? Do they affect the economy?

The Land and People

449

Discussion Questions

1 What kinds of trees grow there?
2 What caused the grasslands to be so fertile?
3 What crops are grown there now?
4 What does the phrase "the nation's breadbasket" mean?

Caption Answer

The tundra lacks forests.

Activity

Botany Booklet

 OBJECTIVES: 1.01, 1.02, 1.03

Students will make a botany book of the plants that grow in the Arctic region. They will use a variety of sources (plant identification books, encyclopedias, and science textbooks) to research these plants. The format for recording the information will be:
• Name of plant:
• Scientific name:
• Location:
• Uses:
• Colored illustration:
Include such plants as Arctic poppy, sea bluebell, whiplash saxifrage, lichens, black spruce tree.
Have students design a cover for their booklet.

Extension Novice ELL students will need to work with partners.

LESSON 2 REVIEW

Fact Follow-Up Answers
1. Canadian winters are very cold. In the Arctic North, the temperature stays at –20° F and colder. Even in southern Canada, the winter gets cold enough in areas away from coastlines to make it dangerous to stay outside long. The areas that are the least cold are located on the Pacific coast of southern Canada.
2. Tundra, forests, and grasslands are the three vegetation areas. Tundra is a dry, treeless plain that can only support mosses and lichens for plant life. Forests grow throughout Canada, except on the Arctic Plains. Forest lands are not as fertile as the grasslands area, which had thousands of years to develop fertile soil through the decay of plant roots.
3. The Prairie Provinces are called Canada's "breadbasket" because the fertile soil of the provinces produces wheat and barley for bread flour as well as hay, corn, and grasses for cattle feed.

Talk About It Answers
1. The West Coast climate is mild because of the warming winds that blow across the area from the Pacific. It is wetter than the rest of Canada. The differences affect the lives of people who live on the West Coast because they are able to grow more crops due to a longer growing season and reliable rainfall and because they can work and play outside year-round. The mild climate attracts tourists who spend money to help the economy.
2. Answers will vary. Students should include examples of how climate affects daily life and the Canadian economy.

OBJECTIVES: 1.05, 1.06, 1.07, 3.04

Discussion Questions

1 What are some of the major problems in tapping the resources of the Arctic Plains?

Caption Answer

It makes it easier for people and goods to travel to the island.

Reading Strategy Activity

Vocabulary Mapping

OBJECTIVES: 1.03, 1.06, 5.02, 6.04, 6.05

Try this vocabulary mapping technique with the key terms in this lesson. Use the Vocabulary Mapping worksheet or notebook paper to draw the graphic organizer below. Divide the class into five groups. Each person in the group chooses a vocabulary word and completes all three parts for the word. Group members may need to help with difficult words. When all participants have finished, each person must teach his word to the group. At the end, paste the group's words on a sheet of colored paper to post in the room.

Definition: _____
_____

WORD

Sentence: _____   **Picture:**
_____
_____
_____

LESSON ③ Canada's Changing Environment

KEY IDEAS

- Canada faces environmental challenges in overfishing, logging, and the development of hydroelectric and petroleum energy sources.

- Opposition to development has caused Canadians to rethink their use of the environment.

KEY TERMS

acid rain
James Bay Project
overfishing

Canada is one of the richest and most advanced countries in the world. Canadians want to be sure that they also protect their environment. Their land is important to them. A Haida Native American artist worried about the effects of Canada's growth on the land. The artist wrote,

This is a great place, but we take it for granted. When I go back to my home, I see the scars of logging everywhere. The abalone is fished out.... It's really scary for me. We don't seem to notice the good things until they are gone.

Often choices are difficult. Cleaner air and water may mean fewer factories and fewer jobs. Canadians look to the North to find more resources. There are challenges there, too.

Canada's Resources

Canadians are slowly beginning to tap the resources of the Arctic Plains. Some of its many resources are found here. It costs a lot of money to mine metals and minerals in weather with temperatures below zero.

Transportation also is a major problem. The Arctic has only a few good roads. Most of the year, northern rivers are frozen solid or clogged with chunks of ice.

At a zinc and lead mine in the Arctic, the only way for workers to get to and from the mine is by airplane. The nearest port is free of ice for only a month and a half in the summer. Then a ship rushes in with enough food supplies for the entire year. The ship carries out all of the zinc and lead mined there.

Even with high pay, a heated underground swimming pool, and a gym, not many skilled workers want to work away from their homes for a long time.

The Confederation Bridge, completed in 1997, replaced a ferry service. The bridge connects Prince Edward Island to mainland Canada. **How could the bridge improve the island's economy?**

Background Information

Good News for Churchill, Canada

Although global warming is a worrisome problem for much of the world, the town of Churchill, population 1,100, hopes the warming trend continues. As Canada's northernmost industrial harbor, it is the only major port on Hudson Bay. For decades most shippers ignored it because it was ice-bound five months of the year. However, over the past 30 years, the ice cover on Hudson Bay has decreased by about one third. Many more oceangoing ships now stop there to pick up wheat shipped by rail from the prairie provinces. They take their cargo to Africa, Europe, and Mexico. "If we...have global warming, then the only way for Churchill to go is up," says Canada's Minister of Transport. Throughout the Arctic region, ice cover has begun to retreat earlier and earlier.

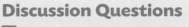

Canada—Economic Activity and Resources

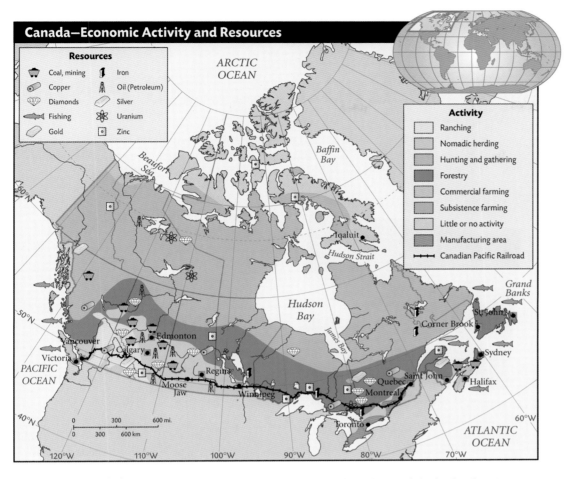

Resources
- Coal, mining
- Copper
- Diamonds
- Fishing
- Gold
- Iron
- Oil (Petroleum)
- Silver
- Uranium
- Zinc

Activity
- Ranching
- Nomadic herding
- Hunting and gathering
- Forestry
- Commercial farming
- Subsistence farming
- Little or no activity
- Manufacturing area
- Canadian Pacific Railroad

Water Wealth

In the last 50 years, Canadians have been tapping another resource. Water resources, like rivers and waterfalls, can be put to use. Much of the energy used in Canada's factories and homes comes from hydroelectric power. It is cleaner for the environment than burning fossil fuels like coal or oil.

But water power is not without problems. Some Canadians are worried that hydro-electric plants will hurt the environment and the people of Canada.

During the building of the hydroelectric *James Bay Project,* large areas of land in Quebec were flooded. Many Native Americans were forced to find new homes.

The government, the Inuit, and the Cree of northern Quebec came to an agreement. The native peoples received 5,400 square miles (14,040 sq km) of land and more than $225 million (Canadian dollars) for their losses.

Several phases of the project have been completed. But other plans were cancelled and others were put on hold. Today, Quebec is planning to build a new dam in a new phase of the project.

The Land and People

451

Discussion Questions

1 What are some of the major problems in tapping the resources of the Arctic Plains?

2 What are the pros and cons of the James Bay project?

Map Activity

Graphing with Symbols

NATIONAL GEOGRAPHY STANDARDS: 1, 3, 4, 15,

GEOGRAPHIC THEMES: Human-Environmental Interaction

OBJECTIVES: 1.06, 5.02, 5.07

Assign groups for all of the different economic resources (ten are shown on the map). Have each group quickly create markers for each of their symbols on the map. For example, the "silver group" would make two markers to represent silver. Using a large chart-paper-sized piece of graph paper, the class will make a graph using the symbols from the map. Have each group place one symbol per grid square for each of the symbols shown on the map. After each group has had its turn, discuss the implications of available resources and how these resources can be utilized in Canada. Point out how dramatically the graph illustrates the scarcity and availability of resources. Next, have students return to their groups and compare the economic activities to the economic resources by regions or sections of the map. Have groups write a pro and con list regarding the mixing of the activities and resources. For example, how does offshore drilling for oil mix with commercial fishing (positively and negatively)?

Writing Activity

Endangered Canadian Animals

OBJECTIVES: 1.02, 1.03, 1.06

Have students pretend to write letters to Canadian officials asking for protection of the species below. Tell them to be sure to include why they think it is important to protect the species and offer any ideas they have for protecting the animals. Review letter-writing skills with students.

- Seal pups—hunted for fur
- Lobsters—overfished
- Cod and other fish off Newfoundland—overfished
- Caribou—pipelines interfering with environment
- Whales—hunted for blubber
- Salmon—overfished

Additional information may be available from marine resources or Canadian environmental groups.

Extension Novice ELL students can write the envelopes to learn or review the address.

Map Activity

The Land and Waters of Canada

NATIONAL GEOGRAPHY STANDARDS: 1, 4

GEOGRAPHIC THEMES: Place

OBJECTIVES: 1.01, 1.02, 1.06

Give each student a blank map of Canada. Have students identify and label each of the following:

Arctic Plains
St. Lawrence River
Canadian Shield
Rocky Mountains
Great Slave Lake
Columbia River
Mackenzie River
Yukon River

Appalachian
  Highlands
St. Lawrence
  Lowlands
Interior Plains
Hudson Bay
Fraser River

The Great Lakes—Ontario, Erie, Huron, Superior, Michigan

Extension Novice ELL students should be able to do this activity using an atlas. Students can write the names of these landforms on their maps.

Harnessing Hydroelectric Power

One resource Canada will not run out of is water. Canada has found ways to use the water to produce energy for its people and to sell to the United States.

Some large power plants are driven by water. They are called hydroelectric plants. Hydro means "water." The plants convert the water power into electricity.

To harness the power of the water, most hydroelectric plants are built near dams. Hydroelectric plants work when some of the water behind the dam rushes through pipes into the plant.

In the plant, water turns a wheel connected to a shaft, or large pole. The shaft runs a turbine where it spins powerful magnets. The magnets spin inside the turbine close to copper wire. This creates a strong electric current.

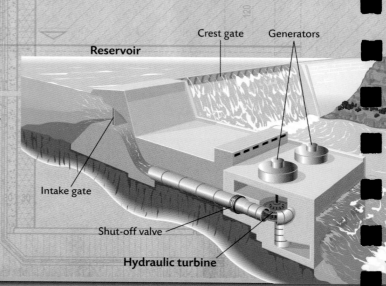

Reservoir

Crest gate   Generators

Intake gate

Shut-off valve

Hydraulic turbine

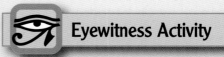

The electricity flows out of the plant on power lines. The electricity is then sent to thousands of homes, factories, and businesses. The power of water meets almost 75 percent of Canada's electricity needs.

The James Bay Project has built several hydroelectric power stations. They are on the La Grande River in northwestern Quebec at James Bay. The courses of La Grande and a few other rivers were moved. Then dams were built to create reservoirs. Water from the reservoirs powers the turbines.

The project covers an area of the size of the state of New York. It is one of the largest hydroelectric systems in the world. It makes enough power to meet the needs of half of Quebec. Planning began in 2004 to build a new dam on the Rupert River.

Eyewitness Activity

Renewable Energy Student Debate

OBJECTIVES: 1.06, 5.01, 5.02, 6.02

Discuss with students that hydroelectric power is a renewable form of energy, similar to solar and windpower. These forms of energy are based on resources that will not run out. Non-renewable energy sources are resources that are used up in the process of making energy, such as oil or coal.

Many people prefer that we use renewable energy resources (called "green" energy) because they cause less impact on the environment and do not contribute to global warming. However green energy forms are not without environmental costs.

Refer to the Guide to Student Debates in the front of the Teacher's Edition. Divide the class into two or four groups. Half of the groups will be the affirmative team. The other half with be the negative team. The students will need to conduct Internet research to support their side of the following resolution: Resolved: That the James Bay Project in Canada is a good example of the benefits of renewable energy sources.

Students on both sides should consider factors including the cost of building the project, the cost of producing electricity, who buys/uses the energy generated in the power plants, the environmental impact of the project, and the cultural impact of the project on the Cree people.

The Land and People

453

 ## Activity

Adjusting to a Harsh Environment

OBJECTIVES: 1.02, 1.06, 1.07

Canada wants to tap the resources of the North. The barriers to Canadians living and working in this area are mostly environmental. Begin this activity by discussing with your class why the environment in northern Canada would be a barrier to "normal life." How might their normal lives be changed in this environment? Next, ask your students to design their own underground cities that would satisfy their desire for normal life in an unfriendly environment. Each student should draw and color his or her underworld city and write a paragraph explaining how it works as an alternative to the unfriendly natural environment.

Discussion Questions

1 What has the Canadian government done to solve the problem of overfishing? What has happened as a result?

2 What environmental problem do Canada, North Carolina, and many other areas of the United States share?

3 What are Canada and the United States doing to solve it?

 **Caption Answer**

Overfishing has dangerously reduced the cod population. Fishing is restricted to give the cod population a chance to grow again.

 **Activity**

Acid Rain Summit

◤ **OBJECTIVES:** 1.02, 1.06, 4.07

Split the class in half. Have one half be Canadians and the other half be United States citizens. Assign roles on both sides as parents, businesspeople, government officials and so on. Have them dress for their specific job. Decorate the classroom with flags of Canada and the United States. Hold a summit to decide ways in which the two countries can work together to solve the acid rain problem.

This could be videotaped. The students need to come up with a compromise. Finally, send your conclusions to both the American and Canadian governments.

The Fishing Crisis

For many centuries, the Grand Banks off the Atlantic coast of Canada (see map, page 451) had many, many fish. It was the center of a huge fishing industry. Fishing boats netted all the fish they could. Few people thought the fish supply would be in danger.

But in the late 1980s, things began to change. Catches got smaller. The region was overfished. *Overfishing* means more fish are caught than hatched each year. Overfishing means that the fish population has dropped.

In the Grand Banks, the fish numbers are dangerously low. Commercial fishermen from around the world have hurt the fish populations. Technology has helped them find and catch the fish.

In 1994, the Canadian government stopped all cod fishing to give the cod population a chance to come back. Although some flounder species have come back, the cod has not. For now, the ban will continue.

In Canada's Atlantic Provinces, the fishing industry employed most people. The ban has caused many to lose their jobs and has hurt the economy.

Acid Rain

Some years back, park officials on Mount Mitchell, North Carolina's highest mountain, noticed trees on the mountain top were dying. Forests on surrounding mountains were already dead.

Scientists said that *acid rain* was the cause. This form of air and water pollution is caused by gasses from cars, factories, and power stations. The gasses mix with drops of water. Lakes, fish, and wildlife can be hurt by acid rain.

Many fishing boats on the Atlantic coast remain idle in harbors of the Appalachian Highlands because the Canadian government restricts cod fishing. **Why is fishing restricted?**

Acid rain is a serious problem for southern Ontario. Pollution comes from the smokestacks of factories and power plants. It is carried by winds to the lakes and forests of Canada. In Ontario alone, the fish in more than 1,000 lakes have been killed off by acid rain. Air pollution also threatens Canada's maple trees, the nation's symbol.

In the 1980s, Canada and the United States blamed each other for this problem, but in the 1990s they began working together to solve it. In 2004, the Canadian government said that in order to protect the environment, more needed to be done. Acid rain is still a problem.

These same sources of pollution also cause global warming. Canada requires power plants to keep harmful gases from leaving factory and power plant smokestacks. The United States is working with Canada to reduce the pollution.

Hard Choices

The James Bay Project has sharpened the debate over the use of Canada's resources. Should projects that bring such huge changes to the environment be repeated? Supporters say that the project brings jobs. It also brings money. Critics argue forests were destroyed and can never be replaced. The project was just too costly. The issues are still not settled.

What would YOU do?

If you lived in Canada, you would have to weigh the importance between people having jobs and the possible destruction of the environment. **What would you do? Would you argue for development? for preserving the environment? or something else?**

During a visit from the Queen of the United Kingdom and Canada to British Columbia, citizens protest against logging in the province. **How have Canadians encouraged protection of the environment?**

LESSON 3 REVIEW

Fact Follow-Up
1. How has Canada's physical environmental changed?
2. What are some of the difficulties of tapping the resources of the Arctic?
3. How do hydroelectric plants affect Canadians?

Talk About It
1. Why is it said there are too many fishermen and not enough fish in Canada?
2. What are some of the hard choices Canada faces? Which choice do you think will be most difficult? Explain why.

The Land and People

455

Caption Answer

They have strongly protested widespread changes to the land, such as the James Bay hydroelectric project.

Teacher Notes

Changes in Fishing Technology
By 1840, the French were responsible for many of the technological innovations that changed the fishing industry. They introduced the *bultow*, or trawl fishing, to replace the traditional handline used from the deck of vessels. The bultow was simply long lines of several hundred meters with hundreds of baited hooks attached at regular intervals. The line was set or moored on the sea floor by fishers operating from chaloupes and flat-bottomed craft called "dories." Though more efficient than the simple hook and line method, trawl fishing was widely criticized for catching too many fish and destroying the stocks. Nevertheless, fishers from New England, Nova Scotia, and Newfoundland soon adopted this technique, as did the Spanish and Portuguese.

LESSON 3 REVIEW

Fact Follow-Up Answers
1. Logging; mining of gold, lead, zinc, and oil; and the building of large hydroelectric plants have all changed the landscape. Overfishing has caused the depletion of certain fish, especially cod.
2. Bitter cold, which makes transportation and living difficult, is a major problem. Ships can reach the ports where the minerals are stored only once a year. Few people want to work and live in lonely, desolate, and cold areas.
3. Hydroelectric plants provide electricity to cities and provide Canada with revenues from the sale of excess power to the United States. But hydroelectric plants require the flooding of land, which often displaces people.

Talk About It Answers
1. Fishing has been a way of life on the east coast of Canada for 300 years, so many people have depended on fishing for their livelihood. Yet because of overfishing, there are no longer enough fish to provide many people with enough income to survive. The government prohibition against cod fishing has added to the problem for fishermen trying to make ends meet.
2. Important points: Encourage students to suggest a variety of hard choices (challenges) faced by Canada, choose the one they think is most difficult, and explain why they chose it. Canada faces choices of extracting resources versus maintaining the environment. Probably the most difficult choices will relate to obtaining energy (oil or hydroelectric) while protecting the land.

Teaching This Skill Lesson

Materials Needed   textbooks, paper, pencils, enough newspapers (not necessarily of the same date) for small group use, marking pens

Classroom Organization whole class, small groups

Beginning the Lesson   Distribute newspapers. Using a newspaper, model for students a search for articles about or announcements of (1) public meetings in the community and (2) evidence of citizen action (as opposed to the action of governments and their agencies).

Lesson Development Organize the class in small groups and assign roles for cooperative work (e.g., reader(s), checker(s), recorder, reporter). Distribute newspapers and marking pens to each group. Circulate as students look for evidence of public meetings and citizen action. When groups report, record information on the chalkboard. Have students read the Skill Lesson, or paraphrase it for them. Then have each small group choose one public meeting of interest and brainstorm ways of finding out more information about the topic of the meeting.

Conclusion Groups should report on (1) which meeting interested them and (2) how they might find out more information about the topic. In a general class discussion, relate their reports to the three ways of deciding whether or not to attend a public meeting.

Extension Invite a civic activist or elected public official to observe the lesson and comment. If possible, a class field trip to observe a public meeting might be arranged. Individual students could be awarded extra credit for attending a public meeting with a parent and writing a report about it.

SKILL GOALS NORTH CAROLINA SOCIAL STUDIES SKILL

skill

Applying Decision-Making and Problem-Solving Techniques to World Issues

Acid Rain in Canada

Imagine that you live in a suburb of Toronto. One day you see a notice on a bulletin board in the shopping mall. It says:

> S T O P
> **ACID RAIN**
> FROM THE SOUTH
> – Public Meeting –
> Tuesday,
> December 12
> 7:30 P.M.
> Room 210
> **Municipal Building**

You must make a choice. As a citizen, should you attend the meeting? How do you decide whether to go? First, you might consider what you already know about the topic (in this case, acid rain.) What do you need to know in order to make good choices? Will this meeting (left) help you learn more?

A second way of deciding is to look at your reasons. List all the reasons to go to the meeting and all the reasons not to go on a piece of paper. Look it over. You can make your choices based on your reasons.

A *third* way of deciding is to find out which group is holding the meeting. Are you likely to learn new information? Will you only hear one side of the issue?

If you are likely to hear only one side of the issue, you might want to learn about the other side. You can read about other points of view or attend other meetings.

If you decide to attend the meeting, you will need to learn about the issue. How will you do this?

First, if there have been any articles about the subject in the newspaper, read them. Write down any questions you have after reading.

Second, watch TV news shows to learn more about the issue. Remember, though, that sometimes people say things on TV that may not be totally true. To get more information, use your school's media center and the Internet. They are good places to start your research.

Here are some facts you may learn about acid rain in Canada:

1. More than $1 billion worth of damage is caused by acid rain each year.

2. Eighty percent of Canadians live in areas of high acid rain levels.

3. More than 80 percent of the most productive agricultural land in eastern Canada receives more than acceptable levels of acid rain.

What do you decide to do to reduce levels of acid rain?

A copper-nickel mine and acid rain killed foliage on a hillside in Ontario.

Skill Lesson Review

1. What are some other ways of deciding whether or not to take civic action? *Besides gathering information, you might also talk with friends and other people whose opinions you respect, or think about your own experiences.*

2. Why is information important for informed civic behavior? *Information helps us in making decisions. It also prepares us to persuade others to our point of view.*

3. Think of an issue in your community. How can you find out about the issue in order to be an informed citizen? *Encourage students to name as many sources of information as they can. The local newspapers, radio, television, political action groups, and local meetings are important sources of information in most communities.*

Talk About It

1. Important points: Students should choose one region and explain their choice. Explanations should include information about climate, population, and location.
2. Important points: Encourage students to suggest a variety of questions, then choose those they think most important. Possible questions would be about clothing, types of houses, languages, recreation, and types of businesses.

 ## Mastering Mapwork

1. The influence of the physical environment on human activity is likely to be greater in Dawson than in Vancouver because Dawson is farther north and is inland, receiving none of the warming winds that Vancouver receives. It is likely that people living in Dawson are more influenced by the physical environment than people living in Vancouver.
2. The environment affects people more. Most land is tundra; no trees can grow. More polar bears, foxes, seals, and caribou than people live in this region. People have done very little to change this physical environment; they have changed the ways they live to cope with the harsh environment.
3. This fact shows more environmental influence on humans. If the physical environment were not so challenging, it is likely that the population would be more evenly distributed given that there are valuable natural resources in northern Canada.
4. You would probably see the same general patterns. They are roughly at the same latitude, and both are in the Interior Plains region. They would be similar to the upper Midwest region of the United States.

CHAPTER 18 REVIEW

Lessons Learned

LESSON 1
Location and Size
Canada is the second-largest country in the world. It includes six physical regions: the Arctic Plains, Appalachian Highlands, Great Lakes-St. Lawrence Lowlands, Canadian Shield, Interior Plains, and Western Mountains.

LESSON 2
Climate and Vegetation
The Canadian climate is cold, except in British Columbia on the West Coast, where the climate is mild. The climate allows the growth of three major types of vegetation: tundra, forests, and grasslands.

LESSON 3
Canada's Changing Environment
Canada faces the environmental challenges of overfishing, logging, acid rain, and discovering safe energy sources.

458

Talk About It

1. Imagine that you and your family are moving to Canada. In which region would you choose to live? Explain your answer in as much detail as you can.
2. Imagine that a visitor from Canada is coming to your school. What questions can you ask the visitor to find out the most about the climate, resources, and people of Canada? Why would you ask these questions? Explain your answer.

Mastering Mapwork

HUMAN-ENVIRONMENTAL INTERACTION
Use the map on page 451 to answer these questions:
1. Locate Vancouver in British Columbia and Dawson in Yukon Territory. How might human-environmental interaction in these two places differ even though both are located in the Western Mountains of Canada?
2. From this map and your reading in Chapter 18 would you say that people in the Arctic Plains region affect the environment more or that the physical environment affects people more? Explain.
3. Eight out of ten Canadians live within 200 miles of the United States border. Does this fact show more environmental influence on people or more human influence on the environment? Explain.
4. Would you expect to see similar patterns of human-environmental interaction in Regina, Saskatchewan, and Winnipeg, Manitoba? Are those patterns similar to or different from those in the United States?

Becoming Better Readers

More Graphic Organizers

Graphic organizers come in a variety of shapes and sizes. Graphic organizers are tools to help organize information. Make a graphic organizer to help organize all the information you learned about Canada in this chapter.

 ## Becoming Better Readers

Important points: Students should choose or create a graphic organizer that is appropriate to the nature of the material covered. Students should be able to demonstrate how it helped them organize information.

Go to the Source

Understanding Rankings

Read the document below from the Environment Canada division of the Canadian Government. Answer the questions using information from the data.

Canadian Cities are Weather Winners!

From St. John's to Victoria, Canadians love to brag about the weather that they endure (or enjoy!). Surely their community must get the most in the entire country! But which Canadian city really is the rainiest, the snowiest or the windiest? And where is the sunshine capital?

To find the answers, David Phillips, Environment Canada's Senior Climatologist, and the nation's favorite weather guru, has analyzed 30 years of recent weather data for Canada's 100 largest cities.

Weather Category*	First place	Second place	Third place
Coldest year-round	Yellowknife NT	Thompson MB	Whitehorse YT
Warmest year-round	Chilliwack BC	Vancouver BC	Abbottsford BC
Wettest (rain and snow)	Prince Rupert BC	Port Alberni BC	Chilliwack BC
Snowiest	Gander NL	Corner Brook NL	Sept-Îles QC
Most foggy days	St. John's NL	Halifax NS	Saint John NB
Sunniest year-round	Medicine Hat AB	Estevan SK	Swift Current SK
Windiest city year-round	St. John's NL	Gander NL	Summerside PEI

*Selected categories

Questions
1. Which city gets the most snow?
2. Which city is the third-wettest in Canada? the second-wettest?
3. Explain the difference between the meaning of the "Wettest" city and the "Snowiest" city?
4. Which city is the windiest and has the most foggy days?
5. Which city is the warmest and one of the wettest?

The Land and People

459

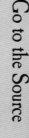

Go to the Source

Go to the Source

Understanding Rankings

OBJECTIVES: 1.02, 103

SOCIAL STUDIES SKILLS: 3.02

NOTE: The document "Canadian Cities are Weather Winners!" is part of an Environment Canada Web page. Web pages can be primary sources too. Visit NCJourneys.com for a link to the Environment Canada Weather Winners Web site. There you can see the top cities in all categories.

Answers
1. Gander NL
2. Third-wettest is Chilliwack BC; second wettest is Port Alberni BC.
3. The snowiest city just counts snow. The wettest city counts both rain and snow.
4. St. John's NL
5. Chilliwack BC

How to Use the Chapter Review

There are four sections in the Chapter Review: Talk About It, Mastering Mapwork, Becoming Better Readers, and Go to the Source. Use the Vocabulary Worksheets and the Chapter Review Worksheet in the Teacher's Resource Guide for additional reinforcement and preparation for the Chapter Assessments. The Chapter and Lesson Reviews and the Chapter Review Worksheets are the basis of the assessment for each chapter.

Talk About It questions encourage students to speculate about the content of the chapter and are suitable for class or small-group discussion. They are not intended to be assigned for homework.

Mastering Mapwork has students apply one or more of the Five Themes of Geography to maps within the chapter.

Go to the Source activities allow students to analyze a primary source that relates to the content of the chapter. The questions and activities familiarize students with different types of primary sources and also build content-reading skills.

Becoming Better Readers focuses on building reading strategy skills necessary for reading comprehension in the content areas.

CHAPTER 19

Settling a Nation

Social Studies Strands

Geographic Relationships

Cultures and Diversity

Historical Perspectives

Economics and Development

Global Connections

North Carolina Standard Course of Study

Goal 1 The learner will apply key geographic concepts to the United States and other countries of North America.

Goal 2 The learner will analyze political and social institutions in North America and examine how these institutions respond to human needs, structure society, and influence behavior.

Goal 3 The learner will examine the roles various ethnic groups have played in the development of the United States and its neighboring countries.

Goal 4 The learner will trace key developments in United States history and describe their impact on the land and people of the nation and its neighboring countries.

Goal 5 The learner will evaluate ways the United States and other countries of North America make decisions about the allocation and use of economic resources.

Teaching & Assessment

- English Language Learner Modified Lesson Plans for this chapter are found in the Teacher's Resource Guide.

- *ExamView® Assessment Suite* is provided at **NCJourneys.com**. It includes customizable assessments for all chapters. Paper tests are also available in the Teacher's Resource Guide. See pages T16–T17 for information about how to use the assessments and the Scoring Guide.

Worksheets

Worksheets and answer keys are found both in the Teacher's Resource Guide and at **NCJourneys.com**, including Reading Guides, Reading Strategies, Chapter Reviews, English Language Learner and others.

Activities and Integrations

SOCIAL STUDIES

- ■ Canada's Geography, p. 460B
- ● Provinces and Territories Memory Drill, p. 460B
- Canada, p. 461
- Changing Lifestyles of Canadian People, p. 463
- Skill Lesson: Population Distribution, p. 467
- Carolina Connection: Raleigh, p. 471
- ● ■ Time To Barter, p. 474
- Read Aloud, p. 476
- Working on the Canadian Pacific Railroad, p. 478
- Recreation for the Railroad Workers, p. 479
- Transcontinental Railway Activities, p. 479
- Setting a Purpose, p. 482

FINE ARTS	FINE ARTS OBJECTIVES
▲ ■ Building a House, p. 460B	2.01, 3.02
● ▲ ■ Inuit Mural Art, p. 463	2.01, 3.02
● ▲ Totem Pole, p. 469	2.01, 3.02
★ ▲ ■ Couriers de Bois, p. 472	2.01, 3.02

MATHEMATICS	MATHEMATICS OBJECTIVES
Making a Mosiac of the Ethnic Groups of Canada, p. 464	1.02, 4.01
Rail System, p. 480	1.02

SCIENCE	SCIENCE OBJECTIVES
★ ▲ ■ Couriers de Bois, p. 472	1.02, 1.05, 1.06

READING/LANGUAGE ARTS	READING/LANGUAGE ARTS OBJECTIVES
Activator: *Brian's Winter,* p. 460	4.03, 5.04
▲ ■ Writing Prompt: Totem, p. 460	4.06, 4.09
Reading Strategy: Making Questions, p. 462	1.02
Reading Strategy: Question Answer Relationships, p. 468	2.02
Julie of the Wolves, p. 469	2.03, 2.06
Exploring a New Land, p. 470	1.03
★ ▲ ■ Couriers de Bois, p. 472	3.06, 4.03
● ▲ ■ Create A Filmstrip, p. 473	2.03
Hudson Bay Explorer, p. 474	4.06, 4.09
Reading Strategy: Higher Level Questioning, p. 478	2.02
Becoming Better Readers, p. 484	2.01
Judging the Accuracy of Historical Fiction, p. 485	3.01

TECHNOLOGY	TECHNOLOGY OBJECTIVES
★ ▲ ■ Couriers de Bois, p. 472	2.13

CHARACTER AND VALUES EDUCATION	TRAITS
★ Problem Based Learning: What Price Development, p. 460B	good citizenship
Fight of the Loyalists, p. 476	courage
"To Build or Not To Build," p. 483	good citizenship

● Basic Activities ★ Challenging Activities ▲ English Language Learner Novice ■ English Language Learner Intermediate

Introductory Activity

Canada's Geography

OBJECTIVES: 1.02, 1.06, 1.07

Before class, collect photos from magazines, newspapers, and travel brochures of the various physical environments that exist in Canada. Include snow-covered mountains, islands, prairie lands, and frozen areas like the tundra. Divide the class into cooperative learning groups. Give each group one photo, paper, a marker, and the following directions:

1. Write a paragraph consisting of at least five sentences describing the environment in the scene. Use vivid adjectives and adverbs. Paint a word picture for your audience.
2. Write the name of the country in the Western Hemisphere where you think this photo was taken. What makes you think this?
3. Humans have to interact with and adapt to the environment, which often means changing it. For example, a town separated by a river might change the environment by building a bridge across the river. An example of adapting to the environment would be to use the available materials in a region to build shelter. Look at your photo again and tell two ways that humans could adapt to this environment or change it.
4. Present your findings to the class.

 Culminating Activity

Provinces and Territories Memory Drill

OBJECTIVES: 1.02, 1.03, 1.06

Divide the class into 13 groups. Assign each group a province or territory (see page 437). Have each group report one interesting fact about their respective province or territory. After each group has reported, call out a province or territory and see how many students can remember the fact. Repeat the activity and as more students remember the fact, pick up the pace until you can get through the list very quickly with the majority of the class repeating the fact. As an extension, ask if individual students can repeat the list alone.

 **Art Activity**

Building a House

OBJECTIVES: 1.02, 1.03, 1.05

After studying the land and environment of Canada, divide the class into 13 cooperative groups. Assign each group a province or territory of Canada. Their task is to design an energy efficient home using the resources of their area. Students may build a model or draw a blueprint. Once projects are completed, have students present them to the class and display their work.

Problem Based Learning Activity

What Price Development

OBJECTIVES: 1.02, 1.03, 1.06

Situation You are a fifth grader living in Calgary, Alberta. You live in a suburb or nice neighborhood and a nice house. The city has a great deal to offer you and your family—shopping, good schools and colleges, many cultural and sporting events, and easy access to other parts of Canada and the world. Your cousin lives in a small village in the northern regions of Alberta. His life is different from yours but he is happy in such an environment. Your cousin's father (your uncle) is a game warden who protects the wildlife in this area and tries to ensure their natural habitats.

Task You learn that a logging company in Calgary is planning to fully log a region in northern Alberta, including the region where your cousin's family lives. The company promotes good jobs and more money for the people involved, but the land would no longer be a useable home for wildlife and nature. In addition, the beautiful countryside of northern Alberta would be gone. What would you do about this situation?

Each student must read the situation and devise his or her own plan of attack.

Reflection

- What is the more important issue in this case: the idea of progress and logging the northern regions of Alberta, or the idea of preservation and saving the natural habitat? Make a list of pros and cons for each of the main issues and sides mentioned and use those reasons to support your answer.
- Who and what would be affected if this takes place? if this does not take place?
- What types of compromises do you see that might accommodate both sides?
- Who should decide whether this proposal is okay or not?

Once the assignment is complete, ask students to share their proposals. Which ones were the best? Which ones might work? Which ones would not be reasonable? Discuss personal feelings as well.

Teaching Strategies

Use graphic organizers to help students compare/contrast the first settlers of Canada with those of the United States. Emphasize how United States history has impacted the development of Canada.

Discussion Questions

1 Have you ever visited a place that you felt belonged more to the animals than to people? Would you say you were a "foreigner" there? Why?

Activator

 OBJECTIVES: 1.02, 1.03, 1.06

Read a passage from *Brian's Winter* by Gary Paulsen (Laureleaf, 1998. ISBN 0440227194). Ask the students what they learned about Canada in Chapter 18.

Writing Prompt

 OBJECTIVES: 1.02, 1.06, 2.08

Writing an Advertisement During the 1800s, Canada opened the western part of the country to settlers by building a railroad and offering free land to pioneers. Write an ad one might have seen in the 1800s for this free land. Make a small poster with your words and original illustrations.

Descriptive Writing Look at the totem on page 469. Native Americans of the Pacific Northwest and Canada made totems as a record of their families. Each section represented a member of the family. Often animals were used to represent the characteristics of the family members. Describe what the totem of your family would look like from the top to the bottom. Include members of your immediate family in your totem. How would you describe each member?

Extension Create your family's totem from construction paper. Display it with your writing.

Novice ELL students may need more explanation.

CHAPTER

19

Settling a Nation

Chapter Preview

LESSON 1
People of Canada
Canada's citizens are diverse. Native American and Inuit peoples, descendants of the French and British settlers, and new immigrants from Asia, Africa, Latin America, and Europe, make up Canada's population.

LESSON 2
First Settlers
Native Americans and Inuit first settled in Canada. Europeans began to arrive about 450 years ago.

LESSON 3
Moving West
Gold and railroads brought settlers to the prairie provinces and the North.

 Timeline of Events

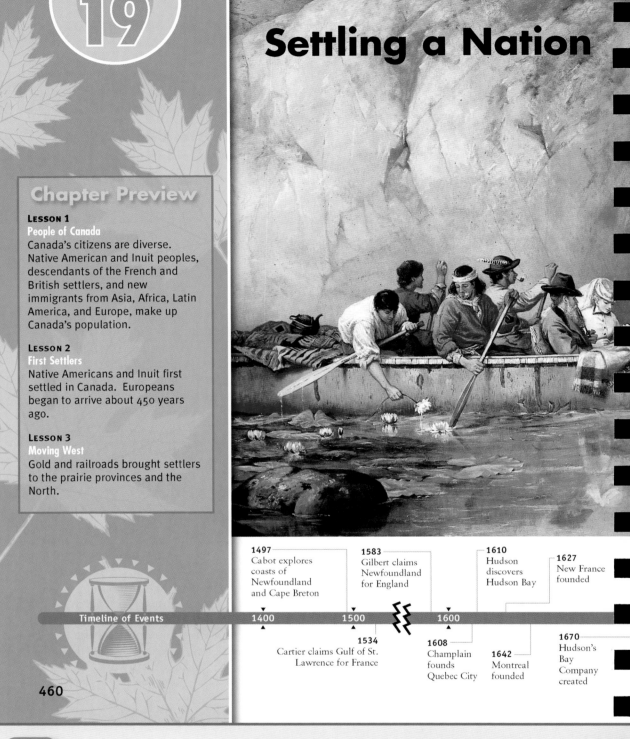

1497 Cabot explores coasts of Newfoundland and Cape Breton

1534 Cartier claims Gulf of St. Lawrence for France

1583 Gilbert claims Newfoundland for England

1608 Champlain founds Quebec City

1610 Hudson discovers Hudson Bay

1627 New France founded

1642 Montreal founded

1670 Hudson's Bay Company created

1400   1500   1600

460

 **Chapter Resources**

Print Resources

Nonfiction

Alexander, Bryan. *What Do We Know About the Inuit?* Peter Bedrick Books, 1995. ISBN 0872263800.

Cordoba, Yasmine A. *Igloo.* Rourke Book Co., 2001. ISBN 1559162775.

Harmon, Daniel E. *Jacques Cartier and the Exploration of Canada.* Chelsea House Publishers, 2001. ISBN 0791059588.

Livesey, Robert. *The Fur Traders.* Stoddart, 1989. ISBN 0773753044.

—. *The Loyal Refugees.* Stoddart Kids, 1999. ISBN 0773760431.

Martin, Jacqueline Briggs. *The Lamp, the Ice, and the Boat Called Fish.* Houghton Mifflin, 2001. ISBN 061800341X.

Mattern, Joanne. *The Travels of Samuel de Champlain.* (Explorers and Exploration series) Steadwell Books, 2001. ISBN 073981494.

Waterman, Jonathan. *Arctic Crossing: A Journey Through the Northwest Passage and Inuit Culture.* Knopf, 2001. ISBN 0375404090.

A photographer walked through a wilderness park in western Canada. He said,

Most places in North America, no matter how far you go into the wilderness, you find signs of people—a fire ring on the shore, the sound of a logging operation, a footpath. But here I've never even seen a jet trail. The birds own the sky and the only footprints come in sets of four.... If you're a person, you're a foreigner."

In some places in Canada, people are the "foreigners." The land is untouched. In other places, Canadians have reshaped the environment. In this chapter you will see ways Canadians have changed the land.

French Voyageurs were accustomed to demanding and difficult work as they transported goods and people from place to place.

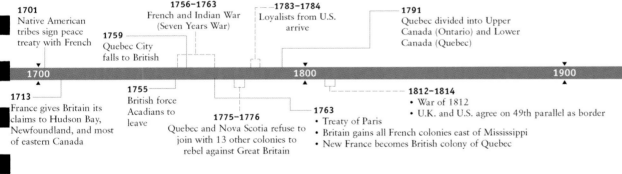

1701
Native American tribes sign peace treaty with French

1759
Quebec City falls to British

1756–1763
French and Indian War (Seven Years War)

1783–1784
Loyalists from U.S. arrive

1791
Quebec divided into Upper Canada (Ontario) and Lower Canada (Quebec)

1700 — **1800** — **1900**

1713
France gives Britain its claims to Hudson Bay, Newfoundland, and most of eastern Canada

1755
British force Acadians to leave

1775–1776
Quebec and Nova Scotia refuse to join with 13 other colonies to rebel against Great Britain

1763
• Treaty of Paris
• Britain gains all French colonies east of Mississippi
• New France becomes British colony of Quebec

1812–1814
• War of 1812
• U.K. and U.S. agree on 49th parallel as border

Fiction

Marceau-Chenkie, Brittany. *Naya, the Inuit Cinderella.* Raven Rock , 2000. ISBN 1894303059.

Norman, Howard. *The Girl Who Dreamed Only Geese: And Other Tales of the Far North.* Harcourt, 1997. ISBN 0152309799.

Reynolds, Jan. *Frozen Land: Vanishing Cultures* (Vanishing Cultures series). Harcourt, 1993. ISBN 0152387870.

Audiovisual

Canada: People and Places. North Carolina State University Humanities Extension/Publications Program. 18 minutes.

Web Sites

Visit NCJourneys.com for links:
• The Beaver Fur Hat
• Canadian Pacific Railway Archives
• The Fur Trade in New France, The Coureurs des Bois
• Sir Humphrey Gilbert's Voyage To Newfoundland, 1583
• Hudson's Bay Company
• Inuit Tapirisat of Canada
• Inuit Art
• The Kids' Site of Canadian Settlement - Library and Archives Canada
• Jacques Cartier settlement rediscovered

OBJECTIVES: 1.07, 2.08, 3.04

Discussion Questions

1 Why do Canadians describe their country as a mosaic?

2 Why do you think people from other countries move to Canada? What things do you think appeal to them about moving there?

3 What opened the way for more English colonists to move to Canada?

Reading Strategy Activity

Making Questions

OBJECTIVES: 4.02, 4.03

Review with the class the question words: Who, What, When, Where, and Why. Discuss how other higher-order question words can be asked such as How, Is, Will, Might, Can, Would, and so on.

List all the question words on the board. Read the first four paragraphs on page 462. Have volunteers ask questions from this paragraph using the higher-order words. You might write the question on an over head and let a volunteer answer the question. Continue reading and asking questions until the students are proficient. Doing this strategy in other subjects during the day will reinforce learning. It helps if students learn to write these types of questions down in a notebook and answer them each time they read something.

To continue with the text, divide the class into groups of three. One student reads the next paragraph, the second asks a question, and the third answers the question. Rotate the jobs to the right and continue reading the lesson.

When they are proficient, challenge the class to use the North Carolina Thinking Skills question stems. These ask a higher level of question. A link to these can be found at **NCJourneys.com**.

LESSON 1 People of Canada

KEY IDEAS

- The first settlers of Canada probably came thousands of years ago from Asia across the land bridge.

- Other Canadians are descendants of French and British settlers and new immigrants from Asia, the Middle East, and Europe.

- Most Canadians live along the United States border.

KEY TERMS

mosaic
New France

Canadian artist Robert Davidson was asked to describe what he liked about his country. "I like to be alone a lot. Canada is a good place to feel alone."

Why would he say this? Canada is a country of wide open spaces. But it does not have many people.

Think about the United States. Canada is bigger than our country. We have about 300 million people. Canada has about 33 million.

Canada's population is not spread out evenly across its land. Eighty percent of Canadians live within 200 miles (322 km) of the United States. The northern two thirds of Canada's land have few people.

Settlement Patterns

Several of the largest cities in Canada are found in the Great Lakes–St. Lawrence Lowlands region. These include Toronto, Montreal, and Ottawa. Ottawa is Canada's capital.

These cities are located close to other large cities in the United States. They are also located on important waterways. This has made them important for transportation and manufacturing.

On the Pacific Coast, Vancouver is in the southern part of British Columbia. It is a busy port city.

The huge spaces of northern Canada have less than 1 percent of Canada's people. Fewer people live in the Northwest, Yukon, and Nunavut Territories combined than in the city of Durham, North Carolina.

Because most of Canada is so thinly populated, even Canada's major cities are not far from the wilderness. In almost all parts of Canada, unsettled lands are no more than a few hours' drive away.

A Mosaic of Peoples

People from all over the world live in Canada today. The 2001 Census found that more than 18 percent of Canada's people were born in other countries.

Canadians compare their country to a mosaic. A *mosaic* is a type of artwork. It is made of many different small pieces. They are put together to create one large image. Canadians come from many different countries with different customs and beliefs. Together, these groups form the Canadian nation.

 Name Origin

Alberta Named after the daughter of Queen Victoria.
Manitoba Named for the chief god of the early inhabitants.
Nova Scotia Latin for "New Scotland"
Ottawa Algonquin word for "place of traders"
Prince Edward Island (PEI) Named for the son of George III who would become

the father of Queen Victoria.
Quebec French form of an Algonquin word meaning "where the river narrows"
Saskatchewan Cree name for "swift current"
Calgary Gaelic for "clear, running waters"
Montreal "Mount Royal"
Saskatoon Native American word for the edible red berries that grow along the river bank
Toronto a Wyandot word for meeting place where two major trails cross
Winnipeg Cree for "muddy water"

Canada–Population Density

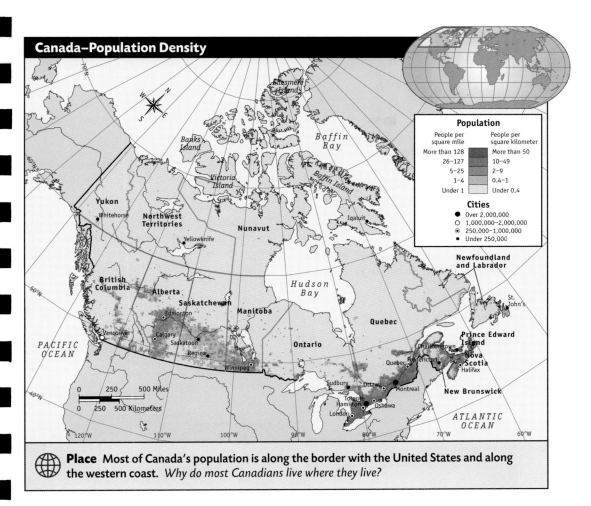

Population

	People per square mile	People per square kilometer
	More than 128	More than 50
	26–127	10–49
	5–25	2–9
	1–4	0.4–1
	Under 1	Under 0.4

Cities

● Over 2,000,000
○ 1,000,000–2,000,000
◉ 250,000–1,000,000
• Under 250,000

Place Most of Canada's population is along the border with the United States and along the western coast. *Why do most Canadians live where they live?*

The First Peoples

As you read in Chapter 4, the first settlers of Canada were Native Americans. The first people most likely walked over the land bridge from Asia. This bridge connected Asia and North America during the Ice Age. Canadians call these peoples the First Nations.

Other people, now known as the Inuit, also came from Asia. But they came near the end of the Ice Age. By then the land bridge was disappearing. Many Inuit probably came in boats.

Today, Inuit mostly live in the northern parts of the Northwest Territories, Nunavut, and Quebec. They make up less than 1 percent of Canada's people. Other Native American groups live in Canada. Many make their homes in the forest lands of the north.

At one time the Inuit and other Native Americans (First Nations) lived mainly by hunting, gathering, and fishing. After the arrival of Europeans, they rapidly lost their land to the new settlers. About 70 percent live on reservations that the government created for them. They work hard to preserve their cultures.

Settling a Nation
463

Discussion Questions

1 What is a land bridge? How could a land bridge disappear?

2 Besides losing their land, what other problems do you think Native Americans faced when Europeans moved to Canada?

3 How did the Inuit and other Native Americans live?

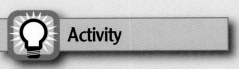

Caption Answer

The population centers are scattered along the southern border with the United States. The climate here is less harsh than farther north, and these cities are near other population and transportation centers.

Activity

Changing Lifestyles of Canadian People

OBJECTIVES: 1.07, 2.07, 3.06

Have students research the following people and their culture: Inuit, French, English, Asians, and Africans. Study the lifestyles of each group. List ways the lifestyles have changed in the last 20 years. Make a bulletin board depicting the old and new ways of life of one group.

Extension Make a bar graph and/or a pie graph showing the percentage of population growth for each group

Activity

Inuit Mural Art

OBJECTIVES: 1.06, 3.06, 3.07

Draw a picture or class mural showing ways the Inuit used the natural environment to meet their needs. Pictures might include gloves, fur skin clothing, fishing in ice. Variations include a class quilt illustrating ways the Inuit adapted to the environment, dioramas depicting village life, or models of shelters built out of plaster.

Discussion Questions

1 If so few people have moved to Canada since the early days of settlement, why do you think Canada's French-speaking population has continued to grow so steadily?

2 Who were the first Europeans to come to Canada? What did they call their colony?

3 What opened the way for more English colonists to move to Canada?

4 Today, how many Canadians have British ancestors?

 Math Activity

Making a Mosaic on the Ethnic Groups of Canada

 OBJECTIVES: 1.07, 3.04, 3.06

Students should use an almanac to find the percentages of ethnic groups making up Canada's population of 33 million people. Round the numbers to total 100 percent.

Draw a large outline map of Canada. Have students cut out circles of various colors to represent the percentage of the ethnic groups. Each ethnic group should have its own color. For example: 25 red circles would represent 25 percent. Glue these circles to the map. The circles should be located primarily within 200 miles of the United States border, where most Canadians live.

 **Caption Answer**

The name of the cafe is French.

The French and British

Except for the Native Americans, almost everyone in Canada at one time spoke either English or French.

The French France was the first European country to explore and claim parts of Canada. French trappers and traders traveled by canoe and sled, learning about the land from Native Americans.

France started a permanent colony called *New France.* About 10,000 people moved there to build the colony. Most of the French people now living in Canada are related to these early colonists.

The number of people in Canada who are French-speaking has continued to grow.

WORD ORIGINS

In 1535, Jacques Cartier first sailed the St. Lawrence River. He asked Huron villagers what their land was called. Thinking he meant their town, they replied, "kanata." *Kanata* is a Huron-Iroquois word meaning "a settlement." Cartier returned to France and claimed discovery of a new land. He called it **"Canada."**

Today, people from many French-speaking countries move to Quebec. The city of Montreal is the second-largest French-speaking city in the world. (Paris, the capital of France, is the largest). About 23 percent of Canada's population is French-speaking.

In the 1700s, France and Britain fought for control of North America in what we call the French and Indian War (Canadians call this the Seven Years War). The British won. The war ended with the Treaty of Paris in 1763.

The British Only a few British colonists moved to Canada before the United States won its war for independence from Britain. Then thousands of Loyalists, colonists who had sided with Great Britain in the revolution, fled to Canada.

Loyalists were soon followed by people from other parts of Britain—especially Scotland and Ireland. By 1867, English-speaking people outnumbered the French. Today, about 25 percent of all Canadians have British ancestry.

This is a cafe in Quebec. **What in this picture shows French culture?**

Chapter 19

Other Europeans

In the late 1800s, Canadians opened up their west to settlers. They built a railroad and offered free land. People from Iceland came to settle. Mennonites from Russia escaping religious persecution also came. People from Norway, Sweden, and Ukraine arrived. They all knew how to survive in a challenging climate.

After World War II ended, people from Italy, Greece, and Portugal settled in Canada. They were joined in the 1950s and 1960s by people from Hungary and Czechoslovakia. These refugees sought freedom in Canada after their countries were taken over by the Soviet Union.

Related to Raleigh
Several members of Sir Walter Raleigh's family explored the New World. Raleigh founded Roanoke. Sir Humphrey Gilbert, his half-brother, founded Newfoundland. Raleigh's son, Walter, was killed exploring South America; his half-nephew founded Fort St. George.

These Russian immigrants came to Canada in the early 1900s. **When did people from Italy, in southern Europe, move to Canada?**

The Canadian Colonies

You will learn more about how Canada formed a government in Chapter 20. But did you ever wonder about Canada's colonies? Were they like the 13 colonies that became the United States?

After the American Revolution, the colonies to the north of the United States were part of British North America. All of today's Canada was ruled by Great Britain.

Eastern Canada New France was founded by the French. After the French and Indian War (Seven Years War), it became a British colony. The British divided it into two parts, Ontario and Quebec. Later, these two colonies became the Province of Canada.

New Brunswick, Newfoundland and Labrador, Nova Scotia, and Prince Edward Island were all separate British colonies before joining Canada. Like the 13 American colonies, they each had their own governments.

Western Canada British Columbia was part of the Oregon Territory given to the United Kingdom and the United States by Spain. It became a British colony.

Manitoba and Northwest Territories were created in 1870 from lands bought from the Hudson's Bay Company. The Northwest Territories at one time covered most of northern and western Canada. Yukon, Alberta, Saskatchewan, and Nunavut were all once part of the Northwest Territories.

Settling a Nation

465

Discussion Questions

1 What other European groups settled in Canada?

2 What is Canada's most important waterway?

3 The text says that more than half of all Canadians live in the Great Lakes–St. Lawrence Lowlands region, partly because of its location. What other reasons can you think of that make this area a desirable place to live?

 ELL Teaching Tips

Be Aware of Culture Shock
The new ELL student in your classroom is probably suffering from culture shock. Imagine how you would feel if you were in his or her shoes! Make sure you create an environment where the ELL student feels safe. This will lessen the intensity and duration of culture shock.

 **Caption Answer**

After World War II

Discussion Questions

1 Which provinces are in the Interior Plains? How are they similar to the area of United States located south of them?

2 Why do you think Asian immigrants are attracted to Canada?

3 How did moving across the Canadian border keep men from serving as soldiers in the United States? Why do you think they went to Canada rather than to another country? Do you agree with their decision to do this? Why or why not?

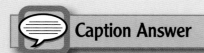 **Caption Answer**

Most Asians move to western Canada, especially Vancouver, Calgary, and Edmonton, and to Toronto in the East. They are looking for new opportunities, and many want to live in communities with other Asians.

Canadians from Asia and Africa

In the 1880s, more than 15,000 Chinese workers helped build Canada's first railroad in the west. They became the first Asian settlers of Canada. From these roots, the Chinese community in Canada has grown.

In recent years, the cities of Toronto, Vancouver, Calgary, and Edmonton have attracted Asian immigrants.

People of African descent make up less than 1 percent of Canada's population. Many have come to Canada from island countries in the Caribbean. Other have come from South Africa, Somalia, and other areas of Africa.

Immigrants from the United States

Before the Civil War, many enslaved African Americans escaped to Canada. Slavery had been outlawed in Canada. Most Canadians were against slavery. Some of them wrote a song about the goals of the runaway slaves:

> I'm on my way to Canada
> That cold and distant land
> The dire effects of slavery
> I can no longer stand—
> Farewell old master,
> Don't come after me.
> I'm on my way to Canada
> Where men are free.

The Vietnam War in the 1960s again brought United States citizens to Canada. More than 32,000 young men moved across the border rather than serve as soldiers in that war. Many stayed and settled. Some did come back to the United States when they were allowed to return several years after the war ended.

Asian immigrants first moved to Canada to help build a railroad across the country. Many wealthy Asians now invest in the country. **To what part of Canada do most Asians move? Why?**

LESSON **1** REVIEW

Fact Follow-Up
1. Who were the first Canadians? Where did they settle?
2. From what areas of Europe have people moved to Canada? When did each group move?

Talk About It
1. What are some challenges facing a country with two or more languages spoken by entire provinces?
2. Why have European and other groups moved to Canada? Has life in Canada lived up to their expectations?

LESSON **1** REVIEW

Fact Follow-Up Answers
1. It is believed that the first Canadians were people who migrated from Asia over the land bridge during the Ice Age. These people came in two groups. The first were Native American; the second were the Inuit.
2. During colonial times in the 1600s and 1700s, settlers came from France, then Great Britain. During the late 1800s, European settlers came from colder parts of Europe, including Iceland, Norway, Sweden, Russia, and Ukraine. In the last century, Greeks, Italians, and Portuguese emigrated to Canada after World War II. Refugees from Eastern Europe, especially Hungary and Czechoslovakia, came to Canada in the 1950s and 1960s.

Talk About It Answers
1. Countries where more than one language is officially spoken face several challenges: schools must teach both (all) languages so that citizens can communicate with each other, governments and businesses must be able to provide information to all citizens, and TV, radio, and newspapers must have programs or papers in both languages.
2. Europeans, Africans, and Asians who arrived in the last century came for safety, better jobs, and political freedom. Earlier Europeans came for the opportunities provided by the resources of fur and fish (in colonial times) and agricultural land (during the 1800s) in Canada. All of these expectations have been for the most part fulfilled.

Analyzing, Interpreting, Creating, and Using Resources and Materials

Population Distribution in Canada

The same information can be shown in different ways. So it is good to learn how to read different kinds of graphs, tables, maps, and charts.

Reading a Table or Graph

Look at these two different charts. They both show the population distribution in Canada. One shows this data in a table. The other shows this data in a bar graph.

The table shows information with words and numbers. It is a list. Look at the table. You can see the percentage of Canada's total population for each province and territory.

You can take data from the table. Use it to make a bar graph.

Reading a Map

The population density map on page 463 gives different information. Colors show you how the population is spread out in different areas. From the map you can learn how many people live in one area.

Using the Information

Being able to see information in different ways can be helpful. For example, suppose that you are opening a business to sell HDTVs in Canada. Your company needs to have one warehouse for each 1 million people. You know that Canada has about 33 million people.

How could you use these tables to figure out how many warehouses you need? Will these tables also help you decide on how many warehouses will be needed in each province? Can you use the map to help locate the warehouses? How?

Canadian Population Distribution, 2001

Province/Territory	Percentage of Total Population
Alberta	9.9%
British Columbia	13.0%
Manitoba	3.7%
New Brunswick	2.4%
Newfoundland	1.7%
Nova Scotia	3.0%
Ontario	38.0%
Prince Edward Island	0.45%
Quebec	24.1%
Saskatchewan	3.26%
Northwest Territories	.124%
Yukon Territory	.095%
Nunavut	.089%

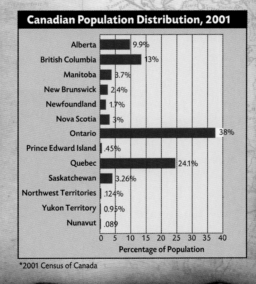

Canadian Population Distribution, 2001

Alberta 9.9%
British Columbia 13%
Manitoba 3.7%
New Brunswick 2.4%
Newfoundland 1.7%
Nova Scotia 3%
Ontario 38%
Prince Edward Island .45%
Quebec 24.1%
Saskatchewan 3.26%
Northwest Territories .124%
Yukon Territory 0.95%
Nunavut .089

Percentage of Population (0 5 10 15 20 25 30 35 40)

*2001 Census of Canada

Settling a Nation

Teaching This Skill Lesson

Materials Needed textbooks, paper, pencils, map of Canada to use on an overhead projector, AV markers of different colors

Classroom Organization whole class, small groups

Beginning the Lesson If a new business has recently opened or closed in your community, ask students' opinions about the event, focusing on why it occurred. Ask what criteria are considered when locating or closing businesses, and record students' responses on the chalkboard.

Lesson Development Direct students to study the population distribution charts in the Skill Lesson and the population density map on page 463. Ask which information is easier to work with, accepting all answers.

Place students in small groups and tell them that they will be deciding the locations of warehouses for a business that will be distributing television sets all over Canada. There will be one warehouse for every 1 million people, and Canada has a total population of 33 million people. Students are to use the population distribution map and the two population distribution charts in making their decisions as to where the warehouses are to be located. Encourage students to use their mathematical skills in making their decisions.

Conclusion As groups make their reports, use different colored markers to locate warehouses. Have students discuss any noticeable similarities or differences in their decisions.

Skill Lesson Review

1. Why might someone use a bar graph instead of printed percentages to present information? *A bar graph can present information that can be seen quickly.*
2. A fast-food company will use only a population density map to choose sites for new restaurants. Why? *They want a site with a sufficient population to support the business. A population density map shows where most people live.*
3. Think of some information you have about Canada, something you want others to know. What is the best way to present information?

Explain. *Important points: Encourage students to suggest several formats; lead them to understand that some formats are better than others depending on the information to be presented. Photographs, maps, bar graphs, pie charts, videos, Web sites, and the written word are possibilities.*

4. What are some problems of using maps and graphs to present information? What are some benefits? *Maps and graphs include no interpretation of information. However, they can be a quick way to present facts.*

LESSON 2 First Settlers

Discussion Questions

1 What does it mean to be "resourceful"? In what ways are the Inuit resourceful?

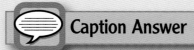

Caption Answer

They learned to fish and hunt. They also used animal skins for clothing and tents.

Reading Strategy Activity

Question Answer Relationships (QAR)

OBJECTIVES: 4.07, 5.04, 5.06

Questioning makes students more involved in any lesson. This means not only answering teacher-made questions but making their own questions as well. QAR is a strategy to help students use background knowledge to develop their own questions.

Use the story *The Three Little Pigs* to introduce four types of questions:
- **Right There** The answer can be found in only one sentence in the text. (What did the first little pig use to build his house?)
- **Think and Search** The answer is in the text, but it is in several sentences or paragraphs. (Describe the house.)
- **Author and Me** The answer is not in the book. You must take what you already know or believe and what is in the book to answer the question. You must read the material to know how to answer the question. (Did the third pig act wisely when the wolf came to his house?)
- **On My Own** The answer is not in the book, but the book makes you think about what you already know. You could answer the question without reading the material. (Would you be afraid if you saw a wolf in the woods?)

After teaching the four questions and giving several examples with each

KEY IDEAS

- Native Americans adapted to Canada's climate.
- European explorers used the land's resources. Fish and furs were important for trade.

KEY TERMS

beavers
coureurs de bois
deportation
Grand Banks
umiaks
wigwams

The wind blows cold. The temperature drops below zero. Six sleds pulled by dogs cross the ice. Everyone is warm inside sealskin coats. The Inuit villagers cross the tundra. Tatatuapik (ta·ta·TOO·ah·pik) signals everyone to stop. He has found a lake under the snow and ice. He takes out his ice-cutting knife. He scrapes away the snow from the ice below him to make a fishing hole. Now there will be fish for dinner.

It is time to stop for the night. Everyone will need a place to sleep. There are few building materials on the treeless tundra. So Tatatuapik and the others use their long bone knives to carve blocks out of the packed snow. They stack the blocks to build a snowhouse.

The Inuit

It takes special skills to live in the Arctic. Knowing which way to go on flat, snow-covered ground takes great skill. An Inuit person will carefully look for the patterns the wind makes on snowdrifts. This helps him or her find their direction.

For thousands of years the Inuit have survived in the harsh environment of the Arctic. They use the resources of the sea and land. They have fished and hunted to get food and clothing.

They have used the skins of seals, caribou, and other animals. They make soft fur-lined jackets and sealskin boots to keep out the cold. They stretch animal skins over a whalebone frame. This makes lightweight summer tents. They use kayaks and **umiaks,** sealskin boats, to cross rivers and oceans. Whale oil gives heat and light. Meat, fat, and bone have their uses, too.

The Inuit have lived in the Arctic for thousands of years. **How do they survive in this environment?**

kind, tell students they are going to be the teacher. Divide the classroom into cooperative groups. Assign one of the four types of questions to each group. Read aloud pages 468–469. Have the groups make a question of the type you assigned to their group. Share questions aloud and call on students to answer each group's question.

Continue with the other sections in this lesson. Change the group's assignment of question types. Make certain each group has different types of

questions by the end of the section. Some groups will have difficulty writing certain types of questions with some sections and may require help.

Natives in the Northern Forests

Like the Inuit, Native American settlers of Canada's forests also lived off the land. The Slave (slah·VAY), Cree, and Ojibwe (oh·JIB·way) hunted, gathered, and fished. The forests gave wood to build homes. But the cold climate and the rocky ground of the Canadian Shield made them work hard to live.

In the northern forests, Native Americans built homes called *wigwams*. These were made from trees and animal skins. Native Americans made clothing from the soft skin of deer, caribou, and elk.

They also made canoes out of bark. Canoes were good boats for small streams and rivers. Paddlers could easily carry the light boats from one body of water to another.

Along the Yukon River, the Athabascan (ah·THAH·bas·kahn) people hunted rabbits. They ate the meat and used the fur for warmth. In summer the Athabascans fished

for salmon. They hunted moose in the fall. In the winter, caribou were hunted for food and fur. The wood of the forests fueled cooking fires and provided logs for cabins.

Both Inuit and other Native Americans respected their environment. They lived close to the land. They taught their children to treat it wisely. These peoples valued its resources. They took only what they needed.

Customs

Bone Game: The Inuit play variations on a bone game. It uses a small caribou leather bag with about 40 seal and bird bones. There are a few different ways to play. In one game, players compete to rebuild the skeleton of a seal's flipper or bird's foot. In another, players try to take bones from the bag using a noose on the end of a leather thong to hook the bones.

This is a replica of a western red cedar totem pole. It was carved by Native Americans of the northern forests. **How else did the native peoples use trees?**

Securing a Nation   469

Discussion Questions

1 What are some of the ways the other Native American tribes lived off the land?

 **Caption Answer**

They made homes and canoes from trees.

 **Activity**

Julie of the Wolves

OBJECTIVES: 1.01, 1.02, 1.03

After reading the book *Julie of the Wolves* by Jean Craighead (HarperTrophy, 1974. ISBN 0064400581.), students will make a map of Alaska.

Use an atlas to make and label the map as follows:
- North Slope (where Julie was lost)
- Brooks Range
- Arctic Ocean
- Chukchi Sea
- Beaufort Sea
- Bering Sea (father presumed lost here)
- Arctic Ocean
- Barrow (where she lived with Daniel's family)
- Nunivak Island (seal camp where she lived with her father)
- Point Hope
- Avalik River (where she met Inuit couple)
- Kangik (Inuit village where her father was)

Activity

Totem Pole

OBJECTIVES: 1.02, 1.06, 1.07

Let students form groups called "clans" to work on individual totem poles. Gather cardboard tubes from gift wrap or paper towels and cut into 6-inch sections. Glue each section to a 3-inch by 3-inch cardboard platform to make it stand alone. Cereal boxes

can be used since tubes are lightweight. Students should draw three or four figures on the tube with pencil and outline the figures with black marker to make them more distinct.

Each group should choose three colors to represent its clan. All members will paint their poles using the colors of the clan. Use white to highlight eyes, mouths, and other features. Caution students to use only small paint brushes and very little paint.

Caption Answer

The St. Lawrence River and the Great Lakes. The French were the first to explore the Great Lakes area, which offered trapping.

 Activity

Exploring a New Land

 OBJECTIVES: 1.06, 1.07, 4.07

Neil Armstrong, the first person to walk on the moon, and John Cabot, the first European to explore North America, are both important figures in our history. Which one made the greatest contribution? Conduct a debate, with one side supporting Neil Armstrong and the other supporting John Cabot. Use the Guide to Student Debates in the Teacher's Edition.

Extension Role-play an encounter between Cabot and Armstrong. Have them compare trips. Interview the two explorers and record it on a cassette tape.

Draw posters showing their similarities and differences

 Activity

Explorers

 OBJECTIVES: 1.07, 4.01, 4.07

Have students imagine that they are John Cabot about to set sail for the rich fishing grounds of the North Atlantic. Students should create an advertisement to recruit sailors for the voyage and exploration.

Extensions
- Role-play a scene that might have taken place on Cabot's ship.
- Role-play a scene on Henry Hudson's ship when Hudson, his son, and loyal followers were put adrift in Hudson Bay.
- Dramatize Cartier's claiming Quebec for France in 1530.
- Research Hudson, Cabot, Cartier, and

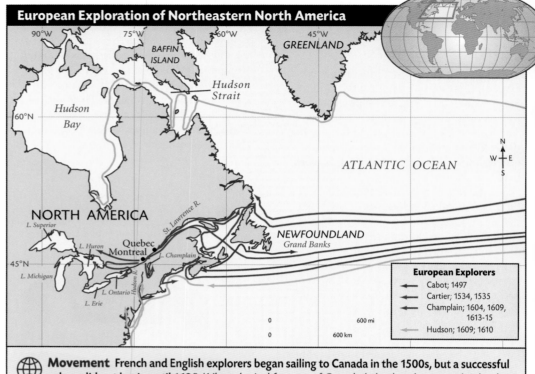

Movement French and English explorers began sailing to Canada in the 1500s, but a successful colony did not begin until 1635. *What physical features of Canada helped explorers reach inland areas? From the map key can you tell why the French were the first Europeans to begin settling Canada?*

John Cabot, in his search for the Northwest Passage, explored the waterways of what is now eastern Canada. **What was the Northwest Passage?**

Champlain. Make a chart showing the country each represented, the area each explored, and the dates of his exploration.

 **Caption Answer**

Europeans believed there was a Northwest water route through North America that would get them to Asia.

European Explorers

Dreams of gold and spices brought the early European explorers to Canada. But fish and furs made them stay.

When the Europeans came, they saw the land differently than the Native Americans did. The Europeans changed Canada's environment. They changed how natural resources were used.

Cabot

One of the first explorers was John Cabot. He sailed in 1497 and claimed the island of Newfoundland for England. He also found the **Grand Banks.** This is a rich fishing area off the Atlantic coast. His men could easily catch many codfish. They just attached baskets to ropes and trailed them over the side of the ship.

Reports of this great fishing spot attracted people from England, Portugal, and France. The coves and bays of the Atlantic coast made good harbors. Fishing boats used them when sailing to or from the Grand Banks.

Almost 40 years after Cabot left, French King Francis I sent Jacques Cartier to Canada. The king wanted him to claim land for a colony called New France.

Cartier

Cartier wanted to find a water route to Asia. Europeans called this legendary route the Northwest Passage. They believed this route would be found in the far north of North America. The nation that could find it first would be very lucky. It would control the trade in silk, jewels, and spices from Asia.

Cartier made three trips to Canada. On the second he went up the St. Lawrence. He sailed more than 900 miles (1,449 km) up the St. Lawrence from where it flows into the Atlantic. His travels were stopped by giant rapids near the hill he called Mont Réal (later called Montreal).

Champlain

In 1608, another French explorer sailed for Canada. Samuel de Champlain followed Cartier's old route up the St. Lawrence. He stopped at the hill the natives called Quebeck, meaning where the river narrows in Algonquian. There he started a colony.

Natives brought the colony food to eat and furs to trade. The fur trade helped the colony do well. This became Quebec City, the capital of New France.

Word Origins

The city of **Montreal** is named for a hill. The hill was near the rapids that kept explorer Jacques Cartier from going farther up the St. Lawrence River. Cartier named the hill Mont Réal. It means "Royal Mountain" in French.

Samuel de Champlain built an outpost for France at Quebec. **How was this French settlement like the English settlement in Massachusetts?**

Settling a Nation

471

Discussion Questions

1 Who was one of the first explorers in Canada? What did he find and report about that caused other Europeans to come to Canada?

2 When and why did Jacques Cartier come to Canada?

3 How many trips did he make?

Caption Answer

Native Americans helped the struggling colonists with food, just as in Plymouth.

Activity

Carolina Connection: Raleigh

OBJECTIVES: 1.07

Have students locate all of the places mentioned in the text that Raleigh's family members visited and explored on a map of the Western hemisphere. Using a Venn Diagram or other graphic organizer, have students compare Newfoundland or Fort St. George with Roanoke using the map and information from Chapter 5 (the end of Lesson 2 and beginning of Lesson 3).

Background Information

Naming Canada

In 1535, Jacques Cartier traveled by ship up the St. Lawrence River as far as the village of Stadacona. This village stood on the site of what is today Quebec City. On his explorations two Native Americans guided him. When Cartier and his expedition arrived in Stadacona, Cartier asked the two men what the village was called. They used the Huron-Iroquois word "Kanata" for Stadacona. Although the word means "village" or "settlement," Cartier thought it was the name of the country; so he returned to France calling the place he had explored "Canada."

Discussion Questions

1 What were *couriers de bois*? What did the Europeans want to buy from them?

2 What were cital? What did the Europeans want to buy from them?

 Eyewitness Activity

Coureurs de Bois

OBJECTIVES: 1.02, 1.03, 1.06

Have students choose one of the animals mentioned in the selection and find out more about its behavior. What is its habitat? How does it get its food? What predators threaten it? How did the settlers use this animal? Draw, paint, or sculpt the animal and share it with the class.

The French and Indian fur traders often used canoes to travel to trapping areas. Each canoe was made of a wood frame covered in bark from a birch tree. The bark was sewn together with spruce tree roots. The canoe was sealed with a sticky substance from spruce or pine trees. Although the canoe could carry a heavy load, it was light enough to be carried by one man. Most canoes would hold about eight people. Designs or marks were etched on the birch bark.

Have students draw a canoe and add their own markings. Color the canoe brown. Have them write a short story about the time they went trapping with the coureurs de bois in the Canadian wilderness.

Extension ELL students can make the canoe and omit the short story.

EYEWITNESS TO HISTORY

Coureurs de Bois

The *coureurs de bois* (coo·RUHR duh bwah) were French scouts. They traded with Native American tribes in Canada. They learned how to live in the Canadian wilderness from the tribes they traded with. *Coureurs de bois* means runners of the woods in English.

The object of the *coureurs de bois'* trade was fur. They traded with native leaders for pelts [furskins] of beaver, mink, otter, and bear. Native Americans got knives, pots, guns, blankets, and new metal fishing hooks.

Beaver pelts

Trading with Native Americans

Coureurs de bois had to know several Native American languages in order to do the trading.

Indians Portaging Furs *by Cornelius Krieghoff*

Activity

Create a Filmstrip

OBJECTIVES: 1.07, 2.07, 2.08

Make a filmstrip using acetate/transparencies or laminating scraps on the overhead projector. On a plain sheet of paper, draw off sections to represent frames for a filmstrip. Give each student or group a copy. Have students research Native American tribes and culture (see list below). Students will plan their oral report and illustrate it on acetate with markers. Tape the frames in order in one single line. The overhead becomes the filmstrip projector. Cover the overhead with a sheet of paper that has a rectangle cut out of it. Pull the filmstrip through as students present their reports. Play Native American (First Nations) music in the background as reports are given.

First Nations	Slave
Cree	Oijbwa
Athabascan	Inuit
topics about Indians	celebrations
homes	food
clothing	religious
beliefs	transportation
way of life	

Extension Intermediate and novice ELL students can work with a partner.

*T*he *coureurs de bois* became skilled woodsmen. Native Americans taught them how to build sturdy shelters. These would protect them from heavy winter snows. They also learned how to make birch bark canoes. The canoes were small, light, and steady. They made traveling Canadian rivers easier. The *coureurs de bois* who paddled the canoes came to be called *voyageurs.*

*E*ven with their skill and new knowledge, *coureurs de bois* were often cold and lonely. One wrote in his diary: "I long to see the smoke from the chimneys of Jonquiere [a colonial settlement] curling up to meet the sky. I am tired and wet... In a month I will rent a room ... and bask before the fire, warming my poor feet and drinking spiced tea."

Hudson's Bay Company voyageurs

Settling a Nation

Discussion Questions

1 What English explorer came to Canada? What large body of water did he claim for England?

2 What treasures did later settlers find in Canada?

Activity

Time to Barter

OBJECTIVES: 1.02, 1.06, 1.07

Discuss the development of the Hudson Bay region. Include the importance of fur trading and trapping in the area. The French trappers and the Native Americans often bartered. To illustrate this economic concept, instruct students to write an advertisement describing what goods or services they are willing to give.

For example, I will clean out your desk and pack your bookbag for two days; I will copy your assignments from the board for a week.

Then have students write what they would like to receive in return. For examples, I would like a new sharpened Number 2 pencil; I would like a candy bar.

Let students carry out the bartering process (one class period). Be sure to review all barters.

Writing Activity

Hudson Bay Explorer

OBJECTIVES: 1.02, 1.06, 1.07

Imagine that you are an explorer in the Hudson Bay area. Create a diary telling what you would find and the sights you would see as you travel.

Extension Include maps of the area and illustrations of its people, animals, and vegetation.

The Fur Trade

European explorers never found gold. They did not find the Northwest Passage to Asia. But, they did find *beavers.* Europeans wanted to buy beaver pelts (skins) because of their special fur.

French traders called *coureurs de bois* loaded their canoes with trade goods. They left New France and searched the forests for furs.

Montreal became the center of the French fur trade. Montreal was located on the St. Lawrence River, the highway of the colony. It was a natural place to store fur pelts, buy supplies, and rest.

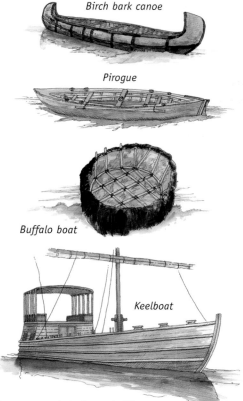

Birch bark canoe

Pirogue

Buffalo boat

Keelboat

The coureurs de bois *used different types of boats to travel North America's rivers.* **Why would they need more than one kind of boat?**

Fur was used in Europe to make clothing, and beaver hats, like this man's cloak and hat. **What city was the center of the French fur trade?**

Hudson's Bay Company

The English saw the success of the French. They also wanted a share of the fur trade. They, too, had colonies in North America. They also had a claim to Canada.

Two centuries earlier, English explorer Henry Hudson had claimed what he thought was a giant sea for England. That sea is called Hudson Bay. Hudson's travels ended badly—his unhappy crew left him to starve to death.

Hudson's explorations did lead to a rich reward for the English. This reward was a share in the fur trade. In the late 1600s, England founded the Hudson's Bay Company. The company became a rival to New France's traders.

Besides beavers, Canada's forests held minks, wolves, and otters. The search for these furs drew both English and French traders farther and farther west.

474

Caption Answer

They had to carry different supplies, and travel through a variety of conditions.

Caption Answer

Montreal was the center for the fur trade.

Tragedy for the Acadians

"Acadian" was the name for the French people who lived in the French colony of Acadia, centered in today's Nova Scotia. They first settled there in 1604 and lived mostly along the coast. Their villages were located on the border of two great colonial empires. They were often caught in the middle of conflicts between the French and British. Acadians tried to stay neutral.

In 1713, the French gave Acadia to the British. The British disliked Acadians for many reasons. One reason was because the French and British had been enemies for hundreds of years. Religion was another reason. The French were Catholics. Most of the British were Protestants.

In 1756, the first year of the French and Indian War (Seven Years War), the British wanted the Acadians to help fight the French. The Acadians refused. So the British decided to make them leave. They burned the Acadians' homes and took their land. About 12,000 men, women, and children were forced onto ships. Most were taken to the southern colonies. Forcing people to leave their homes is called **deportation.**

Later, some of the Acadians made their way back to Nova Scotia. Others headed southwest to Louisiana. There they became known as the *Cajuns*. The word cajun comes from the word Acadian. Many descendants of the Cajuns still live in Louisiana today.

In 2003, Queen Elizabeth II issued a proclamation. It recognized the wrongs the Acadians suffered during the removal. Starting in 2005, Canada's government made July 28 a day to remember the Acadian deportation.

The Acadians were forced to leave their homes right away. They had little time to pack anything, and many had to leave all of their belongings. **How would you feel if you were forced to leave your home and all your possessions?**

Settling a Nation

475

 **Caption Answer**

Answers will vary.

Discussion Questions

1 Why were the Acadian forced to leave?

2 Are there still disagreements and conflicts in the world today involving different religious beliefs?

3 Why do you think people fight over religion?

4 Do you think the word Cajun sounds like the word Acadian? how might they be connected?

 Teacher Notes

The French and British in Acadia

When English explorer John Cabot visited what is now Nova Scotia in 1497, there were two groups of Algonquin-speaking indigenous peoples, the Abnaki and the Micmac, already living there. Although the English were the first modern Europeans to explore Nova Scotia, it was the French who first claimed it in 1524. By 1604, they had established a struggling colony there known as Acadia.

The colony was plagued by infighting among the Jesuit missionaries and the colony's Protestant patrons. Over the next several decades the French were repeatedly challenged by the British for control of the area. In 1621, King James renamed the area Nova Scotia, offering it to Scottish colonists, although the French continued to resist for the remainder of the seventeenth century. Ultimately, the Treaty of Utrecht in 1713 confirmed British control, with a number of French "Acadians" being permitted to remain more or less unmolested by their British landlords.

In 1744, however, the French and British again battled over Nova Scotia, but by this time the Acadians were, for the most part, unwilling combatants, and the British prevailed. Despite their apparent loyalty to the British crown, the Acadians were accused of collaboration and it was decided that they should be deported. Between 1755 and 1760, several thousand Acadians were relocated throughout colonial America, the most sizeable group ending up in Louisiana.

The Story of Evangeline

Discussion Questions

1 What are some other groups of people we have studied this year who have been forced to leave their homes?

2 When we read a fictional story about a historical event, should we believe everything we read in the story?

3 How can we tell the difference between fact and fiction?

Activity

Read Aloud

OBJECTIVES: 3.06, 3.07, 4.02, 4.03

Read aloud selected segments of the poem "Evangeline." After reading, have students illustrate their favorite part of the poem. Encourage students to remember the historic setting of the tale, and to try to depict it accurately.

Activity

Flight of the Loyalists

OBJECTIVES: 1.07, 2.08, 4.07

Have students read a historical novel about the American Revolution, such as *Johnny Tremain* by Esther Forbes or *Sarah Bishop* by Scott O'Dell. Have students pretend that their parents have just told them they are going to have to leave North Carolina. The year is 1783, and the American Revolution has just ended. The American colonists have defeated Great Britain and are no longer under the rule of King George III. Your parents believe that it was wrong for the 13 colonies to break away from the mother country, Great Britain. Because of this belief, your family will move to Canada and start all over again. Some questions they can explore are:

1. What will you miss in North Carolina?
2. What hardships might your family encounter in the move?
3. How will you travel to Canada?
4. What landforms and bodies of water will you see?

Historians write about important events in the past. But sometimes we can also learn from stories of people who lived through those events.

Some poets, novelists, and playwrights write about the past, too. Their stories are fiction. But the setting of the story may be based in history. The setting is where and when the story takes place. Characters in the story show us what life may have been like for people who lived in other times.

Almost 100 years after the Acadians were forced to leave, Henry Wadsworth Longfellow wrote a poem. He imagined what it must have been like for these people. His poem is called "Evangeline." It tells the story of a young Acadian girl named Evangeline Bellefontaine and her love for Gabriel Lajeunesse.

In the story, Evangeline and Gabriel have just become engaged. They look forward to a happy life together. But before they are married, the British navy arrives. The captain tells the villagers that they must move.

Namely, that all your lands, and dwellings, and cattle of all kinds

Forfeited be [given over] to the crown; and that you yourselves from this province
Be transported [moved] to other lands. God grant you may dwell there
Ever as faithful subjects, a happy and peaceable people!
Prisoners now I declare you; for such is his Majesty's pleasure [wish]!"

The British soldiers force everyone in the village from their homes. The Acadians boarded ships to be taken away.

...forth came the guard, and marching in gloomy procession [lines]
Followed the long-imprisoned, but patient, Acadian farmers.

Evangeline stands on the shore and watches as Gabriel and his father sail away. Before she can board a ship, Evangeline's father dies.

Evangeline spends the rest of her life searching for Gabriel. She sails down the Mississippi River. She does not know that Gabriel

has passed by her on a raft going the other way. When Evangeline arrives in Louisiana, she finds Gabriel's father. He tells her his son has gone north to look for her.

Others tell Evangeline that they are sure Gabriel lives in Michigan. So Evangeline travels there. But when she arrives, Gabriel cannot be found.

After wandering for many more years, Evangeline arrives in Philadelphia. There, she decides to become a nun. She spends the rest of her life caring for the poor and the sick.

When many people come down with an illness, Evangeline finds Gabriel among the sick. He is now an old man. Gabriel dies in her arms. Evangeline dies a short time later. She is buried next to Gabriel in a graveyard in Philadelphia.

All was ended now, the hope, and the fear, and the sorrow,
All the aching of heart, the restless, unsatisfied longing,
All the dull, deep pain, and constant anguish of patience!

At the end of the poem, Longfellow reminds the reader that now another people "with other customs and language" lives in Acadia.

Today, this poem helps us think about history. We know that Evangeline was not a real person. We also know that some things in the poem did not really happen.

Yet we can still think about why the British made the Acadians leave. We can also think about other people in history who have been forced to leave their homes. We have read about some of those groups in our study of North America.

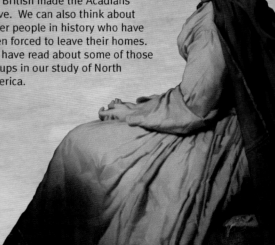

The Loyalists

Supporters of the British in the 13 colonies that became the United States were called Loyalists. They believed the Americans were wrong to separate from Britain.

Many feared for their lives. Some lost their homes. Others were persecuted for their beliefs.

Many fought back. British Captain Banastre Tarleton was the commander of the "loyal legion" of Loyalists. Tarleton was called "Bloody Tarleton" because of his attacks on the Patriots. One historian wrote that Tarleton "wrote his name in the letters of blood all across the history of the war in the South."

After the American Revolution ended, about 40,000 Loyalists moved from the United States to Canada.

The Move North

The Loyalists packed all they could into trunks. Some were wealthy merchants and landowners. Others were carpenters and craftspeople.

They closed their houses, stores, and workshops. When they left, many did not think they would ever see their homes again.

Once they reached the safety of their new homes, many Loyalists had more hardships ahead of them.

In 1783, a young barrelmaker wrote that Loyalists from Virginia and the Carolinas were living in a ship "crowded like a sheeppen." Other Loyalists were lucky to be on shore. They made do with houses "built from sods, where men, women, children, pigs, bugs, mosquitoes and other insects all mingl'd [mingled, or lived together] in society."

Loyalists helped develop the areas where they settled in Canada. They were loyal to the British government.

Loyalists fled the new United States to Canada. **Why did they have to leave their homes?**

Discussion Questions

1 Do you think it was right of the Patriots to force the Loyalists to leave their homes?

2 One of the values of the United States is freedom of speech. Americans believe that you should have the right to express a different opinion. Were the Loyalists allowed to have a different opinion from the Patriots?

 Caption Answer

They wished to remain loyal to Great Britain and American colonists were fighting for independence from Great Britain.

LESSON 2 REVIEW

Fact Follow-Up
1. How did the earliest Canadians interact with their physical environment?
2. Who were the first Europeans to visit Canada? Why did they visit?
3. How did Europeans interact with the physical environment of Canada?

Talk About It
1. The French claimed a large empire in North America and settled it mainly with a few thousand fur traders. Compare this to how the English settled their colonies.
2. Compare and contrast the Loyalists and Acadians.

Settling a Nation

477

LESSON 2 REVIEW

Fact Follow-Up Answers
1. They learned to make warm clothes, build snug shelters, and preserve food for the harsh winters. People of the forest lands built shelters and canoes from trees and animal skins. All learned to hunt the animals of Canada—caribou, rabbit, and moose.
2. The first Europeans were the French, then the British. Dreams of gold and spices first led them to Canada. They stayed because of furs and fishing.
3. Europeans used baskets and metal hooks to fish for cod. Trappers built canoes to paddle inland. There they hunted beaver for fur. They built towns in Canada to trade beaver and later wolf, mink, and otter furs.

Talk About It Answers
1. The English founded colonies with many settlers. They built farming communities and, like the French, trapped and fished.
2. Important points: The Acadians and the Loyalists were both forced from their homes and had to leave everything behind. The Loyalists were forced out by other Citizens (Patriots); the Acadians were forced out by the government. The Acadians largely fled to America; the Loyalists largely fled to Canada. The British welcomed the Loyalists; the British forced the Acadians to leave.

OBJECTIVES: 1.05, 1.07, 4.07, 5.02

Discussion Questions

1 What made the settlement of the plains provinces possible?

 Reading Strategy Activity

Higher-Level Questioning

OBJECTIVES: 1.05, 1.07, 4.07, 5.02

Most often, teachers ask the questions in the classroom. This works great when all the students are focused on the discussion. But what happens if some students are not paying attention? Would they pay more attention if they made up the questions for someone else to answer? Could students be taught to ask high-level questions that make their peers think?

Bloom's taxonomy can be used to ask higher-level questions. Teach an easy form of the types of questions to the class. This can be posted on the wall for easy access.

Knowledge—retelling or repeating facts directly from the text

Analyzing—pulling out details from different sections to make one answer

Generating—taking what you know and adding details to help understanding

Integrating—putting together information and discarding some to make a statement

Evaluating—drawing a conclusion based on evidence from the text

Read Lesson 3 aloud or with partners. Make a transparency or project a copy of the worksheet of question starters. As a whole group, elicit possible questions from the class and write them on the transparency or white board. Let the student call on a classmate to answer the question. Use as many examples as time allows. This method will help students learn to write questions on their own.

 **Caption Answer**

It brought people and new industries to the West.

KEY IDEAS

- Railroads opened Canada's west to settlement.
- The Prairie Provinces and the Western Mountains changed as settlers found new resources.
- The Lowlands changed as Canada became urban and industrial.

KEY TERMS

Canadian Pacific Railway
"last best west"

LESSON 3 Moving West

The first European settlers of Canada found riches in its oceans and forests. Later, settlers found other treasures. They were oil, gold, and wheat.

These resources were hard to reach. Canada is wide. The climate is cold. The landscape can be rough. Yet Canadians met nature's challenges. They changed the environment. They claimed the land's resources.

Opening the West

Canada's prairie provinces are some of the world's top wheat farmlands. But about 100 years ago, this land was almost all grassland. Few people lived here.

This photograph shows an 1876 steam locomotive of the Canada Pacific Railway.
How did the railroad open the west?

Chapter 19

Activity

Working on the Canadian Pacific Railway

OBJECTIVES: 1.05, 1.06, 1.07

Canada is a confederation composed of ten provinces and three territories. In 1867 Canada became an independent nation and began one of its greatest projects—building a railroad to stretch across the entire country. The Canadian Pacific Railway was built in the late nineteenth century. It extends across the vast western prairies and Rocky Mountains through some of the most remote communities to the Pacific Ocean.

Thousands of railroad workers worked hard and spent their lives building the Canadian Pacific Railway. Pretend you are a railroad worker. Keep a daily journal discussing the hardships, the adventures, the towns, the recreation, and the challenges you faced while working to build the Canadian Pacific Railway.

Then the *Canadian Pacific Railway* was built. It opened the land to settlers from Europe and the United States. They settled on the plains. Trains were as important to prairie settlers as canoes had been to the fur traders.

Building the Railroad

Canada's landscape made building the railroad hard work. In the east, builders had to carve the rock in the Canadian Shield to make a place to lay the track. In other places, rock was not a problem. But the muskeg was so soggy the roadbeds sank.

Workers had a different challenge in the West. A way had to be found through the Western mountains. About 15,000 Chinese workers had a dangerous job. They used dynamite to blast tunnels through the mountains. Explosions and falling rocks killed or injured many people.

The map on page 451 shows how the railroad opened the west. Find Toronto and Moose Jaw on the map. It took trappers and traders in canoes three months to make the trip from Toronto to Moose Jaw. The railroad shortened the trip to three days.

The railroad would also help bring new industries to the plains. It linked farms to ports on the Great Lakes and the St. Lawrence River.

New Immigrants

The railroad was finished in 1885. It stretched from the Atlantic to the Pacific Coast. Railroads took out newspaper ads in Europe and the United States. They wanted people to come to the *"last best west."* Many did. They came for free land and the hope of a better life.

Most people came from eastern Canada, the United States, Germany, Italy, Ukraine, and northern European countries. By 1905, enough people had come to create two new provinces, Alberta and Saskatchewan.

CANADIAN PORTRAIT

Mary Ann Shadd Cary
1823–1893

Mary Ann Shadd Cary was a writer, teacher, lawyer, abolitionist and the first African American newspaperwoman in North America. She spoke out against slavery and fought for equal rights for all people.

Cary was born in Wilmington, Delaware. She was the oldest of 13 children. Her family helped runaway slaves when she was young. They moved to Pennsylvania so the children could go to school. Cary became a teacher. She taught African American children in Delaware, New York, and Pennsylvania.

When the Fugitive Slave Law was passed in the United States, Cary moved to Canada with her brother. She wrote a pamphlet, "Notes on Canada West." This was read by many African Americans in the United States. It told about the opportunities for them in Canada. She then founded Canada's first anti-slavery newspaper, the *Provincial Freeman*. She was nicknamed the "rebel" by her friends. During the Civil War, Mary Shadd Cary was made a "Recruiting Officer" for the Union Army. She moved back to the United States. After the war, Cary became active in the women's rights movement. She studied law at Howard University. When she graduated, she became one of the first female African American lawyers in the country.

Discussion Questions

1 From where did most settlers come?

2 What hardships were overcome in order to build the railroad?

3 Why did the completion of the railroad lead to more factories and cities being built?

Activity

Recreation for the Railroad Workers

OBJECTIVES: 3.04, 3.06, 4.07

Railroad workers spent many long hours building the Canadian-Pacific Railway. This left little time for entertainment and recreation. During the harsh winters and the lonely hours away from their families, the workers had to find ways to entertain themselves. Pretend you are a railroad worker and develop a board game or a new group activity to be enjoyed while sitting in a bunkhouse.

Settling a Nation

479

Activity

Transcontinental Railway Activities

OBJECTIVES: 3.04, 4.07, 5.05

Obtain a copy of the poem "Night Journey" by Theodore Roethke, from *The Collected Poems of Theodore Roethke* (Doubleday, 1966. ISBN 0385086016.). Discuss the importance of the railroads to westward expansion. List the landforms the train passes through on this trip west. Have students pretend they are looking out of the train's window. Draw a picture of one of the scenes described in the poem.

Canada is the second-largest country in land area in the world. The Canadian Pacific Railway linked the eastern and western parts of Canada. From the map on pages 454–55, have students list major cities the railroad passed near or through. What were the two terminal points for the railway line? (*Vancouver and Saint John*)

Have students list three ways the railroad helped Canada. Possible answers: making Canadians feel unified; bringing prospectors to the gold mines of the Yukon, helping build Canada, giving access to the resources of the various areas of the country.

Student Presentation Prompt
Imagine you and a friend boarded the railroad at Saint John and disembarked at Vancouver. You have been asked to tell about the geographic diversity of each region at a meeting of a local civic club. Use the maps in your textbook (in Unit 5) and the chart to the left to help you plan your presentation.

Discussion Questions

1 What problems did the farming settlers have to overcome?

2 What discovery changed the province of Alberta?

Caption Answer

Farmers grew wheat.

Caption Answer

Wheat fields gave way to oil fields, small farming towns like Edmonton became large cities.

Activity

Rail System

OBJECTIVES: 1.06, 4.02, 4.07

Consider the building of the Canadian Pacific Railway and the trans-continental railroad in the United States. Both rail systems were built in undeveloped territory and opened up opportunities for many to inhabit the inner land areas of Canada and the United States.

The transcontinental railroad in the United States runs from _____ to _____. The Canadian Pacific Railway runs from _____ to _____.

• Calculate the distance of each railroad. Which covers more land?

• Look at a map (topographical) to recognize landforms that the railroads passed through or around. Be sure to pay attention to the elevation of the mountains. Which railroad do you think was the more difficult to construct? Why?

• What kinds of problems might railroad workers encounter at each land region?

• Why was the Canadian Railway built so close to the United States border?

Industries on the Plains

Agriculture was the first industry on the plains. Oil became another important industry several years later.

Farming

Settlers had to work hard to turn the prairie into farmland. Whole families plowed and planted wheat. They worked from sunup to sunset in the few months of the growing season. Days are long in the summer because of the rotation of the earth. There are more hours of sunlight in Canada in the summer than in lands closer to the Equator (see Chapter 3).

Summer temperatures could reach more than 95°F (35°C). Fires sometimes swept across the fields. They destroyed homes and crops. A season's work could be gone in minutes.

Settlers overcame these problems. They changed grasslands into productive wheat farms. They also raised cattle on ranches.

Ships on the St. Lawrence carried farm products across the Great Lakes to Chicago. They also took Canada's products out and across the Atlantic Ocean to London.

Farming on the Canadian frontier in the 1800s was challenging. **What did settlers grow?**

Oil

In 1947, oil was discovered in Alberta. The wheat fields gave way to oil fields.

Soon Alberta had more than 1,200 oil wells. The oil business boomed. Edmonton, Alberta, turned from a small farm town to a large center. There oil was made into gasoline and other products.

Other cities in Canada also were affected by the oil industry. For example, back east in Hamilton, Ontario, there were steel mills. They rolled out the steel for Alberta's pipelines.

The discovery of oil in Alberta drew people to the Plains Provinces and to the west. **How did oil wells in Alberta change the eastern provinces?**

Teacher Notes

The Grand Trunk Pacific Railway

The Grand Trunk Pacific Railway was a 4,800 km system whose main line ran from Winnipeg, Manitoba, to Prince Rupert, British Columbia. Incorporated in 1903, it was built to allow the Grand Trunk Railway to compete against the Canadian Pacific Railway for the profitable traffic that was developing in western Canada.

The Grand Trunk Pacific line was completed on April 9, 1914. Its route went westerly from Winnipeg to Edmonton, Alberta, through the Rocky Mountains using the Yellowhead Pass, then followed the Fraser and Skeena Rivers to Prince Rupert.

Several branches were built, including ones to Regina, Saskatchewan, and Calgary, Alberta. A connection was built between Sioux Lookout on the National Transcontinental Railway to Fort William (now Thunder Bay), Ontario, to move grain traffic to the great lakes.

To encourage passenger traffic to and from the

Gold Mines

In 1856, Vancouver, British Columbia, and New Caledonia were British colonies on the Pacific coast. They were mainly made up of trading posts for the Hudson's Bay Company. The population was very small. The 700 people in Vancouver, for example, were mostly traders and trappers.

Only a few people had reasons to make the long journey west. But in 1858, that changed. A prospector found gold nuggets the size of marbles in the Fraser River.

Miners search for gold in the Gold Rush. **What is a gold rush?**

The Gold Rush

News of the gold discovery spread. More than 20,000 gold seekers came into the area. They were part of the gold rush.

After the gold rush ended, many stayed anyway. They liked the mild climate of the west coast. Leaders in Canada agreed to extend the railroad to the Pacific coast.

These three colonies joined to form today's province of British Columbia. Mining, forestry, fishing, and farming were the main industries of the region.

The Klondike Gold Rush

Another gold rush happened in 1898. The Klondike Gold Rush brought miners even farther north to the Northwest Territory. Dawson was the closest town to the gold fields. It grew from a few hundred people to 50,000. Most of these people went home when the gold rush ended.

The Canadian government decided to make a second territory, the Yukon, out of the Northwest Territories.

The Pig War of 1859

Which war killed only a pig? The Pig War of 1859, of course!

The 1846 Oregon Treaty set the border between Canada and United States at the 49th parallel of latitude. The border stretched from the Great Lakes to the Pacific coast. Both sides agreed that all of Vancouver Island would stay British. But the treaty was not clear about the other islands in Puget Sound.

The treaty said the border was "in the middle of the channel." But there were two channels of water around the islands. Both nations claimed the Gulf Islands and San Juan Island. There were about 18 Americans on San Juan Island. The British thought they should not be there. They believed the land was owned by the Hudson's Bay Company.

An American settler there named Lyman Cutlar shot and killed a pig that was rooting in his garden. The pig belonged to the Hudson's Bay Company. The British wanted to arrest Cutlar. The Americans asked the United States government to protect them. Soldiers were sent. This made the British angry. They brought in forces, too.

When the British and American leaders far away heard of this, they were shocked. They did not want to fight each other because of a pig. They asked the leader of Germany, Kaiser Wilhelm I, to settle the dispute. The border was finally set in 1872. Today, the San Juan Islands belong to Washington state. The Gulf Islands belong to British Columbia.

Settling a Nation

481

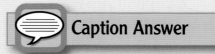

Discussion Questions

1 How did the discovery of gold and the gold rush change the population and regions of Canada's west and northwest?

Caption Answer

A time of high interest and activity mining gold

ELL Teaching Tips

Cooperative Learning Helps ELLs Become More Productive in the Classroom

New ELL students who work in cooperative learning groups learn English more quickly. They are forced to become an important part of the class. They can learn the basic vocabulary of the unit you are teaching to become more active participants. Encourage other members of the group to help them.

---

railway, the Grand Trunk Pacific purchased steamships and provided a service from the port of Prince Rupert along the Pacific Coast to Vancouver, Victoria, Seattle, and Alaska. The company also built and operated the Fort Garry Hotel at Winnipeg and the Macdonald Hotel at Moncton.

The high level of traffic that the railway expected never developed. The lack of revenue, along with the high cost of construction, led the railway into bankruptcy shortly after the outbreak of World War I. The federal government assumed control of the railway in 1919.

Discussion Questions

1 How did railroads help industry grow?

Caption Answer

People moved to the cities as industries grew.

Activity

Setting a Purpose

OBJECTIVES: 1.06, 1.07, 4.07

Students need a purpose for reading. If they are given something fun to do with a friend, the purpose for reading becomes fun, also. Since students love to write notes to friends, why not allow it for this lesson?

For today's assignment, allow students to write a Buddy Letter to a peer discussing what they read in Lesson 3. Give specific instructions for length and content of the letter. Using paper in the shape of a maple leaf or a scroll is better if the letters will be displayed.

Industry Grows

Once fur trappers had paddled canoes on their way west. Today, giant ships filled with grains, steel, and ore docked in the cities.

The railroad was finished in 1885. It gave Canadians a way to move wheat, lumber, iron ore, and many other natural resources. These could be brought from farms, forests, and mines in the west to cities in the east.

The railroads helped industry grow. They opened up new markets for goods. Industries bought western resources. They needed iron, steel, and fuel to run factories.

Factories

New factories were built in the St. Lawrence Lowlands. Lumber from the forests of British Columbia, farm products from the prairie provinces, and oil from Alberta were loaded onto trains. They went by rail to factories in Quebec and Ontario. There these raw materials became cereal, paper, or gasoline for Canada, the United States, and Europe.

The Great Lakes–St. Lawrence Lowlands became Canada's manufacturing center. This region was close to where most of the

Toronto grew as industries grew. **Why did people move to the cities?**

Background Information

Difficult Adjustments

The most pressing issues for most Native American communities in Canada are self-government, control of land, and lack of economic opportunities on the reserves. Many of Canada's reserves, or reservations, are quite small. Native peoples on these reserves continue to struggle with the government over fishing and hunting rights as well as land claims. After the Inuk in northern Quebec settled their land

claims in the James Bay area in 1975, their lives began to change as they developed local businesses. They still eat traditional foods like caribou meat, Zebedee Nungak, a tribal leader, said, but "we are not living in igloos or driving dog sleds any more." Trucks and planes are more common forms of transportation.

country's people lived. It was connected by the Great Lakes and rivers to the Great Plains of Canada and the United States.

Cities Grow

As industry grew, more people came to Canada's cities. The largest, Toronto and Montreal, built highways and subways so that people could live in suburbs and work downtown.

Canada remained a largely rural nation until after World War II. In the 1940s, Canada's manufacturing centers became urban centers. Now about 80 percent of all Canadians live in cities.

Changes for Native Americans

These changes to Canada's open lands also changed life for the native peoples. Not all of these changes were good.

Inuit

Before the 1960s, the Inuit lived in temporary snowhouses or tents. They tracked caribou or seal. They hunted beluga whales. Many Inuit still hunt and trap, but they do it part-time. Now most use snowmobiles instead of dog sleds to cross over the Arctic tundra.

Most of the year the Inuit live in modern houses. Under their fur-lined parkas they wear jeans and T-shirts. Satellites link the Arctic with the rest of Canada. Almost every home has a television. Igloos and tents are used only on hunting trips now.

Many Inuit still hunt and eat caribou, fish from the Arctic, and other traditional foods. They also eat snack foods and hot dogs and drink soda flown to the Arctic. They share the culture of modern Canada. They also work to keep their own culture alive.

Other Native Americans

There are about half a million other Native Americans (First Nations) in Canada. Almost half live on the country's 2,200 reservations. These are owned by the Native Americans but managed by the government. The Canadian government is responsible for the Native Americans' schools, housing, and health care.

Native Americans in Canada and the United States have had a similar history. European settlers moved westward. The claims of Native Americans were often ignored. By the late 1880s, almost all Native Americans had lost their land.

Since the 1970s, many Native Americans have united. They have won more rights and better treatment from the government. The government has had to pay some Native American peoples for the loss of hunting and fishing grounds.

Discussion Questions

1 In what ways has the life of the Inuit changed?

2 Other Native American tribes have united together to gain what rights?

 Activity

"To Build or Not to Build"

◤ **OBJECTIVES:** 3.04, 3.06, 4.07

Organize a class debate to consider the pros and cons of using Inuit hunting and fishing land for the development of natural gas, oil, and hydroelectric projects.

Pros
- Development would bring needed jobs.
- Development would bring in tax money.

Cons
- Development would adversely affect the caribous' habitat.
- Development would create the possibility of oil and chemical pollution.

As a follow-up to the debate, ask your students to write an imaginary conversation between an Inuit fisherman and an oil company executive in charge of researching new sites for development.

LESSON ③ REVIEW

Fact Follow-Up
1. How did building the Canadian Pacific Railroad change Canada?
2. Describe the life of a farm family in the Prairie Provinces.
3. What things happened to turn grasslands into wheat fields and oil fields?

Talk About It
1. How did changes like the building of railroads or the discovery of gold and oil change life for Native Americans?
2. How did these discoveries change life for the Western settlers? for people who lived in eastern Canada? Were all the changes good?

Settling a Nation

483

LESSON ③ REVIEW

Fact Follow-Up Answers
1. The railroad opened the west to settlement, attracting immigrants seeking free land. The resources of land, wheat, and oil were developed because of western settlement. Western towns grew from small outposts to large cities. The railroad connected the huge country from sea to sea. Two new provinces and a new territory were created because of the growth of the west created by the railroad.
2. Acceptable answers include information that relates to the difficulty of life there: grass fires, winter cold, loneliness, hard work, and heat during the growing season.
3. The first settlers began plowing the grasslands and grew wheat on the fertile soil. Then, when oil was discovered in Alberta, oil fields began to be developed where grass and wheat once grew.

Talk About It Answers
1. Important points: Make certain that students answer all parts of the question and explain whether life improved for each group of people mentioned. The lives of Native Americans were changed because they lost their land along the railroad route and were forced to move to reservations, thus losing their hunting and fishing grounds.
2. Important points: Make certain that students answer all parts of the question and explain whether life improved for each group of people mentioned. Traditional ways of life in the West began to change as more people came looking for gold and oil. Because resources brought east by the railroad inspired the development of industry, eastern Canada grew quickly into a manufacturing center. This made people wealthier and life more convenient in the East.

Talk About It

1. Important points: Students should state agreement or disagreement and explain their statement. Possible answers should include information about how any group that has settled in Canada has adapted to and/or changed the physical environment.
2. Important points: Students should choose one event and explain why they chose it. The discovery of gold enriched Canada and brought increased population to British Columbia and the Yukon, causing British Columbia to be named a province and the Yukon a territory. The completion of the Canadian Pacific Railroad united the country, encouraged immigration from other parts of the world, improved transportation and communication, linked western farms to eastern ports, and resulted in the creation of two new provinces, Alberta and Saskatchewan.
3. Important points: Students should choose one group and explain why they chose it. The French coureurs de bois lived much as the Native Americans did, traveling the waterways in birchbark canoes, trading for furs, and building shelters in ways taught them by the Native Americans. The Native Americans, because they increased the numbers of animals killed to sell to the French, may have directly changed the physical environment more than the coureurs de bois.
4. Important points: Students should choose a position and support it with reasons. Much of Canada's west is unsettled, which would be attractive to adventure-seekers. However, its climate is cold and harsh, making it a challenging place to live.

Mastering Mapwork

1. The movement of people into these areas resulted in the changes.
2. This is movement of both people and goods (the goods being the hunted/trapped animals carried on snowmobiles).
3. It was more the movement of goods because the coureurs de bois left almost none of their language and way of life behind them. They adopted the ways of living of the Native Americans.
4. The railroad was the movement of people goods, and ideas.

CHAPTER 19 REVIEW

Lessons Learned

LESSON 1
People of Canada
Canada's first settlers were the early Native Americans and Inuit. Settlers from France and England came in the 1600s. In the past 200 years, immigrants have come from Asia, the Americas, and Europe. Today's population mainly lives along the United States border, especially in the Great Lakes–St. Lawrence Lowlands region.

LESSON 2
First Settlers
The French were the first to use the resources of Canada as trappers. English settlements followed. The British forced the Acadians to leave. Loyalists from the new United States settled in Canada.

LESSON 3
Moving West
The Canadian Pacific Railroad opened the Canadian west to settlement. New settlers changed the environment of the prairies, the West and the North. The area along the Great Lakes and St. Lawrence River became Canada's industrial and population center.

484

5. Coal may move from the West to eastern cities and ports, or from the southwest to western ports. The map most clearly shows east-west movement. The railroad demonstrates this movement.

Talk About It

1. Someone has said that "Canadian history is the history of human environmental interaction." Do you agree or disagree with this statement? Explain why.
2. Which event in Canada's history was more important the discovery of gold in the Fraser River and the Yukon or the completion of the Canadian Pacific Railroad? Explain your answer.
3. Which early Canadian settlers—the French or the Native Americans—lived more within the physical environment? Explain your answer.
4. Given the environmental problems facing Canada today, does the description, "last best west" still apply? Explain.

Mastering Mapwork

Movement
Use the maps on pages 451 and 463 to answer these questions:
1. British Columbia was made a province and the Yukon a territory because of the gold rushes of 1858 and 1898. Which kind of movement—of people, goods, or ideas—caused these changes?
2. Many Inuit still hunt and trap, but they do it part-time, racing snowmobiles instead of dogsleds over the Arctic tundra. What kind of movement is this–of people, goods, or ideas?
3. Was the movement of the *coureurs de bois* into the wilderness the movement of goods or of ideas?
4. The Canadian Pacific Railroad united Canada east to west. Along this route much movement occurred. Was this the movement of people, goods, or ideas?
5. According to the map on page 451, how might coal move across Canada? What type of movement does the map show most clearly? Why do you think this is the case?

Becoming Better Readers

Asking Questions
Good readers continually ask questions as they read. Being able to ask questions shows understanding of what is important in the text. Write two good questions about how the western part of Canada was opened. Refer to pages 478 and 479.

Becoming Better Readers

Important points: Students should have two questions about the opening of the West. These may include questions about the railroad, immigrants, or Mary Ann Shad Cary and her call to African Americans to migrate to Canada's frontier.

Go to the Source

Judging the Accuracy of Historical Fiction

Compare the two quotations below from people involved with the deporation of the Acadians. Think about how these relate to what you read in Lesson 2. Answer the questions with information from the documents.

> *The inhabitants, sadly and with great sorrow, abandoned their homes. The women, in great distress, carried their newborn or their youngest children in their arms. Others pulled carts with their household effects and crippled parents. It was a scene of confusion, despair and desolation.*
>
> —Colonel John Winslow, British officer in charge of Acadian deportment

> *Since these people arrived consumed in wretchedness and in the greatest possible need, through the orders of the French General and mine they were helped immediately with fresh bread and biscuits which had been prepared for the first needy ones who might arrive. I ordered that an ox and a calf, which I had sent for upriver for my own consumption [use], and that of those who are with me, be given to them. This was done on the same night that they had encountered the launch [boat] which was transporting them, and the pilot assured me that immediately upon receiving these animals they slaughtered them and ate the meat raw.*
>
> —Antonio de Ulloa, colonial governor of Louisiana

Questions
1. What is the overall mood or tone of the quotes?
2. How are the sources different from one another?
3. What characteristic would best describe Antonio de Ulloa?
4. Compare these to what you read about the poem "Evangeline." How accurately do you think the poem describes what happened?

Go to the Source

Settling a Nation   485

Go to the Source

Judging the Accuracy of Historical Fiction

OBJECTIVES: 3.03, 3.01, 4.02
SOCIAL STUDIES SKILLS: 3.05, 4.02, 4.03, 4.05

Have students compare these accounts of the deportment of the Acadians to the story of "Evangeline" feature on page 476. Discuss what similarities and differences they find in the versions of events.

Answers
1. The mood was one of sadness, desperation and sorrow. For example "sadly," "women in great distress" "consumed in wretchedness and in the greatest possible need."
2. Colonel John Winslow's account described the inhabitants leaving, whereas Antonia de Ulloa talked about the inhabitants arriving in Louisiana and described their need for food and how they were helped.
3. Important points: Students should identify adjectives that describe him. He was generous, he gave the people food that he had purchased for his own consumption. He was compassionate because he helped the people immediately with fresh bread and biscuits. He was caring.
4. Longfellow describes the Acadians boarding the ships as gloomy but patient. Colonel John Winslow describes them as sad, in great distress, and a scene of confusion, despair, and desolation. Thus Longfellow's description of "gloomy" may fit, but "paitent" may not.

How to Use the Chapter Review

here are four sections in the Chapter Review: Talk About It, Mastering Mapwork, Becoming Better Readers, and Go to the Source. Use the Vocabulary Worksheets and the Chapter Review Worksheet in the Teacher's Resource Guide for additional reinforcement and preparation for the Chapter Assessments. The Chapter and Lesson Reviews and the Chapter Review Worksheets are the basis of the assessment for each chapter.

Talk About It questions encourage students to speculate about the content of the chapter and are suitable for class or small-group discussion. They are not intended to be assigned for homework.

Mastering Mapwork has students apply one or more of the Five Themes of Geography to maps within the chapter.

Go to the Source activities allow students to analyze a primary source that relates to the content of the chapter. The questions and activities familiarize students with different types of primary sources and also build content-reading skills.

Becoming Better Readers focuses on building reading strategy skills necessary for reading comprehension in the content areas.

Economy and Government

Social Studies Strands

Economics and Development

Government and Active Citizenship

Global Connections

Technological Influences and Society

Cultures and Diversity

North Carolina Standard Course of Study

Goal 2 The learner will analyze political and social institutions in North America and examine how these institutions respond to human needs, structure society, and influence behavior.

Goal 5 The learner will evaluate ways the United States and other countries of North America make decisions about the allocation and use of economic resources.

Goal 6 The learner will recognize how technology has influenced change within the United States and other countries in North America.

Teaching & Assessment

- English Language Learner Modified Lesson Plans for this chapter are found in the Teacher's Resource Guide.

- *ExamView® Assessment Suite* is provided at **NCJourneys.com.** It includes customizable assessments for all chapters. Paper tests are also available in the Teacher's Resource Guide. See pages T16–T17 for information about how to use the assessments and the Scoring Guide.

Worksheets

Worksheets and answer keys are found both in the Teacher's Resource Guide and at **NCJourneys.com**, including Reading Guides, Reading Strategies, Chapter Reviews, English Language Learner and others.

Activities and Integrations

SOCIAL STUDIES

Problem Based Learning: Canada's Government, p. 486B
▲ ■ Provinces, p. 487
Carolina Connection: Nortel Networks, p. 487
■ Map of Canada, p. 497
Healthful Living, p. 491
Frederick Banting Profile, p.491
Canada and the Music of Raffi, p. 496
Canadians in the United States, p. 498
● ▲ ■ Government Mobile, p. 500
Canada Day, p. 503
▲ ■ Coins as Symbols, p. 504
Skill Lesson: Government Chart, p. 505

TECHNOLOGY	TECHNOLOGY OBJECTIVES
★ Ad Campaign, p. 492	2.12

VISUAL ARTS	VISUAL ARTS OBJECTIVES
▲ ■ Moose in a Can, p. 486B	2.01
▲ ■ Physical Region Picture Books, p. 486B	4.03
Canadian Economy and Government, p. 486B	2.01
Ad Campaign, p. 492	4.01
▲ ■ National Anthem, p. 502	1.10, 9.05

READING/LANGUAGE ARTS	READING/LANGUAGE ARTS OBJECTIVES
▲ ■ Physical Region Picture Books, p. 486B	4.03
▲ ■ Canadian Economy and Government, p. 486B	4.07
Writing Prompt: Neighbors, p. 486	4.09
Activator: Current Events p. 486	2.01
Reading Strategy: GRASP ,p. 488	3.05
★ Asbestos Dilemma: To Produce or Not Produce, p. 490	3.06
★ Ad Campaign, p. 492	4.03
Reading Strategy: Seed Discussions, p. 493	1.03
St. Lawrence Seaway, p. 496	2.02
● Reading Strategy: Guide-o-Rama, p. 497	2.02
Becoming Better Readers, p.500	
National Symbols of Canada, p. 507	

CHARACTER AND VALUES EDUCATION	TRAITS
● Friendly Neighbors Character Education, p. 495	trustworthiness/integrity
Learning About Leadership, p.502	courage, perserverance

● Basic Activities   ★ Challenging Activities   ▲ English Language Learner Novice   ■ English Language Learner Intermediate

Introductory Activity

Physical Region Picture Books

OBJECTIVES: 1.02, 1.06, 1.07

Have students begin a picture book detailing the six physical regions of Canada. Each book will have a construction paper cover and six sheets of plain paper. Label the pages as follows: Arctic Plains, Appalachian Highlands, Great Lakes-St. Lawrence Lowlands, Canadian Shield, Interior Plains, and Western Mountains.

The title of the book could be A Look at Canada's Physical Regions.

Tell students that as they "travel" through each region, they will draw a picture of the region and write a sentence about it. They will share their picture books with a primary class when completed.

Alternative topics for the picture book might include a map of Canada, first settlers, European explorers, plant life, animal life, symbols, transportation, arts and crafts, resources. This book could be called All About Canada.

 **Culminating Activity**

Canadian Economy and Government

OBJECTIVES: 5.05, 5.06, 5.07

Canada has a strong economy. Using construction paper, glue, scissors, and old magazines, have the class create a collage about things that Canada produces. These items can be raw materials, natural resources, industries, and finished products.

Have the students write a poem about the Canadian economy and why Canada is so productive.

Extension Novice ELL students can contribute to the collage by cutting and pasting pictures. Have them work with a partner for guidance on what items to cut out.

 **Art Activity**

Moose in a Can

OBJECTIVES: 1,02, 1.06, 4.07

Prior to this activity, have students collect clean, empty 46-ounce juice cans or small coffee cans. Have students spray or cover the cans with brown paint or paper. Students will decorate outside of can to resemble the face of a moose. They can use pipe cleaners, paper, or foam sheets (purchased at craft store) to make antlers. Glue antlers with a hot glue gun. Adult supervision is a must! Students may use the can to keep pencils, note cards, and other items as study of Canada continues.

Extension This is a good activity for novice ELL students to review colors and body parts.

 Problem Based Learning Activity

Canada's Government

OBJECTIVES: 2.02, 2.04, 2.08

Situation Have students imagine that they are members of the Canadian government, either in the House of Commons or the Senate. They are not residents of Quebec, but they have many friends who live there and they enjoy the lifestyle that Quebec offers. Regularly they hear in the media that residents of Quebec desire to separate from Canada. Because Quebec is so heavily populated and developed, this province is important to Canada's economy. This helps support less developed provinces like Saskatchewan. The dissension of the Separatists is causing a rift between Quebec and the other provinces and territories of Canada. These areas feel that the Separatists are not considering the nation's needs.

Task Break the students into groups: one group representing the Separatists of Quebec, one representing the residents of Quebec who do not wish to separate from Canada, a commission of individuals representing the other territories and provinces of Canada, and the senators and members of the House of Commons. The government does not have provisions for a province leaving the Confederation. Have students discuss the viewpoints of these groups, answering the following questions:

- If Quebec separates from Canada, how will my particular group feel about this?
- If Quebec is not allowed to separate, how will this affect my group/Canada?
- What is my group's opinion about what is best for Canada?
- What compromise might my particular group offer that others have not considered?
- Who, according to my particular group, should be allowed to make this decision?
- How do we address the concerns of those who oppose the decision?

Reflection Have each group share its points of view with the entire class. Be sure to include both good and bad points. After the groups have shared their points of view, ask students to consider what each group said. Then ask students to imagine that they are members of the Canadian government. Based upon the discussion they have heard in class today, how would they vote? Ask them to state why they would vote this way and what things have influenced them in making their decision.

Teaching Strategies

There are many terms that students will need to know in order to understand the information in this chapter. Therefore, you will need to utilize a variety of vocabulary strategies to ensure that students comprehend the new terms. In this chapter, emphasis should be placed on the structure and components of a parliamentary government. Allow ample time to ensure students' understanding since this may be the first formal introduction on this type of government.

Discussion Questions

1 Why do Canadians believe in a strong partnership between government and business?

2 Traveling from east to west, which major Canadian cities does the Canadian Pacific Railway travel through?

Activator

 OBJECTIVES: 2.02, 2.04, 2.08

Canadian Current Events On the day prior to the activity, assign students to find any mention of Canada in the newspaper or television news. List their findings on the board as headlines. After all headlines are listed, have the class identify categories into which the headlines might be placed. Discuss possible alternative categories as well. Once a final list of categories has been agreed upon, regroup the headlines and discuss what the categories suggest about our relationship with Canada.

Writing Prompt

 OBJECTIVES: 2.04, 5.05, 5.06

Clarification Canada is our nearest neighbor and trading partner. Think about why it is important to get along with one's neighbors. Write a paper that explains your thoughts about this. Give two reasons why you think the way you do.

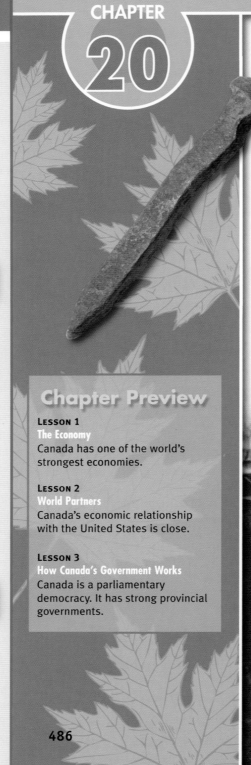

CHAPTER
20

Economy and Government

Canadians believe in a strong partnership between government and business. The building of the railroad across Canada is a good example of this.

There were no private companies that could do the job alone. So the government created the Canadian Pacific Railway. It gave the new company money and land.

This partnership paid off. The railroad united the country. It helped Canada's economy grow into one of the strongest in the world.

Construction of the Canadian Pacific Railroad

Chapter Preview

LESSON 1
The Economy
Canada has one of the world's strongest economies.

LESSON 2
World Partners
Canada's economic relationship with the United States is close.

LESSON 3
How Canada's Government Works
Canada is a parliamentary democracy. It has strong provincial governments.

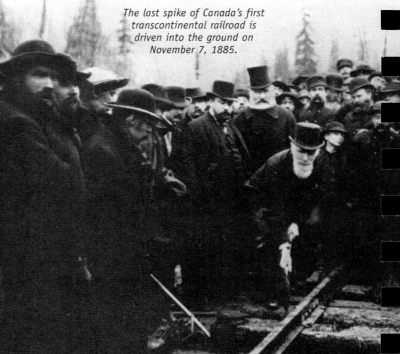
The last spike of Canada's first transcontinental railroad is driven into the ground on November 7, 1885.

486

Chapter Resources

Print Resources
Nonfiction

Gibbons, Gail. *The Great St. Lawrence Seaway.* Morrow Junior Books, 1992. ISBN 0688069843

Granfield, Linda. *Canada Votes: How We Elect Our Government.* Kids Can Press, 1994. ISBN 1550742507.

Kizilos, Peter. *Quebec: Province Divided*

(World in Conflict series). Lerner Publications, 1999. ISBN 0822535629.

Audiovisual

Canada: Economy and Government. North Carolina State University Humanities Extension/Publications Program. 14 minutes.

Canadian Provinces

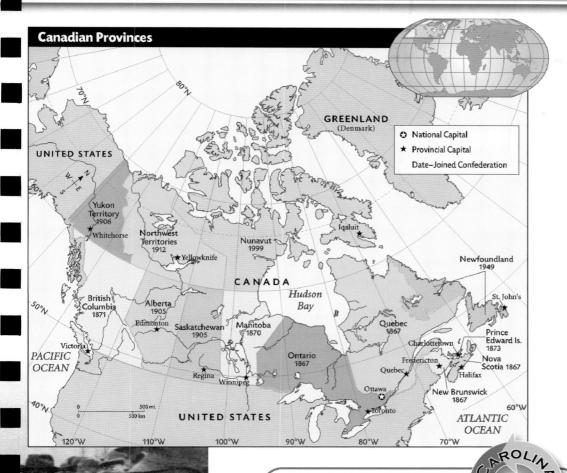

National Capital
★ Provincial Capital
Date–Joined Confederation

GREENLAND
(Denmark)

UNITED STATES

70°N

80°N

Yukon
Territory
1906
★ Whitehorse

Northwest
Territories
1912
★ Yellowknife

Nunavut
1999

Iqaluit
★

CANADA

Hudson
Bay

Newfoundland
1949

St. John's
★

British
Columbia
1871

Alberta
1905
Edmonton
★

Saskatchewan
1905

Manitoba
1870

Quebec
1867

Prince
Edward Is.
1873

Charlottetown
★

Victoria
★

PACIFIC
OCEAN

Regina
★

Winnipeg
★

Ontario
1867

Fredericton
★

Nova
Scotia 1867

Quebec
★

Halifax
★

Ottawa
⊕

New Brunswick
1867

Toronto
★

UNITED STATES

ATLANTIC
OCEAN

500 mi.
500 km

120°W   110°W   100°W   90°W   80°W   70°W   60°W

50°N

40°N

Nortel Networks

North Carolina has a key link with one of Canada's biggest private businesses. Nortel Networks is Canada's largest maker of telephone equipment. It is also one of the largest in the world.

In 1980, Northern Telecom (now called Nortel Networks) chose Research Triangle Park to be one of its research and manufacturing centers.

Research Triangle Park is often called RTP. It is located in between Raleigh, Durham, and Chapel Hill.

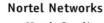

487

Web Sites
Visit **NCJourneys.com** for links to these Web sites:
- Celebrate Canada
- Government of Newfound-land and Labrador: The Grand Banks
- British Commonwealth of Nations
- Canadian Broadcasting Company
- Embassies and Consulates of Canada
- Government Canada
- Great Lakes–St. Lawrence Seaway System
- The Monarchy Today: How the Monarchy works
- Parks Canada - Canada World Heritage Sites
- Statistics Canada
- St. Lawrence River and Seaway

Map Activity

Provinces

NATIONAL GEOGRAPHY STANDARDS: 1, 4
GEOGRAPHIC THEMES: Region
OBJECTIVES: 1.01

Have students illustrate a blank map of Canada with a symbol for each province and territory. They should also identify the capital city of each province and territory. Have them write on the back side of the map a sentence describing what each symbol represents.

Activity

Carolina Connection: Nortel Networks

OBJECTIVES: 5.03, 5.04, 5.05

Visit **NCJourneys.com** for a link to Nortel Networks home page to learn more about the company. Have students discuss why communication technology is an important part of the economies of North Carolina, the United States, and Canada. Review Nortel's mission statement and values statement. Discuss what these are and why an organization would put them on its Web site. What do they tell us about a company?

OBJECTIVES: 5.01, 5.02, 5.03, 5.06, 5.07

 Caption Answer

Canada Post and nuclear power

 Reading Strategy Activity

GRASP (Guided Reading and Summary Procedure)

OBJECTIVES: 5.01, 5.02, 5.03, 5.06, 5.07

Read aloud the lesson introduction. Ask students to tell what they remember without looking at the text. List these suggestions on the board (even if some are wrong). The list might look like this:
• Getting to some of Canada's resources is hard and can cost a lot of money.
• The government lowers taxes.
• The government helps businesses save money in the far north.

Ask students to review the passage and, if they wish, add information like: "The government has built roads, airstrips, and telephone lines." Ask if they see anything on the board they want to change or delete. They may want to change "The government helps businesses save money in the far north." to "The government builds things to help businesses save money where costs are high."

Ask students to read the other sections one at a time. Follow the procedure above. Be sure to read one section at a time. Reading more material than that may make retaining the information difficult.

Extension When the lesson is finished, have students write a brief summary in a notebook about Canada's economy. Encourage students to identify new things they have learned about Canada.

KEY IDEAS

• Crown corporations play a large role in Canada's strong economy.
• Most Canadians work for private businesses.
• Canada has both primary and secondary industries.

KEY TERMS

crown corporations
primary industries
secondary industries

Getting to some of Canada's resources can sometimes be hard. Also, it can cost a lot of money. So the government works closely with private companies. Together, they work to develop the nation's resources.

The government wants private companies to drill for oil and mine for minerals. So it lowers taxes for businesses that do those things. This helps these businesses save some money. They can then use that money to pay for the extra costs of drilling or mining.

The government has done even more to help businesses that will go into the far north. It has built roads, airstrips, and telephone lines. These help companies save money in a place where costs are high.

The government has also invested in Canada's people.

Education

Canada has one of the best education systems in the world. With a good education, people can do many different kinds of jobs. Canada's well-educated people are an important resource.

Many Languages

Each province runs its own educational system. In Quebec, most children go to a school where everything is taught in French. Other provinces have mostly English-speaking schools. In some provinces,

The National Film Board of Canada runs the nation's movie industry. Here a crew makes a film about Canada for an international trade show. **What other Canadian businesses are run by the government?**

Chapter 20

 Teacher Notes

A Few Acres of Snow

"A few acres of snow" is a version of several quotations by Voltaire, the eighteenth-century French philosopher. It shows his view that Canada, and therefore New France, lacked economic value and strategic importance to France. This phrase has become rooted into Canada's popular

culture and it is regularly quoted by Canadians. It is often used ironically, illustrating that Canada's potential for development was worth much more than what Voltaire believed.

parents can choose to send their children to a French- or English-speaking school. Most children in Canada learn both French and English.

In Nunavut, children are taught only in Inuktitut (in·OOK·tih·toot) until they finish fifth grade. Inuktitut is the language of the Inuit. Students are taught in English from then on.

Many Canadians go on to college. Several Canadian universities, such as McGill in Montreal, are world famous. People come from all over the world to study in Canada.

People who graduate from college use what they have learned at work. This helps Canada's economy grow.

Government and Business

Canada's economy is similar to the economy of the United States. It is a free market economy. As in the United States, Canada's government also makes rules for businesses to follow. But it also is slightly more involved in the economy than is the government in our country.

Crown Corporations

Government ownership of businesses has been much more common in Canada than in the United States. Companies owned or controlled by the national and provincial governments are called *crown corporations.*

Canada chooses to own businesses that are important for the country. It used to own more. But the government decided that many businesses could do well on their own. So it sold them. Some of the Canadian businesses that started as crown corporations include Air Canada, an airline; the Canadian National Railway; Petro-Canada, a gasoline company; Nova Scotia Power, and several provincial telephone systems.

Today, crown corporations deliver the mail (Canada Post), oversee the nuclear energy programs, and do other important jobs for the nation.

TV, Radio, and Film

Canada still owns the National Film Board of Canada. It makes movies. The government also makes radio and television shows. The Canadian Broadcasting Corporation broadcasts news and entertainment programs in English and French.

Why does the government own these companies? Canada wants to make sure that its national culture is presented in film and on television. This might not happen if all Canada's television shows and movies were made in other places, like in Hollywood, London, or Paris.

Other Government Aid

The national and provincial governments own about 90 percent of all Canada's forests. Private lumber companies pay the government for the right to harvest trees on publicly owned land.

Look at the Canadian Energy map below. The oil shipped from Norman Wells in the Northwest Territories has a long trip to the cities where it will be used. Pipelines built with government money help carry oil to the United States and Canada.

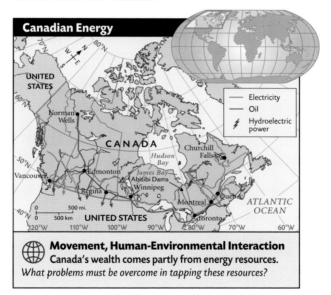

Canadian Energy

Electricity
Oil
⚡ Hydroelectric power

Movement, Human-Environmental Interaction
Canada's wealth comes partly from energy resources. *What problems must be overcome in tapping these resources?*

Economy and Government

Discussion Questions

1 What are crown corporations?
2 What are some of the businesses that are government owned?

Caption Answer

Transportation from remote areas presents a problem. The impact on the environment is another concern.

ℹ **Background Information**

Natural Resources in Newfoundland

Newfoundland and Labrador may one day lose their reputations as Canada's "have-not" provinces. These Atlantic provinces have had high jobless rates. Until recently, Newfoundland's population was shrinking by about 1 percent per year. Now oil fields off the Grand Banks near Newfoundland's coast are aiding these economies. Oil and natural gas from wells in the Canadian Atlantic are lighting homes and fueling factories in the northeastern United States. Canada is the top provider of natural gas to the United States. Only Saudi Arabia sells more oil to the United States. States in the western United States have long imported oil from Alberta province. Eastern states like New York and Pennsylvania are now looking to the Atlantic provinces.

Discussion Questions

1 Explain what is meant by primary and secondary industries. What are some examples of each?

2 What are some of the high-tech developments made by Canadians?

ELL Teaching Tips

Encourage Participation

Encourage ELL students to participate in class. Most ELL students are hesitant to speak even when they know the correct answer. Give them nonverbal opportunities to respond to the questions.

Activity

Asbestos Dilemma: To Produce or Not to Produce

OBJECTIVES: 1.02, 1.03, 1.06

The United States gets metals and metal ores from Canadian mines. The two countries are each other's most important trading partner. Canada is one of the world's major storehouses for minerals and ranks first in the world in mineral production. Asbestos is a mineral that is mined in huge deposits in Quebec, which is the world's largest producer of asbestos. Asbestos has fibers that are soft, flexible, and bendable, which enable it to be woven into cloth. Asbestos is also fireproof and does not conduct electricity. It is used for firemen's gloves, helmets, and suits, as well as for insulation for pipes and lining for automobile brakes. On the other hand, it is an extreme health hazard because the fine fibers can be breathed into the lungs, causing lung disease.

Students will role-play an asbestos miner in Canada. They must decide if they are for or against the continuing production of asbestos. They will choose and complete one of the projects below:

• Linguistic: From the point of view of

the miner, write a persuasive letter to the president of the International Asbestos Company expressing your point of view and concerns. Include suggestions.

• Logical: Research numbers of deaths or illnesses caused by asbestos inhalation. Create a bar graph or pictograph, showing your information.

• Spatial: Design a poster that illustrates your point of view. Be sure to include pictures and words that demonstrate your point and opinion.

• Kinesthetic: Create a mime demonstration

to explain your side.

• Interpersonal: Create a debate with three other friends. Be sure to have all the evidence.

• Intrapersonal: From the point of view of a miner, write a five-day journal, reflecting your ideas.

• Musical: To emphasize your point of view, create a chant that could be sung outside an asbestos company.

• Naturalist: Collect information on how nature is affected by our use of asbestos. Include photos and interviews.

Industry

Canada is a large country with many different natural resources. These resources can be found in different parts of the country. Forests can be found in British Columbia, so timber and paper are important industries there. The oil industry is key in Alberta. Mining is important in Ontario. And fishing is still important along the Atlantic Coast.

Primary Industries

Natural resources are raw materials. They are also called primary products. Businesses that gather them are called *primary industries.*

Some of Canada's primary products include oil and natural gas, timber, and minerals. Farm crops, such as wheat and barley, and fish, such as salmon and cod, are also primary products. Selling these products is important to Canada's economy.

About 100 years ago, 70 percent of Canadian families worked in farming. Look at the pie chart on the next page. Now only about 3 percent do.

Secondary Industries

Industries that make goods from primary products are called *secondary industries.* Look at the pie chart again. About 15 percent of Canada's workforce has jobs in these manufacturing industries.

Canada's top secondary industry is the making of transportation equipment. Canadian iron ore is made into steel and then sold to car and truck manufacturers in Windsor, Ontario, Detroit, Michigan, or elsewhere.

Other important secondary industries are food processing and paper products.

High-Tech

Canadians also have a strong high-tech industry. They have invented diving suits for exploring underwater. They have also written computer programs that control satellites.

Engineers in Ontario built a camera that takes a perfectly clear photo of a car license plate. But it takes the picture from an airplane flying half a mile up in the sky! Police and military officers use this camera for detective work around the world.

Primary and Secondary Industries

Primary industries are those that gather or sell products such as oil and natural gas, timber, minerals, wheat, barley, salmon, and cod. This is a pump drawing oil from a well in Saskatchewan.

Secondary industries are those that make goods from raw materials. Examples of products produced by secondary industries include transportation equipment, processed foods, and paper. This is a food processing plant in Ontario.

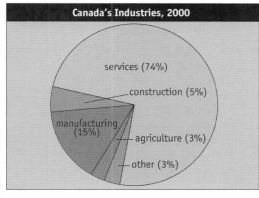

Canada's Industries, 2000

services (74%)

construction (5%)

manufacturing (15%)

agriculture (3%)

other (3%)

Compare this chart to the one on page 329. **How are the economies of Canada and the United States alike?**

Services

Look at the pie chart again. About three fourths of all Canadians work in service jobs. Many of these workers are teachers, doctors and nurses, or lawyers. Others work in banks, hotels, restaurants, or stores.

There is another type of service that is growing in both Canada and the United States. These are businesses that protect the environment. They clean up pollution.

Taxes Pay for Services

We just read that Canada's different regions have different resources and industries. Some of these industries make more money than others.

Canada's government taxes provinces such as Ontario, Alberta, and British Columbia. These provinces have strong economies. The taxes are used to pay for services in the provinces and territories that do not have as much. Some of the services that the government provides with this money are healthcare and education.

Some people want this policy to change. They want each province to pay its own way. Canadians are discussing this issue right now.

Economy and Government

CANADIAN PORTRAIT

Frederick Banting
1891–1941

Frederick Banting was a doctor who won a Nobel Prize. He discovered how to make insulin. Insulin is a product your body makes to turn sugar into energy. People with diabetes (di•ah•BEE•tees) have too much sugar in their bodies. Their bodies cannot make (or do not make enough) insulin. Banting's work brought hope to these people.

Banting was the youngest of five children. He grew up in Alliston, Ontario. While at the University of Toronto, he decided to study medicine. During World War I, he joined the Canadian Army Medical Corps. He was wounded in France, and he won a medal for bravery.

After the war, Banting finished his studies and became a doctor. At the time, diabetics, people with diabetes, faced shorter lives. They often went blind or had to have a foot or leg amputated. They faced many challenges.

Banting read an article about diabetes research. It gave him an idea. He decided to try to find a way to give insulin to people with diabetes.

Banting formed a team of researchers. They found that they could use dogs to make insulin for people. The people they tested the insulin on got much better quickly. With the insulin, diabetics could bring their blood sugar level under control. The discovery did not cure diabetes. But it made life much better for diabetics all over the world.

Frederick Banting

491

Discussion Questions

1 What are some of the resources the public needs that are made available by the Canadian government?

2 About how many Canadians are employed in service industries? What are some of these service industries?

3 How are the poorer provinces able to give their citizens the same services as richer provinces?

 Caption Answer

Most of the industries are service industries, for both countries manufacturing is the second largest industry.

 Activity

Frederick Banting Profile

 OBJECTIVES: 4.03

Divide the class into pairs or groups of three. Each pair of students will visit a variety of Web sites and use classroom and library resources to gather information about Frederick Banting. Distribute appropriate graphic organizers (see the Graphic Organizers in the Teacher's Resource Guide) to help students take notes. Once their research is complete, each pair will create a storyboard about this person's life and work. Using this information they will produce a short digital story (using PowerPoint or other programs) to share the information they have learned with the class.

 Teacher Notes

Healthful Living

The portrait on Frederick Banting is an excellent opportunity to incorporate activities related to Healthful Living Goal 4 for Grade 5 (nutrition and physical activity). In light of the rapid increase in diabetes among children and adults, practicing good nutrition and exercise early is a proven critical preventative measure. Invite a nutritionist or diabetes specialist from a local hospital to talk to the class about diabetes and the importance of good nutrition. If you know of a student in your school or an adult with diabetes invite him or her to share his or her experience about living with diabetes and taking insulin (not all diabetics take insulin) with the class.

Activity

Ad Campaign

OBJECTIVES: 1.02, 1.06, 1.07

Divide the class into cooperative groups. Present the situation below. Then assign each group an industry around which to create an ad campaign: insurance, Canadian Pacific Rail System, Canadian airline, Canadian Broadcasting Corporation, hydroelectric power, food processing, Canadian Film Board, lumber, or paper products. Students will present their ad campaigns to class.

Situation A major advertising company in Canada has just hired you. This company is responsible for many major industrial accounts throughout the country. Your boss is giving you the following account. Develop an ad campaign for this industry. Choose at least three ways to promote your company from the list below:

- A catchy slogan to be published in a magazine or newspaper, on a billboard, or on the side of a bus
- Magazine/newspaper ad with an illustration
- Song or jingle
- TV commercial
- Radio ad
- Web page
- PowerPoint presentation

A Journey to NEWFOUNDLAND AND LABRADOR

The Newest Province

Newfoundland and Labrador is Canada's newest province. It joined the Confederation in 1949. Newfoundland is a large island. Labrador is part of mainland Canada.

About 90 percent of the province's people live in Newfoundland. People get to and from the island and Labrador mostly by airplane or boat.

Labrador is nicknamed "the Big Land." It has a big, open sky and many hours of summer sunlight.

People who live in Newfoundland and Labrador enjoy lots of activities. In the summer, you can watch a boat race called the Royal St. John's Regatta. It is North America's oldest sporting event. You may also kayak, fish, hike, or go iceberg or whale watching. Music lovers enjoy the province's orchestra. There are festivals and cultural events year-round.

Winters here are long. They last from about November to April. It can be a challenge. But winters are a great time for adventure, too! There is a winter snowmobile trail network that runs throughout Labrador. It is almost 932 miles (1,500 km) long.

This province also has important natural resources. Almost 80 percent of eastern Canada's offshore oil resources are located in the ocean off Newfoundland and Labrador.

LESSON 1 REVIEW

Fact Follow-Up

1. What are the differences between crown corporations and privately owned businesses?
2. What are the differences between primary and secondary industries?
3. How many Canadians work in agriculture? in service industries? Explain why.

Talk About It

1. Compare Canadian and American attitudes toward government's involvement in business.
2. In Canada, wealthier provinces pay more in taxes than they receive in government benefits. Why?
3. Why are there fewer crown corporations today?

LESSON 1 REVIEW

Fact Follow-Up Answers

1. Crown corporations are businesses owned by the Canadian government. Privately owned businesses are owned by individuals.
2. Primary industries are industries that gather raw materials, such as oil, gas, minerals, wheat and other agricultural products, fish, and timber. Secondary industries are industries that process those raw materials, such as oil refining, manufacturing, steel processing, paper milling, and food processing.
3. About 3 percent of Canada's workforce is in agriculture. About 75 percent work in service industries. Although Canada is a world leader in agriculture, mechanization and other improvements in agriculture make it highly productive, so not many people are needed to grow a lot of food. In service industries, many workers are needed to do a variety of jobs in education, financial services, health care, tourism, law, and environmental protection.

Talk About It Answers

1. The Canadian attitude is for government to be heavily involved in business. The Canadian government owns businesses in key areas: transportation, medicine, filmmaking. Crown corporations compete with privately owned companies. In the United States, the attitude today is to keep government out of business except in the area of regulation.
2. Canadians believe that all citizens should share in benefits from Canada's economic growth. So resource-rich provinces such as Ontario, Alberta, and British Columbia help poorer provinces.
3. The Canadian government has not had to play as big of a role in developing businesses as it once used to.

LESSON 2 World Partners

The Ambassador Bridge stretches between Windsor, Ontario, and Detroit, Michigan. More than 10,000 trucks cross the bridge each weekday. One quarter of all the goods and services traded between Canada and the United States each year crosses this bridge.

North American Neighbors

The border between the United States and Canada is 5,500 miles (8,855 km) long. It is the longest undefended border in the world. Every day, Canadians and Americans go back and forth across this border. They travel for work and for play.

Good Friends

There are many reasons for this friendly relationship. The United States and Canada share the English language and a similar heritage. They also have similar economic systems and similar ways of doing business. They are important trading partners. *Trading partners* are countries that trade closely together.

Sports bring them together too. Teams from Canada and the United States compete against one another in baseball, basketball, and hockey.

The two countries, as you read in Chapter 18, also work to clean up the environment together. Canada and the United States share waters in the Great Lakes and the oceans. They also share air pollution. So they work together to clean the air and to protect the waters and fish.

KEY IDEAS

- The St. Lawrence Seaway was built by the United States and Canada.
- The economies of Canada and the United States depend on each other.
- NAFTA strengthened those economic ties.
- Canada's trade with Pacific countries is growing.

KEY TERMS

NORAD
St. Lawrence Seaway
trading partners

International Peace Park

Waterton-Glacier International Peace Park was the world's first international peace park. It is a symbol of the cooperation and good will between the United States and Canada. It celebrates the longest peaceful border between two nations in the world.

The park runs along the frontiers of both nations. Glacier National Park is on the American side. It is in northwestern Montana. Waterton National Park is on the Canadian side. It is in Alberta. The parks were joined as an International Peace Park in 1932.

Wolves, bears, big horn sheep, and mountain lions live in the park. There are high mountains and cold lakes. The park reminds us that our natural resources belong to everyone.

Bison in Waterton Park

Economy and Government   **493**

Background Information

Bringing Construction Skills South

One unique sign of interdependence is the jobs held by Mohawk Indians living on the Kahnawake Reservation near Montreal. Many of these men are the sons and grandsons of Mohawk ironworkers who helped build New York's Empire State Building, George Washington Bridge, Henry Hudson Parkway, and World Trade Center. Hired first as laborers, they showed no fear of balancing on narrow rails high above waterways and city streets and soon took on more skilled jobs as iron workers. While working on major steel construction projects in New York City, many spent weekdays in New York, making the 400-mile commute to the reservation for weekends.

OBJECTIVES: 4.08, 5.04, 5.07

Discussion Questions

1 In what ways are Americans and Canadians friendly neighbors?

Reading Strategy Activity

Seed Discussions

OBJECTIVES: 4.08, 5.04, 5.07

This is a group discussion method without the teacher being the facilitator. Begin by telling students they will be leading their own discussions for this lesson. As they read the lesson on the relationship between Canada and the United States, they are to think of one important thing, the "seed," to discuss from the material. They will write the seed in their journal or on a card. Make a list of ideas for seeds, such as something they do not understand, how they feel about something in the text, something interesting or unusual, vocabulary that should be learned, a picture or chart that catches their attention, or something that made them recall something they already know. You may want to model some possible seeds using Lesson 1. Make certain students understand the difference between a good comment or question that starts a discussion and a weak one. Model comments for the students, such as, "I really like your idea . . . ," "I agree with you about . . . but I also think that . . . , " or "I think that part means . . . ."

Read Lesson 2. Sticky notes could be used by students to write seeds while reading. Arrange students into groups and assign one person to act as the leader. Begin with one student introducing one seed. Have the other students respond to that before the next person introduces a seed. If very little can be said about a seed, it is a weak one.

Discussion Questions

1 What did the building of the St. Lawrence Seaway enable ships from the United States and Canada to do?

2 What are some of the things Americans buy from Canadians? that Canadians buy from Americans?

Caption Answer

Canada and the United States are each other's most important trade partner. Both nations see an advantage to trading without the expense of tariffs.

Differences

Canada is a sovereign nation and makes its own decisions. At times, Canadians disagree with the policies and decisions of the United States. Canada did not participate in the the 2003 invasion of Iraq. But it later gave support to rebuild Iraq.

Defense and Terrorism

The United States and Canada want to keep their nations safe. The governments are worried about terrorist attacks. The open border can be a challenge. The freedom of the border is good for citizens and businesses. But the two countries also want to make sure that terrorists or other people doing illegal things do not take advantage of the open border.

The American and Canadian military forces have cooperated for more than 50 years. The North American Aerospace Defense Command **(NORAD)** center was set up during the Cold War. It was designed to protect the United States and Canada from a nuclear weapons attack. In 2006, a new agreement was signed. It will help the two countries fight terrorism, too.

The St. Lawrence Seaway

Canada and the United States have strong economic ties. Ships sail back and forth on the Great Lakes and the St. Lawrence River. They carry wheat from Saskatchewan and ore from northern Quebec. They also carry corn from Illinois, iron pellets from Minnesota, and coal from New York.

Large freighters sail from United States or Canadian ports on the Great Lakes to the Atlantic Ocean. They use the *St. Lawrence Seaway.* Long ago, canals opened a passage from Lake Erie to the Atlantic Ocean for small boats. But large ships needed something deeper.

The seaway has locks and many canals and channels. These help large ships go from

Trade between the United States and Canada all along the St. Lawrence Seaway (above and right) represents a key partnership. **Why have the Canadian and United States governments agreed to trade freely?**

the Great Lakes through the St. Lawrence River and Gulf of St. Lawrence to the Atlantic Ocean.

The United States and Canadian governments planned and built the seaway in the 1950s. Each year, more than 43 million tons of cargo pass through the system, strengthening the economic connection between the United States and Canada. The seaway is the best example of their close cooperation.

Look at the Eyewitness to History on page 496. Find the map of the seaway. It shows how the seaway connects large parts of both countries.

Trade

Relative to size, Canada's population is small. Therefore, it has always needed to find markets outside Canada for its products. Trading primary products with other nations has been important. Canada's exports include wheat, zinc, and newsprint.

The United States and Canada are each other's most important trading partners.

Teacher Notes

Icebreaking

It is the responsibility of the Canadian Coast Guard (CCG) Icebreaking Program to ensure that marine shipping moves in a safe, timely, and efficient manner through or around ice-covered waters. The Great Lakes/St. Lawrence Seaway component of Central and Arctic Region's Icebreaking program supports the activities of two medium duty icebreakers (CCGS Samuel Risley/CCGS Griffon) during the traditional ice season from mid-December to the end of April. After a severe winter, additional support of larger icebreakers may be sought in the early spring after the opening of the seaway locks. Icebreaking efforts during the late fall, winter, and early spring assist the export abilities of the Canadian economy.

Imports and Exports

About 84 percent of all Canadian exports go to the United States. About 56 percent of Canada's imports are from the United States.

Canadians buy many of their winter vegetables and fruit from the United States and Mexico. American automakers have factories in Canada. They make cars, trucks, subway cars, and airplanes for buyers at home and abroad.

The two countries also trade electricity. Hydro-Quebec sells power to New England states. So do electric companies in Canada's Atlantic provinces.

Economy and Government

495

Discussion Questions

1 With what other nations does Canada trade?

 **Activity**

Friendly Neighbors
Character Education

OBJECTIVES: 3.04, 3.06, 4.07

The United States and Canada are friendly neighbors. The 5,500-mile border between the United States and Canada is the longest undefended border in the world.

Canada and the United States have promised to be good neighbors and trading partners. We share the English language, similar economic systems, and some of the same ways of doing business. We share sport teams, too. In basketball and hockey, Canadian and American teams compete with one another. With so many similarities these two countries have developed trust and a stable friendship. This allows the border to be undefended.

In small cooperative groups, have students give examples of when they trusted someone. List some people they trust. How do they know when they can trust someone? What characteristics make them trustworthy? Can students recall a time someone trusted them?

Agreements that are abided by help build trust between nations. For example, Canada and the United States agreed to clean up the Great Lakes. Canada and the United States jointly built the St. Lawrence Seaway. How do agreements help nations build trust? Are there any agreements you would propose to help Canada and the United States become even better neighbors?

Eyewitness Activity

St. Lawrence Seaway

OBJECTIVES: 1.02, 1.06, 4.07

Canadians sometimes call the St. Lawrence River the "Mother of Canada." Although it is not the longest river system, it is Canada's major transportation route for shipping. Before the seaway was built, travelers had to face dangerously swift waters. In 1959, Canada and the United States opened the St. Lawrence Seaway, making travel much easier. Have students use the map on page 497 to trace the route of ships using the seaway. Make a list of cities located along the seaway.

Have students research how a system of canals and locks works. A comparison could be made to the system that moves ships along the Panama Canal.

Whenever the environment is changed by man, although there may be many benefits, there are often environmental disadvantages. Have students brainstorm a list of problems that could have occurred in building the seaway. Answers may include more pollution because of increased use of the seaway, a possibility of oil spills, the destruction of animal habitat, and so on.

Discussion questions to use after reading the selection:

1. When did work on the seaway begin? end? (*1954, 1959*)
2. How long did it take to build the seaway? (*five years*)
3. What bodies of water does the seaway connect? (*Great Lakes and the Atlantic Ocean*)
4. How many locks are used to raise and lower the ships? (*15 locks*)
5. Why is the seaway called "North America's fourth seacoast"? (*The seaway is very important to the economies of the United States and Canada.*)

THE BUILDING OF THE

The Canadian city of Toronto is a long way from the Atlantic Ocean. Yet, thanks to the St. Lawrence Seaway, freighters from Japan, the United Kingdom, and France sail to Toronto and other inland cities. At the same time, other freighters leave Toronto. They sail to places around the world with loads of iron ore, grain, and wood.

Building the St. Lawrence Seaway began in August 1954. Millions of cubic feet of dirt were moved. Workers built 15 locks. These raise and lower ships between the Great Lakes and the Atlantic Ocean.

The seaway was finished in 1959. It is 2,342 miles (3,771 km) in length. It allows ships to travel more than 9,500 miles (15,295 km). They can now reach the North American heartland.

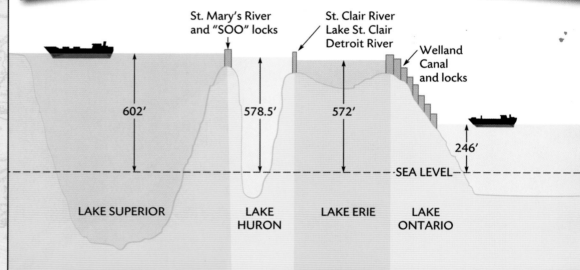

St. Mary's River and "SOO" locks — St. Clair River / Lake St. Clair / Detroit River — Welland Canal and locks

602' — 578.5' — 572' — 246' — SEA LEVEL

LAKE SUPERIOR — LAKE HURON — LAKE ERIE — LAKE ONTARIO

Activity

Canada and the Music of Raffi

OBJECTIVES: 1.06, 3.04, 3.07

Play the song "C-A-N-A-D-A" by Raffi. Provide the lyrics of the song to each student. Have students sing along with the song a few times. Using their lyric sheets, have students underline the following:

- Douglas fir
- bobcat
- lobster
- maple trees
- maple sugar
- wheat
- reversing falls
- tidal bore
- goose (Canada)
- Maple Creek
- snowfall
- magnetic hill
- dollar bill (Queen Elizabeth II currency)
- autumn fall (changing of the seasons)
- timber woods (timber industry)

continued on next page

St. Lawrence Seaway

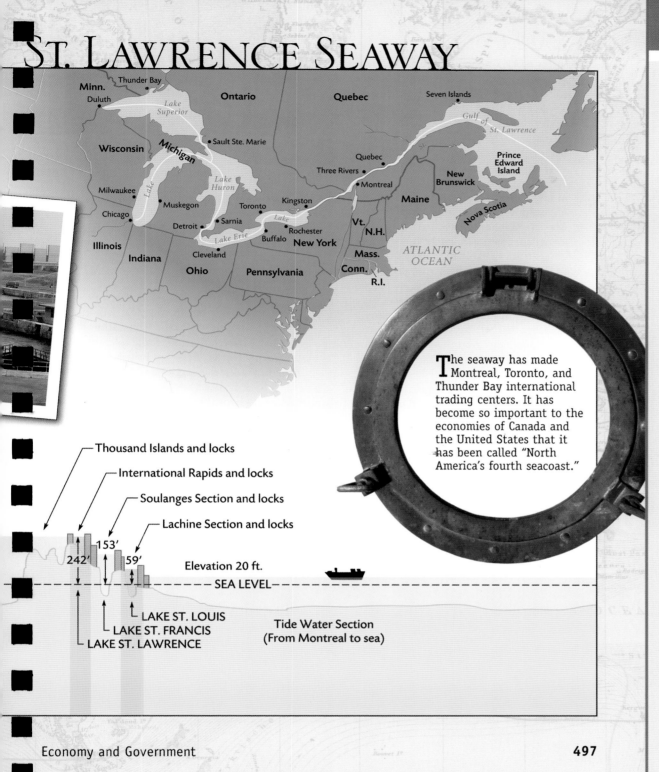

The seaway has made Montreal, Toronto, and Thunder Bay international trading centers. It has become so important to the economies of Canada and the United States that it has been called "North America's fourth seacoast."

— Thousand Islands and locks

— International Rapids and locks

— Soulanges Section and locks

— Lachine Section and locks

242' 153' 59'

Elevation 20 ft.

SEA LEVEL

LAKE ST. LOUIS
LAKE ST. FRANCIS
LAKE ST. LAWRENCE

Tide Water Section
(From Montreal to sea)

Economy and Government

497

Discussion Questions

1 Explain how a lock works. Why do you think it is called a lock?

Map Activity

Map of Canada

NATIONAL GEOGRAPHY STANDARDS: 1, 4, 12

GEOGRAPHIC THEMES: Region, Place, Movement, Human-Environmental Interaction

OBJECTIVES: 1.01, 1.03, 4.02

Give each student a blank map of Canada with the provinces and territories outlined. Have students do the following map tasks:

- Label the provinces and territories.
- Identify where caribou can be found.
- Identify where the Dene settlements are located.
- Identify where the Inuit settlements are located.
- Locate Admiralty Inlet to show where zinc and lead are mined.
- Label the Arctic Ocean and show where the Beluga whales are located.
- Label or show the Arctic Bay area.

Variation Instead of just writing words like "lead" or "Inuit" on their maps, have your students develop symbols to identify and complete the map tasks. Make sure your students include a key to their map symbols.

Put students in pairs (or small groups) and assign a topic from the list for them to research. Remind them that these topics relate to Canada, so the information they seek out has to relate to Canada. (For example, students need to research the amount of snowfall in Canada.)

When a sufficient amount of time has been given for research, instruct the students to prepare a short presentation of their topic. Each pair needs to include a visual aid.

Discussion Questions

1 What are some of the positive things about Canada's standard of living?

Caption Answer

It represents the gateway to the Pacific Rim.

Activity

Canadians in the United States

OBJECTIVES: 4.08

Have students identify prominent Canadians who have successful careers in the United States. Have students speculate why they have come to the United States to work. What does this say about the cultures of the United States and Canada?

A few famous Canadians:
Dan Aykroyd
Jim Carrey
Celine Dionne
Michael J. Fox
Nelly Furtado
Wayne Gretzky
Peter Jennings (deceased)
Avril Lavigne
Rick Moranis
Mike Myers
Matthew Perry
Mary Pickford (deceased)
Keanu Reeves
Mack Sennett (deceased)
Martin Short
Alex Trebek
Shania Twain

NAFTA

In 1993, Canada signed a three-way trade agreement with the United States and Mexico. This was the North American Free Trade Agreement, or NAFTA (nahf·tah). Under this agreement, the three countries cut tariffs, taxes on goods coming into their countries.

Not all Canadians supported NAFTA. Some factory workers feared it would result in fewer jobs for Canadian workers. Factories might move south to the United States or Mexico. Canadian merchants worried their Canadian customers might buy cheaper goods from the United States or Mexico.

But other Canadians support Canada's part in NAFTA. They believe the country must find markets for its products. As one Canadian businessman said, "We are realizing that we are North Americans, not just Canadians. And this is a North American market, not just a Canadian and a United States market."

NAFTA has had some clear effects on Canada's economy. Canadian exports to both Mexico and the United States almost doubled between 1994 and 2000. NAFTA has made Canada more attractive to foreign and domestic investors.

FTAA

Canada is talking with the United States, Mexico, and 32 other democratic

A large archway makes this street look like an entry into a Chinese city, but this is in Victoria, British Columbia. **Why is the archway there?**

governments in the Western Hemisphere. They are working to create a new free trade zone. This would be called the Free Trade Area of the Americas (FTAA).

The Pacific Rim

Canada is strengthening its ties with countries outside North America, too. Like the United States, it is a Pacific Rim nation. Five provinces have important trade relations with the Pacific region. They are British Columbia, Alberta, Saskatchewan, Ontario, and Quebec. Vancouver, British Columbia, is Canada's busiest port for trade with such countries as China and Japan. Canada is working on ways to grow trade with this region.

Canada also has good relations with Australia and New Zealand in the Pacific. They share a similar heritage. They are both important customers for Canadian goods. You will read more about their special relationship in the next chapter.

LESSON 2 REVIEW

Fact Follow-Up
1. Describe North Carolina's connections with Canada.
2. How are the United States and Canada interdependent?
3. Why is NAFTA important to Canada?

Talk About It
1. How do Canada and the United States cooperate for defense?
2. What are some signs of Canada's interdependence with Asia? Does this interdependence affect all Canadians? Why or why not?

LESSON 2 REVIEW

Fact Follow-Up Answers
1. Nortel Networks, a Canadian company, has offices in North Carolina.
2. The countries are interdependent in economy, trade, transportation, and sports. Each country is the other's leading trade partner. The countries are increasingly interdependent because of NAFTA. A symbol of their interdependence is the St. Lawrence Seaway, which was constructed cooperatively by both countries to connect the heartlands of both countries to the world. Citizens of both countries cross the long, undefended border to work in each other's countries. Teams from Canada and the United States play together in four major sports leagues: the Canadian Football League, the National Hockey League, the National Basketball Association, and

Major League Baseball.
3. NAFTA has made Canada more attractive to investors. It has contributed to a huge growth in exports as well.

Talk About It Answers
1. Canada and the United States cooperated during the Cold War to defend each other from missile attacks. Today they work together to prevent terrorism.
2. Signs of interdependence with Asia are the increasing trade with Asian countries conducted from Canada's West coast and the number of Asians moving to western Canada. The interdependence affects mainly western Canadians now but will affect more citizens as the Pacific Rim grows in importance as a trading partner.

Diane France is a Canadian writer. Someone asked her what she liked about Canada. She had no trouble deciding.

Canada is wonderful because it has . . . safe streets. Democracy. Good schools. Phones that work. . . . Roads and bridges that are plentiful and safe. Power at the flick of a switch. Good medical care. Little poverty. Water you can drink.

Many Canadians would agree with this point of view. Canada has one of the world's highest standards of living. Its citizens tend to live longer than citizens of other countries. Fewer Canadian babies die in infancy.

Canada's strong government has helped the country achieve this success.

Role of Government

Americans and Canadians have similar ideas about the rights of citizens. Both believe people's rights should be protected. Both believe that all people have the right to equal treatment under the law.

Different Views

Yet the two nations have different views about the role of government in their lives. Researchers asked people from both countries if government should "help citizens get a job and a good standard of living" or "let each person get ahead on his own." Many more Canadians thought the government should help its citizens. More than half of the United States citizens said government should stay out of people's lives.

These different views can be seen in the different healthcare systems. The Canadian government provides all citizens with healthcare. In the United States, most people pay for healthcare by buying insurance from private companies. Only people older than sixty-five get help with heath care costs from the government in the United States.

KEY IDEAS

- Canada is a parliamentary democracy.
- Provincial governments share power with the national government.
- The Canadian constitution maintains strong ties with the United Kingdom.

KEY TERMS

Canada Day
confederation
Constitution Act of 1982
Dominion Day
governor general
Nunavut
prime minister
Separatists

OBJECTIVES: 2.04, 2.05, 3.06

Discussion Questions

1 What does "equal treatment under the law" mean?

2 Why do you think citizens of the United States and Canada have differing views about government?

Reading Strategy Activity

Guide-o-Rama

OBJECTIVES: 2.04, 2.05, 3.06

This is a good lesson of the textbook to introduce a guided reading strategy called a Guide-o-Rama. Make copies of the Guide-o-Rama worksheet for each student.

A Guide-o-Rama is a reading tool that will help students understand the lesson independently. They are to read it by themselves and follow the instructions exactly as they are written. They will be asked to make predictions about the material before they read. Students should make their best guess. No points will be taken off the paper for their predictions. It is important for them to guess because checking their predictions will keep them focused while they read.

Activity

Government Mobile

OBJECTIVES: 2.02, 2.04, 2.07

Construct a mobile or stabile showing the structure of the Canadian government. Use a coat hanger and show the levels of the government.

Sovereign Head
(king or queen)
governor general

Legislature/ Executive	Judiciary
prime minister	Supreme Court
Parliament	of Canada
cabinet	Government of
Senate	the Day
House of Commons	Opposition
departments and	
agencies	

Extension Novice ELL students can copy from an example. They should look up five of the words in a bilingual dictionary and write the equivalent in their own language. Intermediate students may participate as directed.

500

 It's a Fact

History of a Symbol: The Maple Leaf

1834: The St. Jean Baptiste Society in North America made the maple leaf its emblem.

1836: *Le Canadien*, a newspaper published in Lower Canada, referred to it as a suitable emblem for Canada.

1848: The Toronto literary annual, *The Maple Leaf*, referred to it as the chosen emblem of Canada.

1860: The maple leaf was incorporated into the badge of the 100th Regiment (Royal Canadians) and was used in decorations for the visit of the Prince of Wales that year.

1867: Alexander Muir wrote *The Maple Leaf Forever* as Canada's confederation song ; it was regarded as the national song for several decades. The coats of arms created the next year for Ontario and Quebec both included the maple leaf.

A Parliamentary Democracy

The Canadian and American forms of government are alike in key ways. Both are democracies. The people elect representatives. They are different in other ways.

Parliament

Canada's legislature is the Parliament. It makes laws for the national government. It has two houses. The smaller house is the Senate. The larger house is called the House of Commons.

In the United States, the lawmaking and executive branches are separate. The members of Congress make the laws, and the president and executive branch carry them out. In Canada, the Parliament combines the lawmaking and executive branches of government.

The Prime Minister

Parliament chooses the leader of Canada's government. The leader is called the *prime minister.* He or she is a member of Parliament. The majority party in Parliament gets to pick the prime minister. The parties that do not have a majority are called "the opposition."

In the United States, the president serves a four-year term. He or she must step down if not reelected. A parliamentary system is different.

The prime minister stays in office as long as the House of Commons supports the programs he or she recommends. A prime minister must resign when his or her party no longer has a majority of representatives in the House.

Elections

But sometimes members of the prime minister's party do not support a program important to him or her. A special vote is taken. This is called a "vote of no confidence." If the prime minister loses this vote, a new election must be held. Then the party that wins the most seats will form a new government. That means the majority party will choose a new prime minister.

With support or not, the prime minister must call an election at least once every five years.

The Governor General

Canada still has ties with the United Kingdom. The king or queen of the United Kingdom is also Canada's head of state. The king or queen appoints a *governor general* to represent him or her in Canada.

The governor general, like the king or queen, does not take part in politics. One important job the governor general does is represent the king or queen to officially open Parliament's session. Today, the governor general mostly takes part in ceremonies.

The size and beauty of Canada's Parliament building (left) reflects its importance. **Inside (right), why does it look much like the British Parliament?**

Economy and Government

501

Discussion Questions

1 What is the name of Canada's lawmaking body? How is the Parliament different from the United States' national government?

2 Who is the leader of Canada's government? How is his or her job different from that of the president of the United States?

3 Who is the monarch of Canada?

4 What is the job of the governor general?

 **Caption Answer**

The interior reflects British influence in Canadian government.

1876–1901: The maple leaf appeared on all Canadian coins. The modern one-cent piece (penny) has two maple leaves on a common twig, a design that has gone almost unchanged since 1937.

1917: During the First World War, the maple leaf was included in the badge of the Canadian Expeditionary Force. Since 1921, the Royal Arms of Canada have included three maple leaves as a distinctive Canadian emblem.

1939: Canadian troops used the maple leaf as a distinctive sign, displaying it on regimental badges and Canadian army and naval equipment.

1957: The color of the maple leaves on the arms of Canada was changed from green to red.

1965: The red maple leaf flag was inaugurated as the national flag of Canada.

Discussion Questions

1 Think about the original Articles of Confederation in the United States and the Confederation of Canada. What do you think confederation means?

2 Do you think John Macdonald is like George Washington? Why or why not?

3 How is the way Canada became a new nation different from the way the United States became a nation?

4 Who are the Mounties? Why do you think they are famous?

 **Activity**

National Anthem

 OBJECTIVES: 1.06, 1.07, 2.04

For this activity, you will need a tape of the Canadian national anthem, "O Canada," and copies of the words. As your students enter the classroom, play the tape and give them a copy of the words. Ask students to think about how Canadians might feel about their country, as indicated by the words of "O Canada." What do these words tell them about Canadians? As a follow-up, ask students to write a paragraph or two comparing the feelings expressed in "O Canada" with the feelings of "The Star Spangled Banner."

Extension Novice ELL students can circle the words they recognize in the song or the ones they can read.

CANADIAN PORTRAIT

John A. Macdonald
1815–1891

Sir John A. Macdonald is called the founding father of Canada. He united the French and English-speaking people. He also helped start the Canadian Pacific Railway.

Sir John was born in Scotland. When he was five years old, his father's business was not doing well. The family wanted a new start. They moved to Upper Canada (today's Ontario).

Sir John was well respected and successful in business. When he was 28, he married his cousin Isabella Clark. Soon after the wedding, she became ill. No one knew the cause of her sickness. They had two sons. One died when he was thirteen months old. Isabella died in 1857.

He was elected as a Conservative representative in the Province of Canada's assembly. Later Sir John was chosen to be attorney general. He served as co-premier from 1856 to 1862.

In 1867, Sir John married again to Susan Agnes Bernard. They had one daughter.

About this time, Sir John decided it was important for the colonies in British North America to join together. The colonies in the east did not all agree. But after the American Civil War and other events, they decided it would be best to form a confederation.

Sir John wrote the British North America Act that created Canada. He was chosen to be the first prime minister of this new country. He worked to bring more provinces into Canada.

He served Canada until his death.

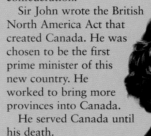

502

Confederation

Do you remember reading in Chapter 19 about the French and Indian War? The Canadians call that the Seven Years War. Great Britain won that war. The French colonies were taken over by the British. Most of North America north of New Spain became a British colony.

Then the 13 southern British colonies rebelled. They became a new nation, the United States of America. The remaining colonies were called British North America. These colonies became today's Canada.

A New Nation

The colonies in British North America were much like the other 13 colonies before the American Revolution. They were not united together. They were each their own colony.

On July 1, 1867, British North America joined together to form a new country. There was no revolution. Instead, Canada became a "dominion." A dominion was a country that governed itself but stayed part of the British Empire.

The provinces joining together to make the country of Canada is called *confederation.* But the new country had only four provinces. They were New Brunswick, Nova Scotia, Ontario, and Quebec.

 **Customs**

Canadian Thanksgiving Canadian Thanksgiving is celebrated on the second Monday of October. Around 1578, the English navigator Martin Frobisher held a ceremony in today's Newfoundland. He gave thanks for surviving his journey.

Around 1750 this celebration of harvest came to Nova Scotia. Settlers from the southern New England colonies brought it with them. At the same time, French settlers were also holding feasts of "thanksgiving."

Activity

Learning About Leadership

OBJECTIVES: 4.03

Some have said that there are six qualities that make a leader: passion, vision, preparation, courage, perseverance, and integrity. Using a graphic organizer, have students find examples (they may need to do additional research on the Internet or in the media center) to illustrate these qualities of John Macdonald.

Next, students should create a day that celebrates the importance of this person. They should name the day and create a symbol and slogan for the day; choose a date significant in the person's life as the day to hold the celebration, and create some special events to celebrate on that day.

Early celebrations of Dominion Day (left) included parades. Today, Canada Day is an event that attracts families to big-city parks. **What does Canada Day celebrate?**

Canada's 1887 constitution created a national government. This gave the United Kingdom of Great Britain and Ireland power over Canada's laws. The **Constitution Act of 1982** put Canadians in charge of their own government.

July 1st is a national holiday. It was called **Dominion Day.** Now it is called **Canada Day.** Which date in American history does this remind you of?

Caption Answer

Canada Day celebrates the nation's peaceful end as a British colony and the beginning of its existence as a dominion in the British Commonwealth.

Activity

Canada Day

OBJECTIVES: 3.07, 4.03

Canada Day is celebrated on July 1 each year. Canadians celebrate in ways similar to United States citizens celebrating their Independence Day on July 4. Hold a Canada Day celebration. Make Canadian flags, share Canadian foods or foods made with maple syrup, and play music by Canadian musicians (Rush, Bryan Adams, Shania Twain, Celine Dionne, and others

The Mounties

The Royal Canadian Mounted Police (RCMP) are nicknamed the Mounties. They are the national police force of Canada. The Mounties are famous for their red uniforms and flat-brimmed hats. They are a symbol of Canada. The RCMP are called mounted police because they used to ride horses. Today, Mounties are a regular police force. Horses are ridden for special ceremonies.

The RCMP began as the North-West Mounted Police. Sir John A. Macdonald, the first prime minister of Canada, created this force. He wanted to bring law and order to the North-Western Territories.

Today, the RCMP enforces federal laws. It also is the provincial or territorial police for Canada's three territories and eight of its provinces. This would be similar to the State Highway Patrol in North Carolina. Ontario, Quebec, and parts of Newfoundland and Labrador have their own provincial police forces. Many towns and cities in Canada also use the RCMP as their local police force.

The RCMP is the largest police force in Canada. The Mounties do many jobs. They patrol towns and cities. They protect the prime minister and other leaders. They enforce federal laws. They fight terrorism. The RCMP often cooperates with police in the United States to solve crimes and protect citizens of both countries.

Economy and Government

503

 Background Information

Quebec and the Separatists

In 1980 and again in 1995, the people of Quebec voted against seceding from Canada. In the first decade of the twentieth century Quebec's Separatist party, the Bloc Quebecois, had fewer representatives in Parliament than in the past. According to polls taken in 2000, only about one fourth of Quebec's citizens want Quebec to become a separate nation. Some political analysts say that the people of Quebec are tired of the fight over this issue. Others question whether the benefits of secession would outweigh the costs.

Discussion Questions

1 How are the governments of the provinces organized?

2 Who are the Separatists? What are they in favor of? What conflict does this cause?

3 When in United States history did states want to break away?

Activity

Coins as Symbols

OBJECTIVES: 1.07, 2.04, 4.07

For this activity, you will need a Canadian penny or other coin for each student in the class (a paper copy of the coin will work as well). You will also need a United States penny for each student. After providing each student with a Canadian coin and a United States coin, ask the class to study them carefully, noting the symbols of each country. What do these tell about each country? Who is the woman on the Canadian coin? Why would Canadians have Queen Elizabeth on their coins? Why would they have the beaver? the moose? the loon? Now ask your students to write a paragraph on the symbols they see and what they think the significance is for Canada. Share the paragraphs in class.

Extension Have novice ELL students place each coin under a white piece of paper. With a pencil go over the coin (as if they were coloring it). The final product is a black-and-white version of the coin. Students can label their rubbings.

Provinces and Territories

Today, Canada has ten provinces and three territories. It took 132 years for all the provinces and territories to join Canada. The provinces work both independently and together. Confederation allows each province to keep its special culture. For example, the many French-speaking people in eastern Canada wanted to keep their language. They did not want to lose their French traditions.

The Federation

Like the United States, the national and provincial governments of Canada have different powers. The national government directs transportation and trade, banking, defense, and relations with other countries. Canada's leaders wanted the new national government to unite the country and strengthen its economy.

Provinces are set up like the national government. But the leaders of provinces are called premiers. Territories have less power than provinces. They are supervised by the national government.

Provincial governments are responsible for education, health, town and city government, and natural resources. Canada's provinces have strong governments. Ontario and Quebec, not the national government, decide how to spend money earned from their sale of hydroelectricity. Alberta decides how it will export oil.

WORD ORIGINS

In April 1999, Canadians redrew the map of their country. The Inuit people were given their own territory. It was carved out of the eastern half of the Northwest Territories. The Inuit chose the name **Nunavut** for the territory. This means "our land."

The Inuit are the people once called Eskimos. The word Eskimo means "eaters of raw meat." Inuit, the name they prefer, means "the people" in their own language.

Quebec

Quebec has a strong French heritage. A large portion of its citizens want Quebec to separate from Canada. They think that Canada's government cannot protect their French culture. These people are called *Separatists.*

In the past 30 years, there have been two votes in Quebec. Citizens were asked if they wanted to stay a part of Canada or separate from it. The Separatists lost both votes, but only by a little. Therefore, Quebec has stayed a part of Canada.

Canada's national government has passed laws to help protect French culture and heritage in Quebec. Many Canadians, particularly in the western provinces, do not like Quebec's requests for special treatment. This sometimes causes conflict among the provinces.

LESSON 3 REVIEW

Fact Follow-Up

1. What is a prime minister, and who elects him or her?

2. How is the Canadian government dealing with native peoples?

3. Explain why Canadians speak of the French and British as "two founding peoples."

Talk About It

1. What are some differences between a parliamentary system of government and the form of government in the United States? some similarities?

2. How are Canadian provinces similar to states in the United States? How are they different?

LESSON 3 REVIEW

Fact Follow-Up Answers

1. The prime minister is the leader of Canada's government. He or she is chosen by members of the majority party in Parliament's House of Commons.

2. Canada's government has paid native peoples for losses they suffered because of land taken from them for building railroads and, later, for building hydroelectric plants. The government also created a new territory from the Northwest Territories for the Inuit people, called Nunavut.

3. Both the French and the British played important roles in settling Canada. Both French and English language and customs are part of Canadian culture.

Talk About It Answers

1. Both are democratic, with two house legislatures. However, the Parliament contains both legislative and executive branches because the prime minister who leads the nation is chosen by the members of the majority party in parliament. Prime ministers can serve as long as the House of Commons supports his or her programs, as compared to the United States, in which the president must run for election every four years and can only serve two consecutive terms.

2. Both provinces and states share power with the national government (federalism), thus provinces and states have authority over education while the national government has the authority to build national transportation systems, conduct foreign policy and trade, and make banking laws. However, Canadian provinces have more power than our states because of their control over the use of natural resources.

Applying Interpreting, Creating,
and Using Resources and Materials

Charting the Organization of Canada's Government

There are many kinds of charts. Charts can tell us different things. The chart below is called an organizational chart. This kind of chart tells us how a group is set up. Usually, the person in the top block is the leader. He or she is responsible for the organization.

Everyone else is listed in the boxes under the leader. They report to him or her. The lines show who supervises, or is the boss of, whom. Different people have different jobs.

Governments also have organizational charts. This chart shows how Canada's government is set up. At the top, the monarch is the king or queen. Next, the governor general is shown. In Parliament, the House of Commons is shown equal to the Senate. The dotted lines show that the prime minister and the cabinet are members of Parliament, too.

Reading the Charts

Compare this chart with the United States Government chart on on page 431. Answer these questions.

1. Compare the position of the president of the United States to the positions of prime minister and governor general in Canada.

2. What are the differences and similarities between the two governments?

3. In Canada, what is "the opposition," and how do Canadians determine what the opposition is?

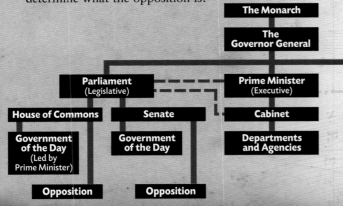

 Skill Lesson Review

1. How can organizational charts be useful? Think of as many ways as you can. *Answers will vary. Organizational charts provide a quick outline of how work gets done and who is responsible for it along the way.*

2. Construct an organizational chart of your school. You need to interview the principal or your teacher to complete the chart. *Answers will vary.*

Teaching This Skill Lesson

Materials Needed textbooks, paper, pencils, a transparency of the organizational chart of your school system, overhead projector

Classroom Organization whole class

Beginning the Lesson Display the organizational chart of your school system. Ask: "Who is in charge, and how is this person chosen to be in charge?" Accept student's responses, correcting any misinterpretations. Note the wide range of activities under the control of the school system.

Lesson Development Have students study the chart in the Skill Lesson. Ask questions such as these:
- Who chooses the monarch, and who is the current monarch?
- How is the governor general chosen, and what is the job of this official?
- Who chooses the prime minister, and how is this person chosen?
- What is meant by the "Government of the Day"? (In Canada, the Government of the Day is formed by the party winning the most votes in a parliamentary election. New parliamentary elections may be called if the party in power loses a vote of confidence in the House of Commons.)
- What are the branches of government, and how many are there?

Compare this chart with the chart on page 431, noting that the chart showing the checks and balances system of the United States government is not an organizational chart. Use the questions in the Skill Lesson for Chapter 20 to begin the comparison. Encourage students to ask questions and make other comparisons. As a homework assignment, have students draw an organizational chart of the United States government, using the Canadian chart as a model.

Conclusion Allow students to compare their charts in small groups. Display charts in the classroom if desired.

Talk About It

1. Important points: Encourage students to suggest as many questions as possible, then choose the three they think most important. Questions might center on the role of government in education.
2. Important points: Encourage students to suggest arguments on both sides of the issue and choose the arguments they think most powerful. Answers should explore the benefits of government regulation as well as the importance of free enterprise.
3. Important points: Students should focus on advantages, not disadvantages, and should distinguish between confederation and federalism. It is possible that confederation works better with 10 provinces than it would with 50 states. Confederation protects the individuality of each province. The federal system may be more efficient since responsibilities and privileges of the national and state governments are clearly defined.

 Mastering Mapwork

1. Regina, Saskatchewan, and Winnipeg, Manitoba, are located nearest 50°N.
2. Important points: Encourage students to suggest a variety of answers. Reasons may include the lack of other obvious boundaries.
3. Alberta and Saskatchewan are divided by 110°W.
4. Toronto is located south and west of Ottawa.
5. Manitoba is bounded by the United States on the south, Saskatchewan on the west, the Northwest Territories on the north, Hudson Bay on the northeast, and Ontario on the east.

 Becoming Better Readers

Important points: Student's answers must involve a strategy for understanding and also for making predictions.

CHAPTER 20 REVIEW

Lessons Learned

LESSON 1
The Economy
Canada has one of the world's strongest economies. It has important primary and secondary industries, plus a growing high-tech industry. Most Canadians work in service industries.

LESSON 2
World Partners
Canada and the United States are good neighbors. They cooperate in things like the St. Lawrence Seaway, defense, and trade.

LESSON 3
How Canada's Government Works
Canada is a parliamentary democracy. It is modeled on the system of the United Kingdom. Provinces share power with the national government.

Talk About It

1. Imagine that a Canadian teacher is coming to visit your class. What are the three best questions to ask your guest in order to learn more about Canadian government? Explain why your questions are the best.
2. Canada and the United States have different beliefs about government involvement in business. Most Canadians believe that government should be involved. Many Americans disagree. Why?
3. Which system of government has more advantages: the confederation of Canada or the federalism of the United States? Explain your answer.

Mastering Mapwork

LOCATION
Use the map on page 487 to answer the following questions.

1. Which two provincial capitals are located nearest 50°N?
2. Latitude 60°N forms the boundary of four provinces and one territory in Canada. Why do you think this is the case?
3. Which two provinces share 110°W as a boundary?
4. Describe the location of Toronto relative to Ottawa, the national capital.
5. Describe the relative location of the province of Manitoba.

Becoming Better Readers

Strategies While Reading
Good readers continually ask themselves if they understand what they read. They make predictions about what they will read. What strategies did you use to understand what you read in this chapter?

Go to the Source

Understanding a National Symbol

Canada's national anthem "O Canada" and coat of arms are symbols that unite Canadians. Canada's motto is on the coat of arms. In Latin it means, "A Mari Usque Ad Mare." In English it means, From Sea to Sea. Read the lyrics below and study the coat of arms. Then answer the questions below using information from the sources.

O Canada!
Our home and native land!
True patriot love in all thy sons command.
With glowing hearts we see thee rise,
The True North strong and free!
From far and wide,
O Canada, we stand on guard for thee.
God keep our land glorious and free!
O Canada, we stand on guard for thee.
O Canada, we stand on guard for thee.

Questions
1. When viewing the Canadian coat of arms, what evidence shows that Canada and the United Kingdom were associated with one another?
2. How is patriotism represented in Canada's national anthem?
3. What do you think is the purpose for putting the motto *From Sea to Sea* on the Canadian coat of arms?

Economy and Government   507

 Go to the Source

National Symbols of Canada

OBJECTIVES: 3.06

SOCIAL STUDIES SKILLS: 3.05

Review with students some of the many other symbols in the coat of arms: the three royal lions of England, the royal lion of Scotland, the royal fleurs-de-lis of France and the royal Irish harp of Tara. On the bottom portion of the shield is a sprig of three maple leaves representing Canadians of all origins. For more infomation on the coat of arms, visit **NCJourneys.com** for alink to the Canadian government's descriptiion of it.

As an extension to this activity, have students design their own coat of arms. You may also compare this coat of arms to the seal of the president of the United States in Chapter 17, Lesson 1.

Answers
1. In the coat of arms there is a British flag and a crown. Students may also identify the lion and unicorn as a British symbol.
2. Students should quote lines or stanzas from the song that demonstrates patriotism such as: "O Canada! Our home and native land! True patriot love in all the sons command." or "God keep our land glorious and free!" "O Canada, we stand on guard for thee."
3. It shows pride in their country' size, because Canada extends from the Atlantic Coast to the Pacific coast.

 How to Use the Chapter Review

There are four sections in the Chapter Review: Talk About It, Mastering Mapwork, Becoming Better Readers, and Go to the Source. Use the Vocabulary Worksheets and the Chapter Review Worksheet in the Teacher's Resource Guide for additional reinforcement and preparation for the Chapter Assessments. The chapter and lesson reviews and the Chapter Review Worksheets are the basis of the assessment for each chapter.

Talk About It questions encourage students to speculate about the content of the chapter and are suitable for class or small-group discussion. They are not intended to be assigned for homework.

Mastering Mapwork has students apply one or more of the Five Themes of Geography to maps within the chapter.

Becoming Better Readers focuses on building reading strategy skills necessary for reading comprehension in the content areas.

Go to the Source activities allow students to analyze a primary source that relates to the content of the chapter. The questions and activities familiarize students with different types of primary sources and also build content-reading skills.

Society and Culture

Social Studies Strands

Cultures and Diversity

Global Connections

Technological Influences and Society

North Carolina Standard Course of Study

Goal 2 The learner will analyze political and social institutions in North America and examine how these institutions respond to human needs, structure society, and influence behavior.

Goal 3 The learner will examine the roles various ethnic groups have played in the development of the United States and its neighboring countries.

Goal 4 The learner will trace key developments in United States history and describe their impact on the land and people of the nation and its neighboring countries.

Teaching & Assessment

• English Language Learner Modified Lesson Plans for this chapter are found in the Teacher's Resource Guide.

• *ExamView® Assessment Suite* is provided at **NCJourneys.com.** It includes customizable assessments for all chapters. Paper tests are also available in the Teacher's Resource Guide. See pages T16–T17 for information about how to use the assessments and the Scoring Guide.

Worksheets

Worksheets and answer keys are found both in the Teacher's Resource Guide and at **NCJourneys.com**, including Reading Guides, Reading Strategies, Chapter Reviews, English Language Learner and others.

Activities and Integrations

SOCIAL STUDIES

● All Aboard!, p. 508B
★ Problem Based Learning: Canada's Society and Culture, p. 508B
Activator: Canadian Speaker, p. 508
People of Canada, p. 509
Carolina Connection: Missionaries in Alaska, p. 509
■ Designing an Underground Mall, p. 512
Quebec City Timeline, p. 516
▲ French-Speaking Canada, p. 519
Calgary Day, p. 522

READING/LANGUAGE ARTS	READING/LANGUAGE ARTS OBJECTIVES
Canadian Cultural Showcase, p. 508B	3.06, 4.03
Writing Prompt: Visit a City, p. 508	4.09
● Reading Strategy: Modeling Notetaking, p. 510	2.01, 2.02
▲ ■ City Plaques, p. 511	3.06
Meet Author Robert Munsch, p. 512	2.02, 3.02, 3.03, 4.07
▲ Radio commercial, p. 514	3.06, 4.07
Reading Strategy: Power notes, p. 515	2.02
Going Separate Ways, p. 517	4.07
● Reading Strategy: Sticky Note Discussions, p. 520	2.01, 2.02
Soap Carving, p. 524	4.07
▲ Skill Lesson: Provincial Flags, p. 525	3.06
Becoming Better Readers, p. 526	2.01

SCIENCE		SCIENCE OBJECTIVES
▲ ■ Soap Carving, p. 524		1.02, 1.06

TECHNOLOGY	TECHNOLOGY OBJECTIVES
Badge of Honor, p. 508B	2.13
Canadian Cultural Showcase, p. 508B	2.13

VISUAL ARTS	VISUAL ARTS OBJECTIVES
Badge of Honor, p. 508B	2.01, 3.02
▲ Radio Commercial, p. 514	
▲ ■ Inuit Dioramas, p. 513	2.01, 3.02
★ Going Separate Ways, p. 517	
▲ ■ Window With a View, p. 523	2.01, 3.02
Analyzing Flags, p.527	
▲ ■ Soap Carving, p. 524	2.01, 3.02

CHARACTER AND VALUES EDUCATION	TRAITS
What Would You Do?, p. 519	fairness
Portrait Activity, p.518	perserverence

● Basic Activities   ★ Challenging Activities   ▲ English Language Learner Novice   ■ English Language Learner Intermediate

Introductory Activity

All Aboard!

OBJECTIVES: 1.06, 1.07, 4.07

Ask your students to draw a long train using mural paper. The train is traveling along the Canadian Pacific Railway. Students should fill in the train windows with their own drawings showing different scenes of Canadian life as the train travels across Canada from the Atlantic to the Pacific. Add a conductor holding a sign announcing the provinces the train passes through on its transcontinental journey. All aboard!

 **Culminating Activity**

Canadian Culture Showcase

OBJECTIVES: 1.05, 3.04, 3.06

Time limit: 5 days, approximately.

Divide the class into cooperative groups. Each group will be assigned one of the major ethnic groups of Canada: Scots, French, Danish, Vietnamese, Russian-Jewish, Chinese, Greek, Japanese. These groups will research the heritage of each ethnic group (the Internet is a good resource). Make a map showing where the groups live.

Research the following:

religion	religious symbols
songs	celebrations/traditions
dances	clothing/costumes
customs	occupational preferences
foods	famous Canadians from
artworks	the group

After research, each group will set up a station in a designated area. In stations there will be displays of students' research topics.

Ideas for displays: art gallery, ethnic dishes for tasting, dolls dressed in ethnic costumes, students wearing ethnic costumes, ethnic music playing in background, posters, reports on items on display, slide show, transparencies, video.

Invite parents, the community, and the school to learn more about Canadian culture.

 **Art Activity**

Badge of Honor

OBJECTIVES: 1.05, 1.07, 3.06

The Northwest Mounted Police has its own badge and motto.

Students will create their own badge. Their badge should use emblems or symbols of their own character traits. The badge can be in the shape of a maple leaf, a circle, shield, or any other design. They can look at clip art for more ideas. Have them create a personal motto to print on the badge.

When making the badges have students use heavy paper and cover with gold or silver foil to give an authentic look. They can glue a pin onto the back of the badge and wear it. Have students share the emblems and mottoes on their badges with the class.

 **Problem Based Learning Activity**

Canada's Society and Culture

OBJECTIVES: 1.05, 3.04, 3.06

There are many different festivals that celebrate the cultural background of Canada. Yet as lives get busier and busier, it becomes more difficult for people to find time and the opportunity to share their customs with others.

Situation As a member of a provincial chamber of commerce how would you propose that community members share their culture with others? Consider ways that may involve technology. Festivals and carnivals could be planned, but people need an opportunity to share their backgrounds more than one day per year. How could you provide an opportunity to do this, and why would this be important?

Task Put students into groups, each group representing one province or territory in Canada. Have students review the map on page 509 so they have an idea about the people of their province and their backgrounds. How might the province create opportunities for individuals to share their culture with others? What could be done, and how might it change the traditional ways to do things? As a group, develop a marketing plan. This means that students need to create a proposal for the officials in the provincial government about how their agency will foster cultural development and positive experiences for the citizens of their province. What events throughout the year should be scheduled? What kinds of things might they change or start? Students should create this plan using PowerPoint or a hyperstudio stack and present it to the class.

Reflection Discuss the proposals as a class. Note the advantages and disadvantages of each plan.

Teaching Strategies

This chapter provides excellent opportunities for students to learn about the culture of Canada. Choose activities that will help students learn about the different aspects of culture in our northern neighbor. During the study of this chapter is an excellent time to ask a guest speaker to make a presentation on Canada.

CHAPTER

21

Activator

 OBJECTIVES: 1.07

"So You're Canadian, Eh?" Identify a person in your school or community with a connection to Canada. Invite him or her to describe that connection to the class (5 minutes). Give students a chance to ask questions.

Writing Prompt

 OBJECTIVES: 1.02, 1.06, 1.07

Clarification Choose a Canadian city that you might like to visit. Give three reasons why you would like to visit there.

Essay The French Canadians have insisted that certain parts of their culture be protected with the help of the Canadian government. They feel certain traditions are important and worth preserving. Think of a tradition your family has. Tell about the tradition and why it is important to you and your family.

Caribana Festival parade in Toronto

Society and Culture

The Caribana Festival brings together thousands of people in Toronto each summer. They dress in glittering costumes and dance through the streets. They beat steel drums and sing songs. This parade celebrates the culture of people from the Caribbean islands who now live in Canada.

This parade also shows us the cultural mosaic of Canada. Other festivals honor this, too. People at the Winnipeg Folkarama celebrate the many different cultures in Canada. The Calgary Stampede celebrates western ranch life. The Inuit, Native American, British, and French cultures continue to have a strong presence in everyday life.

The Winnipeg Folkarama attracts Canadians of many cultures.

Chapter Preview

LESSON 1
A Changing Society
Canada has changed as its major cities have grown.

LESSON 2
Tradition Lives
The British and French heritages still affect the lives of Canadians.

LESSON 3
A Cultural Mosaic
The cultures of Canada are like the different pieces of a mosaic that are part of a whole.

508

Chapter Resources

Print Resources
Fiction

Eckert, Allan W. *Return to Hawk's Hill: A Novel.* Little Brown, 1998. ISBN 0316215937.

Greenwood, Barbara. *A Pioneer Sampler: The Daily Life of a Pioneer Family in 1840.* Houghton Mifflin, 1998. ISBN 0395883938.

Stenhouse, Ted. *Across the Steel River.* Kids Can Press, 2001. ISBN 1550748912.

Nonfiction

Corriveau, Danielle. *The Inuit of Canada* (First Peoples series). Lerner Publications, 2001. ISBN 082254850X.

Hamilton, Janice. *Quebec.* (Hello Canada series) Lerner Publications, 1996. ISBN 0822527669.

Hancock, Lyn. *Destination Vancouver.* (Port cities of North America series) Lerner Publications, 1998. ISBN 0822527871.

Livesey, Robert. *The Railways.* Stoddart Kids, 1997. ISBN 0773759018.

Ethnic Groups in Canada

British/Irish/Scottish (B)
French (F)
German (G)
Ukranian (U)
Italian (I)
Chinese (Ch)
Native American/Inuit (Na)
Scandinavian (Sc)
Dutch (D)
South Asian (Sa)
Caribbean (C)

NOTE: Only top 5 ethnicities in each province are graphed.

F. Blount Drane

In 1915, a young North Carolinian reached the village of Fort Yukon. His name was Frederick Blount Drane. His mission was to minister to Native Americans. They lived along the Yukon River north of the Arctic Circle.

It was a cold place for a man from North Carolina. Drane learned from the villagers. He wore a caribou-skin parka, sealskin boots, and snowshoes. He ate the same foods they ate.

After a decade in the Arctic, Reverend Drane returned to North Carolina. During the rest of his life, he looked back fondly on his days of living in the north.

509

Discussion Questions

1 What are some of the cultural celebrations of Canadians?

2 What is the major ethnic group represented in each province and territory?

Map Activity

People of Canada

NATIONAL GEOGRAPHY STANDARDS: 1, 4
GEOGRAPHIC THEMES: Movement
OBJECTIVES: 1.01

Have students look at the pie charts on the map on this page. Then, using a globe or a large map of the world, as a class, trace the possible routes the various ethnic groups would have taken to get to Canada. Which groups came the farthest? Which groups have been in Canada the longest (don't forget to trace the route of the Inuit and Native Americans across Berengia)? What groups might be included in the "other category"? Discuss how this movement is similar to or different from immigration in the United States.

Activity

Carolina Connection: Missionaries in Alaska

OBJECTIVES: 3.05

Have students search the Internet for information on missionaries who went to Alaska. Their guiding research question should be to compare why missionaries may have gone to Alaska or the far north. Then have them compare these reasons with the reasons that European Christian missionaries came to the Americas in the 1500s.

Rogers, Barbara Radcliffe. *Toronto.* (Cities of the World series) Children's Press, 2000. ISBN 0516220349.

Rogers, Stillman. *Montreal.* (Cities of the World series) Children's Press, New York, 2000. ISBN 0516216376.

Wilner, Barry. *Mark Messier* (Ice Hockey Legends series). Chelsea House, 1997. ISBN 0791045595.

Web Sites

Visit **NCJourneys.com** for links to these Web sites:
- Canadian Heritage
- Christmas Traditions in France and in Canada
- Cool Canada
- Culture.ca, Canada's Cultural Gateway
- Prince Edward Island and Lucy Maud Montgomery
- Quebec 400th
- Royal Canadian Mounted Police

LESSON 1 A Changing Society

Discussion Questions

1 Why do many citizens and immigrants choose to live in Canada's cities?

2 How does Montreal rank among Canada's cities? What features contribute to its "French Flavor"?

Caption Answer

French movies, theaters, and art exhibitions

Reading Strategy Activity

Modeling Notetaking

🏴 **OBJECTIVES:** 1.05, 1.07, 3.04, 3.06

Taking notes is a good way to remember facts for a test. When students write something, they recall the information better. Reading over those notes before the test is a good way to trigger memory about what was read earlier.

Fifth graders have difficulty selecting important facts for notetaking. They usually want to write everything they read instead of the most important things. Modeling the technique will give students a clearer understanding.

Take notes on Chapter 21, Lesson 1, together. First, decide the purpose for taking these notes. Will a test be given on the material? Discuss your purpose with the class.

Read the first section, Montreal. Ask several students what they think the important points are. Accept all answers and don't correct even the ones you consider incorrect. You may say something like, "These are good ideas. Let's read the passage again and decide which ones are the most important and write those."

Use the Think Aloud method to show students how you came up with the important notes: "This sentence is interesting, but I don't think I need to write it down," or "Who can write this sentence with the fewest words and still keep the meaning?" Let students suggest

KEY IDEAS

- Most Canadians live in cities, and each city gives its residents a unique way of life.

- Life has changed in the Arctic for native people because of television, satellites, and airplanes.

Today, 80 percent of all Canadians live in cities. They move there for jobs. City life is also exciting. Canada's cities are some of the safest, cleanest, and best-run in the world.

Most immigrants to Canada move to cities, too. Newcomers look for jobs. But they also want to live near people from their homeland. They share customs and language.

Let's take a walk through five of Canada's cities. Each shows the different ways of life in Canada.

Montreal

Montreal is Canada's third-oldest and second-largest city. It was founded around 400 years ago on the St. Lawrence River.

An Inland Seaport

This location helped Montreal grow. It was once a small settlement in New France. Today it is one of the world's great ports. Montreal is now a major transportation and financial center.

The city is on an island in the middle of the St. Lawrence River. The island is 30 miles (48 km) long and less than 10 miles (16 km) wide. The city was built at a point where the river narrowed. Here rapids stopped boats from sailing farther up the river. Therefore, many early travelers had to leave the river and carry their canoes overland.

Several streets in Montreal look like Paris. **What are some less obvious signs of French culture in Montreal?**

510

Chapter 21

shortened notes. Write them on the overhead for students to copy.

Read the section sentence by sentence and model the procedure. Do more sections of the chapter with the whole class if it is needed. Some classes need more modeling than others. Divide the class into groups and give each group a large piece of paper. Let each group take notes on a different section of the chapter. Bring the class together to share the notes.

This view of Montreal's skyline makes the city look different from Toronto (see below). **Why do you think they do not look alike?**

Many people of British, Irish, Russian, Chinese, and West Indian heritage also make their home there. But the city still has a strong French flavor.

Montreal is a showcase for French culture in North America. It has many theaters, movies, and art exhibits by French and French-Canadian artists. One proud resident stated that it was "possible to see the latest French movies as soon as they see them in Paris. We hear French orchestras and see French theater and ballet."

Until the St. Lawrence Seaway opened, Montreal was the farthest point inland that large oceangoing ships could reach. It is about 1,000 miles (1,610 km) from the Atlantic Ocean. But even so, it is one of the world's largest inland seaports.

People

Montreal has more French-speaking people than any city except Paris, France.

Toronto

Toronto is Canada's largest city. It is also Canada's banking and business center. The city is located on Lake Ontario and the St. Lawrence Seaway. It has many businesses that make and ship products from the mines and forests of the Canadian Shield.

Like many cities, Toronto has an underground shopping center. But Toronto's is the largest in the world. There are 16 miles (26 km) of walkways. You can shop in any of 1,200 stores.

From a distance, Toronto looks like many big cities in the United States. **What has Toronto built underground?**

Society and Culture

511

Discussion Questions

1 If you were to visit Toronto, what would you like to see?

 Caption Answer

Montreal is an older city.

 Caption Answer

Toronto has an underground city with three levels of shops and restaurants and more than 1,000 stores.

 Activity

City Plaques

 OBJECTIVES: 1.02, 1.03, 1.07

Have students research a Canadian city, such as Montreal, Toronto, Vancouver, Winnipeg, and so on. Take notes of natural resources, symbols, vegetation, or other features for which the city is known. Provide construction paper at least 6-inches by 18-inches. Students will write the city's name in large, bold, outline letters. They will draw representations of the city inside each letter. Illustrations can come from industry (banking, fashion design), natural resources (trees, flowers, animals, birds, minerals), history (famous individuals, buildings, battles), sports (hockey, baseball, football, lacrosse, curling), nicknames, and annual events (Blue Jays, Calgary Stampede, City of Roses).

 Teacher Notes

Winnie the Bear

The American black bear after whom the character Winnie the Pooh was named was brought to England in 1914 by a Canadian army officer named Harry Colebourn. Colebourn had been trained at the Ontario Veterinary College and on his way to England for the war, his train stopped at White River, Ontario. There, Colebourn bought a small female black bear cub from a hunter who had killed its mother. Colebourn named the bear Winnie, after his hometown of Winnipeg. When the Brigade was called to action in France, Colebourn took Winnie to the London Zoo for a long loan. Colebourn survived the war and formally presented the London Zoo with Winnie in December 1919. Winnie became a popular attraction and lived until 1934. The bear was the favorite of the son of A.A. Milne, Christopher Robin, at the zoo, and Christopher Robin often spent time inside the cage with it.

Discussion Questions

1 What are some of the ethnic groups living in Toronto?

2 How does Vancouver rank among Canada's cities?

3 What are some reasons people enjoy living there?

4 Which ethnic group is Vancouver's largest?

Caption Answer

Answers will vary. Vancouver has a mild climate, scenic views, and a diverse community.

Activity

Meet Author Robert Munsch

OBJECTIVES: 1.05, 1.06, 3.07

Show students how to use graphic organizers. Read aloud the *Paper Bag Princess* by Robert Munsch (Firefly Books, 1985. ISBN 0920236162.) to a certain point and ask students to predict the ending. Use a Venn Diagram to compare Elizabeth, the main character, with other princesses in other stories, such as Cinderella or Snow White.

In large groups or in smaller cooperative groups have students list and discuss the character traits of Elizabeth, Ronald, and Dragon. Have students team up with a buddy from kindergarten or first grade and read aloud to their buddies other books by Canadian authors.

Culmination Have students write and illustrate their own original picture book about Canada.

People

In Toronto we can see the mosaic of Canada's culture. There are many ethnic groups that call the city home. Greeks, Italians, South Asians, Chinese, and many other ethnic groups have their neighborhoods. You will see restaurants, grocery stores, and gathering places.

Tomson Highway is a Native American who writes plays. He once wrote,

> *In Toronto, I can see the skin colorings of every race on the planet . . . . And I can hear the sound of languages from the four corners of the world . . . . This diversity, this richness of cultures, this electric mixture of so many strands of humanity . . . makes this country so unique, so lovable.*

Sports

Sports fans enjoy the Rogers Centre. Its roof can open and close depending on the weather. Fans can watch games year-round. In the summer they go see the Blue Jays play baseball.

Hockey is Canada's national sport. Fans of the Toronto Maple Leafs can watch them shoot pucks into the net at the Air Canada Centre.

Many tourists from the United States like to visit Vancouver as well as Seattle when they visit the Pacific Coast. **Would you like to travel there? Why?**

Vancouver

Vancouver is on the West Coast. It is the largest city in British Columbia. It is the third-largest urban area in Canada.

The city is located on a peninsula that points into the Pacific Ocean. Vancouver has a mild climate. Its harbor stays ice-free all year. Because of this and its location on the West Coast, Vancouver is a key port. It is Canada's main gateway for trade with Pacific Rim countries and the northwestern United States. It is Canada's busiest port.

Like Toronto, Vancouver is an English-speaking city. Its citizens come from many cultures. People of many faiths live and worship there. Some go to Buddhist temples. Others go to synagogues or churches.

Asian Cultures

Many people of Asian descent live in Vancouver. Its first Asian settlers were from China. They came to mine the gold fields on the Fraser River. Later, more Chinese were brought over to build railroads.

Recently, many Chinese have come from Hong Kong. They left there before the British turned the city over to China in 1997. Chinese residents make up about 17 percent of the city's population. Vancouver also has strong Vietnamese, Japanese, and South Asian communities.

Activity

Designing an Underground Mall

OBJECTIVES: 1.02, 1.06, 3.04

Have students, individually or in cooperative groups, design their own underground malls with entertainment facilities. These could be maplike drawings or clay models. Have individuals or groups share their designs and explain why they designed the mall the way they did.

Winnipeg

Rivers and railroads helped Winnipeg grow. The Hudson Bay Company owned the land in what is now Manitoba. Fur traders and trappers built a trading post at the place where the Red and Assiniboine (as·SIN·ih·BOIN) Rivers meet. This became the town of Winnipeg.

The tracks of the Canadian Pacific Railway were laid through Winnipeg. The new railroad helped the prairie town grow. Farmers brought their grain to the railroad to ship it east.

Winnipeg built farm supply centers and grain elevators. These stored the wheat until the trains came to take it to market. Today, Winnipeg is a large city. Canadians call it the "Gateway to the West."

Winnipeg started as a small prairie town. It is now a big city. **Are there any signs it is a place linked to nearby grain and cattle industries?**

Iqaluit

Canada's newest and most northerly capital city is Iqaluit. Only about 7,250 people live there. It has a unique history.

The Inuit people did not build permanent cities. They followed and hunted game in the summer. In the winter they lived along the coast and hunted seals.

In the 1800s, Europeans came to the area to hunt whales. They built a village that became Iqaluit. Inuit later settled there, too. Some took jobs working for the Europeans.

In the 1970s, the Inuit told the government of Canada that they wanted their own territory. This dream came true. In 1999, Nunavut was created out of land that was part of the Northwest Territories.

Iqaluit is the capital of Nunavut. **Why was it important for the Inuit to have their own territory?**

Discussion Questions

1 How has Winnipeg changed over the years?

2 What caused the change?

3 What are some of the changes and problems facing the Inuit and other Native Americans of Canada?

4 How is the government trying to help?

Caption Answer

There are grain elevators in the picture.

Caption Answer

Their lifestyle and culture is tied to the land.

Art Activity

Inuit Dioramas

OBJECTIVES: 1.05, 1.07, 3.04

Have students make shoe box dioramas showing traditional (prior to 1960) Inuit homes, clothing, and other aspects of Inuit life. Make contrasting dioramas to show modern Inuit homes, clothing, and transportation. Discuss changes in lifestyle and possible reasons for the changes.

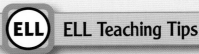

ELL Teaching Tips

Avoid Singling Out ELL Students

If you have some important information to convey, speak to the student one-on-one rather than in front of the class. When they are put on the spot, it is more difficult for them to understand what you expect.

Background Information

Wintry Winnipeg

In spite of winter temperatures hitting –30° F, Winnipeg has a population of more than 680,000. It is the capital of Manitoba province, and one half of all the people living in the province make their homes in this city. The nearest large city, Minneapolis, Minnesota in the United States, is 450 miles away.

Winnipeg's boom years stretched from the 1880s through the 1920s after the Canadian Pacific Railroad brought thousands of immigrants from the United States, Europe, and Iceland. Offers of free farmland drew many settlers, as did the promise of religious freedom. Some of the mansions, banks, warehouses, and other buildings from this era of prosperity remain in Winnipeg's historic district.

Discussion Questions

1 Why is it important that tundra buggies protect the tundra?

Writing Activity

A Radio Commercial

OBJECTIVES: 1.03, 3.06, 3.07

Have students choose their favorite Canadian city and brainstorm what makes that city interesting. Students will create a radio advertisement for their city. The advertisement may include a catchy jingle or popular song with new words, an interview with "a person in the street" in that city, sound effects, slogans, and so on.

Example:

Crack! (sound of bat hitting ball) "Take Me Out to the Ballgame" playing in the background. Text may be: "Hurry right this way. Get your peanuts, popcorn, and see the best ballgame in town: the Toronto Blue Jays versus the Texas Rangers! Remember—Toronto—the place to be! The Sky Dome's the limit!"

The City Today

Iqaluit is the capital of Nunavut. It is Canada's fastest-growing community. It only officially became a city in 2001. Iqaluit's economy is based on being the capital. It now has many government offices. People usually travel to Iqaluit by airplane.

Iqaluit is located on the Arctic tundra on Baffin Island. In the summer, it has 21 hours of sunshine a day. But in the winter, it is extremely cold. During December, days are short. The sun rises and sets within four hours.

Blizzards and high winds can stop travel in the Arctic. So winter visitors sometimes have to spend an extra night or two in the North. This is called being "weathered-in."

Wildlife in Churchill

The Canadian town of Churchill in Manitoba is alive with wildlife.

Each fall, Churchill becomes the polar bear capital of the world. About 1,200 bears gather on the icy tundra. They are waiting for the the Hudson Bay to freeze. Then they will wander out on the ice to find seals.

Special tour buses called tundra buggies take visitors to see the polar bears. The buggies have huge tires. The tires do not hurt the tundra as much as regular bus or car tires can. Bears come right up to the buggies. Bears are beautiful, but dangerous.

In summertime, Beluga whales swim in the Hudson Bay and Churchill River. These are small whales that look much like porpoises. They are born gray, but turn snow-white when adults. Belugas are friendly and curious. They let people swim with them. People enjoy whale watching trips to see the Belugas.

Other species that can be seen in the area are caribou, harp seals, arctic foxes, and ptarmigans (snow chickens).

LESSON 1 REVIEW

Fact Follow-Up
1. What are some similarities among the five cities described in the text?
2. Why is Vancouver a center for Asian culture?
3. How have the changes in arctic life affected the Inuit?
4. What is Churchill, Manitoba, famous for?

Talk About It
1. How do differences among Canada's cities reflect the variety of the nation's people?
2. Why do you think it was important for the Inuit to have their own territory? Explain.
3. How is life in Canada's cities similar to and different from life in cities in the United States?

LESSON 1 REVIEW

Fact Follow-Up Answers
1. All are located in southern Canada, near the border with the United States. All are provincial capitals and large cities, Toronto being the largest. All are located near either freshwater or saltwater, and water has been important in the development of each.
2. In the past, Chinese immigrants came there to work in gold mines. In recent years, many people have moved there from Hong Kong.
3. Traditional ways of life are passing away. Jobs are scarce, and young people must move south to find work.
4. Polar bears and Beluga whales

Talk About It Answers
1. Important points: Encourage students to suggest a variety of differences and link the differences to the mosaic of Canada's people. All cities are home to people from many cultures. In the east, Montreal reflects a definite French influence. In the west, Vancouver shows the influence of Asia.
2. Important points: After having so many things take away from them by Europeans, the Inuit wanted to claim some land as their own to preserve their own culture and way of life.
3. Important points: Students should compare and contrast what they know about American cities with Canadian cities. Both countries have cities that are modern, busy places with tall buildings. Nunavut is different, being in the far north with a small population.

The United States fought a revolution to free itself from Great Britain. The Canadians did not. They loosened their ties slowly and peacefully.

Canadians still have strong British connections. Parts of Canada also have deep roots in French culture. Both traditions are alive today. This unites some people. It also brings challenges.

British Ties

Canada is still part of the **British Commonwealth of Nations.** This group is made up of the United Kingdom and some of its former colonies. Some of the other countries that belong are Australia, India, Kenya, Jamaica, and other nations. They are connected by their history as British colonies.

The British legacy is everywhere in Canada. It can be seen in the English language, the form of government, and the court system. British style has influenced the design of buildings and cities. Ottawa, the nation's capital, and Toronto, Canada's largest city, have many British-style buildings.

During World Wars I and II, the British and Canadians fought side by side. During World War II, Canadian warships escorted supply ships across the Atlantic. They brought badly needed aid to the British.

Is this the United Kingdom? No, it is Canada. The ceremony and uniforms look British. **If you were Canadian, what might you be proud of in Canada's British heritage?**

Society and Culture

515

KEY IDEAS

- Canada has strong ties with the United Kingdom.

- Signs of Canadian culture are the national flag and song.

- Descendants of French settlers preserve their French culture and customs.

KEY TERMS

British Commonwealth of Nations
"God Save the Queen"
"O Canada"

Example A

Power Notes: Sports

    Power 1: Sports
        Power 2: Football
            Power 3: Oblong ball
            Power 3: 100 yard field
        Power 2: Tennis
            Power 3: Racket
            Power 3: Tennis court

Example B

Power Notes: Animals

    1. Animals
      2. Horses
        3. Thoroughbreds
        3. Quarterhorse
      2. Bears
        3. Grizzly
        3. Polar
      2. Cats
        3. Persian
        3. Siamese

 **OBJECTIVES:** 1.05, 1.07, 3.06, 4.07

Discussion Questions

1 How was Canada's independence from Great Britain different from the United States'?

2 What is the British Commonwealth of Nations? Who are members?

3 In what ways are British influences present in Canada?

💬 Caption Answer

Answers will vary. Possibilities include government, courts, and architecture.

📖 Reading Strategy Activity

Power Notes

OBJECTIVES: 1.05, 1.07, 3.06, 4.07

Power notes are a way to help students understand the difference between main ideas and supporting details. It is close to outlining except that main ideas are assigned a 1, and details are assigned a 2, 3, and so on. It is good to use power notes with content materials because it helps students organize ideas.

Show the following diagram:
    Power 1: Main idea
        Power 2: Detail for power 1
            Power 3: Detail for power 2

Choose a familiar topic. Point out that details for the main idea have a 2, and details for a 2 have a 3. See Example A (far left). Choose another topic. Let students supply the power 2s and 3s while you write them in. See Example B (left). Divide the class into groups of four and choose a topic such as music, to be the power 1. Students will work together to fill in the blanks. Check each group's results to see which group is first.

Point out the way the title and subheadings in Lesson 2 are arranged as 1 and 2 power notes. Have students fill in the power 3 notes.

515

Discussion Questions

1 Quebec City turned 400 years old in 2008. Why do you think its French culture has lasted so long when Canada is largely an English-speaking nation?

 Eyewitness Activity

Quebec City Timeline

OBJECTIVES: 3.01, 4.02

Using the information found in the Eyewitness to History as well las outside or Internet sources, instruct students to create a timeline that compares the settlement of Jamestown with the founding of Quebec. They should search on the Internet for a timeline of Quebec's settlement and a timeline of Jamestown's settlement. After students finish their timelines, ask them to write a paragraph describing what each colony did similarly and differently.

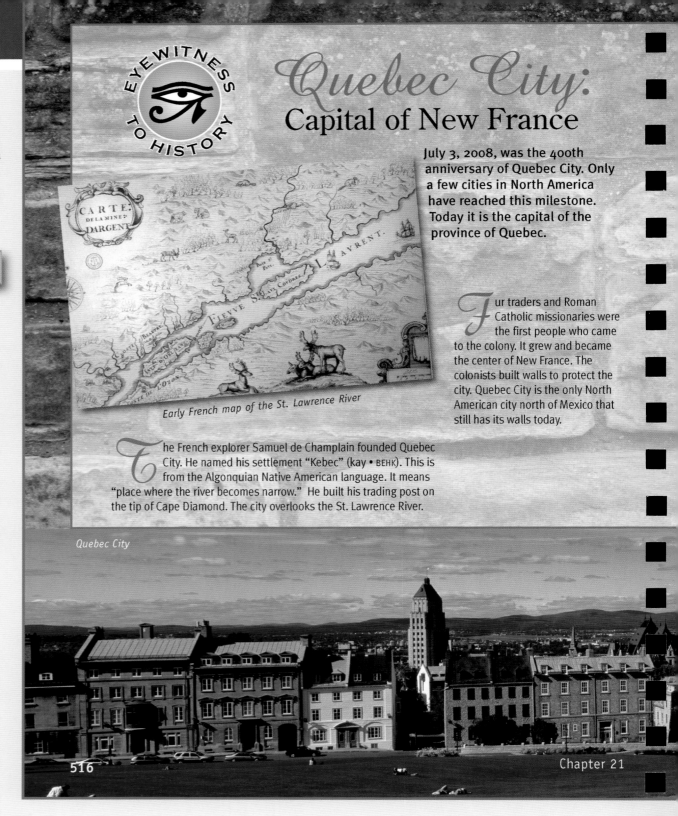

Quebec City: Capital of New France

July 3, 2008, was the 400th anniversary of Quebec City. Only a few cities in North America have reached this milestone. Today it is the capital of the province of Quebec.

Early French map of the St. Lawrence River

Fur traders and Roman Catholic missionaries were the first people who came to the colony. It grew and became the center of New France. The colonists built walls to protect the city. Quebec City is the only North American city north of Mexico that still has its walls today.

The French explorer Samuel de Champlain founded Quebec City. He named his settlement "Kebec" (kay • BEHK). This is from the Algonquian Native American language. It means "place where the river becomes narrow." He built his trading post on the tip of Cape Diamond. The city overlooks the St. Lawrence River.

Quebec City

516

Quebec City has a long and rich history. In 1759, the British and French fought a famous battle on the Plains of Abraham. The British won and took control of the city. This led to France's surrender of North America in the Seven Years War (French and Indian War).

Illustration of Quebec City in the 1700s

After Great Britain controlled the colony, parliment passed the Quebec Act. It gave religious freedom to the people of Quebec. This was one reason why the French there chose not to join in the American Revolution. So the 13 colonies invaded Quebec instead. In the winter of 1775–1776, American troops tried to capture Quebec City. But they failed. The walls protected the city until more British troops arrived in the spring.

In World War II, two conferences were held in Quebec City with the leaders of the United States, the United Kingdom, and Canada. There they made plans for the invasion of Europe in 1944.

United States President Franklin Roosevelt and the Prime Minister of the United Kingdom Winston Churchill (standing, right) met with other officials at the Quebec Conference in 1943.

Society and Culture

517

Writing Activity

Going Separate Ways

OBJECTIVES: 1.05, 1.07, 2.04

Discover how Canada and the United States handled the separation from Great Britain differently. Simulate the early colonial days of both Canada and the United States just before the United States separated from Britain. Have half of the class be Canadian colonists and the other half be United States colonists. Have students research the events of both periods and how the British homeland influenced the events. Create timelines, do story boards, and stage historical re-enactments showing how they break from the "mother country." Finally, have students write a story about their new country from the point-of-view of a citizen, culminating with how the separation from Britain occurred. Be sure to have them include the feelings that their citizen would have felt relating to particular historical events, such as the Boston Tea Party. Their feelings might explain why the separation of the United States from Britain was so much sharper than Canada's separation. Present-day Canadians still maintain loyalty to the United Kingdom, but the United States does not.

Discussion Questions

 In what ways are French influences present in Canada?

 **Caption Answer**

Canadians were working to build a national identity.

 **Activity**

Portrait Activity

OBJECTIVES: 4.03

Divide the class into pairs or groups of three. Each pair of students will visit a variety of Web sites and use classroom and library resources to gather information about Lucy Maud Montgomery. Distribute appropriate graphic organizers (see the Graphic Organizers in the Teacher's Resource Guide) to help students take notes. Once their research is complete, each pair will create a storyboard about Montgomery's life. Using this information they will produce a short digital story (using PowerPoint or other programs) to share the information they have learned with the class. Have students read aloud sections of Montgomery's writings that describe life on Prince Edward Island or in Canada.

CANADIAN PORTRAIT

Lucy Maud Montgomery
1874–1942

Lucy Maud Montgomery was born on Prince Edward Island. Her mother died before she turned two. After his wife's death, her father went to live in the western territories of Canada. Montgomery went to live with her grandparents. When she turned sixteen, she was to Saskatchewan to live with her father and stepmother. She only stayed one year. Then she returned to Prince Edward Island.

Montgomery went to Prince of Wales College in Charlottetown on the Island. She graduated with a teaching certificate and taught at several schools on the Island. She also briefly worked for two newspapers for a short time. Then Montgomery moved back home to care for her grandmother.

During this time she began to write stories and poems. In 1908, she published her first book, *Anne of Green Gables*. She wrote more than 500 short stories and poems and 20 novels. Nineteen of the novels were set on Prince Edward Island.

After her grandmother's death, Montgomery married Ewan Macdonald, a minister, and they moved to Ontario. They had three sons. One died at birth. She lived in Ontario for the last years of her life.

Montgomery's stories are still read by people around the world. After World War II, *Anne of Green Gables* was translated into Japanese. Today, people join Lucy Maud Montgomery book clubs in Japan. They meet to read and talk about her books. Thousands of people from Japan and other nations visit her home on Prince Edward Island each year.

518

This is the Maple Leaf flag. It replaced the Union Jack as Canada's national symbol. **Why did Canada want a new flag?**

New Symbols

Canada's first flag was called the Union Jack. It also showed Canada's close ties with the United Kingdom. The United Kingdom's flag is also called the Union Jack.

For many years, Canadian bands played *"God Save the Queen"* at official ceremonies. Children sang it in school. This song is the United Kingdom's national anthem.

Canadians thought it was important to create their own national symbols. In 1965, Canada chose the Maple Leaf flag to be its new symbol. *"O Canada"* became Canada's national anthem in 1980.

French Identity

French language and French customs also have a long tradition in Canada. It was a French colony for more than 150 years. It only became a British colony in 1763.

Quebec Province was the home of French settlers. It is still home to the majority of French-speaking Canadians today (see map, page 509).

WORD ORIGINS

The Montreal **Canadiens** are an NHL hockey team. But why do they call themselves the Canadiens and not the Canadians?

People who live in Canada call themselves by two different names. English speakers call themselves "Canadians." People who speak French use the word "Canadien." It is the French spelling.

To French speakers, the name and the team are symbols of their ties with France.

I Remember

Many French Canadians take great pride in their French ancestry, culture, and language. The provincial flag has four white *fleur de lis*, the symbol of France. Quebec's motto is *Je me souviens.* This means "I remember" in English. It means that the people of Quebec remember their French heritage.

A French-Canadian businessman spoke proudly of Quebec's ties with France:

> *Our French-Canadian writers are published in France, our best students go to France . . . . Even for the average person, Paris is just around the corner. In the last 30 years we have grown back together with France.*

He and others want to make sure that Quebec stays French in culture. More than 80 percent of the people in Quebec speak French as their first language. Only about 10 percent of people who live in Quebec consider English their first language. Most live around Montreal. Many of them speak French as well.

Until 1974, both English and French were official languages of Quebec. That year, Quebec voters decided to make French the only official language. All children must attend French-speaking schools.

Some large businesses did not like this. **So they moved their headquarters from** Montreal to Toronto. Many English-speaking families left as well.

About 40 percent of Canada's population is Roman Catholic. Membership in that church is a reminder of the strong French culture in Canada.

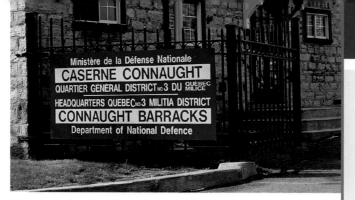

Signs in Quebec are written in French and usually do not include an English translation, such as the one at left. **Why do you think that sign is written in both English and French?**

What would YOU do?

If you walk down a street anywhere in Quebec, you might have trouble finding your way unless you speak French. Due to a law passed in the 1980s, all signs must be written in French.

Supporters of the law say it is fair. Most of the province's residents speak French. Some of Quebec's English speakers disagree. They feel discriminated against. They have asked for the law to be repealed. **What would you do? Why?**

LESSON 2 REVIEW

Fact Follow-Up
1. How do both British and French traditions persist in Canada today?
2. What are Canadian connections to Britain? to France?
3. What are some signs of British culture in Canada? of French culture?

Talk About It
1. Why do you think some French-speaking Canadians might want Quebec to separate from Canada?
2. Why might the British and French cultures not always fit together? How can the government help people get along?

Society and Culture   **519**

OBJECTIVES: 3.04, 3.06, 3.07

Discussion Questions

1 If you and your family were able to attend any of the celebrations of cultural differences mentioned in the book, which would you choose? Why?

Caption Answer

It is an acknowledgment of the importance of different cultures in a nation.

Reading Strategy Activity

Sticky-Note Discussions

OBJECTIVES: 3.04, 3.06, 3.07

Sticky-notes work great to help students take an active part in reading. Students stay focused on the material and comprehend more when they are assigned a specific task.

Small sticky-notes work best. Instead of throwing away the notes when this lesson is complete, ask students to place their notes on the inside cover of their textbook to use again when reading another lesson.

Students should place a sticky-note on any area or picture they either think is interesting and would like to discuss, don't understand and would like to ask a question about, or have something they know more about and would like to share with the class. Modeling always helps students understand what is expected. As you read page 520 aloud, stop when you come to a place where you would place a sticky note and explain why you would place it there.

When students have the concept, have them read the remainder of the lesson. Suggest they place one note per subheading. Discussion begins by having students talk about a place they marked and explain why they marked it. Discussions can be done in small groups with one person acting as the leader.

KEY IDEAS

- Canadian culture is called a mosaic.
- Each ethnic group maintains its important traditions.
- Canadians share a love for the outdoor life and hockey.
- Inuit and Native American art is highly valued today.

KEY TERMS

Calgary Stampede
ice hockey
Stanley Cup

Many people who have studied Canada and its people say that Canadian culture is hard to define. It includes the favorite sports, art, music, festivals, and other ways Canadians enjoy themselves. Canada's culture is a mosaic made of many people and traditions.

A Year of Festivals

Throughout the year, many Canadian cities hold festivals. These highlight the customs of different groups and regions in Canada.

Icelandic The largest settlement of Icelanders outside Iceland is in Gimli, Manitoba. They hold a three-day festival to celebrate that town's Icelandic heritage.

Scottish Nova Scotia means "New Scotland." The community of Antigonish there holds the Highland Games. They are the world's longest running highland games outside of Scotland.

Chinese Vancouver hosts North America's largest Chinese fair each January. The festival is the biggest of its kind anywhere in the world outside of China.

There are other festivals that celebrate things unique to Canada.

These are scenes from Scottish (left) and Icelandic (below) festivals. The festivals celebrate those cultures in Canada. **Why is it important to celebrate different cultures?**

39

520

Chapter 21

ℹ Background Information

Celebrating the Viking Past

A tiny fishing village in Newfoundland hopes to raise awareness of its place in the history of the Americas by attracting tourists to L'Anse aux Meadows, on the northernmost tip of Newfoundland. This site holds the remains of a thousand-year-old Viking settlement, the first in the Americas. The town has a sod-covered church and a chieftain's hall that is part of a replica of a Norse port. These tourist attractions sit close by the ruins of the real Viking village, which was declared a UNESCO World Heritage Site.

Maple Sugar

The maple leaf is Canada's national symbol. Maple festivals in Quebec, Ontario, and the Maritimes are popular. Many communities host these festivals each spring. The sap runs in maple trees in March. It is tapped and boiled down to make maple syrup.

Eastern Canada produces 85 percent of the world's maple syrup. The rest is made in the northeastern United States.

Calgary Stampede

In early July. Calgary, Alberta hosts the *Calgary Stampede.* It is Canada's' largest annual event. It is also the world's largest outdoor rodeo. It celebrates Canada's western heritage.

The stampede has many events in addition to the rodeo. There are concerts, agricultural competitions, chuckwagon races, Native American exhibits, and other things to do. You can eat at one of the many pancake breakfasts held around the city, too.

Canadians show their pride in their heritage and their country in all of these special celebrations.

The Calgary Stampede features chuckwagon races and other events to celebrate the western heritage of Canada. **If your town had a festival, what would it be like?**

Society and Culture

CANADIAN PORTRAIT

Wayne Gretzky
1961–

Wayne Gretzky's nickname is "The Great One." He is the greatest hockey player of all time and a member of the Hockey Hall of Fame.

Gretzky grew up in Ontario. His father was an immigrant from Poland. When Gretzky was six years old, he was good enough to play on a team with ten-year-olds. His jersey was too big, so his father tucked in the back right side. He played all his games that way from then on.

As a youth, Gretzky always played with older, bigger, faster players. "I could never beat any people with my strength," he said. "My eyes and my mind have to do most of the work."

When Gretzky was seventeen, he became a professional. The next year he joined the Edmonton Oilers. After playing there for nine years, he was traded to the Los Angeles Kings. Many Canadians were upset to see him play for a team in the United States.

Gretzky had an amazing career. He helped win four Stanley Cup Championships and three Canada Cups. He was the National Hockey League's (NHL) all-time goal, assist, and points leader. He retired in 1999.

He is the only player who will ever wear the number 99. The NHL retired that number for all its teams.

Gretzky is still active in hockey. He managed the Canadian men's hockey team for the 2002 Winter Olympics. He became a coach for the Phoenix, Arizona, Coyotes NHL team in 2005.

521

 **Caption Answer**

Answers will vary. Celebrations might center on a cultural tradition, a unique part of the landscape, or a local product.

Discussion Questions

1 What are some activities that Canadian families do that are the same as American families? What are some that are different?

 **Activity**

Calgary Day

📐 **OBJECTIVES:** 1.06, 1.07, 4.07

Invite students to dress in cowboy attire on the designated day. Treat the class to a pancake and maple syrup breakfast. After eating the pancakes and cleaning up, explain to the students they are going to be treated to a morning similar to the Calgary Stampede in Calgary, Alberta. The children will participate in games that reenact events similar to what is held at the Calgary Stampede.

Wild Horse Race Rules: Divide your class into equal teams. Set up an obstacle course using cones or milk jugs. Each team will have one "wild horse"—a broom or stick pony to ride. When the whistle blows, each contestant rides the pony down through the obstacle course and back. Once they cross the starting line, the pony is passed to the next contestant on the team and the race continues until every rider has gone through the obstacle course. The first team to successfully ride the pony in the shortest amount of time will be declared the winning team.

Bucking Bronco Rules: Keep the same teams as in the previous game. Give each team an old sheet and one nerf ball (the Bronco). Each team member will position himself or herself around the sheet. They must hold the sheet with both hands and stretch it until it is tight and at waist level. Place a nerf ball in the center of the sheet. At the signal, each team will fan the sheet in an up-and-down motion trying to keep the nerf ball on the sheet. The object of the game is to keep the ball on the sheet as it is being fanned. The team that keeps the ball moving and on the sheet the longest will be declared the winner.

Rope the Steer Rules: Keep the same teams. Place cones, milk jugs, bowling pins, or any item to represent the steer to be "roped." Place the items to be roped at a desired distance from the starting line. Give each team three hula hoops. Most PE teachers have hula hoops and will loan them out. Students will have three chances to rope the steer by throwing the hula hoop around the cone or whatever item you have chosen to represent the steer. The team that ropes the most steers wins the game.

Chuckwagon Race Rules: Keep the same teams and run relays. Each team will be given a wagon. Place food items in the wagon, such as canned foods, a loaf of bread, bottled water, pots and pans, and so on. All wagons must have the same number of items. At the start signal, each student must "drive" (pull) their wagon through the obstacle course and back. They are not allowed to lose any items out of their wagon. If an item falls out, they must stop and reload the wagon. Then they may continue the race. The first team to success-fully complete the race first wins.

The team that wins the majority of the relays listed above becomes the Calgary Champs. Suggested prizes: blue ribbons, Canadian coins, school supplies, medals, candy, a bandanna. Following the events of the "stampede" teach the children a square dance and serve lemonade and cookies.

Being Canadian

Canada is a proud nation. Its citizens enjoy their lifestyle. They also appreciate the quality of life that their nation provides.

But Canadians also face challenges. Some come from having such strong provincial governments. Other challenges come from having strong but different cultural backgrounds.

First Nations

Canadians call the Native Americans who live in their country the First Nations. Canada has tried to be more respectful of First Nations cultures than it has in the past. Inuit peoples are not part of the First Nations.

Canadians appreciate and showcase Native American arts and crafts. In British Columbia at a Kwakiutl (kwa·ki·YOO·tul) village, carvers make woodcarvings known as totem poles. These carvings honor their ancestors.

Regional Loyalties

Within regions like the prairie provinces or the Atlantic provinces, people have much in common. Some Canadians may feel greater loyalty to their province than to the country as a whole.

It is as though, said one Canadian, "there is an Ontario patriotism, a Quebec patriotism, or a western patriotism, but there is no Canadian patriotism." These loyalties have made it harder for Canadians to come together as a nation.

But Canadians are united by a love of hockey and the outdoors.

Ice hockey is the perfect game for Canada. Its frozen lakes are great places to learn to ice skate in the winter. Ex-Montreal Canadien goalie Ken Dryden described hockey. He said it was a game that grew from "long northern winters uncluttered by things to do." With a net, a stick, and a small disk called a puck, it can be played on frozen ponds and in snow-covered streets.

The Outdoors

There is a saying, "Scratch a Canadian and you'll find a backwoodsman." This describes how Canadians enjoy the outdoors. Even though it is cold, winter is not a stay-inside season. People wear warm hats and coats and put on boots. They put snow tires on cars. Canadians make sure snow plows are ready to roll.

Canadians ski in the mountains, ice skate on frozen lakes, or play ice hockey on neighborhood rinks. The Rideau Canal in Ottawa freezes solid each winter. It then becomes the world's longest skating rink.

Many Canadian families spend their summer vacations at the beach or in the woods. One Canadian woman remembered how she felt when her family first arrived at their summer cabin. She wrote about their vacation on a lake in the Manitoba woods:

Cool fresh air of the woods hit me: a strong smell of spruce and balsam, pine needles, . . . wildflowers, rotting logs, wet moss, and beneath it all, the cold, slightly fishy smell of the lake.

Customs

Ice Hockey

Canada gave the United States and the world ice hockey. It has dominated the sport. The National Hockey League awards the **Stanley Cup** trophy to the champion each year. Since 1927, Canadian teams have won it 41 times.

Canada's teams are the Toronto Maple Leafs, Edmonton Oilers, Calgary Flames, Ottawa Senators, Vancouver Canucks, and Montreal Canadiens.

Society and Culture

523

  **Activity**

Window with a View

OBJECTIVES: 1.01, 1.06, 4.07

Give each student an 18-inch by 12-inch sheet of white construction paper. Tell them that this is a window. Have students cut out paper from old wallpaper books in the shape of curtains for the window. Glue the curtains to the window. Have students choose a scene to sketch illustrating some aspect of life in Canada.

Possible scenes:

1. People dressed in costumes of feathers and sequins dancing through the streets in a Carnival parade in Toronto.
2. An ice sculpture at the Winter Carnival in Quebec.
3. A chuck wagon race at the Calgary Stampede.
4. A Royal Canadian mounted policeman guarding Parliament in Ottawa.
5. The fourteen-story-high roller coaster at the the West Edmonton Mall in Alberta.
6. An oil well in Alberta.
7. A large oceangoing vessel traveling the St. Lawrence Seaway.
8. Toronto's famous CN Tower.
9. The Toronto Blue Jays playing at the Sky Dome.
10. An Inuit snowmobiling across the tundra.

When sketches are completed, have students share their views of Canada with the class. Place "windows" on display in the class or hallway.

Extension Have students write several sentences below their window describing their scene.

Discussion Questions

1 Other than art, what purpose do totem poles serve?

2 Why is it important to preserve this form of art?

 Activity

Soap Carving (Soapstone Carving Simulation)

OBJECTIVES: 1.06, 3.04, 3.06, 3.07

If possible, obtain photographs or drawings of Inuit soapstone carvings to show students. Discuss how the Inuit interacted with the environment. Note the importance of such animals as the seal, walrus, and whale. Have students choose an animal and write how that animal helped the Inuit by providing food, clothing, and/or shelter. Then have students make a paper pattern of their animal. The pattern should be the size of a bar of soap. Have students carve their animal using the safest instruments possible. Check craft stores for proper tools. Create a classroom display of carvings and written information gathered by students.

Extension Have students write a legend about their animal.

Research Questions

- What are the major features of the animal's habitat?
- How does it get its food?
- What predators threaten it?
- How do the Inuit hunt it?
- What uses do they make of this animal?

A Journey to • NUNAVUT •

Inuit Art: From Drawings to Stone to Cloth

Canadian artist and art collector James Houston helped start interest in Inuit art. He began the West Baffin Inuit Co-operative. There Inuit sculptors and artists make carvings and prints.

Cape Dorset artist Pitaloosie Saila (pih·tah·LOOS·ee SAY·lah) (shown here) drew a scene called "Stopping to Rest." It showed two women. They each had a young child.

Eegyvudluk Pootoogook (EE·gie·vud·luk poo·TOO·gook) then traced the drawing onto a smooth stone. He inked the stone and carved the design. Then he covered the stone with paper. He rubbed the paper with his fingers. This put the design on the paper.

On Holman Island, Stanley Eloknak Klengenberg's (el·o·NAHK KLEN·gen·BERG) made a stencil called "Cold and Hungry." It shows the hardships his ancestors faced to survive life in the Arctic. He named another of his stencils "Ancestors' Song for Survival." It shows how Inuit want to preserve their traditions.

Klengenberg's drawings were printed on paper by Louis Nigiyok (NIG·ee·yok). Some artists, however, do both parts of the printmaking process.

In other communities in the Arctic, the Inuit transformed drawings into beautiful tapestries. Other Inuit carve traditional scenes in stone or walrus ivory. They also use bones from whale and caribou.

All of their creations help us learn about the Inuit way of life.

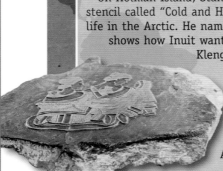

LESSON **3** REVIEW

Fact Follow-Up
1. What are some bonds that bind Canadian provinces together? that bind all of Canada together?
2. Why is the maple important to Canada?
3. What are some developments in Inuit art?

Talk About It
1. Why might it be said of Canadians, "Scratch a Canadian and you'll find a backwoodsman"?
2. Why might it be said that Canadians celebrate differences?

LESSON **3** REVIEW

Fact Follow-Up Answers
1. Some bonds include a common history, common experience in dealing with the living conditions of Canada, hockey, and Native American art.
2. Eastern Canada produces 85 percent of the world's maple syrup. The maple leaf is Canada's national symbol.
3. Sculpting stone, bone, and ivory, woodcarving, and printmaking are all practiced by Inuit artists today.

Talk About It Answers
1. Important points: Encourage students to suggest a variety of reasons that will support this statement. Most early European settlers of Canada lived in wilderness areas. Many Canadians are interested in outdoor life, and even urban areas are close to wilderness.
2. Through festivals such as those celebrated by Icelanders and Danes as well as the Highland Games in Nova Scotia and the Calgary Stampede, Canadians support the expression of the variety of cultures that are present in their country.

Accessing a Variety of Sources; Gathering, Synthesizing, and Reporting Information

Learning about Canada and Its Provinces Using Flags

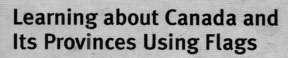

Study the flags on this page. What can we learn from them about the people of North Carolina, the United States, and Canada?

First, look closely at the colors in the flags. Did you know that blue is the most popular flag color in the world? Blue can stand for loyalty or patriotism. Red can stand for courage. What else could blue and red represent? What might white represent?

By the colors they use in their flags, nations, states, or provinces tell us what they think is important about themselves.

Patterns on flags, like the colors, can also tell us about the places they represent. The flag of the United States has stars and stripes. The Canadian flag has a maple leaf. What do these symbols mean?

Flags are Symbols

Look now at the North Carolina flag. What colors are used? There are two dates written on the flag. What do they represent?

The Canadian flag has changed from the Union Jack to the Maple Leaf. Why? How has the flag of the United States changed? Has the flag of North Carolina changed?

Look now at the figures on the province flags. Many province flags contain symbols of the United Kingdom, such as a lion or parts of the British flag. The rampant, or rearing, lion on Nova Scotia's flag is a symbol of Scotland. Scotland is part of the United Kingdom.

What do the *fleurs-de-lis* symbolize on Quebec's flag? How does Alberta's flag represent its landforms? What do the symbols on Ontario's flag mean?

You will study more about Canada's flags in Go to the Source in the Chapter Review.

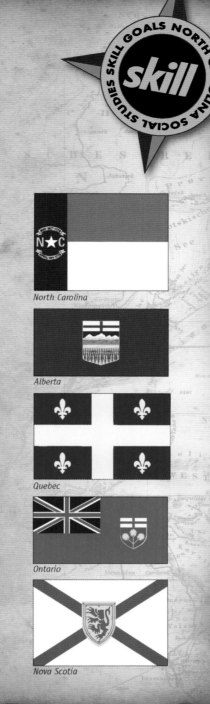

North Carolina

Alberta

Quebec

Ontario

Nova Scotia

Access to the Internet will help this lesson. Students may use any search engine, enter the word "Canada," and follow a path, with your guidance, to locate the flags and their history of Canadian provinces. If this is not possible, locate and print this information for student use.

Materials Needed textbooks, chart paper, markers, an assortment of flags (North Carolina, United States, Canada, and city or county flags)

Classroom Organization whole class, small groups

Beginning the Lesson Have students examine the assortment of flags, noting similarities and differences. Record these statements about similarities and differences. Ask students to speculate about how colors and designs were chosen and by whom.

Lesson Development Either allow students to use the Internet to search for information about provincial flags of Canada or organize small groups, giving each group information about one province. Have students examine these flags and comment on similarities and differences among them, comparing these statements with earlier statements already recorded. Encourage students to read the Skill Lesson for more information and questions about flag colors and designs.

Distribute chart paper and markers and have each group design a classroom or school flag.

Conclusion Display students' flags and discuss their varying choices of color and design.

Extension If you have a city or county flag, invite a city or county official to tell the class why the flag was designed as it was. This may also be an opportune time to discuss proper flag etiquette with a representative of a veterans' organization such as the American Legion.

 Skill Lesson Review

1. Does the North Carolina flag contain more information than the United States flag? Is the same true of Canadian provincial flags when compared to the Maple Leaf flag? *The North Carolina flag contains dates and a quotation. Provincial flags also contain more information. Local symbols must be more specific to distinguish smaller areas.*

2. What are some important symbols other than flags? *Responses should include anthems, seals such as the state and national seals, symbols such as Uncle Sam.*

Talk About It

1. Important points: Students should make a choice and explain it. Many French-speaking residents of Quebec favor separation as the only way to preserve their culture. Others disagree, and do not want to run the risk of isolating Quebec from the rest of Canada.
2. Important points: Students should agree or disagree and give reasons for their answer. The mosaic quality of Canada's cultures and provincial loyalties are a barrier to unity.
3. Important points: Encourage students to suggest various places, giving reasons for their suggestions, and choose one, explaining their choice. Many Russians live in Manitoba, and that might be an important factor in choosing a place to live.
4. Important points: Students should state an opinion that takes into account both Canada and the United States. Forms of government may be a factor, and Canada's huge size may have an effect on the feeling of national identity. Many people in Canada feel a stronger bond with their provinces or regions than with the nation as a whole.
5. Important points: Students should choose one answer and explain their choice. Likenesses include large size, rich resources, democratic governments, diverse societies, nearness to oceans and to each other. Differences include temperature, population size, history, and closeness to cultures of other nations.

Mastering Mapwork

1. Quebec is largely French in terms of ethnic groups. It would be logical to expect the French language and French customs to be major characteristics of place
2. New Brunswick, where French is the second most common ethnic group, would be likely to have the French language as a cultural characteristic of place.
3. Newfoundland has the largest percentage of British ethnic heritage
4. The most important Native American and Inuit presences are in the Northwest Territories and Nunavut.
5. British Columbia has the most people of Chinese heritage.

Lessons Learned

LESSON 1
A Changing Society
Most Canadians live in cities. Vancouver, Montreal, Toronto, Winnipeg, and Iqaluit show different parts of Canada's culture.

LESSON 2
Tradition Lives
Canada's culture is influenced by the British and French.

LESSON 3
A Cultural Mosaic
Each province celebrates unique ways of living. Canadian ethnic groups celebrate their own customs. Together, Canadians share an appreciation for the outdoors and ice hockey. Canada calls its Native Americans First Nations.

526

Becoming Better Readers

Important points: Students should choose one important element and support their choice with details from the reading.

Talk About It

1. In 1980 and 1995, the people of Quebec voted not to separate from Canada. The issue may come up again. Imagine that you are a French-speaking resident of Quebec. Will you favor separation or not? Explain your choice.
2. It has been said that each Canadian province has its own culture but that Canada as a nation does not have a "Canadian culture." Do you agree or disagree with this statement? Give reasons for your answer.
3. Imagine that you are a Russian who plans to move to Canada. Where will you choose to live? Explain the reasons for your choice.
4. "Canadians identify with their regions and United States citizens identify with their country." Do you agree or disagree with this statement? Why or why not?
5. Is Canada more like the United States than it is different, or is it more different than it is similar? Explain your answer.

Mastering Mapwork

PLACE
Use the map on page 509 to answer these questions:
1. Examine the ethnic groups in Quebec. Given what you know about Canada and Quebec, what cultural characteristics of place would you expect to observe in Quebec?
2. Which province other than Quebec would be most likely to have the French language as a major cultural characteristic of place?
3. In which province is the British ethnic group most important as a cultural characteristic of place?
4. In which province or territory is there the most important Native American or Inuit presence?
5. Which province has the most people of Chinese heritage?

Becoming Better Readers

Taking Notes
We become better readers so that we can become better learners. Good readers know how to read a text and pull out the important information. What was the most important information about Canada's culture? What were the important details you wanted to remember?

Go to the Source

Flags of Canada

Study the provincial flags of Quebec, Nunavut, and British Columbia, and answer the questions below.

Quebec

Blue and the *fleur-de-lis* were chosen by King Louis VII of France in the twelfth century and were on the French flag at that time. The cross represents the cross that was on the banner flying from Jacques Cartier's ship in 1534.

Nunavut

The colors, blue and gold, symbolize the riches of the land, sea, and sky. Red is a reference to Canada. The inuksuk (in·NUK·shuk) symbolizes stone monuments which guide people on the land and mark special places. The star is the North Star. It is the traditional guide for navigation. It is symbolic of the leadership of elders in the community.

British Columbia

The Union Jack, or British flag, on the shield symbolizes its colonial origins. Its geographic location between the Pacific Ocean and the Rocky Mountains is represented by the wavy blue and silver bars and the setting sun.

1. How are the three flags above different?
2. On British Columbia's flag, what do the wavy blue and silver bars and the setting sun symbolize?
3. What is the significance of the North Star on the Nunavut flag?
4. What symbol on the Quebec flag was also on the banner that was flying on Jacques Cartier's ship in 1534?

Society and Culture

527

(vertical tab) Go to the Source

 Go to the Source

Flags of Canada

OBJECTIVES: 3.05, 1.07, 1.03
SOCIAL STUDIES SKILLS: 3.05

This Go to the Source builds on the Skill Lesson in this chapter. Many of Canada's provincial and territorial flags showcase the symbols of their citizen's cultural heritage. As an extension to this activity, have students design their own flags for Canada and North Carolina showcasing the cultural heritage of these places.

Answers

1. The differences among the flags are in the symbolizism of the different origin of each place's heritage. Quebec is French, Nunavut is Inuit, and British Columbia is British. Quebec is blue. The fleur-de-lis symbol was chosen by King Louis VII of France in the twelfth century; they were on the French Flag at that time. On the Nunavut flag, the colors blue and gold symbolize the riches of the land, sea, and sky. British Columbia shows the Union Jack (flag of the United Kingdom) on the shield symbolizing its colonial origins.
2. It represents British Columbia, the geographic place/location between the Pacific Ocean and the Rocky Mountains.
3. The significance is that it is a traditional guide for navigation. It is symbolic of the leadership of the elders in the community.
4. It was a cross.

 How to Use the Chapter Review

There are four sections in the Chapter Review: Talk About It, Mastering Mapwork, Becoming Better Readers, and Go to the Source. Use the Vocabulary Worksheets and the Chapter Review Worksheet in the Teacher's Resource Guide for additional reinforcement and preparation for the Chapter Assessments. The Chapter and Lesson Reviews and the Chapter Review Worksheets are the basis of the assessment for each chapter.

Talk About It questions encourage students to speculate about the content of the chapter and are suitable for class or small-group discussion. They are not intended to be assigned for homework.

Mastering Mapwork has students apply one or more of the Five Themes of Geography to maps within the chapter.

Becoming Better Readers focuses on building reading strategy skills necessary for reading comprehension in the content areas.

Go to the Source activities allow students to analyze a primary source that relates to the content of the chapter. The questions and activities familiarize students with different types of primary sources and also build content-reading skills.

Unit **6** Mexico

This unit opens with a picture of folk dancers in bright costumes in Mexico. In this unit, your students will take a close look at the land and people of Mexico, tracing the changes in its environment and the traditions that have shaped its culture.

Students also will learn what political and economic challenges face Mexico, the United States' southern neighbor.

UNIT LESSON PLAN

	LESSON 1	LESSON 2	LESSON 3
CHAPTER 22 **The Land and People**	Located south of the United States, Mexico has varied landforms. **Essential Question:** Where is Mexico located, and what are its geographical features? **Suggested Time:** 1 day	Mexico has warm deserts and cool mountains. It also has rain forests and evergreen forests. **Essential Question:** How can we describe the climate and vegetation found in Mexico? **Suggested Time:** 1 day	Mexico's population descends mainly from Native Americans and Spanish settlers. **Essential Question:** What do we know about the people and culture of Mexico? **Suggested Time:** 1–2 days
CHAPTER 23 **People and Environment**	Mexico was the center of two great Native American civilizations: the Mayan and the Aztec. **Essential Question:** Why was Mexico at the center of two great Native American civilizations—the Maya and the Aztec? **Suggested Time:** 1–2 days	Mexico was part of the Spanish colony of New Spain, which was organized to benefit the economy of Spain, not the Native Americans who lived in Mexico. **Essential Question:** Why was New Spain organized? **Suggested Time:** 1–2 days	The colonization of New Spain changed the environment and the way of life of many Native Americans. **Essential Question:** How did the colonization of New Spain change the environment and the way of life for many Native Americans? **Suggested Time:** 1–2 days
CHAPTER 24 **Economy and Government**	After Mexico won independence in 1820, strong leaders took charge. During most of the twentieth century, one party ruled the country. New election laws have encouraged democracy. **Essential Question:** What kind of government has Mexico had since winning its independence in 1820? **Suggested Time:** 1–2 days	After the revolution, Mexico's government controlled the chief industries. Now NAFTA has increased free enterprise in Mexico. **Essential Question:** What is NAFTA, and how has it affected Mexico? **Suggested Time:** 1 day	NAFTA offers hope for Mexico's economic future. Still, health and environmental problems must be solved before all Mexicans can benefit from the treaty. **Essential Question:** What challenges must Mexico face to help its citizens? **Suggested Time:** 1 day
CHAPTER 25 **Culture and Society**	Mexico City, Acapulco, and Monterrey are exciting cities that are each unique. Together, they show the variety of Mexico today. **Essential Question:** What is it like in the cities of Mexico City, Acapulco, and Monterrey? **Suggested Time:** 1 day	Most Mexicans are Roman Catholic. Many Native Americans still keep their own religious traditions, or blend them with Catholicism. **Essential Question:** What religions are important to the people of Mexico? **Suggested Time:** 1 day	Music and art are important to Mexican culture. Soccer, wrestling, and baseball are the most popular sports. **Essential Question:** What are important cultural activities to the people of Mexico? **Suggested Time:** 1 day

Preparing the Unit

- Worksheets, assessments, and reproducibles for this unit are found in the Teacher's Resource Guide and at **NCJourneys.com** See the list of Cultural Resources in the Teacher's Edition.
- Because of the number of students moving into our state from Mexico, allot ample time for the study of this unit. If you have any students in your classroom or families in your community from Mexico, ask them to make presentations to the class and/or bring in artifacts from Mexico to display in the classroom.
- Decorate your room with pictures and posters that illustrate the geography, tourist attractions, people, and culture of Mexico. Share some resources and activities listed in the Teacher's Edition with your cultural arts teachers to integrate their lessons.

Unit Teaching Strategies

- Use the ideas in the wrap-around as suggestions to help you meet the needs of your students and your teaching style. There is a lot of material to be covered and you must pace yourself in order to teach the curriculum.
- The variety of suggested activities are included to help you differentiate your instruction to meet the needs of your students. Use these activities to best enhance your instruction. Do not feel that you should implement them all.
- If time is a factor, use this unit with Units 5 and 7 for student projects culminating with a festival of nations. Preview the list of suggested projects throughout the units, prepare a list of choices for the students, and assign the topics to the students to complete. Students can teach each other by giving presentations on various topics from the units. Students will be actively involved and you will save instructional time.
- Check **NCJourneys.com** for updates and materials.

Unit Projects

Students will have ten days to complete their project. They have the option of choosing from five different projects, and should choose only one. The projects offer variety so students can pick areas that interest them. Suggested report format: Reports should be one page in length, typed, and double-spaced.

PROJECT CHOICES

OBJECTIVES: 1.02, 1.06, 1.07

Postage Stamps

Explain the purpose of postage stamps and the information they contain (country, place, person, event or item identified, and price of stamp in the country's currency). Have students design a set of three Mexican stamps: an important person, a historic event, and a cultural aspect.

Extension Show ELL students a model.

Trade Route

Using a physical map of Mexico, have students plot an itinerary for a trading expedition, identifying what products from colonial Mexico could be traded to Europe. If you would prefer to have them create a more involved project, you could form groups and have them create trade companies and decide what types of goods they will trade for what European goods in return.

Pack Your Bags

Have students plan an imaginary ten-day trip to Mexico. They need to plan an agenda that will allow them to see and experience as much as possible. In their research, they might want to talk to a travel agent, interview a person in the community who has traveled to Mexico, or visit a local library. After they have planned the trip, they will put together an itinerary for their trip, listing the places they will visit and their transportation to those places. They should be able to explain why they selected those places.

Timeline

Have students create a timeline showing the types of government, leaders, cultures, and important facts for various time periods in Mexican history. Students should illustrate their timeline with artwork depicting people and/or scenes relevant to events that occurred.

Natural Resources Map

Mexico's future depends on good use of its rich natural resources. Students will construct a physical/political map of Mexico and will locate and label the following information on the map: mountains, major cities, bodies of water, and natural resources. Students will give the map a title, develop symbols for the natural resources, and provide a key for the map.

Extension Novice ELL students can label the map and give the map a title

Bulletin Board Ideas

Mexico

Use a large map of Mexico as the centerpiece. Have students bring in pictures and words that describe Mexico. Place the items around the edges of the map. Draw arrows from the items to the regions of Mexico described by the words and pictures.

On the Menu

Create a bulletin board focusing on Mexican foods. Give students paper plates to illustrate with the foods of Mexico. Have students write the names of the food on the plates. You may want students to do further research and include recipes of regional dishes. Students may also create a menu for an imaginary restaurant with an appropriate name and prices in the appropriate currency.

Match Game

Create cards with the names of famous Mexican men and women throughout history. Create separate cards with brief biographical descriptions and/or pictures, and post them on the bulletin board. Challenge students to match the descriptions to the person. Provide the answers under the cards.

Unit Activities

 Introductory Activity

Mexico Map Puzzles

 OBJECTIVES: 1.01, 1.03, 1.06

Distribute a blackline state map of Mexico to the class, and have students label and color each state. Then have each student carefully cut out each state and place the pieces in a plastic bag. Assign each student a partner and have them exchange bags. Students will then reassemble their partner's map.

 **Culminating Activity**

Class Magazine

OBJECTIVES: 1.05, 1.07, 3.04

Tell the class that they are the publishers of a new magazine about North America. They must come up with a title for their magazine, and decide how many pages each issue will be.

After studying each unit in their social studies textbook, they are to publish an issue of their magazine. As a class, discuss what articles should be included in the issue. Use some of the story ideas suggested below or create your own. What maps and illustrations will be needed? What types of charts and statistics will be necessary to help readers understand the information? Break the class into editorial teams of writers, cartographers, illustrators, statisticians, and designers. The writing team (this can be a larger group) will be responsible for writing the articles. The cartography team will be responsible for drawing the maps to go with the articles. The illustrators will be responsible for finding or drawing pictures to illustrate the articles. The design team will be responsible for putting the magazine together. Remind students that each group needs to coordinate with the others so that their final project will look professional and be easy for readers to understand.

Make several copies so that your students can share their magazine with the other classes in your school. Students should keep copies of the magazines from each unit so that they will have a complete set of magazines on North America at the end of the year.

Unit 6 story ideas: Mexico's Native American cultures, the Spanish in Mexico, Mexico's major industries, the people of Mexico, the Mexican Revolution, the *caudillos* of Mexico

 Science Activity

Landscapes of Mexico: Environmental Diorama

 OBJECTIVES: 1.01, 1.03

Students will create an environmental diorama to illustrate the geography of Mexico. They should refer to Chapter 22 for information about the climate, landforms, and vegetation of Mexico. Students will present their diorama to the class explaining their depiction.

Extension ELL students may complete the project by labeling the parts of the diorama they have created.

 Technology Activity

Music of Mexico

OBJECTIVES: 1.06, 3.04, 3.07

Divide the class into cooperative groups. Using the Internet, CDs, tapes, or MP3s, have the groups research the music of Mexico. Students should pretend that they are running a Mexican radio station and must create a play list for a 10-minute segment. Students should locate the music and arrange to play it in their presentation. Each group should present its radio show to the class. The "DJs" should explain the types of music selected, identify the performer(s), and provide some background information about the performers and/or the music itself.

Extension Have Mexican novice ELL students bring in music from Mexico if they have some at home and/or show classmates how to dance to the music.

 Math Activity

Exchange Rate Problem

 OBJECTIVES: 1.06, 5.04, 5.06

Mexico is a major market for the United States. Convert the dollar price to the Mexican price for the item. Use the newspaper or almanac to find the current exchange rate. Have the class come up with other products to calculate.

1 liter cola	$1.09
chocolate bar	$0.50
bicycle	$250.00

Extension Assist ELL students by showing them examples first.

Unit Resources

See also the Resources for Chapters 4, 5, 26, and 27 and Unit 7 for additional Latin America materials.

Print Resources

Fiction

Anacona, George. *Pablo Remembers: The Fiesta of the Day of the Dead.* Lothrop Lee & Shepard, 1993. ISBN 0688112498.

Coburn, Jewell Reinhart, and Connie McLennan. *Domitila: A Cinderella Tale from the Mexican Tradition.* Shen's Books, 2000, ISBN 1885008139.

George, Jean Craighead. *Shark Beneath the Reef.* HarperCollins, 1989. ISBN 0064403084.

O'Dell, Scott. *The Black Pearl.* Houghton Mifflin, 1995. ISBN 0395069610.

Trevino, Elizabeth Borton de. *El Guero: A True Adventure Story.* Farrar, Straus, Giroux, 1991. ISBN 0374420289.

Nonfiction for Students

Baquedano, Elizabeth, and Michel Zabe. *Eyewitness: Aztec, Inca & Maya.* DK Publishing, 2000. ISBN 0789461153.

dePaola, Tomie. *Legend of the Poinsettia.* Putnam Pub. Group, 1994. ISBN 0399216928.

Harvey, Miles. *Look What Came from Mexico.* Franklin Watts, 1999. ISBN 0531159396.

Illsley, Linda. *Mexico* (Food & Festivals). Raintree/Steck Vaughn, 1999. ISBN 0817255532.

Jermyn, Leslie and Fiona Conboy. Welcome to Mexico (Welcome to My Country). Gareth Stevens Publishing, 1999. ISBN 0836823982.

Kalman, Bobbie, and Jane Lewis. *Mexico from A to Z* (Alphabasics Series). Crabtree Pub., 1999. ISBN 0865054126

MacDonald, Fiona, and Mark Bergin. *How Would You Survive as an Aztec?* Franklin Watts, 1997. ISBN 0531153045.

Mexico (Fiesta! series). Grolier Educational, 1999. ISBN 0717291103.

Olawsky, Lynn Ainsworth, and Janice Lee Porter. *Colors of Mexico* (Colors of the World). Carolrhoda Books, 1997. ISBN 1575052164.

Rummel, Jack. *Mexico* (Major World Nations series). Chelsea House, 1999. ISBN 0791047636.

Sola, Michele, and Jeffrey Jay Foxx. *Angela Weaves a Dream: The Story of a Maya Artist.* Disney Press, 1997. ISBN 0786800739.

Stein, R. Conrad. *Mexico* (Enchantment of the World series). Children's Press, 1998. ISBN 0516206508.

Winter, Jonah, and Ann Juan. *Frida.* Arthur A. Levine, 2002. ISBN 0590203207.

Nonfiction

Crosby, Alfred W. *The Columbian Exchange: Biological and Cultural Consequences of 1492.* (30th Anniv. ed.) Praeger Paperback, 2003. ISBN 0275980928.

Diamond, Jared. *Guns, Germs, and Steel: The Fates of Human Societies* (2nd ed.). W. W. Norton, 2005. ISBN 0393061310.

Mann, Charles C. *1491: New Revelations of the Americas Before Columbus.* New York: Alfred A. Knopf, 2005.

Restall, Matthew. Seven Myths of the Spanish Conquest. Oxford University Press, 2003. ISBN 0195160770.

Back issues of magazines

Mayan Culture. Cobblestone Publishing Company. ISBN 0382443950.

Mexico in Ancient Times. Cobblestone Publishing Company. ISBN 0382405331.

Mexico, People & Cultures. Cobblestone Publishing Company. ISBN 0382445899.

Audiovisual

National Geographic Special Presentation: *Guns, Germs, and Steel.* 2005. PBS Video.

Web Sites

Visit **NCJourneys.com** for links to these Web sites:

- AncientMexico.com
- The Geography of MesoAmerica, Metropolitan Museum of Art: Timeline of Art History
- Guns, Germs, and Steel companion Web site
- Latin American Network Information Center, University of Texas
- Mexico Connect
- National Museum of Mexican Art

Paideia Seminar

The Story of Colors

OBJECTIVES: 1.05, 1.06, 3.04

La Historia de Los Colores. (The Story of Colors) by Subcomandante Marcos and Anne Bar Din. (Cinco Puntos, 1999. ISBN 0938317458.)

Theme Equality. The book is presented in English and Spanish. The book has a moral and has lavish pictures for the students to explore. The moral shows the merit of many cultures and a belief in diversity.

Pre-seminar Have students read a typed version of the book and if possible study the pictures in a copy of the book.

Opening Questions

- In this folktale the world is black and white until the gods find colors. What does the word color mean to you?

Core Questions

- What does the text teach us about diversity of people?
- Based on the text what is meant by color?
- Are there things in the text that support your opening statement about color?
- In what ways are you and the people in the book alike? Different?

Closing Questions

- If you were the artist, how would you have represented color? Explain.
- Have you ever had an experience with color as explained in the text?

Post-seminar Students will take a piece of art paper and draw a picture under the title, Color My Day.

Map Activity

Mexico

NATIONAL GEOGRAPHY STANDARDS: 1,2

GEOGRAPHIC THEMES: Location

OBJECTIVES: 1.01, 1.05

Have the students look at the map on page 529. Ask:

In which hemispheres does Mexico lie? *the Northern and Western Hemispheres*

What is the relative location of Mexico? *Northern and Western Hemispheres, south of the United States, shares a border with the United States, north of Central America, bordered on the east by the Gulf of Mexico, and on the West by the Pacific Ocean*

Based on Mexico's relative location, what do you think the climate is like? *hot, including desert, steppe, tropical savanna climates*

Based on your last answer, would you like to live in Mexico? Why?

Now have the students close their books and sketch Mexico in 10 minutes. When the students complete their maps, analyze the reasons the maps look like they do.

Unit 6

Waves from the Gulf of Mexico and the Pacific Ocean both crash upon Mexico's shores. Tall mountains divide the nation from north to south. The land has plains and deserts. It also has rain forests.

Mexico's history goes back to the Maya and Aztecs. The Maya people lived at the same time as ancient Egyptians. Hundreds of years later the Spanish brought their customs to the Americas. Today Mexico looks forward to a bright future with the other nations of North America.

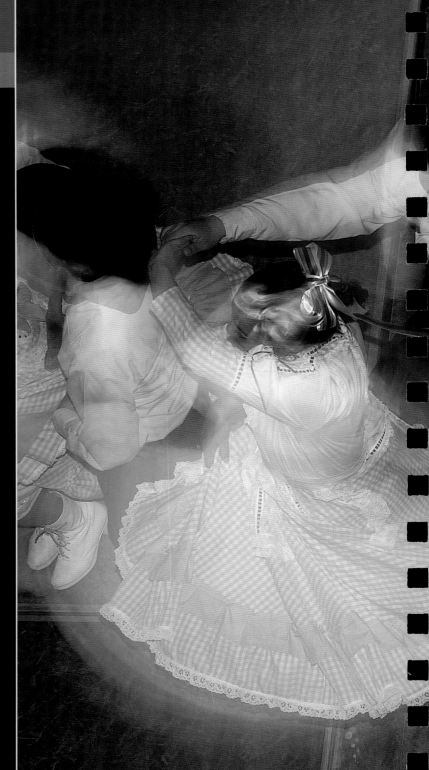

Mexican folk dancers

528

Social Studies at Work

Exhibit Designer

An exhibit designer is someone who researches and creates meaningful learning exhibits at museums of all kinds.

Meet Linda Dallas
Vice President, Design and Production, Exploris Museum

It's hard not to love a job where you get to use an atlas every-day. That's what Linda Dallas tells her friends when they ask her how she likes her job. It's a rare day that Dallas, who is vice president of design and production at Raleigh's Exploris Museum, doesn't use her atlas. Her work is all about learning about the various corners of the world and the people who inhabit them.

Even though social studies was always one of Dallas' favorite subjects, she choose to major in mathematics in college at Howard University in Washington, D.C. While living in the nation's capital, she worked for the Smithsonian Institute at both the American Museum of African Art and the Hirshhorn Museum.

She came to North Carolina to attend the School of Design at North Carolina State University. There she earned a master's degree in product design. It's also where she started teaching college-level drawing and design courses and where her own drawings started receiving critical acclaim.

Mexico

Unit Preview

CHAPTER 22
The Land and People
Mexico is located south of the United States. It is a nation rich in resources.

CHAPTER 23
People and Their Environment
The Native Americans and the Spanish colonists have changed Mexico over hundreds of years.

CHAPTER 24
Economy and Government
Mexico's economy is growing. Mexico has had to slowly develop into a democracy.

CHAPTER 25
Culture and Society
Mexico's society is a mixture of Native American and Spanish cultures. The Roman Catholic Church also has a strong influence.

529

Dallas' connection with Exploris began when she worked as a volunteer coordinator for the museum's Anne Frank exhibit. Now she is responsible for coordinating the content, design, and fabrication of all Exploris exhibits and educational products. She also keeps busy designing educational products for the museum to sell to other museums and exhibit in its own gift shop.

The best part of the job for Dallas is that she gets to explore other places, people, and cultures to her heart's content. Sometimes her curiosity is satisfied by research alone. Other times, the research makes her want to actually see the places she's learning about. Every once in a while she gets to do both. No matter if it's through a book, an interview, or a jaunt around the world, though, Dallas considers any day a good one when research is involved.

Exhibit Designer for a Day
Start your own classroom museum by asking each student to contribute one "artifact" that reflects something they've learned in your class this year. Artifacts can be actual objects or a student-designed contribution such as a time line, a drawing, or a photograph. Students must include a short description for their artifact and come up with a creative way to display it.

Find Out More
For information about the Exploris Museum and exhibits and programs, go to the link at **NCJourneys.com.**

The Land and People

Social Studies Strands

Geographic Relationships

Historic Perspectives

Cultures and Diversity

Global Connections

North Carolina Standard Course of Study

Goal 1 The learner will apply key geographic concepts to the United States and other countries of North America.

Goal 3 The learner will examine the roles various ethnic groups have played in the development of the United States and its neighboring countries.

Goal 4 The learner will trace key developments in United States history and describe their impact on the land and people of the nation and its neighboring countries.

Goal 6 The learner will recognize how technology has influenced change within the United States and other countries in North America.

Teaching & Assessment

- English Language Learner Modified Lesson Plans for this chapter are found in the Teacher's Resource Guide.

- *ExamView® Assessment Suite* is provided at **NCJourneys.com.** It includes customizable assessments for all chapters. Paper tests are also available in the Teacher's Resource Guide. See pages T16–T17 for information about how to use the assessments and the Scoring Guide.

Worksheets

Worksheets and answer keys are found both in the Teacher's Resource Guide and at **NCJourneys.com**, including Reading Guides, Reading Strategies, Chapter Reviews, English Language Learner and others.

Activities and Integrations

SOCIAL STUDIES

Scavenger Hunt, p. 530B
★ Problem Based Learning: Ancient America, p. 530B
▲ ■ 3-D Map, p. 531
▲ ■ Twisting on Mexico, p. 534
● Relative Location, p. 535
Read the Label, p. 546

READING/LANGUAGE ARTS	READING/LANGUAGE ARTS OBJECTIVES
★ ▲ ■ Pop-up Book, p. 530B	4.07
▲ ■ Activator: *Quetzalcoatl Tale of the Ball*, p. 530	2.03
Writing Prompt: Interviewing, Poem, p. 530	4.07
Carolina Connection: James K. Polk, p. 531	2.03, 4.07
Reading Strategy: Cornell Method, p. 532	3.02
● Volcano Legend Literature, p. 533	3.02
● Reading Strategy: Attribute Analysis T Chart, p. 536	2.01
● Reading Strategy: Highlighting, p. 540	3.05
■ Selling Mexico, p. 544	3.06, 4.07, 4.09
The Meeting of Cortes and Moctezuma, p. 542	4.07, 4.09
● Mezcla, p. 541	2.03, 4.07
People, p. 541	2.03, 3.06, 4.07
Skill Lesson: Comparing Regions of North America, p. 547	2.09, 3.02, 3.06
Becoming Better Readers, p. 548	2.01
Gathering InformationFrom Letters, p.549	2.02, 2.04

MATHEMATICS	MATHEMATICS OBJECTIVES
Mountains of the Mexican Mainland, p. 539	1.02, 4.01

SCIENCE	SCIENCE OBJECTIVES
Mexico: Climate and Vegetation, p. 537	1.01, 3.04
Indigenous Plants and Animals, p. 538	1.01
Animal Migration in North America, p. 539	1.01

TECHNOLOGY	TECHNOLOGY OBJECTIVES
Carolina Connection: James K. Polk, p. 531	2.13
★ Meeting of Cortes and Moctezuma, p. 542	2.13
Animal Migration in North America, p. 539	2.13

VISUAL ARTS	VISUAL ARTS OBJECTIVES
▲ ■ Constellation Viewers, p. 530B	3.02
● Mezcla, p. 541	5.03, 5.04
★ Selling Mexico, p. 544	2.01, 3.02

CHARACTER AND VALUES EDUCATION	TRAITS
What Would You Do?, p. 538	good judgement, self-discipline
Learning About Leadership: Portrait Activity, p. 545	perserverance, courage

● Basic Activities ★ Challenging Activities ▲ English Language Learner Novice ■ English Language Learner Intermediate

Introductory Activity

Scavenger Hunt

OBJECTIVES: 1.02, 1.05, 1.06

This is a good activity to get students motivated. They will use their skimming skills, and it is competitive. Prepare questions and answers from the chapter. Divide the class into two teams. Tell the class that questions will be asked from particular pages. Students should have their books open to those same pages.

On the board, put a scoring chart, labeled Team A and Team B. Ask a question to the whole class. Whoever finds the answer first puts his or her hand up. Call on the first hand you see. If the answer is correct, that team gets a point. If the answer is incorrect, choose from the hands of the other team. If that is incorrect, give the answer, and no team scores.

 Culminating Activity

Pop-Up Book

OBJECTIVES: 1.02, 1.06, 3.04

Ask each of your students to create a children's pop-up book on one of the following topics:

Maya or Aztec culture, Maya or Aztec gods, Tenochtitlán, Teotihuacán, Maya pyramids, Religion of Aztecs, Christopher Columbus, Explorers of Middle America, Middle American homes, or a tourist book on Mexico. Be sure to provide them with some models of pop-up books from home or the library. A resource book on pop-up

bookmaking is *How to Make Pop-Ups*, by Joan Irvine. Morrow, William & Co., 1988. ISBN 0688079024.

Some sample pop-up books are:
Teammates, by Peter Golenbock. Harcourt, 1992. ISBN 0152842861.
Jackie Robinson and Breaking the Color Barrier, by Russell Shorto. Millbrook Press, 1991. ISBN 1878841351.
Baseball Saved Us, by Ken Mochizuki. Lee & Low Books, Inc., 1995. ISBN 1880000199.

Extension ELL novice students will need an example. It may take ELL students longer to complete.

 Art Activity

Constellation Viewers

OBJECTIVES: 1.06, 1.07, 5.05

The Maya civilization was known for its knowledge and use of astronomy in everday religious life. The Maya built great observatories to study the stars and constellations.

Materials empty soup or vegetable cans, tracing paper, pencil, scissors, large nail and hammer, sky map of constellations, materials to cover cans, black spray paint

Directions Have students choose a constellation. Be sure there are no duplicates. On the tracing paper, trace around the outside of the closed end of the can. Draw dots representing stars inside the circle on the tracing paper. Turn tracing paper over, so one sees the reverse image of the constellation. Place image over the closed end of the can. Use a nail and hammer to punch holes in the end of the can where the dots are.
Spray the inside of the can and the outside end with black spray paint. Students should cover the outside of the can with material and decorate it. To view constellations, face a light source and hold viewer to the eye.

Problem Based Learning Activity

Ancient America

OBJECTIVES: 1.02, 1.05, 1.06

Situation The Mexican Plateau in central Mexico sits high above the other land regions and is surrounded by tall mountains. The Aztecs chose this region for their empire. The protection that a plateau and mountains provided was important.

Task Have students discuss the strategic benefits for people in the early days of what is today's Mexico. Why would they seek out land such as this to build upon? If you were a foe, why would it be difficult to attack a civilization located in this type of land region?

The Aztecs truly had the advantage against the enemy. After the discussion, ask the class to research the exact location, elevation, and climate of the Mexican Plateau. In small groups they will draw the location on a poster board and surround the plateau appropriately with the tall mountains. They must get the general direction of north, south, east, and west correct.

Then each group will evaluate the geography of the land and pretend that they must protect this area. Which parts of the plateau would be most vulnerable to attack from the ground (hundreds of years ago)? Which parts of the plateau are the most naturally protected? Which areas of the border would you reinforce the most, and why? On the poster, they should indicate their strategy for defending the plateau, and explain why this would have been beneficial.

Reflection Ask students to consider how location played such an important part in the lives of early Native Americans. Location often determined whether people survived. Ask students to reflect upon how location affects daily life.

Teaching Strategies

Because geography is the focus of this chapter, a variety of maps should be available for students to use during the instruction of the chapter. The use of graphic organizers will also enable students to organize the information from the chapter.

Bring in native foods from Mexico to give students a taste of the crops grown in Mexico. Take time to dispel any misinformation or preconceived ideas that students might have about Mexico.

Discussion Questions

1 How did Hernán Cortés describe the land of Mexico to King Carlos I of Spain?

 Activator

OBJECTIVES: 1.06, 1.07, 3.06

Read *A Quetzalcoatl Tale of the Ball* by Marilyn Parke and Sharon Panik, illustrated by Lynn Castle (McGraw-Hill Children's Publishing, 1992. ISBN 0866539603.). The bold colors and unique illustrations will surely attract students' attention. Every illustration is bordered with symbols, creatures, plants, and architecture that are renderings of glyphs from pre-Columbian Mesoamerica.

Model the game that the two gods play, using the book as a guide. Also, using the glyphs that border each picture, a lesson can be introduced about the glyphs and their place in Mesoamerican culture.

 Writing Prompt

OBJECTIVES: 1.05, 1.07, 3.04

Interviewing Create a list of questions you might ask someone about his or her experience eating in a Mexican restaurant. Be sure to ask about the decorations in the restaurant as well as the ingredients of the food and the names of the dishes. Find someone to ask your questions to and write the results. Share it with your classmates.

Poetry Write the name of Mexico's famous volcano, Popocatepetl, vertically on your paper. As you study Mexico, write facts you have learned beside each letter in an acrostic. Illustrate your poem and display with those of your classmates.

Example:

P eople of Mexico are mainly Roman Catholic and speak Spanish.

O axaca is the name of a state and city in Mexico.

CHAPTER

22

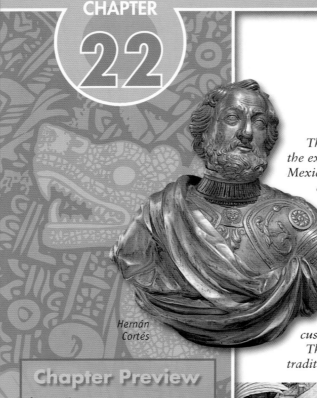

Hernán
Cortés

Chapter Preview

LESSON 1
Location and Size
Located south of the United States, Mexico has many landforms.

LESSON 2
Climate and Plant Life
Mexico has warm deserts and cool mountains. It also has rain forests and evergreen forests.

LESSON 3
People of Mexico
Mexico's people descend mainly from Native Americans and Spanish settlers.

530

The Land and People

There is a story that the king of Spain once asked the explorer Hernán Cortés to describe the land of Mexico. Cortés simply took out a sheet of paper. He crumpled it and laid it out before the king. The bumps and ridges on the wrinkled paper showed the king the great variety of landforms in Central Mexico.

The people of Mexico are just as different as its landforms. They are united by a Spanish colonial heritage dating back more than 500 years. This European influence can be found in religion and government. It is also in the language and customs.

This influence has blended with Native American traditions to form modern Mexico.

 Chapter Resources

Print Resources

Fiction

Alarcon, Francisco X. *From the Bellybutton of the Moon and Other Summer Poems/Del Imbligo de la Luna: Y Otros Poemas de Verano.* Children's Book Press, 1998. ISBN 0892391537.

Johnston, Tony. *My Mexico/México mío.* Paper Star, 1999. ISBN 0698117573.

Nonfiction

Crisfield, Deborah. *The Travels of Hernán Cortés* (Explorers & Exploration series). Steadwell Books, 2000. ISBN 0739814885.

Haskins, Jim. *Count Your Way Through Mexico.* Carolrhoda Books, 1990. ISBN 0876145179.

Milord, Susan. *Mexico: 40 Activities to Experience Mexico Past & Present.* Williamson Publishing, 1999. ISBN 1885593228.

Mexico—Political/Physical

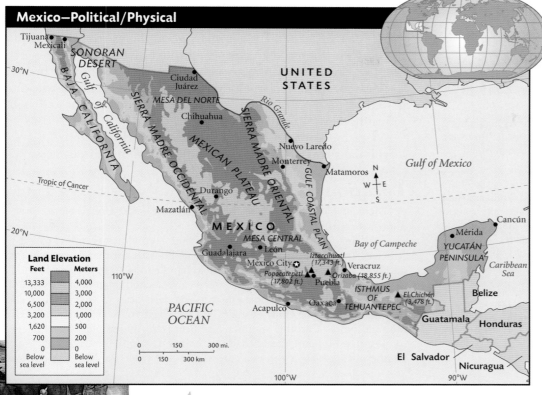

Land Elevation

Feet	Meters
13,333	4,000
10,000	3,000
6,500	2,000
3,200	1,000
1,620	500
700	200
0	0
Below sea level	Below sea level

James K. Polk

James K. Polk was born in North Carolina in 1795. He was elected the eleventh president of the United States in 1844. One of his goals was to expand the size of the United States. Texas had gained its independence from Mexico in 1837. In 1846, President Polk sent United States troops to help the Republic of Texas settle a border dispute. This turned into the Mexican War.

Texas became a state. The United States won the war. The territories that would become New Mexico, Colorado, Arizona, Utah, and California became part of the United States. This war caused bad feelings between the two countries for many years.

531

Discussion Questions

1 What did James K. Polk want to do when he sent troops to help the Republic of Texas?

Map Activity

3-D Map

NATIONAL GEOGRAPHY STANDARDS: 3, 5
GEOGRAPHIC THEMES: Place
OBJECTIVES: 1.01, 1.02, 4.07

Have students make a three-dimensional map of Mexico using clay or salt and flour. Show all landforms including mountain ranges, deserts, plateaus, rain forests, and bodies of water. Make tiny labels and attach them to toothpicks which may be inserted while the material is wet. If using flour, let the map dry before painting the various sections. Major cities could be labeled if space is available.

Extension Assist ELL students by modeling the activity.

Activity

Carolina Connection: James K. Polk

OBJECTIVES: 1.05, 1.07, 4.03

The James K. Polk Memorial Association's Web site has an educational resources link. The page contains an online quiz, a journal writing activity, a debate activity, map exercises, and a closer look at nineteenth century education. The site also includes a list of resources for further reading. A 12-minute video about the James K. Polk home is available for purchase. Accompanying the video is an educational materials packet. Visit **NCJourneys.com** for a link to the site.

Olawsky, Lynn Ainsworth. *Colors of Mexico* (Colors of the World series). Carolrhoda Books, 1997. ISBN 1575052164.

Winter, Jonah and Frida Kahlo. *Frida* (English language edition). Arthur A. Levine, 2002. ISBN 0590203207.

Audiovisual

Mexico. International Video Network (IVN.com).

Web Sites

Visit **NCJourneys.com** for links to these Web sites:

- Geography of Mexico, Mexico for Kids
- Mexican Earthquake Disaster (19 September 1985), British Council
- Mexico Geography and Environment, Library of Congress

 **OBJECTIVES:** 1.01, 1.02, 1.03

Discussion Questions

1 How does North Carolina benefit from being close to Mexico?

2 What is Mexico's relative location to North Carolina?

Reading Strategy Activity

Cornell Method

OBJECTIVES: 1.01, 1.02, 1.03

Textbooks contain different types of information. It is often a difficult task deciding what facts are important to include. This method of note-taking requires students to reflect on the lesson after completing their note-taking.

Using a sheet of notebook paper, students are to section the paper as illustrated in the graphic (below). The date and page number are to be written at the top left, and a horizontal line extending the width of the page is to be drawn beneath.

The middle section of the paper will be in two parts: A vertical line is to be drawn about 2 inches from the left margin. A horizontal line extending the width of the page is to be drawn under that a few inches from the bottom of the page.

After the reading is complete, let students read their notes. As they look over what was written, key words and ideas should be written on the left side of the paper. On the right side of the paper should be details from the text that relate to the key words and ideas on the left side.

The bottom section is for students to reflect upon their reading to build understanding.

Date____ Page____	
Key Words and Ideas	Information In Text

Try this method with other subjects such as science. The more students practice, the better they will be at note-taking.

KEY IDEAS

- Mexico is located south of the western United States.

- Mexico has highlands and plateaus. There are also mountains and deserts.

- The Mesa Central offers the best farmland. The Aztecs and other ancient peoples made their home there.

KEY TERMS

Mesa Central
Mesa del Norte

LESSON 1 Location and Size

North Carolinians get many good things from Mexico. In the winter, vegetables are brought by truck to the United States. Factory products are also shipped from Mexico. American truck drivers often meet Mexican truck drivers at the border. There they exchange their freight and return home.

Mexicans come to North Carolina to work. North Carolinians travel to Mexico on both vacation and business.

Location

Mexico is located south of the western part of the United States. It is almost three times larger than Texas.

Let's imagine that your family is driving from North Carolina to Mexico. To drive through Mexico, you will need a car that can climb up and down high mountains. It must also handle long stretches of flat and dry plains. You will pass through steep canyons and open country. You will see areas with few people and large modern cities as well. High in the mountains it will be chilly at night. On the coast you will be reminded of a humid North Carolina summer. The heat is dry in the plains.

Just like Brendan and his dad in Chapter 1, you will cross many southern states. Then you will enter Texas and reach the Mexican border.

Mexico City is the largest city in Mexico. **What landforms might these people see in Mexico?**

Chapter 22

 Caption Answer

Mountains, canyons, and plateaus

Driving Through Mexico

The border between the United States and Mexico is 2,000 miles (3,220 m) long. This is one of the busiest borders in the world.

On your trip you cross the border near Brownsville, Texas. The first Mexican city you reach is Matamoros (ma·tah·MOR·as). The highway becomes a black ribbon running through miles of sand. You have reached the Mesa del Norte.

You continue to take the highway south. Once you reach the capitol of Mexico City, you begin to travel southeast.

South of Mexico City, the highway enters the Isthmus of Tehuantepec (teh·WAHN·ta·PEK). An isthmus is a narrow land bridge. The isthmus lies between the Gulf of Mexico and the Pacific Ocean. If you continue on this road you will reach the countries of Central America. The nations of Guatemala and Belize border Mexico to the south.

WORD ORIGINS

The word "Mexico" comes from a Native American language. The word *mexica* was the name of a group that lived in the Mesa Central before the Spanish arrived.

The Copper Canyon—Barranca del Cobre—is part of the Sierra Madre mountains.
What two bodies of water border Mexico?

The Land and People

533

Mexico's Regions

Like the United States and Canada, Mexico can be divided into regions. These are the Mesa del Norte, the Mesa Central, and Southern Mexico.

Mesa del Norte

Mountains rise along the eastern and western sides of the **Mesa del Norte.** To the southeast there are low and rolling mountains like those of the eastern United States. These are the Sierra Madre Oriental. Little rain falls here and in the southeastern area of the plateau. Mexico's western mountains are tall with deep canyons. Mountain streams created the canyons over many years. These mountains are called the Sierra Madre Occidental.

Throughout much of the Mesa del Norte, the climate is dry. Cactus and wild scrub are the only plants that can survive in areas that receive only 2 inches of rain a year. Some dry areas have been changed into farmland through modern watering systems.

Farmers grow things like beans, corn, and chili peppers. They also grow cotton and wheat. Ranchers raise cattle in some parts of the Mesa del Norte. Beef has become an important industry. Large numbers of sheep and hogs are raised as well. Livestock has been raised in Mexico for almost 500 years.

Discussion Questions

1 What is the Mesa del Norte like?
2 What mountains are beside the Mesa del Notre?
3 What has made farming more productive on the Mesa del Norte?

 Caption Answer

The Pacific Ocean and the Gulf of Mexico

 Writing Activity

Volcano Legend Literature

OBJECTIVES: 1.01, 1.02, 1.06

Mexico City sits between two volcanoes, Popocatepetl, which means "White Woman," and Iztaccihuatl, which means "Smoking Mountain." A famous legend exists about these twin volcanoes that rise more than 17,000 feet. Iztaccihuatl was named after a beautiful princess. Her father, the king, offered her hand in marriage and his kingdom to any man who could defeat all his enemies.

Popocatepetl, Ixy's sweetheart, came forward and agreed to fight the king's enemies. While Popo was away fighting, Ixy was told by a jealous suitor that Popo had been killed. She died of grief before Popo returned. Popo was so brokenhearted when he returned, he built a tall pyramid and placed her body on top. He also built a second one in which to sit and hold a torch to light his lost love's sleep. Today, when Mexicans see the volcano smoke, they say Popo is lighting his torch for Ixy.

A version of the legend may be found in the library or it could be retold to the class. Have students compare the legend with another legend, such as the one about the Blowing Rock, and then compose a brief legend about a particular landform in North Carolina.

Background Information

Aztec Agriculture

The Aztecs were skilled farmers. They practiced irrigation by diverting water from streams to fields. They built elaborate walls to terrace slopes and prevent erosion. On their lands, they grew corn, sweet potatoes, tomatoes, squash, cacao, and tobacco. These crops were unknown to Europeans at that time. Today Mexican farmers still terrace their fields at higher elevations where flat land is scarce. Terrac-ing involves forming the land on a mountainside into a series of flat steps. This allows a farmer to grow crops on inclines that otherwise would be too steep. This practice is a reminder of Aztec agriculture.

Discussion Questions

1 Where are the silver mining centers of Mexico?

2 Where is Mesa Central?

3 What two large cities are located there?

 Caption Answer

Much of the Mesa del Norte has a desert climate. The Mesa Central's high elevation gives the region a cooler climate. Some of Mexico's best cropland is in the Mesa Central.

 **Map Activity**

Twisting on Mexico

NATIONAL GEOGRAPHY STANDARDS: 1, 4, 5

GEOGRAPHIC THEMES:

OBJECTIVES: 1.01, 1.02, 1.03

Materials shower curtain liner, overhead projector, masking tape, small index cards, and markers

On the index cards write the name of the countries of Middle America and the large bodies of water: Caribbean Sea, Gulf of Mexico, Atlantic Ocean, Gulf of California, and Pacific Ocean.

Project the Middle America transparency onto the shower curtain liner and trace the countries' outlines onto the curtain. Do not write in names of the countries; they are on the index cards. Tape the shower curtain onto the floor.

How to play: Six people may play the game. Four people (of the same sex) are the twisters. The twisters place their hands and feet on the countries that the fifth person calls out. Using the map on page 393, the sixth person checks to make sure that the player touches the correct country or body of water. A twister is eliminated when he or she falls or fails to touch the correct country or body of water. The winner is the last one left in the game.

Mexico's Spanish settlers forced Native Americans to dig for silver. Today, the nation's silver mines continue to produce this precious metal. Much is used for jewelry. In this region the Mexican states of Zacatecas (zah·kah·TAY·kas) and San Luis Potosi are silver mining centers. Northern states such as Sonora and Chihuahua have large mining operations.

Mesa Central

The *Mesa Central* is the middle region of the Mexican Plateau. It is an area of high plateaus near tall mountains. This region is cool and dry. Mexico City and Puebla are the two large cities located in this region.

Near Mexico City is an active volcano, Popocatepetl (po·pah·KAH·teh·peht·l). It stands almost 18,000 feet (5,400 m) tall. Popocatepetl is an important symbol of Mexico.

Years ago in this region, melting snow formed large lakes. Many of these lakes have been drained to create more land for living.

Some of Mexico's best cropland is found in the Mesa Central. Most Mexicans eat a lot of corn and beans. These crops grow well here. Squash and chili peppers grow well on the plateau, too. A large portion of Mexico's people have lived on the rich farmland of the Mesa Central since before the Spanish came.

When you leave the Mesa Central you begin a steady descent from the plateau to the Isthmus of Tehuantepec and the Yucatán Plain. The highway then takes you directly to southern Mexico through the city of Oaxaca (wah·HAH·kah).

Southern Mexico

The Yucatán Plain is part of Southern Mexico. Look at the map on page 531. The Yucatán Plain begins at the edge of the Mexican Plateau south of the Bay of Campeche (kam·PEE·chee). It stretches through the Yucatán Peninsula and into the countries of Guatemala and Belize.

Here the elevation is lower and the land flatter. Oak and pine trees grow alongside cactus. Rain forests thrive in the hot and humid climate of the southern Yucatán Plain.

A farmer in Oaxaca walks among dry corn stalks. **What are some differences between the Mesa del Norte and the Mesa Central?**

 Background Information

Mexico and the Ring of Fire

Mexico is about one fourth the size of the United States; the third-largest country in Latin America after Brazil and Argentina. The mountains in central and southern Mexico include many active volcanoes, such as Popocatepetl and Pico de Orizabas in the Central Mesa, part of the Ring of Fire (a circle of volcanic peaks around the rim of the Pacific Ocean). Along the Ring of Fire earthquakes are more frequent.

Both volcanic eruptions and earthquakes occur at places where tectonic plates meet. Mexico sits on the western edge of the North American plate that bumps up against the Pacific, Cocos, and Caribbean plates. The scraping and sliding of the plates causes earthquakes. Mexico's most devastating quake occurred in September 1985 in Michoacan, Mexico. More than 9,000 people lost their lives.

The ground beneath the Yucatán Plain is made of limestone. Rainwater seeps through limestone quickly. No rivers run through the Yucatán Plain. Instead there are holes in the limestone called *cenotes* (say·NO·tays). These holes collect and provide water for the people. The ancient lowland Maya people built cities here using the *cenotes* for water.

During the dry season farmers grow wheat and alfalfa. They harvest their crops during the wet season. Farmers also grow cotton and sisal, a fiber used to make rope and textiles. These are plants that do not require a lot of water. Farmers grow sugar and coffee further south.

At Mexico's most southern tip is the state of Chiapas (CHEE·ah·pahs). There you will find another range of tall mountains and some volcanoes. This is also the home of the modern highland Maya. The Highland Maya split away from the lowland Maya centuries ago.

Coffee and corn are important crops here. Logging and beef production are major industries.

In the south, the state of Guerrero (GWAH·reh·ro) has silver, copper, and iron. Oil is found in the humid lowlands along the Gulf of Mexico. Mexico exports some of these raw materials. Most are used in Mexico's own factories.

These men are drying sisal fibers on racks in Yucatán, Mexico. Sisal is an important crop. **What are the other important crops in Mexico?**

Discussion Questions

1 How is the land in southern Mexico different from the land in the north?
2 What are *cenotes*?
3 What are some of the crops that are grown in the south?

Caption Answer

Coffee, corn, wheat, alfalfa, and sugar.

Map Activity

Relative Location

NATIONAL GEOGRAPHY STANDARDS: 1, 4
GEOGRAPHIC THEMES: Location
OBJECTIVES: 1.01, 1.02, 1.03

This activity can be done individually or in cooperative groups. Give out markable laminated blackline maps of North America that include latitude and longitude. Pass out marking pens to students. Call out a relative location. Students must decide the country to which you are referring based on the relative location and circle that country. Students then should raise their hand so that you can check for accuracy.

LESSON ① REVIEW

Fact Follow-Up
1. What is an isthmus?
2. What are the three regions of Mexico?
3. In which region is Mexico City located?
4. Which region has the best cropland?
5. What are the features of Southern Mexico? of the Mesa del Norte? of the Mesa Central?

Talk About It
1. If you could visit one of the three regions of Mexico, which would you choose? Why?
2. Why do no rivers run through the Yucatán Plain?
3. How does relative location contribute to trade between the United States and Mexico? What factor might discourage trade?

The Land and People

LESSON ① REVIEW

Fact Follow-Up Answers
1. An isthmus is a land bridge lying between two bodies of water.
2. The Mesa del Norte, the Mesa Central, and Southern Mexico are the three regions.
3. Mexico City is located in the Mesa Central.
4. The Mesa Central has some of the nation's best cropland.
5. The Mesa del Norte's features include: the Sierra Madres Oriental, plateau, and the Sierra Madre Occidental. The Mesa Central's feature include: the Mexican Plateau, Popocatepetl, and large lakes. Southern Mexico's features include: rain forests and the Yucatán Plain.

Talk About It Answers
1. Important points: Students should choose one region and explain why. Reasons could include landforms, climate, products, economic activities, or history/culture.
2. The ground below the Yucatán Plain is made of limestone. Because limestone is very absorbent, rainfall seeps through it and does not run off to form rivers.
3. The closeness of the countries helps the shipment of foodstuffs, raw materials, and manufactured goods. Other factors might discourage trade, for example, farm vehicles need to drive up and down the mountains and over long sections of flat, dry plains to reach markets.

LESSON 2 Climate and Plant Life

Discussion Questions

1 How does Mexico's temperature compare with the temperature of the United States?

2 What are some factors that affect Mexico's climate?

3 What is the climate like in the western parts of the Mesa del Norte? along the northern coast?

4 What is the climate like on the Mesa Central? in the Yucatan Plain? in the highlands of the south?

Caption Answer

Elevation and nearness to water

Reading Strategy Activity

Attribute Analysis: T-Chart

OBJECTIVES: 1.02, 1.03, 1.06

A T-Chart can help students compare climate and vegetation. Make a chart like the one below. As the students read the lesson, have them list the characteristics of climate on one side and vegetation on the other. This can also be done in groups. Have them share their charts when finished.

CLIMATE	VEGETATION

KEY IDEAS

- Mexico is warmer than most of the United States. In Mexico's mountains and plateaus, the climate is much cooler.

- Mexico contains forests, grasslands, and deserts.

- Rain forests grow on Mexico's low plains. Evergreen forests are found at higher elevations.

Mexico is warmer than most parts of the United States. As in the United States, elevation and nearness to water affect the climate. The highest mountain peaks may have snow. Other places in Mexico have more tropical climates with miles and miles of thick plants.

There are also places with dry, sandy deserts that get little rain. Here, cactus and scrub grasses grow. There are even places in Mexico with many pine trees. There the countryside looks similar to the Appalachian Mountains of western North Carolina.

Climate

As you climb higher into the mountains, you'll feel it get cooler. You will also notice differences in rainfall and humidity. These differences are linked to elevation, as you read in Chapter 3.

In the western parts of the Mesa del Norte the land is flat and the climate is hot and dry. The mountains have cooler weather. Along the eastern coast of the Mesa del Norte, near the Texas border and Gulf of Mexico, the damp winds blow off the water. These winds and low elevation create warm temperatures and humid conditions.

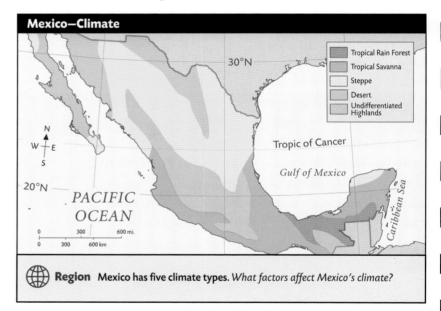

Region Mexico has five climate types. *What factors affect Mexico's climate?*

ELL Teaching Tips

Avoid Singling Out ELL Students

If you have some important information to convey, speak to the student one-on-one rather than in front of the class. When people are put on the spot, it is often more difficult for them to understand what you expect if they have limited language ability.

The Mesa Central is dry and cool. Most people live at an elevation of more than 8,000 feet (2,400 m). People in the Mesa Central live near the Equator. But they enjoy a pleasant climate due to the higher elevation.

People living on the Yucatán Plain have homes very close to sea level and not far north of the Equator. Their climate is hot. Since they also are near the ocean, the air is moist. Rain falls often.

Farther south in the highlands of Chiapas, the climate is once again cool. That is due to their higher elevation.

Plant Life

Mexico also has many kinds of plant life. It has forests and grasslands. There are also plants in the desert. These are three of the four main types of plant life you learned about in Chapter 3. Climate and elevation affect what types of plants grow in each region.

Grasslands in Mexico are much less common than forests and desert plants. Do you remember reading about deserts? Deserts receive less than 10 inches of rain per year. Yet you will find a great variety of plant life in these areas. Some of the driest areas have

cactus, scrub brush, and even small trees. These plants are able to bud and bloom when it rains.

The Mesa del Norte sits at a high elevation, around 6,000 feet (1,800 m) and is quite level. The plateau is mainly covered with evergreen and leafy forests. The highest mountain ranges are cool and dry. Only small hardy trees and some grasses grow in this region. People have a hard time growing crops here.

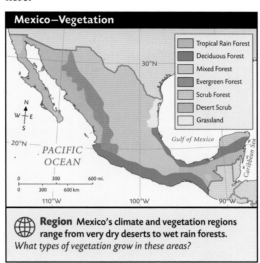

Mexico—Vegetation

Legend:
- Tropical Rain Forest
- Deciduous Forest
- Mixed Forest
- Evergreen Forest
- Scrub Forest
- Desert Scrub
- Grassland

Region Mexico's climate and vegetation regions range from very dry deserts to wet rain forests. *What types of vegetation grow in these areas?*

Plants and Elevation

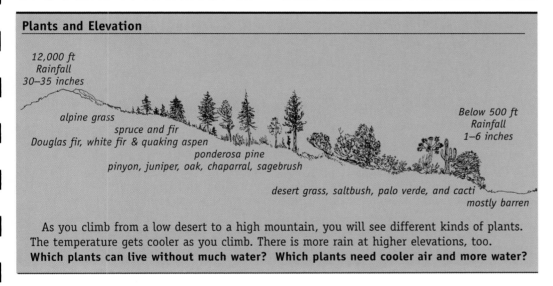

12,000 ft
Rainfall
30–35 inches

alpine grass
spruce and fir
Douglas fir, white fir & quaking aspen
ponderosa pine
pinyon, juniper, oak, chaparral, sagebrush

Below 500 ft
Rainfall
1–6 inches

desert grass, saltbush, palo verde, and cacti
mostly barren

As you climb from a low desert to a high mountain, you will see different kinds of plants. The temperature gets cooler as you climb. There is more rain at higher elevations, too. **Which plants can live without much water? Which plants need cooler air and more water?**

The Land and People

537

Discussion Questions

1 What are the main types of vegetation found in Mexico?

2 What types of vegetation are found in Mexico's deserts?

3 What characteristic is common to all deserts?

Caption Answer

Desert scrub grows in the desert and tropical rain forest vegetation grows in the rain forest regions.

Caption Answer

Desert grass, saltbush, palo verde, and cacti grow with little water. Alpine grass, and spruce, firs, and aspen trees need more water.

Map Activity

Mexico—Climate and Vegetation

NATIONAL GEOGRAPHY STANDARDS: 1, 4, 8
GEOGRAPHIC THEMES: Place
OBJECTIVES: 1.02, 1.03, 1.06

After reading the text on Mexico's climate and vegetation, have students match climate types with vegetative types. Have student compare the maps on pages 536 and 537 section by section to see where the regions overlap (ex: steppe with scrub forest).

Assign one pair of a climate and vegetation region to each student. Provide each with a paper lunch bag (brown or white). Instruct them to decorate one side of the bag with symbols or pictures of the climate and vegetation types.

On index cards or small pieces of paper, have students write characteristics of their assigned regions. When all are finished, have them share clues in their bags one at a time until their classmates can guess the climate and vegetative type.

Finally, discuss how climate and vegetation are related, and how and

Background Information

Mexico's Rain Forests

Although 14,640,994 acres of Mexico's rain forest disappeared between 1990 and 2005, the deforestation rates decreased 15.3 percent since the close of the 1990s. In 1996, Mexico enacted its first-ever national environmental plan.

The Selva Lacandona in the state of Chiapas is one of North America's last remaining tropical rain forests. It is home to many animal species including jaguar, spider and howler monkeys, harpy eagles and many migratory songbirds. It is part

of a larger rain forest ecosystem that extends to Belize. It is the second-largest rain forest system in the Americas. Only the Amazon rain forest is larger.

Mexico is one of the world's top five nations for biodiversity. It has at least 26,071 species of vascular plants (of which 48 percent are native) and to 2,765 known species of amphibians, birds, mammals, and reptiles (34 percent of which are indigenous).

Discussion Questions

1 Which region is like the Mesa del Norte? How?

2 What is the vegetation like in Southern Mexico?

Caption Answer

The wheat field shows how people farm the land.

Science Activity

Indigenous Plants and Animals

OBJECTIVES: 1.01, 1.02, 1.03

From the list below of plants and animals indigenous to Mexico, have each student choose one to research. Find out where the animal or plant lives or grows. What are the uses of the plant or animal? Share the findings with the class.

Examples: sapodilla tree, guayule, agave, poinsettias (called Nochebuenas), the saguaro cactus, the giant dagger cactus, prickly pear cactus, maguey cactus, vanilla plant, cocoa pods, ocelot, jaguarundis, jaguars, cacomistle, margay, the green iguana, chihuahuas, sidewinder rattlesnake, armadillo, tapir, quetzal bird, roadrunner, kangaroo rat, monarch butterfly, California porpoise, axolotl, gray whale, Bolson Tortoise, and Kemp's Ridley Sea Turtle.

In Mexico's Mesa Central, climate and plant life are much like those of the Mesa del Norte. On land cleared of the forests people grow corn and wheat.

Southern Mexico is not far north of the Equator, but climates and plant life change with height above sea level. Tropical rain forests and moist plains grow on the low, hot lands of the Yucatán Plain. Rain forests are also found at higher elevations.

At the southern tip of Mexico the state of Chiapas has several different elevations so different types of plants grow there. Tropical rain forests grow in some areas. Forests also grow there. Some even have oak trees.

Changing the Land

At the higher elevations of Mexico, a few people terrace the land. Terracing is when a mountainside is shaped into a series of flat steps. Terraces let farmers grow crops on slopes that otherwise would be too steep.

What would YOU do?

You have an opportunity to live with your family for a year in a small town in Mexico. You will learn Spanish and go to the local school. What should you do to prepare? How would you make sure you are ready for life in a new place?

A saguaro cactus grows in a wheat field in the Baja area of Mexico. **How does this photograph show human-environmental interaction?**

LESSON 2 REVIEW

Fact Follow-Up
1. How does elevation affect climate in Mexico?
2. Of the four main types of plant life, which three does Mexico have?
3. Where in Mexico are there tropical rain forests?
4. Why have mountainsides been terraced?

Talk About It
1. Southern Mexico lies in the Tropics. How is it possible that there are snowcapped mountains in Mexico?
2. Where in Mexico would you go to visit an area least like the southeastern United States? What type of plants would you find there?

LESSON 2 REVIEW

Fact Follow-Up Answers
1. In general, higher elevations have cooler climates.
2. Mexico has forests, grasslands, and desert.
3. There are tropical rain forests on the Yucatán plain and southward into Chiapas.
4. Terraced mountainsides allow farmers to grow crops on inclines that otherwise would be too steep.

Talk About It Answers
1. Elevation influences climate so that even in tropical climates high mountains can be topped with snow.
2. Important points: Students should choose one area and explain their choice. Climate, vegetation, and elevation should be mentioned.

San Cristobal de las Casas

The state of Chiapas is in the southern part of Mexico. There the city of San Cristobal de las Casas lies in a valley more than 7,000 feet (2,133 m) high. The mountains rise to more than 9,000 feet (2,743 m). A Spanish settler founded the city in 1528.

At first the town was called San Cristobal. "Las Casas" was added to the city's name later. It honors Father Bartolome de las Casas. Many years earlier he fought for the rights of the Native Americans in the Spanish colonies.

Today, San Cristobal de las Casas is a center of highland Maya culture. It is also a vacation spot for tourists from all over the world. Around the city lay many Maya villages. San Cristobal is the area's market town.

In the hills and valleys around San Cristobal, the Maya grow their crops on terraces. Most dress in traditional clothes. Most Maya speak their own languages and Spanish.

Visiting San Cristobal can be a journey into the past. Many of the streets in the town are made of cobblestones. This makes for a rough ride in a car or truck.

Yet modern technology is also present here. Computers and satellite dishes bring news of the world. Airplanes from Mexico City land at the local airport every day.

Math Activity

Mountains of Mexico

OBJECTIVES: 1.01, 1.02, 1.06

Divide the class into cooperative groups and give these directions to students:

1. Using available resources, identify the seven highest mountains in Mexico and rank them from the lowest to the highest.
2. Estimate to the nearest thousands, hundreds, and tens the heights of the seven mountains.
3. Write five word problems using the seven mountains and their given heights. Include addition, subtraction, estimation, greater than, and less than.
4. Exchange word problems. Each group solves problems from other groups.
5. Use the information to make a bar graph of the mountains from highest to lowest.
6. Make a relief map of Mexico and place the seven mountains in the proper location. Label and include an elevation key.

Extension Intermediate ELL students can do activities but may take longer to do them. Novice ELL students can copy the order of height, copy the height estimations, make a bar graph, and do the relief map.

Science Activity

Animal Migration in North America

OBJECTIVES: 1.01, 1.02, 1.03

Before reading the lesson, ask students to share their ideas about what types of plants grow in Mexico. From the last lesson, many will remember that cacti and other tropical plants grow there.

Give each student a map of Mexico. Tell them to read the lesson on the vegetation of Mexico. As they read they are to sketch the different plants on the map in the places where they belong. Remind them to not spend an excessive amount of time on the drawings. A key could also be made on the bottom for the plants. Give examples to use such as scrub grasses, cacti, small trees, evergreen trees, deciduous trees, and tropical rain forest plants. Pictures of these plants would also help with visualization.

OBJECTIVES: 1.05, 1.06, 1.07, 3.04

Discussion Questions

1 What does *mezcla* mean?

2 What are the main languages spoken in Mexico today?

3 What does *mestizo* mean?

Caption Answer

Mezcla means mixture. Modern Mexico is a combination of Native American and European people and cultures. The is a small number of Africans in the mezcla.

Reading Strategy Activity

Highlighting

OBJECTIVES: 1.05, 1.06, 1.07, 3.04

Highlighting is sometimes called selective underlining because some students do better with underlining with a pencil instead of using a highlighter pen. If colored pens are used, caution students to color lightly. A heavy hand defeats the purpose.Modeling is the key to student understanding. Make a transparency of a sample lesson and show students how to choose important parts to highlight.Explain that underlining is effective in understanding a lesson. Most people can't remember everything they read, but organizing the material helps. Underlining is a way to see main ideas and details at a glance. Develop your own steps for underlining. See the suggestions in the box.

On Their Own

Make a copy of Lesson 3 for each student (or hand out clear transparencies and let students paperclip them to their textbook) to highlight or underline. Arrange the class into groups of four. One student underlines what the group decides are the main ideas and details. Groups present their work aloud to the class. Discuss as a class what they underlined and why.

Extension Novice ELL students can copy the information given by the teacher.

KEY IDEAS

- Most Mexicans live in the cities of the Mesa Central.

- Mexico's culture combines Native American customs with Spanish traditions.

- Trade is bringing Mexico and the United States closer together.

KEY TERMS

mestizo
mezcla
tiendas

People from Europe and North America came together to build Mexico. The Mexican people descend mainly from Native Americans and the Spanish. A small population with African ancestors lives along the Gulf of Mexico.

Mexican writers and artists began calling themselves *La Raza Cosmica* (the Cosmic Race) after the revolution. They believe each ethnic group helps make their nation strong.

Where People Live

The most densely settled area of Mexico is the Mesa Central. Its four largest cities are all located here.

This region is also the home of Mexico's ancient cities. People have lived and worked there for thousands of years. Mexico has a thinly populated northern desert region. But the northern region's border towns have growing populations. Their closeness to the United States draws people and businesses to the border.

Much of Mexico is a patchwork of open spaces mixed with urban areas. In the southern highlands there are fewer people than in the Mesa Central. The rain forests of the Yucatán Peninsula are also thinly populated.

As you drive along you might find yourself alone on long stretches of isolated highway. But you might also find yourself in crowded places along the coast. Many people live there, too.

Mexico City's Paseo de la Reforma shows how Mexico honors its past while being a busy, modern city. **What does *mezcla* mean? How does it describe Mexico?**

540

Highlighting Suggestions

- Read the first paragraph. (Some suggest reading the entire lesson first. Use what works best.)
- Reread and start underlining.
- Never underline the entire sentence.
- Search for key terms or key ideas. (Younger students need more structure. You may need to be more specific and say underline names, dates, places, and so on.)
- Make certain the main idea of a paragraph is underlined.
- Consider using a different color pen to stress the difference between the main idea and details (such as red for main idea and green for details). Extra notes can be written in the margins to clarify ideas.

Guadalajara's cathedral is one sign of European influence in Mexico. **What is another sign of Spanish influence?**

A Mezcla of Peoples

The Spanish word *mezcla* means mixture. It describes the population of Mexico. Before the Spanish came, Mexico was home to the Maya and Aztec empires. Everyone spoke their own Native American language and worshiped their own gods.

Language

The Spanish brought their language and the Roman Catholic Church. So modern Mexico is mostly a combination of Native

Americans and Europeans. There is also a small number of Africans.

The majority of Mexicans speak Spanish. Ninety-one percent use Spanish as their principal language. There are several Native American languages spoken there as well. More than 6 percent of Mexicans speak one of these Native American languages.

Native American languages have given us both Spanish and English words. The words chocolate and tomato come from Nahuatl words. Throughout Mexico, Spanish is mixed with Native American words for places and animals. The same is true for many plants.

About half of the Mexican people are *mestizo,* or persons of mixed Native American and European ancestry. Around one third of the population is Native American. About 15 percent are European. About 1 percent of the population falls into other categories.

Customs

Mexicans celebrate the coming of Christmas with a *posada*. Posada is a Spanish word that means "shelter." Sometimes they have a little pageant where children portraying Mary and Joseph knock at three doors and ask to come in. They are turned away at the first and second doors. They are welcomed in and offered special foods and drinks at the third door. The children break open a *piñata*. Out pours all kinds of candy. There might also be some fruit and coins in the *piñata* as well.

WORD ORIGINS

The word "**mestizo**" refers to Americans of both Native American and European background. The phrase comes from the Spanish word *mestizar* and means "to mix" or "cross." *Mestizo* people have ancestors who are both European and Native Americans.

The Land and People   541

 Activity

People

OBJECTIVES: 2.08, 3.04, 3.06

People, written and illustrated by Peter Spier, is a great way to introduce culture and diversity to students. Have students read the book through completely, and then read the book a second time noting one interesting statement or picture for each of the following words or phrases (listed in the order they appear in the book):

Babies; colors of eyes; noses or lips or ears; hair; clothing; beauty; wise, foolish, decent; noise, quiet, or fun; games/fun; tastes; homes; laugh, cry, or excel; doing things with others or by ourselves; pets; celebrations; foods; religions; gods; work; rich or poor; languages; writing; power; ranks; and remembered by.

Students may choose to write a paragraph describing the purpose of the book, select one or more of the things that they encountered in the book to research further, or write a letter to the author telling him their opinions of the book.

 Caption Answer

The Spanish language and the Roman Catholic Church

 Activity

Mezcla

 OBJECTIVES: 1.05, 3.04, 3.06

Mexico is like "a cake with many ingredients." After students have read the lesson, list on the blackboard the many different people who have come to Mexico: Spanish, African American, French, and Native Americans.

1. Share with the class photos, artwork, and videos of the many cultures of Mexico. Discuss the various visual products. Students will then create a mural depicting an aspect of a given culture, such as religion, history, traditions, or work. Students should be prepared to be interviewed by a fellow classmate about the subject of their mural.
2. Using a variety of resources, find a game from Mexico. Learn the rules of the game and be prepared to teach the game to a younger grade. It will be your responsibility to gather all materials necessary for the lesson.
3. Find a folktale from Mexico. Practice reading the folktale aloud. Create props to use with the story (such as puppets, posters, pictures, and so on) as you read or retell it to the class or a younger class. Ask fellow classmates to assist in the presentation if needed. Record the folktale ahead of time if you would like to manipulate the props.
4. Select a culture from Mexico. Create a poem with details and images that describes the culture. Acrostic poems work really well with this activity.

Eyewitness Activity

The Meeting of Cortés and Moctezuma

OBJECTIVES: 1.02, 1.03, 1.06

Go to **NCJourneys.com** for a link to a lesson plan about Cortés and Moctezuma. This unit can be used in part or in its entirety. The following is a lesson summary:

Lesson 1 The Aztecs Establish a Sacred City—Early history of Tenochtitlán and Aztec religion basics.

Lesson 2 Spain's Standing in the World—Conquests of the Spanish leading up to and influencing the clash with the Aztecs.

Lesson 3 Moctezuma's Preparation for Leadership—Information on Moctezuma's training as a priest, astrologer, and warrior.

Lesson 4 The Meeting of the Two Cultures—Defines the accounts of each group and offers a chance to compare and contrast the two cultures.

Lesson 5 The Fall of Tenochtitlán—Defeat of the Aztecs led to the fusion of the two cultures.

Some of the activities include reenacting of Aztec myths, creating story maps that reveal the importance of the Aztec gods in founding Tenochtitlán, writing, recognizing point of view, and writing scripts that highlight Cortés and Moctezuma's dialogue.

The Meeting of Cortés and Moctezuma

EYEWITNESS TO HISTORY

Hernán Cortés was the leader of the Spanish forces that conquered the Aztec Empire. Moctezuma II was the Aztec emperor at that time. The meeting of these two leaders was one of the most dramatic moments in the history of Mexico.

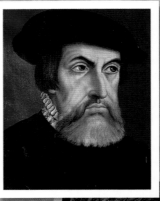

In 1519, the Spanish governor of the island colony of Cuba sent Hernán Cortés (left) to the mainland. Cortés' goal was to make contact with the people there. His orders were to explore, not to conquer. Cortés did not follow his instructions. He conquered the Aztecs.

Moctezuma II (left) was the Aztec ruler. In 1517, when Moctezuma first heard of the Spanish landing on the coast, he posted people to watch the foriegners and to let him know when more arrived. When Cortés arrived in 1519, Moctezuma's people told him about the newcomer. Moctezuma sent gifts and people to meet Cortés.

542

Background Information

Mexican Megalopolis

Population is unevenly distributed in Mexico. Mesa Central has the three largest cities in Mexico. With a population of 18 million, Mexico City is one of the twenty largest cities in the world. Only Tokyo, Japan, has more people. Guadalajara, Mexico's second-largest city, has 3 million and Puebla, the third-largest, has about the same. In recent years, pollution, the high cost of living, and crime have led many people to move from Mexico City to smaller cities nearby. These places have become suburbs. Workers now commute to jobs in Mexico City from as far as 100 miles away. The cities of the region are growing together. "Towards the middle of the twenty-first century," predicts demographer Gustavo Garza, "this megalopolis will [hold] approximately 50 million people."

Aztec Empire

Teotihuacán

Tenochtitlán

Cortés and the Spanish brought many things that the Aztecs had never seen. They had guns, huge fighting dogs, horses, and steel armor.

Cortés fought his way from the coast to the Mesa Central. The Spanish made an alliance with enemies of the Aztecs. Then Cortés traveled to the Aztec capital. The two men met.

Cortés meets Moctezuma

Moctezuma II was dressed in a great cape of colorful feathers. Cortés wore shiny armor. Cortés gave Moctezuma II a necklace of pearls and diamonds. Moctezuma II gave Cortés a chain hung with large gold figures. Moctezuma invited the Spanish to stay with him in his palace.

Eventually Cortés kidnapped Moctezuma II. With the help of the Aztecs' enemies, the Spanish soldiers, and European diseases, the Aztec empire fell. Moctezuma was killed in a battle with the Spanish, but it is unclear whether he was killed by the Spanish or his own people.

Cortés conquers the Aztecs

The Land and People

543

Discussion Questions

 1 From where are other immigrants to Mexico?

 **Caption Answer**

The Aztec culture

 **Activity**

Selling Mexico

OBJECTIVES: 1.02, 1.05, 1.06

Assign each student a state in Mexico. They will design a real estate sales brochure for it. The goal is to create a brochure that would make someone want to move to and purchase real estate in that state.

Using physical maps and other resources, students need to gather information on major landforms, major bodies of water, plant life, animal life, climate, population, and major cities. Give each student an 8½-inch by 11-inch piece of construction paper and these directions: Fold the paper into three equal columns. On one side label columns 5, 6, and 1 from left to right. Flip the page over and number the columns 2, 3, and 4 from left to right. Students should create a catchy title and an illustration about the assigned state on panel, and include their name as the selling agent.

Panels 2, 3, and 4 will be a "property description." They should write well-developed paragraphs describing the physical landforms and other features of the state. Across all three panels, students should draw an illustration of the physical features described in the paragraph. In column 5, they should write a paragraph persuading the buyer to buy property in the given state. In column 6, they should list factual information about the climate, major cities, and population.

Have students fold the brochure in alternate directions so that the pages appear in correct order.

The Roman Catholic Church has been an important influence in Mexico for almost 500 years.
What culture did the European explorers encounter when they first arrived?

Native Americans

Chapter 4 explained how the first settlers of the Americas moved from Asia. Many of these people traveled as far south as modern Mexico. They built great cities in the Mesa Central and Yucatán Peninsula.

Others remained nomads for a time or moved about the land according to the season. There were also highly advanced cultures that developed in other parts of Mexico.

Europeans and Africans

The Spanish came to Mexico in 1519. They conquered the Aztecs. Over time many more Spanish people came to Mexico. They started the colony of New Spain. Its capital was Mexico City. Then the Spanish spread out across the land. They built cities in many places. Most of these cities exist today.

Few people from places other than Spain came to Mexico. Over the years some Asians and other Europeans made the journey. Africans arrived in Mexico as free men and women. Sometimes they came as the result of shipwrecks in the Gulf of Mexico.

Others escaped slavery on Caribbean islands and then came to Mexico. A small number were brought to Mexico as slaves. More recently, some Africans have moved to Mexico.

544

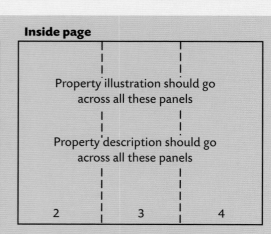

Outside page				Inside page		
Why should you buy this property		Catchy title		Property illustration should go across all these panels		
Persuasive paragraph	Informational panel	Selling Agent: Student name		Property description should go across all these panels		
5	6	1		2	3	4

Mexico Today

Beginning in the 1980s, many Central Americans began to flee to Mexico. They left political conflicts in their own countries. Many of these people spend time in Mexico on their way to the United States. They travel north seeking work and freedom.

There are also some communities in Mexico with a large number of United States citizens. Many of these are retired people. There are 9,000 foreigners in the state of Guanajuato (gwan·ah·WA·to) alone. About 350,000 United States citizens live in Mexico today.

Mexico is a country of young people. More than half of its people are under 20 years of age. The nation's total population is almost 110 million.

In the second half of the 1900s, many Mexicans moved from the country to the cities. Today Mexico is an urban nation. Around 71 percent of the population lives in cities or towns.

This modern building is the stock exchange in Mexico City. **Do more Mexicans live in urban or rural areas?**

The Land and People

Benito Juarez
1806–1872

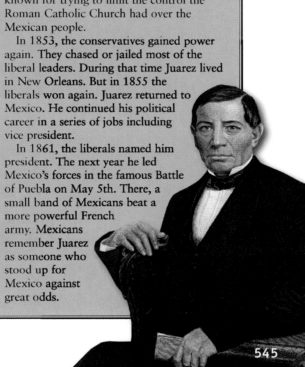

Benito Juarez was the son of Native Americans. He served as president of Mexico for two terms (1861–1863, 1867–1872). He is the only Native American to ever hold that position. Juarez was orphaned when he was three years old. He then lived with his sister in Oaxaca while he went to school.

At first Juarez thought of becoming a priest. He later changed his mind and decided to study law. He began practicing law and soon entered politics. First he served as a judge. Then he became governor of Oaxaca in 1841.

Juarez was a member of the "liberal" party. The liberals tried to improve the living conditions of the native people. He became known for trying to limit the control the Roman Catholic Church had over the Mexican people.

In 1853, the conservatives gained power again. They chased or jailed most of the liberal leaders. During that time Juarez lived in New Orleans. But in 1855 the liberals won again. Juarez returned to Mexico. He continued his political career in a series of jobs including vice president.

In 1861, the liberals named him president. The next year he led Mexico's forces in the famous Battle of Puebla on May 5th. There, a small band of Mexicans beat a more powerful French army. Mexicans remember Juarez as someone who stood up for Mexico against great odds.

545

Discussion Questions

1 Why have people from Central America come to Mexico?

2 Why have people from the United States settled in Mexico?

3 What is one Mexican town that has many retired and foreign people?

Caption Answer

Urban areas

Activity

Learning About Leadership: Portrait Activity

OBJECTIVES: 2.04, 3.06

Some have said that there are six qualities that make a leader: passion, vision, preparation, courage, perseverance, and integrity. Using a graphic organizer, have students find examples (they may need to do additional research on the Internet or in the media center) to illustrate these qualities of Benito Juarez.

Next, students should create a day that celebrates the importance of Juarez. Have the create a symbol and slogan for the day; choose a date significant in the person's life as the day to hold the celebration, and create some special events to celebrate on that day.

Teacher Notes

Benito Juárez

Benito Juárez served as president of Mexico from 1858 to 1872. Juárez's rise is particularly significant because he was born a indigenous Zapotec villager who did not learn to read or speak Spanish until he was a teenager. He eventually went to law school and became a champion of liberal democracy. Juárez had to continually battle the vested interests of Mexican aristocracy. A friend of Abraham Lincoln, Juárez, like Lincoln, is now regarded as one of the most influential statesmen of nineteenth-century North America.

Discussion Questions

1 Why are Mexico and North Carolina becoming more closely linked?

2 What is a *tienda*?

 **Caption Answer**

Produce and manufactured goods

 **Activity**

Read the Label

 OBJECTIVES: 5.01, 5.02, 5.07

Have students visit a *tienda* or Latin American store in your area. (If there are none, students can go to the section of their local supermarket where the Mexican food is displayed.) Ask them to select one product and carefully read the label. Have them report on the following:

• Is the label bilingual?
• Is there a similar product available through conventional United States distribution?
• What addresses, if any, are on the label?
• What other useful information is on the label?

Relations with North Carolina

Mexico is one of North Carolina's biggest trade partners. Several of North Carolina's textile companies have started partnerships with Mexican firms. Some have built new factories there and closed other factories in the United States.

Industries here export a number of products to Mexico. North Carolina also buys produce and manufactured products from Mexico. Truckers travel long distances hauling these goods.

Coming Closer

The people of Mexico and North Carolina come into contact with one another all the time. Mexicans are learning to speak English and North Carolinians are studying Spanish.

In the cities and small towns of North Carolina you see *tiendas,* or shops selling food and magazines from Mexico. The country that seemed so far away only 20 years ago has come to the very doorstep of North Carolina.

These women are sewing clothes at a Mexican factory. **What do Americans buy from Mexico?**

LESSON 3 REVIEW

Fact Follow-Up
1. What is the most densely settled area of Mexico?
2. How does the Spanish word *mezcla* describe the population of Mexico?
3. Describe the diversity of the population of Mexico.
4. What is a *tienda*?

Talk About It
1. Which country is more a country of youth: Mexico or the United States? Explain why.
2. More and more United States citizens are moving to Mexico to live and work. Why?
3. What might be some effects of a North Carolina company building a new factory in Mexico?

LESSON 3 REVIEW

Fact Follow-Up Answers
1. The Mesa Central is the most densely settled area.
2. Mezcla means mixture, and the Mexican population is mostly descended from Native Americans, Spanish, and Africans.
3. About half of the Mexican people are mestizo, of mixed Native American and European ancestry. About one third of the population is Native American, while approximately 15 percent are of European descent. About 1 percent of the population falls into other categories.
4. Tienda is the Spanish word for a shop that sells food and magazines.

Talk About It Answers
1. Important points: Students should mention that more than half of Mexico's population is under twenty years old.
2. Because Mexico has a lot of industries and Mexico is one of the biggest trade partners of the United States.
3. Important points: Effects might include the loss of jobs in North Carolina, the creation of jobs in Mexico, the saving of the company money, or the possibility of keeping the price of the finished goods low for American consumers.

Analyzing, Interpreting, Creating, and Using Resources and Materials

Comparing the Regions of North America

Just as you have learned about regions of the United States and Canada, you have now begun to learn about the regions of Mexico. In your studies of regions in the United States and Canada, you learned about both physical and political regions. You may even remember learning about cultural and language regions.

Do you recall any differences between French-speaking and English-speaking regions in Canada?

Let's compare the regions of Canada, the United States, and Mexico. This will help you learn about the things these three countries share and about their differences. To begin these comparisons, you will need to make two important decisions.

First, you will need to choose which regions you will study. Choose one region from each country. They are listed below.

A. The United States regions: New England, the Mid-Atlantic, the Southeast, the Midwest, the Southwest, the West, and the Pacific.

B. The Canadian regions: the Arctic Plains, the Appalachian Highlands, the Great Lakes-St. Lawrence Lowlands, the Interior Plains, the Canadian Shield, and the Western Mountains.

C. The Mexican regions: the Mesa del Norte, the Mesa Central, and Southern Mexico.

The Mesa del Norte in Mexico

You might use the maps in Chapters 14, 15, 16, 18, and 22 to refresh your memory of these regions. You will need to decide the best way to compare these regions. You might choose landforms, climate, minerals, and other economic resources. What other things might you use? population? economic activities? You could even use recreation as one of the things you compare.

Your teacher will guide you as you make these decisions and compare the regions of the United States, Canada, and Mexico.

Teaching This Skill Lesson

Materials Needed textbooks and other reference materials, chart paper, rulers, pencils and markers

Classroom Organization whole class, individual

Beginning the Lesson Ask how the United States, Canada, and Mexico are alike and different. Accept all answers, recording them on the chalkboard. Follow the general question with probing questions such as "Are landforms in Mexico, Canada, and the United States similar or different?"

Lesson Development Tell students they will be comparing regions of Canada, Mexico, and the United States to understand similarities and differences among the three countries. Direct students to the Skill Lesson on page 547 to select one region from each of the three. (Students may choose any region from each country to compare.) Emphasize the importance of choosing criteria for comparison, noting the criteria mentioned in the Skill Lesson. To avoid confusion, all students should choose the same criteria. Once criteria have been chosen, sketch a simple data retrieval chart on the chalkboard for students to use as a model for reporting their comparisons, or refer students to data retrieval charts used previously. Students may complete data retrieval charts as a homework assignment.

Conclusion When students have completed their comparisons, allow them to discuss and compare their work in small groups. Post charts in the classroom.

Skill Lesson Review

1. Which criterion was best for showing similarities among the regions? *Encourage students to discuss criteria. Landforms and minerals will likely be mentioned.*

2. Were any criteria you chose not useful? If so, why? *It is likely that criteria having to do with physical features and basic economic resources would have been more useful than cultural characteristics.*

Talk About It

1. Important points: Students should choose one of the two and explain their choice. Answers should refer to landforms, mineral wealth, soils, the availability of water, and population.
2. Africans arrived as escapees from other Spanish colonies, as free men and women, and as the result of shipwrecks in the Gulf of Mexico. More recently some Africans have emigrated to Mexico.
3. Important points: Students should take a position and explain it. The Mexican population is largely a mixture of Spanish, mestizo, and Native American people. The population of the United States includes large numbers of people from many European, Asian, African, and Central and South American countries.
4. Reasons include the exchange of goods, improved transportation, the need for workers, and agreements between governments that encourage increased contacts.
5. Important points: Encourage students to speculate, supporting their speculation with reasons. If Cortés had not appeared before Moctezuma, another Spanish explorer might well have done so. Cortés was well supplied; other Spanish explorers would have been well supplied as well.

Mastering Mapwork

1. Veracruz lies on relatively flat terrain on the border of the Bay of Campeche and is located south of the Tropic of Cancer. One would expect to find a warm to hot climate and tropical vegetation and plant life.
2. Ciudad Juarez lies on the Rio Grande River, a border between Mexico and the United States. It is located on Mexico's Central Plateau at an elevation between 6,500 and 10,000 feet. In Ciudad Juarez one would expect to find a relatively cool climate because of its elevation and nearness to the Tropics. In spite of its location on the Rio Grande, the city is not likely to be humid because of its nearness to desert regions. Because it is located on an international border, Ciudad Juarez is likely to be an active city with many people crossing the border and considerable traffic.
3. Because Mexico City is a national capital, one would expect to find many government buildings and government workers in this place
4. Merida is located on a peninsula, has an elevation between 0 and 700 feet above sea level, and is located south of the Tropic of Cancer. Here one would expect to find a

CHAPTER 22 REVIEW

Lessons Learned

LESSON 1
Location and Size
Mexico lies south of the western United States. It includes many highlands. The best land for farming is in the Mesa Central, where the Aztecs and other ancient peoples settled.

LESSON 2
Climate and Plant life
Although Mexico's climate is warmer than most of the United States, the air is cooler in the mountains and plateaus. Rain forests grow on the low plains, and evergreen forests grow in the highlands.

LESSON 3
People of Mexico
The cities of the Mesa Central are highly populated. Mexico's culture is a mixture of Native American and Spanish traditions. In recent years, trade has brought the United States and Mexico closer together.

hot, wet climate as well as tropical vegetation and animal life.
5. Because of its low elevation and nearness to the Tropics as well as to the Gulf of Mexico and Bay of Campeche, one would expect to find a warm, moist climate, flat land, and much vegetation.
6. Although Mexico City is located in the Tropics, it is likely to be cooler than Chihuahua because it lies at a higher elevation.
7. Monterrey is likely to be warmer than Mazatlán even though Mazatlán is located farther south because Mazatlán can receive cooling breezes blowing off the Pacific Ocean.

Talk About It

1. Which region, the Mesa Central or Southern Mexico, do you think has more valuable resources for Mexico's future? Explain why.
2. How did Africans arrive in Mexico?
3. Is the word *mezcla* a more accurate description of the population of Mexico or the United States? Explain.
4. Why have contacts between North Carolina and Mexico increased in recent years?
5. Suppose Hernán Cortés had not disobeyed orders and kidnapped Moctezuma II. How do you think life in Mexico might have been different? Explain why.

Mastering Mapwork

Movement
Use the maps on page 531, 536, and 537 to answer these questions:
1. Locate Veracruz. What physical characteristics of place would you expect to find in Veracruz?
2. Locate Ciudad Juarez. What physical and cultural features of place would you expect to find in this place?
3. Using only the information from this map, what cultural features of place would you expect to find in Mexico City?
4. Locate Merida on the Yucatán Peninsula. What physical features of place would you expect to find in this location?
5. Locate the Gulf Coastal Plain. What physical features of place would you expect to find in this place?
6. Which of these cities is likely to be cooler: Chihuahua or Mexico City? Explain why.
7. Which city is likely to be warmer: Monterrey or Mazatlan? Explain why.

Becoming better readers

More on Taking Notes
In order to remember what they read, good readers will sometimes take notes. To take notes, good readers write the main idea and one or two details that tell more about the main idea. Reread the portrait of Benito Juarez on page 545. Write down the key points of his life and one or two details that support those points.

Becoming Better Readers

Important points: students should have the most important idea listed in their notes. Some should have supporting details. Notes may include:

- Juaez was a Native American.
- He was president for two terms.
- Juarez became a lawyer.
- Juarez entered politics.
  He was a Judge; he was the governor of Oaxaca.
- Juarex tried to improve conditions for native people.
- He led Mexico to victory at the Battle of Puebla.

Go to the Source

Gathering Information from Letters

Letters to friends and family can be primary source documents. They describe people, places, and events at a particular point in time. People often also write of their thoughts and feeling about things that are happening. Historians often use letters to learn more about a culture or other things that may have been happening during a a particular period of time.

Read the letter from the pen pal to her friend below. Answer the questions using information from the letter.

Translation:

> Hi, how are you Christian? Good, I hope. I am from Mexico and I live in the state of Querétaro in the town of Jalpan, and my name is Ana Guadalupe. I am going to explain a little about Mexico. Mexico is a place where there are many ecosystems: aquatic, aerial, terrestrial. In the aquatic live fish, serpents, and more other things. In the air live birds, butterflies, and other things. On land there live horses, mountain lions, turkey, snakes, spiders and other things. Now I have explained Mexico to you. I would like you to tell me about California and about your customs and I hope that we will be good friends.
>
> Sincerely,
> Your new friend:
> Ana Guadalupe

Questions

1. Where does Ana live?
2. What are the three ecosystems in Mexico that Ana describes?
3. Why would Ana want Christian to tell her about customs in California?
4. What is Ana's purpose in writing this letter?
5. What is Ana's tone in this letter?

The Land and People   549

  Go to the Source

Gathering Information from Letters

OBJECTIVES: 1.03

SOCIAL STUDIES SKILLS: 3.05, 4.06

Penpals are a good way for students to learn about other places and cultures. As an extension to this activity, have student write letters to imaginary pen pals or match students with penpals from Mexico or another place in North America.

Answers

1. Jalpan, Queretaro, Mexico
2. Acquatic, aerial, and terrestrial
3. Possible answer: Ana is Cristian's pen pal and she wants to learn about the customs where he lives.
4. Possible answer: Ana is introducing herself to her new penpal. She is telling him a little about herself and where she lives.
5. Ana's tone is friendly.

 ### How to Use the Chapter Review

There are four sections in the Chapter Review: Talk About It, Mastering Mapwork, Becoming Better Readers, and Go to the Source. Use the Vocabulary Worksheets and the Chapter Review Worksheet in the Teacher's Resource Guide for additional reinforcement and preparation for the Chapter Assessments. The chapter and lesson reviews and the Chapter Review Worksheets are the basis of the assessment for each chapter.

Talk About It questions encourage students to speculate about the content of the chapter and are suitable for class or small-group discussion. They are not intended to be assigned for homework.

Mastering Mapwork has students apply one or more of the Five Themes of Geography to maps within the chapter.

Becoming Better Readers focuses on building reading strategy skills necessary for reading comprehension in the content areas.

Go to the Source activities allow students to analyze a primary source that relates to the content of the chapter. The questions and activities familiarize students with different types of primary sources and also build content-reading skills.

People and Environment

Social Studies Strands

Cultures and Diversity

Historic Perspectives

Technological Influences and Society

Economics and Development

North Carolina Standard Course of Study

Goal 2 The learner will analyze political and social institutions in North America and examine how these institutions respond to human needs, structure society, and influence behavior.

Goal 3 The learner will examine the roles various ethnic groups have played in the development of the United States and its neighboring countries.

Goal 4 The learner will trace key developments in United States history and describe their impact on the land and people of the nation and its neighboring countries.

Goal 5 The learner will evaluate ways the United States and other countries of North America make decisions about the allocation and use of economic resources.

Teaching & Assessment

- English Language Learner Modified Lesson Plans for this chapter are found in the Teacher's Resource Guide.

- *ExamView® Assessment Suite* is provided at **NCJourneys.com.** It includes customizable assessments for all chapters. Paper tests are also available in the Teacher's Resource Guide. See pages T16–T17 for information about how to use the assessments and the Scoring Guide.

Worksheets

Worksheets and answer keys are found both in the Teacher's Resource Guide and at **NCJourneys.com**, including Reading Guides, Reading Strategies, Chapter Reviews, English Language Learner and others.

Activities and Integrations

SOCIAL STUDIES

- ★ Problem Based Learning: *Haciendas*, p. 550B
- Settling Far from Home, p. 550B
- Activator: Travelling Trunks, p. 550
- Mayan Mysteries, p. 555
- Talk to an Archaeologist, p. 561
- ● Spanish Settlement with Plaza, p. 558
- Food Report, p. 564

READING/LANGUAGE ARTS	READING/LANGUAGE ARTS OBJECTIVES
★ Mexican Ruins Tour, p. 550B	4.03
Writing Prompt: The Perfect Maya, p. 550	4.09
Reading Strategy: Directed Reading, Thinking, p.552	2.05, 3.02
▲ ■ Legend of the Mayan Gods, p. 553	4.07
★ Aztec/Maya Comparison, p. 554	3.02
Mexican Codex Books, p. 556	4.03
Reading Strategy: Think-Pair-Share, p. 557	2.09
● Mexico Bingo, p. 562	1.03
Reading Strategy: Herringbone Outline for the Main Idea and Details, p. 563	2.09
Point of View Essay: The Hacienda, p. 564	4.09
Night of the Jaguar, p. 565	3.06, 4.07
■ Skill Lesson: Columbian Exchange?, p. 566	3.01, 3.07, 4.09
Becoming Better Readers, p. 568	2.01
Understanding Legends, p. 569	

MATHEMATICS	MATHEMATICS OBJECTIVES
Silver Jewelry, p. 560	1.02

SCIENCE	SCIENCE OBJECTIVES
Silver Mining in Mexico, p. 560	2.07

TECHNOLOGY	TECHNOLOGY OBJECTIVES
Silver Mining in Mexico, p. 560	2.13
Recipes of Colonial Mexico, p. 561	2.13
Carolina Connection: Mexican Taste Test, p. 565	2.13

FINE ARTS	FINE ARTS OBJECTIVES
▲ ■ A Plate of History, p. 550B	3.02
Legend of the Mayan Gods, p. 553	3.02
▲ ■ Silver Jewelry, p. 560	3.02

CHARACTER AND VALUES EDUCATION	TRAITS
● ▲ ■ The Maya Character Education, p. 552	kindness
What Would You Do?, p. 556	good judgment
■ Skill Lesson: Columbian Exchange?, p. 567	respect

● Basic Activities   ★ Challenging Activities   ▲ English Language Learner Novice   ■ English Language Learner Intermediate

Introductory Activity

Mexican Ruins Tour

OBJECTIVES: 1.01, 1.03, 1.07

Have students create a brochure, Web site, or digital presentation for a seven-day tour of Mexican ruins. They need to calculate how much time should be spent at each site as well as travel time between sites. Encourage them to use photos from the Web or travel magazines to illustrate their brochure.

Culminating Activity

Settling Far From Home

OBJECTIVES: 1.02, 1.06, 4.07

Divide students into groups to plan the necessities of a new settlement in the New World. The Spanish government will be sending its explorers and settlers to start a permanent settlement in Mexico. They will be one of its members. They are part of the team preparing for the voyage and the start-up of the settlement. In the planning phase, students should think about the occupations of people that should travel to the New World to start up a settlement. Would some occupations be more helpful than others? Students should develop a plan and consider the following:

- Who should go?
- What should be the maximum number of people? the minimum number of people?

- What supplies need to be taken?
- What preparations are necessary for starting up a settlement in the New World?
- What climate can be expected?
- What about the crew?

After the plans are developed have the groups present them to the class as though they were presenting them to the government of Spain. Ask the rest of the students to think of what the group may have left out as well as the strengths that they brought out. Make a master list of items to plan for and prepare for.

Art Activity

A Plate of History

OBJECTIVES: 3.04, 3.06, 3.07

Have students design and illustrate their own piece of "historical pottery" on paper plates, displaying information on an aspect of Aztec or Mayan culture. Use sturdy white paper plates (without wax coating) and colored pencils. Display on a bulletin board when completed. You can stain plates with tea to give an older look.

Problem Based Learning Activity

Haciendas

OBJECTIVES: 1.06, 2.08, 3.06

Situation The *hacienda* system in Mexico during the colonial era seriously impacted Mexico and its way of life during that time and even still today. A few individuals owned the *haciendas.* They were considered wealthy and privileged. These individuals often abused their privilege and many others suffered as a result. The idea that so few own so much and control what others have is something that many societies have had to deal with for many generations. Today, Mexico still deals with the legacies of this system. How could the *hacienda* owners have done things differently during colonial times? What kinds of things could these individuals have done to encourage people to work for them?

Task Ask students to read about the *haciendas* on page 559 of their text. After discussing as a class how the *hacienda* system worked, ask students to individually brainstorm ways in which these landowners could have accomplished their tasks with the mines, provided food for the towns-people, and shared the wealth with the workers. Students will brainstorm on one piece of paper. On a second piece of paper, the students will draw a web with the center circle being "*hacienda.*" The "legs" coming from the center will be the many benefits that *haciendas* provided. On a third piece of paper, have students evaluate the web and conclude how changes in society might have changed history in Mexico. Have students share their own perceptions with the class.

Reflection Have students discuss how the lifestyle of a few can affect the lifestyle of many. Why is it important for people as a whole to be concerned about others rather than just themselves? Does this philosophy in the end make things better for all? Have the students write about ways in which they can consider the feelings and opportunities of others in their lives.

Teaching Strategies

Activate prior knowledge by reviewing what students learned about the Native Americans of Middle America in Chapter 4 and the first contact with the Spanish in Chapter 5. The teacher notes in both of those chapters will also help you frame class discussion and understanding of the relationships between the native people and the Europeans.

Students will be fascinated by the early Mexican cultures. Compare these early civilizations with other early civilizations from around the world.

This chapter provides excellent opportunities for integration activities in science and math.

Activator

OBJECTIVES: 1.02, 3.04, 3.06

Traveling Trunks Divide students into several groups and assign a city in Mexico to each group. After studying their city, they will make or collect artifacts from the city and place it in their trunk (shoebox). Each trunk should also contain a fact sheet listing the items in the box with a short explanation so the trunk can travel without its owners. Students may want to decorate the trunks with travel stickers. After each group presents its trunk to the class, set up a check-out system where the trunks can travel to other grades or other fifth grade classes.

 Writing Prompt

OBJECTIVES: 1.07, 3.04, 3.06

Writing a brochure Choose one Native American group, either the Maya, the Aztecs, or the Zapotecs. Research your group. Fold a piece of construction paper in thirds lengthwise and create a brochure called "How to be a Perfect Maya" (or Aztec or Zapotec). Be sure to include how a person would dress, what he or she would eat, the jobs he or she might have, where and what homes would be like, and other interesting facts.

Personal narrative This chapter talks about the Spanish and their desire to find valuable minerals in the New World. They did find much gold and silver in Mexico.

Think about a time when you found something valuable. It might not have been as valuable as gold or silver, but something that was special, or valuable, to you. Tell what you found, where you found it, and what you did with it.

CHAPTER 23

People and Their Environment

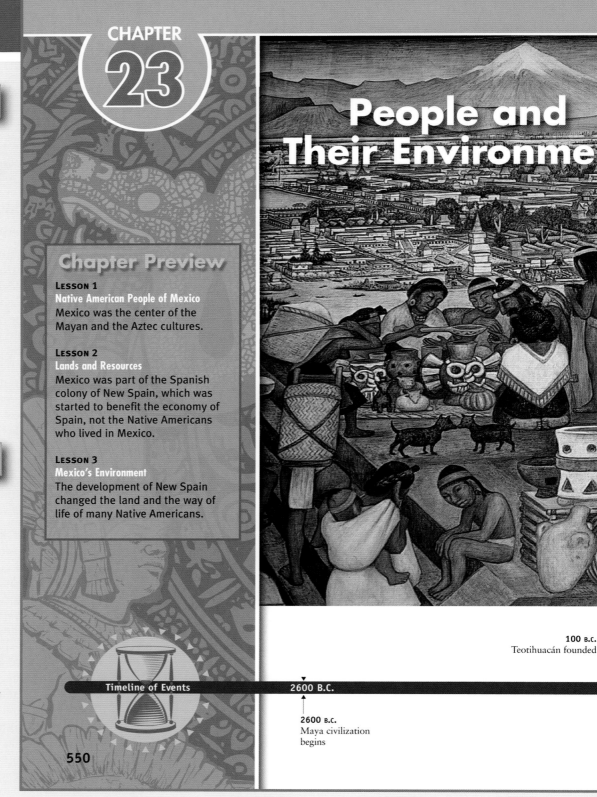

Chapter Preview

LESSON 1
Native American People of Mexico
Mexico was the center of the Mayan and the Aztec cultures.

LESSON 2
Lands and Resources
Mexico was part of the Spanish colony of New Spain, which was started to benefit the economy of Spain, not the Native Americans who lived in Mexico.

LESSON 3
Mexico's Environment
The development of New Spain changed the land and the way of life of many Native Americans.

 Timeline of Events

2600 B.C.
Maya civilization begins

100 B.C.
Teotihuacán founded

2600 B.C.   100 B.C.

550

 Chapter Resources

Print Resources

Nonfiction

Baquedano, Elizabeth. *Aztec, Inca & Maya* (Eyewitness series). Dorling Kindersley, 2000. ISBN 0789465965.

Dawson, Imogen. *Clothes and Crafts in Aztec Times* (Clothes and Crafts in History series). G. Stevens, 2000. ISBN 083682735X.

Day, Nancy. *Your Travel Guide to Ancient Mayan Civilization* (Passport to History series). Runestone, 2001. ISBN 0822530775.

Johnson, Sylvia A. *Tomatoes, Potatoes, Corn, and Beans: How the Foods of the Americas Changed Eating Around the World.* Atheneum Books for Young Readers, 1997. ISBN 0689801416.

Macdonald, Fiona. *How Would You Survive as an Aztec?* (How Would You Survive? series). F. Watts, 1995. ISBN 0531143481.

Rees, Rosemary. *The Aztecs* (Understanding People of the Past series). Heinemann Library, 1999. ISBN 1575728885.

In the center of the Mexican flag is a picture of an eagle. It is sitting on a cactus with a snake in its mouth. This was a sacred symbol to the Aztecs. They had once wandered the earth searching for a place to build their homes.

They believed that the gods would give them a signal when they reached the right place. When they saw the eagle with the snake in its beak, they would know that they had reached the right place.

Diego Rivera's The Gran Tenochtitlán

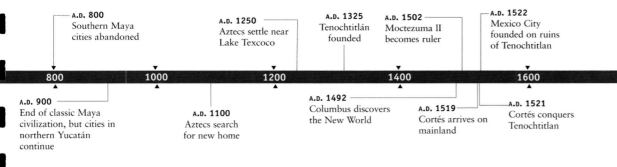

A.D. 800 Southern Maya cities abandoned

A.D. 1250 Aztecs settle near Lake Texcoco

A.D. 1325 Tenochtitlán founded

A.D. 1502 Moctezuma II becomes ruler

A.D. 1522 Mexico City founded on ruins of Tenochtitlan

800   1000   1200   1400   1600

A.D. 900 End of classic Maya civilization, but cities in northern Yucatán continue

A.D. 1100 Aztecs search for new home

A.D. 1492 Columbus discovers the New World

A.D. 1519 Cortés arrives on mainland

A.D. 1521 Cortés conquers Tenochtitlan

Stein, R. Conrad. *The Aztec Empire* (Cultures of the Past series). Benchmark Books, New York, 1996. ISBN 0761400729.

Audiovisual

Conquistadors. 2001. PBS Video.
Lost Kingdoms of the Maya. National Geographic Video, 1997.

Web Sites

Visit **NCJourneys.com** for links to these Web sites:
• Ancient American Artifacts, Discovery Channel Discovery School
• Ancient Mexican Art, Smithsonian Institute exhibit
• Aztec Mexica
• Conquistadors companion Web site
• Discovery of America, Mexico for Kids
• Maya Adventure
• Maya.Mexico for Kids
• Mexican Gold: Corn and its Many Connections Lesson Plan
• Mexico: Splendors of Thirty Centuries
• Sad Night,Mexico for Kids
• Teotihuacan Home Page

LESSON 1 Native American People of Mexico

Discussion Questions

1 What are two of the most important Native American groups that built great civilizations in Mexico?

2 What three crops grow well together in Mexico?

3 Once people were successful in farming and created a food surplus, what were they then able to do?

Caption Answer

Because they grow well together

Reading Strategy Activity

Directed Reading Thinking Activity

OBJECTIVES: 1.07, 3.04, 3.07

A Directed Reading Thinking activity involves guiding the students through reading material. An oral DRTA can be used as a class or group activity, with small groups, or with individuals. This is a written DRTA, Students are led to interact with the information in an active problem-solving manner. Using the worksheet, prepare students to read by answering prereading questions. During reading, the students independently read a small, manageable part of the selection and answer questions for comprehension.

Make copies of the DRTA worksheet in the Teacher's Resource Guide. Students should follow the directions, answering the questions.

Activity

The Maya Character Education

OBJECTIVES: 1.02, 1.06, 4.07

The Maya had a civilization that lasted for 1,000 years and then broke apart. No one knows why the people left. Some anthropologists (who study old societies and ways of life) think there may have been drought, a time when crops could not get enough water

KEY IDEAS

- Mexico was the center of the Maya and Aztec cultures.

- The Maya developed a written language. They were also skilled in farming and math.

- The Aztecs built great cities that were centers of religion and culture.

KEY TERMS

drought
obsidian
rituals
slash-and-burn farming
specialization

Long before the Spanish came there were already several great cultures in today's Mexico. Two of the most important were the Aztec and the Maya. These ancient peoples built great cities. Both had a complex system of laws. Like other great civilizations, both knew how to farm native plants and best use their natural resources.

The Aztecs had created a huge empire by the time the Spanish arrived. Sometimes the empires fought wars just as European kingdoms did. Kings ruled these empires. The kings claimed the gods chose them to rule.

Native American Culture

The Spanish conquered the Native Americans. But they did not destroy all of their culture. Native American traditions still have a great influence in Mexican society.

The Three Sisters

Corn and beans were very important to the early people of Mexico. They also grew different kinds of squash. These plants grow well together. The wide leaves of the corn plant shade the beans and squash from the harsh sunlight.

The bean and squash vines can climb the corn stalks. The squash plant's leaves and vines in turn cover the ground. This protects the soil and keeps it moist. It also prevents weeds from growing. The beans put nutrients in the soil that helps the corn and squash grow. This combination of plants even attracts certain insects that feed on other more harmful insects.

Successful farming means people have plenty of food. A community that has extra food allows people to share the work. This is called *specialization.* This means that people can divide the work, or specialize, based on their skills and talents. When the Native Americans became successful farmers, more people in their empires could do other jobs. Some people were able to do special jobs in the cities. They could be priests, or make pots, or build pyramids.

The people planted corn or maize, squash and pumpkins, and beans together. **Why are these crops called the "three sisters?"**

Chapter 23

to grow. Others think it may have been a war that caused the people to leave their cities.

In modern times, people sometimes have to leave their homes. Floods, hurricane winds, and tornadoes are a few of the reasons people must leave their homes. Sometimes their homes are destroyed and they cannot return, for example, many people have left New Orleans after Hurricane Katrina and not returned. Many people who come to the United States from other countries have also suffered losses. Their homes may have been destroyed by war or by a famine (a time of

mass hunger). During the bad times, people need understanding, caring, and strength. Courage can help someone get through a hard time.

Activity Working as cooperative groups, think of ways that people can help one another in times of trouble. What would be a compassionate response to families in times of flood? a fire? an earthquake? Have each cooperative group choose one of the compassionate responses and draw a picture to represent that action. Place the pictures on a bulletin board with the

The Lowland Maya

The Lowland Maya people lived in the Yucatán Peninsula. They had to prepare the land there to plant crops. They used a *slash-and-burn* method to clear the land. They cut down plants and trees and burned what they had cut. The burning helped return nutrients to the soil.

The Lowland Maya built a system of canals to bring water from rivers to their fields. After a while, Mayan farmers began to produce more food than they needed to feed everyone.

A market system tied Maya towns together. Priests were important because people believed that the priests brought messages from the gods. The messages told them when to plant crops and predicted the weather. Priests also led the people in *rituals* (special ceremonies) and prayers for successful farming.

In the cities of the Yucatán Plain, the Maya built pyramids of stone for religious rituals. The rituals sometimes included a human or animal sacrifice.

The Maya also created a written language. They wrote in picture-symbols called hieroglyphs.

The Maya used astronomy to create an accurate calendar. This means that they studied the position of the sun, moon, and stars. This helped them keep track of the seasons. They even invented an advanced system of mathematics.

The Decline of the Maya

The Maya way of life thrived for nearly 1,000 years. The Maya left their cities around A.D. 900. That was about 600 years before the Spanish arrived. Historians still do not know why they did this. But they have some theories about what happened.

Some think that the Maya population grew too fast. Not enough people were farming and too many poeple were doing other jobs. The Maya system of farming may have used up too much land. Maya farmers might not have been able to grow enough food to feed everyone in the cities. The problem with this theory is that we know that Maya farmers often grew more food than they needed.

Another theory is that a severe *drought,* or lack of rain, may have hurt food production and caused starvation. People may have moved away to find food.

Others think that a war within the Maya society caused many to flee into the jungle. Some moved to the highlands of modern Guatemala and the Mexican state of Chiapas. There they had to adapt to life in the mountains.

Today, more than 3 million people continue the Maya way of life. They are still adapting to the modern world while trying to keep many of their ancient ways. These are the Highland Maya. We will learn about their culture in Chapter 26.

This statue was used as a marker in a Maya ball game.
Why do you think the figure is wearing knee pads?

People and Their Environment

Discussion Questions

1 What is slash-and-burn agriculture?

2 How did the Maya bring water to their fields?

3 What were some of the accomplishments of the Maya?

4 What are some theories as to why the Maya left their cities around A.D. 900?

Caption Answer

For protection during the game

Activity

Legends of the Mayan Gods

OBJECTIVES: 1.03, 2.08, 3.07

The Maya perfected a written language. Their system of writing was hieroglyphics, which means they wrote with pictures. Some Maya writing details important events and ceremonies in their culture. Other writing deals with legends concerning Mayan gods and famous warriors.

Have students write their own legend that explains a natural phenomenon concerning a Maya god or a famous Maya warrior. They should make a collage of clippings from newspapers and magazines that will serve as a visual interpretation of their legend.

Extension Have students write their legends in glyphs instead of English. Pass the legends around and have a different student interpret the legend for the class. This activity will demonstrate the difficulty in correctly interpreting "written" documents from earlier cultures when we have no convenient key.

words kindness in large letters across the top.

Extension Have pictures depicting types of natural disasters for novice ELL students to learn the vocabulary. If possible, find photos of people helping people. Have students use bilingual dictionaries to learn adjectives and verbs relating to kindness.

Get the addresses of the American Red Cross from their Web site. Choose a place in the United States where there has been a disaster of some kind. As a class write letters of encouragement to the children of that area. Send your letters to the American Red Cross. Ask them if they might share those letters with the children of the stricken area. You might wish to draw pictures to cheer up the children. Have novice ELL students copy a sample letter and draw pictures.

Discussion Questions

1 Where and when did the Aztec live?

2 How were the Aztec able to farm on a lake?

Caption Answer

Encourage students to speculate about the relationship between the importance of religion and the building of cities.

Activity

Aztec/Maya Comparison

OBJECTIVES: 1.07, 2.08, 3.06

Have students examine similarities and differences between the lives of the Aztec and the Maya using Venn diagrams that illustrate these contrasting characteristics. They should revise their lists of similarities and differences and the Venn diagrams as necessary through the study of the unit.

1. housing and settlements
2. occupations
3. advancements
4. agriculture
5. language and communication
6. foods
7. clothing

  Answers may include:

Mayan culture: 1. mud mixed with straw; thatched roofs; small, widely scattered villages, some cities; 2. merchants, farmers, priests; 3. astronomy, mathematics; 4. slash and burn, then move to a new area; 5. hieroglyphics, picture symbols; 6. corn, beans, squash, fish; 7. animal skins, natural materials.

Aztec culture: 1. stone apartments in large windowless buildings around a patio; 2. stone masons, farmers, priests, doctors, merchants, soldiers; 3. drainage systems, schools; 4. used irrigation; built artificial islands on which to grow crops; 5. no written language; 6. maize, squash, beans, peanuts, manioc, fish, frogs, salamanders; 7. animal skins, woven natural materials.

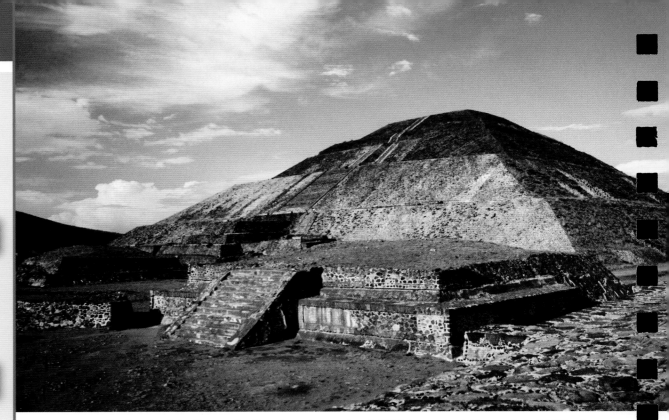

The Temple of the Moon at Teotihuacán took more than 7,000 laborers about 15 years to build. **Why do you think the temple was important to Native Americans?**

The Aztecs

The Aztec way of life developed on the Mexican plateau around the year A.D. 1300. There the Aztecs began to farm and work as soldiers in the other nearby cities. They lived around a series of large connected lakes. In the middle of one lake was a large island. There they built the splendid city of Tenochtitlán (tay·noke·tee·LAHN).

The Native Americans began free schools where children could learn different professions. Some learned astronomy. Others learned to be doctors or priests. Schools also taught young girls the necessary skills for running a household or serving the religious community.

Farming

The Aztecs created a special way of farming the wet land. They dammed the lakes in certain spots and drained them in other places. Then they cut thick mats of floating water plants into long strips. They piled these on top of one another. As they added more strips, the water plants sank to the bottom.

The farmers kept piling on strips until the last was above the water. Then they scooped the rich mud from the lake bottom and covered the mat of water plants. Here they planted crops. These gardens were called *chinampas*. The Aztecs also created ways to bring water from the lake to their crops.

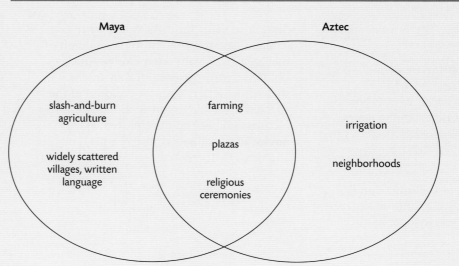

Maya   Aztec

slash-and-burn agriculture

widely scattered villages, written language

farming

plazas

religious ceremonies

irrigation

neighborhoods

Aztec Cities

The Aztecs were good at taking the ideas of other peoples and improving them. They borrowed ideas about building and farming from their neighbors.

A nomadic people, the Aztecs invaded the Valley of Mexico looking for a new home. They often were brutal and violent rulers. They built great cities, but also made many enemies. More than 300,000 people lived in Tenochtitlán by the mid-1400s. It was one of the largest cities in the world. The ruins of Tenochtitlán lie beneath present-day Mexico City.

Ruins of the Past

Today the ruins tell us how Native Americans lived before the Europeans came. The ruins were once painted bright colors. Tall pyramids have Native American carvings that tell us about the animals they saw. You can see the domed buildings the Maya used to observe the stars. There are even huge open courts where the people played ball games.

The lakes where the Aztec cities began are now gone. The canals used by the Maya to water their fields are covered by centuries of plant growth. But you can still imagine cities with thousands of people. The squares were busy markets filled with buyers and sellers trading goods from across the region.

This stone marked a boundary of a Maya court game.
What do you think happened to the Maya?

The City of the Gods

Teotihuacán (tay·oh·tee·wah·KAHN) was, at the time, the largest city in the Americas. It had a population of more than 100,000 at its peak.

Historians are not quite certain which Native American group originally founded the city. It may have been the Toltecs or the Tolonacs. But many different Native American peoples, including the Aztecs, lived in the city over several centuries.

Teotihuacán was carefully laid out in blocks like our modern cities. It had many temples. Its pyramids influenced the Maya and Aztec cultures. There was even a drainage system under the streets to carry away the rainwater from sudden storms.

The city became a trading center. Merchants traded things like obsidian knives and tools used to cut beautiful feathers and precious stones. **Obsidian** is a mineral created by volcanoes. It looks like black glass. Obsidian was the hardest substance known to the Native Americans. When chipped, it made a sharp edge that was excellent for cutting.

Discussion Questions

1 What are two large cities of the Aztec?

Caption Answer

Students should speculate based upon the following theories: Maya farmers used too much land and could no longer grow enough food to support the cities, or war within the Maya society caused people to flee.

Activity

Maya Mysteries: Inquiring Minds Want to Know... Probing the Past

OBJECTIVES: 1.05, 1.06, 3.04

Working in small groups, have students review Chapter 23 for references to artifacts or look at photos of artifacts from Mexico. They should add them to a graphic organizer like the one below.

Have the groups write several sentences describing each category. They should list one or more artifacts that may be seen in each category, and add a drawing for each category.

Category	Description	Artifact
Language		
Arts and Crafts		
Sports		
Foods		
Architecture		

Background Information

Maya Pyramids

Unlike the pyramids of Ancient Egypt, Maya pyramids were not mainly tombs for royalty. Maya pyramids, some as high as 20-story buildings, were temples. A single flight of steep stairs led to a platform on top where a temple sat. Priests conducted ceremonies there that were probably private and secret. The rooms inside the temple building were so small that only a few people could fit inside them at one time. At the base of some pyramid temples, the Maya sometimes buried nobles and priests, but the main activities took place at the top.

ELL Teaching Tips

Become an Active Listener!

When listening to ELL students speak, give lots of non-verbal feedback and praise. Give students all of your attention and try to understand their comments. Be sure your body language is patient and inviting.

Activity

Mexican Codex Books

 OBJECTIVES: 1.05, 1.06, 4.07

Mexican Codex Books were created by folding fig bark paper, cloth, or deerskin into the shape of an accordion. Maya Codices contained calendars used for planting and harvest times or stories about such events as the creation. Some codices, such as the Aztec Codex, were used for record keeping. They contained beautiful pictographs and told a story.

Have students fold 6-inch by 15-inch construction paper into four equal sections accordion style.

Have them record facts learned in another subject, such as a science, or write a story using pictures. They should make the drawings colorful.

A Journey to MEXICO'S ANCIENT CIVILIZATIONS

The Calendars of Mexico

Astronomy and religion were closely linked for both the Aztecs and the Maya. They believed that the movement of the sun, moon, and stars told them the will of the gods. Both cultures developed an advanced system of mathematics to help them in track this movement. They used it to make accurate calendars. The calendars allowed them to predict things such as eclipses and comets.

The priests and royalty were astronomers. This means that they studied the stars. They used their learning in colorful rituals. They wore special costumes made of beautiful feathers and golden cloth.

These ceremonies were held in huge temples or on the great pyramids. We know that structures of that size could not have been planned and built without a strong knowledge of math and geometry.

The calendar was important to life in ancient Mexico. People believed that time moved in a great circle. Their calendars were even round. Knowing when to expect the

dry or rainy season or when to look for storms helped them survive. Knowing the best times to plant or harvest were also important for farming.

Their knowledge of astronomy and math made the priests powerful. They held high positions in society. Understanding the ancient calendar is important to many of the descendants of the Aztecs and Maya

LESSON ❶ REVIEW

Fact Follow-Up
1. Describe the relative location of the Lowland Maya and Aztec cultures.
2. What crops did both the Maya and Aztecs grow?
3. How did they make use of their water resources?
4. What were the major cities of the Aztec people?

Talk About It
1. How did the farming practices of the Maya and Aztecs help them develop cities?
2. What were some of the similarities between the Maya and Aztecs?
3. What is specialization? Why is it important for creating civilizations?
4. What happened to the Maya culture?

LESSON ❶ REVIEW

Fact Follow-Up Answers
1. The Lowland Mayan civilization developed on the Yucatán Peninsula on the east coast of Mexico. The Aztec civilization developed on the Mesa Central.
2. Both cultivated corn, beans, and squash.
3. The Maya built a system of canals to carry water from cenotes to their fields. The Aztecs lived around a series of large connected lakes that they both dammed and drained for agriculture. They also built aqueducts and elevated causeways to carry water from lakes to fields.
4. Tenochtitlán once had more than 300,000 residents. The city lies beneath present-day Mexico City. The Aztecs also incorporated Teotihuacán, built by an earlier civilization, into their empire.

Talk About It Answers
1. Both civilizations were able to produce a surplus of food so that

workers could be freed to work as traders, miners, craftspersons, and builders, and in other jobs.
2. Important notes: Encourage students to name as many similarities as they can. Some similarities: both were built on agriculture, both made innovative use of water resources, both had a market system and traded, both developed advanced systems of mathematics, both had highly developed religious practices led by priests, both left large buildings.
3. Specialization is when each person in a society can do the think they like best for a job rather than only farming to feed his or her family.
4. Students should speculate based upon the following theories: Mayan farmers used too much land and could no longer grow enough food to support the cities, or war within the Maya society caused people to flee.

LESSON 2 Lands and Resources

In the 1490s the Spanish and other Europeans were searching for a water route to Asia. They wanted to trade with China and the islands in Southeast Asia. Europeans believed that the earth was round. They thought if they sailed west they would eventually reach Asia. Europeans did not know that America lay in between Asia and Europe.

Finding the Americas was a surprise to the Europeans. They were also surprised to find that there were people and many valuable natural resources in this New World. The Spanish started colonies in the Americas in order to take the resources back to Spain.

The Spanish Arrive

The Spanish first colonized the islands of the Caribbean. Next they sent missions to the west to explore. They did not know whether they would find more islands or a new continent. They hoped they would find a route to Asia and its spices and other riches. Instead, the mainland of North America blocked their way.

The Spanish forces led by Cortés and his Native American allies conquered the Aztec empire. Then Spanish colonists started to move onto the mainland. The sights they saw dazzled them.

The Spanish learned a great deal from the Native Americans. The Spanish enjoyed eating the chili peppers and corn grown by Native American farmers.

Ships like this Spanish galleon brought explorers and colonists to Mexico. **Why did trading ships need cannons?**

People and Their Environment

557

KEY IDEAS

- Mexico was part of the Spanish colony of New Spain.
- Spain started the colony to benefit Spain rather than the Native Americans.
- The Spanish built large silver mines and large farms to supply the mine workers.
- Catholic priests from Spain worked to convert Native Americans to Christianity.

KEY TERMS

haciendas
plaza

OBJECTIVES: 1.07, 3.06, 3.07

Discussion Questions

1 What were the Spanish and other Europeans looking for? Why?

2 Why did they set up colonies in the Americas?

3 Where did the Spanish first colonize? Then where did they explore?

 Caption Answer

To defend themselves from pirates

Reading Strategy Activity

Think-Pair-Share

OBJECTIVES: 1.06, 3.06, 4.07, 6.01

This strategy engages all students into a discussion. The idea is to ask a broad question with several answers from the lesson. Have all students "Think" about the answer they would give to the question. Next, students "Pair" up with a classmate to quickly discuss their answer to the question. Partners "Share" with the class the answer they concluded was best. An example for this lesson is below.

Use this strategy at the **beginning** of the lesson to engage background knowledge. After previewing the lesson and preteaching the vocabulary, read the introduction on page ask, "Why do you think the Europeans were surprised to find the American continents?"

In the **middle** of lessons a question encourages student participation. Questions could be: "Why did the Spanish start colonies?" "Why did Spain restrict what the colonies could do?" "How did the Spanish treat the Native Americans?"

At the **conclusion** of the lesson ask this question to summarize the information. "How did Spain benefit from its colonies in New Spain?" Always make the think and pair times short to keep the lesson moving at a swift pace.

Discussion Questions

1 How were the Spanish cities in the New World constructed?

2 What was at the center and heart of the town's life?

3 What was the colony, now called Mexico, named?

4 What things did the Spanish export from the colony?

5 Why did the Spanish insist that most items used in the colony be bought from Spain?

6 What are some of the things that were regulated by the Spanish and sold for a high price to the colonies?

Caption Answer

The Spanish colonists wanted to bring their idea of order to the New World.

Activity

Spanish Settlement with Plaza

OBJECTIVES: 1.06, 1.07, 4.07

Divide the class into cooperative groups. Ask each group to create a Spanish colonial settlement constructed around a square called a plaza. Around this plaza, the settlement should include a church, a town hall, and marketplace. Provide the groups with the following materials: cardboard for the bottom or base; various sizes of milk cartons, juice boxes, shoe boxes, clay, construction paper, paint, markers, glue, scissors, pipe cleaners, and any other extras. When they have completed their model settlement, each group should name it and write a brief description of life in their village. Have each group share the information about their settlement with the class.

This drawing shows the design of a village planned by Spanish colonists. The church faces the plaza. You can also see the grid pattern of the streets. **Why were the villages so carefully planned?**

New Towns and Settlements

The Spanish believed in an orderly world. This affected the way they built towns. Buildings were placed around a central square called a *plaza.* This is where the people gathered in the evenings. There were strict rules about how a town should be built. Streets were laid out in a grid pattern. The Catholic Church and town hall were built around the plaza.

These two large buildings reminded everyone that the Catholic Church and the Spanish Crown were the two most powerful things in the colony.

The marketplace was the heart of the town's life. People went there to buy food and other necessities. There they could have their wagons repaired. Goods were brought in from the countryside to be sold in the market.

Colonial Economy

The Spanish called Mexico "New Spain." Mexico was a colony of Spain. It helped Spain grow rich and powerful.

Trade

Spain made Mexico and other Spanish colonies in the Americas ship all goods such as sugar and gold back home. Fleets of Spanish ships armed with cannon brought this wealth across the Atlantic Ocean. The cannon protected the ships from pirates. Twice each year Spanish ships arrived in New Spain and other colonies full of cargo from Spain. They then returned to Spain filled with gold, silver, and sugar.

Spain insisted that its colonies buy all their goods from Spain. The Spanish government also limited what the people in its colonies could produce. The colonists were only allowed to raise food and make some types of rough clothing. Everything else had to come from Spain. This helped Spain make money from their exports to the colonies in addition to the things the colonies shipped back to them.

Buying goods from Spain cost a lot of money. For example, the colonists needed wine for rituals in their Catholic churches. Many places in Mexico were suitable for growing wine grapes. But this was forbidden. They had to be grown in Spain and only by wine growers approved by the Spanish government. Gunpowder and tobacco were controlled in much the same way. These controls prevented the colonies from taking business away from Spain.

Spain wanted its colonies to increase production. The colonies expanded sugar plantations on Spain's islands in the Caribbean and in the humid land along Mexico's coast.

558

Teacher Notes

Sor Juana Inés de la Cruz

A Carmelite nun, Sor Juana Inés de la Cruz (1648–1695) was a central intellectual figure in colonial Mexico. By 1680, her suite of rooms and substantial library had become the base of scholarly pursuits in Mexico City. She had an insatiable desire to understand everything around her and she fiercely asserted a woman's right to fully participate in scholastic inquiry.

The three volumes of her works were printed in Spain with several editions published by the eighteenth century. In 1693, she gave up all contact with the world, signed a confession with her own blood, sold her books, scientific and musical instruments, distributed the money to the poor, and devoted her time exclusively to religious duties. She died the victim of an epidemic while nursing her sister nuns.

Mining

Spain also wanted all the gold and silver in Mexico. Soon thousands of Native Americans were digging for precious metals from mines in the ground.

Mining had a great effect on the wealth of the growing colony. The mines required many workers. Therefore, they also needed plenty of such supplies as food and building materials.

The areas around the mines supported the miners. Food was grown to feed the miners. The mine shafts were braced with lumber and stone. The miners used leather to make containers to carry water and earth out of the mine shafts. They also needed candles. These materials had to be brought to the mines.

Haciendas

The farms where these mining supplies were produced were called **haciendas.** The Spanish owners of *haciendas* usually had a house on the farm as well as one in town. Owning a *hacienda* made a colonist wealthy and powerful.

A *hacienda* was a large piece of land, like a ranch or farm. The main role of the *hacienda* was to feed the people in the cities and keep the mines supplied. There

were always plenty of horses and cows on a *hacienda*. They needed a lot of land for grazing. Native Americans had never seen so many large animals. The largest ranches were in the northern Mexico.

At first, Native Americans were given to the landowners as virtual slaves. Later, Spain's government allowed colonists to make Native Americans work on the *haciendas* without paying them. But the colonists were responsible to educate and convert Native Americans to Christianity. It was not much of an improvement for the Native Americans.

The owners also had to provide food and shelter for the workers. The owners of the *haciendas* did not always keep their word. Sometimes they treated the Native Americans on their land well. But sometimes they mistreated them. Owners forced the Native Americans to work long hours at very hard jobs. Many died of disease and overwork.

The *hacienda* system had another long-lasting effect. Native Americans had lived on the land that became *haciendas* long before the Spanish arrived. The newcomers took that land. As a result, much of the land in Latin America is still owned by a limited number of people today.

Haciendas like this were once centers of wealth. **How did mining affect the local economy?**

People and Their Environment

559

Discussion Questions

1 What other economic systems grew in the colonies as a result of mining operations?

2 What is a *hacienda*? What activities took place there?

3 What happened to the Native American population because of the Spanish *hacienda* system?

Caption Answer

Mines created an extensive new demand for labor, supplies, and mining equipment.

Background Information

A Devastating Impact

Throughout the Spanish colonies, the Native American population declined sharply following the Spanish conquest. In central Mexico, in less than 100 years the number of Native Americans fell from around 25 million in 1519 to slightly over 1 million in 1605. Diseases such as small-pox brought by the Europeans were the major cause of this drastic decline. Overwork and malnutrition also played a part. Those who survived faced other threats. *Hacienda* owners used legal and illegal means to take land from Native American pueblos, or towns. Sometimes they offered to buy the land. Other times they simply took it. A third method involved forcing Native Americans to move to new, smaller communities. *Hacienda* owners included high royal officials, church officials, and wealthy merchants.

Eyewitness Activity

Silver Mining in Mexico

OBJECTIVES: 1.06, 5.01, 5.02

The Kentucky Coal Council's Coal Education program has an extensive Web site. Visit **NCJourneys.com** for a link. One of the lessons there is "Minerals and the Products of Mining." (This lesson covers many more minerals besides silver.)

The objectives are to plot on a map the source of some mineral products, identify some mineral products used every day, watch a soil demonstration, and complete mineral puzzles.

The lesson has a multiple-choice quiz, activity sheets, and complete information and instructions.

Activity

Silver Jewelry

OBJECTIVES: 1.02, 1.06, 3.07

Materials: silver craft wire (available at craft or art supply stores), paper, pencil

Native Americans mined silver and fashioned jewelry to adorn themselves. Ask students to bring in silver jewelry or bring in some examples. Have each student design on paper a piece of silver jewelry such as a bracelet, earrings, or necklace. Students should estimate the amount of silver craft wire needed for their design. Students can then create and wear their piece of jewelry.

Extension Novice ELL students can learn the vocabulary for jewelry from pictures. Students should write or copy the names of each piece as many times as necessary and practice pronunciation.

SILVER MINING in Mexico

The Spanish seized the gold and silver of the Aztecs and the other peoples of Mexico. Then they looked for more. The deposits of gold in Mexico were soon gone. But silver existed in great amounts. In northern Mexico, large deposits of silver ore were found.

The Spanish made the Native Americans work in the mines. Most of the time their labor was forced. Often they were made to stay deep within the mine for a week at a time. They were forced to journey long distances from their homes to work in the mines.

The conditions in the mines were poor. The mines were damp. The air was bad. The hours were long. The mines sometimes caved-in on the workers.

Native American miners

In the sixteenth century, Judge Alonso de Zorita described these conditions of the Native American workers to the Spanish king. "They died in the mines or along the road, of hunger and cold or extreme heat, and from carrying enormous loads of implements for the mines or other extremely heavy things; for the Spaniards, not satisfied with taking them so far away to work, must load them down on the way."

Spanish coins made from Mexican silver

560

Chapter 23

Teacher Notes

Taxco Silver

New Orleans architect, artist, and writer William Spratling is recognized as the key figure of modern silver art in Mexico. Spratling, who was well connected to the literary and arts communities in New Orleans, moved to Mexico in 1929 and immediately made similar connections there. In 1931, the United States Ambassador to Mexico, Dwight Morrow, commented that

Taxco had once been the center of a thriving silver industry. Spratling immediately moved to Taxco, and with the assistance of some skilled silversmiths, he began to design and produce finely crafted silver jewelry. Spratling's shop soon expanded and became a hub in a network of highly regarded silver jewelry producers. By the end of World War II, the demand for Mexican silver jewelry was stronger than ever, and Taxco again became the center of the silver jewelry industry in Mexico.

Etching depicting harsh conditions in the mine

Activity

Talk to an Archaeologist

OBJECTIVES: 4.01, 6.01

Invite an archaeologist to visit the classroom. Write the North Carolina Archaeology Office at 421 N. Blount Street, Raleigh, NC 27601, or call the office at (919) 733-7342; fax: (919) 715-2671 (**www.arch.dcr.state.nc.us**) for more information. Ask them to talk about tools used by archaeologists to uncover the past. Ask that they bring in artifacts to share with the class.

Silver belt buckle

Today mining is still hard work. But Native Americans are no longer enslaved and forced to work in the mines. Modern techniques and machinery are used throughout northern Mexico. They produce not only silver but also copper, iron, zinc, lead, and gold.

Modern silver mine in Mexico

People and Their Environment

561

Activity

Recipes of Colonial Mexico

OBJECTIVES: 1.06, 3.04, 3.06

Majorca Bread
2 cups flour
1 cup warm water
Small pinch of salt

Roll dough 2 inches thick. Cut with circular biscuit cutter. Bake on cookie sheet at 350° for 30 minutes. Flip pieces and bake till golden brown. Keep in dry place for two weeks.

Cocido de Garbanzo
1 cup chopped pork
1 cup sausage, well cooked
2 cups cooked garbanzo beans
   (chickpeas), drained
1 small onion, chopped small
2 cloves garlic, minced
1 teaspoon dried oregano
salt and pepper

Brown pork and onion. Add garlic and fried sausage and garbanzos. Add spices and simmer for 1 hour, adding water as needed.

Discussion Questions

1 What tradition reminds you of Mexican new year?

2 Why would some people call Dona Marina a traitor and others call her a heroine?

Activity

Mexico Bingo

OBJECTIVES: 2.08, 3.04, 4.07

At the beginning of the chapter give students a list of vocabulary words from the chapter. Have them look up the definitions. After they have completed this task give them time to review. Next, make an empty sample bingo card for each student. Write the names, places, or phrases on the board and ask them to put one in each blank. Call out the definition and have the students find the word.

WORD ORIGINS

Mesa is a Spanish word that means "table." Spanish people called high plateaus in Spain and in parts of the Americas mesas because they are high and flat, like a table.

MEXICAN PORTRAIT

Dona Marina: "La Malinche"
1496—c.1529 or 1551

In 1519, Cortés and his men were making their way across Mexico. In one place he received a gift of 20 slave women from a Maya king. Cortes had the women baptized as Christians.

One woman was given the Spanish name Dona Marina. Her family was Aztec, but they had sold her to the Maya as a slave when she was young. She was the only one who spoke the language of the Maya and the language of the Aztecs. In Cortés' party there was a Spanish priest who also spoke Maya. This meant that when Cortés reached the Aztec capitol he could communicate with King Moctezuma II through the priest and Dona Marina.

She helped Cortés understand Aztec culture. She also convinced him not to kill so many Aztecs. Because she helped Cortés, some people called her a traitor. Others think she is a heroine because she saved many lives.

Dona Marina translates for Cortés

Customs

Mexican families gather on December 31 to celebrate the coming of the new year. They have a special tradition. When the clock starts to strike twelve, everyone eats twelve grapes. Each person must finish the grapes before the clock stops striking. The grapes represent the twelve months of the coming year. Finishing all the grapes as the clock strikes is said to give one good luck all through the new year.

LESSON 2 REVIEW

Fact Follow-Up
1. What goods did the Spanish government require to be shipped from New Spain to Spain?
2. What products were the people of New Spain required to buy from Spain?
3. What were *haciendas*?

Talk About It
1. Describe the cultural features of place in the towns of New Spain.
2. Why was the *hacienda* system developed?
3. Which people did the *hacienda* system serve better: the Spanish or the Native Americans? Explain why.

LESSON 2 REVIEW

Fact Follow-Up Answers
1. The Spanish government demanded that Mexico and other Spanish colonies in the Americas ship all sugar, gold, and silver to Spain's home ports.
2. Spain insisted that the colonies buy all imported goods, such as wine and gunpowder, from Spain and limited what the people in New Spain could produce.
3. *Haciendas* were farms where materials—food, building materials, fuel, and leather—were produced to support the mining industry.

Talk About It Answers
1. Central square called a plaza, where their was a market. Catholic church and town hall were built around the plaza. Streets were laid out in a grid pattern from the plaza.
2. The *hacienda* system was developed to assure a supply of the materials needed to keep the silver and gold mines operating and feed the people in the cities.
3. Important points: Students should choose one group and explain their choice. The Spanish received all necessary goods for running the silver mining operations. *Hacienda* owners were able to get land from Native Americans without paying for it. Native Americans worked both on the *haciendas* and in the mines and were reduced to slavery. Native Americans did receive the benefits of the large animals introduced into New Spain, though these large animals put a huge burden on the previously untouched grasslands and forests.

LESSON 3 Mexico's Environment

When Cortés and his army of Spanish *conquistadors* arrived in Mexico, they brought with them many things that the people there had never seen. One of the most amazing things they brought was the horse. The Native Americans had never seen an animal so large. The horses were covered in shining armor. They were also fast.

At first the Native Americans even believed that the rider and horse were one animal and that they could not be killed. The Native Americans were frightened. Horses gave the Spanish a great advantage over the Aztecs and other Native Americans.

Changes to the Environment

Both before and after colonization, human beings altered and changed the land of Mexico. The Spanish used more wood in building houses than had the Native Americans. They had mostly used stone and adobe. Using timber meant trees were cut. Slowly but steadily, forests began to disappear in the Spanish colonies. This problem expanded over time.

The Spanish also brought livestock such as cattle and horses to New Spain. These animals required great amounts of grazing land. Overgrazing soon ruined the vast grasslands of Mexico. The Spanish brought with them new crops like wheat and barley. These crops soon replaced fields that were once corn.

Changes in Diet

In general, the *haciendas* worked well to support the operation of mines and plantations. They also supplied food that the Spanish liked to eat. But *haciendas* cut into the production of traditional Native American foods.

Many Native Americans had to work in mines and on *haciendas*. They worked on sugar plantations, too. They no longer had as many chances to grow food for themselves. They were working full-time for the Spanish. Many Native Americans had lost their land. Others lost the water that they needed for their crops when the Spanish set up their own watering systems. So fewer traditional foods were raised.

Sometimes Native Americans living on *haciendas* were allowed to grow crops for their families. Yet they rarely could raise what they needed. The plots of land were usually very small and of poor quality. These changes led to a decrease in the production of food by the Native American people. The richness of the Native American diet was gone within decades of the Spanish conquest.

People and Their Environment

KEY IDEAS

- The colonization of Mexico changed the environment.

- Many Native Americans lost their lands to the Spanish *haciendas*.

- The Spanish brought to the New World animals and technology that Native Americans had never seen.

- Many Native Americans died of diseases brought by the Europeans.

KEY TERMS

Columbian Exchange

This figure of a conquistador *on a horse, was made around 1650.* **What do you think life was like in America before there were horses?**

563

OBJECTIVES: 1.06, 4.07, 5.01, 5.02, 6.01, 6.02

Discussion Questions

1 Why were the horses the Spanish brought so amazing to the Native Americans?

2 In what ways did the Spanish change Mexico's environment?

3 How did the Native American diet suffer because of the Spanish?

Caption Answer

It took longer to get places because you had to walk or use dogs.

Reading Strategy Activity

Herringbone Outline for Main Idea and Details

OBJECTIVES: 1.06, 3.06, 4.07, 6.01, 6.02

This strategy will help students record the main idea and supporting details in a condensed manner. The main idea is written in the center while supporting details are written on the adjacent lines.

The main idea of the first organizer is Native Americans. On the vertical lines, ask students to write things the Native Americans gave to the Spanish or that the Spanish took from the Americas. Students should find three facts in the textbook and write them on the horizontal lines.

The main idea of the second organizer is the Spanish. On the vertical lines, ask students to write what the Spanish gave or brought to the Native Americans. Students should find three facts in the textbook about each of those and write them on the horizontal lines. Share these when the students finish.

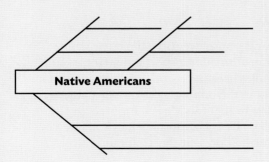
Native Americans

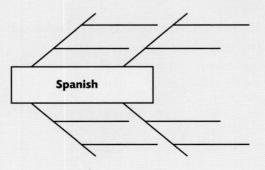
Spanish

Discussion Questions

1 What was the Colombian Exchange?

2 What were some crops brought by the Europeans?

3 What were some crops grown in the Americas?

Caption Answer

Gold, silver, and riches

Writing Activity

Point of View Essay:
The Hacienda

OBJECTIVES: 1.07, 2.08, 3.04

Review with students the nature of the *hacienda* system and have them write two descriptions. The first will be from the point of view of a Spanish colonist whose family owns the *hacienda*. The second will be from the point of view of a Native American whose family works on the *hacienda*.

Writing Activity

Food Report

OBJECTIVES: 1.06, 3.02

Have students choose a food (for example corn, beans, tomatoes, or others) mentioned in this section that came from North America. They should research the food they chose.

Have them write the results of their research on a large index card. On a large piece of construction paper, they should cut out the shape of the food and paste the index card on the food. Students should describe their food to the class.

The Columbian Exchange

The Spanish and the Native Americans exchanged, or shared, many things. This process was called the **Columbian Exchange.** It was named after Christopher Columbus. The Columbian Exchange involved plants and animals. It also involved ideas and even diseases.

Plants and Farming

Europeans brought many different grains, vegetables, and fruits from Europe. The Americas gave Europe foods like corn and potatoes. Fruit such as tomatoes and avocados also were first found in the Americas.

Three other important American plants became popular throughout the rest of the world. Cacao (cah·COW), from which chocolate is made, and vanilla beans are still important crops today. People in Europe also became fond of another plant, tobacco.

New ways of growing plants were shared between the people of Europe and the Americas. Africans made contributions as well. Europeans and Africans showed the Native Americans how to plow the ground, toss seeds, and then cover them with dirt. Native Americans taught the Europeans and Africans how to carefully select seeds and plant them in combinations that complemented one another.

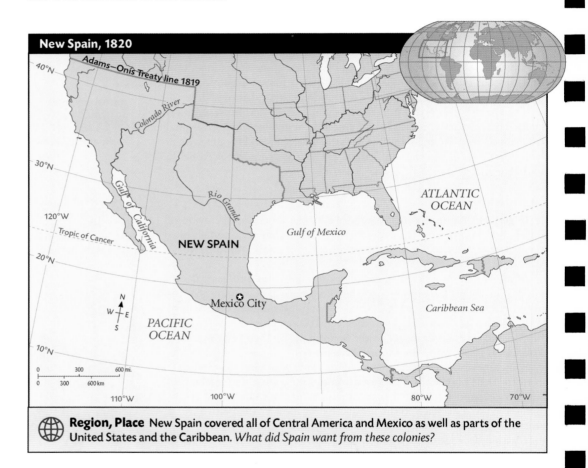

New Spain, 1820

Adams–Onis Treaty line 1819

Colorado River

ATLANTIC OCEAN

Gulf of California

Rio Grande

Tropic of Cancer

Gulf of Mexico

NEW SPAIN

Mexico City

Caribbean Sea

PACIFIC OCEAN

Region, Place New Spain covered all of Central America and Mexico as well as parts of the United States and the Caribbean. *What did Spain want from these colonies?*

Background Information

Horses and the Columbian Exchange

One of the most important animals in the Columbian Exchange was the horse. Horses greatly aided the Spanish in their conquests in the Americas. "After God," Spanish soldiers used to say, "we owe the victory to the horses." Spanish soldiers mounted on horseback terrified the Aztecs. They had the same effect on millions of other Native Americans. Over time the horse completely transformed transportation. Horses and mules became essential for turning machinery in the mining industry. Mustangs were first brought to Mexico for breeding in 1535. By 1600, mustang herds roamed as far north as present-day Colorado.

Animals from Europe

The Americas had few large animals. Only the llama in South America and the buffalo in northern North America were large. The buffalo were too difficult to tame. The llama, because of its spindly legs, could not carry as much weight as a man. Neither animal lived in Mexico or Central America.

Even the dogs in the Americas were small. Almost all farm animals such as chickens and cows came from Europe. Only the turkey and a few other species of birds were raised by the Native Americans before the arrival of the Spanish.

Exchange of Ideas

Spanish *conquistadors* brought new ideas to the Americas. One of the most powerful was Christianity. Priests of the Roman Catholic Church began to convert Native Americans wherever the Spanish founded colonies.

The Spanish idea of government also had a great effect on the Americas. For the first time, from the southwestern United States through Mexico to South America, all the people (except in Brazil) were brought under the same type of government. This was New Spain.

The Spanish language unified the region. For the first time the majority of the people spoke the same language. Today almost all of Latin America shares a common heritage of church and state from their colonial rulers.

Technology

Technology was also shared. The Spanish brought gunpowder and explosives and great wagons pulled by large work animals. This gave Native Americans a better understanding of the wheel. The Spanish also brought the knowledge of how to create stronger metals such as iron and steel.

The Native Americans taught the Europeans new ways to water and farm the land. Native Americans also helped Europeans

People and Their Environment

better understand the movement of the stars and planets.

Disease from Europe

Unfortunately for the Native Americans, Europeans also brought diseases. Deadly diseases such as smallpox, malaria, yellow fever, measles, cholera, typhoid, and the bubonic plague were new to the Americas. The Native Americans had no natural immunities to these diseases. This means that their bodies could not fight these illnesses.

Historians still debate how many native people lived in the Americas before the Europeans arrived. They are also unsure exactly how many died due to these diseases. But they do know that diseases did kill many, many native people. This may have made it easier for Europeans all over the Americas to conquer and settle the region.

Signs of Mexican Culture in North Carolina

You probably can see signs of Mexican life in North Carolina in your local supermarket. Many grocery stores stock Mexican products and fruit. People from Mexico and other parts of Latin America enjoy tropical fruit and vegetables that are not grown here. "Many of our best customers are people from Mexico and Latin America," said one grocery store manager. "They miss the foods that they grew up with and have become used to. We try to fill that gap."

Now most products made in the United States have both English and Spanish directions on them. This helps Spanish-speaking customers buy and use them.

565

Discussion Questions

1 What animals were raised in Europe and brought to the Americas? Which were original to the Americas?

2 What were some major ideas the Spanish brought that changed the Native American's way of life?

3 What were some technological advances of each group?

 **Writing Activity**

Night of the Jaguar

OBJECTIVES: 1.02, 1.03, 1.06

Using encyclopedias and the Internet, have students research the use of jaguar imagery throughout Aztec, Maya, and Mexican culture. Have them write a paragraph on their findings on a piece of paper cut into the shape of a jaguar.

Writing Activity

Carolina Connection: Mexican Taste Test

OBJECTIVES: 3.03, 3.04, 3.06

Go shopping in a local Mexican grocery store or in the Mexican food section of the grocery store. Bring in mangos, beans, tortillas, and other foods to share. Have a taste test and have students vote or take a survey to see which foods they like the best.

Discussion Questions

1 Do we exchange ideas with other cultures today?

2 What is your favorite "American" food? does it have any indigenous American ingredients?

Caption Answer

Corn, chocolate, vanilla, potatoes, and tomatoes and tobacco

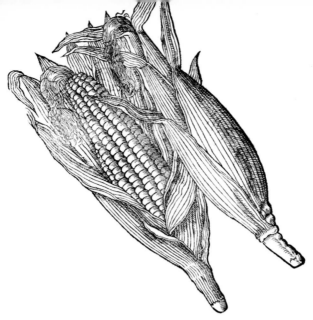

This drawing of maize, or corn, appeared in a European book in 1633. **Along with corn, what were the other important plants that originated in America?**

The Colonial Legacy

Imagine Mexico before the arrival of the Spanish. There was no wheat with which to make bread, only corn for tortillas. No peaches or pears or sugar to sweeten the daily diet. There were no large animals to carry heavy burdens.

Now think about Europe and the rest of the world without chocolate, vanilla, corn, potatoes, and tomatoes. Exchanges of ideas and technology have changed people's lives in positive ways on both sides of the Atlantic.

There is also a negative side to this exchange. Disease killed millions of Native Americans in the years after contact with the Europeans. Many Native Americans lost their land and were made to work as slaves.

These legacies still sometimes cause prejudice. They led to great inequalities of wealth in the region that exist today. The story of people, the environment, and Mexico is a complex one. It is filled with positives and negatives. People often disagree about how to measure the value of colonization.

What would YOU do?

Throughout Middle America, a major issue is deciding how to best use limited farmland. Imagine you are in charge of deciding how land is to be used. If you allow the land to be always growing crops, the soil will lose all its nutrients. It will be useless for farming. But if you let the land rest, farmers and their families will suffer. What would you do?

LESSON 3 REVIEW

Fact Follow-Up
1. What large animals did the Spanish bring to New Spain?
2. What new crops did the Spanish bring to New Spain?
3. How did Spanish building practices and large animals change the physical environment of New Spain?
4. What was the Columbian Exchange?

Talk About It
1. Describe human-environmental interaction in New Spain after the Spanish conquerors arrived.
2. How did the Columbian Exchange give almost all the people of Latin America a common heritage?
3. What are the costs and benefits to the region of the Columbian Exchange?

566

Chapter 23

LESSON 3 REVIEW

Fact Follow-Up Answers
1. The Spanish brought cattle, sheep, and horses—animals the Native Americans had never seen.
2. Crops such as wheat, barley, oats, and rye were brought by the Spanish.
3. The Spanish used much more wood in construction than did the Native Americans; land soon became deforested. The large animals required much land for grazing and threatened the grasslands.
4. The Columbian Exchange was the exchange of plants, animals, ideas, technology, and diseases between Spanish conquerors and Native Americans.

Talk About It Answers
1. Important points: Students should include the increased use of wood for building that contributed to deforestation and the introduction of large animals that contributed to overgrazing.
2. The introduction of the Spanish language, Spanish forms of government, and Roman Catholicism laid the basis for a common heritage.
3. Important points: possible answers include:Costs: illness wiped out most of the Native Americans; forced work on haciendas. Benefits include: new foods, shared farming techniques

Analyzing, Interpreting, Creating, and Using Resources and Materials

Was the Columbian Exchange an Exchange?

You read in Chapter 22 about the encounter between Hernán Cortés and Moctezuma II, and you have been reading in this chapter about the Columbian Exchange. After reading Chapters 22 and 23, you might be left with this question: Was the Columbian Exchange really an exchange, or was it something else?

What is an exchange? Have you ever traded lunch treats or stuffed animals or sports cards with a friend? If you have, you have engaged in an exchange.

When you trade with your friends, both sides must be willing to trade. If you have something your friend wants but you want to keep, you will not be willing to trade it away. If you have something someone wants and that person simply takes it from you, giving you nothing in return, there has been no trade. There has been a theft.

Finally, you would never consider trading something you already have for another object that you don't even want, would you? Of course not! You would never make a trade like that, would you?

A true exchange then has three parts:

1. **A willingness to exchange:** Both sides have to be willing to trade or exchange.
2. **Reciprocity:** Each side exchanges something and gets something else.
3. **Satisfaction:** Unless both sides are pleased with the exchange, it doesn't go through.

Using these three parts, can you decide whether the Columbian Exchange was an exchange or something else? This is a question you must consider carefully before making a decision. There are a number of questions to be answered beginning with these:

1. What was exchanged, and for what was it exchanged?
2. Was the Columbian Exchange planned (intentional), or did it just happen?
3. If the exchange was not intentional, was it really an exchange?

People and Their Environment   5

Skill Lesson Review

1. Which criterion for an exchange was satisfied in the Columbian Exchange? *Encourage students to discuss the three criteria.*
2. How did the role play of an exchange help you understand the criteria for an exchange? *Encourage student discussion, noting the importance of willingness to exchange as a criterion.*
3. Was it easier to argue that the Columbian Exchange was an exchange? *Encourage student discussion, focusing on reasons behind their opinions.*

Teaching This Skill Lesson

Materials Needed textbooks, paper, pencils, items for exchange to begin the lesson

Classroom Organization whole class, individual

Beginning the Lesson Offer to exchange an item of little value (such as a sheet of paper, pencil) for an item of greater value (such as a book bag, a sports ball) owned by a student. When the student refuses to exchange (probe until the student refuses, or consult with the student on the role play before beginning the lesson), ask class why the student did not want to exchange. Lead students to suggest that the student was not required to exchange (willingness to exchange); that it was not a fair exchange because the value of items was unequal (reciprocity); and that only one side would be pleased with the exchange (satisfaction).

Lesson Development Ask students what was exchanged in the Columbian Exchange. Encourage students to skim Chapters 22 and 23 as they mention items. Draw a line down the middle of the board separating two lists, with headings "Exchanged by Europeans" and "Exchanged by Native Americans." Record items students mention on the chalkboard. Students should copy the lists. When lists are relatively complete, remind students of the three criteria for an exchange (willingness to exchange, reciprocity, satisfaction). Refer them to the Skill Lesson. Ask whether the Columbian Exchange was really an exchange, accepting students' responses and probing for reasons behind those responses. As a homework assignment, have students write a point-of-view essay of no more than three paragraphs arguing that the Columbian Exchange was or was not a genuine exchange.

Conclusion Allow students to share their essays in small groups. Post essays in the classroom.

Talk About It

1. Important points: Students should choose one of the two and explain their choice citing technological and other achievements.
2. Important points: Encourage students to suggest as many achievements as possible, choose one, and explain it. Among the achievements were agricultural innovation, the building of cities, a written language, and the use of water, astronomy, mathematics, metal working, and a calendar.
3. Similarities include the facts that Aztec and Spanish cities were centers of trade, government, and religion. Both used adobe (the Spanish used more wood in construction than the Aztecs). Differences include religions, styles of religious architecture (the pyramid versus the cathedral), and the sophisticated use of water resources of the Aztecs.
4. Important points: Students should choose one of the three and explain their choice. The *hacienda* system still influences land ownership patterns. Sugar plantations changed the environment. Silver mines resulted in many deaths.
5. Important points: Encourage students to state a point of view and explain it with examples. Responses should mention agriculture, technology, religious and political life, plant and animal life, and diseases.

Mastering Mapwork

1. The border runs along about 43 degrees North of the Equator.
2. The United States/Mexico border
3. 1,800 miles

Lessons Learned

LESSON 1
Native American People of Mexico
Mexico was the center of two great Native American cultures: the Maya and the Aztec. The Maya developed farming, mathematics, and a written language. No one knows why the Maya left their cities. The Aztec built great cities that were centers of religion and culture. They irrigated their crops.

LESSON 2
Lands and Resources
Mexico was part of the Spanish colony of New Spain. Spain set up the colony to benefit its own economy. The Spanish built large silver mines and *haciendas*. Silver and farm products were sent to Spain. Goods the colony needed had to be gotten from Spain. Catholic priests from Spain worked to convert Native Americans to Christianity.

LESSON 3
Mexico's Environment
Spain's colonization of Mexico changed the environment. The Spanish brought animals and technology to the New World. Native Americans taught the Spanish new farming techniques. Many Native Americans died of diseases brought by the Europeans.

Talk About It

1. Which of the civilizations—the Mayan or the Aztec—do you believe was more creative? Explain your choice.
2. What do you think was the greatest achievement of the Maya and Aztec civilizations? Explain why.
3. Both the Aztecs and the conquering Spanish planned complex cities. In what ways were their cities similar and different?
4. Which do you think had the greatest consequence for Mexican society today: the *hacienda* system, sugar plantations, or the silver mines? Explain why.
5. Was the Columbian Exchange a benefit or a burden for America? Explain your answer.

Mastering Mapwork

LOCATION
Use the map on page 564 to answer these questions:
1. Describe the absolute location of the northwestern border of New Spain.
2. What is where the Rio Grand runs today?
3. Esitmate how far it is from the Adams-Onis Treaty Line to Mexico City using the scale.

Becoming Better Readers

More Strategies While Reading
Good readers do not try to memorize all the details of what they read. Instead they look for key ideas and some important details that support the key ideas. Reread the "Eyewitness to History" on pages 560–561. Write two or three main ideas of this article. Then write one or two details that support the main idea.

Becoming Better Readers

Main ideas:
1. The Spanish took the Native Americans' gold and silver.
2. The gold ran out, so they mined silver.
3. The Native Americans were forced to work in he mines.
   a. The conditions were bad in the mines.
   b. Many Native Americans died in the mines.
4.. Today, mining is hard.
   a. Machines help.
   b. No one is forced to work in a mine.

Go to the Source

Understanding Legends

Corn was the most important food crop in Mexico for hundreds of years. Maya, Aztecs, and other Native Americans worshiped corn gods and developed myths and legends about growing and harvesting corn. Read the legend below. Answer the questions using information from the legend.

Many years ago, a man and his son went from Aramberri to Tamulipas to look for work. They came back with 20 burros (donkeys) loaded with corn. On the way, night fell. They unloaded the burros, and tied the 20 bushels of corn, all together, to a big tree trunk. Later, they started a fire to make dinner and, after that, they went to bed behind where they had left the 20 bushels of corn.

The next morning, they got up before dawn, had breakfast and went to get their burros to feed them. Then they looked for the corn to load it onto the burros, but they couldn't find it. All they found was a very big trail. The man and his son gathered the burros and followed the trail the bushels left. After several hours on the road, they found a very large snake carrying all of the corn. Then they realized that they had tied the corn not to a tree trunk, but to the snake.

At night, when the beast was hungry, it went looking for food and dragged the 20 bushels of corn after it. Legend has it that the trail left by the snake and the bushels of corn is now the road going from Aramberri to La Boquilla.

Questions

1. What is the significance of the snake dragging 20 bushels of corn?
2. Based on the selection, what will most likely happen?
3. What part of the selection is exaggerated?

Go to the Source

Go to the Source

Understanding Legends

OBJECTIVES: 1.03
SOCIAL STUDIES SKILLS: 3.05, 4.05, 4.06

Twenty Bushels of Corn

People in different cultures make up stories to explain both common and uncommon events. Folktales and legends are popular because they have mythic elements that explain how something came to be. "Twenty Bushels of Corn"is one of the most popular legends in Mexico today.

Answers

1. It left a trail that is now the road going from Aramberri to La Boquilla.
2. People in Mexico most likely will use the road going from Aramberri to Boquilla.
3. Tying 20 bushels of corn to a snake, and the snake dragging the corn to make a road. are both far fetched and untrue.

How to Use the Chapter Review

There are four sections in the Chapter Review: Talk About It, Mastering Mapwork, Becoming Better Readers, and Go to the Source. Use the Vocabulary Worksheets and the Chapter Review Worksheet in the Teacher's Resource Guide for additional reinforcement and preparation for the Chapter Assessments. The chapter and lesson reviews and the Chapter Review Worksheets are the basis of the assessment for each chapter.

Talk About It questions encourage students to speculate about the content of the chapter and are suitable for class or small-group discussion. They are not intended to be assigned for homework.

Mastering Mapwork has students apply one or more of the Five Themes of Geography to maps within the chapter.

Becoming Better Readers focuses on building reading strategy skills necessary for reading comprehension in the content areas.

Go to the Source activities allow students to analyze a primary source that relates to the content of the chapter. The questions and activities familiarize students with different types of primary sources and also build content-reading skills.

CHAPTER 24

Economy and Government

Social Studies Strands

Economics and Development

Historic Perspectives

Government and Active Citizenship

Global Connections

Technological Influences and Society

North Carolina Standard Course of Study

Goal 2 The learner will analyze political and social institutions in North America and examine how these institutions respond to human needs, structure society, and influence behavior.

Goal 4 The learner will trace key developments in United States history and describe their impact on the land and people of the nation and its neighboring countries.

Goal 5 The learner will evaluate ways the United States and other countries of North America make decisions about the allocation and use of economic resources.

Goal 6 The learner will recognize how technology has influenced change within the United States and other countries in North America.

Teaching & Assessment

- English Language Learner Modified Lesson Plans for this chapter are found in the Teacher's Resource Guide.

- *ExamView® Assessment Suite* is provided at **NCJourneys.com.** It includes customizable assessments for all chapters. Paper tests are also available in the Teacher's Resource Guide. See pages T16–T17 for information about how to use the assessments and the Scoring Guide.

Worksheets

Worksheets and answer keys are found both in the Teacher's Resource Guide and at **NCJourneys.com**, including Reading Guides, Reading Strategies, Chapter Reviews, English Language Learner and others.

Activities and Integrations

SOCIAL STUDIES

Problem Based Learning: Rural Development, p. 570B
Activator, p. 570
Caudillo Compare and Contrast, p. 575
Mexican States, p. 577
Portrait Personality, p. 579
● Houses in Mexico, p. 583
▲ Make a Passport, p. 586
Who are the Zapatistas?, p. 588
▲ Life in Mexico City, p. 589
Comparing Maps Over Time, p. 593

READING/LANGUAGE ARTS	READING/LANGUAGE ARTS OBJECTIVES
"Sure It's Sequencing," p. 570B	3.05
● Mexico Photomania, p. 570B	4.03
Mexican Biographies, p. 570B	4.03
● Reading Strategy: Recognizing, Genres, p. 572	2.08
Writing Prompt, p.570	4.01, 4.02, 4.03
★ Independence Comparison Time Line, p. 573	3.02
● Presidential Comparison, p. 578	3.02
Reading Strategy: Recognizing Themes, p. 579	1.03
★ NAFTA Debate, p. 581	1.03
Reading Strategy: Understanding Tone, p. 584	2.09
Skill Lesson: Analyzing Mexico's Economic and Political Development, p. 590	2.02, 2.05
Becoming Better Readers, p. 592	2.01

MATHEMATICS	MATHEMATICS OBJECTIVES
Time in Mexico, p. 583	1.02
Deforestation Math, p. 587	1.02

SCIENCE	SCIENCE OBJECTIVES
Environmentally Friendly Development, p. 580	2.07

TECHNOLOGY	TECHNOLOGY OBJECTIVES
■ *Caudillos* of Mexico, p. 574	2.13
Carolina Connection: Daniels, p. 578	2.13
■ Natural Resources, p. 582	2.13

VISUAL ARTS	VISUAL ARTS OBJECTIVES
Mexican Biographies, p. 570B	3.02
★ Mexican National Anthem, p. 576	9.03, 9.04, 9.05 (music)

CHARACTER AND VALUES EDUCATION	TRAITS
What Would You Do?, p. 588	good judgement

● Basic Activities ★ Challenging Activities ▲ English Language Learner Novice ■ English Language Learner Intermediate

Introductory Activity

"Sure, It's Sequencing"

OBJECTIVES: 2.02, 2.04, 2.08

Prepare a list of main ideas from Unit 6. From the list, write out a main-idea sentence on sentence strips. Make enough copies of the same sentence for each cooperative group. Then cut apart the sentences word by word, and put them in envelopes. Give each group one envelope with the same sentence. When you say "go," the groups empty their envelope, and put the sentences together as quickly as they can. Students will raise their hands when finished. The first team wins a point, after they read it aloud to the class. Collect the envelopes, pass out a second one, and play until all envelopes have been used. Have students copy the list and put in their notebooks.

 ## Culminating Activity

Mexico "Photomania"

OBJECTIVES: 2.02, 2.04, 2.08

Have the class imagine that they have just returned from a trip to Mexico. Have them create a photo album of pictures taken with their new camera and include captions under each picture, giving some details. Each student will present his or her album to the class, and discuss each picture.

Extension Novice ELL students can do the pictures and label them.

 ## Art Activity

Mexican Biographies

OBJECTIVES: 1.07, 2.08, 4.01

Have each student cut out an oval from a sheet of posterboard, the cutout large enough so that the student can peer through it. Have students draw the body of a historical figure, and decorate with the appropriate clothes for the period with hats, buttons, pieces of fabric, or decorative braid. In the blank background space on the poster, students should print facts about the person's life.

Next, they should write a report about the person in the first person (I am Santa Anna, I was born . . .). Have students present their reports to the class. Hang the posters along with the biographies in the hall or media center.

Extension Novice ELL students can draw and label the picture of the person.

 ## Problem Based Learning Activity

Rural Development

OBJECTIVES: 1.07, 3.04, 4.07

Situation Mexican cities today are suffering from overcrowding. People have flocked to these cities from rural areas hoping for a better way of life. The population shift has put a tremendous strain on the cities of Mexico. The new Mexican government also has committed to trying to make the living conditions and economy of Mexico better. The cities do not have enough jobs, resources, or housing for all of the people, and the problem has made life dangerous in the city for the residents and those who live nearby.

Task Have students break into small cooperative groups. The groups should come up with a way to entice people to leave the city. What kind of campaign would be effective in order to get individuals to move to the countryside? What incentives could they provide? Students will need to consider what types of jobs might be found in the countryside of Mexico and how they could encourage employers to set up shop in rural areas. As students develop their ideas, have them design the city/village/town out of poster-board and clean empty milk cartons. They can cover the cartons with construction paper and lay out the village on the poster paper so that people can see that they have included all the necessities in a Mexican village. Is leaving the city really better for the people? Why or why not? How would these villages benefit the Mexican economy and what would be the consequences? How hard would it be for Mexico to get something like this to happen?

Reflection Videotape students while they share a "public service announcement" about the importance of living in a healthy environment and strong economy. The students will share their reflections about why individuals who have moved to Mexican cities might be happier in planned, supported areas of rural Mexico. How does quality of life affect people's happiness, and why?

Teaching Strategies

This chapter will represent the history and heritage of some of your students.

The information in this chapter will also help students gain a better understanding of economics in Mexico as well as in the United States. Discuss the impact of a globalizing economy, represented by NAFTA, on North Carolina's economy, especially the textiles and furniture industries.

Also, discuss the significant differences in Mexico's economy and educational system between the middle class and wealthy families and poorer families. Discuss what economic factors in Mexico might influence people to emigrate to the United States.

Activator

 OBJECTIVES: 4.08

Show students pictures of the Alamo in Texas, and recount for them the story of Texas' break with the new nation of Mexico. You may want to play the song "The Ballad of Davy Crockett" and describe Crockett's role at the Alamo.

Writing Prompt

 OBJECTIVES: 1.02, 1.06, 1.07

Personal Narrative

This chapter describes Mexico's struggle to be free from the rule of Spain. Write about a rule, either one at home or at school, that you think is unfair. Be sure to tell why you think the way you do. Give at least three reasons.

Essay

Independence is something that most countries and people cherish. Mexico wanted to be independent of Spain's rule. Think of something that you will be glad that you can do for yourself someday. Write an essay describing why you want to be independent and do this for yourself.

CHAPTER

24

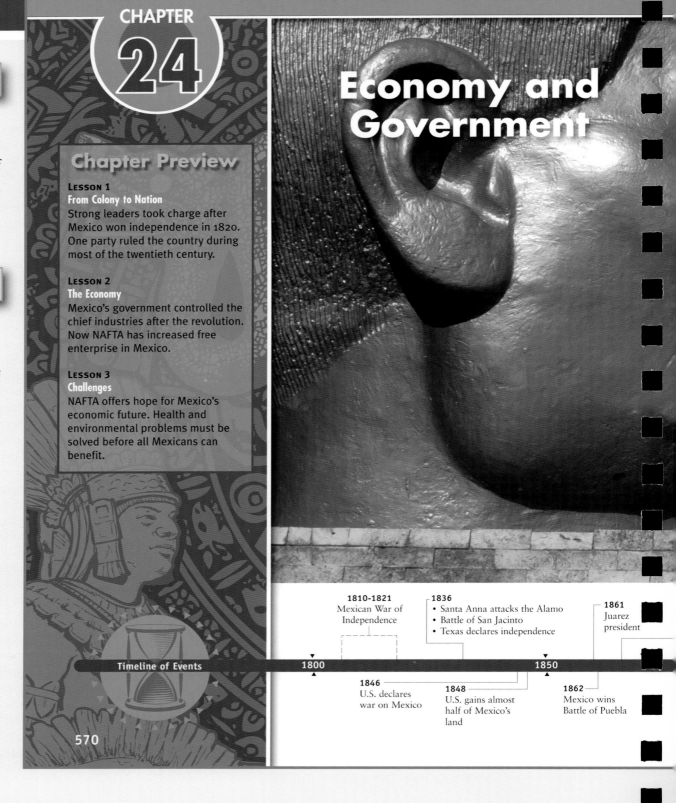

Economy and Government

Chapter Preview

LESSON 1
From Colony to Nation
Strong leaders took charge after Mexico won independence in 1820. One party ruled the country during most of the twentieth century.

LESSON 2
The Economy
Mexico's government controlled the chief industries after the revolution. Now NAFTA has increased free enterprise in Mexico.

LESSON 3
Challenges
NAFTA offers hope for Mexico's economic future. Health and environmental problems must be solved before all Mexicans can benefit.

Timeline of Events

1810-1821
Mexican War of Independence

1836
• Santa Anna attacks the Alamo
• Battle of San Jacinto
• Texas declares independence

1861
Juarez president

1800

1850

1846
U.S. declares war on Mexico

1848
U.S. gains almost half of Mexico's land

1862
Mexico wins Battle of Puebla

570

One of the most famous of New Spain's leaders was Bernardo de Galvez. Galvez was the Spanish governor of the territory of Louisiana. Galvez helped the 13 colonies become independent from Great Britain. He led Spanish troops against British forts from Florida to Louisiana.

Galvez became viceroy of New Spain in 1784. He died of yellow fever only two years later. He had lots of ideas about how New Spain could be governed better. Many were put into practice.

The United States honored Galvez' descendants. It named them members of the Sons and Daughters of the American Revolution.

In Baja California, Mexico, stand sculptures of some of Mexico's important political leaders: Venustiano Carranza, Benito Pablo Juares, and Miguel Hildalgo y Costilla.

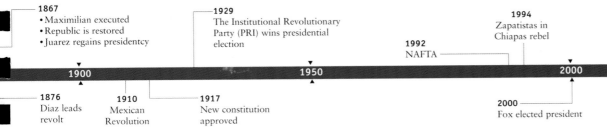

1867
• Maximilian executed
• Republic is restored
• Juarez regains presidentcy

1929
The Institutional Revolutionary Party (PRI) wins presidential election

1992
NAFTA

1994
Zapatistas in Chiapas rebel

1900

1950

2000

1876
Diaz leads revolt

1910
Mexican Revolution

1917
New constitution approved

2000
Fox elected president

Chapter Resources

Print Resources

Fiction
Bunting, Eve. *A Day's Work*. Houghton Mifflin, 1997. ISBN 0395845181.

Nonfiction
Cedeno, Maria. *Cesar Chavez: Labor Leader*. Econo-Clad Books, 1999. ISBN 0785742727.

Harvey, Miles. *Look What Came from Mexico*. Franklin Watts, Inc., 1999. ISBN 0531159396.

Web Sites

Visit **NCJourneys.com** for links to these Web sites:
• MexOnline
• Presidencia de la Republica (with English translations)
• United States Embassy in Mexico
• NAFTA Secretariat

:

OBJECTIVES: 1.04, 2.04, 3.06, 4.06

Discussion Questions

1 What similarities exist between the United States and Mexico in their struggles for independence?

2 Who was the father of Mexican Independence?

3 What did the Creoles think about Father Hidalgo's move for independence from Spain? Why?

4 When did Mexico become free from Spanish rule?

 Caption Answer

Because the Spanish government imposed higher taxes and sent more troops to Mexico

Reading Strategy Activity

Recognizing Genres

OBJECTIVES: 1.04, 2.04, 3.06, 4.06

The ability to read for pleasure, to gain information, or to support an opinion requires students to know different types of literature. Students should be exposed to a variety of genres and should understand their uses. Social studies and history are types of informational writing. This strategy takes several days to complete. Introduce literature strands and give specific examples. Use the Literature Strands worksheet to practice identifying genres (this is best done as a whole-group activity or in cooperative groups).

Literature Strands Bingo Make a blank bingo board with 12 squares for each student. List 11 types of literature on the board and let students randomly fill in their board, including a free space. Call out examples of different types of literature and play bingo. Explain why the titles fit each strand. Using other examples, play the game until students have a good understanding.

Extension Display books in the classroom labeled with their literature strand. ELL students can write strand names on index cards to practice at home. Have them practice pronunciation.

LESSON **1** From Colony to Nation

KEY IDEAS

- Mexicans won independence from Spain in 1821. They fought against taxes.

- Mexico's constitution provided for free public education and land reform. It also provided for fair wages and a system of health and welfare.

- The Mexican–American War and civil war weakened Mexico's economy. President Porfirio Díaz brought economic development to Mexico.

- One party ruled Mexico for most of the twentieth century.

KEY TERMS

Creoles
caudillo
Institutional Revolutionary Party (PRI)

PEOPLE TO KNOW

Bernardo de Galvez
Father Miguel Hidalgo
Porfirio Díaz
Francisco Madero
Venustiano Carranza
Vicente Fox Quesada
Emiliano Zapata
Antonio Lopez de Santa Anna

By 1800, the Spanish colonists had become tired of the lack of freedom. Much like the American colonists, they were unhappy with heavy taxes. The examples of the American and French Revolutions helped them decide to form their own nation.

Mexico Wins Independence

Father Miguel Hidalgo was a priest. He was called the "Father of Mexican Independence." In 1810 he and other rebels began to resist Spanish rule. Thousands of poor farmers followed Father Hidalgo. These followers were not an organized army. They were just people who believed that Spain had not treated them fairly. They believed a county run by Mexicans would be better.

Hidalgo's followers armed themselves. They attacked the Spanish leaders. At first, the rebels had support from many people. But later they could not unite all the Mexican people. The Creoles (KREE·ohls), did not want Father Hidalgo's followers to gain power. *Creoles* were wealthy Spanish people born in New Spain.

Creoles owned Mexico's *haciendas*. Their families had become important leaders in Mexican affairs. The Creoles wanted Spain to give Mexican leaders more freedom to run the colony. They did not support Father Hidalgo's call for independence at first.

Spanish troops crushed the unrest. They killed its leaders, including Father Hidalgo. The Creoles made no protests. But the Spanish king made the mistake of thinking that all Mexicans were traitors.

He ordered the Creoles to pay more taxes. He also ordered a large army to stop any trouble. These actions made the Creoles decide that they could no longer trust Spain.

In 1820, there was political unrest back in Spain. The king faced a revolt. Juan Odonojú (oth·on·oh·HOO) was the commander of Spain's army in Mexico. He was convinced that the colony should be free. He made no effort to keep Mexicans from declaring their independence. By the end of the next year, the last Spanish officials went home. Mexico had gained the freedom to govern itself.

Father Miguel Hidalgo wanted Mexico to be free from Spain. **Why did the Creoles finally join the revolution?**

Examples:
The moral of the story: Jealousy is bad.
"Paul Bunyan's Story"
"Why Bats Hunt at Night"
George Washington's Friend
The Story of Beth Mace by Beth Mace
The Story of Beth Mace by Marjorie Brown
"The Talking Frog"
"The Day the Martians Were Defeated"
"John White and the New Land"
"New Boy in Class"

Sample Bingo Board

Information Text	Tall Tale	Biography	Autobiography
FREE SPACE	Fable	Historical Fiction	Science Fiction
Myth	Legend	Realistic Fiction	Fantasy

Portrait of a Gentleman, *artist unknown, shows a Creole gentleman of Mexico in the 1700s.* **How was Mexico's fight for independence similar to that of the United States?**

Independent Mexico

Becoming independent from Spain in 1821 was easier for Mexico's new leaders than creating a new government.

The Early Years

The leaders could not agree on the type of government they wanted. Some wanted a strong central government. They also wanted the Roman Catholic Church as Mexico's official religion. Others wanted Mexico's states to have more power than the central government. This group also wanted religious freedom.

Mexico's leaders adopted a constitution. It called for a president and a congress heading the national government. Each of Mexico's states was to have a governor and legislature.

Mexico's leaders had never made laws or governed themselves. Military men often revolted against the young country. One of them was General Antonio Lopez de Santa Anna. He was a *caudillo* (kaw·DEE·yo). Caudillo means strong man. Santa Anna was the president 11 times between 1833 and 1855. He also commanded the Mexican army during the Mexican–American War.

The United States won this war. The treaty of Guadalupe Hidalgo brought peace, but Mexico had to turn over almost half of its territory to the United States.

The Mexican–American War left Mexico broke. Its people were bitterly divided. Then civil war broke out. French troops took control for a short time. Several groups revolted against the government.

The Porfiriato

Porfirio Díaz seized power in 1876. He was a hero in the fight against the French. Díaz formed good relations with some of Mexico's important leaders. He used his army to control those who opposed him. He began a dictatorship that ruled Mexico until 1911.

Díaz's long rule is called the Porfiriato (por·fee·ree·AH·toh). The Porfiriato brought economic development to Mexico. Díaz built railroads and improved the mining industry. He also invited people from other countries to invest in Mexico.

Most people stayed loyal to Díaz for a long time. Many believed that the economic development helped the whole country. But later they learned that the only people who made money were a few wealthy Mexicans and people from other countries. Díaz's opponents saw that the people who spoke out against Díaz were usually violently attacked. Mexicans got tired of the government's failure to bring democracy.

Economy and Government

573

Discussion Questions

1 What problems did Mexico have in establishing its new government?

2 What is a *caudillo*?

3 What was the result of the Mexican-American War?

4 Who was Porfirio Díaz?

5 What economic developments did he bring to Mexico during his rule?

 Caption Answer

Both were colonized by a European nation, and both had trouble deciding what kind of government they wanted and faced problems strengthening their new government.

Activity

Independence Comparison Timeline

OBJECTIVES: 1.07, 2.02, 2.04

Have students create a timeline representing the 13 colonies' struggle for independence from Britain (see Chapter 6). Next, have them construct a similar timeline representing Mexico's struggle for independence from Spain. Once the timelines are complete, create a graphic organizer on the board in which the similarities and differences of the two can be clearly displayed.

Extension Novice ELL students can label a time line from an example and copy from the board the graphic organizer.

Teacher Notes

Battle of San Jacinto

In February of 1836, 189 Texans were finally overwhelmed at the Alamo after defiantly standing for 13 days against more than 2,000 Mexican soldiers led by General Santa Anna. Just two months later, Sam Houston led 750 Texans in the Battle at San Jacinto, which is now regarded as the turning point in the Texas Revolution. Caught unprepared, Santa Anna's men were overtaken in less than half

an hour, and Santa Anna—who described himself as the "Napolean of the West"—was captured. Later, Santa Anna agreed to withdraw Mexican troops from the Texas territory. The defeat at San Jacinto, ten years of instability in the Mexican government, and the entry of Texas into the Union in 1845 set the stage for the final confrontation between the United States and Mexico (1846–1848), ultimately opening the west for United States expansion

Discussion Questions

1 Who was General Antonio López de Santa Anna?

Activity

Caudillos **of Mexico**

OBJECTIVES: 1.07, 2.08, 3.04

This Web site about the *caudillos* of Mexico will impress your students because it has been created by high school students (visit **NCJourneys.com** for a link).

The students have answered three basic questions with their Web site: Who were the *caudillos?* Which countries did they rule? How did the *caudillos* affect the people they ruled? The information is straightforward and easy for students to understand.

Have your students use a graphic organizer to take notes and answer the three questions.

The CAUDILLO
in Mexican History

In the nineteenth century, men with military backgrounds led many Latin American governments. Most had shown bravery in battle. These leaders usually had powerful personalities. Their word was law. Each leader believed that only he knew what was best for his nation. These types of leaders were called *caudillos* (koh·DEE·yohs).

General Antonio Lopez de Santa Anna was one of the first Mexican *caudillos*. From 1824 to 1853, Santa Anna was the center of Mexican government. He was brave in battle. He lost half of his left leg to a cannon ball. Santa Anna commanded the army that lost the Mexican–American War.

General Antonio Lopez de Santa Anna

The mural People in Arms *by David Siqueiros*

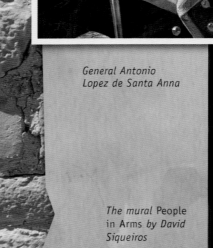

574

General
Porfirio Díaz

eneral Porfirio Díaz was another great *caudillo*. He was a hero when Mexico defeated the French invasion. He ruled Mexico from 1876 to 1911. Mexico made economic progress during his rule. But his government was not democratic. It neglected the poor.

ecause of this, the Mexican people rose up against Díaz. This rebellion is known as the Mexican Revolution. During the revolution, Emiliano Zapata became an important figure. He was also a *caudillo*. Zapata led Native American farmers to defend their land.

apata died in 1919, but he is still a hero to many Mexicans. His rallying cry was "Land and Liberty." It inspires the modern-day Native American rebels in Chiapas. The *caudillo* tradition is still important in Latin America.

Emiliano Zapata

Activity

Caudillos **Compare and Contrast**

OBJECTIVES: 1.07, 2.08, 3.04

Have students compare Mexican *caudillos* with the founding fathers of the United States using a Venn Diagram. This can be done individually, in small groups, or as a class. Students can do additional research and compare such leaders as George Washington, Benjamin Franklin, Thomas Jefferson, Andrew Jackson, John Adams, Samuel Adams, Patrick Henry, and others to the Mexican leaders studied in this lesson. Discuss the similarities and differences as a class.

575

Discussion Questions

1 What was the cause of the Mexican Revolution? When did it begin?

2 Who became the leader of Mexico in 1916?

3 What did the Constitution of 1917 provide for?

4 What is the PRI?

5 How long was the PRI in power in Mexico?

6 What happened to Mexico during its rule?

Caption Answer

He led Native American farmers in defending their land.

Activity

Mexican National Anthem

 OBJECTIVES: 1.07, 2.04, 3.04

Have students look at the words to the Mexican national anthem in Spanish, and make two lists. The first will be a list of those words they recognize immediately, such as "Mexicano" or "canon." The second list will be of the words they might be able to guess in English, such as "oliva." Encourage students to guess even if they are unsure. Discuss the meaning of the anthem.

Ask the ELL teacher or a Spanish speaker in your school (preferably a student) to help.

Mexicanos, al grito de guerra
El acero aprestad y el bridon,
Y retiemble en sus centros la Tierra
Al sonoro rugir del canon.

Mexicans, at the cry of battle
lend your swords and bridle;
and let the earth tremble at its center
upon the roar of the cannon.

Cina, jioh Patrial tus sienes de oliva
De la paz el arcangel divino,
Que en el ciela tu eterno destino
Por el dedo de Dias se escribio.
Mas si osare un extrano enemigo
Profanar con su planta tu suelo,
Piensa, jioh Patria querida! Que el cielo

Emiliano Zapata and Pancho Villa ride into Mexico City in 1910 during the Mexican Revolution. **What did Zapata do in the Mexican Revolution?**

The Mexican Revolution

In 1908, Díaz told the country that he would allow elections. Francisco Madero was a wealthy Mexican businessman. He challenged Díaz. Madero wanted to fix the government and create a democracy.

The Mexican assembly said that Díaz won the election. Madero decided that violence was the only way to remove the dictator. He called for a national revolt against Díaz.

The Mexican Revolution began in November 1910. The Mexican people united against Díaz. They quickly won their freedom. Several months later, Díaz quit and fled to Europe. Then the fighting started again. The revolution became a war between Mexicans with different ideas about their country's future.

By 1916, most Mexicans saw Venustiano Carranza (veh·noos·tee·AH·noh kah·RAHN·zah) as their leader. Carranza called a meeting to write a new constitution. The Constitution of 1917 used Carranza's ideas and those of his rivals.

The constitution said that there must be free public education. It also contained a system of public health and welfare. Limits were also placed on the ownership of land and businesses by people who did not live in Mexico. The constitution called for the president to serve only a single term. The government took over all of Mexico's oil resources. The Roman Catholic Church also had new government controls.

Customs

On May 10, Mexican school children honor their mothers with a celebration. The students invite their mothers to school, which has been decorated for the occasion. In a special ceremony students recite poetry. They also sing and dance to show their love for their mothers. At the end of the program the students give their mothers something they have made.

The PRI

From 1921 until 2000 a single political party ruled Mexico. It is called the *Institutional Revolutionary Party,* or *PRI.* For many years the PRI worked for the ideas of the revolution. The government took over the privately owned *haciendas.* It split them up among millions of landless farmers.

The development of new industry was also supported by the PRI. Labor unions were allowed to set up. A national school system was created. Many hospitals and housing projects were built. The Roman Catholic Church agreed to stay out of politics. The government supervised Catholic churches and schools.

The presidents of Mexico between 1921 and 2000 were all members of the PRI. Candidates for other offices who did not belong to the PRI had little chance of being elected.

Un soldado en cada hijo te dio.

Your forehead shall be girded, oh fatherland, with olive garlands by the divine archangel of peace, For in heaven your eternal destiny has been written by the hand of God. But should a foreign enemy Profane your land with his sole, Think, beloved fatherland, that heaven gave you a soldier in each son.

Patria, Patria! Tus hijos te juran
Exhalar en tus aras su aliento,
Si el clarin con su belico acento

Los convoca a lidiar con valor.
Para ti las guirnaldas de oliva!
Un recuerdo para ellos de gloria!
Un laurel para ti de victoria!
Un sepulcro para ellos de honor!

Fatherland, fatherland, your children swear to exhale their breath in your cause, If the bugle in its belligerent tone should call upon them to struggle with bravery. For you the olive garlands! For them a memory of glory! For you a laurel of victory! For them a tomb of honor!

Mexican States

Place Mexico's government, like that of the United States, is a federal system. *What is a federal system?*

Map labels: UNITED STATES, 110°W, 100°W, 90°W, 30°N, 20°N, Baja California Norte, Sonora, Chihuahua, Coahuila, Baja California Sur, Gulf of California, Durango, Sinaloa, Nuevo León, Monterrey, Tamaulipas, Gulf of Mexico, Zacatecas, Tropic of Cancer, PACIFIC OCEAN, Nayarit, San Luis Potosí, Guanajuato, Querétaro, Bay of Campeche, Yucatán, Aguascalientes, Guadalajara, León, Jalisco, Hidalgo, Mexico City, Tlaxcala, Campeche, Quintana Roo, Michoacán, Puebla, Veracruz, Caribbean Sea, Colima, Puebla, Veracruz, Tabasco, México, Morelos, Guerrero, Acapulco, Oaxaca, Chiapas, Federal District, Caribbean Sea

Legend: ✪ National Capital — State Boundary. Scale: 0 150 300 mi. / 0 150 300 km. Compass: N W E S

New Direction

People wanted more political parties from which to choose leaders starting in the 1980s. In 1988, the PRI's critics claimed the PRI stole the presidential election. Opponents also blamed the PRI for serious economic problems. Some Maya in southern Mexico revolted.

New election laws gave other parties a chance to compete with the PRI. The PRI lost seats in one of the houses of Congress. In 2000, Vicente Fox Quesada of the National Action Party became Mexico's new president.

This is a PRI rally in Mexico City in 1982. **Why did the PRI lose support?**

Economy and Government

577

Discussion Questions

1 Why did the people oppose the PRI in the 1980s and 1990s?

2 Who became the President of Mexico in 2000?

Caption Answer

In a federal system, power is shared between the national government and the state or provincial governments.

Caption Answer

The party was charged with stealing the presidential election and blamed for serious economic problems and an uprising of Native Americans in southern Mexico.

Map Activity

Mexican States

NATIONAL GEOGRAPHY STANDARDS: 1, 4
GEOGRAPHIC THEMES: Region, Place, Location
OBJECTIVES: 1.03, 2.04

Have students rank Mexico's states from largest to smallest. Have students compare this map to the ones on page 536 and 537. Have students describe and compare the climate, landforms, and vegetation of the larger states in the north with the larger states of the south. Have students identify the landlocked states. How many states of the United States are landlocked in comparison?

Background Information

Vicente Fox Quesada

Vicente Fox's election in 2000 ended 71 years of rule by the PRI. Before becoming Mexico's president, Fox was a successful business executive who worked for 15 years for Coca-Cola de Mexico. He once called the soda manufacturer "my second university education." "I learned," he said, "that the heart of business is out in the field, not in the office . . . I learned not to accept anything but winning." After leaving

Coca-Cola, he became a successful manufacturer of cowboy boots. Fox's previous political experience was as governor of the Mexican state of Guanajuato. When a serious economic recession gripped the United States and Mexico in 2001, many of Fox's plans for change had to be put on hold.

Activity

Presidential Comparison

 OBJECTIVES: 2.02, 2.04, 2.08

Have students construct a graphic organizer comparing and contrasting the current presidents of the United States and Mexico. Allow students to develop their own categories for comparison, but suggest the following possibilities:

- Age
- Education
- Family
- Work experience
- Accomplishments

Extension Novice ELL students can copy the information given by the teacher.

Activity

Carolina Connection: Daniels

 OBJECTIVES: 2.02, 2.04, 2.08

Have students research what an ambassador is. They can then write to the Mexican ambassador and describe a few of the things they have learned about Mexico this year. Students should practice good letter writing skills.

MEXICAN PORTRAIT

Emiliano Zapata
1879–1919

Emiliano Zapata was born during the dictatorship of Porfirio Diaz. At this time Mexico's economy centered on the *hacienda*. Almost all of Mexico's wealth was controlled by a few landowners. Zapata spoke Spanish but he also spoke the Native American language. He became a leader in his town. Everyone understood him when he spoke up for the peasants. When he saw the *hacienda* owners burn the village of the peasants he got angry.

Then the revolution began. Zapata became a popular hero. He helped take control of the *haciendas*. The new leaders divided the land equally among the people.

Zapata was killed in an ambush in 1919, by people wanted to go back to the old way of life before the revolution. Today there are groups who call themselves Zapatistas. That name means that they follow his idea that everyone should have a small piece of land, rather than a few people having most of it.

Josephus Daniels, Journalist and Diplomat

CAROLINA CONNECTION

Josephus Daniels was born in 1862 in Washington, North Carolina. When he was thirty-three he became the editor of *The Raleigh Observer* (*The News and Observer* today). His paper supported public-funded schools and universities.

From 1913 to 1921, Daniels served as President Woodrow Wilson's secretary of the navy. Daniels became the ambassador to Mexico when Franklin Roosevelt was elected president in 1932.

The United States' relationship with Latin America was called "The Good Neighbor Policy" under FDR. This policy called for the United States to cooperate with Latin American nations. Daniels helped make this policy a success. He is remembered as one of our best ambassadors to Mexico.

LESSON 1 REVIEW

Fact Follow-Up
1. In Mexico, who were the Creoles?
2. Why was Father Miguel Hidalgo known as the "Father of Mexican Independence"?
3. What is the PRI?

Talk About It
1. Why did the Creoles, who had not supported Father Hidalgo, finally turn against Spain?
2. Which *caudilló*—Santa Anna or Díaz—was more important to Mexico? Explain why.
3. Why do you think the *caudillo* tradition developed in Mexico?

LESSON 1 REVIEW

Fact Follow-Up Answers
1. The creoles were Spanish people born in America who were in the upper class of society and were the wealthy owners of Mexico's *haciendas*.
2. Father Hidalgo was a priest who plotted with other rebels against Spanish rule. At first they enjoyed considerable popularity, but they failed to win the united support of the Mexican people.
3. The PRI is the Institutional Revolutionary Party. They held power from 1921 to 2000.

Talk About It Answers
1. Because Spain taxed them and sent troops to Mexico.

2. Important points: Students should choose one of the two and explain their choice. Santa Anna was *caudillo* during the Mexican-American War and held the presidency 11 times between 1833 and 1855. Díaz seized power and remained in power until 1911. His Porfiriato brought economic development to Mexico.

3. Important points: Encourage students to suggest as many reasons as possible. Among possible reasons are the following: the lack of any tradition of democracy, inexperience in government, the fact that most strongmen in the beginning had been successful and celebrated military leaders, the support of the wealthier classes for the strongmen.

LESSON 2 The Economy

American movies and television often show Mexico as a land of farmers in sombreros. But Mexico has changed greatly in recent years. It has become a nation of huge cities with high-tech factories. There are also modern farms. Tourist resorts attract people from around the world. Mexico changed a great deal economically as well as politically in the twentieth century.

But Mexico's economy also faces many challenges. There is a large gap between the rich and poor. Many people are unemployed or do not have jobs that pay enough to support their families. Mexican states in the south with large Native American populations are usually poorer than states in northern Mexico.

KEY IDEAS

- After the revolution, the Mexican government controlled the key industries.
- NAFTA has had an important effect on free enterprise in Mexico.
- Assembling parts of machinery into finished products is the leading industry in Mexico today.
- Farming and tourism continue to be important parts of Mexico's economy.

KEY IDEAS

maquiladora
globalization

Many poor people move to cities for jobs. The Petroleum Mexico (PEMEX) refinery near Mexico City is one business that attracts them. **What type of economy does Mexico have?**

Economy and Government

579

OBJECTIVES: 5.01, 5.02, 5.03 5.04, 5.06, 5.07

Caption Answer

It is now a free market economy.

Reading Strategy Activity

Recognizing Theme

OBJECTIVES: 5.01, 5.02, 5.04

The theme of a story is the main idea or main subject that the author wants to explore. Often, the theme of a story carries a "moral," or lesson about human nature. In "The Little Red Hen" the theme could be that hard work pays off in the end. Stories like "The Little Red Hen" can have several themes, like "never give up," or "there is no reward for laziness." Choose other stories and discuss possible themes.

After reading Lesson 2, teach a lesson on theme. Although informational reading is different from fiction, a theme is still there. Ask if anyone can think of one for this lesson. If students have difficulty, ask for a statement that makes sense outside of the social studies text. Possible themes:

1. Mexico has a varied economy.
2. It faces many challenges.
3. The economy is a free market system.
4. Manufacturing is an important part of the industries of Mexico.
5. Tourism and agriculture are also important.

Activity

Portrait Personality

OBJECTIVES: 4.03

Divide the class into pairs or groups of three. Each pair of students will visit a variety of Web sites and use classroom and library resources to gather information about the person in this Portrait. Distribute appropriate graphic organizers (see the Graphic Organizers in the Teacher's Resource Guide) to help students take notes. Once their research is complete, each pair will create a storyboard about this person's life and work. Using this information they will produce a short digital story (using PowerPoint or other programs) to share the information they have learned with the class.

Discussion Questions

1 Today, where do most Mexicans live? What types of jobs do they have?

2 What are some of the industries in Mexico that were state-owned? Why?

3 What did Mexico's government do to encourage the growth of private industry?

Caption Answer

Petroleum

Writing Activity

Environmentally Friendly Development

 OBJECTIVES: 1.02, 1.06, 1.07

Materials: small sandboxes, construction paper cut into strips for roads and rectangles for parking lots, model houses from Monopoly, clean, empty milk cartons, drinking straws, watering can

Have students in small groups design an environmentally friendly cities where habitats are protected and in which safe energy sources are nonpolluting. Inform them that water will be sprinkled onto their final creation, therefore their city needs to be aware of forces of nature. Then have the students plan their city, make a mountain, designate forest areas with straws and a river or coastline with blue construction paper. Then they should build their city. Have them examine their city for possible environmental problems. For example, if the students cut down the forest on the side of the mountain, their city will have trouble with erosion and mud slides. Have the groups present and explain their cities' design. Then create a rainstorm with the watering can and watch the effects on the cities.

The Mexican Economy

Before the revolution of 1910, most Mexicans lived in the countryside. Today most Mexicans live in cities and work in manufacturing or service industries. The political system has moved from one run by *caudillos* to a democratic republic. The Mexican economy has also changed. A state-controlled economy has become a free-market system. Trade agreements with more than 40 nations now guide Mexico's economy.

Mexico has a tradition of state-owned industry. After the revolution, the government owned most utilities and factories. Many of these industries needed a lot of money to help them run. The Mexican government became the only source of funding. This was because the constitution stopped businesses from other countries from owning businesses in Mexico.

Growth of Private Industry

During the 1990s, the Mexican government began to sell the state-owned businesses to private citizens and corporations. Some of these were foreign. This was part of the PRI's plan to open trade. They wanted to bring the Mexican economy more into line with that of the United States.

The government made it legal for foreigners to own land and resources in 1993. NAFTA went into effect in 1994. This further reduced the Mexican government's participation in the economy.

This new emphasis on free enterprise has also affected the way privately owned industries operate. Until recently, the government closely watched privately owned businesses. Mexico's government once decided which resources a business might have and what types of products it might make. These rules have now been loosened.

The Mexican government has sold many industries to private citizens and companies. United States' businesses have invested in Mexico. **What is Mexico's most important natural resource?**

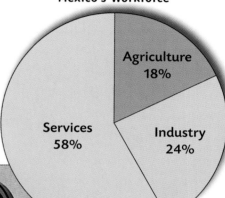

Mexico's Workforce

Agriculture 18%

Industry 24%

Services 58%

Compare this chart to the charts on pages 329 and 491. **How is Mexico's workforce different from that of the United Sates and Canada?**

Chapter 24

Caption Answer

More people in Mexico work in agriculture and fewer people work in services.

Industry

Early in the last century, Mexico's economy began to develop. An iron and steel plant in Monterrey was built. During the 1950s other factories were built, especially around Mexico City. Products such as textiles and glass were made. Goods made using Mexico's own oil have been important. Look at the pie chart on page 580. Today, about 24 percent of the workforce works in industry.

Mining is still important (see map, page 583). Iron, copper, and some less well-known minerals are mined as well. Mexico produces about 15 percent of the world's silver.

Oil is now the most important natural resource. Large deposits of natural gas and petroleum mean that Mexico has enough energy for now. Most of the oil and natural gas deposits are located along the coast of the Gulf of Mexico. Mexico's minerals are largely found in the northern parts of the country.

New Factories

The *maquiladora* (mah·kee·lah·DOH·rah) factories are one of Mexico's most important industrial activities. *Maquiladoras* assemble parts or raw materials that come from the United States. Products that are built here range from electronic equipment to clothing and furniture.

There are thousands of such plants on the Mexican side of the border. Before NAFTA, companies paid small fees to ship the finished goods back into the United States. NAFTA ended these fees. Goods and people steadily flow back and forth between border cities and the two nations.

There are more than 1 million people, mostly women, working in the *maquiladoras*. This is about one third of Mexico's industrial labor force.

These changes are part of globalization. This means that the economies of many countries are connected and depend on one another. But globalization brings challenges.

Just as jobs from the United States and North Carolina moved to Mexico, now jobs are leaving Mexico for other places, such as China.

Maquiladoras are slowly expanding southward into the heart of Mexico. Mexico's government and people hope that the foreign companies will build more than assembly plants. They would like to have factories that manufacture and assemble parts. This type of expansion has already taken place in the auto industry. Big car companies have built large manufacturing plants in Mexico.

Another key part of Mexico's economy is electronics. **What effect have the *maquiladoras* had on the border?**

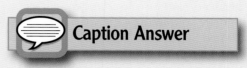

Discussion Questions

1 Today, where do most Mexicans live? What types of jobs do they have?

2 What are some of the industries in Mexico that were state-owned? Why?

Caption Answer

Good flow back and forth steadily across the border.

Activity

NAFTA Debate

OBJECTIVES: 5.01, 5.02, 5.05

Organize a class debate on the positive and negative aspects of NAFTA. Students should use newspapers and the Internet to find information to support their positions. A debate is a formal public argument for or against a proposal. The affirmative side supports the idea. The negative side opposes it. Both sides take part. The proposal must be stated in a positive way. It should be something that is debatable, is of interest to the audience, states only one problem, has clear wording, and suits the age of the debaters. Use the Guide to Student Debates in the Teacher's Edition

---

Background Information

Mexico and NAFTA

Since it took effect in 1994, NAFTA has sparked billions of dollars of United States investment in Mexico, especially in manufacturing. Larger Mexican companies and industries have benefited most from these changes, particularly businesses that export goods. Mexico sells roughly 85 percent of its exports to the United States.

Small and medium–size businesses have gained less. NAFTA agreements ended the protection these firms had from foreign competition. President Fox believed NAFTA would eventually allow for the free movement of people as well as goods and services across North American borders.

Discussion Questions

1 What sights in Mexico do tourists want to see?

2 What are some of the food crops and animals raised in Mexico?

3 What are some vegetables and fruit grown on large-scale commercial farms that are sold to the supermarkets of the United States and Canada?

Caption Answer

Ancient ruins, art, and music

Activity

Natural Resources

NATIONAL GEOGRAPHY STANDARDS: 1, 11, 16

GEOGRAPHIC THEMES: Human-Environmental Interaction

OBJECTIVES: 5.01, 5.04, 5.07

The object of this activity is to create a large replica of the map on page 583. Have the students research and present information related to the map.

Create a large blank map of Mexico on bulletin board paper or a shower curtain (a shower curtain map can be reused). After discussing Mexico's economic activities and resources, assign each student an economic activity or resource. Each student will research his or her assignment and create a short presentation.

The students who are assigned resources will make the appropriate number of symbols to place on the map. For example, there are five natural gas symbols shown on the map, so the student assigned to that resource would create five symbols to represent natural gas.

The students who are assigned an economic activity will color in the region on the map to represent their economic activity.

When all preparations are made, have the students make their presentations and place the symbols on the map.

Discuss the patterns of land use in the cities and rural areas. Analyze with the students how these places and regions may change over time.

Cancún's beaches are crowded year-round. **What are some of the other tourist attractions in Mexico?**

Tourism

Tourism is Mexico's third-largest industry. Mexico's beautiful beaches and climate are major attractions. Wintertime travelers from the United States and Canada visit resorts like Acapulco and the Yucatán Peninsula. The beaches of Cancún and Cozumel attract travelers from around the globe.

The wonders of ancient Native American cultures also attract tourists. The ruins of the ancient Aztec and Maya cultures in such places as Teotihuacán and Chichén Itzá also bring thousands of visitors to Mexico every year. People come to see the other unique cultures found in the country.

Farming

Mexican farming has a colonial heritage. About 18 percent of the population works in a job related to agriculture. Many of these people are small farmers. In the south corn is Mexico's leading crop (see map, page 583). Much of it is used to make tortillas. They are a part of most Mexican meals.

The cattle industry has also been important since the Spanish arrived. Most ranches are found in the north. Sheep and goats are raised in some of the higher elevations.

Large-scale commercial farming is also important in Mexico. Some of the crops feed the Mexican people. Most of it goes north. Much of the fresh vegetables and fruit on the shelves of supermarkets in the United States and Canada during the winter come from Mexico.

Much of this food enters the United States in air-cooled trucks through Nogales, Arizona. All of it is usually sold to supermarkets before it even arrives. When you have a tomato on your sandwich or salad this winter, it may have passed along this same route.

Mexico—Economic Activity and Resources

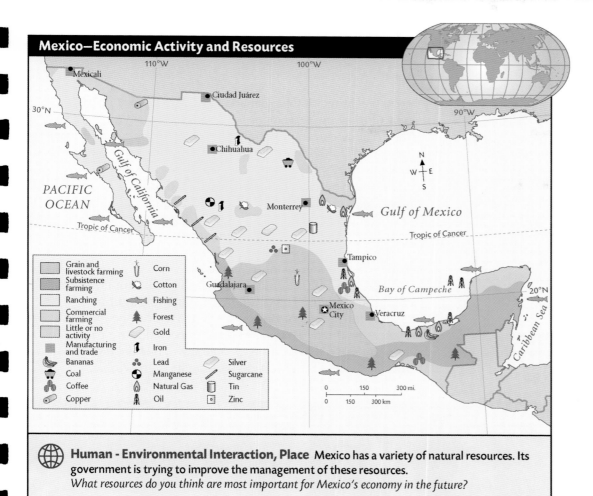

Human - Environmental Interaction, Place Mexico has a variety of natural resources. Its government is trying to improve the management of these resources.
What resources do you think are most important for Mexico's economy in the future?

LESSON **2** REVIEW

Fact Follow-Up
1. What industries were owned by the government after the Mexican Revolution?
2. What is Mexico's most important natural resource?
3. In what part of the country are Mexico's non-petroleum mineral resources mostly found?

Talk About It
1. Why did the Mexican government begin to sell state-owned industries?
2. How did NAFTA change the Mexican economy? Explain your answer.
3. Describe the *maquiladoras*.

Economy and Government

583

Caption Answer

Petroleum, iron, or silver are possible answers.

Math Activity

Time in Mexico

OBJECTIVES: 1.01, 1.02, 1.05

The city of Chihuahua, Mexico, is located in the Mountain Standard Time Zone. Show a map of the time zones and remind students that Chihuahua is one hour behind Central Standard Time and one hour ahead of Pacific Standard Time. To help students practice the time difference, give them some math problems such as the following:
- If you wake up at 6:00 A.M. in North Carolina, white time is it in Mexico? (4:00 A.M.)
- It is 1:00 P.M. in California; what time is it in Mexico? (2:00 P.M.)
- It is noon in Mexico; what time is it in Florida? (2:00 P.M.)
- It is 5:00 P.M. in Mexico; what is the time in Texas? (5:00 P.M.)

LESSON **2** REVIEW

Fact Follow-Up Answers
1. The government owned and managed the oil, telecommunications, electricity, mining, railroad, steel, and food processing industries.
2. Petroleum is Mexico's most important natural resource.
3. These resources are chiefly found in the northern parts of the country.

Talk About It Answers
1. Government leaders wanted to open trade and bring the Mexican economic system more in line with that of the United States.
2. Important points: Encourage students to suggest as many changes as possible. Among the possible changes are the following: more manufacturing jobs, movement of more jobs into the interior of Mexico, the possibility of fewer people leaving Mexico to find jobs, increasing pollution, stress on water resources.
3. *Maquiladoras* are factories in Mexico that assemble parts of raw materials from the United States into finished products.

Discussion Questions

1 Why did Mexico want to link its economy with that of the United States and Canada?

Caption Answer

Encourage Canadian and United States companies to build plants in Mexico, and encourage Mexican exports.

Reading Strategy Activity

Understanding Tone

OBJECTIVES: 4.07, 5.04, 5.06

The tone of a writer lets us know more about how that person feels about his or her subject. Even the people who write our textbooks have a tone in their writing.

As you read Lesson 3, have students make a list of all the words, phrases, or sentences that show the textbook author's tone toward his or her subject, the challenges facing Mexico. Sample words or phrases from pages 584 and 585 might include:
1. But only a few Mexican people profitted
2. the gap between those on the outside looking is is growing
3. unrest makes life difficult
4. neighborhoods have become dangerous and unhealthy
4. cities are overcrowded

After you have made a class list, discuss the tone of each of the words. What words could the author have chose that would have a similar meeting but a different tone?

LESSON 3 Challenges

KEY IDEAS

- Increased trade among the nations of North America helped improve Mexico's economy.
- The Mexican economy continues to reform.
- Many Mexicans are moving to the cities and to the United States to improve their lives.
- Mexico faces serious problems.

KEY TERMS

guerilla war

The United States, Canada, and Mexico signed an important agreement in 1993. It was called NAFTA. The Mexican government wanted to link its economy to those of the United States and Canada. Taxes on goods moving across the two borders are to be taken away by 2009.

The government's leaders believed that NAFTA would get companies from the United States and Canada to build plants in Mexico. They were right. The agreement also made it easier to export Mexico's products to its northern neighbors.

In these ways, NAFTA has helped the economy grow and provide jobs for a growing population.

This was not the first time that the Mexican government encouraged growth. The *caudillo* Díaz had brought new industries into Mexico. But only a few Mexican people and foreigners profited. The government expected more people to benefit under NAFTA. Many people have, but the gap between them and those on the outside looking in is growing.

North American leaders (standing) Carlos Salinas, George H.W. Bush, and Brian Mulroney sign the North American Free Trade Agreement in 1992. **What did they hope NAFTA would accomplish?**

Chapter 24

Teacher Notes

NAFTA

Evaluating NAFTA is difficult because one can apply a variety of criteria and thus can come to numerous conclusions. There are those who claim, for example, that the remarkable expansion of the United States economy after 1994 was due, at least in part, to the NAFTA agreement. Others are less positive about its effects. Certainly, at first glance it is easy to say that Mexico and the

wealthiest major United States companies such as General Motors and the former Burlington Industries (with plants now in Mexico) have received the most benefit from the agreement. On the other hand, it may appear that the American job market has suffered the greatest loss. Along with the moving plants and jobs to Mexico, however, comes the creation of a much larger Mexican middle class market demanding a host of consumer goods. Unfortunately, those consumer goods—particularly electronics— are produced primarily in Asia, rather than in the United States.

Ciudad is one of Mexico's growing cities. **How has Mexico's economy changed since NAFTA?**

Movement

Great numbers of people are moving away from the Mexican countryside. People leave rural areas because pay is low and work is scarce. Healthcare and education can also be hard to find in the country.

In some places political unrest makes life difficult. They hope to find in a city all of the things that are missing in rural communities.

Migration to the Cities

Mexico's cities do not have enough resources to provide for everyone. Mexico City is one of the world's largest 20 cities. It does not have enough places for newcomers to live.

Water and electric services cannot be built fast enough to keep up with its growing population. Smoke and exhaust fumes have polluted the air. Many of the city's neighborhoods have become dangerous and unhealthy places to live.

At least 71 percent of Mexico's people live in cities today. Guadalajara and Puebla are growing rapidly. The border cities of Ciudad Juárez and Monterrey each have more than 1 million residents. All of these cities are overcrowded.

WORD ORIGINS

Every day of the year more than two thousand Mexican people pack up their belongings. They move to Mexico City in search of a better life. Mexico City dwellers call them *paracaidistas* (pah·rah·cay·DEES·tahs), or "parachutists." There are so many people arriving in Mexico City every day that they just seem to fall out of the sky.

Economy and Government

585

Discussion Questions

1 Why are so many people moving from the Mexican countryside to the cities?

2 What problems do the cities face because of their growing populations?

3 Why can't the manufacturing plants be easily moved from the cities to smaller towns?

 Caption Answer

Industry was privatized.

 Activity

Houses in Mexico

 **OBJECTIVES:** 1.07, 2.08, 4.07

Although some ranch-style homes are found in certain areas of Mexico today, ranch style is not the predominant house style of the country. There are common characteristics in most buildings. Many homes are built with a courtyard or patio surrounded by a wall. Few houses in Mexico are built of wood. Other materials are used. Adobe, or mud bricks are customary for walls and roofs, and now concrete blocks are replacing adobe bricks. Thatch, a type of straw made from maize, is a roofing material used in some villages, and bamboo or palm is used in others.

Explain how this is an example of human-environmental interaction. How are adobe bricks beneficial in the hot climate? thatch? palm? bamboo?

How are the houses in the area where you live another example of human-environmental interaction?

Discussion Questions

1 Why are immigrants coming to the United States?

2 How much of Mexico's water is undrinkable?

3 What is one solution President Fox has for Mexico's water pollution problem?

4 What are push factors? What are pull factors?

5 For how many years do Mexican children attend school?

 **Caption Answer**

Answers will vary

 **Activity**

Make a Passport

 OBJECTIVES: 1.06, 3.04, 3.06

Using the Passport pattern in the Teacher's Resource Guide, have students design their own passport. Discuss how passports are used and why. Visit **NCJourneys.com** for a link to the State Department's passport information Web site.

 **Caption Answer**

Jobs, higher-pay, access to healthcare, quality of life, opportunity, political freedom

Migrant farmworkers load watermelons in Mississippi. **Who would harvest crops in the United States if the migrant farmers stayed in Mexico?**

Push and Pull Factors of Immigration

UNITED STATES

PULL
- Jobs
- Higher pay
- Access to healthcare
- Quality of life
- Opportunity
- Political freedom

PUSH
- Poverty
- Unemployment
- Lack of opportunity
- Insecurity
- political oppresssion

MEXICO

Push factors are things that might influence a person to emigrate, or leave, their country. Pull factors are things that attract a person to move to a particular country. Immigrants weigh the costs and benefits of all these factors when they make a decision to move. **What pull factors attract Mexican immigrants to North Carolina?**

Moving to the United States

People move to the United States for the same reasons that some others move to Mexico's cities. Some Mexicans come to the United States to make it their permanent home. Others come only at certain times of the year to work during harvests.

Still others commute every day between the towns on the border. Mexicans enter the United States because they can't make enough money in Mexico to support a family.

Mexicans who come to work in the United States usually send money home each month to Mexico. The sacrifices made by the workers help improve the lives of their families back home.

586

Chapter 24

Going to School in Mexico

In Mexico, all children between the ages of five to fifteen must attend school. They go to school from first grade to ninth grade. Just like students in most American schools, Mexican children must pass tests.

At the age of eleven, students must pass the *Certificado de Educación Primaria* (Primary Certificate) exam. It is a national test. Then the student goes on to one of two different schools for three more years. One school prepares students to go on to college. The other prepares students to work in a trade. They study to be nurses, mechanics, secretaries, or other jobs.

In rural areas students attend these schools by watching lessons on TV. It is called *Telesecondaria*.

At sixteen, students who want to go to college or have a special trade go to school for another three years.

Mexico's school systems face many challenges. About 15 percent of children do not go to school. The federal government funds the schools. But schools in rural areas do not have as many resources as schools in the cities. Many people move to cities so their children can go to better schools.

Private schools are better than public schools. Families that can afford it send their children to private schools. They get a better education and can get better jobs.

Mexico continues to improve it schools. More people in Mexico can read than ever before. This attracts more high-tech and other businesses to Mexico.

Mexican classroom

The Environment

Mexico's environment is being affected by the nation's rapid growth.

Water Pollution

Mexico has a problem with water pollution. This is true not only in the cities. It is also true in the country. The government of Mexico calls this problem one of "national security."

More than 12 million Mexicans have problems getting safe drinking water. Almost 75 percent of Mexico's water is unsafe to drink. Farms and cattle ranches receive their water free of charge. So do the mines.

Deforestation

Mexico's shrinking forests are also part of the "national security" problem. Trees help hold the soil in place during rainstorms. When many trees are cut, soil washes away. Farmland is ruined. This abuse of the land means even more people are being forced to move to the cities and the United States. When people cannot farm their land they must move to find work.

Some people in Mexico cut trees illegally. The Mexican government says that people cutting the trees threaten violence or actually fight if someone tries to stop them. That makes other people afraid to try.

Discussion Questions

1 Why has the cutting of too many trees become a "national security issue"?

2 What does the government intend to do about the deforestation of Mexico?

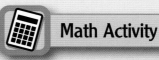
Math Activity

Deforestation

 OBJECTIVES: 1.06, 5.02

In countries that use the metric system, large tracts of land are often measured in *hectares*. A *hectare* is the area equivalent to 10,000 square meters, or 2.47 acres. Between the years 1993 and 2000, about 8 million hectares of Mexican forests were lost. (An area about the size of Ireland). That means that the forest is being destroyed at a rate of about 1.1 million hectares per year. At that rate, how many hectares would, on average, be destroyed in a single day?
1,100,000 ÷ 365 = 3,013 hectares (7410 acres or 11.5 sq m) per day.

Extension Assist ELL students by setting up the problem for them.

Background Information

Pollution Problems Along the Border

Some of Mexico's major air and water pollution problems are along the United States-Mexico border, where more than 10 million people live on both sides. The Rio Grande, which provides water for many communities in both countries, has often been used by Mexican cities as a dump site for human and industrial waste. Mexican cities along the border have begun building local sewage treatment plants using funds set aside by NAFTA side accords to solve air and water pollution problems. One major source of air pollution in this area is the coal-fired electricity plants in northern Mexico. Smog from these plants often moves north to settle over Big Bend National Park in Texas

Discussion Questions

1 Why did some Native Americans of Chiapas protest NAFTA?

2 By what name were they called?

3 What happened to the uprising?

 Caption Answer

Their community-owned land is being privatized.

 Activity

Who are the Zapatistas?

 OBJECTIVES: 1.06, 1.07, 3.06

Have students research the Zapatista movement with specific emphasis on one of the following figures:

- Subcomandante Marcos
- Francisco Madero
- Venustiano Carranza
- Francisco Villa
- Alvaro Obregón
- Emiliano Zapata

As an extension, consider showing a clip from the Hollywood bio-pic *Viva Zapata!* starring Marlon Brando.

This group of Zapatista supporters in Chiapas are protesting Mexico's federal government. **Why are the Zapatistas against NAFTA?**

The Zapatista National Liberation Army

On January 1, 1994, NAFTA went into effect. On that same day, a radical group of Maya farmers began a **guerrilla war** against the Mexican government. They named their group after Emiliano Zapata, the hero of the Mexican Revolution and of Native Americans in Mexico.

They wore masks to hide their faces and protect their families. The Zapatistas protested the parts of NAFTA that they believed threatened the land reform promised by the Constitution of 1917 and the Mexican Revolution. They were also worried about self-government and the survival of their Native American culture.

The Mexican army reacted swiftly to the uprising. The rebels were driven back into the forests.

The Zapatistas, who are mainly from Chiapas, are concerned that the poorest parts of the country are being left out by NAFTA's free trade reforms. The rebels fear losing control of their traditional, community-owned lands through privatization. Their spokesman, Subcomandante Marcos, has delivered many speeches and messages to Mexico and the world pleading for greater respect for the civil and human rights of Native American people.

What would YOU do?

In January of 1994 hundreds of armed guerrillas took over a small town in southeastern Mexico. They claimed that the Mexican government had ignored the region's extreme poverty. Imagine you are either the leader of the guerrillas or in the Mexican government. How would you have handled the conflict? Why?

A Journey to MEXICO CITY

Dealing with Population and Pollution

Mexico City is one of the fastest-growing cities in the world. The city's population is growing so fast that utility companies have to ration water and electricity.

Water and power to one area of the city are sometimes shut off. This allows water and power service to flow to another area. Most people save jugs of water to use when water service is cut off to their area. Even when the water does come out of the tap, it often comes out at a trickle instead of a stream. Filling the jugs takes a long time.

The Mexican author Carlos Fuentes wrote a book about Mexico City. Fuentes describes polluted air that can stay trapped over the city for days. It is not uncommon for pollution to be so bad that people can see only halfway across the city.

The snowcapped volcano Popocatepetl (po·po·CAH·teh·pet·l) is often hidden by smog. On really bad days the air begins to leave a taste in your mouth like metal. Breathing it for extended periods of time can cause headaches and chest pains for some people.

LESSON 3 REVIEW

Fact Follow-Up
1. What three nations signed the NAFTA treaty?
2. Why did Mexico want NAFTA?
3. Why are Mexican people moving from the countryside to cities?

Talk About It
1. Why does the Mexican government describe problems of water pollution and cutting too many trees as a threat to "national security"?
2. What did the Zapatistas want? Why were they worried about NAFTA?

Economy and Government

589

LESSON 3 REVIEW

Fact Follow-Up Answers
1. Canada, the United States, and Mexico signed the treaty.
2. Mexicans believed the agreement would encourage United States and Canadian firms to build factories in Mexico. Also, it would be easier to export Mexican products to the United States and Canada.
3. People leave rural areas because pay is low, work is scarce, health and educational services are poor, and in some places political disorders threaten lives.

Talk About It Answers
1. The government calls them "national security problems" because they are such severe problems, and they threaten the health and safety of the Mexican people.
2. The Zapatistas took Zapata's name because he was a great hero to poor people and is remembered today. The Zapatistas fear that the benefits of NAFTA will not reach all Mexicans and that land reform will be threatened by privatization.

Teaching This Skill Lesson

Materials Needed textbooks, paper, pencils

Classroom Organization whole class, individual, small groups

Beginning the Lesson Ask "When has Mexico's government been most democratic?" Accept all responses. Next, ask "Are you sure you are right?" Probe students' responses.

Lesson Development Tell students they will be reviewing and recording information from Chapter 24 about Mexico's economic and political development and making a chart so they can give better answers to the questions you have just asked. Place students in pairs to complete a chart such as the one in the Skill Lesson. One member of the pair is to focus on government; the other, on economic development.

Conclusion Allow students to compare completed charts in small groups before you conduct a general class discussion around questions such as those posed in the Skill Lesson. Post charts in the classroom.

Analyzing, Interpreting, Creating, and Using Resources and Materials

Studying Mexico's Economic and Political Development

Mexico has been an independent country for nearly 200 years. In that time there have been many changes in government. Let's look at the relationship between the kind of government Mexico has had and how well its economy works.

Government and the Economy in Mexico		
Government	**Dates**	**Economic Development**

To help you answer this question, you will need to compare different periods in Mexican history. A chart like the one shown above will help you do this. You will need to make some notes on two kinds of information before you make the chart.

1. What are the different governments that have been in power since the country became independent?
2. What economic changes have taken place in Mexico since independence?

Remember to note specific dates whenever you can. Dates are convenient "hooks" for hanging ideas on. You will notice that the middle column of the chart on this page has spaces for dates and time periods.

Your notes will give you the information you need to complete the chart. You can think about questions such as these:

590

 Skill Lesson Review

1. Was it easier to find information about government or economic development? *Accept student responses, probing for reasons. It is likely that students found it easier to find information about government.*

2. How important was the "Dates" column in the chart? *Encourage students' responses, noting the importance of linking governments with economic development for comparison purposes.*

- When has Mexico's government been most democratic?
- When has Mexico's economy been strongest? When has it been the weakest?
- Which groups in Mexico have generally held political power?
- Have the people in power in government generally been wealthier than other Mexicans?
- At what times have poorer people benefited most?
- Finally, is there a relationship between Mexico's government and how well its economy works?

Palacio de Bellas Artes, Mexico City

Economy and Government

591

Talk About It

1. Among possible answers are these: The Spanish had occupied Mexico for longer (roughly 1500–1800) than the British occupied the colonies that became the United States; in the British colonies, colonial assemblies gave colonists opportunities for some limited self-government whereas Mexico had no such experience. For Spain, Mexico was an extremely valuable colony with rich deposits of precious metals. British North America had no such wealth. Spain systematically stripped Mexico of this wealth; in British North America the colonies fairly early developed their own independent economies.

2. Important points: Encourage student responses. Among the possible reasons are: there was no tradition of local self-government in Mexico; many *caudillos* had at one time been honored military leaders and thus were popular at least in the beginning; and the alliance between the *caudillos* and *hacienda* owners helped the *caudillos* remain in power.

3. Important points: Encourage students to speculate as to reasons. Among the reasons: Producing goods from start to finish will create more jobs than just assembling them.

4. Important points: Students should choose either government or the economy and explain their choice. Government changes include revolution, internal warfare, constitutional government, a long period of single-party (PRI) rule, an uprising of Native Americans in southern Mexico, and the victory of the National Action Party in 2000. Economic changes include a massive movement to the cities, movement of jobs from ranching and farming to manufacturing; movement from state-owned to privately owned businesses; the growth of foreign investment; and the signing of NAFTA.

5. Important points: Encourage students to name challenges facing Mexico, choose one to solve, and explain their choice. Among the challenges: migration to the cities, migration out of Mexico, water pollution, deforestation, air pollution, and the challenge of the Zapatistas.

CHAPTER 24 REVIEW

Lessons Learned

LESSON 1
From Colony to Nation
Mexicans won their independence from Spain in 1821. Their constitution provided free public education and land reform. It also provided for fair wages and health care. Strong leaders ruled Mexico after the revolution. A single party has remained in power during most of the time since the revolution.

LESSON 2
The Economy
The Mexican government controlled chief industries after the revolution. Now Mexico's businesses belong to individuals or companies. *Maquiladoras* form the most important part of Mexico's industry today. Farming and tourism also continue to be important parts of Mexico's economy.

LESSON 3
Challenges
NAFTA has generally improved the Mexican economy by making trade easier and less expensive. Mexico must now improve its environment. The problems of overcrowding and pollution are important challenges for Mexico today.

592

Talk About It

1. In earlier chapters you read that the United States after its revolution against Great Britain successfully developed democratic institutions that worked fairly well. Why do you think Mexico's revolution against Spain did not have the same results?
2. Why do you think the *caudillo* system lasted so long in Mexico?
3. Maquiladoras provide employment for many Mexican workers. Why do many Mexicans want to produce goods from start to finish rather than assemble products in the maquiladoras?
4. Which do you think changed more during the twentieth century: the Mexican economy or the Mexican government? Explain your answer.
5. If you could solve one of the problems facing Mexico today, which would you choose? Explain why.

Mastering Mapwork

LOCATION
Use the map on page 583 to answer these questions:
1. Which economic activity is more widely practiced: ranching or family farming?
2. What economic activities and resources are located nearest Guadalajara?
3. What economic activities and resources are located nearest Mexico City?

Becoming Better Readers

Using Literature Techniques
Good readers recognize genre and theme when they are reading. Social studies books usually are one genre: nonfiction. A technique you can use to help you understand what you are reading is to read as though your book were a story that is unfolding. It is! Write a story about Father Miguel Hidalgo. Use factual information to tell your story.

Chapter 24

Mastering Mapwork

1. Ranching is more widely practiced.
2. Guadalajara lies in an area of manufacturing and trade surrounded by grain and livestock farming. There are forests and silver resources nearby.
3. Mexico City lies in an area of manufacturing and trade surrounded by grain and livestock farming. Silver, forests, oil and natural gas are available near Mexico City.

Becoming Better Readers

Important points: students should have a story with a beginning, middle and end. The story should use facts mentioned in the textbook about Father Miquel Hidalgo.

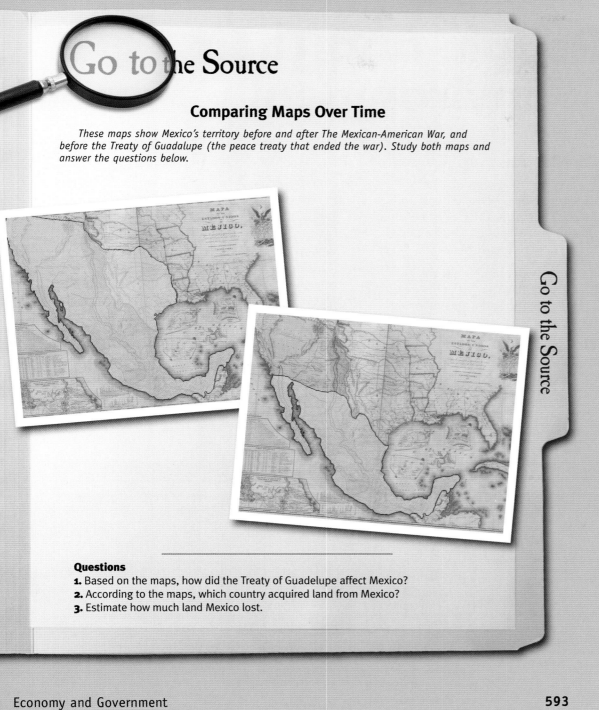

Go to the Source

Comparing Maps Over Time

These maps show Mexico's territory before and after The Mexican-American War, and before the Treaty of Guadalupe (the peace treaty that ended the war). Study both maps and answer the questions below.

Go to the Source

Questions
1. Based on the maps, how did the Treaty of Guadelupe affect Mexico?
2. According to the maps, which country acquired land from Mexico?
3. Estimate how much land Mexico lost.

Go to the Source

Comparing Maps Over Time

OBJECTIVES: 1.07
SOCIAL STUDIES SKILLS: 3.01, 3.05

The Treaty of Guadalupe
The Treaty of Guadalupe Hidalgo ended the Mexican-American War. Under it, Mexico ceded 1.36 million km² (525,000 square miles) to the United States in exchange for $15 million. The United States also took over $3.25 million in debts Mexico owed to American citizens.

The land shown on the map includes: parts of Colorado, Arizona, New Mexico, and Wyoming, and all of California, Nevada, and Utah. The remaining parts of what are today the states of Arizona and New Mexico were later ceded under the 1853 Gadsden Purchase.

Answers
1. Mexico lost a large portion of land and became a smaller country
2. The United States
3. Mexico lost about half of its land.

Economy and Government

How to Use the Chapter Review

There are four sections in the Chapter Review: Talk About It, Mastering Mapwork, Becoming Better Readers, and Go to the Source. Use the Vocabulary Worksheets and the Chapter Review Worksheet in the Teacher's Resource Guide for additional reinforcement and preparation for the Chapter Assessments. The Chapter and Lesson Reviews and the Chapter Review Worksheets are the basis of the assessment for each chapter.

Talk About It questions encourage students to speculate about the content of the chapter and are suitable for class or small-group discussion. They are not intended to be assigned for homework.

Mastering Mapwork has students apply one or more of the Five Themes of Geography to maps within the chapter.

Becoming Better Readers focuses on building reading strategy skills necessary for reading comprehension in the content areas.

Go to the Source activities allow students to analyze a primary source that relates to the content of the chapter. The questions and activities familiarize students with different types of primary sources and also build content-reading skills.

People and Their Environment

Social Studies Strands

Cultures and Diversity

Economics and Development

Global Connection

Individual Developments and Identity

North Carolina Standard Course of Study

Goal 2 The learner will analyze political and social institutions in North America and examine how these institutions respond to human needs, structure society, and influence behavior.

Goal 3 The learner will examine the roles various ethnic groups have played in the development of the United States and its neighboring countries.

Goal 6 The learner will recognize how technology has influenced change within the United States and other countries in North America.

Teaching & Assessment

- English Language Learner Modified Lesson Plans for this chapter are found in the Teacher's Resource Guide.

- *ExamView® Assessment Suite* is provided at **NCJourneys.com.** It includes customizable assessments for all chapters. Paper tests are also available in the Teacher's Resource Guide. See pages T16–T17 for information about how to use the assessments and the Scoring Guide.

Worksheets

Worksheets and answer keys are found both in the Teacher's Resource Guide and at **NCJourneys.com**, including Reading Guides, Reading Strategies, Chapter Reviews, English Language Learner and others.

Activities and Integrations

SOCIAL STUDIES	
● Balloon Burst Relay, p. 594B	
Mexico Population Density, p. 597	
★ Cultural Research: Mexico, p. 599	
Holiday Crossover, p. 600	
Literature Connection, p. 603	
Culture Collage, p. 610	
▲ ■ Skill Lesson: What is "Mexican Culture?," p. 612	

READING/LANGUAGE ARTS	READING/LANGUAGE ARTS OBJECTIVES
Interviews, p. 594B	3.01, 4.03
Problem Based Learning: Cultural Understanding, p. 594B	2.02, 3.07
▲ ■ Activator: Mexican Travel Magazines, p. 594	4.09
▲ ■ Writing Prompt: Music, Our Lady of Guadalupe, p. 594	4.09
Reading Strategy: Types of Resource Material, p. 596	2.06, 3.02
● Reading Strategy: Using Print Materials, p. 602	2.06
★ ■ Celebrations in Mexico, p. 604	3.02, 3.06
El Dia de los Muertos, p. 605	3.02
● Reading Strategy: Using the Internet, p. 607	2.02
Becoming Better Readers, p. 614	2.01
Reading Newspaper Articles, p. 615	2.05, 2.07

MATHEMATICS	MATHEMATICS OBJECTIVES
Mexico: Predominant Ethnic Groups, p. 595	1.02

SCIENCE	SCIENCE OBJECTIVES
Making a Butterfly Garden, p. 601	1.05, 1.06

TECHNOLOGY	TECHNOLOGY OBJECTIVES
Guanajuato, p. 598	2.13

VISUAL ARTS	VISUAL ARTS OBJECTIVES
▲ ■ Novel Neckties, p. 594B	3.02
Activator: Mexican Travel Magazines, p. 594	2.01
Carolina Connection: Native American Artifacts, p. 595	5.01, 5.03, 5.04
Musicana, p. 600	1.01, 5.03
Mariachi Time, p. 607	2.06, 6.07
● ▲ ■ Cultural Poster, p. 611	2.01, 5.03
Making Murals, p. 609	2.01, 3.02

CHARACTER AND VALUES EDUCATION	TRAITS
What Would You Do?, p. 604	good citizenship
★ Missions, p. 603	good citizenship

● Basic Activities   ★ Challenging Activities   ▲ English Language Learner Novice   ■ English Language Learner Intermediate

Introductory Activity

Balloon Burst Relay

 **OBJECTIVES:** 3.04, 3.06, 3.07

Develop a list of vocabulary words from this chapter and give it to students. Have students define the words. Provide 10 minutes during one class for students to practice the words and definitions. Draw up a set of questions and multiple-choice answers based on the vocabulary list, and make two copies. Cut apart the questions and answers, keeping the multiple-choice answers with their questions, and insert each question and its answer into a balloon. Blow up the balloons, tie the ends, and put the balloons in large trash bags, keeping the two sets separate. Tell students in advance that they will be running a relay race and will need to wear long pants so the bursting balloons will not sting their legs.

On the day of the relay, divide the class into two groups. Set out two chairs. This could be played outdoors or in a large, empty room. Have the teams line up, beginning about 20 feet (6 m) from the chairs, and give each child a balloon. Stand between the chairs. When you yell "Go!" the first students in line are to run with their balloon to the chairs in front of the team, sit on the balloons, and burst them. The first student to pop his or her balloon reads the question out loud for all the students to hear and chooses one of the multiple-choice answers. If the answer is incorrect, the student from the other team reads his or her question and answer. After students give the correct answers, the next in line run to the chairs and repeat the process. The first team that finishes wins.

If a student is not wearing long pants or does not want to burst the balloon, another teammate can sit on the balloon, but after the balloon bursts the student must read and answer the question without help from the teammate.

 ## Culminating Activity

Interviews

OBJECTIVES: 1.07, 2.08, 4.01

Divide the class into pairs. Each pair is to create an interview, with both questions and answers, of a famous person from Mexican history. Interviews must consist of at least ten questions and answers and should leave the class with a solid understanding of who this person was and why he or she is significant to the study of Mexico. Interviews should be performed for the class, with costumes and props.

Art Activity

Novel Neckties

OBJECTIVES: 1.07, 2.08, 3.04

Tell students: "You have just returned from a trip to Mexico, and brought back a special souvenir necktie for your favorite uncle. You were very careful to select one that would teach him as much as possible about Mexico."

Then have students design souvenir ties on folded strips of white construction paper, about 30 inches by 4 inches. Have them sketch pictures, symbols, flags, or anything else about Mexico using colorful markers to color in the illustrations. Display on a bulletin board.

 ## Problem Based Learning Activity

Cultural Understanding

OBJECTIVES: 3.04, 3.06, 3.07

Situation Have students pretend that they have been asked to develop a cultural center for Mexican immigrants who have moved into their community. After reading Chapter 25, reflect as a class upon what makes up Mexican culture. Use the book as a guide and then brainstorm. Help students categorize the cultural information into groups, such as:

music	the arts
literature	sports
festivals	recreation time
food	

Task Divide students into small groups and assign each group one cultural area. They are to research the importance of their area of culture to Mexico and consider ways to introduce these same items into the local Mexican community in North Carolina. Students will present their research and ideas to the class. They must include a discussion about why it is important for people to participate and enjoy their native culture. What might be the consequence in the local community as a result of a different culture being introduced? Discuss this with students, and consider education programs for the local community about Mexican culture. What would be important to share, and why might this be beneficial?

Reflection Ask students to reflect upon their own culture. What does culture do for a person, and what would it feel like if everything you knew about culture were to be taken away? How might that affect a group of people? What might be the consequences of those feelings?

Teaching Strategies

It is important to allot ample time to the study of this chapter because it will help build pride and self-esteem in many of your students with Mexican ancestry.

Plan a Mexican Culture Day where students can display projects, foods, and dress that they have learned about during research.

Discussion Questions

1 What are the names of some of the holidays (festivals) that Mexicans celebrate?

Activator

OBJECTIVES: 3.04, 3.06, 3.07

Mexican Travel Magazines Bring in travel magazines for examples and share them with the class. Have students choose a particular region of Mexico. They are to write a paragraph for a travel magazine encouraging people to visit the area of their choice. Tell them to make their place as inviting as possible. Students could draw a picture to illustrate the paragraph.

Writing Prompt

OBJECTIVES: 3.07

Response to music Listen to some music from Mexico. While you are listening, write words that describe how you feel. Write the words randomly all around your paper. Illustrate your words and display them with your classmates' papers.

Creative writing Read the story of the Virgin of Guadalupe in this chapter. Discuss with your classmates the characters, setting, and plot. Either alone or with a group, create a story about a person who tries to get someone to do something for him/her (like the building of the church in the story). What magical means could the person use?

CHAPTER

25

"Little burro" piñata

Culture and Society

Festivals are a big part of Mexican culture. Each town has a holiday each year to honor its patron saint. Mexicans celebrate Easter and Christmas as Christians do in the United States.

There are some other holidays that Mexicans celebrate. The Day of the Dead and the Day of the Virgin of Guadalupe (gwah·deh·LOO·pay) are special. There is also Cinco de Mayo and Independence Day. Holidays are both serious and joyful. They can include fireworks and live music.

People like to dance and eat on Mexican holidays. There are often religious ceremonies, too. People in the country celebrate in more traditional ways. Native American customs are often part of the festivities. Celebrations in the cities are more modern.

Chapter Preview

LESSON 1
A Tale of Three Cities
Mexico City, Acapulco, and Monterrey are exciting cities. They show the variety of Mexico today.

LESSON 2
Tradition and Religion in Mexico
Most Mexicans are Roman Catholic. Many Native Americans still keep their own religious traditions.

LESSON 3
Culture in Mexico
Music and art are important to Mexican culture. Soccer and baseball are popular sports.

Worshippers carry a picture of Our Lady of Guadalupe in Chiapas.

594

Chapter Resources

Print Resources

Fiction

Coburn, Jewell Reinhart. *Domitila: A Cinderella Tale from the Mexican Tradition.* Shen's Books, 2000. ISBN 1885008139.

Soto, Gary. *Chato's Kitchen.* Paper Star, 1997, ISBN 0698116003.

Nonfiction

Ancona, George. *El piZatero/The PiZata Maker.* Harcourt, 1994. ISBN 0152000607.

Frazier, Nancy. *Frida Kahlo: Mysterious*

Painter (The Library of Famous Women series). Blackbirch Marketing, 1994. ISBN 1567110126.

Gedes, Bruce and Paloma Garcia. *Lonely Planet World Food: Mexico.* Lonely Planet, 2000. ISBN 1864500239.

Barbash, Shepard. *Oaxacan Woodcarving: The Magic in the Trees.* Chronicle Books, 1993. ISBN 0811802507.

Trenchard, Kathleen. *Mexican Papercutting: Simple Techniques for Creating Colorful Cut-Paper Projects.* Lark Books, 1998.

Mexico—Predominant Ethnic Groups

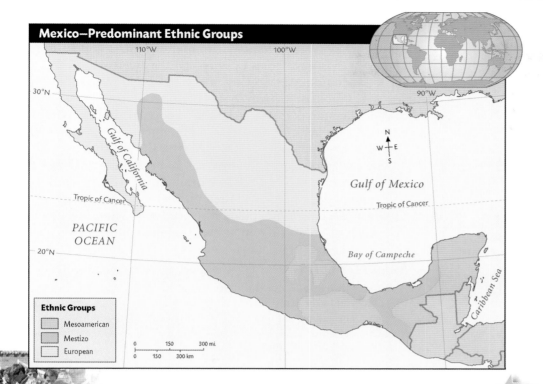

Ethnic Groups
- Mesoamerican
- Mestizo
- European

0   150   300 mi.
0   150   300 km

Native American Artifacts

The largest museums in North Carolina have art and artifacts from the Maya and Aztec cultures. These works show the importance of nature to the Native Americans of the time.

Works of art tell the tales of the people who made them. They are important primary resources.

Art made today about people and places long ago are also important. They **tell stories**, too. But the artists were not there when what they painted or sculpted happened. So these are secondary sources.

Exhibits of modern works of art by Latin American painters and sculptors can also help us understand Latin America.

CAROLINA CONNECTION

595

Map Activity

Mexico—Predominant Ethnic Groups

OBJECTIVES: 2.08, 3.04, 4.07

Provide the students with almanacs or visit the *CIA World Factbook* online (visit **NCJourneys.com** for links).

Have students look up Mexico and then Ethnic Groups. They can then collaborate with a partner or in small groups to come up with a creative way to show the different ethnic groups in percentages or fractions. For example, students could demonstrate the total ethnic population using dried beans in a narrow clear glass container: 60 pinto beans (for 60 percent Mexican), 30 black beans (for 30 percent Amerindian), 9 lima beans (for 9 percent white), and 1 red bean (for 1 percent other). Try to leave your directions to the class open-ended so students can come up with their own ideas.

After the students have created their representations, have them share and discuss them with their classmates.

Ask students why they think these ethnic regions are relatively uncomplicated and uninterrupted. Compare Mexico's ethnic diversity with the United States.

Activity

Carolina Connection: Native American Artifacts

OBJECTIVES: 3.07, 6.04

Visit **NCJourneys.com** for links to Web sites of museums in North Carolina with Native American artifacts. The links include the North Carolina Museum of Art, the Mint Museum of Art and the Duke University Museum of Art.

You may view examples of art from Latin America with your class. Also, you may contact the museums' education staff via the Web sites for additional programs.

ISBN 1579900119.
Behrens, June. *Fiesta!* (Special Holiday Books). Children's Press, 1988. ISBN 0516488155

Audiovisual

Food for the Ancestors. PBS Video. (Day of the Dead and Mexican foods).

Web Sites

Visit **NCJourneys.com** for links to these Web sites:

- Discovery Channel lesson plan for Mexican holidays
- *Food for the Ancestors* companion Web site
- Friday and Friends: A Prospectus of the Mexican Family through Children's Literature
- Mexico—Language, Culture, Customs and Etiquette
- The Virtual Diego Rivera Web Museum

OBJECTIVES: 1.02, 1.06, 3.04, 3.06

Caption Answer

Museums of anthropology, medicine, and art, or one dedicated to the revolution.

Reading Strategy Activity

Types of Resource Material

OBJECTIVES: 1.02, 1.06, 3.04, 3.06

Use the following example:

What if your best friend told you he was moving to Hyde County. Do you know how far away he or she will be from you? If you don't know the location of Hyde County, what book would you look in to find it?

There are several different types of research materials that can be found in the library. If readers know what these materials contain and how to use them, they can find the answers to many of the questions you may have.

Bring in examples of references in the table below as they are taught. Use the Types of Resource Materials worksheet in the Teacher's Resource Guide to practice this skill.

Textbook References

The **table of contents** is located at the beginning of textbooks. It is a list of the units, chapters, and page numbers of the book.

Textbooks, along with other books, have a section at the back of the book called the **Appendix**. It contains a small atlas, a dictionary of geographic terms, a gazetteer (an alphabetical list of geographical names), and other items.

Most texts have a **glossary** located at the back. The glossary listed alphabetically is a small dictionary giving meanings of words used in the text.

An **index** is another list located at the back of the book. It has topics found in the book and the page numbers where they are located.

LESSON 1 A Tale of Three Cities

KEY IDEAS

- Mexico City is the capital of the country. It mixes ancient and colonial cultures with modern ways.
- Acapulco was once an important port. Now tourists enjoy the city.
- Monterrey is the third-largest city in Mexico. It is an important manufacturing center.

KEY TERMS

El D.F.

Mexico City is home to over 25 million people. **What are some of the museums you can visit in Mexico City?**

Mexico is a country with many cultures and customs. It has huge areas of open space as well as growing cities. Mexico City is rich in ancient history. But it also has a modern subway system.

Acapulco (ah·kah·POOL·koh) is a popular tourist spot. It has beautiful beaches and exciting entertainment. The daring Cliff Divers of La Quebrada (lah keh·BRAH·dah) are famous.

The very modern Lighthouse of Commerce is in Monterrey. It shines its gleaming green laser beam out across the city.

Regional differences are often distinct in Mexico. Mexico City is in the center. Acapulco is in the west. Monterrey is in the east. Each offers its own individual flavors and lifestyles.

Mexico City

Most Mexicans do not call their capital Mexico City. They call it *"El D.F."* (ehl day effe). That is short for Federal District. This is similar to Americans calling our capital "D.C." for District of Columbia. Mexicans sometimes call the capital simply Mexico. Mexicans refer to their country as "the Republic."

Old and New

Mexico City was built on the ruins of the Aztec city Tenochtitlán. When the Spanish conquerors arrived there, they smashed almost every piece of Aztec culture. They even drained the lakes and filled them in. But visitors can still see signs of Aztec culture in the city today.

The Plaza of Three Cultures shows this history. Here are the ruins of the Aztec village of Tlatelolco. There are also Spanish colonial churches

596

Chapter 25

Reference Material	Definition	Can Be Used to Find
atlas	collection of many kinds of maps	location, boundaries, climate, land formations, population, and more
almanac	a book of facts published yearly	national and state information (resources, government), population, and events of the year
dictionary	alphabetical listing of words, pronunciation, and meaning	spelling, pronunciation, word derivations, grammar
encyclopedia	collection of information on many topics, sometimes published in several volumes	information about people, history, ideas, inventions, and events
magazine	a short collection of essays, usually with photos	articles on people, events, and ideas

WORD ORIGINS

Plaza in Spanish means simply "place." But in Mexico the plaza is the center of activity. People gather in the plaza daily to sell goods and just be together in a shared space.

and a modern high-rise apartment building. Ancient and colonial houses are still used in modern Mexico.

People visit the Floating Gardens of Xochimilco (so·chee·MIL·koh) to experience Old Mexico. It is the last of the Aztec lagoons. These were the lakes around which the Aztecs built their culture.

At Xochimilco you can hire a boat and a pilot to guide you around the chinampa (chee·NAHM·pah) flower gardens. There are

boats selling tacos and drinks. Strolling musicians offer to play favorite songs for visitors.

To experience twenty-first century Mexico, visitors go to Reforma Avenue in the Zona Rosa. It is the heart of modern Mexico. There they shop and stay in lovely hotels.

Mexico has one of the world's finest subway systems. The Metro can quickly take you to one of Mexico City's many museums. The most famous are the museums of Anthropology and Modern Art. There is another museum dedicated to the Revolution.

The National Palace is like the White House in the United States. Leaders of Mexico from New Spain to today's president have made this their home. Diego Rivera painted beautiful murals here.

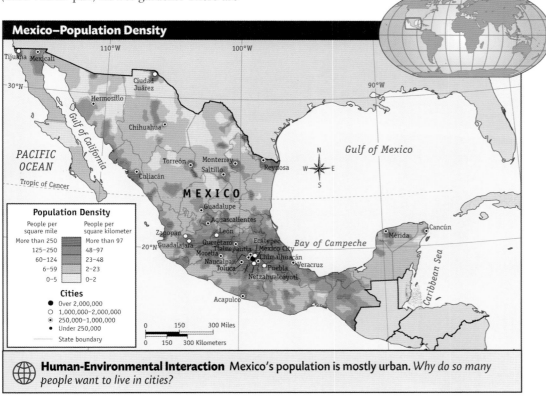

Mexico–Population Density

Population Density

People per square mile	People per square kilometer
More than 250	More than 97
125–250	48–97
60–124	23–48
6–59	2–23
0–5	0–2

Cities
- ● Over 2,000,000
- ○ 1,000,000–2,000,000
- ◉ 250,000–1,000,000
- • Under 250,000
- State boundary

0   150   300 Miles
0   150   300 Kilometers

Human-Environmental Interaction Mexico's population is mostly urban. *Why do so many people want to live in cities?*

Culture and Society

597

Discussion Questions

1 What are some sights you might see while visiting Mexico City?

💬 Caption Answer

Cities offer more opportunities for jobs and education.

🧭 Map Activity

Mexico Population Density

NATIONAL GEOGRAPHY STANDARDS: 1, 9, 12

GEOGRAPHIC THEMES: Movement, Human-Environmental Interaction

OBJECTIVES: 1.05, 1.06, 1.07

Enlarge the map on page 597 to 8½ inches by 11 inches and give a copy to each student. Provide the students with stackable markers such as pennies.

Students are to come up with a scale for markers comparable to the colored population legend on the map. Stress that their scale should be comparable to the scale in the book. (For example, 5 markers = 2 to 59 people per square mile.)

Have students study the map in the book and place the appropriate number of markers on their copy of the map according to scale.

When they have finished, have them record their observations. Next, have students record why they feel there are more people in some areas than in others. Have students share their recorded observations and discuss the exercise.

ℹ️ Background Information

Mexico's Baseball Capital

Monterrey is sometimes called the "Pittsburgh of Mexico" because steel making is an important industry there. But it also has another claim to fame. With Mexico's largest stadium and the nation's Baseball Hall of Fame, it is Mexico's baseball capital. It also has 50 Little League networks and its own national team, the Monterrey Sultans. In April 1999, it became the first city to host a Major League Baseball season

opener outside of the United States or Canada. Fans hoped the game played between the San Diego Padres and the Colorado Rockies would one day lead to placement of an expansion team in Monterrey.

Eyewitness Activity

Guanajuato

OBJECTIVES: 1.02, 1.06, 4.07

Beautiful pictures and informative text make up this Web site on World Heritage Sites in Mexico (visit **NCJourneys.com** for a link).

The first link leads the user to text that tells about the history of Guanajuato and what the city is like today. One interesting fact is that the name of the town translates into "Hill Of Frogs." The indigenous people called it that because they thought that only frogs were fit to live there!

The third link gives more information about World Heritage cities around the world. Links are available for different cities, including Guanajuato. The information at the link is interesting and informative. There are also more links available at the bottom of Guanajuato's page.

EYEWITNESS TO HISTORY

Guanajuato

Rich silver and gold deposits surround Guanajuato (gwah·nah·HWAH·toh). It was the wealthiest city in Mexico for centuries. The city is located on the Mesa Central, north of Mexico City. Guanajuato was built on the hillsides of a valley. The town's roads are steep and rolling (below). Some are actually alleyways with stairs.

In 1988, the United Nations named Guanajuato a World Heritage Zone. Because of this, the town bans traffic lights and neon signs. Buildings that do not fit with its colonial design are not allowed. The landscape of the valley means that there is little room for new buildings anyway.

598

Guanajuato was the site of one of the first battles of the Mexican War for Independence. On September 29, 1810, Father Hidalgo's followers attacked the place where people loyal to Spain had taken refuge. The building was burned to the ground. Many were killed. Later, Hidalgo was captured and executed. His head was displayed here to remind people not to go against Spain.

The name Guanajuato comes from the Nahuatl language. the word Quanax-huato (qua·nas·HWAH·toh) means "Hill of Frogs." Because of the Native American name, the image of the frog is can be seen throughout the town. This is similar to ways that a Ram, a Wolf, or a Blue Devil might be seen in Chapel Hill, Raleigh, or Durham.

The Basillica Nuestra Señora

Writing Activity

Cultural Research: Mexico

OBJECTIVES: 2.08, 3.06, 3.07

Divide the class into six groups to conduct research on Mexican fiestas, carnivals, music, sports, and painting and sculpture. Each group is to share its findings with the class in oral reports and demonstrations.

Alternate: Use six groups in a jigsaw cooperative learning format to help the class learn about the six topics.

Whichever approach is taken, it is useful to have a summarizing discussion in which students explore relationships between Mexican cultural activities and cultural activities in Canada and the United States. The discussion should focus on likenesses and differences and the possible reasons for them.

599

Discussion Questions

1 How has the port city of Acapulco changed through the years?

2 What are some sites you would enjoy visiting in Acapulco?

 Caption Answer

For its beaches, nightlife, and entertainment

 Activity

Holiday Crossover

OBJECTIVES: 1.07, 2.08, 3.06

As a class, make a list on the board of holidays celebrated in the United States.

Ask students which they think are also celebrated in Mexico. Circle those and then add other major Mexican holidays that are not celebrated in the United States.

JANUARY
- January 1—Año Nuevo (New Year's Day)
- January 6—Día de los Santos Reyes is the day when Mexicans exchange Christmas presents in accordance with the arrival of the three gift-bearing wisemen to Jesus Christ.
- January 17—Feast Day of de San Antonio de Abad is a religious holiday.

FEBRUARY
- February 5—Día de la Constitución commemorates Mexico's constitution.
- February 24—Flag Day honors the Mexican flag.

MARCH
- March 5—Carnaval kicks off a five-day celebration before Lent.
- March 21—The Birthday of Benito Juárez, a famous Mexican president and national hero.

APRIL
- Semana Santa—Semana Santa is the holy week that ends the 40-day Lent period. This week includes Good Friday and Easter Sunday.

MAY
- May 1—Primero de Mayo is equivalent to Labor Day in the United States.
- May 5—Cinco de Mayo honors the Mexican defeat of the French army at Puebla de los Angeles in 1862.
- May 10—Mother's Day

JUNE
- June 1—Navy Day

SEPTEMBER
- September 15 and 16—Mexican Independence Day celebrates the day that Miguel Hidalgo announced the Mexican revolt against Spanish rule.

OCTOBER
- October 12—Día de la Raza celebrates Columbus's arrival to the Americas.

NOVEMBER
- November 1 and 2—Día de los Muertos honors Mexico's dead.
- November 20—Mexican Revolution Day celebrates the Mexican Revolution of 1910.

DECEMBER
- December 12—Día de Nuestra Señora de Guadalupe honors Mexico's patron saint.
- December 16—Las Posadas celebrates Joseph and Mary's search for shelter in Bethlehem.
- December 25—Navidad (Christmas day)

Acapulco

Acapulco is a port city on the Pacific Ocean. It is a popular tourist spot. In the 1500s it was one of the most important harbors in the Spanish empire. It was a major port for ships from Asia. These brought silks and spices to Mexico. From Acapulco these treasures were taken overland to Veracruz. Then they were shipped to Spain.

The riches attracted pirates. Acapulco's port was raided many times. The Spanish built the Fortress of San Diego at the harbor entrance. Today you can visit this star-shaped fort.

Tourism

Acapulco became a quiet fishing village after Mexico's independence. In the late 1920s, the Mexican government built a road

Acapulco has long been an important vacation spot in Mexico. **Why do tourists vacation in Acapulco?**

and airport. It wanted to promote the city to tourists because of its beauty.

The government also brought in electricity and a drainage system. Then nice hotels were built. Hollywood stars in the 1930s and 1940s began to visit Acapulco. The city has grown from a population of barely 20,000 in 1950 to more than 2 million people today. More than 1.5 million tourists visit every year.

People visit Acapulco for its beaches and nightlife. Visitors enjoy many forms of entertainment. There are also parks where people can go boating and roller-blading. They watch trained dolphins and go on water rides.

Cliff Diving

Acapulco is famous for the Cliff Divers of La Quebrada. La Quebrada is a steep mountain ledge overlooking the bay.

Daring young men put on diving shows several times a day. They dive gracefully into the water from a height of 140 feet (42 m). They must time their dives with the tide and waves. If they were to hit the water at low tide they would get hurt. The final diver of the day dives holding a pair of flaming torches.

Monterrey

Monterrey is the third-largest city in Mexico. It is a center of international trade and manufacturing. The city is located near the border with the United States. It is surrounded by mountains. A famous one is Cerro de la Silla, or Saddle Mountain.

Monterrey is a modern city. But the heart of the old city is the colonial Plaza Zaragoza. It is also known as the Macroplaza. It has beautiful fountains and statues.

Monterrey has a twenty-first-century side as well. The Lighthouse of Commerce is a stunning, bright red tower. It stands over the entire town. The Lighthouse flashes a laser beam across the city at night. To some it resembles a red hot iron bar.

The Alfa Cultural Center is an example of modern architecture. Some people think it looks like a telescope pointing to the sky. It symbolizes the importance of science to the city. Inside is the Science and Technology Museum. It has an interactive center where students can study astronomy and physics. There is also a planetarium there.

The mountains are only 30 miles (48 km) from Monterrey. Twelve miles (19 km) to the south is the Mesa de Chipinique (CHEE·pee·NEE·keh). You can drive through a cool forest of oak and pine to reach that plateau. There visitors enjoy a beautiful view of the city.

Just a bit farther south is the Cola de Caballo (kah·BIGH·yoh) waterfall. The Boca Dam forms an artificial lake near the waterfall. There people sail and water ski.

Driving west from Monterrey you will pass through dry plains and great mountains. You will arrive at some caves called Garcia Grottos (gar·SEE·ah GROHT·tohs). In the caves are a series of interesting rock formations. Their names come from their shapes, such as "Indian Head" or "Hand of the Dead."

The modern Faro del Comercio, translated as the Lighthouse of Commerce, is a monument to business. It mixes the old and the new in Monterrey. **What is another example of modern architecture there?**

LESSON 1 REVIEW

Fact Follow-Up
1. What holidays do Mexicans celebrate?
2. Most Mexicans do not call their capital Mexico City. What do they call it?
3. In the past Acapulco was a seaport. What is it known for today?
4. Which city is known as a center of trade and manufacturing?

Talk About It
1. If you could visit one of these four cities, which would you choose? Why?
2. Which of the four cities described in this lesson do you think is most modern? Explain why.
3. How do these cities blend Native American and European cultures?

Culture and Society

601

Discussion Questions

1 How is the city of Monterrey different from Acapulco?

2 What would you plan to see if you were to visit Monterrey?

Caption Answer

The Alfa Cultural Center

Activity

Making a Butterfly Garden

◀━ **OBJECTIVES:** 1.02, 1.06, 2.08

Monarch butterflies migrate from the United States each autumn to spend the winter in Mexico. Different species of butterflies have different preferences of nectar, in both colors and taste. Students can plant a garden on the school grounds to attract butterflies. Plant like colors together to make it easy for the butterfly to find. Some suggestion of plants that attract butterflies are aster, black-eyed Susan, butterfly weed, daylilies, hibiscus, marigold, and pink azalea.

LESSON 1 REVIEW

Fact Follow-Up Answers
1. They celebrate Easter, Christmas, the Day of the Dead, the Day of the Virgin of Guadalupe, and Independence Day.
2. El D.F.
3. People visit Acapulco for the beaches and nightlife.
4. Monterrey is an industrial hub and is near enough to the United States border to be linked closely with the expanding trade spurred by NAFTA.

Talk About It Answers
1. Important points: Students should choose one city and explain their choice using details of life in the city. Physical and cultural characteristics of place should be mentioned.
2. Important points: Encourage students to suggest criteria for deciding which city is most modern (criteria might include housing, transportation, health care, education, technology), then evaluate the modernity of the three cities using the criteria they chose.
3. Important points: Architecture, art, parks, and people are all aspects of cities that blend native American and European culture.

OBJECTIVES: 1.03, 1.07, 2.08, 3.06, 3.07

Discussion Questions

1 In what ways were the Catholic Church and the native religions blended? Why?

2 How did the priests go about converting the Native Americans to Catholicism?

3 What is a mission?

Reading Strategy Activity

Using Print Materials

OBJECTIVES: 1.03, 1.07, 2.08, 3.06, 3.07

As you assign research projects to your students, be sure that they understand how to find information and cite the print materials as sources in their projects. Provide opportunities for students to use the table of contents and the index of resource books and magazines. Teach them to cite their sources including the author, title, publisher, and date. Arrange time for your school librarian to show students how to use the card catalog and how to find books and magazines on specific subjects. Although the Internet has changed the way we research, students should be taught how to find their way around a library.

Teacher Notes

Mayan Religion

The Mayan religion centered around the worship of a large number of nature gods. Chaac, a god of rain, was especially important in popular ritual. Among the supreme deities were Kukulcan, a creator god closely related to the Toltec and Aztec Quetzalcoatl, and Itzamna, a sky god. An important Mayan trait was their complete trust in the gods' control of certain units of time and of all peoples' activities during those periods. The Mayans believed in many gods. The following are the main ones:

KEY IDEAS

- Mexican tradition includes many reminders of Native American religions.

- Some Native Americans helped Catholic priests convert people.

- The Virgin of Guadalupe is an important religious symbol for Mexicans.

- Masks play a dramatic part in Mexican cultural traditions.

KEY TERMS

Day of the Dead
missions
patron saint
Virgin of Guadalupe

The Spanish monarchy and the Roman Catholic Church were closely linked. Missionaries from Spain were among the first to settle in Latin America.

They came because Spain wanted to convert Native Americans to Christianity. The priests arrived with the explorers. The native people managed to blend parts of their own religions with those from Europe. This can be seen throughout Mexico and Central America today.

Native American Beliefs

In Mexico there are many reminders of Native American religions. Some people still worship the old gods. Some have merged them with Catholic Christian beliefs. The missionaries looked for common themes in the Catholic and native religions. They used these similarities to teach the native peoples.

The story of the Aztecs wandering in search of a homeland is one example of this. Priests may have compared it to the Bible story of the Jews searching for the Promised Land. Priests also built churches in places that were already sacred to the Native Americans. Sometimes they even destroyed old temples and used the same materials to build new churches.

The old religions were difficult to erase from the hearts and minds of the Native Americans. There are still reminders of these older religions. A trip to Mexico would not be complete without visiting the Aztec and Mayan pyramids.

You can also see the observatories where these people studied the stars. You have read how the stars and planets were part of their religion. People in rural areas still watch the movements in the sky. These help the farmers know when to plant and harvest crops. Although their numbers are small, a few people still worship the old gods and follow the old religion.

Catholicism in Mexico

In the early years of the conquest two or three priests would travel to a Native American village. They explained the Christian religion to Native Americans. They baptized them. Then they built a church. These priests were the first to learn the Native American languages. They taught the Native Americans how to speak Spanish.

The priests also built *missions.* The missions were centers of worship and learning. They were built to convert and educate Native Americans. Spanish settlers built towns around the missions.

602

Kinich Ahau—the Sun god. He was the patron god of the city Itzamal. He was believed to visit the city at noon everyday. He would descend as a macaw and consume prepared offerings.

Chaac—the god of rain. He was a benevolent god for Mayans, who often sought his help for their crops. Chaac was associated with creation and life.

Yumil Kaxob—the maize god. In certain areas of Middle America, like Yucatán, the maize god is combined with the god of flora. The maize god is principally shown with a

headdress of maize and a curved streak on his cheek.

Yum Cimis—the god that would lead you to heaven.

Kukulcan—the wind god—was also known as the feathered-serpent god Kukulcan

Most Native Americans did not like the idea of giving up their religious beliefs for Christian ones. Many fled into the surrounding countryside. Others stayed in the villages but did not follow the priests' teachings.

Other Native Americans wanted to convert to Christianity. Many helped the missionaries convert others. They traveled with the priests to other villages. There they translated and taught Spanish. They also protected the priests from harm.

Over time, the Catholic religion in Mexico and Central America came to combine Catholic beliefs with Native American religious views. Catholic saints replaced Aztec and Mayan gods. Often the two came to be associated with one another. Some Catholic holy days were arranged to fall on Aztec and Mayan feast days.

This drawing shows a Catholic missionary preaching to Native Americans. **What role did Spanish missions play in colonial Mexico?**

Small churches are at the center of village life. This one was built in the early 1800s in San Luis Potosí, Mexico. **How is this church different from other churches you have seen?**

Culture and Society

603

Caption Answer

Spanish missions were there to convert and educate Native Americans and serve as centers for communities of Spanish settlers.

Caption Answer

It is smaller and simpler.

Activity

Missions

⬤ **OBJECTIVES:** 2.08, 3.06, 3.07

In the early days of the Catholic Church in Mexico, missions were built as a way to convert the native people to Catholicism. The missions included farms, living quarters for priests, schools, and villages. The missions were built for the Native Americans to provide what the priests thought was a better way of life. Today many types of mission activities continue under the auspices of the Catholic Church as well as churches of many other denominations. These missions may include schools, housing, and medical assistance and support groups. Today's missions are designed to reach out to where people are. Ask students to identify any mission groups and activities in their community. Through this discussion, determine what the missions are trying to accomplish. Ask students if they see any other needs in their communities that the mission organizations are not addressing or that could be met by a mission organization if they are unaware of any missions in their community. How might these needs be met? Have students create an agency list, hours of operation and contact personnel

Activity

Literature Connection

⬤ **OBJECTIVES:** 1.07, 3.06, 3.07

Use the book *Fiesta!: Mexico's Great Celebrations* by Elizabeth Silverthorne, illustrated by Jan Davey Ellis (Millbrook Press, 1994. ISBN 1562948369).

Read some of the book, which gives a wealth of information about the many celebrations enjoyed by our neighbors to the south. As an extra resource, the book contains easy recipes that can be helpful to students.

Help the class make some of the simple art activities supplied with the book and choose a festival to celebrate. Dress in traditional costumes and decorate the classroom to make the occasion a special day.

Discussion Questions

1 What is a patron saint?

2 What is the story of Juan Diego and the Virgin of Guadalupe?

 Caption Answer

Many Catholic holy days correspond to Aztec feasts.

 Caption Answer

She is a symbol of Mexico.

 Research Activity

Celebrations in Mexico

➤ **OBJECTIVES:** 1.07, 3.06, 3.07

Divide your class into cooperative groups. Give them a list of holidays and celebrations in Mexico. Assign or have groups choose one celebration. Each group will research their chosen celebration and will present the information in an interesting way.

Possible celebrations:
- Carnival
- Lent, Holy Week, and Easter
- Feast of Our Lady of Guadeloupe
- Cinco de Mayo
- Day of the Dead
- Dia de la Raza

Possible activities:
- floats and parade
- create a video program
- posters with some form of presentation
- role-playing
- compare/contrast activities with United States and/or Canadian celebrations.

What would YOU do?

Many Catholics in Mexico say the Catholic Church must help the people wherever it can. Others say the Church should support the government more. They fear the Church will become too powerful if it does too much on its own.

Imagine you are a government official serving a poor community. Would you let the Church try to help them? Why or why not?

The Virgin of Guadalupe appears to Juan Diego. **In what ways has Mexico blended Catholic and Aztec traditions?**

The Virgin of Guadalupe's image appears on candles and other religious artifacts. **Why is her image seen in many places?**

The Virgin of Guadalupe

The Virgin Mary is a sacred figure in the Roman Catholic religion. She is the mother of Jesus Christ.

Every Mexican child learns the legend of the Virgin of Guadalupe. It is one of the most popular stories in Mexico. It takes place in the early years of New Spain.

Juan Diego was a Native American who had converted to Christianity. In December of 1531, he was walking to the new Catholic church in Tlatelolco. He climbed a hill that had been a sacred spot to an Aztec goddess. He heard someone singing.

Then he saw a brilliant vision of the Virgin Mary. Mary told Juan Diego to go to the Spanish bishop and tell him to build a church on the hill. She spoke to him in his native language. Bishop Zumarraga did not believe Juan Diego. A few days later the Virgin Mary reappeared. She told Juan Diego to gather roses from the top of the hill and take them to the bishop. This seemed impossible because roses did not bloom at that time of the year. But Juan Diego found bright red roses growing on the hill. He gathered them in his cloak and took them to the bishop.

He opened his cloak to remove the roses and they tumbled out. But the image of the Virgin Mary was imprinted on the cloth of his cloak. This Virgin Mary was dark-skinned and Native American. The cloak today hangs above the altar in a giant church built to honor the Virgin.

No one is sure why the name Guadalupe was given to the Virgin Mary vision Juan Diego saw. But that vision has become a symbol of Mexico.

The *Virgin of Guadalupe* is the *patron saint* of Mexico. Patron saints are special guardians of a person, place, or activity. You will see the Virgin of Guadalupe's image among the Mexicans living in North Carolina.

604

Chapter 25

ELL Teaching Tips

Encourage Social Interaction

ELL students need to interact with real speakers of English. Give them a variety of activities. Limit the amount of time ELL students spend completing nonverbal tasks. Acceptance is an excellent motivational tool!

A family decorates a tomb on the Day of the Dead.
On what day is the Day of the Dead?

The Day of the Dead

The day after North Carolinians celebrate Halloween, Mexicans celebrate a holiday called the **Day of the Dead.** Some people go to the cemetery and honor their dead ancestors at midnight.

Everything that day has the theme of death. People wear masks resembling skulls. They eat candy and special bread shaped like bones. People also cover graves with yellow marigolds. They leave small amounts of the dead person's favorite foods. The towns of Pátzcuaro (PAHTZ·kway·roh) and the state of Michoacán (mee·chah·wah·KAHN) are famous for their festivals.

Mexican Family Life

Families are the center of Mexican life. In many homes, grandparents, parents, and children may live together. Families in rural areas might be large.

Most Mexican families are traditional. The father is the head of the family. Mothers are greatly respected, but the father usually makes most decisions. In the cities, many women have jobs. Women who live in rural areas work on the farms.

Mexican girls do not have as much freedom as do girls in the United States and Canada. Boys in rural areas work in the fields. Young people in the cities sometimes have part-time or full-time jobs.

Mexicans believe that they should help family members. They might help a family member find a job or go to school.

Culture and Society   605

Discussion Questions

1 In what ways are Halloween and the Day of the Dead similar? How are they different?

 Caption Answer

November 1, the day after Halloween

 Activity

El Días de los Muertos

 OBJECTIVES: 2.08, 3.06, 3.07

To introduce the Day of the Dead, use a graphic organizer such a three-ringed Venn Diagram to compare Memorial Day, Halloween, and the Day of the Dead.

Invite a Mexican guest speaker to share their experiences of the Day of the Dead.

Ask students to volunteer to bring pictures and share stories about an ancestor.

Background Information

Festival of Our Lady of Guadalupe

All over Mexico, the festival of Our Lady of Guadalupe is celebrated on December 12. The national celebration is held at the Basilica de Guadalupe in Mexico City, but fiestas also take place at churches named for the Virgin throughout the country. On the day of the festival, thousands gather at the Basilica early in the morning bringing flowers to celebrate the mass. Outside the church, Native American dancers in traditional dress perform native dances. Tecate, in Baja California Norte holds a parade in which charros, or cowboys, on horseback take part. The Tzotzil and Tzeltal Indians in San Cristóbal de Las Casas participate in a two-day celebration that includes fireworks and music by marimba and string bands. A parade takes celebrants to the Hill of Guadalupe where the church dedicated to the Virgin stands.

Discussion Questions

1 Why do you think masks are important in celebrations in Mexico?

Caption Answer

Answers will vary. Both feelings will be shared by many people.

Masks

In Mexico, masks are worn not only for the Day of the Dead but for other holidays, too. Some Mexicans wear happy masks at Christmas. Some wear sad masks at Easter.

The Native Americans wear masks while dancing. These special dances tell tales of the conquest and their fight against the Spanish. Other dances tell fables and legends.

Masked dancers at a carnival in Huejotzingo, Mexico. **Do you think the dance about the fight with the Spanish would be happy or sad?**

LESSON **2** REVIEW

Fact Follow-Up
1. Why did Roman Catholic priests and missionaries arrive in Mexico so early?
2. What elements of Native American religions can still be observed in Mexico?
3. What are patron saints, and who is the patron saint of Mexico?

Talk About It
1. Why does Catholicism in Mexico blend ancient traditions with Christian teachings? Is it the same in other countries?
2. Which of all the religious holiday celebrations would you most like to experience? Explain why.

LESSON **2** REVIEW

Fact Follow-Up Answers
1. They came because Spain wished to convert Native Americans to Christianity. The priests marched alongside the conquistadors.
2. Some people still worship the old gods or have merged them with Catholic beliefs. Reminders exist in monuments, astronomical observatories, and temples. Native Americans wear masks while performing dances during Christmas and Easter.
3. Patron saints are special guardians of a person, place, or activity. The Virgin of Guadalupe is the patron saint of Mexico.

Talk About It Answers
1. Important points: Encourage students to identify examples of blending—building churches on ancient temple sites, the fact that the Virgin of Guadalupe was seen on a hill that had been sacred to an Aztec goddess, the image of the Virgin of Guadalupe as dark-skinned and Native American. This is an example of the movement of ideas. Students may share examples of different Christian celebrations or traditions from European, African, or Asian cultures.
2. Important points: Encourage students to suggest holiday celebrations and choose one based on physical and cultural characteristics of place.

LESSON 3 Culture in Mexico

Mexico is large. It has many states and regions. Each area of the country has a special culture, much like the United States and Canada.

The areas of Mexico closest to the northern border are a lot like the southwestern United States. Southern Texas or Arizona might seem much like the northern Mexican states of Coahuila (koh·HWEE·ah) or Sonora (soh·NOHR·rah).

The culture is more international in the Mesa Central. In the more isolated southern states Native American customs are common.

Sports and the arts are important in Mexico. The brightly colored costumes of the mariachi and the rhythms of Latin dance music often fill the air. There are also soccer and wrestling fans.

Music

Ranchero (rahn·CHAH·roh) music is very popular. It might remind a person from North Carolina of country music. It has a similar rhythm and tells sad stories. Another popular form of music is *mariachi.* You may have seen a mariachi band on television or even playing in North Carolina. The musicians dress in silver-studded pants and jackets. They wear wide-brimmed sombreros. They look like Mexican cowboys of old.

Another Mexican musical tradition is the *conjunto* (coh·HOON·toe). Small groups of musicians play conjunto. They play accordions and a special kind of guitar called a bajo (BAH·hoe) sextos. This folk music is popular in northern Mexico.

City streets are often filled with the sounds of music coming from stores and shops. Bands play in the town plaza on Sunday evenings and for special occasions. Children learn to dance at an early age. Boys and girls are generally not shy at all about dancing. Young people and adults often attend the same dances. Most popular music in Mexico is created with dancing in mind.

Culture and Society

KEY IDEAS

- Mexican music has many forms, from traditional to rock 'n' roll.

- Literature, art, and film are important in Mexican culture.

- Soccer and baseball are the most popular sports. Wrestling is very popular, too.

KEY TERMS

fútbol
mariachi

Senorino Alvarez, age ninety, plays in a mariachi band in Mexico City's Garibaldi Square. **Have you heard mariachi music?**

607

Activity

Mariachi Time

OBJECTIVES: 1.07, 2.08, 3.06

Have students make rattles to play in a mariachi band. They can use plastic eggs or hosiery containers as the rattles and fill the containers with seeds or small beads. The containers can then be attached to craft sticks or small dowels, and students can decorate the rattle. Play a CD or tape of mariachi music and let the class play along with their rattles.

Extension Ask a local Hispanic group if they know of bands that could perform mariachi music from Mexico at your school.

 **OBJECTIVES:** 2.08, 3.06, 3.07

Discussion Questions

1 How is mariachi music different from other kinds of music?

2 How do you know that music is important to Mexicans?

 Caption Answer

Answers will vary. Ask students to describe what they heard.

Reading Strategy Activity

Using the Internet

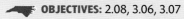 **OBJECTIVES:** 2.08, 3.06, 3.07

The Internet has changed the way we research. With information literally at our fingertips it is important to teach our students how to surf the web to research information about topics in social studies. Be sure students are familiar with how to research online as well as safety rules for using the Internet. In the classroom or in the school computer lab, restrict the students to these search engines or another that you know you can trust for kid friendly sites.

Part of educating students on Internet use is to be sure that they are familiar with terms like: Internet, search tools, search engine, browser, online, navigational tools, file server, Web, site, Web site, address, bookmark, navigate, and browse. Create many opportunities for students to become fluent with these terms. You may want students to create a picture dictionary defining these key terms.

Discussion Questions

1 What is a mural?

2 Where might you find a mural in Mexico?

Activity

Music and Dance

 OBJECTIVES: 3.07

Students will research music and/or dances of Mexico. Look for instructions on how to do a specific dance. If instruction is not available, they should create their own movements to the music. Then teach the original or the "new" dance to fellow classmates. You may want a music or dance instructor to help on this assignment. To add authenticity to the lesson, try to dress in the cultural costume of the dance.

  Suggested dances and music:

Bolero: A Spanish national dance created in Cádiz, Spain, in 1780. It has many swirling steps; the dancer keeps time with castanets.

Fandango: A couple dances in triple time to guitars, castanets, and singing.

Flamenco: A Spanish dance brought by colonists. Colorful dresses and suits worn by gypsies.

Teacher Notes

Rivera at Rockefeller Center

In 1933, the Rockefeller family sought to install a series of murals in the lobby of Rockefeller Center in New York City. Diego Rivera was selected from a larger field of candidates (including Matisse and Picasso) on the recommendation of Nelson Rockefeller. Rivera was openly left in his political leanings. His mural, "Man at the Crossroads Looking with Uncertainty but with Hope and High Vision to the Choosing of a Course Heading to a New and Better Future," had a laborer who strongly resembled Lenin. A major controversy erupted. Rivera was asked to alter the mural. He refused, and John D. Rocke-

MEXICAN PORTRAIT

Diego Rivera
1886–1957

   Diego Rivera was born in the town of Guanajuato. He began drawing at an early age. Soon he began to paint. He married Frida Kahlo. She was an equally important Mexican artist. She was the subject of many of his paintings and murals.

   Diego Rivera was a master of painting. He could imagine how his paintings would look before he had finished them. His subjects rarely had to even be in the same room with him once he began to paint.

   To Diego Rivera, art was public. He wanted it to be displayed where everyone could see it. He also wanted his work to be enjoyed by Mexicans from all walks of life. Painting murals was the way he brought his art to all people.

   A mural is a large picture painted directly on the walls or ceilings of buildings. Rivera liked using murals because many people could see the painting at one time.

   Diego Rivera's murals are colorful. They most often show Mexico's people past and present. Aztec warriors and Spanish conquistadors are featured in some murals. Others portray people working in fields or factories.

   There are several of Rivera's murals in this book. Look at them and think about which ones you like best and why.

Diego Rivera,
Self-Portrait, 1941

The Fine Arts

   In Mexico you will also find a rich tradition of painting and sculpture. After the Mexican Revolution, the government hired artists to paint great murals in many places. Diego Rivera and José Clemente Orozco (oh·ROH·skoh) were famous muralists. They painted scenes of Mexican history and daily life on the walls of public buildings.

   Frida Kahlo was another famous Mexican artist. She painted a fantasy world full of strange images. These were paintings of Mexican life as she saw it. These artists were all inspired by the ancient paintings and buildings around their nation.

   There is also a great craft tradition in Mexico. Pottery is painted with beautiful designs copied from the walls of ancient pyramids and temples. The Mexican government helps make sure these traditional crafts continue.

   Taxco is located in the state of Guerrero (geh·REH·roh). It is famous for beautiful silver jewelry. Around the lakeside city of Pátzcuaro, coppersmithing has been a trade since before the Spanish conquest.

Architecture

   Architecture is also an important art in Mexico. Mexicans take great pride in the way their buildings look. In cities like Monterrey you will see buildings decorated with glass and colored tiles. Some are built in new and interesting shapes. In other places like Guanajuato, the architecture will be in the beautiful Spanish colonial style.

This silver bracelet is an example of one of Mexico's many fine arts. **What other crafts does Mexico produce?**

feller, Jr., (Nelson's father) was so angered that Rivera was dismissed and several months later the mural was destroyed.

Caption Answer

Pottery and coppersmithing.

Movies and TV

Mexico has an important film and television industry. Mexican films are shown all over Latin America and Europe. There have been many films made about the Mexican Revolution. Just as many have been made about singing cowboys (rancheros). These have introduced Mexican music to the rest of the world.

Cantinflas (kahn·TEEN·flahs) was a Mexican comedian who made more than 80 films. They were shown all over the world. When he died in 1986, thousands of people and presidents from other countries in Latin America attended his funeral.

This is a self portrait of Frida Kahlo, a famous Mexican artist. **When did the Mexican government begin promoting the arts?**

MEXICAN PORTRAIT

Frida Kahlo
1907–1954

Frida Kahlo was the most famous female Mexican painter of the twentieth century.

Kahlo's mother was Mexican and her father was German. Her early life was difficult because she suffered from polio when she was six.

When she was eighteen, she was in a very serious bus accident. This caused health problems for the rest of her life. She started to paint because she was bored from staying in bed after the accident.

Kahlo decided to change her studies from medicine to painting after the bus accident. She often chose Maya and Aztec themes for her paintings. She liked the bold colors and costumes of the native people.

The Mexican Revolution began when Kahlo was three years old. She was interested in politics her whole life. She supported the working class. She did not want only a few people to have all the power.

Kahlo also painted many self-portraits. She frequently showed herself in some sort of physical or emotional pain. In 1933 she married Diego Rivera. He was a famous muralist. Their marriage was difficult. They later divorced and then remarried a few years later.

Rivera said of his wife, "Frida Kahlo is the greatest Mexican painter. Her work is destined to be multiplied by reproductions and will speak, thanks to books, to the whole world."

Culture and Society

609

Discussion Questions

1 What other forms of art can be found in Mexico?

2 How are these art forms different from art we usually see in North Carolina?

 Activity

Making Murals

 OBJECTIVES: 1.07, 3.06, 3.07

In Mexico the art of Diego Rivera is often visible in murals. Rivera painted these murals so that many people from many walks of life could see and enjoy them. Many works of Mexican art have bright colors often used in Mexican clothing and fabrics. As a class create a mural as Diego Rivera might have done. Decide upon a theme, for example, the working family, festivals, foods, customs, history, and so on, and carry it out throughout the entire mural. Each student should research one aspect of the theme, and draw and paint it into the overall mural. The students must consider the types of colors and designs that might have been used in Mexico. Once the mural is completed, place it in the school hallway or the school cafeteria.

 Caption Answer

After the Mexican Revolution.

 Background Information

Frida Kahlo

Today painter Frida Kahlo is well known throughout the Americas, but during her lifetime her husband Diego Rivera was far more famous. Born in 1907, her life was greatly changed by a bus accident at age eighteen. The accident left her with severe back problems. She often had to stay in bed or move about in a wheelchair. Her career as an artist began when she was recovering from this injury. She started drawing the self-portraits that became a major part of her later work. "I paint myself because I am so often alone and because I am the subject I know best," she once said. She liked to dress in traditional Mexican folk dress. She enjoyed wearing the costumes of Tehuantepec, an area known for its strong-minded, outspoken women.

Discussion Questions

1 What is a social conscience?

2 Why do people say Latin American literature has a social conscience?

3 What is the most popular sport in Mexico?

4 How is baseball in Mexico like that in the United States?

Caption Answer

Today's writers are addressing problems and suggesting solutions to them by writing about Latin American history.

Activity

Culture Collage

OBJECTIVES: 2.08, 3.04, 3.06

Culture: (as defined by *Exploring Your World*, the Adventure of Geography by the National Geographic Society) "A culture is the entire way of life shared by a group of people. It is learned behavior passed from one generation to the next. Because of this, people with one group have the same language and similar customs, beliefs, ceremonies, and habits. They are accustomed to certain foods, types of housing, and kinds of clothing. A culture is also a plan for living that allows a society to function smoothly and fulfill its needs."

Write the following words on the board: language, customs, beliefs, ceremonies, habits, foods, housing, clothing. Discuss culture with students. Review cultural information in Chapter 25.

Divide the class into groups and have them collect pictures that deal with one of the various topics in Lesson 3 (music, arts, literature, sports). Each group should make a collage of the collected pictures, and then write a brief explanation for the bottom of the collage.

Mexican poet Octavio Paz won the Nobel Prize in Literature in 1994. **Why do people say that Latin American literature has a social conscience?**

Literature

Mexico has produced great writers. Both Octavio Paz (ahk·TAH·vee·oh PAHZ) and Carlos Fuentes (foh·EHN·tehz) are world famous for their books and essays. Paz won the Nobel Prize in Literature in 1990. In their books they explored the theme of what it means to be a Mexican.

Paz and Fuentes, like many Latin American authors, write about the history of their nation. They want readers to think about solutions to Mexico's problems. Because of this, people say that Latin American literature has a social conscience.

Customs

Mexican Names First names are used only for family and close acquaintances. Mexican children are generally given two last names. The first is their father's family name (the last name he gained from his father). The second is their mother's family name (the last name she gained from her father). Many Mexicans refer to themselves using the last name gained from their father.

Sports

Soccer is the most popular sport in the world. It is number one in Mexico as well. Soccer is called *fútbol* throughout Latin America. There are many professional leagues across Mexico. Teams from the big cities play annually for a national championship. One of the biggest games is Mexico City versus Guadalajara (GWAH·dah·lah·HAH·rah).

The national team has participated in the World Cup Tournament many times. The World Cup tournament was held in Mexico in 1970 and 1986.

Baseball is also played in Mexico. Teams from Mexico's major cities play in the Mexican League. More than 80 players born in Mexico have played in the major leagues in the United States. In the 1980s, Fernando Valenzuela was a star pitcher for the Los Angeles Dodgers. Roberto Avila led the American League in batting in 1954.

Wrestling

One of the most popular forms of entertainment in Mexico is professional wrestling. They call it lucha libre (LOO·chah LEE·brah). Almost every night of the week in major cities there are matches. Thousands of fans go to watch. Mexican wrestlers are

610

divided into two groups. The *rudos* (ROO·dohs) are the bad guys. The *técnicos* (TEHK·nee·kohs) are the good guys. Most Mexican wrestlers wear masks.

One Mexican wrestler was more famous than all the others. His name was El Santo (ehl SAHN·toh), "The Saint." El Santo was a *técnico* and wore a silver mask. He made more than 20 movies. A series of comic books were written about him.

Mexican wrestlers have begun to come out of the ring and act almost like real super-heroes. One wrestler named Superbarrio (SOO·pehr BAH·ree·roh) (Super neighborhood) began trying to help people who rented apartments in Mexico City. They fought for fair rent and decent housing in the months after the 1985 earthquake. Today he speaks out about other political issues.

Superecologista Verde (SOO·pehr eh·koh·loh·HEE·stah) (Super Ecologist Green) protests damage to the environment. Another masked wrestler named Superanimal (SOO·pehr·ah·nee·MAHL) (Super Animal) speaks out against cruelty to animals.

A wrestler in costume meets with children at a match in Mexico City. **What have some Mexican wrestlers begun to do?**

Discussion Questions

1 How have professional wrestlers of Mexico shown that they, too, have a social conscience?

 **Caption Answer**

Some wrestlers act almost like real superheros.

 **Activity**

Cultural Poster

◀ OBJECTIVES: 2.08, 3.06, 3.07

Choose one of the cultural areas discussed in Chapter 25. These include music, sports, art (painting/sculpture), and religion. Have the students reread that section. Use the textbook and other research materials to create a cultural poster of Mexico. They should use their own artwork or find pictures to illustrate their posters.

LESSON 3 REVIEW

Fact Follow-Up
1. Describe music in Mexico.
2. After the Mexican Revolution the government promoted the painting of great murals in many places. Who were famous muralists?
3. In what places are the people known for their beautiful silver jewelry and copper work?
4. What is the most popular sport in Mexico, and what is it called?

Talk About It
1. Which sport in Mexico is of most interest to you? Explain why.
2. Why do people say that Latin American literature has a social conscience?
3. Why is visual art important in Mexican culture?
4. To what extent are Mexico and the United States dependent on one another?

Culture and Society

611

LESSON 3 REVIEW

Fact Follow-Up Answers
1. Mexican music ranges from "ranchero," a type of country music, to contemporary rock 'n roll. "Mariachi" continues to be popular.
2. The most famous were Diego Rivera, and Jose Clemente Orozco.
3. Taxco is known for silver jewelry. Around Patzcuaro coppersmithing has been a trade since before the Spanish conquest.
4. Soccer, called fútbol, is the most popular sport in the world and is number one in Mexico as well.

lesson, choose the one of most interest to them, and explain their choice.
2. Today's writers are addressing problems and suggesting solutions to them by writing about Latin American history.
3. Important points: Students should point to the traditions of the Native Americans. Speculate that in a nation where literacy has been low, visual art is a way to communicate with everyone.
4. Important points: Students should consider all they have all they have learned about Mexico and the United States. Possible connections might include ecomomy, immigrants, and shared history.

Talk About It Answers
1. Important points: Students should name the sports described in this

Teaching This Skill Lesson

Materials Needed textbooks, chart paper, pencils, markers

Classroom Organization whole class, small group, individual

Beginning the Lesson Ask "What are the cultural characteristics of Mexico?" Record students' responses on the board. Next, write the names of the four cities featured in Chapter 25 on the chalkboard, asking "Do all of the four cities have the cultural characteristics you described?"

Lesson Development Tell students they will be making web charts on each of the four cities to help themselves answer the question "What are the cultural characteristics of Mexico?" Divide the class into four groups and assign one of the four cities to each group. Next, work with the whole class to decide on the categories they will use in the web chart, since all groups should use the same characteristics. Once categories have been established, each group is to complete its own web charts (with one copy for each student in the group) using information from Chapter 25. (Note: Encourage students in each of the four groups to become as informed as possible about the characteristics of "their" cities.) Once the web charts are complete, regroup with four students in each group, each student with a web chart of one city.

Conclusion Allow time for students to share information about each city in their small groups. Again, ask the question "What are the cultural characteristics of Mexico?" Students should have more informed responses to the question as a result of their research.

Extension If desired, have each student write a paragraph describing the cultural characteristics of Mexico.

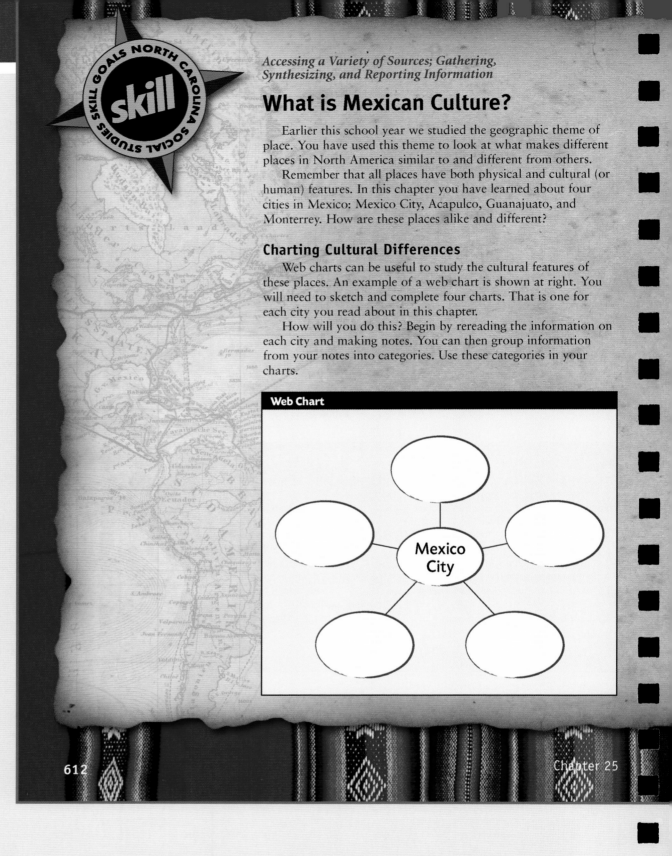

Accessing a Variety of Sources; Gathering, Synthesizing, and Reporting Information

What is Mexican Culture?

Earlier this school year we studied the geographic theme of place. You have used this theme to look at what makes different places in North America similar to and different from others.

Remember that all places have both physical and cultural (or human) features. In this chapter you have learned about four cities in Mexico: Mexico City, Acapulco, Guanajuato, and Monterrey. How are these places alike and different?

Charting Cultural Differences

Web charts can be useful to study the cultural features of these places. An example of a web chart is shown at right. You will need to sketch and complete four charts. That is one for each city you read about in this chapter.

How will you do this? Begin by rereading the information on each city and making notes. You can then group information from your notes into categories. Use these categories in your charts.

Web Chart

Mexico City

For example, there is information about important buildings in every city; so one of your categories might be Buildings. What other categories can you use? Should you use the same categories for each city?

Once you have completed the web charts, try to answer the question: What is "Mexican culture"?

Review Lessons 2 and 3 closely. These might help you answer the question more completely. Can you construct a web chart using information from all the lessons in this chapter? Can you write a paragraph describing Mexican culture? Are there other ways you can describe Mexican culture? What might some of these ways be?

Finally, is Mexican culture so diverse that you cannot explain it in just one paragraph? Is there other information that you need?

Playing soccer in Mexico

Culture and Society

613

 Skill Lesson Review

1. Which category helped you see most similarities among the four cities? *Encourage student discussion. Language, food, and/or religion are likely choices.*

2. Can you think of other ways of comparing four cities that would be easier or just as effective? *Encourage students to explore other means of comparison, discussing the positives and negatives of each.*

Talk About It

1. Important points: Students should choose one of the cities (Mexico City, Acapulco, Monterrey, and perhaps Guanajuato) and explain why they chose it. Explanations should refer to both physical and cultural characteristics of place.
2. Important points: Students should state an opinion and explain it. Mexico is predominantly Roman Catholic today; however, Catholicism is blended with Native American traditions and pockets of Native American religion remain. Roman Catholic schools remain under the supervision of the government, and there are public schools.
3. Important points: Students should express an opinion and explain it. Music is played in outdoor spaces all over Mexico at least once a week. Murals are outdoor paintings that can be seen by people walking along the sidewalks. Architecture is an art form, and buildings can be seen by all.
4. Important points: Encourage students to suggest as many questions as they can, then choose the three that would elicit the most information. Explanations might refer to various aspects of life in Mexico City including recreation, the arts, government, education, pollution, and drinking water problems.
5. Important points: Students should state an opinion and explain it. Rivera's murals depicted events from Mexican history as well as scenes from the daily lives of working people, such as people harvesting sugarcane and factory workers. Rivera also chose the mural form because murals are often on the exterior of buildings so more people can see them.

Mastering Mapwork

1. European ethnic group
2. Mesoamerican
3. Mestizo
4. European
5. Mesoamerican
6. Mestizo
7. European

Lessons Learned

LESSON 1
A Tale of Three Cities
Mexico's cities offer variety in atmosphere and culture. Mexico City is the capital of the country. Acapulco attracts many tourists. Monterrey is a manufacturing and trade center.

LESSON 2
Tradition and Religion in Mexico
Most Mexicans are Catholic. Many Native American religious traditions survive today. Some religious traditions mix Roman Catholic and Native American cultures. The Virgin of Guadalupe inspires devotion and pride.

LESSON 3
Culture in Mexico
Mexicans art is known around the world. The most popular sports are soccer and baseball. Wrestling is popular, too.

Becoming Better Readers

Important points: Students should list and describe the ways they find information. The topics do not need to be social studies related. they should, however, show good research planning and organization about the research process. Judgements about the quality of the source are important, too.

Talk About It

1. Which of the cities described in this chapter do you think best reflects the nation of Mexico? Explain why.
2. The Roman Catholic missions established in Mexico had two purposes: to convert and educate Native Americans. Did they accomplish these purposes? Explain.
3. Do you think art is more a part of everyday life in Mexico than it is in the United States? Explain your answer.
4. If a visitor from Mexico City were to come to your classroom, what three questions would you ask him or her in order to learn the most about the city? Explain why you would choose these three questions.
5. Mexican writers are said to have a social conscience. Do you think that other artists have a social conscience as well? Consider Diego Rivera. Explain your answer.

Mastering Mapwork

LOCATION
Use the map on page 595 to answer these questions:
1. Which ethnic group is concentrated in northern Mexico?
2. Which ethnic group is concentrated in southern and southeastern Mexico?
3. Which ethnic group is concentrated in western and central Mexico?
4. Which ethnic group is most numerous in the area surrounding Monterrey?
5. Which ethnic group is most numerous in the area surrounding Merida?
6. Which ethnic group is most numerous in the area around Acapulco?
7. Which ethnic group is most numerous in Tijuana and Ciudad Juárez?

Becoming better Readers

Using Resource Materials
Good readers use many sources to gather information. Sometimes they read a book. Sometimes they use the internet. What are some of the ways you find information about topics that interest you?

Go to the Source

Newspaper Articles

Read the newspaper article below. Answer the questions using the information from the article.

> Cinco de Mayo
> U.S. celebrates holiday more than some parts of Mexico
>
> by Paul Huggins
>
> Jesus Chavez grew up in Mexico but never witnessed a Cinco de Mayo celebration until he came to the United States.
>
> Alberto Carbajal grew up in Mexico and practiced months to march in Cinco de Mayo parades.
>
> The contrasting experiences of the two restaurant managers can be as confusing as the origins of the holiday itself, which many Americans mistakenly believe is Mexican Independence Day. It actually commemorates Mexico's 1862 victory over the French at the Battle of Puebla.
>
> But don't let any misunderstanding stop you from enjoying dinner and drink specials local Mexican restaurants will offer Thursday. Truth is, American's enjoyment of those discounts is part of the tradition.
>
> "It's just a bigger holiday here than in Mexico," he added with a clueless shrug. "When I got to the United States is when I started celebrating Cinco de Mayo."
>
> Some Spanish students in Elizabeth Cheatham's class at Calhoun Community College came to the same conclusion.
>
> Because she knew many of the students mistakenly believed Cinco de Mayo was like the Fourth of July in the United States, Cheatham assigned them to research the origins of the holiday.
>
> "One student said 'When I was doing my research on Cinco de Mayo, I learned it is really an American tradition,'" Cheatham said.
>
> World Book Encyclopedia agreed. It has no mention of Cinco de Mayo in its vast Mexico section, but does list it under Mexican-American cultures.

Questions

1. What holiday do Americans mistakenly believe Cinco de Mayo represents?
2. Why is Cinco de Mayo a bigger holiday in the United States than in Mexico?
3. When did Jesus Chavez start celebrating Cinco de Mayo?
4. What are the professions of Jesus Chavez and Alberto Carbajal?
5. Explain what one student meant when she said, "When I was doing my research on Cinco de Mayo, I learned it is really an American tradition"?

Go to the Source

Culture and Society

615

 Go to the Source

Newspaper Articles

➤ **OBJECTIVES:** 1.03, 1.07

SOCIAL STUDIES SKILLS: 3.05

Cino de Mayo

Discuss as a class the differences between Independence Day in the United States (July 4th) and Cinco de Mayo.

Answers

1. Mexican Independence Day
2. Americans believe Cinco de Mayo is like the Fourth of July in the United States, so it is a bigger holiday in the United States than in Mexico.
3. When he moved to the United States.
4. They are both restaurant managers.
5. More Americans celebrate Cinco De Mayo because they enjoy dinner and drink specials found in local restaurants.

? How to Use the Chapter Review

There are four sections in the Chapter Review: Talk About It, Mastering Mapwork, Becoming Better Readers, and Go to the Source. Use the Vocabulary Worksheets and the Chapter Review Worksheet in the Teacher's Resource Guide for additional reinforcement and preparation for the Chapter Assessments. The chapter and lesson reviews and the Chapter Review Worksheets are the basis of the assessment for each chapter.

Talk About It questions encourage students to speculate about the content of the chapter and are suitable for class or small-group discussion. They are not intended to be assigned for homework.

Mastering Mapwork has students apply one or more of the Five Themes of Geography to maps within the chapter.

Becoming Better Readers focuses on building reading strategy skills necessary for reading comprehension in the content areas.

Go to the Source activities allow students to analyze a primary source that relates to the content of the chapter. The questions and activities familiarize students with different types of primary sources and also build content-reading skills.

Central America and the Caribbean

The face you see in this unit opener is of a woman dressed for carnival, an important cultural festival in the Caribbean. In this unit, your students will study the land and people of Central America and the Caribbean. The relationship between people and the land in these environmentally significant areas is important for students to understand.

UNIT LESSON PLAN

	LESSON 1	LESSON 2	LESSON 3	LESSON 4
CHAPTER 26 **Central America**	Central America's mountains run like a spine along the region. The climate is hot and humid along the coast and cooler in the mountains. **Essential Question:** How is the climate of Central America affected by its physical features and elevation? **Suggested Time:** 1 day	During colonial times, Europeans used the rich land and resources of Central America for themselves. **Essential Question:** In what ways did Europeans use the land and resources to their benefit during colonial times? **Suggested Time:** 1 day	After independence, many Central American leaders were dictators. Now the region is becoming more democratic. **Essential Question:** How has leadership changed in Central America over the years? **Suggested Time:** 1 day	Central America's cultures are diverse but share a Spanish heritage. The Catholic Church is also a strong bond between cultures. **Essential Question:** How can we describe the culture of Central America? **Suggested Time:** 1 day
CHAPTER 27 **The Caribbean Islands**	The three island groups of the Caribbean enjoy warm weather all year. **Essential Question:** Where are the Caribbean islands, and how can we describe the geographical features found there? **Suggested Time:** 1 day	The culture of the Caribbean is a mixture of Native American, African, and European influences. **Essential Question:** What do we know about the culture of the Caribbean Islands? **Suggested Time:** 1 day	The plantation system and mining changed the environment of the Caribbean. **Essential Question:** How did the plantation system and mining affect the environment of the Caribbean? **Suggested Time:** 1 day	The food, sports, and music of the Caribbean show the influence of many cultures. **Essential Question:** How do the food, sports, and music of the Caribbean reflect a blend of cultures? **Suggested Time:** 1–2 days

Preparing the Unit

- Worksheets, assessments, and reproducibles for this unit are found in the Teacher's Resource Guide.
- See the list of Cultural Resources in the Teacher's Edition.
- Before you begin the Unit, decorate your room with pictures and posters that illustrate the geography, tourist attractions, people, and culture of the regions.
- Preview the list of suggested resources in this unit and set up a resource library in your classroom for students to use for research projects or during reading time.

Unit Teaching Strategies

- Share some of the suggested resources and activities listed in the Teacher's Edition with your cultural arts teachers so that they can integrate their lessons.
- Use the ideas in the wrap-around as suggestions to help you meet the needs of your students and your teaching style. Please consider that there is a lot of material to be covered and that you must pace yourself in order to teach the curriculum. The variety of suggested activities are included to help you differentiate your instruction to meet the needs of your students. Utilize these activities to best enhance your instruction, and do not feel that you should implement them all.
- If time is a factor, use this unit in addition to units 5 and 6 for students to do projects that culminate with a festival of nations. Preview the list of suggested projects throughout the units, prepare a list of choices for the students, and assign the topics to the students to complete. Students can teach each other by giving presentations on various topics from the units. By using this type of instruction, students will be actively involved and will save instructional time.
- This unit as well as Units 5 and 6 should be used as an adventure for the students to allow them to explore our neighboring countries. It also provides ample opportunities for comparing and contrasting these areas with what they have just learned about the United States.
Check **NCJourneys.com** for updates and materials.

Students will have ten days to complete their project. They have the option of choosing from the different projects, and should only choose one of the five projects. The five projects offer a lot of variety so students can pick an area which interests them. Suggested report format: one page in length, typed, and double-spaced.

PROJECT CHOICES

 OBJECTIVES: 1.05, 1.07, 3.07

Design a Flag
Have students select a country in the Caribbean or Central America with an ethnically diverse population. Have them design a new flag for that country, one that incorporates something that represents each ethnic group. They should write a paragraph explaining their design.

Where Would I Like to Visit?
Have students choose one nation that they would like to visit. Students will write a short essay describing why that country interests them, why they would like to visit it, and what aspects of the country they would like to know more about—food, culture, religious practices, government, and so on.

A Study of Diverse Regions
Students will select a country or countries to research. They can choose the format to display their research: giant book, poster, graphic organizer, or other ideas. Information for each country should include four or more of the following: location, landforms, languages, religions, foods, ethnic groups, holidays and/or cultural events, landmarks and/or attractions, recreation, famous people, climate, plants, and animals. They should include a map of the country.

Extension Novice ELL students can do a map and label it, or make a poster of the plants and animals and draw and label them.

Poem of a Country
Have students choose a country in Central America or the Caribbean. They should identify its neighboring countries, important bodies of water, important physical features, and climate and vegetation and record this on a graphic organizer. Using this information, students are to write a poem describing the physical characteristics of the country studied. Have students write their poems on an outline map of their designated country.

Mobile with Attitude
Students will design and create a mobile illustrating influential people from the region. Mobile attachments should be cut in the shape of people and include their name. An attachment to each person should include biographical information and contributions.

Bulletin Board Ideas

Movement of People
Using a map of Central America and the Caribbean as your centerpiece, trace the origins of the people who live there. Students could illustrate with outlines or drawings of people.

Regions
Using a map of Central America and the Caribbean as the centerpiece, color each nation and territory a different color and label each one. On slips of paper, put pictures or names of various items that are representative of each place. Have "items" (pictures or names of items on paper slips) available to represent each place. Have students place items in the proper location on the map as you study the unit.

Introductory Activity

Menu Mania

> **OBJECTIVES:** 2.08, 3.05, 3.07

Geography and resources dictate the diet of a region. Have students create two menus: one that might be found in a restaurant in Central America and another that might be found in a restaurant in the Caribbean. Include drawings of the geography of the regions on the covers of the menus. Inside the menus, students should list items that people in these regions enjoy.

Have students design two tabletop settings from these regions. Create food dishes from construction paper and markers. Cut them out and glue them on posterboard. Set out on desks in the classroom. Classmates can take turns sitting at each desk and explaining the foods and regions.

Extension Novice ELL students can make the foods and label them on the plate.

Culminating Activity

Class Magazine

> **OBJECTIVES:** 1.06, 1.07, 2.08, 3.06, 3.07

Tell the class that they are the publishers of a new magazine about North America. They must come up with a title for their magazine and decide how many pages each issue will be.

After studying each unit in their social studies textbook, they are to publish an issue of their magazine. As a class, discuss what articles should be included in the issue. Use some of the story ideas suggested below or create your own. What maps and illustrations will be needed? What types of charts and statistics will be necessary to help readers understand the information? Break the class into editorial teams of writers, cartographers, illustrators, statisticians, and designers. The writing team (this can be a larger group) will be responsible for writing the articles. The cartography team will be responsible for drawing the maps to go with the articles. The illustrators will be responsi-

ble for finding or drawing pictures to illustrate the articles. The design team will be responsible for putting the magazine together. Remind students that each group needs to coordinate with the others so that their final project will look professional and be easy for readers to understand.

Make several copies so that your students can share their magazine with classes in your school. Students should keep copies of the magazines from each unit so that they will have a complete set of magazines on North America at the end of the year.

Unit 7 story ideas: Native American cultures, the Spanish in Central America, European influence in the Caribbean, African influence in the Caribbean, the region's major industries, the peoples of different countries, or music and dance from the region.

Science Activity

The Parts of a Rain Forest

> **OBJECTIVES:** 1.01, 1.02, 1.03, 1.06

The rain forest is divided into four layers: the floor, the understory, the emergent layer, and the canopy. Divide the class into groups. Assign each group a layer. Students will research and collect data on the animals, insects, and plants living in their layer. Students should also find information on the temperature, soils, heights of layers, rainfall amounts, and human influences as well. For the human impacts, have some students record their findings on human-shaped forms. Have students cut out of construction paper shapes of animals or plants that live in the rain forest. Have them record their findings on the shapes. Allow students to report their findings to the class. As students report their findings, create a mural or diagram on the wall with various animal and plant shapes. When students finish you will have a completed cross section of a Central American rain forest.

Technology Activity

The Parts of a Rain Forest

> **OBJECTIVES:** 5.01, 5.02, 5.06

Students will select a country in this region and use the Internet to research six products, three that the country exports and three that it imports. Students should also identify countries that produce the imported products. (Be sure all countries in the unit are selected.) When the Trade Market Day arrives, students will write on paper strips two of their country's export products and where they go and two of their country's import products and from what countries they come. Collect the strips, mix them up and redistribute them to students. Give a student a ball of yarn and ask him or her to read a strip. The student will say, for example, "My Costa Rican pineapples go to Saudi Arabia." The student with a Saudi Arabian product will raise his or her hand. The student with the yarn will hold one end and throw the ball to the student with the strip reading "Saudi Arabia." That student will say "My Saudi Arabian oil goes to Puerto Rico," and the game continues. When they finish they will have a web of yarn and understanding of interdependence. Other examples include Puerto Rican sugar to India, Indian tea to Panama, Panamanian bananas to Poland, and so on.

Math Activity

Scavenger Hunt Graphing

> **OBJECTIVES:** 1.07, 3.07, 5.06

To demonstrate the importance of the area's economy, assign students to look for items at home (clothing, appliances, toys, and so forth) that were made in Central America or the Caribbean. Classify the items by category as they are identified. Have the class determine what percentage of the total of all of the items is in each category. Graph this on the board. Students can make graphs of their own individual findings.

Unit Resources

Print Resources

Fiction

Bernier-Grand, Carmen T. *In the Shade of the Nispero Tree*. Orchard Books, 1999. ISBN 0531301540.

Cole, Joanna. *The Magic School Bus Inside a Hurricane* (Magic School Bus series). Scholastic Trade, 1996. ISBN 0590446878.

Gonzalez, Lucia M. *Señor Cat's Romance: And Other Favorite Stories from Latin America*. Scholastic, 2001. ISBN 0439278635.

Young, Richard. *Stories from the Days of Christopher Columbus: A Multicultural Collection for Young Readers* (American Storytelling series). August House, 1992. ISBN 0874831989.

Nonfiction

Albert, Toni. *The Remarkable Rainforest: An Active-Learning Book for Kids*. Trickle Creek Books, 1996. ISBN 0964074206.

Atkinson, Stuart. *Storms and Hurricanes* (Understanding Geography series). E D C Publications, 1996. ISBN 0746020120.

Burleigh, Robert. *Chocolate: Riches from the Rainforest*. Harry N. Abrams, 2002. ISBN 0810957345.

Chessen, Betsey. *Rainforest*. Econo-Clad Books, 1999. ISBN 0613178459.

Coe Sophie D. and Michael D. Coe. *The True History of Chocolate*. Thames & Hudson, 2000. ISBN 0500282293.

Farmer, Jacqueline. *Bananas*. Charlesbridge Publishing, 1999. ISBN 0881061158.

Pratt, Kristin Joy. *A Walk in the Rainforest*. Dawn, 1992. ISBN 1878265539.

Wardlaw, Lee. *Bubblemania: A Chewy History of Bubble Gum*. Aladdin Paperbacks, 1997. ISBN 0689817193.

Back issues of magazines

Costa Rica. Cobblestone Publishing Company. ISBN 0382445252.

Dominican Republic. Cobblestone Publishing Company. ISBN 0382443837.

El Salvador. Cobblestone Publishing Company. ISBN 0382443802.

Haitians. Cobblestone Publishing Company. ISBN 038240548.

Guatemala. Cobblestone Publishing Company. ISBN 0382407881.

Puerto Rico. Cobblestone Publishing Company. ISBN 0382409035.

Web Sites

Visit **NCJourneys.com** for links to these Web sites:

- Central American/Caribbean Political Resources
- Government links for Central America and the Caribbean, University of Michigan Library Documents Center
- Central and South America resource links, State Road Elementary Library, Webster, New York (includes Caribbean)
- Internet Resources for Latin America, New Mexico State University Library
- Latin American & Iberian Resources, Duke University Libraries
- Latin American Government Documents Archive
- Latin American Public Opinion Project
- Mesoamerican Civilizations: Maya and Inca
- News Link (links to hundreds of U.S. and world newspapers)
- Political Database of the Americas, Georgetown University
- Teaching about the Americas

Paideia Seminar

Mama and Papa Have a Store

OBJECTIVES: 2.08, 3.04, 3.06, 3.07

Mama and Papa Have a Store by Amelia Lau Carling. Penguin Putman Inc., 1998. ISBN 0803720440. The book shows a typical day as the author's parents operate their store in Guatemala City. They have emigrated from China.

Theme kindness, trustworthiness, perseverance, change, immigration

Pre-seminar Have students read a typed version of the book. Have them look for the ways that Mamma and Papa have adapted to their new environment while keeping some traditions from their own culture.

Opening Questions

- What word or phrase would you use to summarize the changes that the family in the story have undergone?

Core Questions

- Based on the text, how did the people of Guatemala City accept or reject the new family from China?
- What traditions from China were kept by the family?
- What do you think is very hard about moving to a new country with a different culture?
- If you had to move to another country (or have moved) how would (do) you feel?

Closing Questions

- What things did you learn during this discussion? What prompted your learning?

Post-seminar Have students interview classmates in the school to see if they have moved from another country. After the data is collected students can graph the school population according to country of birth. They can also color a world map showing the places represented.

Map Activity

Central America & the Caribbean

NATIONAL GEOGRAPHY STANDARDS: 1,2

GEOGRAPHIC THEMES: Location

OBJECTIVES: 1.01, 1.05

Have the students look at the map on page 617. Ask:

- Which hemispheres do Central America and the Caribbean lie within? *Northern and Western Hemispheres*
- Describe the relative location of Central America and the Caribbean. *Northern and Western Hemispheres, south of Mexico, northwest of South America, bordered by Caribbean Sea (Central America) or the Atlantic Ocean (Caribbean) on the east and the Pacific Ocean (Central America) or the Gulf of Mexico (Caribbean) on the west.*
- Based on the relative location, what do you think the climate is like? *tropical rain forest and tropical savanna*
- Based on the last question, where would you like to live and why? *Answers will vary.*

   Now have the students close their books and sketch Central America and the Caribbean in 10 minutes. When the students complete their maps, analyze the reasons the maps look like they do.

Unit 7

Central America and the Caribbean

Central America and the Caribbean are regions of contrasts. Volcanoes, rugged mountain ranges, steaming rain forests, deserts, and hurricanes can make life difficult. But there are also areas with fertile soil, great natural beauty, and year-round, springlike weather.

Central America and the Caribbean are in the Tropics. Central America is made up of temperate mountains, volcanoes, and hot, coastal lowlands. Islands formed from volcanoes and coral deposits make up the Caribbean.

The diverse geography in this region is matched by the variety in the histories of the nations and territories found there.

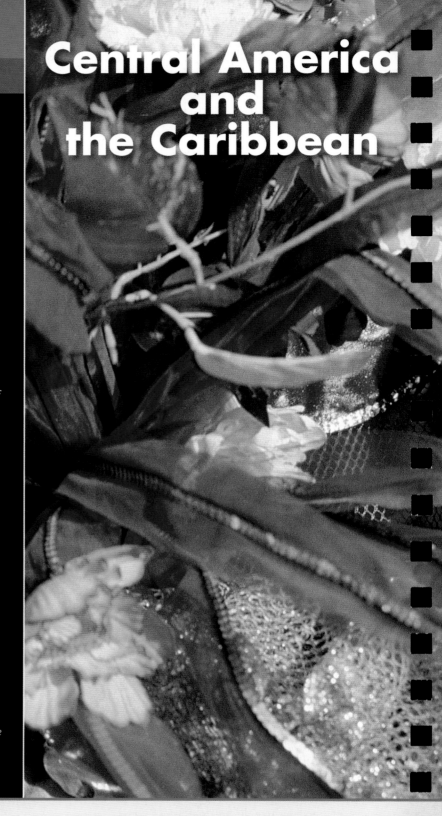

Carnival, Martinique

Social Studies at Work

Artistic Director

An artistic director is someone who directs the creative work of a performing arts company.

Meet Chuck Davis

Founder and Artistic Director of the African American Dance Ensemble.

   Peace, love, and respect. Those words represent the values behind Chuck Davis's work as founder and artistic director of the African American Dance Ensemble. After graduating from Ligon High School and serving a two-year stint in the navy, the

North Carolina native went on to pursue a degree in theater and dance at Howard University.

   New York was the next destination on his career path. There he studied all forms of dance with some of the most renowned masters in the field. He also began to dance professionally and received rave reviews wherever he went. With a growing national and even international reputation as a dancer, Davis decided to come home to North Carolina, where he joined the faculty of the American Dance Festival in Durham and eventually founded the African American Dance Ensemble.

   That was back in 1980. Today, Davis and his dance troupe

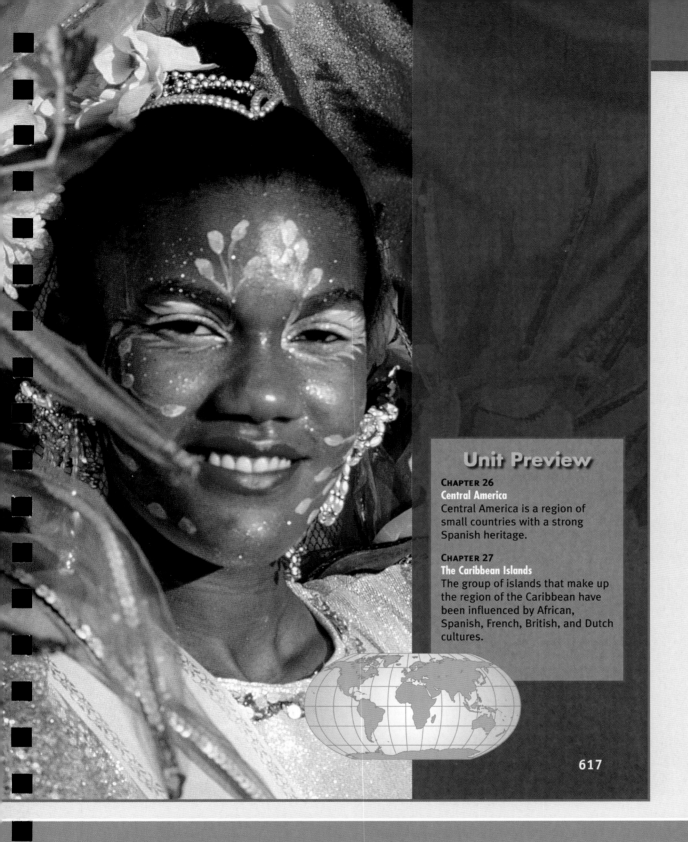

Unit Preview

CHAPTER 26
Central America
Central America is a region of small countries with a strong Spanish heritage.

CHAPTER 27
The Caribbean Islands
The group of islands that make up the region of the Caribbean have been influenced by African, Spanish, French, British, and Dutch cultures.

617

are widely regarded as the premier dance company of its kind. Davis himself has been honored as one of America's 100 irreplaceable dance treasures, officially by the Dance Heritage Coalition and unofficially by just about anyone who has seen his work.

Davis regards his work as much more than art. It's a way to share his heritage and pass on an important cultural legacy to people all over the world. Davis' work celebrates traditional African culture, aesthetics, and values while encouraging inter-racial cooperation and cross-cultural understanding.

Artistic Director for a Day
Ask teams of students to make up new words for a favorite song that reflects what they are learning in social studies. Allow time for each group to perform their songs for the entire class, adding choreography in accordance with the groups' comfort level.

Find Out More
Go to **NCJourneys.com** for a link to explore the work of Chuck Davis and the African American Dance Theater.

Central America

Social Studies Strands

Geographic Relationships

Historic Perspectives

Economics and Development

Government and Active Citizenship

Global Connections

Cultures and Diversity

North Carolina Standard Course of Study

Goal 1 The learner will apply key geographic concepts to the United States and other countries of North America.

Goal 2 The learner will analyze political and social institutions in North America and examine how these institutions respond to human needs, structure society, and influence behavior.

Goal 3 The learner will examine the roles various ethnic groups have played in the development of the United States and its neighboring countries.

Goal 5 The learner will evaluate ways the United States and other countries of North America make decisions about the allocation and use of economic resources.

Teaching & Assessment

- English Language Learner Modified Lesson Plans for this chapter are found in the Teacher's Resource Guide.
- *ExamView® Assessment Suite* is provided at **NCJourneys.com.** It includes customizable assessments for all chapters. Paper tests are also available in the Teacher's Resource Guide. See pages T16–T17 for information about how to use the assessments and the Scoring Guide.

Chapter Worksheets

Worksheets and answer keys are found both in the Teacher's Resource Guide and at **NCJourneys.com**, including Reading Guides, Reading Strategies, Chapter Reviews, English Language Learner and others.

Activities and Integrations

SOCIAL STUDIES

Problem Based Learning: Central America, p. 618B
Activator: Changing the Environment, p. 618
● ▲ I am a Country, I am a Capital, p. 619
Adopt a Rain Forest, p. 623
Artifact History, p. 627
Economic Activity, p. 628
Nature's Dyes, p. 630
Are Dictators *Always* Bad?, p. 635
Developed versus Developing, p. 641

READING/LANGUAGE ARTS	READING/LANGUAGE ARTS OBJECTIVES
Central American United Nations, p. 618B	1.03
■ Writing Prompt: Building the Panama Canal, p.618	4.09
Carolina Connection: O Henry, p. 619	3.07
Quetzal Bird, p. 624	1.04, 1.05, 3.06
Reading Strategy: Test Taking Techniques, p. 620	3.05
Reading Strategy: Test Taking Vocabulary, p. 626	1.03
Reading Strategy: Looking Back, p. 631	2.06, 3.02
Reading Strategy: Review and Recall, p. 637	2.01, 2.02
★ Developing Countries, p. 638	4.02
Skill Lesson: Thinking About Population, p. 643	1.03
Becoming Better Readers, p. 644	2.01

MATHEMATICS	MATHEMATICS OBJECTIVES
★ ▲ ■ A Trip Around Central America, p. 618B	1.02
Butterfly Migration, p. 624	4.01, 4.02
Banana Graphs, p. 632	4.01
Cooking with Fractions, p. 639	1.03
Understanding Statistics, p. 645	1.02

SCIENCE	SCIENCE OBJECTIVES
Growing a Rain Forest, p. 622	1.01, 1.02, 1.03, 1.07
★ Climate and Vegetation, p. 663	1.07, 3.03, 3.06
Butterfly Migration, p. 624	1.02, 1.03

TECHNOLOGY	TECHNOLOGY OBJECTIVES
Carolina Connection: O Henry, p. 619	2.13
▲ ■ Butterfly Migration, p. 624	2.13
Panama Canal, p. 634	2.13

VISUAL ARTS	VISUAL ARTS OBJECTIVES
● ▲ ■ Beach Towel, p. 618B	2.01, 3.02
Growing a Rain Forest, p. 622	2.01, 3.02
● ▲ Banana Mania, p. 632	2.01, 3.02
★ Central America: Economic Activities and Resources, p. 629	2.01, 3.02

CHARACTER AND VALUES EDUCATION	TRAITS
What Would You Do?, p. 625	responsibility, caring, good citizenship
Keeping Peace, p. 636	good citizenship
Missions, p. 640	caring, responsibility

● Basic Activities ★ Challenging Activities ▲ English Language Learner Novice ■ English Language Learner Intermediate

Introductory Activity

A Trip Around Central America

 OBJECTIVES: 1,01, 1.02, 1.06, 3.04

Using a large wall map, ask your students to plot an imaginary trip to Central America. In each country your students visit, they should identify its capital, one custom, its monetary system, its cultural origins, and one point of interest. They may choose one of the following:

1. Create a timeline with pictures and writing to determine how long it will take them to travel from place to place.
2. Calculate rate, time, and distance to travel from place to place as well as through the entire country.
3. Send messages to Central American students via the Internet to find out what they might expect on their trip.
4. Investigate vegetation and geographic landforms in each country.
5. Consider what items they will need as they travel from place to place.

As a follow-up, discuss how hard it is to travel from place to place in Central America. Consider the physical, cultural, and political barriers that exist there.

Extension Intermediate and novice ELL students can label the cities and countries on a map.

Culminating Activity

Central American United Nations

OBJECTIVES: 2.05, 3.04, 4.07, 4.08

Have a mock United Nations conference of Central American countries with an ambassador from each country, modeled on the conference held in Costa Rica in 1987 (see page 636). Encourage a discussion of the benefits of democratic governments, where citizens have the right to vote in free elections. Discuss the democratic process in society.

- Why might countries refuse to participate in a democratic society?
- What are the benefits of a democratic society?
- How would democracy help promote peace in Central America?

Students should prepare their points of view, pro and con, before the conference is held. At the end, have the nations sign the treaty much like they did for Arias's peace plan.

Art Activity

Beach Towel

OBJECTIVES: 1.06, 1.07, 2.08, 3,02, 3.04, 3.06

Student Directions You have just returned from a trip to Central America. You could buy only one souvenir. You chose a large beach towel, covered with all kinds of interesting information.

Give each student a large sheet of white paper. Using the text and other resources, students will design a beach towel with pictures, maps, symbols, and so on to illustrate the culture of the region. Color brightly and glue colorful strips of tissue paper on the two short ends. Hang on the walls.

Extension Show ELL students an example.

Problem Based Learning Activity

Central America

OBJECTIVES: 5.04, 5.06, 5.07

Situation Central America has struggled with many challenges since its freedom from Spain. Only recently has this region freed itself from the rule of dictators. Today democracy is still a new idea. Consider what it might be like to be a businessperson from the United States desiring to do business with a farmer in Central America. Unfortunately, you can not depend upon the political system of the nation in which this farmer lives. There is no other place that you can find this product, yet sometimes the government demands extra money, or prohibits the export, and sometimes you simply loose contact. The unpredictability of the business will directly affect your business in the United States. What are you to do?

Task Using two empty coffee cans home have students place items from home in the cans that signify the costs and benefits of continuing this business relationship (play money, bananas, ships symbolizing the Panama Canal, coffee, cocoa, and so on). The cans can be labeled or decorated. These cans will help students make decisions about dealing with unpredictable business circumstances. Students will bring the cans to class and share. Discuss how the business situation could be resolved using the "costs" can and the "benefits" can. Some reasons tend to "outweigh" others.

Reflection Ask students to consider how decisions sometimes have to be made because of circumstances—even though you may not want to make a decision. Many decisions affect a large amount of people beyond the ones making the decisions.

Teaching Strategies

If students are not already assigned a country for research, you might want to consider assigning a Central American country to students for research projects that will culminate in a Central American Festival of Nations. Use a variety of maps and hands-on activities to help students identify the countries and geographical features in this region. If possible, invite a guest to make a presentation to the class who is from one of the Central American countries or who has traveled to one of them.

Discussion Questions

1 Why is the quetzel a symbol of freedom in Central America?

Activator

OBJECTIVES: 2.08, 5.01, 5.02, 5.06

Changing the Environment Display the following items in front of the class: Bag of coffee beans, bag of sugar, bunch of bananas, and a pineapple. Ask the class what these items have in common. Then start a discussion on how these items are grown on plantations in Middle America and the effects plantations have had and still have on the environment.

Writing Prompt

OBJECTIVES: 1.06, 5.05, 6.01, 6.02

Writing Directions Read the Eyewitness to History section: Building the Panama Canal (see pages 634–635). It was a tremendous building project. Think of a project you have constructed. It might be something you have made with your parents or friends. It might have been made at school or at home. Write in detail each step you used to build your project.

Clarification There is much controversy about whether the United States should offer help to developing countries. Write a paper stating your position on this. Be sure to tell why you think the way you do.

Clarification Think of a cultural tradition you and your family enjoy. It might be music, sports, art, storytelling, or religious events. Write about why you enjoy this tradition. Be sure to give at least two reasons why.

Extension Intermediate ELL students can participate in the clarification.

CHAPTER 26

Central America

The most magnificent bird in Central America is the quetzal (KET·sahl). This bird was sacred to the Maya. The Aztecs prized its bright red and green feathers. The quetzal cannot live in captivity. For this reason it is a symbol of freedom in Central America. It is the national bird of Guatemala.

Its tail feathers can be up to 5 feet (1.5 m) long. Because poachers have killed and captured so many of these birds, it is difficult to spot one today. But there are some protected zones where, with luck, one might see a quetzal perched among the high branches of the forest.

A male quetzal

Chapter Preview

LESSON 1
Land and People
Central America's mountains run like a spine along the region. The climate is hot and humid along the coast and cooler in the mountains.

LESSON 2
People and Environment
During colonial times, Europeans used the rich land and resources of Central America for themselves.

LESSON 3
Economy and Government
After independence, many Central American leaders were dictators. Now the region is becoming more democratic.

LESSON 4
Society and Culture
Central America's cultures are diverse but share a Spanish heritage. The Catholic Church is also a strong bond between cultures.

618

Mayan temple in Tikal, Guatemala

Chapter Resources

Print Resources

Fiction

Ada, Alma Flor. *Three Golden Oranges.* Atheneum Books, 1999. ISBN 0689807759.

Palacios, Argentina. *The Hummingbird King: A Guatemalan Legend* (Legends of the World series). Troll, 1993. ISBN 0816730520.

Rohmer, Harriet (contrib.), Octavio Chow and Morris Vidaure (eds.). *The Invisible Hunters/Los Cazadores Invisibles: A Legend from the Miskito Indians of Nicaragua.* Scott Foresman, 1993. ISBN 089239109X.

Skarmeta, Antonio. *The Composition.* Groundwood Books, 2000. ISBN 0888993900.

Whitton, Eduardo Thiers, Miguel Angel Asturias, and S.A. Santillana. *El Señor Presidente.* Santillana Pub., 1998. ISBN 8429435905.

Nonfiction

English, Peter (ed.). *Panama in Pictures* (Visual Geography series). Lerner Publica-

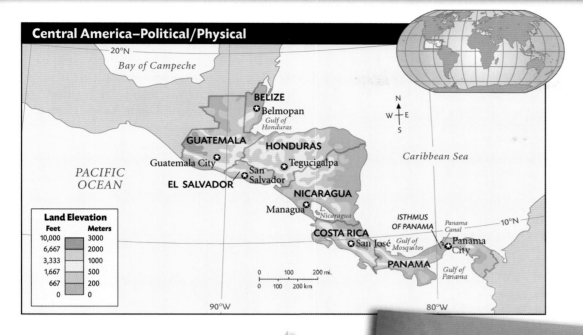

Central America–Political/Physical

20°N
Bay of Campeche

BELIZE
⊛Belmopan
Gulf of Honduras

GUATEMALA
HONDURAS

Guatemala City⊛
⊛San Salvador
Tegucigalpa⊛

Caribbean Sea

PACIFIC OCEAN

EL SALVADOR

NICARAGUA

Managua⊛
L. Nicaragua

ISTHMUS OF PANAMA
Panama Canal

10°N

COSTA RICA
San José⊛
Gulf of Mosquitos
⊛Panama City

PANAMA
Gulf of Panama

Land Elevation

Feet	Meters
10,000	3000
6,667	2000
3,333	1000
1,667	500
667	200
0	0

0   100   200 mi.
0   100   200 km

90°W   80°W

O. Henry and Honduras

William Sydney Porter was born in Greensboro in 1862. He is one of North Carolina's most famous authors. He used the pen name O. Henry. His stories usually had surprise endings. You may have read his Christmas story "The Gift of the Magi."

While O. Henry lived in Texas he was accused of stealing. Instead of going to jail, he fled to Honduras. He learned that his wife was sick. So he returned to the United States. He was arrested. In prison he wrote a book of short stories set in Honduras. The book, *The Cabbages and Kings*, was published in 1904.

CAROLINA CONNECTION

COUNTRIES of Central America

- Belize
- Costa Rica
- El Salvador
- Guatemala
- Honduras
- Nicaragua
- Panama

619

tions, 1996. ISBN 082251818X.
Schlesinger Arthur Meier and Fred L. Israel (eds.). *Building the Panama Canal: Chronicles from National Geographic.* Chelsea House, 1999. ISBN 0791051021.

Audiovisual

La Vida Pura: Meet Yesinia, A Costa Rican Youth. North Carolina State University Humanities Extension/Publications Program.

Modern Marvels: Panama Canal. New Video Group, 1994.

National Geographic's Really Wild Animals: Totally Tropical Rain Forest. National Geographic Video. 1994.

Web Sites

Visit **NCJourneys.com** for links:
- Central American Newspapers
- The Panama Canal
- Belize Field Guide for Ambergris Caye

Map Activity

I am a Country, I am a Capital

NATIONAL GEOGRAPHY STANDARDS: 1
GEOGRAPHIC THEMES: The World in Spacial Terms
OBJECTIVES: 1.01, 1.03

Write the names of the countries and capitals of Central America on separate index cards. There will be 14 in all. If necessary, make duplicates so each student in the room has a card. Tell the students they have 1 minute to locate their word on the map and to decide if the word is a country or a capital. Assist students by explaining that names of countries are written in all capital letters and cities are written in both capital and lowercase letters.

Tell the students to refer to the pronunciation in the gazetteer in their textbook to learn how to pronounce their word.

Students with country cards move to one side of the room while "city cards" move to another. Then have them match the city and country cards. Post them on a map.

Extension Novice ELL students can participate if they understand the difference between the two or has classmates to help.

Activity

Carolina Connection: O. Henry

OBJECTIVES: 1.06, 1.07, 2.08

Divide students into six groups to research O. Henry's life. Have students read the information on the Web sites and try to find an author's particular "slant." For example, the North Carolina article spends more time talking about O. Henry's youth in North Carolina. Have the students identify the "slant" and share with their classmates. The students should indicate which articles show no bias toward any particular time in O. Henry's life. Visit **NCJourneys.com** for links to Web sites on O. Henry.

LESSON 1 Land and People

Discussion Questions

1 What is the Pacific Ring of Fire?

2 What benefit to the soil do volcanoes bring?

Caption Answer

It has many volcanoes and earthquakes. It is part of the Ring of Fire.

Reading Strategy Activity

Test Taking Techniques

OBJECTIVES: 1.01, 1.02, 1.03, 1.06

With all the testing that is required today, test taking techniques are an important reading strategy to teach your students. Here are some of the basic strategies.

- Do a quick survey of the test so that you can budget your time and have a good idea what is on the test.
- Do the easiest problems first. Come back to the problems that require more thought.
- Read the entire question before answering.
- With multiple choice questions, read all the answers before choosing one.
- With writing/essay questions, write down an outline, or some main ideas and supporting details that you want to be sure you include in your answer before you start to write. This way you will not forget them as you are writing
- If you finish the test early, read back over the test to be sure that you understood each question.
- If you start to get nervous, take a deep breath.

KEY IDEAS

- The nations of Central America lie in southern North America. They are close to South America.
- Many of the mountains of Central America are volcanoes.
- Central America is hot and humid in areas close to the coast and in valleys. In the mountains, the climate is cool or very cold.
- Central America is rich in plant and animal life.

KEY TERMS

ecotourism
Ring of Fire
Tierra Caliente
Tierra Fria
Tierra Helada
Tierra Templada

Some people have called Central America "the Land of the Shaking Earth." It has many volcanoes and earthquakes. People get used to living near volcanoes. Even small children know what to do if the ground begins to shake beneath their feet.

In Central America you will see corn planted almost everywhere, even on the side of a volcano. Warm weather vegetables and cool weather vegetables both grow year-round. Central Americans are trying to make a living through preserving their forests and wildlife.

This market in Antigua, Guatemala falls in the shadows of the Pacaya Volcano. **Why is Central America nicknamed the "Land of the Shaking Earth."**

620

Chapter 26

Teacher Notes

Masaya National Park

Managua, with an estimated population of over 1 million, is the capital of Nicaragua and is located on the Central American volcanic axis. Masaya is perhaps the most interesting volcano in Nicaragua as well as the most visited. It was made into a national park by the Sandinistas in 1979. The Spanish discovered Masaya in 1524 and subsequently climbed to its highest point. They built a wooden cross there to deter the Native Americans from throwing people into it as a sacrifice (the cross is still there and a flight of stairs lets you climb up to it). Masaya is a basaltic volcano, which has non-typical explosive eruptions. An eruption in April 2001 sent tourists and scientists scurrying. No one was killed, but there were some injuries.

Location and Landforms

The nations of Central America are on a narrow strip of land called an isthmus. The isthmus separates the Caribbean Sea and the Pacific Ocean. It also connects North and South America. High mountains and volcanoes run along this land like a pointy spine.

Central America is part of a huge ring of volcanoes. This is called the Pacific *Ring of Fire.* The ring circles the Pacific Ocean. It reaches from Asia to Alaska to the tip of South America. In this circle volcanic eruptions and earthquakes are common.

Volcanoes have helped and harmed Central America. The ash from volcanoes has enriched the soil. This helps plants grow. But earthquakes have also destroyed cities and taken lives.

Elevation and Climate

Central America lies in the Tropics. This means that temperatures remain fairly stable throughout the year.

In between its two coasts, the land rises to mountains more than 12,000 feet (3600 m) above sea level. The mountains are a barrier to transportation, communication, and agriculture. But their elevation provides a climate with spring-like weather all year.

The map on page 623 shows the three main climate types. They are tropical rain forest, tropical savanna, and highlands.

The rainy season lasts from May until November. Every year it brings storms and flooding to many areas. Hurricanes from the Caribbean Sea often destroy crops, bridges, and buildings and sometimes kill many people.

In 1998, Honduras was devastated by Hurricane Mitch. For more than two days the winds howled at speeds of more than 150 miles (241.5 km) per hour. Four feet (1.2 m) of rain fell. Floods and mudslides killed thousands. The homes of more than 1 million people were destroyed.

Ring of Fire

- Earthquake

Region The Ring of Fire rims the Pacific Ocean. *What benefits and challenges do the volcanoes bring to Central America?*

A family inspects a parched cornfield in Los Rojos, Nicaragua. **What do you see in the background of this photo?**

Central America

621

Discussion Questions

1 How do major cities in Central America compare in elevation to places in North Carolina?

2 What other natural disasters threaten Central America?

Caption Answer

Volcanic ash enriches the soil, but earthquakes can destroy cities and take lives.

Caption Answer

A dormant volcano

Teacher Notes

Climate Zones of Central America

The *tierra caliente* is a zone embracing the tropical rain forest and tropical savanna climates. In this hot, wet environment crops are often grown on plantations. Many of the descendants of Africans brought to the New World as slaves are concentrated in the tierra caliente zone.

The *tierra templada* is most notably the zone of the coffee tree. The upper limits of this zone— approximately 6,000 feet (1,800 m) above sea level—are generally also the upper limit of plantation agriculture in Central America. Six cities exceeding 2 million in population—São Paulo, Belo Horizonte, Caracas, Medellin, Cali, and Guadalajara—are in this zone.

The *tierra fría* at 6,000–10,000 ft (1,800 m–3,200 m) experiences frost and is often inhabited by Native American populations. Such hardy crops as potatoes and barley grow there.

The *tierra helada* consists of the alpine meadows along with still higher barren rocks and permanent fields of snow and ice. This zone has some grains and animals. This area is characterized by small settlements.

Discussion Questions

1 What elevation zones are in Central America?

2 What are their characteristics?

3 What is grown there?

4 How does it help the environment?

5 What are some important birds of Central America? Have you seen any of these? If so, where?

Caption Answer

Chewing gum

Activity

Growing a Rain Forest

OBJECTIVES: 1.02, 1.06, 1.07

This activity takes several days. Before beginning, ask students to bring in books, encyclopedias, and Internet articles about the rain forests of Central America. Gather these materials to use for research and illustrations. In one section of the room, hang black bulletin board paper to create the background for the rain forest. Explain to the students that over the next few days you will be "growing" a rain forest and will need their help. Have vivid, colorful construction paper to construct the rain forest. Label the parts of the rain forest with word cards.

Background The layers of the rain forest are the emergent, canopy, understory, and floor. The emergent layer is made up of the tops of the tallest trees. The canopy is very high and thick where the vegetation grows together, with only a few emergent trees breaking through the top. Sunlight cannot penetrate through this abundant foliage to reach the dark floor below. The canopy is where most of the plants and wildlife exist. There are buttress roots that support the tall trees. Vines go from tree to tree connecting all vegetation. Smaller amounts of sunlight reach the understory, where plants compete for survival. Sapling and midsize trees are also part of the

The *Tierras*

Central America also has several elevation zones (see map, page 619).

Along the coasts, from sea level up to about 2,500 feet (750 m), is the zone called **Tierra Caliente,** or Hot Land. Here temperatures are hot, like summer in the Coastal Plain of North Carolina. The main crops are bananas, sugarcane, and rice.

The next elevation zone, the **Tierra Templada,** or Temperate Land, is found at elevations between 2,500 feet (750 m) and 6,000 feet (1,800 m). Major crops here include coffee, corn, wheat, and vegetables. The temperatures are mild, like spring in North Carolina.

Most people live in this zone. Several capital cities are above 3,000 feet (900 m) in elevation. North Carolina's capital, Raleigh, is 434 feet (130 m) above sea level. Asheville, North Carolina, is 2,140 feet (642m) in elevation.

At 6,000 feet (1,800 m) above sea level is the **Tierra Fria,** or Cold Land. Fewer people live here. They grow potatoes and grains. They raise livestock such as sheep for wool.

The last zone is the **Tierra Helada,** or Icy Land. It is above 12,000 feet (3,600 km). In Central America there is very little land at this elevation.

This ceiba *tree grows in a tropical rain forest in Guatemala.* **What is made from a sapodilla tree?**

Plant Life

People around the world believe certain trees are sacred. For the Vikings it was the ash tree. For the Native Americans in North Carolina it was the elm.

One of the special trees of Central America is the *ceiba* (SAY·bah). It grows wide, above-ground roots. Above its huge trunk, its branches stretch up 130 feet (39 m) high. To the ancient Maya people, the *ceiba's* roots represented the underworld. Its branches represented the heavens. Its trunk represented human life on earth.

The *sapodilla* (sah·poe·DEEL·yah) tree is famous for its juice, called *chicle* (CHEE·clay). The Maya boil and harden *chicle.* You may know it as chewing gum.

A third important tree of Central America is the *caoba* (cah·OH·bah), or mahogany tree. Its hard and beautiful wood is prized for making furniture. Sadly, most of the caoba trees in Central America have been cut down to make furniture.

Deforestation

Like nations around the world, Central American nations have cut down much of their forests for logging, fuel, and farmland. Now they are now facing the problems of deforestation.

The country of Costa Rica leads the way in preserving its forests. It has established a national network of parks and wildlife refuges. Tourists from all over the world come to visit these parks.

The entry fees to these national parks help pay for programs to protect plants and animals. This new kind of tourist industry is called ecological, or **ecotourism.**

understory. Plants such as violets, pitcher plants, orchids, and bromelaids grow here. Mosses, mushrooms, and decomposers are among the plants living on the floor.

After reading the Vegetation and the Wildlife sections in the text let students research and create the plants and animals of the rain forest.
- Trees: ceiba (kapok), sapodila, caoba, mahogany
- Birds: quetzal, parakeet, scarlet macaw, toucan, long-legged egret, and laughing falcon
- Mammals: jaguar, pizote, monkeys (howler and spider)
- Insects and Reptiles: butterflies, army ants, tarantula, frog, caiman, alligator, snakes (fer-de-lance and boa constrictor)

Students may find other additions to your rain forest through their research.

Extension Compare the plants and animals of the rain forest to those found in North Carolina. Research medicines and products made from the plant life of the rain forest. Illustrate the results of deforestation by turning the completed mural over to reveal only black paper. This will be the result if we are not responsible with the rain forest!

Central America—Climate

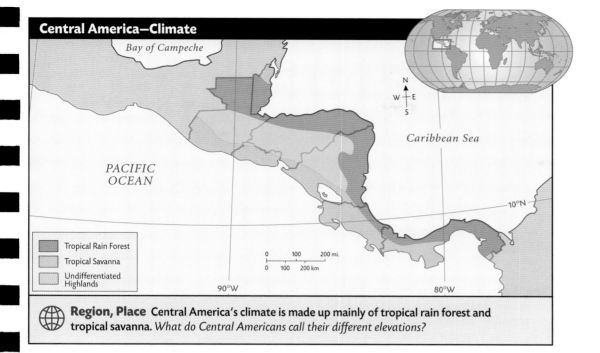

Region, Place Central America's climate is made up mainly of tropical rain forest and tropical savanna. *What do Central Americans call their different elevations?*

Tropical Rain Forest
Tropical Savanna
Undifferentiated Highlands

0   100   200 mi.
0   100   200 km

Bay of Campeche
Caribbean Sea
PACIFIC OCEAN
10°N
90°W
80°W

Central America—Vegetation

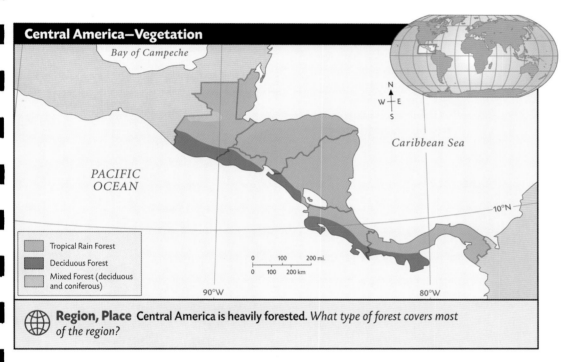

Region, Place Central America is heavily forested. *What type of forest covers most of the region?*

Tropical Rain Forest
Deciduous Forest
Mixed Forest (deciduous and coniferous)

0   100   200 mi.
0   100   200 km

Bay of Campeche
Caribbean Sea
PACIFIC OCEAN
10°N
90°W
80°W

Central America

Background Information

Deforestation

Scientists estimate that Brazil has the most rapid rate of deforestation in the world, followed by Mexico and Indonesia. In Costa Rica, cattle ranching and agriculture are major sources of deforestation. The failure of national and state governments to strictly enforce environmental protection laws is another problem. Cattle ranching causes forest losses because ranchers slash and burn forest land to grow grass as pasture for cattle. Farmers also cut down forests and clear land for new or expanding farms. When old-growth forests are cut down, habitats of plants and animals are lost and soil erodes. Strategies for stopping deforestation include governments cracking down on illegal logging and encouraging or requiring reforestation of land for commercial and other uses.

Caption Answer

Tierra Caliente (hot land), *Tierra Templada* (temperate land), *Tierra Fria* (cold land), and *Tierra Helada* (Icy land).

Caption Answer

Rain forest

Map Activity

Climate and Vegetation

NATIONAL GEOGRAPHY STANDARDS: 1, 4
GEOGRAPHIC THEMES: Place
OBJECTIVES: 1.01, 1.02, 1.04

Assign one of the seven countries to small groups. Ask them to use the section on Elevation and Climate and the climate map to determine which of the four elevation zones are in their country. Share their findings.

Extension Have students make a mini poster of the major crops of their country. Encourage them to use symbols and original illustrations. Compare the mini posters and display them in the classroom.

Activity

Adopt the Rain Forest

OBJECTIVES: 1.01, 1.02, 1.03, 1.06, 1.07

After studying about the unique plants and animals that live in the rain forest and learning their importance to our own survival, students may be willing to do something to preserve it as a service project. There are organizations that work to protect these areas, including The Nature Conservancy's Adopt an Acre program (**nature.org/adopt/**; (800) 842-3678). To date they have protected more than 600,000 acres of rain forest throughout Latin America and the Caribbean. Your classroom will receive a certificate to frame describing the location of the land. The area will be protected as part of a refuge in that country. The cost is about $75 an acre.

Discussion Questions

1 What is ecotourism? How might it help protect these endangered species?

Caption Answer

They are losing their habitats when humans cut down trees where they nest.

Activity

Quetzal Bird

🔖 **OBJECTIVES:** 1.01, 1.02, 1.06

After reading the chapter introduction on page 618, and discussing the quetzal bird, each student will be given a long, green feather made of construction paper, resembling one of the bird's. On one side of the feather, have students write what they already know about the countries of Central America. On the back of their feather, students should write what they want to know about the countries of Central America. In small groups, discuss what they know and want to know about Central America. Have each group share with the class. Have a student artist draw a large quetzal bird for display in the class-room, or make a bulletin board.

Attach the feathers with the "what I want to know" side of the feather showing. As students finish daily assignments and need other activities to do, let them go to the board and find some questions to research. This is a great way to differentiate for gifted learners.

Wildlife

Central America has thousands of remarkable birds, mammals, reptiles, and insects. In Costa Rica alone, there are more than 850 kinds of birds. This is more than in the United States and Canada combined.

Birds

The quetzal is only one of many beautiful birds in Central America. On the Pacific Coast, parakeets live in the wild. Toucans with multicolored, banana-shaped beaks share the skies with the long-legged egret, a shore bird. Can you guess how the laughing falcon got its name?

The scarlet macaw, a noisy parrot with brilliant red, yellow, and blue feathers, looks like a rainbow perched in the treetops. It is a strong bird that can fly up to 35 miles (56.4 km) per hour. Though it has very few natural enemies, humans have cut down the trees where it builds its nests.

Today only 300 scarlet macaws remain in Central America. Because of this, the governments of Belize and Guatemala have started programs to protect them.

The jaguar (right) is sacred to the Maya. The scarlet macaw (left) is a type of parrot. **What is the problem facing these animals?**

Mammals

Central America's most magnificent animal, the jaguar, is sacred to the Maya. It is a large tiger-like cat, yellow-brown with black spots. Sometimes it is all black.

Like the quetzal and the scarlet macaw, however, the jaguar has become rare. It is in danger of extinction due to hunting and loss of habitat.

The pizote (pee·zoe·tay) has a striped tail. It might remind you of a raccoon. But its long snout and way of running make it seem like a cousin of both the anteater and house cat.

There are also several types of monkeys in Central America. Species include the spider monkey and the howler monkey. Despite its small size, the howler monkey can make a huge racket. Once you have heard it screaming in the jungle night, it is impossible to forget.

WORD ORIGINS

The name "**quetzal**" comes from the Aztec word *quetzalli*. It means "brightly colored tail feathers." The feathers of the quetzal are vivid green, with red and blue flashes underneath.

Activity

Butterfly Migration

🔖 **OBJECTIVES:** 1.02, 1.06, 1.07

Among the many species in Central America are butterflies. Some butterflies are endangered. The Saint Francis' Satyr butterfly, native to North Carolina, is endangered. Visit **NCJourneys.com** for links to Web sites with information and photos.

In the spring have a butterfly count. Make graphs to show the numbers reported each day. Discuss the places and time of day the students saw the greatest number.

Extension Have students make a sequence chart of insect metamorphoses:
- Stage 1: eggs
- Stage 2: larva
- Stage 3: pupa
- Stage 4: butterfly or moth

ELL students can complete each activity if working with a partner.

Insects, Spiders, and Reptiles

There are many insects, spiders, and reptiles in Central America. Army ants and tarantula spiders live in the thick forests. There are thousands of types of butterflies.

Central America is home to many frogs. Some of them are poisonous to the touch. Alligators and their cousins, caimans, are found along some Central American waterways. Many large snakes live here. Species include the fer-de-lance and the bushmaster. The bushmaster is the largest poisonous snake in the Americas. The boa constrictor is another native snake.

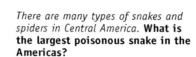
There are many types of snakes and spiders in Central America. **What is the largest poisonous snake in the Americas?**

Discussion Questions

1 If you were in charge of animals for a zoo featuring Central America, which animals would you have?

2 What are some of the insects and reptiles found in Central America? Which would you like to see?

Caption Answer

The bushmaster

What would YOU do?

Ecotourism gives Central American nations a way to preserve their wildlife while they earn money. Imagine that you are placed in charge of a national preserve. What rules would you lay down for visitors to the preserve? How would you explain the importance of these rules to your visitors? What consequence would there be for breaking the rules?

LESSON 1 REVIEW

Fact Follow-Up
1. Describe the climate of Central America.
2. What are Central America's elevation zones? What crops are grown in each zone?
3. What are some important trees in this region?
4. What are some important birds, mammals, and insects and reptiles of Central America?

Talk About It
1. How can the location of Central America be a hazard to its people?
2. How might deforestation threaten animal life in Central America?
3. What do the quetzal, the scarlet macaw, and the jaguar have in common?

Central America

625

LESSON 1 REVIEW

Fact Follow-Up Answers
1. Central America's climate is mainly made up of tropical rain forest and tropical savanna. The mountainous regions of Central America have a Highlands climate, which is often broken down into four zones.
2. Bananas, sugarcane, and rice grow in the *Tierra Caliente,* or hot land. Coffee, corn, wheat, and vegetables grow in the *Tierra Templada,* or temperate land. Potatoes, gains, and livestock are raised in the *Tierra Fria,* or cold land. No crops are raised in the highest zone, the *Tierra Helada,* or icy land.
3. The ceiba tree has wide, above-ground roots, a huge trunk, and branches stretching up to 130 feet (39 m). The sapodilla tree is valued for its chicle, which is harvested and used in making chewing gum. Another native tree is the caoba, or mahogany tree, which has been largely destroyed to make furniture.
4. Animals, birds, insects, and reptiles include: toucans, scarlet macaws, jaguars, pizotes, spider and howler monkeys, spiders, alligators, caimans, and the bushmaster.

Talk About It Answers
1. Because they live in the earthquake and volcanic zones and because of the annual threat of hurricanes, Central Americans live in a location that is hazardous.
2. Animals depend on the forest for both food and protection.
3. They are rare and losing their habitat.

LESSON 2 People and Environment

 OBJECTIVES: 1.07, 2.08, 3.06, 3.07

Discussion Questions

1 Why did the Spanish bring African slaves to the Caribbean and Central America?

 Caption Answer

Tikal's people may have used too many of the area's natural resources, or their civilization may have collapsed after wars with rival Mayan cities.

Reading Strategy Activity

Test-Taking Vocabulary

 OBJECTIVES: 1.07, 2.08, 3.06, 3.07

The ability to do well on tests is vital to success in school. Over the years the language of tests has become more and more sophisticated. By fifth grade **most** students understand the meaning of this new and complicated terminology, but **most likely** your students need a review lesson on test-taking vocabulary.

These are the terms and definitions students need to be taught and should practice for End Of Grade testing:

• **About/Approximately:** almost the same as, close to, but not equal to; used in estimation items in mathematics

• **Best:** an evaluative term meaning exceeding all others in terms of quality and correctness

• **Except:** with the exclusion of; but; to leave out; exclude

• **Least/Least Likely:** an evaluative term meaning lowest in rank or importance; meaning smallest in degree or magnitude

• **Mainly:** an evaluative term meaning the greatest in number, quantity, size, or degree

• **Most/Most Likely:** an evaluative term meaning the principal or most important part or point

A Test-Taking worksheet is provided in the Teacher's Resource Guide to practice the skill with this lesson.

KEY IDEAS

• The Maya have lived in Central America for more than 2,500 years.

• *Mestizos* have a mixture of Native American and Spanish heritage.

• Many descendants of Africans live along Central America's Caribbean Coast.

KEY TERMS

garifuna
indigo

Central America is not rich in gold or silver. Because of this, Spanish colonists there had to look for other products to send back to Spain. Native Americans taught the Spanish many things about the environment.

The People

People have lived in Central America for thousands of years. Native Americans were the first people here.

In the 1500s the Spanish came as conquerors. They stayed as settlers. They forced people from Africa to come to Central America as slaves. All of these people, Native Americans, Spanish, and Africans, have influenced Central America's culture.

Tourists can visit the Temple of the Giant Jaguar in Tikal, Guatemala. **What do you think happened to the people of Tikal?**

626

Chapter 26

These Miskito children are first graders at a school near the Hondoran-Nicaraguan border. **Which group makes up the majority of people living in Central America?**

Native Americans

The Maya lived in much of the northern part of Central America. The ruins of Tikal (tee·KAHL) have been found in the jungles of Guatemala. Tikal was the center of a civilization of great builders and astronomers. It flourished between 1,000 and 2,500 years ago.

No one knows for certain why this great city was abandoned. Perhaps the people used too many of the area's natural resources. Perhaps their civilization collapsed after wars with rival Maya cities.

Today, the ruins have become a national park. People from around the world visit it. They can climb the Pyramid of the Masks and see the magnificent Pyramid of the Jaguar.

The Highland Maya still live in the mountains of western Guatemala. They created their own complex civilization. Though the Spanish conquered them in the early 1500s, their culture was not destroyed.

The Highland Maya continue to live in the *Tierra Templada* and the lower elevations of the *Tierra Fria*. They maintain many of their traditions. They do not mix much with other people.

Other Native Americans live in Central America, too. The Chibcha live in southern Costa Rica and Panama. Today, these groups are struggling to maintain their culture. The ancestors of the Miskito people of Honduras and Nicaragua married Africans but kept their way of life.

Mestizos

In every Central American nation except Belize, *mestizos* make up the majority of the population. *Mestizos* is the name for people who have both Native American and Spanish ancestors. Their communities mix their ancestors' different cultures.

Garifuna

Garifuna are people of mixed African and Native American descent. They live in communities along the Caribbean coast from Belize to Nicaragua. They have their own language. They keep a strong connection with African traditions.

In Belize, the *garifuna* culture is changing. *Mestizos* and Maya have arrived from neighboring countries. These newcomers are adding their ways of life to those of the *garifuna*.

Central America

627

Discussion Questions

1 What are some other Native American groups of Central America and the Caribbean?

2 Who are the garifuna? What is their way of life?

 **Caption Answer**

The Highland Maya

 **Activity**

Artifact Mystery

OBJECTIVES: 1.07, 3.06, 3.07

Have students choose a Native American artifact from a Central American country. It might be one that they have seen in a picture in the textbook or at a museum. Have the students write a descriptive paragraph about the artifact. Remind them to include a sense of order and to use strong verbs and adjectives in their description. Place them into small groups and have them read their descriptions to one another without revealing what the artifact is. After everyone has read, the groups will try to guess the item being described. Have each group report to the class on how hard or easy it was to guess the artifact based on the description.

 Background Information

The Garifuna

The garifuna are descendants of a group of African slaves who escaped from two Spanish slave ships that wrecked near the island of St. Vincent in the Caribbean. They are also descendants of Native Americans from South America, the Arawak and Caribs. The garifuna culture reflects its African roots in its music, dance, and storytelling. Its religious beliefs blend European, Africa, and Native American sources in a mixture of Catholicism, traditional African religions, and Native American beliefs. November 19 is a special day for garifuna communities throughout Central America. Called garifuna Settlement Day, it marks the arrival of the garifuna on the coast of Central America after being forced to leave St. Vincent by the British. In addition to garifuna communities in Guatemala, Honduras, and Belize, small numbers live in Los Angeles, New Orleans, and New York City.

Discussion Questions

1 What are the different classes of people in Central America?

Caption Answer

People from different ethnic groups are sometimes treated differently.

Caption Answer

The Pacific Ocean

Map Activity

Economic Activity

NATIONAL GEOGRAPHY STANDARDS: 1, 16

GEOGRAPHIC THEMES: Human-Environmental Interaction

OBJECTIVES: 5.02, 5.07

Have students compare the map on this page with the map on page 619. Have students classify the economic activities in each of the elevation zones. Discuss the roles that landforms and climate play in economic development.

Ethnic Heritage in Society

People in Central America today do not always treat one another as equals. This inequality is partly based on a person's ancestry, or ethnic heritage. As you have read, Central America's people are descended from different ethnic groups and nationalities. Many groups have their own language and ways of life. They also differ in wealth and social standing.

As in all the Americas, the most powerful people have mainly been of families whose only ancestors were Spanish or other Europeans. They are generally the ones with the most wealth. They also have better educations.

Few Native Americans, *mestizos*, or *garifuna* have become rulers of Central American nations. Some, though, have gained wealth and high social standing.

Many Central Americans experience discrimination because of their ethnic group. Some of this discrimination came from the way the original European settlers treated them. Gaining a better life has been harder for people who face these prejudices.

The Belize woman makes a simple meal in her home.
How does ancestry affect social standing?

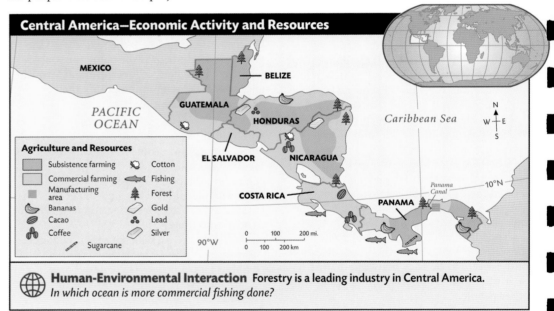

Central America—Economic Activity and Resources

MEXICO
BELIZE
GUATEMALA
PACIFIC OCEAN
HONDURAS
Caribbean Sea
EL SALVADOR
NICARAGUA
COSTA RICA
Panama Canal
10°N
PANAMA

Agriculture and Resources

- Subsistence farming
- Commercial farming
- Manufacturing area
- Bananas
- Cacao
- Coffee
- Sugarcane
- Cotton
- Fishing
- Forest
- Gold
- Lead
- Silver

90°W
0   100   200 mi.
0   100   200 km

N W E S

🌐 **Human-Environmental Interaction** Forestry is a leading industry in Central America. *In which ocean is more commercial fishing done?*

628

Land and Resources

Since the Spanish did not find much gold and silver in Central America, they concentrated on agriculture. As in Mexico, the Spanish carved large *haciendas* out of land occupied by Native American people. Native Americans and enslaved Africans were put to work on plantations.

Unlike in Mexico, these *haciendas* were not used to feed people working in mines. Instead, their products were shipped to Spain. As you will see, these *haciendas* became Central America's biggest and most important businesses.

Chocolate

Colonists found three Central American products to export. The first of these was chocolate.

Chocolate is made from cacao (cah·COW) beans. Europeans knew nothing about cacao or how the beans could be used. Then they saw Native Americans growing cacao trees and making a drink from their seeds.

Europeans quickly found that they liked chocolate, too. They began drinking huge quantities of chocolate after mixing it with sugar, cinnamon, vanilla, and milk.

Other Exports

By the 1800s, cacao was being grown in other parts of the world. Central America lost many of its cacao markets.

To replace them, the Spanish turned to the fruit of the *xiquilite* (see·key·lee·tay) plant. From this fruit they made a deep-blue dye called *indigo.* A red dye called cochineal (coh·KEE·neel) was made from the dried skeletons of a native bug. It became the third major export.

These cacao beans and pods are important products of Central America. **According to the map on page 628, where does cacao come from?**

LESSON 2 REVIEW

Fact Follow-Up
1. What group of people makes up the majority of the population in most Central American nations?
2. Who are the *garifuna*, and where do they live?
3. What products replaced cacao as important exports?

Talk About It
1. What three groups of people have influenced Central America's culture?
2. Why do the *garifuna* mostly live along the Caribbean coast of Central America?
3. How did the *hacienda* systems in Central America and Mexico differ?

Central America

629

Discussion Questions
1 What is chocolate made from?
2 What were *haciendas* used for in Central America?

 Caption Answer

Costa Rica

 Activity

Central America's Economic Activities and Resources

◆ **OBJECTIVES:** 5.01, 5.02, 5.07

After reading the text about chocolate on page 629, have students identify where cocao is grown in Central America. Next, share with students the Chocolate History Timeline (visit **NCJourneys.com** for link).

To learn more about chocolate, assign each student one of the periods from the timeline. Provide them with white drawing paper. Instruct them to use colored pencils to illustrate the topic of their assigned time period. Instruct the students to write the date and title in bold, black letters on their completed picture.

When students have completed their illustrations, arrange the pictures around the room in chronological order. Have each student stand near his or her picture and explain the poster.

Alternatively, students can use the information the gather to create a digital timeline presentation using PowerPoint or other appropriate software.

LESSON 2 REVIEW

Fact Follow-Up Answers
1. Mestizos, descendants of Spanish and Native Americans, make up the majority of the population of the nations of Honduras, El Salvador, Costa Rica, Panama, Guatemala, and Nicaragua.
2. Garifuna are people of mixed African and Native American descent who live in communities along the Caribbean coast of Central America from Belize to Nicaragua.
3. The fruit of the xiquilite plant was used to make a deep blue dye called indigo. A red dye called cochineal made from the dried carcass of an insect also was a valuable export.

Talk About It Answers
1. Spanish, Native Americans, and Africans have influenced the culture of the region.
2. The most plausible explanation is that the garifuna are descended from Africans taken to Central America from the Caribbean islands to work on sugar plantations. Sugar plantations are located in the *Tierra Caliente,* or Hot Land, region found at sea level.
3. In Mexico the *hacienda* system was begun to support the operation of the silver mines. In Central America because there were no precious metals to be mined, the *hacienda* system was used to produce agricultural goods for export to Spain

Activity

Nature's Dyes

OBJECTIVES: 1.07, 5.01, 5.04

After reading about cochineal and reading the section Other Exports, discuss natural dyes. Ask students who are wearing blue jeans to stand. Most likely these were dyed with the color indigo. Have students brainstorm things in nature that they think might be used as dye. Have them collect these items and bring them to class. Buy unbleached muslin and cut it into strips. Experiment to see which items could actually dye the muslin.

Extension Have students further research cochineal and indigo and the importance of these two dyes in the economic development of Central America.

Cochineal

Cochineal is an insect that lives on the Prickly Pear Cactus. The cochineal's body is bright red. Native Americans used the dye to color robes, weapons, and even their bodies.

European red dyes were not as bright as that of cochineal. Cortés saw the Aztec nobles dressed in this color. He knew that Europeans would want it. He immediately shipped bags of the dried skeletons of the cochineal to Spain. By 1600, cochineal was the second most valuable export.

In Europe, cochineal dye was used to color the robes of Roman Catholic Cardinals and royalty. Even the jackets of the "Redcoats" in the British army were dyed with cochineal.

The Spanish tried to keep the source of cochineal a secret. For years they made people believe that it came from a seed. They even called it the "cochineal grain." A Dutch scientist finally viewed one of these "seeds" under a microscope. He saw that it was an insect.

In the late 1800s, a substitute for the dye was discovered. For a time less cochineal was produced. Recently, cochineal production has grown. It is a natural and safe coloring for foods and lipstick.

Cochineal dye

Cochineal on a Prikly Pear-Cactus

630

Chapter 26

LESSON ③ Economy and Government

Spain ruled Central America as a colony for more nearly 300 years. During that time, Spain controlled the economy. Everything was done to benefit the Spanish empire and its rulers.

Much of the food and other agricultural products were sent overseas. Spanish merchants shipped cacao, indigo, and cochineal to a new European markets.

The countries of the region are now independent. Central Americans are no longer forced to send everything to Spain. They can sell it for their own profit.

Yet Central America's economy still is the same in some ways. Much of their income comes from agricultural products. There are few factories. Many goods must be imported.

Along with cacao, bananas are a major export of Central America.
What are some other exports?

Central America

631

KEY IDEAS

- Under Spanish rule, Central America produced crops for export to Europe.

- After independence, Central American nations continued to have plantation economies. Some Central American countries were ruled by dictators.

- Now Central American nations are working to build stable governments and economies.

PEOPLE TO KNOW

Anastasio Samoza
Oscar Arias Sanchez

OBJECTIVES: 2.04, 5.01, 5.02

Discussion Questions

1 What type of economy does Central America have?

 **Caption Answer**

Coffee, sugar, and beef

Reading Strategy Activity

Looking Back

OBJECTIVES: 2.04, 5.01, 5.02

After reading a lesson or a chapter, good readers will look back and think about what they learned. One strategy to use is called 3-2-1. Students are to think about 3 things they learned, 2 interesting facts, and 1 question they still have. For example in this lesson, students might write about the exports of Central America, the government run by caudillos, and the growing and fragile democracy. They might tell 2 facts about the Panama Canal. They might have a question about how Central America might be able to strengthen their democracy to prevent the rich and powerful from running the country. By looking back using the 3-2-1 strategy, students will build understanding of the information provided in the text.

Discussion Questions

1 Why do many Central American people continue to live in poverty?

2 What are some foods that are grown in Central America that are enjoyed throughout the world?

Caption Answer

Companies from the United Kingdom and the United States

Caption Answer

With government backing, plantation owners did not need to increase wages or improve working conditions.

Activity

Banana Mania

OBJECTIVES: 1.07, 2.08, 5.01, 5.02

Ask students to brainstorm ways they enjoy bananas (banana splits, on cereal, sandwiches . . .). List on the overhead or board. Assign each of these to a student artist. Give students a 10-inch pattern of a large banana and some yellow construction paper. Have them make paper bananas. Ask other students to look up facts about the banana industry and write these on the paper bananas. Arrange the bananas in bunches and display in the classroom.

Extension Make a huge banana tree and display in the hallway.

Extension Novice ELL students can write words like banana, banana tree, leaves, and other terms on a construction paper banana.

Math Activity

Banana Graphs

OBJECTIVES: 1.07, 2.08, 5.01, 5.02

Have students use the following information to construct 1) a pie graph, 2) a

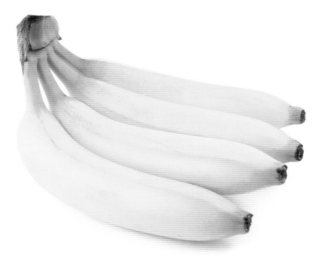

The United States imports bananas from Central America. **Who owned the banana plantations in the 1800s and 1900s?**

The Export Economy

Plantation agriculture grew after the Spanish gave up their colonial empire in 1821. By the late 1800s, plantation owners in Guatemala, Honduras, and Costa Rica were making a profit by exporting coffee beans.

Plantation owners grew rich. They could afford to buy imported goods from other countries. The rest of the people were not so lucky. Many worked for very low wages on the coffee plantations.

At this same time, governments wanted foreigners to invest in banana plantations. The governments offered these people money or land. Some offered the foreigners low taxes. Others promised that people would work for low wages.

British and American companies rushed into Central America to make money growing bananas. Foreign companies set up plantations in Guatemala, Panama, Honduras, and Costa Rica. The foreign owners took most of their earnings out of these countries.

632

Today's Economy

Today, in addition to coffee and bananas, Central America exports sugar, cacao, and beef.

The problems of plantation agriculture still have not been solved. Profits from the plantations have enriched wealthy local or foreign owners.

Wages for plantation workers are still low. Those who have managed to buy their own small farms are also poor.

Some industries and businesses have opened in cities. They do not have enough jobs, however, for all those who want to work. This means that the majority of Central America's people continue to live in poverty.

Government

Spain granted independence to these nations in 1821. Afterward, Central American leaders tried to unite the region into one country. When the effort failed, the region

Anastasio Somoza was a Nicaraguan caudillo. *This photo was taken prior to becoming president in 1937.* **How did the caudillos bring wealth to local landowners?**

Chapter 26

bar graph and 3) a line graph. Then have them answer the questions that follow.

Country from Middle America	Value of bananas exported (in U.S. dollars)
Costa Rica	$200 million
Guatemala	$80 million
Honduras	$220 million
Panama	$60 million

1. Which country exported the most bananas? *Honduras*

2. Which countries exported fewer bananas

than Honduras, but more than Panama? *Guatemala, Costa Rica*

3. Which country exported the fewest bananas? *Panama*

4. Did Guatemala and Panama together export as many bananas as Honduras? *No*

5. How many dollars worth of bananas were exported by all four countries? *$560 million*

Extension This is a good activity for intermediate ELL students. Novice ELL students can work with a partner.

split into nations named Guatemala, El Salvador, Honduras, Nicaragua, and Costa Rica. Panama joined the group later when it broke away from Colombia.

Only recently has Central America become home to democratically elected governments.

Caudillos and Military Dictators

The new nations of Central America tried to set up democracies but they had no experience. Spain was not a democracy. It did not run its colonies democratically. As a result, control was taken by strongmen *caudillos*. *Caudillos* often made alliances with other powerful landowners to protect their own interests.

In the twentieth century, *caudillos* were often military dictators who controlled the country with military force. They made sure that their private partners could get cheap land and cheap labor. With this support, plantation owners did not think they needed to pay workers more or to improve working conditions.

Many times these leaders were backed by the United States especially during the Cold War. The United States supported dictators who promised not to make the country Communist.

The powerful military dictators and their partners grew rich. They were often not willing to use their profits to help most of the people. For example, a dictator might promise to build a railroad to help small townspeople and farmers. In reality, the railroad usually helped only the plantation owners by carrying coffee or banana to ports where it was loaded on ships for export.

Most people continued to live in poverty on small farms and in isolated towns. Governments did little to provide public education or health care. Many people suffered from disease and poor nutrition. Most Central Americans could not read or write.

Central America

Guerrilla Wars

At times the people banded together to fight the government. These conflicts are called guerrilla wars. Guerrilla comes from the Spanish word for war, *guerra*. It means "little war."

Sometimes people have fought because they wanted democratic government. Other times they wanted a different system of government, such as communism or socialism. Often they just want a chance to feed and educate their families.

The men are part of the Sandinista army in Nicaragua. **What are some reasons for guerilla wars in the region?**

633

Discussion Questions

1 What is a *caudillo*? a military dictator?

2 How did these leaders hurt the economy of Central America?

3 What do you think the military and government leaders could have done to help the people of Central America?

4 Where does the term guerrilla come from?

Caption Answer

People banded together to fight the government. Sometimes they wanted a new, more democratic government, sometimes a Communist or socialist governments.

Name Origin

Belize Formerly British Honduras, the name comes from an old French word for "beacon."

Costa Rica "rich coast"

El Salvador Named by Columbus, "the Savior."

Guatemala from an ancient native language, "land of trees" or "land of eagles"

Honduras "deep water"

Nicaragua Named after a native chief, Nicara, whom the Spanish conquered in the 1500s.

Panama Guarani word for "butterfly"

Eyewitness Activity

Panama Canal

OBJECTIVES: 1.07, 4.07, 5.05, 6.02

The New York Times Learning Network (visit **NCJourneys.com** for link) has a Web site for teachers that is packed with lesson plans. One lesson that can be found at the URL listed above is *Changing the Channel*—a lesson about the Panama Canal. The objectives include assessing the new responsibilities of the Panamanians, exploring the history of the canal, and taking a closer look at Panama itself to examine how the canal changed the region forever. The lesson plans include opportunities for essay writing, reading news articles, group collaboration, and research.

EYEWITNESS TO HISTORY

Building the Panama Canal

The Panama Canal crosses the Middle American mainland at its narrowest point. It was one of the largest building projects in the world. It is the most direct route between the Atlantic and Pacific Oceans. Thousands of ships pass through its locks every year.

In the early part of the twentieth century, United States President Teddy Roosevelt (left) made the South American country of Colombia an offer. In exchange for a 10-mile-wide strip of land, the United States would give Colombia $10 million. Columbia owned the land in the Isthmus of Panama. Roosevelt wanted to build a canal. It would connect the Caribbean Sea with the Pacific Ocean. Colombia refused the offer. The United States then helped a group of rebels in the area win independence. The new government called this country Panama. It agreed to Roosevelt's offer.

634

Chapter 26

Background Information

Illness and Building the Canal

Workers arriving to help build the Panama Canal faced many obstacles, but one of the most deadly was also one of the smallest. Pools of stagnant water in the jungle environment provided the perfect breeding ground for mosquitoes. Clouds of mosquitoes were everywhere. They carried a variety of diseases, most notably malaria and yellow fever. "Mosquitoes get so thick

you get a mouthful with every breath," is how one worker described conditions. In order for the project to succeed, the threat of infectious disease had to be eliminated. Dr. William Gorgas, who had helped eradicate yellow fever in Havana, directed the sanitation efforts. Workers drained swamps, swept drainage ditches, paved roads, and installed plumbing. They

also sprayed pesticides by the ton. These efforts were successful. The last case of yellow fever was reported in Panama on November 11, 1906, and malaria cases also declined significantly from a peak of 7.45 per 1,000 workers in 1906 to .30 per 1,000 workers in 1913.

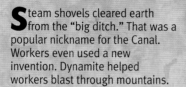

Steam shovels cleared earth from the "big ditch." That was a popular nickname for the Canal. Workers even used a new invention. Dynamite helped workers blast through mountains.

The Panama Canal took more than 43,000 workers eight years to dig. It took two more years to install machines to control the flowing water. Many of the workers came from the Caribbean. Workers earned only 10 cents an hour. They worked nine to ten hours a day.

The Canal cut the distance between San Francisco and New York City by almost 9,000 miles (14,490 km). In 1978, a treaty was signed between Panama and the United States. It passed control of the Canal Zone from the United States to Panama in 1979. This same treaty transferred the ownership of the Canal from the United States to Panama in 2000.

San Francisco

New York City

6,100 miles

15,000 miles

Panama Canal

Activity

Are Dictators *Always* Bad?

OBJECTIVES: 2.02, 2.04, 4.06

Write the words bribe, military power, and dictator widely spaced on the chalkboard. As students scan Lesson 3, have them contribute to a set of class notes linking the three words.

Have students contribute to a list of costs and benefits of dictatorships and link the costs and benefits to specific groups in the population, such as plantation owners or farmers.

Discuss some positive and negative effects of guerrilla movements. Are there other ways to end dictatorships?

Emphasize the importance of Oscar Arias Sanchez and his nation of Costa Rica, which has a democratic tradition.

Ask students why dictatorships have been a problem in Middle America but not in Canada or in the United States.

Extension The video *La Vida Pura—Meet Yesenia, a Costa Rican Youth* (see Resources section) offers excellent insights into the benefits of living in a Middle American nation that spends its national wealth for education and economic development rather than for military power.

Central America

Discussion Questions

1 In a 1987 meeting with rulers of Central American countries, what did Carlos Arias Sanchez say?

2 What type of government do all Central American countries have now?

 **Activity**

Keeping the Peace

📍 **OBJECTIVES:** 2.02, 2.04, 2.05, 2.08

Hold a classroom Peace Conference. Ask students to sit in a circle on the floor or move their desks into a circle. Have a copy of your class (or school) rules to review. Ask students to take turns explaining how each rule ensures peace in the classroom. Explain that the leaders of countries meet occasionally to discuss ideas for keeping their countries safe. One idea is for the people to have a voice in the government. They do this by voting on issues that concern them. Discuss times when students have been able to vote (for class or student council officers).

Think of an issue that your students have been concerned with (such as people breaking in line or saying harmful words). Ask students to take turns offering solutions for these problems. Vote on which solution they think will work best to keep peace in the classroom

Growing Democracy

Nicaragua, Guatemala, El Salvador, Panama, and Honduras were ruled by dictators until recently. In Nicaragua, Guatemala, and El Salvador, long guerrilla wars were fought to end the rule of dictators.

In 1987, Oscar Arias Sanchez, the president of Costa Rica, invited the leaders of Nicaragua, Guatemala, Honduras, and El Salvador to a meeting in San Jose. He wanted to talk about democracy.

In the meeting Arias said Central American governments were wasting their resources on the military. He urged them instead to improve their countries. He said governments ought to be peaceful. He said Central Americans should have the right to vote in free elections.

Today, democratically elected officials lead all the countries of Central America.

However, this has not solved the old problems. A few people still own most of the land. Powerful people control resources. This limits the growth of equality and democracy.

Oscar Sanchez

CENTRAL AMERICAN PORTRAIT

Oscar Arias Sanchez
1940–

In 1941 Oscar Arias Sanchez was born into one of Costa Rica's richest coffee-growing families. As a young man, he studied briefly in the United States and then in Britain, where he earned a law degree. After returning to Costa Rica, he held several government positions. In 1986, voters elected Arias president of Costa Rica. As president, he began his work as a peacemaker in the region. He worked tirelessly to end armed conflict and bring stability to the war-torn region. He convinced the leaders of Guatemala, El Salvador, Honduras, and Nicaragua to talk to him and to each other. In 1987 he proposed a regional peace plan. It called for free elections in Central American countries and other things to bring peace. For his efforts, Arias won the 1987 Nobel Peace Prize. In his acceptance speech Arias said, "I accept for Costa Rica, for peace and for Central America, where 25 million human beings deserve to look to the future with optimism and some hope of progress."

LESSON **3** REVIEW

Fact Follow-Up
1. What products have Central American nations exported to the rest of the world?
2. What, in general, have Central American nations imported?
3. What are caudillos, and how did they become successful?

Talk About It
1. Although many Central American countries are now democratic, their democracy is fragile. Why?
2. What are guerrilla wars?
3. Did *caudillos*, military dictators, and landowners cause guerilla wars? Explain.

LESSON **3** REVIEW

Fact Follow-Up Answers
1. Major exports have included coffee, bananas, sugar, cacao, and beef.
2. With the exception of manufacturing related to agriculture, most Central American nations have imported most manufactured goods.
3. *Caudillos* are strongmen who came to dominate the governments of newly independent Central American countries. They often made alliances with landowners. In the twentieth century they gave way to military dictators.

Talk About It Answers
1. As long as a few people own most of the productive land, the alliance among dictators, military forces, and landowners will threaten democratic governments.
2. Guerrilla wars means "little war." Guerrilla wars have been fought by people who have banded together to fight against dictators.
3. Important points: Students should take a position and explain it. Responses should focus on conditions of workers and alternatives available to them.

LESSON ④ Society and Culture

A long Central America's Caribbean and Pacific Coasts are cultures much like those of the Caribbean islands. The Maya culture survives in the volcanic mountains. In the *Tierra Templada* cities are centers of *mestizo* culture.

Plantation-style farming has left its mark in coffee and banana plantations throughout Central America. Central Americans look more and more to manufacturing and assembly industries to make a living, but farming is still important.

A Tale of Three Nations

Central America is a region of diverse climates and natural resources. Yet the nations of Central America also share a common Spanish heritage and economic base. Let's look at the similarities and differences in three Central American countries.

San José, Costa Rica, is a modern city. **In what ways is Costa Rica different from other Central American countries?**

Central America

637

KEY IDEAS

- Costa Rica is a Central American country with a long history of democracy.

- Nicaragua and Guatemala have suffered from dictatorships and civil war.

- The Catholic Church and cultural traditions form a strong bond among the people of Central America.

- Central America is growing closer to the United States.

KEY TERMS

fiesta patronal
marimba

PEOPLE TO KNOW

Daniel Ortega

 Caption Answer

Costa Rica has a long history of free elections and no army, and has the most developed system of public education in Central America.

 Reading Strategy Activity

Review and Recall

 OBJECTIVES: 2.08, 3.04, 3.06, 3.07

This strategy helps students review and recall information. Have them read the lesson aloud individually, with a buddy, or in small groups. Divide the class into groups and assign each group a subheading or part of the lesson from which to find important facts. Each student should find one fact or key concept from their section and write it on an index card. Groups are to help one another find a fact for each person in the group, making certain all important information in the section is covered.

Form two even-numbered concentric circles. Each student on the outside faces a student on the inside. Both students are to use their cards to take turns explaining the fact to the person opposite them. They may quiz each other to make certain they know the information. The teacher calls time to switch cards with the person opposite them, and the circles move clockwise one person. Each student now has a new partner and a new fact to describe. The activity continues until each student receives his or her original card. This exercise could also be used to study for an upcoming test.

Discussion Questions

1 What makes Costa Rica different from the other Central American countries?

2 Why is Nicaragua one of Central America's poorest countries?

 Caption Answer

Instead of selling their natural resources, countries invite people to visit their natural areas and spend money.

 Caption Answer

The Sandinistas were a leftist guerrilla group that controlled Nicaragua from 1979 to 1990.

 Writing Activity

Developing Countries

OBJECTIVES: 1.02, 1.04, 1.06, 1.07

Divide your class into cooperative groups. Ask each group to research and write an editorial about the conditions of a developing country in Central America and whether the needs of the people are being met by the government. Your students should include possible solutions to the problems.

Tourists ride through the middle layer of a rain forest canopy in Costa Rica. **What is the idea of ecotourism?**

A cornfield ruined by drought in La Jagua, 200 miles north of Managua, Nicaragua. **Who were the Sandinistas?**

Costa Rica

Costa Rica differs in several ways from the rest of Central America. The biggest difference is the nation's long history of free elections. Only twice since 1889 has Costa Rica strayed from democracy.

Costa Rica abolished its army in 1948. Costa Rica also has the most developed public education system in Central America.

Most of the people in Costa Rica live in the *Tierra Templada*. That is where the capital of San Jose is located. There are hot lowlands near the Atlantic coast. There farm families live on whatever they can grow. In the west, along the Pacific, bananas were the major crop between 1930 and 1960.

Recent efforts have been made to help farmers. Farmers are getting help to try planting new crops. One of Costa Rica's most important economic projects is developing the ecotourism industry.

The country has stopped destroying its beautiful rain forests. Costa Rica now encourages tourists to visit its forests and relax on its beaches. Costa Ricans used to make money by selling the lumber from trees. Now, instead of cutting trees down, they take tourists on nature walks and charge money. The plan is working. People from all over the world are visiting Costa Rica. Ecotourism provides money to preserve the environment and create jobs for Costa Ricans.

Nicaragua

Nicaragua is Central America's poorest country. It was ruled by dictators for much of the last century. One family, the Somozas, ruled Nicaragua with the military and a small group of landowners. Foreign companies owned huge coffee and banana plantations.

Most Nicaraguans had few opportunities to improve their lives. This caused an uprising beginning in the 1960s. The fighting lasted for almost 30 years. Many people were killed. Others were forced to flee the fighting. The fighting also destroyed bridges, roads, and crops. It drained the nation's wealth and energy.

In 1979, a group known as the Sandinistas overthrew the Somoza dictatorship. They wanted to re-distribute land more evenly to citizens. Not all Nicaraguans supported the Sandinistas. People argued over land redistribution. The United States supported Nicaraguans fighting against the Sandinista government. In 1990, the war ended. Nicuragua became democratic. An anti-Sandinista government was elected. Several years later, in 2006, the leader of the Sandinistas, Daniel Ortega, was elected president. He has vowed to work within the democratic system.

Nicaragua is a beautiful country and her people are hard workers. Still, Nicaragua has many obstacles in the path to prosperity. Solutions to basic problems, such as feeding the population, are most important.

Guatemala

Guatemala has Central America's biggest population and also the largest Native American population.

Throughout the 1800s, *caudillos* ruled Guatemala. A revolution created a democratic government in 1944. It was overthrown in 1954. From that point until 1986, Guatemala was again ruled by a military dictatorship. Since 1986, Guatemala has been a democracy.

Elections alone have not brought political stability. Guatemala suffered from guerrilla warfare between 1961 and 1996. Maya make up half of the nation's population. They are discriminated against by *mestizos* and people of European ancestry. Poor farmers resent the wealth of rich plantation owners.

Guatemala has great potential. Volcanic ash makes the soil in the *Tierra Templada* fertile. Mineral wealth, such as oil, lies beneath the ground. There are beautiful volcanoes and waterfalls, beaches and lakes. The ruins of the ancient Maya cities and the culture of the modern Maya could also attract tourists.

Central America

Customs

During the week before Easter, in Antigua, Guatemala, people create carpets of colored sawdust and flower petals. These carpets are prepared for a procession of people who will carry statues representing the saints. After the procession is over, the sawdust and petal carpets are destroyed.

Many Maya traditionally carry bundles in tzutaes, or carrying cloths, on their heads. **How are the Maya important to Guatemala?**

639

Discussion Questions

1 What country is Central America's most populous country?

2 What are some problems Guatemala faces?

3 What are some things that might attract tourists to Guatemala?

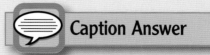
Caption Answer

The Maya make up half of Guatemala's population. The ruins of ancient Maya cities and modern Maya culture could attract tourists.

Activity

Cooking With Fractions

OBJECTIVES: 2.08, 3.04, 3.06

Have students bring to class recipes that contain fractions and use products from Central America. Some examples are: chocolate milkshakes, fruit salads, and recipes with coconut or nuts. Divide the class into groups and have students estimate how many times the recipes must be multiplied to feed the entire class. They will need to multiply the ingredients by that number. Check their math. Ask students to bring in the needed ingredients and cooking utensils. Allow time in class for groups to prepare the food and have a tasting party.

Discussion Questions

1 In what ways do churches, and especially the Roman Catholic Church, help Central American society?

Caring for the poor and education

Missions

OBJECTIVES: 1.02, 1.03, 1.06, 2.08

The Spanish started Catholic missions to convert the native peoples to the Catholic faith. Many felt that the European colonial leaders were harsh to the Native Americans. The Catholic Church became a defender of human rights for Native Americans. Consider all the organizations in your community that defend the human rights of people. Make a list of these organizations. These may include government agencies, nonprofit organizations, churches, hospitals, and so on. Ask students to research these agencies and list the types of help they provide the people of the communities. If possible ask the agencies to provide the students with statistics on how many individuals they serve in a year. Discuss with the students how valuable these types of services are to communities. Ask some of the leaders of these organizations to come in and discuss the importance of what they do. Ask how important it is for community members to support them and volunteer for them. Ask if students might be able to participate.

This Catholic priest is celebrating Semana Santa (Holy Week) in Guatemala.
What challenges face both the Catholic Church and governments in Central America?

Religion in Society

The Roman Catholic Church is the largest Christian denomination in Central America. Roman Catholics and Protestants still work to convert the Native Americans. They send missionaries to work with and teach the poor.

Some religious missionaries teach new farming methods. Others work against drug abuse. Still others take care of the large numbers of homeless children found in many Central American cities.

Private church schools are an important alternative to public schools in Central America. Overcrowding is a problem in public schools in the larger cities. Schools in rural areas sometimes close due to lack of money. Church schools provide a good education to many children at a low cost.

Central American governments look to the Catholic Church to help them give aid to poor citizens. This can lead to problems between the government and the Church.

Priests in poor areas have encouraged citizens to request services that the government cannot provide. Government authorities fear that these requests will cause poor people to rise up against them. Uprisings like these have already happened in some poor areas of Guatemala.

Culture

Central American festivals overflow with games and music. There is also lots of food and dancing. Religious services are important to many festivals.

Patron Saints

Many towns in Central America are named for saints. The patron saint of a town is honored every year with a celebration called a *fiesta patronal.* The feast of San Jose is celebrated on March 19 in Costa Rica.

A *fiesta patronal* usually starts with a service in the town church. The townspeople parade through the streets carrying a statue of the patron saint. The mayor of the town and other important citizens such as priests participate. In some regions a local *mariachi* or *marimba* band will march in the parade.

The *marimba* is a kind of xylophone played by several people at once.

People gather in the plaza to celebrate after the parade. This means there is lots of singing and dancing. Firecrackers and rockets are also set off.

Eating is a big part of the *fiesta patronal.* The foods reflect many centuries of combined Spanish and Native American cooking. Corn is an important part of the diet of Central Americans.

Corn tortillas and tamales are filled with meat, cheese, and beans. They are prepared and eaten by the basketful. If you visit someone's home on fiesta day, you can expect to be served a local specialty.

Bands continue to play past sundown. People dance far into the night. There is often a carnival in the plaza with a Ferris wheel and rides. *Futbol* (soccer) and other games are played. Fireworks light up the night sky.

These dancers take part in a festival in Masaya, Nicaragua. **What celebration in the United States does the description of the *fiesta patronal* bring to mind?**

Central America

Discussion Questions

1 What is a fiesta patronal?

2 What parts of the festival would you enjoy?

Caption Answer

Possible answer: the Fourth of July

Activity

Developed versus Developing

OBJECTIVES: 1.04, 5.02

Using a graphic organizer such as a T-Chart, have students compare the concept of a developing nation with that of a developed nation. They should label one side Developed and the other Developing. Ask students to list social and economic characteristics of Central America under Developing. Have them consider the corresponding characteristic of each one they have listed as it is in the United States and describe it.

Discuss as a class the difference between developed and developing.

Teacher Notes

Fiesta Patronal

Fiesta is the shortened form of fiesta patronal, the Spanish term meaning "patron saint festival". There is a fiesta patronal being celebrated nearly every day somewhere in the Spanish-speaking world. Some characteristics of fiestas are costumed street dancers, parades, lively musical performances, fireworks, and games. Every city in Latin America has its own patron saint and celebrates a fiesta for its patron saint. Some of the fiesta patronals celebrated by Spanish speakers in the United States are *El Dia de los Muertos* (The Day of the Dead) on November 1, Day of the Virgin of Guadalupe, which begins the week before December 12, and *La Fiesta de los Reyes Magos* (Three Kings' Day) celebrated on January 6.

Discussion Questions

1 What makes Costa Rica different from the other Central American countries?

2 Why is Nicaragua one of Central America's poorest countries?

Caption Answer

The new free trade agreement may increase trade further.

Central America's Future

Most of Central America is poor. But there is hope for Central America's future. Governments and private organizations are cooperating to give people a better chance. Democratic elections are giving more people a say in their government. Governments have begun to pass laws against discrimination based on ethnic heritage or skin color.

But much hard work lies ahead. One of the toughest problems is land distribution. Some governments have tried to redistribute the land among the poor. Many landowners oppose this type of solution. Sometimes, governments have to seize private property to redistribute the land. This could easily lead to war. It did in Nicaragua.

Central America is important to the United States. There is growing trade with the United States because of more investment in the region by American companies. The Panama Canal has also increased our nation's economic and political interest in this region.

Another important link between Central America and the United States is people. Many people leave their Central American nations to seek a better life in the United States. Others fled to the United States to escape the military dictatorships and wars.

As you have read, the three big nations of North America signed a free-trade agreement called NAFTA in 1994. A similar agreement went into effect in Central America in 2006. Some people believe that this will open up new markets for Central America and improve their economies. Others see it only as a way to increase profits for large American companies while straining Central American's already weak economies.

Central America is an important trading partner for the NAFTA nations. **What might happen to further these relationships?**

LESSON 4 REVIEW

Fact Follow-Up
1. In what ways does Costa Rica differ from other Central American countries?
2. What events in the twentieth century have contributed to Nicaragua being Central America's poorest country?
3. What is the largest religious denomination in Central America?

Talk About It
1. Why are religious rituals a part of many celebrations in Central America?
2. Of all the promising signs, which one offers the greatest hope for the future of Central America? Explain your choice.
3. Why is Guatemala said to have great potential?

LESSON 4 REVIEW

Fact Follow-Up Answers
1. Costa Rica has a long history of free elections. It has abolished its army and has the most developed system of public education in Central America. It also has pioneered in ecotourism that provides money to preserve the environment and give jobs to Costa Ricans.
2. For many years, one family (the Somoza family) in alliance with the military and a small group of landowners ruled Nicaragua as dictators. Beginning in the 1960s, there was an uprising against the Somoza family, and in 1979 the family was overthrown by the Sandinistas, a leftist guerrilla group that ruled until 1990, when an anti-Sandinista government was elected. Almost 30 years of war (resulting in loss of life, people fleeing the fighting, and the destruction of bridges, roads, and crops) drained Nicaragua of much wealth and energy.
3. The Catholic Church is the largest.

Talk About It Answers
1. Because the Catholic Church established so many towns and villages in Central America and many towns have patron saints, religion is a part of many festivals, especially the fiesta patronal celebrated every year to honor the patron saints of the many towns named for saints.
2. Important points: Students should choose one and explain their choice. Among the promising signs are increased democracy, cooperation between governments and private organizations to make people's lives better, laws against discrimination on the basis of skin color, efforts to redistribute land, and possibilities brought by free trade.
3. Volcanic ash makes the soil in the Tierra Templada rich and fertile. Great mineral wealth lies beneath the ground, especially oil in the north. The beautiful volcanoes, waterfalls, beaches, and lakes could make the country a prime tourist attraction, and the ruins of ancient Maya cities and the culture of the modern Maya could also be great attractions.

Analyzing, Interpreting, Creating, and Using Resources and Materials

Thinking About Population

By now you have had lots of experience in reading maps and graphs. This table provides you with some information about population in four countries of North America that you have studied this year. They are Canada, Mexico, Costa Rica, and Nicaragua.

What do the population figures in the graph below mean? What does it mean that life expectancy in Costa Rica is nearly the same as the life expectancy in Canada? Does it mean that Costa Rica is a wealthier country and better able to care for its elderly citizens?

What does it mean that about one third (36 percent) of Nicaragua's population is under the age of fourteen while less than one fifth (16 percent) of Canada's population falls in that category? Does it mean that Nicaragua values children more than Canada does?

How can these population figures be used? How can decision makers in government use this information? What might nations like Costa Rica be doing to provide for their elderly population? What might nations like Nicaragua be doing to provide for their youthful population?

Young school children in Managua, Nicaragua

Comparing Population Statistics

Countries	Age 1–14 years	Age 15–64 years	Age 65 years and older	Life expectancy at birth
Canada	16%	70%	14%	81.4 years
Mexico	28%	66%	6%	77.3 years
Costa Rica	26%	68%	6%	79.4 years
Nicaragua	36%	60%	4%	77.3 years

*2010 estimate, United Nations Population Division

 ## Skill Lesson Review

1. What information other than these population figures would you need to determine if Costa Rica is as wealthy as Canada? *Responses should include information about average income.*
2. How could you find out how the United States compares to these four nations? *Student suggestions should include census figures, information from almanacs, and information from Internet sources.*
3. Which is easier: reading a table such as the one in this skill lesson, or making a table? *Encourage student responses. It is likely that in this case making a table would be easier.*

Teaching This Skill Lesson

Materials Needed textbook, paper, pencils; a collection of obituary columns from newspapers, sufficient for each small group of no more than five students

Classroom Organization small groups, whole class

Beginning the Lesson Divide students into small groups and distribute obituary columns. Have students tally the ages of deceased persons using ten-year periods. Ask for their comments on whether they think Americans live long lives, accepting all responses.

Lesson Development Have students look at the table in the Skill Lesson. Ask if the obituary announcements in a newspaper in Nicaragua would be similar to or different from the same announcements in a newspaper in the United States. (Remind students that the table shows national figures while the obituary announcements they have seen represent relatively few people.)

Have students rank percentages from lowest to highest by country for each age category, asking questions such as "Which country has the largest percentage of population under 14 years, between 15 and 65 years, 65 years and older?" Accept all answers, probing for correct answers when necessary.

Ask "Which country needs to build more hospitals and nursing homes?" and "Which country needs to build more schools?" Accept answers, probing for correct answers.

Focus on the questions raised in the second paragraph of the lesson, probing to encourage students to suggest a variety of reasons behind the statistics.

Conclusion Ask students to suggest what organizations other than governments might be interested in these population statistics. Encourage students to include such industries as sports, television and motion picture companies, fast food companies, automobile makers, and clothing manufacturers.

Extension Have students write letters to the governments of the three countries suggesting how they might need to provide for various age groups in their populations.

Talk About It

1. Important points: Students should choose one of the three groups and explain their choice. Students should consider language, religion, economy, government, and social life.
2. Important points: Students should choose one and explain their choice., using economic and political examples.
3. Important points: Students should choose one of the three and explain their choice using specifics such as historical and cultural resources, or natural beauty.
4. Important points: Spanish influences are shown by the parade honoring the priest and the worship service. Native American influences can be seen by the music and perhaps the dancing. The combined influences can be seen in foods.
5. Important points: Students should choose one change and explain their choice. Changes include the work of missionaries in agriculture, drug abuse prevention, care for homeless children, education, and encouraging citizens to request services from the government.

Mastering Mapwork

1. Panama City, Panama, is located nearest 80°W.
2. San Jose, Costa Rica, is located nearest 10°N.
3. This line of longitude passes near Guatemala City, Guatemala; San Salvador, El Salvador; and Belmopan, Belize. Belmopan is located in central Belize, east of Guatemala and south of Mexico.
4. Belmopan is located in central Belize, east of Guatemala and south of Mexico.
5. The Panama Canal is located on the Isthmus of Panama, in central Panama, connecting the Atlantic and Pacific Oceans.

CHAPTER 26 REVIEW

Lessons Learned

LESSON 1
Land and People
Central America contains coastal plains and valleys. It also has mountains and volcanoes. The climate is hot and humid in low-lying areas. It is cooler in the mountains. The region's animal and plant life is rich and diverse.

LESSON 2
People and Environment
The Maya have lived in Central America for thousands of years. During colonial times, Europeans and Africans came to the region. *Mestizos* are descendants of Native Americans and Europeans.

LESSON 3
Economy and Government
Central American resources were used for European gain during colonial times. After independence, plantations grew crops for other countries. Now Central American nations are building their own stable economies.

LESSON 4
Society and Culture
Some Central American nations have a long history of democracy. Others have struggled under dictators. The region is now becoming more democratic. All Central American governments are democracies today. But conditions relating to plantation-style farming and poor land distribution still exist.

Becoming Better Readers

Student's questions should use one of the following words: best, except, least likely, more likely. The student should be able to explain how that word changes the question.

Talk About It

1. Native Americans, Spanish, and Africans have all influenced the culture of Central America. Which do you think has influenced the culture most? Explain your answer.
2. Mexico and Central America had different hacienda systems. Which do you think had the greater lasting influence? Explain.
3. Of the three nations—Costa Rica, Guatemala, and Nicaragua—which would you prefer to visit? Explain your choice.
4. How does a celebration such as a fiesta patronal show both Spanish and Native American influences on Central American society?
5. The role of the Catholic Church in Central America has changed over the years. Which change do you think will be most beneficial to the future of Central America? Explain why.

Mastering Mapwork

Movement
Use the map on page 619 to answer these questions:

1. Which Central American capital city is located nearest 80°W?
2. Which Central American capital city is located nearest 10°N?
3. 90°W passes near which three Central American capital cities?
4. Describe the relative location of Belmopan.
5. Describe the relative location of the Panama Canal.

Becoming Better Readers

Taking a Test
When taking a test, good readers read slowly to be sure they understand the questions. Good readers look for key words that provide clues to the answers. Words like *best*, *except*, *least likely*, and *more likely* all provide clues to the test taker. Write a test question using one of these words. Do you see how the word changes the question?

Go to the Source

Panama Canal Statistics

An average of 40 vessels pass through the locks of the Panama Canal each day. Compare the information in the bar graph and the data about what type of ships carry cargo to the canal. Answer the questions below using specific information from the documents.

Vehicle Trips Through the Panama Canal*	
1999	14,336
2000	13,653
2001	13,492
2002	13,183
2003	13,154

Most Important Cargo by Percentage–2003	
Type of Cargo	**Percentage**
Containerized cargo (goods shipped in large containers)	24.9%
Grain	18.9%
Petroleum and petroleum products	8.6%

Questions

1. Which year had the most number of trips through the Panama Canal?
2. Which year had the least number of trips though the canal?
3. Is the number of trips through the canal each year increasing or decreasing?
4. What item is shipped the most in Panama Canal?
5. In 2003, which item made up 18.9 percent of all materials shipped in the canal?

Source: 2001 and 2003 Annual Reports, Panama Canal Authority

Go to the Source

Go to the Source

Panama Canal

OBJECTIVES: 1.07, 5.04, 5.05
SOCIAL STUDIES SKILLS: 3.02, 3.05

Reading Graphs

This graph and chart show the recent trips and cargo percentages for the Panama Canal. Based on the Panama Canal Authority's projections, during the next 20 years, the canal's cargo volume will grow at an average of three percent per year, doubling 2005's tonnage by the year 2025. in 2006, to address this need, Panamanian voters approved a Canal expansion project to add a third lane that will take larger vessels.

Answers
1. 1999
2. 2003
3. Decreasing
4. Containerized cargo
5. Grain

How to Use the Chapter Review

There are four sections in the Chapter Review: Talk About It, Mastering Mapwork, Becoming Better Readers, and Go to the Source. Use the Vocabulary Worksheets and the Chapter Review Worksheet in the Teacher's Resource Guide for additional reinforcement and preparation for the Chapter Assessments. The chapter and lesson reviews and the Chapter Review Worksheets are the basis of the assessment for each chapter.

Talk About It questions encourage students to speculate about the content of the chapter and are suitable for class or small-group discussion. They are not intended to be assigned for homework.

Mastering Mapwork has students apply one or more of the Five Themes of Geography to maps within the chapter.

Becoming Better Readers focuses on building reading strategy skills necessary for reading comprehension in the content areas.

Go to the Source activities allow students to analyze a primary source that relates to the content of the chapter. The questions and activities familiarize students with different types of primary sources and also build content-reading skills.

The Caribbean Islands

Social Studies Strands

Geographic Relationships

Historic Perspectives

Economics and Development

Government and Active Citizenship

Global Connections

Cultures and Diversity

North Carolina Standard Course of Study

Goal 1 The learner will apply key geographic concepts to the United States and other countries of North America.

Goal 2 The learner will analyze political and social institutions in North America and examine how these institutions respond to human needs, structure society, and influence behavior.

Goal 3 The learner will examine the roles various ethnic groups have played in the development of the United States and its neighboring countries.

Goal 5 The learner will evaluate ways the United States and other countries of North America make decisions about the allocation and use of economic resources.

Teaching & Assessment

- English Language Learner Modified Lesson Plans for this chapter are found in the Teacher's Resource Guide.

- *ExamView® Assessment Suite* is provided at **NCJourneys.com.** It includes customizable assessments for all chapters. Paper tests are also available in the Teacher's Resource Guide. See pages T16–T17 for information about how to use the assessments and the Scoring Guide.

Worksheets

Worksheets and answer keys are found both in the Teacher's Resource Guide and at **NCJourneys.com**, including Reading Guides, Reading Strategies, Chapter Reviews, English Language Learner and others.

Activities and Integrations

SOCIAL STUDIES

- ■ Trade Wind Cookies, p. 646B
- ★ Caribbean Cruise, p. 646B
- Activator: Pirates, p. 646
- ■ Island Hopping, p. 647
- Caribbean Compare and Contrast, p. 650
- European Influences in Middle America, p. 658
- ▲ ■ Sugar, p. 662
- ★ The Caribbean—A Research Project, p. 662
- Castro, p. 663
- Grilled Jerk Chicken, p. 667
- Wrap it Up Party, p. 670

MATHEMATICS	MATHEMATICS OBJECTIVES
▲ ■ Ships to Scale, p. 655	1.02

SCIENCE	SCIENCE OBJECTIVES
★ ■ Windward and Leeward, p. 551	3.06, 1.02, 1.03, 1.04, 1.06
Coral Reefs, p. 652	

TECHNOLOGY	TECHNOLOGY OBJECTIVES
Carolina Connection: Hurricane Warning, p. 647	2.13
Slave Rebellions, p. 656	2.13

READING/LANGUAGE ARTS	READING/LANGUAGE ARTS OBJECTIVES
Problem Based Learning: Hurricane Warning, p. 646B	3.02
Writing Prompt: Storms, p. 646	3.02, 4.09
● Reading Strategy: SQRRR, p. 648	1.05, 4.07
★ Beach Umbrellas, p. 649	3.05
Reading Strategy: SCROL, p. 648	1.03
Reading Strategy: Bringing It All Together, p. 661	2.06, 3.02
Three Facts, p. 665	3.05
Reading Strategy: Writing What You Know, p. 666	3.05
Literature Connection–Poetry, p. 666	2.03, 2.04
Folktales, "Anansi", p. 667	2.03
Skill Lesson: How Diverse is North America?, p. 671	2.02, 2.09
Becoming Better Readers, p. 672	2.01
Writing to Government Leaders, p. 673	2.10

FINE ARTS	FINE ARTS OBJECTIVES
▲ ■ Steel Drum Mini-Band, p. 646B	(music)
★ Dialect Fun, p. 653	2.01, 3.02
●▲ ■ Tabletop Plantation, p. 659	2.01, 3.02
Caribbean Musical Chairs, p. 668	(music)
●▲ ■ Caribbean T-Shirt Design, p. 669	2.01, 3.02

CHARACTER AND VALUES EDUCATION	TRAITS
What Would You Do?, p. 660	fairness

● Basic Activities ★ Challenging Activities ▲ English Language Learner Novice ■ English Language Learner Intermediate

Introductory Activity

Trade Wind Cookies

OBJECTIVES: 1.01, 1.02, 1.03

Give each student a paper plate and a large sugar cookie. Have them read the section called "Trade Winds" in Lesson 1. Put the cookie in the middle of the paper plate. On the plate with a red marker, label the cardinal directions N, S, E, and W; and a green marker for the intermediate directions NE, SE, SW, and NW. In the NE section of the plate use a blue marker to label the trade winds with arrows coming from the NE toward the "cookie island." On the NE half of the cookie, spread green icing to represent lush vegetation on the windward side of the island. Spread vanilla icing on the leeward half of the cookie (the side toward which the wind is blowing). Use chocolate pieces to represent a mountain range separating the windward and leeward sides of the island cookie. Add tiny chocolate sprinkles to the vanilla icing (leeward) side to represent desert scrub. Label each part on the paper plate.

 **Culminating Activity**

Caribbean Cruise

OBJECTIVES: 1.02, 1.06, 1.07, 3.04, 3.06

As a culminating activity, turn your classroom into a cruise ship for a day. Brainstorm with students all the activities there are to do on a cruise. Some might include such onboard activities as shuffle board, mini-pin bowling, gourmet dining, buffets, music, movies, dancing, and swimming. Other activities are on shore, like sightseeing. Arrange the desks in the shape of a ship. Cover them with white paper and paint portholes on the side. On the walls around the room, display students' work done about the different island countries of the Caribbean. On the floor space around the ship, have different cruise activities and "ports" to visit. Some of these might be: scuba equipment to try on, shuffleboard, a volcano site, a beach, market place for shopping, a table with food from the Caribbean, and so on. Music (steel drum) should be playing in the background. On this day, children may dress as though they are on a cruise, with sunglasses, hats, and tropical-print clothes.

 **Art Activity**

Steel Drum Mini-Band

OBJECTIVES: 3.04, 3.06, 3.07

Ask students to bring in clean, empty cans of varying sizes with labels removed. (Maybe you can get some large ones from the cafeteria.) Have parents bring hammers to help you and the students make the top of the cans concave. Let students decorate the cans with artwork of the Caribbean. Acrylic paint will adhere to the can sides. Bring in CDs or recordings of steel drum music. Most public libraries have these. Let the students play on their "steel drums."

 **Problem Based Learning Activity**

Hurricane Warning

OBJECTIVES: 1.02, 1.06, 2.07, 2.08

Situation Hurricanes often ravage the Caribbean islands. Many people are always prepared for a hurricane and the damage it might cause. The cost of preparing for a hurricane is tremendous. If you worked for the weather advisory service in the Caribbean and it was your job to notify people of an impending hurricane, it would be important to consider people's safety. However, sending a hurricane warning when unnecessary could severely damage the economy of the islands.

Task Have students brainstorm a list of people who would be involved in the preparation and/or evacuation if a hurricane warning was given. Make another list of what types of preparations would be needed. Then discuss/brainstorm what the effects would be if a hurricane were to hit and no preparations had been made. Who would be affected, how would they be affected, and what would be the effect?

With these lists, ask students to evaluate when to issue a hurricane warning. What would happen if they were wrong? On a piece of paper list the jobs of people who would be affected by the hurricane. Cut up the paper and give each student a slip with the name of an affected job written on it. Ask students to write two journal articles from the point of view of this person (the student can give the person a name), one about how the unnecessary preparation would have upset his or her day, and the other about how the lack of preparation would be a problem.

Reflection Have the students discuss how difficult decisions that have no clear-cut answer must be made each day. There are consequences if the wrong decision is made. How can students make the "best" decision possible with the least risk of errors?

Teaching Strategies

Because of the emphasis on hurricanes and weather in this chapter, it provides an excellent opportunity for integrating science and social studies. You might even consider using this chapter or parts of it during hurricane season. If students are not already assigned a country to research, you might want to consider assigning a Caribbean Island for students to complete a research project on to present to the class. Ask a travel agent to come make a presentation on cruises that visit the Caribbean. A travel agent might also be able to provide posters and travel brochures for students to use in the class.

Discussion Questions

1 Who was Blackbeard?

2 What different groups of people live in the Caribbean?

Activator

 OBJECTIVES: 2.08, 5.01, 5.02, 5.06

Pirates Share stories of pirates of the Caribbean with students (Blackbeard, Anne Bonny, Mary Read, and Bartholomew Roberts are a few examples). Discuss why the Caribbean was an important "hide out" for pirates.

Writing Prompt

 OBJECTIVES: 1.02, 1.06, 3.04, 3.06

Teacher Notes: Many students may not have experienced hurricanes and tropical storms. Their writing should reflect their own experiences and can be about any storm that scared them.

Personal narrative Think of a time when you were in a scary storm. Write a story about your experiences. Be sure to include where you were, whom you were with, and what you felt during the storm.

List writing Generate a list of items a family might need in their home in case a violent storm occurs.

Interview Interview an older person who has experienced a hurricane. Remember to ask who, what, when, where, and how questions about their experience. Write your interview in a question and answer format.

CHAPTER 27

The Caribbean Islands

In the sixteenth and seventeenth centuries, pirates used the islands of the Caribbean for their winter headquarters. Blackbeard often sailed between the coast of North Carolina and Port Royal, Jamaica.

The islands and the waters of the Caribbean have been the site of hundreds of encounters between pirates, European navies, merchants, and Native Americans. Naval battles, accidents, and storms caused many ships to sink. Millions of dollars of gold and silver from the mainland lie buried in shipwrecks beneath the Caribbean's waves.

But for the world's tables, the real treasure of the Caribbean has been sugarcane. Europeans brought it to the region from Asia. The Caribbean islands were an ideal place to grow sugarcane.

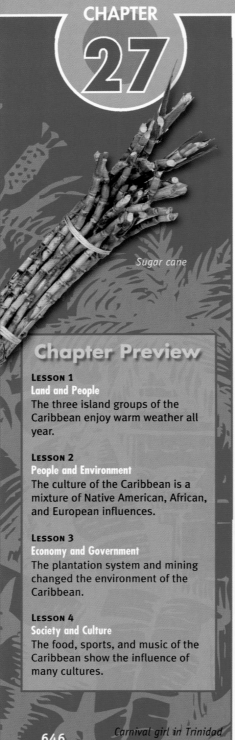

Sugar cane

Chapter Preview

LESSON 1
Land and People
The three island groups of the Caribbean enjoy warm weather all year.

LESSON 2
People and Environment
The culture of the Caribbean is a mixture of Native American, African, and European influences.

LESSON 3
Economy and Government
The plantation system and mining changed the environment of the Caribbean.

LESSON 4
Society and Culture
The food, sports, and music of the Caribbean show the influence of many cultures.

646

Carnival girl in Trinidad

Chapter Resources

Print Resources
Fiction

Bernier-Grand, Carmen T. *Juan Bobo: Four Folktales from Puerto Rico.* HarperTrophy, 1995. ISBN 0064441857.

Crespo, George. *How the Sea Began: A Taino Myth.* Clarion, 1993. ISBN 0395630339.

Gantos, Jack. *Jack's New Power: Stories from a Caribbean Year.* Farrar Straus & Giroux, 1995. ISBN 0374336571.

Ramirez, Michael Rose. *The Legend of the Hummingbird: A Tale from Puerto Rico* (Mondo Folktales) Mondo Pub., 1998. ISBN 1572552328.

Silva Lee, Alfonso (trans.). *Coquí y sus amigos/Coquí and His Friends.* Pangaea, 2000. ISBN 192916503X.

Wallner, Alexandra. *Sergio and the Hurricane.* Henry Holt, 2000. ISBN 0805062033.

Nonfiction

Ancona, George. *Cuban Kids.* Marshall Cavendish Corp, 2000. ISBN 0761450777.

Dash, Paul. *Traditions from the Caribbean.* Raintree/Steck Vaughn, 1999. ISBN 0817253844.

Davis, Gary. *Coral Reef.* Children's Press, 1997. ISBN 0516203754.

Jacobs, Francine. *The Tainos: The People Who Welcomed Columbus.* Putnam, 1992. ISBN 0399221166.

Jamaica. (Welcome to My Country). Franklin Watts Ltd., 2005. ISBN 0749660198.

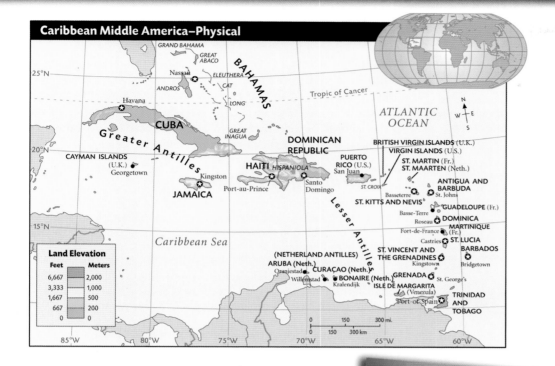

Caribbean Middle America–Physical

25°N
GRAND BAHAMA
GREAT ABACO
Nassau
ELEUTHERA
BAHAMAS
ANDROS
CAT
LONG
Tropic of Cancer
Havana
CUBA
GREAT INAGUA
ATLANTIC OCEAN
Greater Antilles
20°N
CAYMAN ISLANDS (U.K.)
Georgetown
DOMINICAN REPUBLIC
BRITISH VIRGIN ISLANDS (U.K.)
VIRGIN ISLANDS (U.S.)
Kingston
HAITI
HISPANIOLA
PUERTO RICO (U.S.)
San Juan
ST. MARTIN (Fr.)
ST. MAARTEN (Neth.)
JAMAICA
Port-au-Prince
Santo Domingo
ST. CROIX
Basseterre
St. Johns
ANTIGUA AND BARBUDA
ST. KITTS AND NEVIS
GUADELOUPE (Fr.)
Lesser Antilles
Basse-Terre
Roseau
DOMINICA
15°N
Caribbean Sea
Fort-de-France
MARTINIQUE (Fr.)
Castries
ST. LUCIA
(NETHERLAND ANTILLES)
ARUBA (Neth.)
Oranjestad
CURAÇAO (Neth.)
Willemstad
BONAIRE (Neth.)
Kralendijk
ST. VINCENT AND THE GRENADINES
Kingstown
GRENADA
St. George's
BARBADOS
Bridgetown
ISLE DE MARGARITA (Venezuela)
Port-of-Spain
TRINIDAD AND TOBAGO

Land Elevation

Feet	Meters
6,667	2,000
3,333	1,000
1,667	500
667	200
0	0

0   150   300 mi.
0 150 300 km

85°W   80°W   75°W   70°W   65°W   60°W

Hurricanes

Occasionally a major hurricane hits the North Carolina coast. Many hurricanes gain strength in the warm Caribbean Sea after forming off the coast of Africa. Some come ashore on the islands in the Caribbean.

In 1996, Hurricane Fran first skirted north of Cuba and brushed the Bahamas. In 1999, Hurricane Floyd blew through the Bahamas but managed to miss most of the other Caribbean islands. In 2003, Hurricane Isabel passed Caribbean islands but created a new inlet near Cape Hatteras.

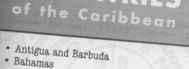

CAROLINA CONNECTION

COUNTRIES of the Caribbean

- Antigua and Barbuda
- Bahamas
- Barbados
- Cuba
- Dominica
- Dominican Republic
- Grenada
- Haiti
- Jamaica
- St. Kitts and Nevis
- St Lucia
- St. Vincent and the Grenadines
- Trinidad and Tobago

647

Discussion Questions

1 What are the names of the largest islands in the Caribbean?

2 What three sets of islands are in the Caribbean Sea?

 Map Activity

Island Hopping

NATIONAL GEOGRAPHY STANDARDS: 1, 4
GEOGRAPHIC THEMES: Region, Location
OBJECTIVES: 1.01, 2.04

Divide the class into pairs. Using the chart and map on this page, each pair will classify each island listed on the chart according to its island group. The students should mark the islands that are independent nations with a star. Students should write the name of the nations that the other islands are territories of next to the territory. Discuss as a class the advantages and disadvantages of being a territory using a graphic organizer.

Activity

Carolina Connection: Hurricane Warning

OBJECTIVES: 1.06, 6.02

Have students visit the U.S. National Hurricane Center's Web site (visit **NCJourneys.com** for a link). This site has current and historical information about hurricanes as well as real-time satellite images and answers to questions. They can also see a list of storm names for the next few seasons.

Audiovisual

International Video Network (IVN.com)
Bahamas.; Caribbean.; Jamaica.
National Geographic's Jewels of the Caribbean Sea. National Geographic Video, 1997.

Web Sites

Visit **NCJourneys.com** for links to these Web sites:
- AfroCuba Web Resources
- The Carib Indians

- Caribbean Studies Centre, London Metropolitan University
- Columbus' Sailing Ships
- Coral Reefs Overview, Center for Sponsored Coastal Ocean Research, NOAA
- A Country Study: Commonwealth of Caribbean Islands
- Cuban Heritage Collection, University of Miami
- European Exploration of the Southeast and Caribbean

- History of Calypso Music
- History of Steelpan Music
- History of St. Kitts
- The Online Dictionary of the Taino
- The Taino

OBJECTIVES: 1.01, 1.02, 1.03, 1.06

 Caption Answer

Cuba

 Reading Strategy Activity

What Good Readers Do: SQRRR

OBJECTIVES: 1.01, 1.02, 1.03, 1.06

Review SQRRR to help students read and learn about the uniqueness of the Caribbean. First students **survey**, or preview, the lesson. They look at the title, subheadings, pictures, boldface words, and any other sections that give the general idea of the information.

Make a **question** with each subheading to help students keep their minds focused on what they are reading. Have each student write the question on notebook paper. **Read** the first section to answer the question a student made. Make a question and read each section of the lesson one after the other.

When finished reading each section, the student reads the question and **recites** the answers from memory. You may want students to write down the answer. If they have difficulty remembering, have them reread that section again. Have students **review** or go back over the assignment. After completion, discuss the generated questions and which ones best suit the material.

 Teacher Notes

KEY IDEAS

- The Caribbean contains three island groups: the Bahamas, the Greater Antilles, and the Lesser Antilles.

- The Caribbean climate is warm all year, with dry and rainy seasons.

- Hurricanes can bring destruction to the region.

- Tourism is an important industry in the Caribbean.

KEY TERMS

asphalt
bauxite
leeward
trade winds
windward

The Caribbean Islands lie between the Atlantic Ocean and the Caribbean Sea (see map, page 647). The islands spread out in a curve. The northern end of the curve is near the coast of southern Florida. The curve stretches southeast to the islands of Trinidad and Tobago. These two islands are very close to the northern coast of South America.

Location and Landforms

The island at the western tip of this curve is Cuba. It points into the Gulf of Mexico at 85°W. Barbados is the most eastern island at 59°W. The most northern island in the region is in the Bahamas at 28°N. The most southern island nation is Trinidad and Tobago at 10°N.

Some of the islands are much larger than the others. The largest is Cuba. The next largest is Hispaniola. Puerto Rico is followed by Jamaica.

But even the largest island is much smaller than North Carolina. Cuba would fit within North Carolina with about 8,000 square miles (20,800 sq km) left over.

Other islands, such as Dominica and St. Kitts and Nevis, are tiny specks of land. Some measure only a few square miles. All the rest of the Caribbean islands together would fit inside of Cuba with room left over!

The Bahamas are in the northern area of the Caribbean Sea. **What is the largest Caribbean island?**

Saffir Simpson Hurricane Intensity Scale

Category One (minimal)
Winds: 74–95 mph (119–153 km/h)
Minimum surface pressure: >980 mbar
Storm surge: 3–5 feet

Damage primarily to shrubbery, trees, and unanchored homes. Low-lying coastal roads flooded, minor pier damage, some small boats torn from moorings. Example: Hurricane Ophelia (2005)

Category Two (moderate)
Winds: 96–110 mph (154–177 km/h)
Minimum surface pressure: 979–965 mbar
Storm surge: 6–8 feet

Damage to tree foliage; some trees blown down. Minor damage to building roofs, windows, and doors. Minor flooding of coast roads. Considerable damage to piers. Evacuation of some shoreline and low-lying areas. Example: Hurricane Bob (1991)

Category Three (strong)
Winds: 111–130 mph (178–209 km/h)
Minimum surface pressure: 964–945 mbar
Storm surge: 9–12 feet

Some large trees blown down. Some structural damage to small buildings. Serious flooding at coast. Many small structures near coast destroyed; larger structures near coast damaged by battering waves and floating debris. Evacuation of lowlying residences. Example: Hurricane Fran (1996), Hurricane Alex (2004)

*Many islands in the Caribbean have volcanoes. These on St. Lucia are dormant. **What two nations share one island?***

Caption Answer

Haiti and the Dominican Republic

Three Island Groups

The Caribbean Sea contains three sets of islands. To the north lie the Bahamas. Farthest to the west lie the Greater Antilles. To the southeast lie the Lesser Antilles.

The Bahamas to the north are made up of about 700 islands. Only two islands have large populations. They are called Grand Bahama and New Providence. The Bahamas are warmed by the Gulf Stream. They share the tropical climate of the islands to the south.

South of the Bahamas is the group of islands called the Greater Antilles. These are the largest islands in the Caribbean. They include Jamaica, Cuba, Puerto Rico, and Hispaniola. The two countries of Haiti and the Dominican Republic share the island of Hispaniola. The French colonized Haiti. The Dominican Republic was a colony of Spain.

The third group is the Lesser Antilles. These islands extend east from Puerto Rico. Then they curve southeast to the coast of Venezuela in South America. They include the U.S. Virgin Islands, the British Virgin Islands; St. Martin/St. Maarten, St. Christopher (St. Kitts) and Nevis, Antigua and Barbados, St. Vincent and the Grenadines, and Grenada.

Trinidad and Tobago are two islands. Together they form one country. That is also true of St. Kitts and Nevis, as well as Antigua and Barbuda.

Curving around westward are the Netherlands Antilles. They are made up of the three islands of Aruba, Bonaire, and Curaçao. These islands are sometimes called the "ABC" islands. These three islands still maintain a close relationship with the Netherlands. The Netherlands cares for their defense and foreign relations.

Activity

Beach Umbrellas

OBJECTIVES: 1.02, 1.03, 1.06

Ask students to bring old umbrellas from home. You will need one per group. Open the umbrella and make a pattern of the sections. Use the pattern to cut pieces of paper in different colors, one for each section of the umbrella. Assign groups of students an island country of the Caribbean to research. Have them write facts and draw original illustrations that represent their research. Open the old umbrella and glue the paper sections onto it. Display in the classroom.

Possible topics for the sections of the umbrella: people, geography, tourist sites, economy, landforms, interesting facts.

The Caribbean Islands

649

Category Four (very strong)
Winds: 131–155 mph (210–249 km/h)
Minimum surface pressure:
  920.08–944.80 mbar
Storm surge: generally 13–18 feet

Some roofs fail, extensive damage to doors/ windows. Shrubs, trees, and signs blown down. Mobile homes destroyed. Near shore, major damage to lower floors of buildings. Land lower than 10 feet above sea level may be flooded. Low-lying roads may be cut by rising water 3–5 hours before arrival of hurricane's eye. Massive evacuation as far

inland as 6 miles. Example: Hurricane Floyd (1999), Hurricane Charley (2004)
Category Five (devastating)
Winds: >155 mph (249 km/h)
Minimum surface pressure: < 920.08 mbar
Storm surge: >18 feet above normal

More wider-reaching, extreme, and severe damage as described in Category Four storm plus: Complete roof failure on many residences and industrial buildings. Some complete building failures with small utility buildings blown over or away. Evacuation within 5–10 miles of shore may be required.

Example: Hurricane Isabel (2003), Hurricane Katrina (both Isabel and Katrina peaked at but did not make landfall as a category Five), Hurricane Andrew (1992)

Discussion Questions

1 What is the climate like in the Caribbean?

2 What are some crops grown there?

3 What are trade winds?

Caption Answer

Broad-leafed palms grow on the windward side and needle-like palms grow on the leeward side.

Activity

Caribbean Compare and Contrast

OBJECTIVES: 1.07, 2.07, 2.08

Interview an adult or classmate who has traveled to the Caribbean. Remember to ask who, what, when, where, and how questions about their visit. Write the results of your interview in the form of a news report. Make an illustration to go with your report.

Find a person who has moved to your community from the Caribbean. Talk with him or her about life in the homeland and the new life in America. Create a chart comparing and contrasting life in each place. Write a summary paragraph about your chart.

	Home Country	U.S.A.
type of house		
schools		
foods		
jobs		

Caption Answer

Answers will vary.

Palm trees of many varieties grow on Caribbean Islands. Some palms have thin, needle-like leaves. Other palms have broad, fan-shaped leaves. **On what side of an island do you think the broad-leafed palms grow? the needlelike palms?**

Climate and Plant Life

Most of the Caribbean Islands are south of the Tropic of Cancer. The weather stays warm all year. Instead of being either cold or warm, the seasons are either rainy or dry. Most places in the islands never have chilly temperatures. Rainfall is heavy, especially from April to December.

Because the islands are warm year-round, farmers are able to harvest several crops a year. Sugarcane, bananas, coffee, and spices are grown on large plantations. Other farmers raise corn, beans, squash, and peppers on smaller plots of land.

Many plants and trees that grow on the Caribbean Islands have wide and heavy leaves. This helps them absorb large amounts of rain and sunshine. Tall palm trees line the streets of many Caribbean towns and villages.

Parrots are endangered species in the Caribbean. **How do you think they should be protected?**

650

Brightly colored birds fly from tree to tree.

Many of islands in the Caribbean are volcanic. Many have mountains. On some, there is little flat land to farm.

As you learned in Chapter 3, elevation affects the climate. The tops of these mountains are cool. Farmers make good use of the cooler climate and fertile soil of the hillsides.

Trade Winds

Winds blowing toward the Caribbean Islands from the northeast are called *trade winds.* European sailors gave them that name many years ago. These winds filled the sails of ships traveling from Europe.

Columbus reached the Caribbean by first sailing south to the Canary Islands. They are a small group of islands owned by Spain off the coast of Africa. From there he turned west and picked up the trade winds. They carried him across the Atlantic Ocean.

Ships driven by engines do not need those winds today. Yet trade winds remain important. They keep steady breezes blowing over many of the Caribbean islands. This cools the tropical heat and makes the islands pleasant to live on or to visit.

Trade winds also pick up moisture as they blow over ocean water. Islands located in the path of the trade winds are called the Windward Islands. They receive rainfall during most of the year. Vegetation on these islands is thick and green all the time.

High mountains divide some of these Windward Islands. Do you remember reading about the rain shadow effect in Chapter 3?

Chapter 24

It's a Fact

The Caribbean

Aruba, which belongs to the Netherlands, used to be a haven for piracy and smuggling. It uses desalinated water, as little freshwater exists on the island.

The Bahama Islands were used as a Civil War base for Confederate ships. While 3,000 islands make up the Bahamas, only 30 are inhabited.

About 80 percent of the people of Barbados are descended from slaves. The island has a 98 percent literacy rate and is home to the oldest secondary school in the Americas, Warwick Academy, which opened in 1626. Bermuda shorts were first worn as part of the police officers' uniforms here.

Thomas Jefferson could have purchased Cuba but instead used the money to finance the Lewis and Clark expedition.

The mountains cause the rain shadow effect on the islands. They act as a block to the winds. Most of the rain falls on the *windward* side. That is the side that the winds first hit.

The opposite side is called the *leeward* side. On the leeward side little or no rain falls. Desert scrub plants and palm trees with needlelike leaves grow there. Some islands receive so little rainfall that food must be imported.

Hurricanes

The sea brings food and money. The sea also creates the conditions that form powerful hurricanes. The word hurricane is the name Native Americans gave to these storms.

Tropical storms develop in the Atlantic Ocean off the coast of Africa during the summer. They often move west across the Atlantic and into the Caribbean Sea. The warm water of the Caribbean feeds the dangerous storms.

The storms build strong winds. The high speed of the wind destroys life and property. An average hurricane measures about 250 miles (403 km) across. Its winds blow from 75 to 150 miles (121 to 242 km) an hour.

Hurricanes drive the level of the ocean up as they approach the coastline. This is called the storm surge. Waves get higher and higher as the storm gets closer. The storm surge floods coasts and small, low islands. This causes even more damage than high winds.

Many of these storms stay in the Caribbean. They pound islands and the mainland of Middle America and the United States. Sometimes they turn northward and move out of the Caribbean. They move along the Atlantic coast of North America. Sometimes they strike North Carolina.

Weather forecasters today can often predict the paths of these storms. This cuts the loss of life. People can take shelter or move out of a storm's path.

Customs

From December through January 6, Puerto Ricans celebrate what is called *Parrandas Navideñas,* a kind of surprise Christmas caroling. A family goes to the house of another family. They play music or sing Christmas carols. Soon the other family invites the group in. After they visit for about an hour, the two families go to another house of a relative or friend.

Hurricane Michelle hit the Bahamas in November 2001. **What causes the most damage during a hurricane?**

The Caribbean Islands

651

- The Dominican Republic is about the size of Vermont and New Hampshire combined. Lack of irrigation creates limited agriculture. It has the Americas' oldest university, founded in 1538.
- Haiti is the second-oldest independent nation in the Americas (1804). Its average farm size is two acres; its literacy rate 45 percent.
- Jamaica is the pirate capital of the Caribbean.

- Port Royal was destroyed by an earthquake in 1692 when most of it fell into the sea.
- Puerto Rico has no poisonous snakes. About two thirds of its population is urban and 90 percent is literate.
- Trinidad and Tobago are separated by 20 miles. The islands have substantial petroleum reserves. Pitch Lake on the island of Trinidad supplies most of the world's natural asphalt.

Discussion Questions

1 What are some reasons tourists come to the Caribbean?

Caption Answer

More than 25 million

Science Activity

Coral Reefs

 OBJECTIVES: 1.06

Have students conduct research on coral reef ecosystems. This may be done in pairs or cooperative groups. Students should answer the following questions in their research:
1. Where are most of the Caribbean coral reefs found?
2. How long does it take to create reef?
3. What are the major kinds or coral?
4. How are light and temperature important to coral reef development?
5. What organisms depend on the reef?
6. Give an example of interdependence in a coral reef ecosystem.
7. How do humans effect coral reefs?
8. What do scientists believe should be done to protect coral reefs?

Students should display their answers to the questions on a drawing of a coral reef.

Many cruise ships stop in the harbor of Charlotte Amalie, St. Thomas, U.S. Virgin Islands. **How many tourists visit the Caribbean each year?**

Tourism

The waters surrounding the islands of the Caribbean are an important resource for the people.

The sea has always been a source of food. The sea now brings tourists to the Caribbean. Tourists love to swim in the sparkling saltwater and walk along the clean, sandy beaches.

There are beautiful coral reefs in the Caribbean. Tourists who enjoy adventure scuba dive and snorkel there.

More than 25 million people vacation in the Caribbean every year. Many arrive aboard cruise ships that sail among the islands. Visitors from around the world spend money. This helps support the Caribbean nations' economies.

After 1950, tourism became the way most people earned money in the Caribbean. It is particularly important on islands where farming is difficult or impossible. Many Caribbean islanders work in hotels, restaurants, and shops that serve tourists.

Coral Reefs

Coral reefs are spectacular, living marine ecosystems. Reefs are built up over many years from the skeletons of dead coral. Coral reefs are a habitat for many kinds of sea life. They also help the Caribbean economy. The animals that live on the reef are a source of food. Reef tourism provides jobs. The reefs also help protect the coastline from storms.

Scientists studying coral reefs have found that reefs all over the world have been rapidly declining. Many of the problems coral reefs face are caused by humans. These problems combine with natural events such as hurricanes, high water temperature, and disease to stress corals and hurt or destroy reef habitats.

Puerto Rico is surrounded by over 3,107 miles (5,000 km) of coral reef ecosystems (below). However, the island's high population density, pollution, overfishing, and other factors have hurt the reefs. The United States government and the other organizations are working to save and protect the coral reefs of Puerto Rico.

652

Chapter 27

Background Information

Tourism in the Caribbean

Tourism is crucial to the economies of most Caribbean nations. In the Bahamas tourism accounts for $1.8 billion in revenue, half of the nation's income. Since the 1980s, tourism has replaced sugar production as the major income earner for the Dominican Republic. The terrorist attacks on the World Trade Center on September 11, 2001, disrupted life in the Caribbean nations as well. American's fears of air travel led to a sharp drop in United States tourism to the region. Hotels and resorts saw bookings drop by as much as 80 percent. Taxi drivers, street vendors, and fishing boat operators also felt the effects. The economies of Caribbean nations suffered. During this time tourist agencies in Caribbean countries worked to attract more tourists from Europe and Canada, where fewer trip cancellations had occurred.

A bauxite mine in Jamaica provides the mineral to make aluminum. There are a few other minerals in the Caribbean. **What important mineral is refined in the Caribbean but is found in nearby South America?**

Other Resources

Few minerals have been found in the Caribbean Islands. Trinidad mines and exports asphalt. *Asphalt* is a black, sticky material that is used to pave roads. Pitch Lake is one of that island's most famous sights. It is a reservoir of black tar. During colonial times, this natural material was used to coat the hulls of ships.

In Jamaica a large deposit of bauxite was found. *Bauxite* is the mineral from which aluminum is made. Huge shovels scoop the ore from open pit mines. It is loaded into train cars and taken to port. From there the ore is shipped to the United States and Canada.

Bauxite is Jamaica's most important export. The United States and Canada buy most of their bauxite supplies from Jamaica.

Oil is refined on several islands. Antigua and Barbuda, Aruba and Curaçao, and Trinidad and Tobago ship petroleum products to world markets. Some oil is found in these islands. Most of the petroleum refined there comes from nearby South American oil fields.

Most metals and other industrial raw materials are brought to the Caribbean from other places. Mexico provides much of the raw materials for the small amount of Caribbean manufacturing.

LESSON ① REVIEW

Fact Follow-Up
1. Describe the relative location of the Caribbean Islands.
2. What are the largest of islands?
3. What is the importance of the trade winds for the Caribbean Islands?
4. What is the importance of tourism?

Talk About It
1. Why did pirates make use of the Caribbean Islands in the sixteenth and seventeenth centuries?
2. Describe how the climate can be both a benefit and a hazard for the Caribbean Islands.

The Caribbean Islands

653

Discussion Questions
1 What are some of the minerals found in the Caribbean?
2 What are they used for?

 Caption Answer

Petroleum

 Activity

Dialect Fun

 OBJECTIVES: 2.08, 3.04, 4.07

Read and discuss *The Cay* by Theodore Taylor (HarperCollins, 1991. ISBN 038000142X.) with the class over a period of several days while studying Chapter 27. Define dialect, and discuss the dialects of different regions in the United States. Using examples from the book, discuss the dialect of Timothy. Ask students to take turns reading it aloud. Have students write a short story with the Caribbean as the setting. Tell them to include dialogue with dialect that might be heard there. Have them create an original glossary for their story.

LESSON ① REVIEW

Fact Follow-Up Answers
1. The Caribbean Islands divide the Atlantic Ocean from the Caribbean Sea in a crescent-shaped arc. They stretch eastward off the southern Florida coast and curve southeast to the islands of Trinidad and Tobago just off the northern coast of South America.
2. Cuba, Hispaniola, Jamaica, and Puerto Rico are the largest of the islands.
3. Islands that receive the trade winds have steady breezes blowing. This air movement cools the tropical heat and makes the islands pleasant places to live or visit. Trade winds also ensure a year-round rain supply.
4. Tourism is the way most people in the islands earn money, especially where farming is difficult or impossible.

Talk About It Answers
1. Reasons include warm winter temperatures, the trade winds, and the fact that there were so many islands it was easy for pirates to move about and escape capture.
2. Climate is a benefit in that more than one crop a year can be grown and temperatures are warm, encouraging the tourist industry. Climate is a hazard because of the frequency of hurricanes.

OBJECTIVES: 1.06, 1.07, 3.04, 3.06

Discussion Questions

1 What were the most numerous Native American tribes in the Caribbean?

 **Caption Answer**

Dominica

Reading Strategy Activity

What Good Readers Do: SCROL

OBJECTIVES: 1.06, 1.07, 3.04, 3.06

SCROL is another technique for previewing a lesson, but it includes writing as well.

The first two steps of SCROL should be done as a whole-group activity.

S stands for survey. Ask students what should be looked at when surveying a lesson.

C stands for connect. Ask students to look at the subheadings and how these connect to each other. Also, ask them what they already know about Cthe Caribbean from Lesson 1 or their prior knowledge. List these on the board, even though some may be incorrect.

R stands for read. Let students read the lesson independently.

O stands for outline. Students write the subheadings on their paper, leaving room for details to be listed under each heading.

L stands for Look back. Have students look back over their notes to see if they make sense and are accurate. Share the notes in small groups.

LESSON 2 People and Environment

KEY IDEAS

- Native Americans, Africans, and Europeans make up the Caribbean's culture.

- Today, most Caribbean people are of African descent.

- The plantation system and mining changed the environment of the Caribbean.

The Caribbean Islands are a meeting ground. People from many backgrounds have settled there. Descendents of Native Americans, such as the Caribs and the Tainos, have mixed with people from Africa, Spain, Portugal, France, the United Kingdom, the Netherlands, Asia, and India. They have formed unique combinations of culture, language, cooking, and music.

Many Peoples

People from across the world have influenced the farming, building, government, and religion of the Caribbean. When thinking about these islands, we must remember that each one is unique.

Native Americans

Tainos and the Caribs were two of the most numerous Native American groups in the Caribbean when Europeans arrived. Under the Spanish, many Native Americans died from disease, overwork, and starvation. Some survivors from both groups mixed with Europeans and Africans.

Tainos were the first Native Americans to be incorrectly called "Indians" by Columbus. As you read in Chapter 5, he believed that he had reached Asia's East Indies. The Tainos welcomed the Europeans and helped them survive. The Tainos introduced the hammock and tobacco to the Europeans. The word barbecue also comes from the Taino language.

Today, the Taino's descendants are found in many places in the Caribbean. They live in Cuba, Puerto Rico, the Dominican Republic, and the Virgin Islands.

The Caribs were another Native American group in the region. They came to the islands from South America. They traveled on canoes with sails. The Caribs arrived around the same time as the Spanish.

The Spanish and the English accused the Caribs of being cannibals. Cannibals are people who eat human flesh. There is little evidence that this was true. But this claim was used as an excuse to attack and enslave the Caribs.

Today, about 3,000 Caribs live on the island of Dominica. Their ancestry is mixed with that of Europeans and Africans.

This eighteenth century engraving of a Carib Indian of the Antilles shows what Caribbean Native Americans looked like when the Europeans arrived.
Where can you find descendants of the Caribs?

Chapter 27

 Background Information

Treasures of the Taino

The discoveries of two Cuban fishermen are helping archaeologists learn more about the Taino Indians. In the small coastal town of Punta Alegra, about 200 miles (322 km) from Havana, a Canadian archeologist has uncovered a large wooden building and parts of its thatch roof dating back 500 to 700 years. The site may hold the remains of as many as 25 Taino houses. The archaeologist learned about this site from a Canadian fly fishing tour group that vacationed in the area in the early 1990s. On their trip, the

Canadians met Pedro Guerra and Nelson Tom. For more than a decade the two fishermen had collected some 200 artifacts that had washed up on the beach near their homes. The pieces included wooden stools and 8-inch-tall idols carved out of a heavy black wood. When the Canadian tourists returned home, they contacted the Canadian archaeologist, who went to Cuba, met with the two fishermen, looked at their collection, and began working with Cuban officials on the current excavations.

These two Carib girls are wearing their school uniforms. They live on Dominica. **Why are most people in the Caribbean today of African descent?**

African Heritage

Most people in the Caribbean have African ancestors. Spain brought Africans to the Caribbean as slaves as early as 1502. Africans were brought to replace Native Americans who had died or escaped into the mountains of the islands. The Africans served as builders and craftsmen. They also fished and farmed.

Just three years after Africans arrived on the island of Hispaniola, there was a huge slave rebellion. Native Americans and Africans joined forces against their Spanish masters.

Many escaped to live in the mountains, forests, and swamps. Some went to Cuba or Puerto Rico. Others made it to Jamaica and the smaller islands. In these safe havens, African culture survived. It blended with Native American ways of life.

Today, Afro-Caribbean culture is rich all over the Caribbean. In every Caribbean nation the food, music, and traditions are very much based on African culture.

Spanish Heritage

The first Spanish ships brought soldiers, priests, and craftspeople to the colony. Later they brought tools, seeds, livestock, and other items to run a colony.

The Spanish laid the first claims to most of the Caribbean islands. The first to gain independence from Spain was the Dominican Republic. As you read in Chapter 11, Cuba and Puerto Rico remained colonies until the Spanish–American War.

Cuba gained independence from Spain in that war. But it came under United States supervision. The United States took possession of Puerto Rico. It is still a territory of the United States. Spanish influence remains strong in language, law, architecture, and religion.

Spain wanted colonies that supplied gold and silver. Very little of these metals were found in the Caribbean. Mexico, however, filled ship after ship with treasures bound for Spain. To reach Spain the ships had to sail through the Caribbean.

The Caribbean Islands

655

Discussion Questions

1 Why were Africans brought to the Caribbean? What jobs did they have? What happened to them?

2 Which countries have heavy Afro-Caribbean cultures?

3 Why was Spain mainly interested in having colonies?

The slave trade brought many Africans to the Caribbean.

Ships to Scale

OBJECTIVES: 1.06, 1.07, 5.05

Draw Columbus's ships to scale in the school parking lot using sidewalk chalk.

Draw a 24-inch circle to represent each crew member. Calculate how much food, water, and other supplies each ship would need. Have students see how much space remains.

- Santa Maria: 82 feet long, 33 feet wide, crew of 40
- Pinta: 72 feet long, 26 feet wide, crew of 20
- Niña: 74 feet long, 24 feet wide, crew of 24

Eyewitness Activity

Slave Rebellions

OBJECTIVES: 1.05, 2.08, 3.06, 4.06

The PBS series *Africans in America—Brotherly Love* is the foundation for the Web site of the same name.

Visit **NCJourneys.com** for a link to the Web sites.

The Haitian Revolution is explained, and links are provided for further information on Toussaint L'Ouverture; Declaration of the Rights of Man; "Revenge Taken by the Black Army"; Tobias Lear to Madison; Douglas Egerton on the Haitian Revolution, Toussaint L'Ouverture and Jefferson; Julius Scott on John Brown Russworm and the Haitian Revolution. The accompanying lesson plans enhance the video program, but two activities do not necessitate watching the video series.

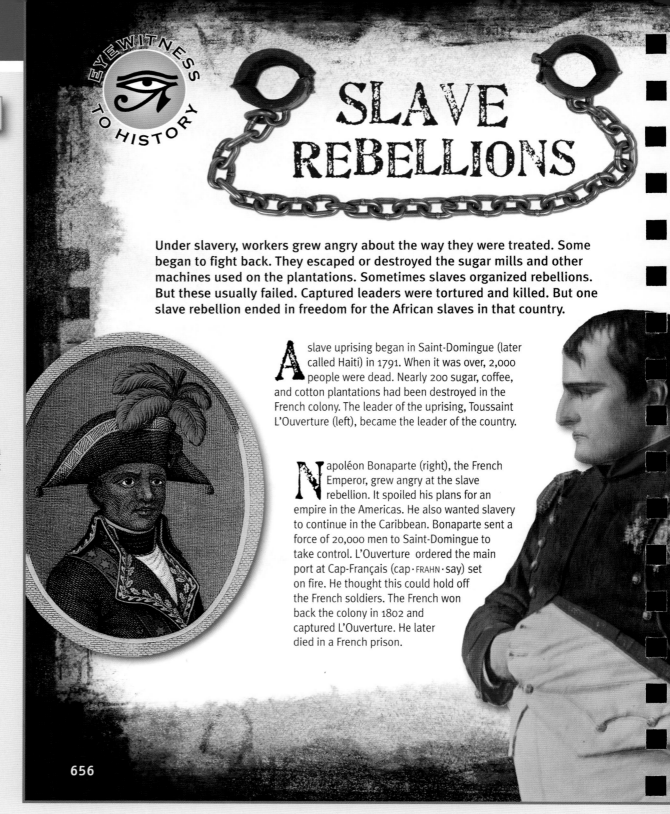

EYEWITNESS TO HISTORY

SLAVE REBELLIONS

Under slavery, workers grew angry about the way they were treated. Some began to fight back. They escaped or destroyed the sugar mills and other machines used on the plantations. Sometimes slaves organized rebellions. But these usually failed. Captured leaders were tortured and killed. But one slave rebellion ended in freedom for the African slaves in that country.

A slave uprising began in Saint-Domingue (later called Haiti) in 1791. When it was over, 2,000 people were dead. Nearly 200 sugar, coffee, and cotton plantations had been destroyed in the French colony. The leader of the uprising, Toussaint L'Ouverture (left), became the leader of the country.

Napoléon Bonaparte (right), the French Emperor, grew angry at the slave rebellion. It spoiled his plans for an empire in the Americas. He also wanted slavery to continue in the Caribbean. Bonaparte sent a force of 20,000 men to Saint-Domingue to take control. L'Ouverture ordered the main port at Cap-Français (cap·FRAHN·say) set on fire. He thought this could hold off the French soldiers. The French won back the colony in 1802 and captured L'Ouverture. He later died in a French prison.

656

The French tried to reestablish slavery but failed. Slaves continued their struggle. At this point, British and Spanish troops invaded the island. These European powers also were against slaves taking over a country.

An army of freed slaves and native-born mulattoes (people of mixed European and African heritage) formed. Jean-Jacques Dessalines led the group. They finally won independence in 1804 after years of fighting. The leaders did not want the name Saint-Domingue. They renamed their new country a native word, Haiti. It means "land of the mountains."

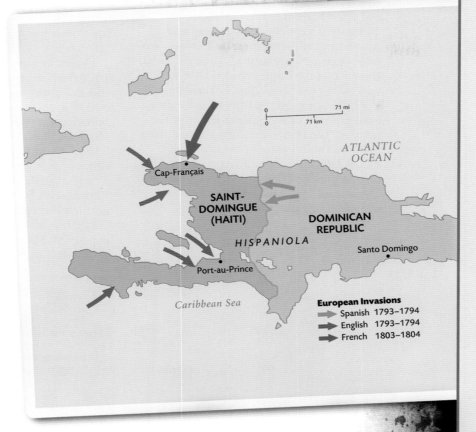

ATLANTIC OCEAN

Cap-Français

SAINT-DOMINGUE (HAITI)

DOMINICAN REPUBLIC

HISPANIOLA

Santo Domingo

Port-au-Prince

Caribbean Sea

European Invasions
→ Spanish 1793–1794
→ English 1793–1794
→ French 1803–1804

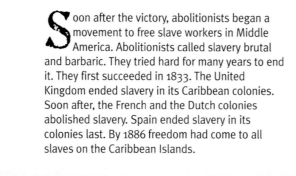

Soon after the victory, abolitionists began a movement to free slave workers in Middle America. Abolitionists called slavery brutal and barbaric. They tried hard for many years to end it. They first succeeded in 1833. The United Kingdom ended slavery in its Caribbean colonies. Soon after, the French and the Dutch colonies abolished slavery. Spain ended slavery in its colonies last. By 1886 freedom had come to all slaves on the Caribbean Islands.

657

 Teacher Notes

Hispaniola: 1492 to 1844

Since 1492 when Columbus first landed on Hispaniola, the history of the island—now divided into two nations, Haiti and Dominican Republic—has been a complicated series of colonial contests for power, intermingled with popular revolts and struggles among the indigenous peoples. After 300 years of colonial occupation and exploitation by Spain, Britain, and France, the slave rebellion in 1791 initiated a series of events allowing Haiti to finally declare independence from France in 1804. Jean-Jacques Dessalines declared himself emporer, but his power was short lived. He was assassinated in 1806 and succeeded by one of his lieutenants, Henri Christophe (who apparently conspired in the plot).

Meanwhile, on the eastern end of the island, a popular revolt aided by the British seized Santo Domingo from French control in 1808. In 1821, a revolt in the Dominican Republic, lead by Jose Nunez de Caceres, managed to gain independence from Spain. One year later the Dominican Republic again fell under Haiti's control. In 1844, a group lead by Juan Pablo Duarte was able to wrest control from Haiti and finally establish the Dominican Republic as a true and independent country.

Discussion Questions

1 What was the purpose of fortifying (making stronger) the harbors in the Caribbean?

2 What do the governments of Cuba and the Dominican Republic have in common?

3 What other European countries had colonies in the Caribbean?

4 Where were these colonies?

 Caption Answer

During the Spanish-American War

 Caption Answer

Aruba, Bonaire, and Curaçao

 **Map Activity**

European Influences in Middle America

NATIONAL GEOGRAPHY STANDARDS: 1, 17

GEOGRAPHIC THEMES: Movement

OBJECTIVES: 1.07, 3.06, 3.07, 4.07

From the time of the earliest Spanish explorers in 1492, Middle America has felt the impact of European culture. On the mainland, the majority of the region was influenced by the Spanish; on the islands, various European nations were influential. Some islands changed hands as a result of wars between European nations. Because of disease, famine, and bloodshed the native populations of the islands were reduced dramatically, and the importation of Africans as slaves had an important impact on the culture. As the United States grew in importance in the region, the United States influenced and controlled some areas of the region.

Students will complete an outline map of Middle America (found in the Teacher's Resource Guide) showing European control of the region in 1700 after Spain began losing territory. Students should create a key and color in those islands or lands controlled by each of the nations active in Middle America.

Spain's Legacy

To guard these treasure ships, the Spanish built fortresses. They built them in the best and safest harbors in the Caribbean. There the treasure ships could be repaired and stocked for the long journey to Europe. San Juan, Puerto Rico; Havana, Cuba; and Santo Domingo in the Dominican Republic were three of the most important colonial ports.

Both Cuba and the Dominican Republic have experienced the Spanish legacy of the *caudillo*. The Dominican Republic was ruled more than thirty years by the strongman Rafael Trujillo. Cuba suffered under the dictatorships of Gerardo Machado and Fulgencio Batista. Cuba today is ruled by another strongman, Fidel Castro.

This turret is part of El Morro Fort, built by the Spanish in Puerto Rico. **When did Puerto Rico gain independence from Spain?**

Other European Influences

France, the Netherlands, and England colonized some Caribbean islands. In the late 1500s, Spain's power in Europe weakened. These other European nations began to slowly take possession of Spanish territories.

During its war for independence from Spain, the Netherlands seized the islands of Aruba, Bonaire, and Curaçao. It also took some of Spain's other islands. Denmark controlled the other Virgin Islands for a time, before the United States came to govern them in 1917. Great Britain gained some of the Virgin Islands from the Dutch.

Spain lost the islands of Guadeloupe and Martinique to the French in 1635. Haiti became a French colony in 1677. The Netherlands and France share ownership of the island of St. Martin (which the Netherlands call St. Maarten) in the Lesser Antilles.

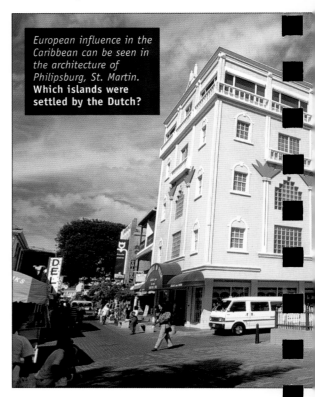

European influence in the Caribbean can be seen in the architecture of Philipsburg, St. Martin. **Which islands were settled by the Dutch?**

Settlement Patterns of Middle America

ATLANTIC OCEAN

THE BAHAMAS

YUCATÁN PENINSULA

MEXICAN PLATEAU
Teotihuacán
Tenochtitlán
Chichén Itzá
Tikal

GREATER ANTILLES

LESSER ANTILLES

PACIFIC OCEAN

Caribbean Sea

Tropic of Cancer

30°N
20°N

Native Americans
- Arawak
- Aztecs
- Carib
- Maya

European Settlers
- ← Dutch
- ← English
- ← French
- ← Spanish

0   300   600 mi.
0   300   600 km

90°W   80°W   70°W

🌐 **Movement** Several European nations established settlements in the Caribbean. *Which European nation had the most settlements?*

💬 **Caption Answer**

Spain

💡 **Activity**

Tabletop Plantation

OBJECTIVES: 1.06, 1.07, 2.08, 3.06

Assign groups of students to research coffee, sugar, and cotton plantations. There could be two groups for each plantation. Ask students to collect small boxes about the size of toaster pastry boxes. Use a desk or table in your room covered with construction paper to represent fields. Make miniature plantation buildings with the small boxes. The owner's home could be constructed with a shoe box or other larger box. Use construction paper to make workers, animals, docks, and other details of plantation life. Ask students to label the parts of the plantation.

Have them bring in some products made from what is grown on their plantation.

The English settled the uninhabited islands of Barbados and St. Kitts-Nevis in the early 1600s. Between 1647 and 1802, they took control of the Bahamas, Jamaica, St. Vincent, and Trinidad and Tobago.

The Environment

Each group of Europeans brought its own way of life to the Caribbean. Yet, like the Spanish, they found that the tropical environment changed their food and housing.

Plantations

Throughout the Caribbean, Europeans started plantations to grow sugar, cotton, and coffee. At first the Spanish used Native Americans to search for gold. After gold supplies ran out and Native Americans died, they turned quickly to plantations and sugar production.

The Caribbean Islands

Discussion Questions

1 Which countries have heavy Afro-Caribbean cultures?

2 How has the plantation system changed the environment of the Caribbean?

3 What other ways have humans changed the Caribbean Islands' environment?

Caption Answer

Polluted land, water, and air

The Spanish already knew that operating plantations with slave labor would make money. They had operated plantations on islands near the African coast. The other Europeans hoped to repeat Spain's success.

Plantations were Europe's most important way of changing the Caribbean environment. Many plantations are there still. Sugar grows in lowland areas. Coffee is raised at higher elevations. Cuba and Puerto Rico grow sugar. Hispaniola and Jamaica's high hills produce coffee.

These farmers are loading harvested sugarcane onto trucks on a plantation in San Germán, Puerto Rico. **What has been the cost of development in the Caribbean?**

Challenges

The system of plantation agriculture has sometimes damaged the Caribbean's land. Soil erodes quickly when it is over planted. It is also lost when trees are cut down and not replaced.

In Haiti, people suffer great poverty. They have had long years of undemocratic government. To survive, people cut down trees for fuel and building homes. There is now a huge problem with deforestation. Thousands of acres of land have become useless.

Humans changed the environment in other parts of the Caribbean. Wherever mining and industry developed, the land, water, and air became polluted. The bauxite mines of Jamaica and the oil refineries of Trinidad bring jobs to those places. But those areas have a hard time keeping the air, water, and land clean.

What would YOU do?

Imagine that your father is a Spanish plantation owner in the Caribbean during colonial times. He thinks he treats the workers well, but you see that the plantation system is unjust. Would you leave your comfortable home and try to change the system?

LESSON 2 REVIEW

Fact Follow-Up
1. What were the most numerous Native American groups when the Spanish arrived in the Caribbean?
2. What is the most numerous population group in the Caribbean today?
3. What were the three most important fortified ports during colonial times?

Talk About It
1. Why did the Spanish import African slaves to the Caribbean islands?
2. Why were plantations important? How did they change the landscape?
3. How did the Caribbean Islands become important ports? How did the Spanish use the ports?

LESSON 2 REVIEW

Fact Follow-Up Answers
1. The Carib and the Taino were the most numerous groups. The Tainos were the first Native Americans to be incorrectly called "Indians" by Columbus.
2. Today, the majority of the people in the Caribbean are of African descent.
3. The most important were San Juan, Puerto Rico; Havana, Cuba; and Santo Domingo in what is now the Dominican Republic.

Talk About It Answers
1. Africans were brought to the islands as early as 1502 to replace the rapidly dwindling labor supply as the Native Americans either died from overwork and diseases brought by the Spanish or fled into the interior mountains of the islands to escape enslavement.
2. The system of plantation agriculture has sometimes damaged the land since soils erode quickly if they are overplanted or if trees are cut down and not replaced. Wherever mining and industry developed, the land, water, and air became polluted.
3. The islands served as safe harbors where Spanish treasure ships could be repaired and resupplied.

Many people from North Carolina and around the world vacation in the Caribbean. You may know people who went there on their honeymoon. Before tourism, farming was the most important industry. Farmers grew mainly sugar, coffee, and tobacco. Today, both farming and tourism are important to the livelihoods of the people of many of the islands.

The Sugar Economy

Christopher Columbus brought sugar to Hispaniola in 1493. The crop grew well there. But it was over a hundred years before there was a strong demand for sugar in Europe. That happened when Europeans began to enjoy drinking coffee and chocolate.

By the 1600s, sugarcane plantations began to spring up across the Caribbean. Growing sugar required a huge investment. Large plots of land had to be cleared and planted. Mills had to be built to process the sugar. Storehouses and transportation were needed.

Sugar also needed many hands to harvest it. Turning the sugarcane into a finished product was hard work. The Native American population was too small. Therefore, Africans were brought to the Caribbean. They were enslaved to do the work.

The cane was cut during the dry season, between January and May. It was crushed in a mill. The juice left from the crushing was boiled in a huge vat. After the liquid sugar cooled, it became either molasses or sugar crystals. Rum was made from molasses. The sugar crystals were packed in great barrels and shipped to Europe.

Governments and *Caudillos*

Plantation farming has sometimes led to undemocratic rule by governments in the Caribbean. Plantation owners supported governments headed by dictators. In return, the dictator helped owners pay little for land and labor. Workers stayed poor. The owner did not have to increase wages or improve the workers' living conditions.

As in Central America, dictators and plantation owners in Caribbean nations formed alliances. These often resulted in brutal dictators coming to power. *Caudillos* and military dictators have ruled a number of Caribbean islands. They were helped by a few rich countrymen and foreign companies.

KEY IDEAS

- Plantation agriculture brought hardships to the Caribbean.
- Cuba's Castro led a revolution but has not allowed free elections.
- Deforestation and erosion are problems in Haiti. Trinidad and Tobago has a successful economy.

These people are harvesting sugarcane on Guadaloupe in 1905. **Why did it take 100 years for the sugar industry to develop?**

 OBJECTIVES: 2.02, 2.04, 5.04, 5.07

Discussion Questions

1 Who brought sugar to Hispaniola? Why is growing sugar such a large investment?

Caption Answer

Only after coffee (and tea) and chocolate became popular in Europe was there a large market for sugar.

Reading Strategy Activity

Bringing It All Together

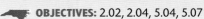 **OBJECTIVES:** 2.02, 2.04, 5.04, 5.07

Ask the students to talk about the reading strategies they have learned through their social studies reading. What strategies have been the most helpful? What organizers do you use when reading a nonfiction text? Explain to students that reading is a lifelong skill that continues to improve as it is practiced. Have students read the Caribbean Portrait about Fidel Castro in this lesson. Ask them to summarize the main idea. Encourage the students to write the key facts in the least amount of words.

The Caribbean Islands

Discussion Questions

1 What is the most important crop in Cuba?

2 Who is Cuba's ruler?

3 Why did the United States government become upset with the government of Fidel Castro?

 **Caption Answer**

The United States Congress banned all American trade with Cuba because of Fidel Castro's relationship with the former Communist Soviet Union.

 **Activity**

Sugar

OBJECTIVES: 5.07

Have students research the history of sugar. They should also examine the different types of sugar products (brown sugar, confectioner's sugar, and others). Visit **NCJourneys.com** for links to possible sources.

Have students make a mural depicting the story of sugar. Follow up by tasting samples of different types of sugar.

 **Activity**

The Caribbean—a Research Project

OBJECTIVES: 1.02, 1.06, 5.03, 5.06

Students will research a nation island of their choosing.
They should research the following:

- history/culture
- currency
- government
- tourist information
- land/water and geography
- language
- climate
- demographics
- weather

Additional information:

Students may present the information in the form of a brochure or poster.

A Tale of Three Countries

Some islands have continued close relationships with their former colonial masters. In other places, moves have been made to bring democracy. In Cuba, however, the government went yet another way.

Cuba

Cuba is the largest island in the Caribbean. It has a blend of Spanish and African heritage. More than half of the Cuban population is descended from both African and European ancestors.

Cuba remained a Spanish colony until 1898. The United States stepped into the Cuban war for independence (the Spanish-American War). After Spain lost, the United States ran the Cuban government for several decades. American forces were stationed there, too.

Sugar has always been the most important crop in Cuba. For years dictators and plantation owners worked together and shared the profits. These dictators ruled with the help of the Cuban army. Foreign companies were happy with the situation and supported the dictators.

Castro In 1959, a group of Communist guerrillas won a victory over the dictator, Fulgencio Batista. These guerrillas were led by Fidel Castro. Castro promised to distribute the wealth of Cuba more fairly. Many Cubans were tired of being ruled by dictators. They supported Castro and his ideas.

Castro's new government redistributed the land and wealth. Some Cubans did not agree with this. They fled the island. Many came to the United States.

Years passed. Castro continued to rule. He became an ally of the Soviet Union. This upset the Americans. Congress banned all trade with Cuba. But still Castro continued to rule.

A tour bus near a sugarcane field symbolizes Cuba's changing economy. **What has prevented tourism from growing in Cuba?**

 Background Information

Plantation Agriculture

Both the plantation and *hacienda* are forms of landownership brought to Central America by Europeans. On the Caribbean islands, the plantation system is more common than the *hacienda*. Plantations typically produce a single crop, such as sugar or coffee, almost entirely for export. In the past the money to finance large-scale plantation operations usually came from outside the islands. Foreigners owned most plantations, and profits from these operations typically did not have a major impact on the local economy. Because crops grown on plantations are sold on world markets, prices for these commodities tend to go up and down as a result of events far from the Caribbean.

Colorful masks are a popular art form throughout the Caribbean. These are from Cuba. **In what way is Cuban culture similar to that of Central America?**

Caption Answer

Both were strongly influenced by Spanish colonists.

Activity

Castro

◀ **OBJECTIVES:** 3.04, 4.08, 5.06

Dived the class into pairs or groups of three. Each pair of students will visit a variety of Web sites and use classroom and library resources to gather information about Fidel Castro. Distribute appropriate graphic organizers (see the Graphic Organizers in the Teacher's Resource Guide) to help students take notes. Once their research is complete, each pair will create a storyboard about the Cuban revolution and life in Cuba today.. Using this information they will produce a short presentation (using PowerPoint or other programs) to share the information they have learned with the class. After their research, students should decide if Cubans are better off under Castro's rule than under Batista.

CARIBBEAN PORTRAIT

Fidel Castro
1926–

Fidel Castro became the absolute leader of Cuba after the revolution there in 1959. Long before the revolution, Castro was politically active while he was studied at the University of Havana in the 1940s. After his marriage, he began practicing law.

During the 1950s, he became more interested in communism. He became a champion of the poor and disadvantaged. At this same time, he began to publicly question the role of United States businesses in Latin America and Cuba. He gained popular support by calling attention to corruption and injustice in Fulgencio Batista's government. Castro led the rebels that forced Batista out in 1959.

Castro is a hero to some and a cruel dictator to others. He has dealt with all United States presidents since Eisenhower in the 1950s.

The most important event in American-Cuban relations was the Cuban Missile Crisis in 1962. You may remember reading about this in Chapter 12. President Kennedy threatened to use military force if Cuba and the Soviet Union did not remove nuclear weapons from Cuba. The missiles were removed. But Castro continued to oppose the United States.

With the fall of the Soviet Union in 1991, Cuba lost its greatest sponsor. Because of America's restrictions on trade with Cuba, the island nation is cut off from a great deal of trade. So Cuba's economy does not grow as quickly as other North American nations. Despite these hard economic times for Cuba, Castro's family today enjoys great wealth and privilege. These are some of the same things Castro fought against in the revolution.

The Caribbean Islands

Discussion Questions

1 What are some of the problems of Haiti?

2 What is the problem with Haiti's government?

3 What type of economy does Haiti have?

 Caption Answer

Francois Duvalier and then his son, Jean-Claude Duvalier.

 Teacher Notes

Haiti: 1844–2000

Since the division of Hispaniola into Haiti and the Dominican Republic in 1844, Haiti has been plagued by political unrest. In 1915, the United States Marines arrived to establish order and to prevent Germany from gaining a foothold in the Caribbean. Without clear political objectives, the United States forces languished there for almost twenty years. Finally, in 1934, the Marines were withdrawn. Still troubled by political instability and with growing unrest in nearby Cuba, another dictator, Francois Duvalier, took power in 1957.

For the next 30 years, Duvalier and subsequently his son, Jean Claude, oversaw a period of repression and corruption that drove the once-rich Haiti to become the poorest nation in the Western Hemisphere. The younger Duvalier fled in 1986. Since then, a series of interventions (including another visit from the United States military) and United Nations peacekeepers have attempted to promote democratic rule—particularly in the election and later re-election of Jean-Bertrand Aristide. Despite these efforts, political killings and other forms of repression have persisted.

Workers sift stones from a rice crop in Haiti. Rice is one of its staple foods. Deforestation has decreased the rice crop. It has hurt the soil and irrigation systems. **Who ruled Haiti from 1957 until 1986?**

Haiti

Haiti occupies the western portion of the island of Hispaniola. The Dominican Republic covers the eastern two thirds of the island. Haiti is one of the poorest countries in the world.

Haiti became a French colony in 1677. Haitians speak a form of French called creole. Haiti was the second European colony in the Western Hemisphere, after the United States, to win independence.

About 95 percent of the population is of purely African descent. The rest are of mixed African and European descent. But this small minority holds most of the important jobs in government and business.

About 70 percent of the people work in farming. There is a severe shortage of fertile land. Deforestation and erosion are major problems.

In the cities almost half the people have no work. For those with jobs, the pay often is not enough to survive.

Dictators In the years since independence, Haiti has seen a long line of dictators and unstable governments. During the nineteenth century there was much unrest. United States Marines occupied the country from 1915 to 1934.

Between 1957 and 1971, François Duvalier ruled Haiti with the help of the military. His son, Jean-Claude Duvalier, ran the country from 1971 until he was overthrown in 1986. The Haitian military ruled the nation until elections were held in 1990.

The 1990 elections were won by a Roman Catholic priest, Jean-Bertrand Aristide. He promised to halt corruption. He wanted to end poverty and bring democracy to the people.

Wealthy business and land owners did not support Aristide. His government was overthrown in 1991. Once again the military ruled Haiti. The United States helped him regain the presidency. In 2000 Aristide was reelected president. But then four years later there was another uprising. Elections were supposed to be held in 2006, but were delayed. Only time will tell whether democracy will succeed in Haiti.

The Haitian economy is almost completely based on farming. Yet in recent years the sugar harvest has gone way down. Deforestation has spoiled the land. Because of the nation's instability, tourism is almost zero.

 Teacher Notes

Dominican Republic: 1844–2000

During the period of the United States occupation of Haiti, the Marines also controlled the Dominican Republic (1916 to 1924). In 1930, strongman Rafael Trujillo assumed power and brought a measure of stability to the country at the cost of personal freedom. Border disputes with Haiti and feuds with other Carribean nations caused much bloodshed during the Trujillo period, which ended with his assassination in 1961. The following years brought marked steps toward democratization, punctuated by conflicts including an open civil war in 1965. President Lyndon Johnson ordered the United States military in to quell the unrest, and relative stability ensued. Since 1974 there have been several peaceful elections.

This oil rig is drilling in Princess Town, Trinidad.
Why are there Indians on Trinidad and Tobago?

Trinidad and Tobago

Trinidad and Tobago is one nation made up of two islands. The islands are located close to the coast of Venezuela. They lie in the southernmost part of the Caribbean. The capital is Port of Spain. It is on Trinidad.

Trinidad is larger and has a more ethnically diverse population. Most of the nation's industry is in Trinidad. Tobago has a much more easygoing pace. It attracts tourists because of its beautiful natural environment.

Columbus claimed Trinidad for Spain in 1498. Europeans did not settle there until 1592. Late in the 1700s, the Spanish king wanted more people to colonize Trinidad. He offered free land to any Roman Catholics who would settle there. Some French planters moved in and built sugar and cacao plantations.

In 1797, the British seized Trinidad. They seized Tobago in 1814. African slaves were brought in to work the plantations. Then in 1838, the United Kingdom outlawed slavery in its territories. So large numbers of laborers were brought to Trinidad from India. These Indians signed contracts to work for five years. After that time they could choose either 5 acres of free land or free passage home. Many stayed.

Multiculturalism Today, about 40 percent of the population of Trinidad and Tobago is Indian. People of African heritage make up another 40 percent. The remaining people are Europeans, Chinese, Southwest Asians, and South Americans. This makes the nation one of the most multicultural in the Caribbean.

Trinidad and Tobago has one of the most successful economies in the region. This is partly due to its supply of oil and natural gas.

The islands gained their independence from the United Kingdom in 1962. It became a member of the British Commonwealth in 1976. Healthcare and education are generally available to most of the population. Overall, the democratic government is stable.

Discussion Questions

1 Where is Trinidad and Tobago?

2 What is its capital?

3 Who claimed Trinidad for Spain?

4 What crops are grown there?

5 Why does Trinidad and Tobago have a successful economy?

 Caption Answer

The British brought laborers from India to replace the slaves who had been freed in 1838.

 Activity

Three Facts I Didn't Know

 OBJECTIVES: 1.02, 1.06, 3.04, 3.06

Give each student an index card. Ask them to write "Native Americans, Africans, Spanish and Other Europeans" on the card, leaving several lines between each group's name. Read the sections about each group in the text. Have them write on their cards three facts about each group they did not know before reading. After all have finished, have students share their facts one at a time. All students listen to what is shared. If someone mentions a fact that is on his or her card, the students make a check mark beside the fact. As a fact is shared and checked off, that fact may not be repeated. Students must listen so they don't repeat facts that have already been shared. When all facts are shared, the activity is complete.

LESSON 3 REVIEW

Fact Follow-Up

1. What was the basis of the Caribbean economy before tourism became important?

2. What guerrilla leader came to power in Cuba in 1959? What strongman did he replace?

3. What measures does the United States government take against Cuba? What are the effects of these measures?

Talk About It

1. Which of these nations, Cuba or Haiti, do you think has greater chance of economic success? Explain why.

2. How did Trinidad and Tobago become one of the most multicultural nations in the Caribbean?

The Caribbean Islands

LESSON 3 REVIEW

Fact Follow-Up Answers

1. Agriculture, mainly sugar, coffee, and tobacco, formed the basis of the Caribbean economies.

2. Fidel Castro replaced Fulgencio Batista.

3. The United States has banned trade with Cuba. Cuba's economy does not grow as quickly as that of other nations.

Talk About It Answers

1. Important points: Students should choose one of the two nations and explain their choice. Cuba has made advances in education, health care, and in the battle against poverty and has a larger land area. Cuba's Communist government is, however, a problem. Haiti has a severe shortage of fertile land, and deforestation and erosion are major problems.

2. The country was ruled by Spain and The United Kingdom before gaining independence in 1976. Both the Spanish and British imported Africans for labor, but after The United Kingdom ended slavery in 1838, large numbers of laborers were imported from India. Today the population is divided among people of African heritage (40 percent), Indians (40 percent), and Europeans, Chinese, Southwest Asians, and South Americans.

OBJECTIVES: 2.08, 3.04, 3.06, 4.07

Discussion Questions

1 What countries contribute to the culture of the Caribbean?

2 What major religions can be found in the Caribbean?

3 What foods are enjoyed throughout the Caribbean?

 **Caption Answer**

The British colonists established Protestant churches and some follow African religions.

Reading Strategy Activity

Writing What You Know

 OBJECTIVES: 2.08, 3.04, 3.06, 4.07

Helping students bring together all they know so that they are able to summarize their learning in writing is difficult. This strategy needs to be modeled several times in several different contexts. Students need lots of opportunities to practice this skill.

Ask students to read this lesson and write a paragraph telling the main idea and the important facts of the lesson. Have them reread their paragraphs. Does the paragraph include the important facts? If not, students should add. If students have included more than the key facts, they should delete the additional information. Model this process for the students. Then have the students work in pairs to create good summary paragraphs.

LESSON 4 Society and Culture

KEY IDEAS

• The culture of the Caribbean is very diverse.

• Caribbean food is a mixture of African, European, and local ingredients.

• Afro-Carribbean music includes reggae, steelpan, and calypso.

• The people of the Caribbean enjoy water sports, baseball, and cricket.

KEY TERMS

calypso
Carnival
Lent
Mardi Gras
reggae
steelpan

People from many places in the world have come to live in the Caribbean. The culture there is diverse. There is great variety in religious customs, food, music, and recreation. Many languages are spoken. The Caribbean is a crossroads of world culture.

The people of the Caribbean have taken contributions of Africa and Europe, Asia and the Americas. They have created distinct societies and cultures on their islands. The roots of Caribbean culture lie in North and South America, Spain, Portugal, England, France, the Netherlands, Africa, and Asia. There is no one true Caribbean culture. But all of the islands show a common African thread in their societies.

Food

Food in the Caribbean will often be a combination of European and African recipes and local ingredients. Seafood is always available, since they are surrounded by the ocean. Lobster and crab are the base of many dishes. So are octopus and clams. Native fruits are important to the Caribbean diet. Have you ever eaten a guava, mango, or plantain?

Religion

Religion plays a big role in people's lives in the Caribbean. Roman Catholicism is a powerful force. This faith came mostly with settlers from France and Spain.

Unlike Central America and Mexico, Catholicism is not the only major religion. There are many followers of Protestant Christian religions. Many are in the former British colonies. On some islands there are also followers of African religions.

A Catholic priest leads an outdoor mass in the Dominican Republic. **In what way is the religious tradition in the Caribbean unlike Central America?**

666

Chapter 27

 Activity

Literature Connection— Poetry

 OBJECTIVES: 1.01, 1.02, 1.03, 1.06

Use the book *Not a Copper Penny in Me House: Poems From the Caribbean* by Monica Gunning, illustrated by Frane Lessac (Wordsong/Boyds Mills Press, 1993. ISBN 1563977931.).

Read some of the poems about a Caribbean youngster living in Jamaica. The book gives a vivid description of the language, architecture, and marketplaces. The reader will gain a realistic picture of life in the Caribbean. The lively portrayal is the next best thing to being in a tropical island.

After students hear some of the poems, save time for discussion. Let students draw a scene from the book, or have them write a descriptive poem of their own about where they live, using the poems from the book as an example.

These children are celebrating Carnival in the streets of Jacmel, Haiti. **When is Carnival celebrated?**

Carnival in the Caribbean

Not everyone is Roman Catholic. But Roman Catholicism has contributed the tradition of carnival to the entire region. *Carnival* (CAR·nih·vahl) is a winter festival. In some places it begins on January 6 and ends about two months later.

The final celebration is on *Mardi Gras,* the day before Lent begins. **Lent** is a time of solemn prayer as Catholics prepare for Easter. The Carnival season is a time of many parties and parades before the quiet season of Lent.

Mardi Gras is the climax of carnival season. People dress in fancy costumes called *mas* (from the word masquerade). These costumes can take months to make and sew. People dressed as butterflies, dragons, and birds fill the streets. Bands play on floats pulled through the streets. Bystanders dance to the beats of Caribbean music.

French Catholic settlers brought the tradition of Carnival to the island of Trinidad. There, clubs called "mas camps"

work together. They create costumes with the same theme. The mas camps perform their street dances as if they were on stage.

In the days leading up to the parades, bands compete in contests to find the best group. They compete in different categories. During the celebrations there are parties lasting late into the night.

WORD ORIGINS

Mardi Gras means "Fat Tuesday." The French words describe the day before the beginning of Lent. This day is the last time many Catholics enjoy meat and other rich foods before the 40 days of Lent.

The Caribbean Islands

667

Activity

Folktales, "Anansi"

OBJECTIVES: 2.08, 3.04, 3.06, 4.07

Review literature strands with the students and give specific examples of each. In your library locate stories about the Caribbean folktale character "Anansi." Decide which type of folktale it most resembles according to the definitions. If the students enjoyed the story,

check to see if your library has other stories with folktales from the Caribbean or from Mexico and Central America. One example is *Stories From Mexico* by Edward Dolch (Garrard Publishing, 1960. ISBN 0811625516.).

Discussion Questions

1 What is carnival?
2 What parts of carnival would you enjoy?

 Caption Answer

January 6 through Mardi Gras

 Activity

Grilled Jerk Chicken

OBJECTIVES: 1.06, 2.08, 3.04, 3.06

"Jerk" is a Caribbean cooking method of flavoring foods with spices. Have students prepare this in class, or bring in to share.

½ cup vegetable oil
1 onion, coarsely chopped
2 scallions, coarsely chopped
1 large pepper, stem and seeds removed
1 tablespoon fresh ginger, grated
3 cloves garlic, coarsely chopped
1 tablespoon finely chopped fresh thyme
2 tablespoons red wine vinegar
1 tablespoon light brown sugar
¼ teaspoon ground cinnamon
¼ teaspoon freshly ground nutmeg
Pinch of ground cloves
1 teaspoon ground allspice
½ teaspoon salt
¼ teaspoon freshly ground black pepper
1 teaspoon fresh lime juice
4 chicken thighs, skin on, bone in
4 drumsticks, skin on

To prepare the jerk chicken: Puree all the ingredients, except the chicken, in a food processor until almost smooth. Pierce the chicken with a fork to make tiny holes. Place the chicken in a large shallow baking dish and rub the marinade into the chicken. Cover and refrigerate for 24 to 48 hours, depending on how intense you want the flavor to be. Preheat grill. Grill chicken on each side for 5 to 6 minutes or until cooked through.

Discussion Questions

 What kinds of music are from the Caribbean?

 What are some sports enjoyed by the people of the Caribbean?

Caption Answer

Calypso and steelpan music; the mambo, merengue, and limbo dances

Activity

Caribbean Musical Chairs

OBJECTIVES: 3.06, 3.07

Bring in samples of different types of Caribbean music to play musical chairs. Add a twist by assigning people who are "out" to teams. The teams must identify the type of music you are playing. The first team to identify correctly receives a point. The team with the most points at the end of playing musical chairs wins.

Bob Marley of Jamaica made reggae music world famous. He spread Caribbean culture wherever he performed. **What other kinds of culture come from the Caribbean?**

Afro-Caribbean Music

Long ago, Caribbean plantation owners tried to destroy the traditions of the African slaves. The owners wanted to control the slaves. They wanted to keep them from revolting. So plantation owners made the slave workers wear European clothing. They made them learn the language of the masters.

One way that the African people saved their culture was through their music. The music was based on complex drumming and other percussion instruments. The Africans made their own instruments. They continued to play music that came from their African heritage. They kept alive their sacred African rhythms.

Reggae and Steelpan

Today, Jamaica is known as a center of *reggae* music. The strong, steady African beats and chanted words of reggae are popular in the Caribbean. In other parts of the Caribbean, **steelpan** music is a favorite. Steelpan musicians make their music on oil drums that have been hammered into shiny, rounded bowls.

Calypso

Calypso is also another type of music that was invented in the Caribbean. Calypso is distinctive because of the lyrics rather than the instruments played. In one type of calypso, called picong, the words are made up on stage. They usually tease a well-known person or even someone in the audience. Calypso songs even mock local politicians.

In some ways, calypso may be considered an ancestor to rap music.

The Caribbean has also given the world some of the most popular types of dance music and dance. *Mambo, merengue,* and the *limbo* were created in the Caribbean. People all over the world learn these dances.

Sports in the Caribbean

Beaches and clear blue water offer the people of the Caribbean opportunities for fun. Fishing, swimming, and sailing are popular pastimes. Caribbean people also enjoy sports brought to the island from other parts of the world.

Baseball

Baseball came from the United States. But it is even more popular in the Caribbean than in our country. If you are a baseball fan, you already know that many of the great players in our major leagues come from the Dominican Republic, Puerto Rico, and Cuba.

Sammy Sosa, the only baseball player to hit more than 60 home runs in back-to-back seasons, is from the Dominican Republic. Roberto Clemente, an outstanding Puerto Rican outfielder for the Pittsburgh Pirates, was elected to baseball's Hall of Fame in 1972.

In all, there are regularly close to 100 players from the Caribbean playing major league baseball in a given season. Even the tiny islands of Curaçao and Aruba have sent players to the major leagues.

Today, major league teams from the United States run clinics and camps in places like the Dominican Republic. Baseball scouts go there to search for the next Sammy Sosa or Roberto Clemente. Often young boys see baseball as a way out of poverty.

Cricket

Cricket is a sport similar to baseball. It uses a ball and a bat. Cricket is mainly popular in former British colonies like Jamaica, Barbados, and Antigua. There cricket is followed with a passion, like college basketball is in North Carolina. Calling themselves the West Indies, the best players from the Caribbean team up. They challenge larger members of the British Commonwealth, including Australia, New Zealand, India, and Pakistan.

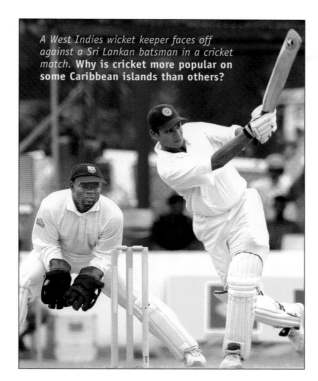

A West Indies wicket keeper faces off against a Sri Lankan batsman in a cricket match. **Why is cricket more popular on some Caribbean islands than others?**

Derek Walcott
1930–

Derek Walcott is the most important living Caribbean author. He won the Nobel Prize for Literature in 1992.

Walcott was born on the island of St. Lucia. His father was a painter who died when Derek was still quite young. He first attended St. Mary's College in St. Lucia. His mother was a teacher there. He got a love of poetry from his mother. He was soon very familiar with the great works of English literature. Walcott got a scholarship to study at the University College of the West Indies in Jamaica. He studied Latin, French, and Spanish.

He also started writing plays about European influence in Caribbean culture. Walcott moved to New York for a time, and then settled in Trinidad to teach and write. He later became a professor of poetry at Boston University.

Walcott is the author of more than twenty plays. He has been a central figure in Caribbean theater throughout his life. His plays often use the island music and storytelling traditions that form the core of Caribbean culture.

The Caribbean Islands

669

Discussion Questions

1 Who are some of the famous sports figures of the Caribbean?

2 What is cricket?

3 Why do you think cricket is played in so many places in the world, and especially in the Caribbean?

 Caption Answer

Cricket is mainly popular in former British colonies because it is a British game.

 Art Activity

Caribbean T-Shirt Design and Tie Dye

OBJECTIVES: 3.04, 3.06, 4.07

Materials: plain white T-shirt (one for each student), variety of dying colors, rubber bands, buckets, water, place to dry T-shirts (clotheslines, hangers), paper, pencil, markers, crayons, colored pencils

Divide students into two groups. Group A will work in small groups to create a possible design to print on a T-shirt. Group B will arrange rubber bands on their shirts and then dip portions of T-shirt into the desired colors. When they finish dying the shirts, they will hang them up to dry. Then group A and group B will switch activities.

While students work, play a recording of reggae music.

 Background Information

The Cricket Craze

Cricket is the most popular spectator sport in the English-speaking Caribbean. During cricket season fans who are not cheering at the stadium are listening to the games on the radio. As in Britain, in Jamaica cricket is the national sport. A cricket team consists of 11 players. On each team there are bowlers, batsmen, wicket keepers, and fielders. Two teams play against each other on a field marked off with wickets, (stakes or sticks) set in the ground. Players take turns at batting and bowling. As in baseball, there are runs, innings, and umpires, but these do not resemble the ones in baseball. The goal is to score the most runs. To score a run, a player has to hit the ball and run to the far wicket or hit the ball to or beyond the marked boundaries of the field. Soccer, also known as football, is second in popularity to cricket on the islands with a British colonial heritage.

Activity

Wrap It Up Party!

📌 **OBJECTIVES:** 3.03, 3.04

Now that you have completed your study of North America, celebrate! Divide the class into pairs and assign (or have them choose out of a hat) each pair a region: Quebec, English-speaking Canada, Nunavut, Northeastern United States, Southeastern United States, Southwestern United States, Western United States, Pacific United States, Alaska and Hawaii, Mexico, Central America, and the Caribbean.

Each pair should prepare a snack for the class that features a recipe or agricultural product of their region. They should also prepare three trivia questions for the class about their region. Encourage students to dress in clothing (historical or contemporary) that relates to their region.

On the day of the party, while you enjoy snacks, play music from all of the regions. Divide the class into two or three teams. Have the teams compete in answering the trivia questions written by the class, getting one point for each correct answer. (You may add harder questions as well that are worth more points). The team with the most points wins an appropriate prize.

Discuss as a class how all these cultures have influenced one another.

A Journey to Curaçao

An Island of Historic Beauty

Imagine you are sailing into Saint Anna Bay harbor in Curaçao's capital city of Willemstad. The first thing you notice are the bright yellow, pink, and green Dutch row houses along the waterfront.

The city was recently added to the United Nations' World Heritage List for its history and beauty. It is home to Mikve Israel Synagogue. This is the oldest continuously used Jewish temple in the Western Hemisphere.

Curaçao is the largest island in the Netherlands Antilles. The island is dry. The land is covered with cactus and short divi-divi trees. These are twisted and bent by the constant ocean winds.

You can explore caves with ancient paintings. The crystal clear water is ideal for diving. Christoffel Park is perfect for a day of watching tropical birds.

The explorer Amerigo Vespucci landed on the island in 1499. He claimed it for Spain. The Spanish built very little on the island. In 1634, the Dutch seized Curaçao. The Dutch West India Company turned Curaçao into one of the main slave ports in the Caribbean.

People of Spanish, Portuguese, Dutch, and African origin came to Curaçao. While Dutch is the official language of the island, everyone speaks Papiamento. Papiamento is a new language. It is a blend of the various languages brought to the island by each wave of immigrants.

In 1918, Curaçao opened its first oil refinery. This industry brought prosperity to the island. Today the inhabitants have many more comforts than do most of their neighbors in the Caribbean.

LESSON 4 REVIEW

Fact Follow-Up
1. What is one common thread in the cultural makeup of Caribbean societies?
2. What is Carnival, and how does it end?
3. What are reggae, steelpan, and calypso?
4. Who are two great major-league baseball players native to the Caribbean?

Talk About It
1. Why can the Caribbean be said to be a crossroads of world cultures?
2. Why was music an important way enslaved Africans Africans preserved their culture?
3. What is your favorite part of Caribbean culture? Why?

LESSON 4 REVIEW

Fact Follow-Up Answers
1. In every society African culture is present.
2. Carnival is a winter festival that begins on January 6, 12 days after Christmas, and ends on Mardi Gras, Fat Tuesday, the day before Lent begins. Mardi Gras is a great festival day.
3. All are styles of music popular in the Caribbean.
4. Roberto Clemente, a Hall of Famer and great outfielder for the Pittsburgh Pirates, was born in Puerto Rico. Sammy Sosa, the only player to hit over 60 home runs in back-to-back seasons, is from the Dominican Republic.

Talk About It Answers
1. Because people from so many places in the world have settled there, the culture is very diverse. The roots of Caribbean culture lie in Africa, Spain, Portugal, England, France, The Netherlands, and Asia.
2. European owners wanted to control the slaves to keep them from revolting so they regulated clothing and language in an effort to destroy African traditions. Slaves could preserve some parts of their culture through music based on drumming, and other percussion instruments. Many objects could be used for drumming including oil drums hammered into round bowls for steel drum music.
3. Important points: Students should support their choice with examples.

Analyzing, Interpreting, Creating, and Using Resources and Materials

How Diverse is North America?

Y ou have learned this year about many societies in North America, Central America, and the Caribbean. You have read about the word "diverse" just as many times. Do you remember studying diverse landforms and climates, diverse plant and animal life, diverse governments and national histories, and diverse peoples and traditions?

The United States has the most diversity in climate and landforms because of its large size. The states of Alaska and Hawaii also add to our country's diversity.

But of all the societies you have studied this year, which has the most diversity in its people and their lives? Here is information about five countries. This will help you begin to answer this question. What conclusions can you draw from this information?

*2006 CIA World Factbook
** U.S. Census Bureau, 2005 American Community Survey.

COUNTRIES	ETHNIC GROUPS	RELIGION	LANGUAGES
United States 300,500,000	White 74.7%, Hispanic** 12.1%, African American 12.1%, Asian 4.3%, Native Americans and Alaska Natives .8%, Native Hawaiian or Other Pacific Islander .1%, two or more races 1.9%	Protestant 52%, Roman Catholic 24%, Mormon 2%, Jewish 1%, Muslim 1%, other 10%, none 10%	English 82.1%, Spanish 10.7%, other Indo-European 3.8%, Asian and Pacific island 2.7%, other 0.7%
Canada* 33,098,932	British Isles origin 28%, French origin 23%, other European 15%, Amerindian 2%, other 6%, mixed 26%	Roman Catholic 42.6%, Protestant 23.3%, other Christian 4.4%, Muslim 1.9%, other 11.8%, none 16%	English (official) 59.3%, French (official) 23.2%, other 17.5%
Mexico* 107,449,525	*mestizo* (Amerindian-Spanish) 60%, Amerindian 30%, white 9%, other 1%	Roman Catholic 89%, Protestant 6%, other 5%	Spanish, various Maya, Nahuatl, and other regional indigeous languages
Costa Rica* 4,075,261	white (including mestizo) 94%, black 3%, Amerindian 1%, Chinese 1%, other 1%	Roman Catholic 76.3%, Evangelical 13.7%, Jehovah's Witnesses 1.3%, other Protestant 0.7%, other 4.8%, none 3.2%	Spanish (official), English
Haiti* 8,308,504	black 95%, mulatto and white 5%	Roman Catholic 80%, Protestant 16% (Note: roughly half the population practices Voodoo)	French (official), Creole (official)

The Caribbean Islands

671

Skill Lesson Review

1. Which column was easiest? most difficult to use? Explain why. *Invite student responses, probing for reasons. Probably the "Religions" column was most difficult.*

2. Do you think you would have been able to deal with so much information when you began the school year? *Encourage students to discuss their increasing abilities to deal with complex information.*

Teaching This Skill Lesson

Materials Needed textbooks, paper, pencils; collection of foods from different countries that illustrate diversity

Classroom Organization whole class

Beginning the Lesson Explore the meaning of the word "diversity" with students, noting diversity in the population of your community and/or school, religious diversity in the community, ethnic diversity represented by foods of various ethnic origins in the supermarket.

Lesson Development Ask students which nation of the five shown on the chart in the Skill Lesson for Chapter 27 is the most diverse. Accept responses, probing for reasons.

Next, ask students to examine the "Ethnic groups" column. If they do not notice differences in terminology and origin, point out discrepancies. Ask students to decide which country is most, and which is least, ethnically diverse. Repeat this procedure for the "Religions" and "Languages" columns.

Ask students to state which country is most diverse, accepting all responses and probing for explanations. Ask what additional information they might need to reach such a conclusion, again accepting all responses and probing for explanations.

Conclusion As a homework assignment, ask students to write a one-to-three-paragraph essay stating which country in their judgment is most diverse. After allowing students to compare papers and perhaps helping each other strengthen writing style as well as arguments, post papers in the classroom.

671

Talk About It

1. Important points: Students should state an opinion and give reasons for it. The sugar economy has depleted the soil and contributed to deforestation. Enslaved Africans and Indians were brought to the island to support the sugar economy. The sugar economy, however, has provided jobs and continues to do so in a region with scarce mineral resources.

2. Important points: Encourage students to suggest a variety of places and choose one. Explanations should include both physical and cultural characteristics of place.

3. Comparisons should include political beliefs and the results of strongman rule in terms of the lives and well being of the inhabitants. It should be noted that Castro came to power as the result of guerrilla warfare while the others achieved power with the support of large landowners and the military.

4. Important points: Encourage students to suggest a variety of resources. Oil and human resources should be mentioned.

5. Important points: Encourage students to recall as many European "imports" as possible, then choose the one thing they think most important and explain their choice. Among the "imports" were Christianity (Roman Catholicism, in particular), the importation of Africans and Indians as laborers, diseases, the system of cash crops, language, and architecture.

 Mastering Mapwork

1. Santo Domingo is the national capital of the Dominican Republic.
2. Havana, Cuba.
3. Willemstad, Curaçao, and Port-of-Spain, Trinidad and Tobago, are the capitals and islands.
4. Nassau, the capital of the Bahamas, is located at 25°N.

CHAPTER 27 REVIEW

Lessons Learned

LESSON 1
Land and People
The Caribbean Islands lie between southern Florida and the northern coast of South America. The three island groups are the Bahamas, the Greater Antilles, and the Lesser Antilles. The climate is warm all year, with dry and rainy seasons.

LESSON 2
People and Environment
Each island in the Caribbean is different, but all are diverse. Native Americans, Africans, and Europeans have all played a part in the history of the region. Their descendents live in the islands today.

LESSON 3
Economy and Government
Plantation agriculture brought slavery to the Caribbean. Sugar has been an important crop. Today's Caribbean economy depends on both agriculture and tourism. Since independence, many Caribbean nations have continued to struggle with poverty and injustice.

LESSON 4
Society and Culture
The Caribbean is a crossroads of world culture. Festivals, food, music, and sports combine many cultural influences in unique ways.

Talk About It

1. Has the sugar economy been a benefit or a burden for the people of the Caribbean? Explain.
2. If you could visit one place in the Caribbean, where would you choose to visit? Explain why.
3. Compare Fidel Castro with other such Caribbean strongmen as Trujillo, Duvalier, and Batista.
4. What resource of the Caribbean Islands do you think will be most important in the future? Explain why.
5. Europeans, especially the Spanish, brought many things with them when they conquered the Caribbean Islands. Which of these things do you think has had the most impact on the people living on the islands today? Explain why.

Mastering Mapwork

LOCATION
Use the map on page 647 to answer these questions:

1. The national capital of a Caribbean nation is located at 70°W. What is the capital, and what is the nation?
2. What national capital is located nearest the Tropic of Cancer?
3. The national capitals of two countries are located very near the northern coast of South America. What are the capitals, and what are the nations?
4. What national capital is located at 25°N?

Becoming Better Readers

What Good Readers Do
Congratulations! You have become a better reader this year. You have learned how to preview a chapter, how to look for main ideas, and how to find important details to support your main idea. What reading strategy do you use the most when reading a nonfiction text?

 Becoming Better Readers

Important points: Students should choose one strategy and describe why they like to use it and how it helps them.

Go to the Source

Writing to Government Leaders

Fidel Castro wrote this letter to President Franklin Roosevelt on November 6, 1940. FDR had just been elected to a third term as President. Read Castro's letter below. Answer the questions using information from the letter.

My good friend Roosevelt I don't know very English but I know as much as to write to you. I like to hear the radio and I am very happy because I heard in it that you will be president for a new (periodo). I am twelve years old. I am a boy but I think very much but do not think that that I am writing the President of the United States.

If you like, give me a ten dollar bill green american, in the letter, because never I have not seen a ten dollar bill green american and I would like to have one of them.

My address is: Sr. Fidel Castro Colegio de Bolover Santiago de Cuba Oriente, Cuba

I don't know very English but I know very much Spanish and I suppose you don't know very Spanish but you know very English because you are American but I am not American.

Thank you very much, Good by. Your friend, Fidel Castro

If you want iron to make your ships I will show you the bigest [sic] mines of iron of the land. They are in Mayori, Oriente Cuba.

Questions

1. How old was Fidel Castro when he wrote this letter?
2. Was Fidel Castro supportive of Roosevelt?
3. What was the goal of Fidel Castro for writing this letter to President Roosevelt?
4. Based on the information in the letter, do you think Castro will keep a positive attitude toward the United States. Why?

Go to the Source

Writing to Government Leaders

➤ **OBJECTIVES:** 3.02, 4.03, 4.06
SOCIAL STUDIES SKILLS: 3.05

Letter from Castro to Franklin D. Roosevelt

Archivists who work for the presidents save all of the mail that the president is sent. One just never knows who might be famous one day! This letter tells us about Castro as a child. What did he seem to value most?

Answers

1. He was twelve years old.
2. Yes, because he said he was happy that he would be president for a new period. He offered to show him where the biggest mines were in Cuba for building ships.)
3. He wanted to show Roosevelt that he liked him and he really wanted an American ten dollar bill, because he had never seen one before.
4. Important points: Accept any answers as evidence as long as they give examples.

How to Use the Chapter Review

There are four sections in the Chapter Review: Talk About It, Mastering Mapwork, Becoming Better Readers, and Go to the Source. Use the Vocabulary Worksheets and the Chapter Review Worksheet in the Teacher's Resource Guide for additional reinforcement and preparation for the Chapter Assessments. The chapter and lesson reviews and the Chapter Review Worksheets are the basis of the assessment for each chapter.

Talk About It questions encourage students to speculate about the content of the chapter and are suitable for class or small-group discussion. They are not intended to be assigned for homework.

Mastering Mapwork has students apply one or more of the Five Themes of Geography to maps within the chapter.

Becoming Better Readers focuses on building reading strategy skills necessary for reading comprehension in the content areas.

Go to the Source activities allow students to analyze a primary source that relates to the content of the chapter. The questions and activities familiarize students with different types of primary sources and also build content-reading skills.

Appendix

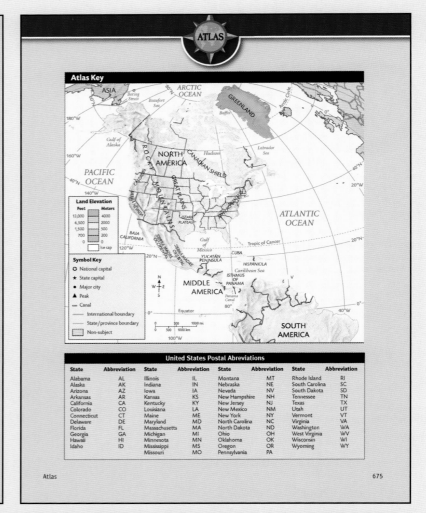

Atlas Key

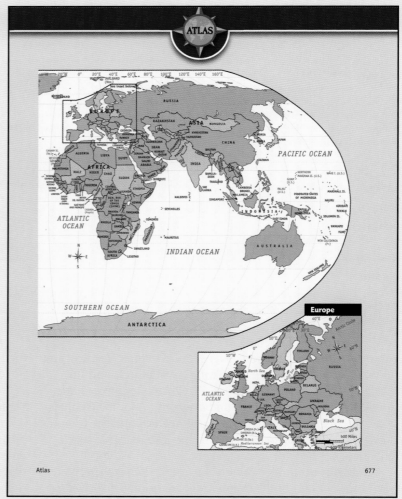

United States Postal Abreviations

State	Abbreviation	State	Abbreviation	State	Abbreviation	State	Abbreviation
Alabama	AL	Illinois	IL	Montana	MT	Rhode Island	RI
Alaska	AK	Indiana	IN	Nebraska	NE	South Carolina	SC
Arizona	AZ	Iowa	IA	Nevada	NV	South Dakota	SD
Arkansas	AR	Kansas	KS	New Hampshire	NH	Tennessee	TN
California	CA	Kentucky	KY	New Jersey	NJ	Texas	TX
Colorado	CO	Louisiana	LA	New Mexico	NM	Utah	UT
Connecticut	CT	Maine	ME	New York	NY	Vermont	VT
Delaware	DE	Maryland	MD	North Carolina	NC	Virginia	VA
Florida	FL	Massachusetts	MA	North Dakota	ND	Washington	WA
Georgia	GA	Michigan	MI	Ohio	OH	West Virginia	WV
Hawaii	HI	Minnesota	MN	Oklahoma	OK	Wisconsin	WI
Idaho	ID	Mississippi	MS	Oregon	OR	Wyoming	WY
		Missouri	MO	Pennsylvania	PA		

World–Political

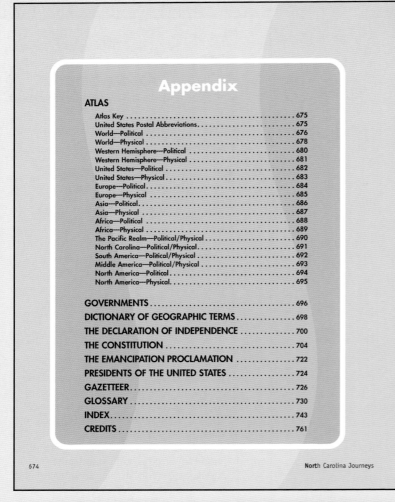

Middle America

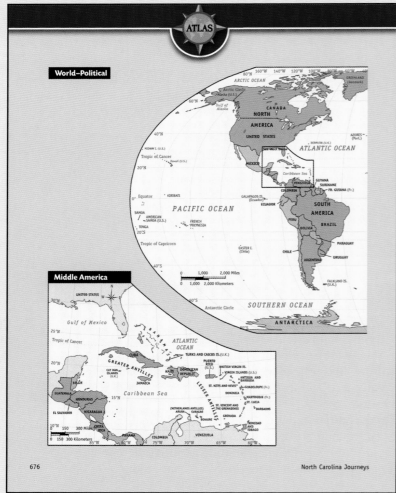

Europe

674–677

World–Physical

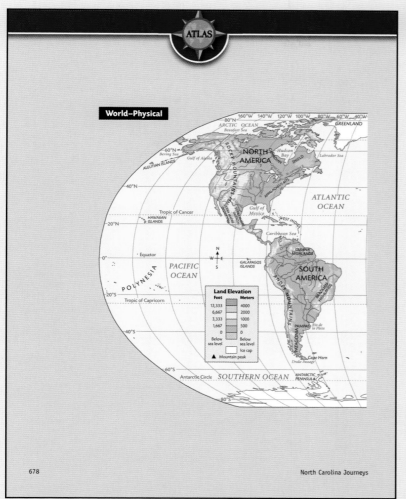

Land Elevation

Feet	Meters
13,333	4000
6,667	2000
3,333	1000
1,667	500
	0
Below sea level	Below sea level
	Ice cap

▲ Mountain peak

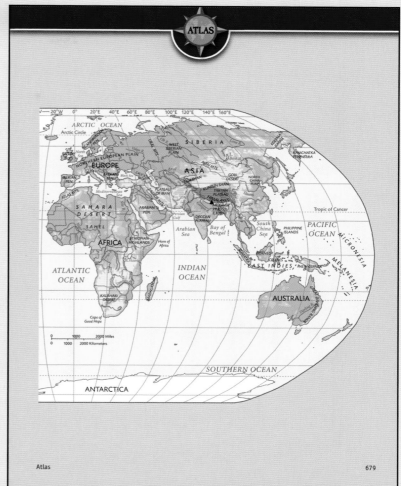

Western Hemisphere–Political

West Indies

○ National capital
● Major city

Western Hemisphere–Physical

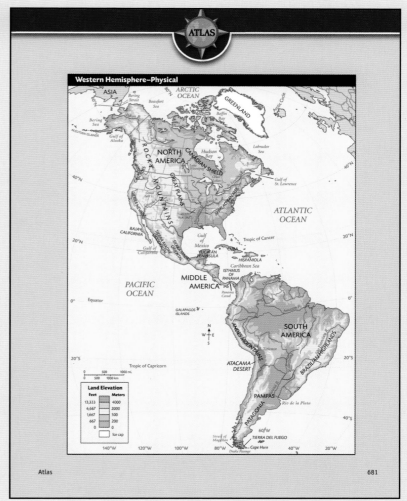

Land Elevation

Feet	Meters
13,333	4000
6,667	2000
1,667	500
667	200
0	0
	Ice cap

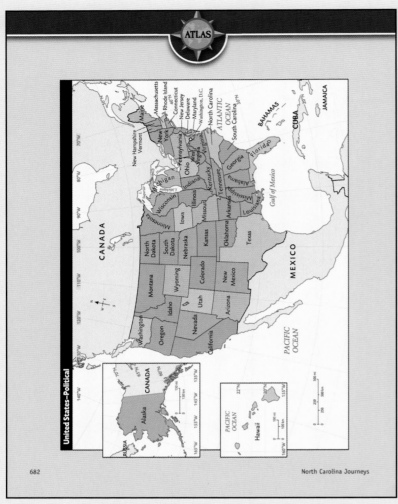

United States–Political

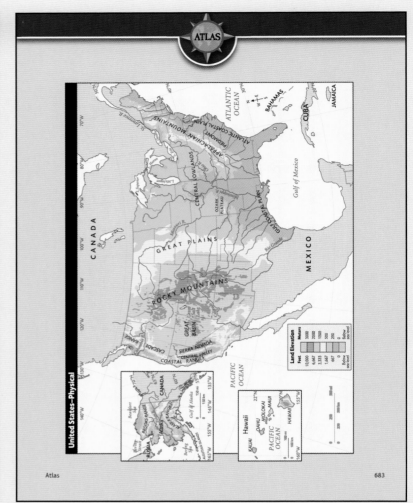

United States–Physical

Europe–Political

National capital
International boundary

Europe–Physical

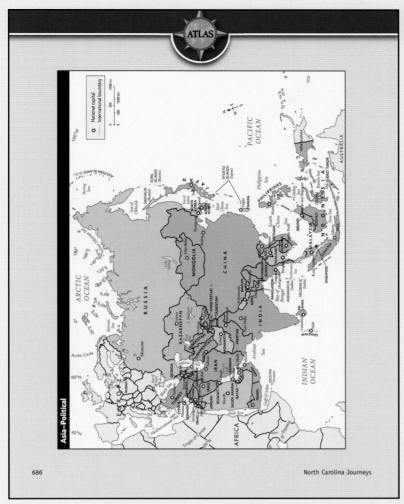

North Carolina Journeys

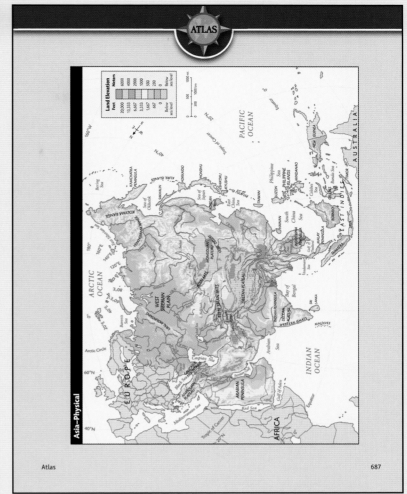

Atlas

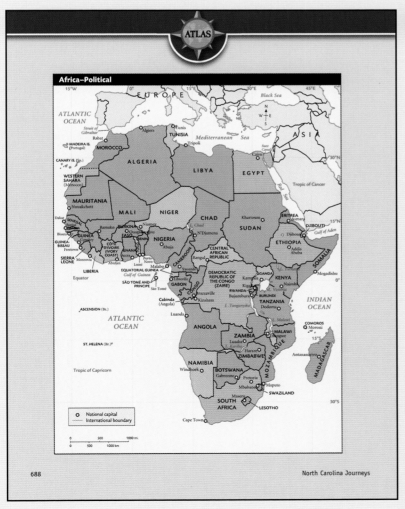

Africa–Political

- ○ National capital
- ‥‥‥ International boundary

North Carolina Journeys

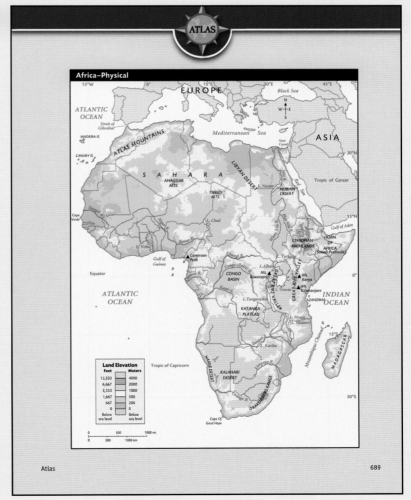

Africa–Physical

Land Elevation

Feet	Meters
13,333	4000
6,667	2000
3,333	1000
1,667	500
667	200
0	0
Below sea level	Below sea level

Atlas

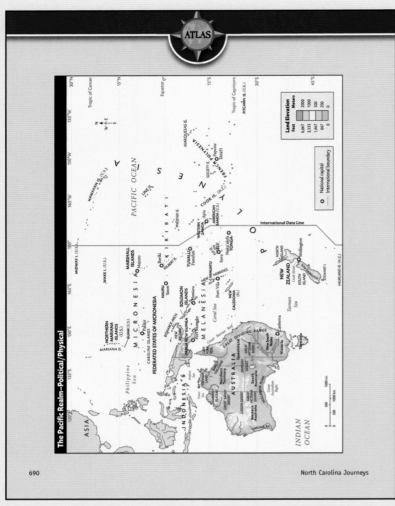

The Pacific Realm—Political/Physical

North Carolina Journeys

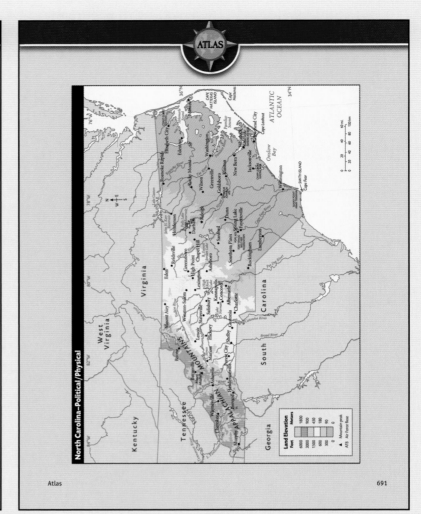

North Carolina—Political/Physical

Atlas

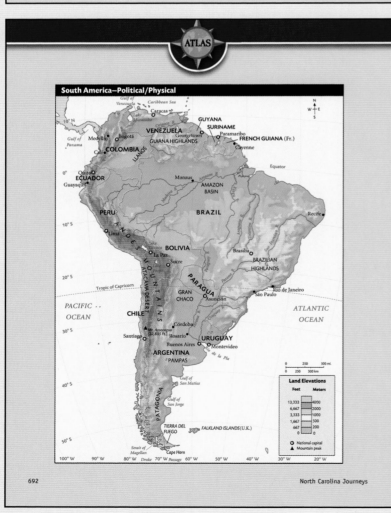

South America—Political/Physical

North Carolina Journeys

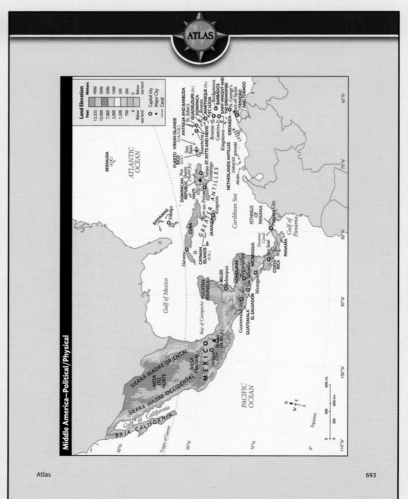

Middle America—Political/Physical

Atlas

North America—Political

○ National Capital
● Major City

694
North Carolina Journeys

North America—Physical

Land Elevation

Feet	Meters
10,000	3000
6,667	2000
3,333	1000
1,667	500
667	200
0	0
Below sea level	Below sea level

~~~ Canal

Atlas
695

TYPES OF GOVERNMENT

There are many types of governments in the regions of the world we study. Many governments use similar terms to describe different functions and organizational structures. This guide reviews the basic structures of constitutional governments, including constitutional monarchies and republics. It also reviews non-constitutional governments, including autocratic and totalitarian regimes.

A constitution is a set of fundamental customs, traditions, rules, and laws that set forth the basic way a government is organized and operated. A nation may have a constitution, but that does not mean it has a constitutional government.

Constitutional Governments

A constitutional government is a government whose actions are limited by law and institutions. If a constitution permits unlimited political power held by one person, a few people, or only one political party, then it is not the basis of a constitutional government. If a constitution does not include ways to enforce limits on the power of government, it is also not the basis for a constitutional government. The separation of powers and the checks and balances system set forth in the United States Constitution are examples of limits of the actions of government. Each branch of the United States government—executive, legislative, and judicial—has the responsibility and the power to "check," or limit, actions taken by the other branches.

In a constitutional government, the constitution is considered a higher law. The constitution, or higher law, provides for the protection of the rights of the individual against unfair and unreasonable infringement by the government and other individuals. This typically includes establishment of a private domain into which the government may not intrude. The individual also typically has "due process of law"—the right to follow the formal procedures written into the law which protect the rights of both innocent and guilty from the arbitrary power of the state. In the United States, these rights are set forth in the Bill of Rights and the due process clause of the Fourteenth Amendment.

President George W. Bush addresses Congress. The United States is a republic with a presidential system of government. The president is not a member of Congress, but is elected by the people through the electoral college.

696
A Journey Through North America

TYPES OF GOVERNMENT

Power is also limited by informal means. These include such group pressure as lobbying and demonstrations, and publicity given to government actions by the media. Another effective restraint is the awareness of citizens and public officials of the traditional limits of power on the government. When a person knows that they have certain rights they are more likely to both exercise them and protect them.

Nearly all constitutional governments are representative democracies. Most are either constitutional monarchies or republics.

Constitutional Monarchies and Republics

Some governments have a monarch as head of state and are called constitutional monarchies. Great Britain, the Netherlands, and Sweden are examples of this form of government. Australia, Botswana, and Canada, as members of the British Commonwealth, accept the British monarch as their own and are considered constitutional monarchies as well.

Constitutional states that have no monarch are called republics. Examples include Germany, the United States, Israel, and Venezuela.

In both constitutional monarchies and republics, the practice and process of governing is by representative democracy. The type of representative democracy is either a parliamentary system or a presidential system.

In a parliamentary system, the chief executive is chosen from among members of the legislative body and is directly responsible to them. Often, this chief executive is called the prime minister. Great Britain, India, and Japan are examples of parliamentary systems.

In presidential systems, the chief executive is not a member of the legislative body and is independently chosen. The president is not directly responsible to the legislature, and is removable by the legislative body only in extraordinary circumstances. A good example of the presidential system is the United States. France has a modified presidential system, combining a strong presidency with elements of a parliamentary system.

Constitutional governments may operate under either a unitary or federal system. In a unitary system, power is concentrated in a central government. France and Japan are examples of unitary systems. In a federal system, power is divided between a central government and territorial subdivisions. Australia, Canada, and the United States are examples of federal systems. In the United States, the Tenth Amendment reserves the rights not granted to the national government to the states and to the people, thus creating the federal system.

Non-Constitutional Governments

In non-constitutional governments there are no effective means available to the general public for limiting the powers of the rulers. In general, rulers are not effectively restrained by law in the exercise of their powers. Often, the government's rulings, actions, and decisions are made arbitrarily. In the Soviet Union under Joseph Stalin, for example, the fate of whole ethnic groups was decided by the dictator.

Under a non-constitutional government, any rights of the individual may be violated by the ruler or rulers. Typically there is no private domain where the individual is protected from the power of the state. Whatever rights the individual may be considered to possess, rather than being protected by stringent standards of due process of law, are subject to arbitrary deprivation. In Uganda, under Idi Amin, the people were terrorized by the Bureau of State Research, which arrested and tortured people at will.

Autocracies and totalitarian states are forms of non-constitutional governments.

Autocracies, or autocratic regimes, may take various forms. These are characterized by the unlimited power exercised by one person or a small group of people. Some autocracies are military, others are civilian. Many present-day autocracies call themselves republics, but many do not have the characteristics of a true republic. Examples of historic autocratic regimes are Haiti under the Duvaliers, the Philippines under Ferdinand Marcos, and Spain under Franco. Contemporary examples are Cuba under Fidel Castro and Libya under Muammar Qaddafi.

Dictatorships that attempt to exercise absolute control over all spheres of human life are called totalitarian dictatorships. The classical examples of totalitarian dictatorships are the Soviet Union under Josef Stalin, Germany under Adolf Hitler, and China under Mao Zedong. Contemporary examples are North Korea under Kim Il Sung and after his death under Kim Jong Il. Iraq under Saddam Hussein is another example.

Non-constitutional governments may also have constitutions that set forth the basic way they are—or are said to be—organized and operated. They also may be organized as parliamentary or presidential governments and may call themselves federal rather than unitary systems. These names, however, are used only to obscure the true nature of the autocratic or totalitarian state. One must study the actual functioning of a government on a daily basis to determine its true nature.

Types of Government
697

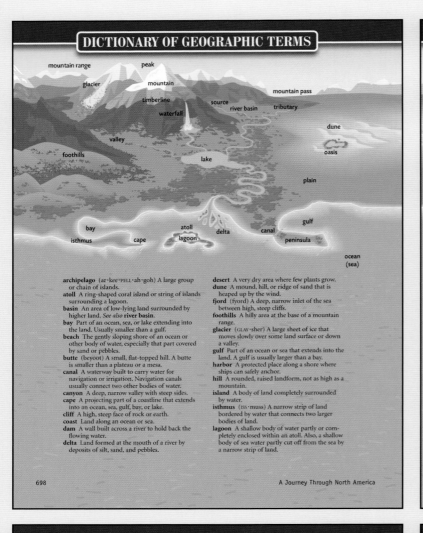

archipelago (ar·kee·PELL·ah·goh) A large group or chain of islands.

atoll A ring-shaped coral island or string of islands surrounding a lagoon.

basin An area of low-lying land surrounded by higher land. *See also* river basin.

bay Part of an ocean, sea, or lake extending into the land. Usually smaller than a gulf.

beach The gently sloping shore of an ocean or other body of water, especially that part covered by sand or pebbles.

butte (beyoot) A small, flat-topped hill. A butte is smaller than a plateau or a mesa.

canal A waterway built to carry water for navigation or irrigation. Navigation canals usually connect two other bodies of water.

canyon A deep, narrow valley with steep sides.

cape A projecting part of a coastline that extends into an ocean, sea, gulf, bay, or lake.

cliff A high, steep face of rock or earth.

coast Land along an ocean or sea.

dam A wall built across a river to hold back the flowing water.

delta Land formed at the mouth of a river by deposits of silt, sand, and pebbles.

desert A very dry area where few plants grow.

dune A mound, hill, or ridge of sand that is heaped up by the wind.

fjord (fyord) A deep, narrow inlet of the sea between high, steep cliffs.

foothills A hilly area at the base of a mountain range.

glacier (GLAY·sher) A large sheet of ice that moves slowly over some land surface or down a valley.

gulf Part of an ocean or sea that extends into the land. A gulf is usually larger than a bay.

harbor A protected place along a shore where ships can safely anchor.

hill A rounded, raised landform, not as high as a mountain.

island A body of land completely surrounded by water.

isthmus (ISS·muss) A narrow strip of land bordered by water that connects two larger bodies of land.

lagoon A shallow body of water partly or completely enclosed within an atoll. Also, a shallow body of sea water partly cut off from the sea by a narrow strip of land.

lake A body of water surrounded by land.

mesa A high, flat landform rising steeply above the surrounding land. A mesa is smaller than a plateau and larger than a butte.

mountain A high, rounded or pointed landform with steep sides, higher than a hill.

mountain pass An opening or gap through a mountain range.

mountain range A row or chain of mountains.

mouth The place where a river empties into another body of water.

oasis A place in the desert made fertile by a steady supply of water.

ocean One of the earth's four largest bodies of water. The four oceans are really a single connected body of salt water that covers about three fourths of the earth's surface.

peak The pointed top of a mountain or hill.

peninsula A body of land nearly surrounded by water.

plain A large area of flat or nearly flat land.

plateau A high, flat landform that rises steeply above the surrounding land. A plateau is larger than a mesa or a butte.

port A place where ships load and unload goods.

reef A ridge of sand, rock, or coral that lies at or near the surface of a sea.

reservoir A natural or artificial lake used to store water.

river A large stream of water that flows across the land and usually empties into a lake, ocean, or other river.

river basin All the land drained by a river and its tributaries.

sea A large body of water partly or entirely surrounded by land. Another word for ocean.

source The place where a river or stream begins.

strait A narrow waterway or channel connecting two larger bodies of water.

timberline An imaginary line on mountains above which trees do not grow.

tributary A river or stream that flows into a larger river or stream.

valley An area of low land between hills or mountains.

volcano (vol·KAY·no) An opening in the earth through which lava, rock, gases, and ash are forced out.

waterfall A flow of water falling from a high place to a lower place.

The Declaration of Independence

The printed text of the Declaration of Independence below shows the spelling and punctuation of the actual document. The signers are listed with the names of their states. Most members signed the declaration on August 2, 1776.

In Congress, July 4, 1776. The unanimous Declaration of the thirteen united States of America,

Preamble

When in the Course of human events, it becomes necessary for one people to dissolve the political bands which have connected them with another, and to assume among the powers of the earth, the separate and equal station to which the Laws of Nature and of Nature's God entitle them, a decent respect to the opinions of mankind requires that they should declare the causes which impel them to the separation.

impel to force by moral pressure

Declaration of Natural Rights

We hold these truths to be self evident, that all men are created equal, that they are endowed by their Creator with certain unalienable Rights, that among these are Life, Liberty and the pursuit of Happiness.—

That to secure these rights, Governments are instituted among Men, deriving their just powers from the consent of the governed,—

That whenever any Form of Government becomes destructive of these ends, it is the Right of the People to alter or to abolish it, and to institute new Government, laying its foundation on such principles and organizing its powers in such form, as to them shall seem most likely to effect their Safety and Happiness. Prudence, indeed, will dictate that Governments long established should not be changed for light and transient causes; and accordingly all experience hath shewn, that mankind are more disposed to suffer, while evils are sufferable, than to right themselves by abolishing the forms to which they are accustomed. But when a long train of abuses and usurpations, pursuing invariably the same Object evinces a design to reduce them under absolute Despotism, it is their right, it is their duty, to throw off such Government, and to provide new Guards for their future security.—

endowed provided

Despotism absolute power and control over a people by one person, for example, a ruler.

List of Grievances

Such has been the patient sufferance of these Colonies; and such is now the necessity which constrains them to alter their former Systems of Government. The history of the present King of Great Britain is a history of repeated injuries and usurpations, all having in direct object the establishment of an absolute Tyranny over these States. To prove this, let Facts be submitted to a candid world.

He has refused his Assent to Laws, the most wholesome and necessary for the public good.

He has forbidden his Governors to pass Laws of immediate and pressing importance, unless suspended in their operation till his Assent should be obtained; and when so suspended, he has utterly neglected to attend to them.

He has refused to pass other Laws for the accommodation of large districts of people, unless those people would relinquish the right of Representation in the Legislature, a right inestimable to them and formidable to tyrants only.

He has called together legislative bodies at places unusual, uncomfortable, and distant from the depository of their public Records, for the sole purpose of fatiguing them into compliance with his measures.

He has dissolved Representative Houses repeatedly, for opposing with manly firmness his invasions on the rights of the people.

He has refused for a long time, after such dissolutions, to cause others to be elected; whereby the Legislative powers, incapable of Annihilation, have returned to the People at large for their exercise; the State remaining in the mean time exposed to all the dangers of invasion from without, and convulsions within.

He has endeavoured to prevent the population of these States; for that purpose obstructing the Laws for Naturalization of Foreigners; refusing to pass others to encourage their migrations hither, and raising the conditions of new Appropriations of Lands.

He has obstructed the Administration of Justice, by refusing his Assent to Laws for establishing Judiciary powers.

He has made Judges dependent on his Will alone, for the tenure of their offices, and the amount and payment of their salaries.

He has erected a multitude of New Offices, and sent hither swarms of Officers to harrass our people, and eat out their substance.

He has kept among us, in times of peace, Standing Armies without the Consent of our legislatures.

He has affected to render the Military independent of and superior to the Civil power.

usurpations seizures or possessions by force or without right

relinquish to give up, yield

inestimable priceless, too valuable to be measured

Annihilation destruction

convulsions violent disturbances

Naturalization of Foreigners allowing people from other countries to become citizens

tenure term

quartering providing lodging or shelter

render to make

abdicated give up responsibility for

perfidy treachery

insurrections rebellions or revolts against civil authority

Petitioned for Redress sent formal written requests asking that wrongs be corrected

unwarrantable jurisdiction unjustifiable power or right to exercise authority over someone

consanguinity descended from the same ancestor

He has combined with others to subject us to a jurisdiction foreign to our constitution, and unacknowledged by our laws; giving his Assent to their Acts of pretended Legislation:

For Quartering large bodies of armed troops among us:

For protecting them, by a mock Trial, from punishment for any Murders which they should commit on the Inhabitants of these States:

For cutting off our Trade with all parts of the world:

For imposing Taxes on us without our Consent:

For depriving us in many cases, of the benefits of Trial by Jury:

For transporting us beyond Seas to be tried for pretended offences:

For abolishing the free System of English Laws in a neighbouring Province, establishing therein an Arbitrary government, and enlarging its Boundaries so as to render it at once an example and fit instrument for introducing the same absolute rule into these Colonies:

For taking away our Charters, abolishing our most valuable Laws, and altering fundamentally the Forms of our Governments:

For suspending our own Legislatures, and declaring themselves invested with power to legislate for us in all cases whatsoever.

He has abdicated Government here, by declaring us out of his Protection and waging War against us.

He has plundered our seas, ravaged our Coasts, burnt our towns, and destroyed the lives of our people.

He is at this time transporting large Armies of foreign Mercenaries to compleat the works of death, desolation and tyranny, already begun with circumstances of Cruelty & perfidy scarcely paralleled in the most barbarous ages, and totally unworthy the Head of a civilized nation.

He has constrained our fellow Citizens taken Captive on the high Seas to bear Arms against their Country, to become the executioners of their friends and Brethren, or to fall themselves by their Hands.

He has excited domestic insurrections amongst us, and has endeavoured to bring on the inhabitants of our frontiers, the merciless Indian Savages, whose known rule of warfare, is an undistinguished destruction of all ages, sexes and conditions.

In every stage of these Oppressions We have Petitioned for Redress in the most humble terms: Our repeated Petitions have been answered only by repeated injury. A Prince whose character is thus marked by every act which may define a Tyrant, is unfit to be the ruler of a free people.

Nor have We been wanting in attentions to our Brittish brethren. We have warned them from time to time of attempts by their legislature to extend an unwarrantable jurisdiction over us. We have reminded them of the circumstances of our emigration and settlement here. We have appealed to their native justice and magnanimity, and we have conjured them by the ties of our common kindred to disavow these usurpations, which, would inevitably interrupt our connections and correspondence. They too have been deaf to the voice of justice and of consanguinity. We must, therefore, acquiesce in the necessity, which denounces our Separation, and hold them, as we hold the rest of mankind, Enemies in War, in Peace Friends.

Resolution of Independence by the United States

We, therefore, the Representatives of the united States of America, in General Congress, Assembled, appealing to the Supreme Judge of the world for the rectitude of our intentions, do, in the Name, and by Authority of the good People of these Colonies, solemnly publish and declare, That these United Colonies are, and of Right ought to be Free and Independent States; that they are Absolved from all Allegiance to the British Crown, and that all political connection between them and the State of Great Britain, is and ought to be totally dissolved; and that as Free and Independent States, they have full Power to levy War, conclude Peace, contract Alliances, establish Commerce, and to do all other Acts and Things which Independent States may of right do. And for the support of this Declaration, with a firm reliance on the protection of divine Providence, we mutually pledge to each other our Lives, our Fortunes and our sacred Honor.

rectitude rightness, moral integrity

John Hancock
President, from Massachusetts

Georgia
Button Gwinnett
Lyman Hall
George Walton

North Carolina
William Hooper
Joseph Hewes
John Penn

South Carolina
Edward Rutledge
Thomas Heyward, Jr.
Thomas Lynch, Jr.
Arthur Middleton

Maryland
Samuel Chase
William Paca
Thomas Stone
Charles Carroll of Carrollton

Virginia
George Wythe
Richard Henry Lee
Thomas Jefferson
Benjamin Harrison
Thomas Nelson, Jr.
Francis Lightfoot Lee
Carter Braxton

Pennsylvania
Robert Morris
Benjamin Rush
Benjamin Franklin
John Morton
George Clymer
James Smith
George Taylor
James Wilson
George Ross

Delaware
Caesar Rodney
George Read
Thomas McKean

New York
William Floyd
Philip Livingston
Francis Lewis
Lewis Morris

New Jersey
Richard Stockton
John Witherspoon
Francis Hopkinson
John Hart
Abraham Clark

New Hampshire
Josiah Bartlett
William Whipple
Matthew Thornton

Massachusetts
Samuel Adams
John Adams
Robert Treat Paine
Elbridge Gerry

Rhode Island
Stephen Hopkins
William Ellery

Connecticut
Roger Sherman
Samuel Huntington
William Williams
Oliver Wolcott

Constitution of the United States of America

The following text is a transcription of the Constitution showing the spelling, capitalization, and punctuation of the original. Parts of the Constitution that have been altered by amendment are crossed out.

The **Preamble** sets out the origin, scope, and purpose of the Constitution. It declares that the power of the government comes from the citizens of the United States.

Article I: The Legislative Branch
Section 1: Congress A two-house legislature is established. Powers are granted by the people to their government. Some powers are denied the government.

Section 2: House of Representatives
1. Election and Terms Representatives are elected by the voters every two years.
2. Qualifications of a Representative Representatives must be at least twenty-five years old, United States citizens for at least seven years, and residents of the state they represent.
3. Divisions of Representatives Among the States The number of representatives a state has is based upon population. The total number of representatives was set at 435 in 1929. Each state must have a minimum of one representative. Each state is divided into congressional districts of equal population. States may lose or gain a representative based upon population decreases or increases. This clause was changed by the Fourteenth Amendment. Before it was changed, Native Americans were not counted at all and only three fifths of a state's slave population was counted.
A law enacted in 1967 abolished all "at-large" elections except in those less populous states entitled to only one representative. An "at-large" election is one in which a representative is elected by the voters of the entire state rather than by the voters in a congressional district within the state.

Preamble

We the People of the United States, in Order to form a more perfect Union, establish Justice, insure domestic Tranquility, provide for the common defense, promote the general Welfare, and secure the Blessings of Liberty to ourselves and our Posterity, do ordain and establish this Constitution for the United States of America.

Article I
Section 1

All legislative Powers herein granted shall be vested in a Congress of the United States, which shall consist of a Senate and House of Representatives.

Section 2

1. The House of Representatives shall be composed of Members chosen every second Year by the People of the several States, and the Electors in each State shall have the Qualifications requisite for Electors of the most numerous Branch of the State Legislature.

2. No Person shall be a Representative who shall not have attained to the Age of twenty five Years, and been seven Years a Citizen of the United States, and who shall not, when elected, be an Inhabitant of that State in which he shall be chosen.

3. Representatives and direct Taxes shall be apportioned among the several States which may be included within this Union, according to their respective Numbers, ~~which shall be determined by adding to the whole Number of free Persons, including those bound to Service for a Term of Years, and excluding Indians not taxed, three fifths of all other Persons.~~ The actual Enumeration shall be made within three Years after the first Meeting of the Congress of the United States, and within every subsequent Term of ten Years, in such Manner as they shall by Law direct. The Number of Representatives shall not exceed

one for every thirty Thousand, but each State shall have at Least one Representative; ~~and until such enumeration shall be made, the State of New-Hampshire shall be entitled to chuse three,~~ Massachusetts eight, Rhode-Island and Providence Plantations one, Connecticut five, New-York six, New Jersey four, Pennsylvania eight, Delaware one, Maryland six, Virginia ten, North Carolina five, South Carolina five, and Georgia three.

4. When vacancies happen in the Representation from any State, the Executive Authority thereof shall issue Writs of Election to fill such Vacancies.

5. The House of Representatives shall chuse their Speaker and other Officers; and shall have the sole Power of Impeachment.

Section 3

1. The Senate of the United States shall be composed of two Senators from each State, chosen ~~by the Legislature thereof~~ for six Years; and each Senator shall have one Vote.

2. Immediately after they shall be assembled in Consequence of the first Election, they shall be divided as equally as may be into three Classes. The Seats of the Senators of the first Class shall be vacated at the Expiration of the second Year, of the second Class at the Expiration of the fourth Year, and of the third Class at the Expiration of the sixth Year, so that one third may be chosen every second Year; and if Vacancies happen by Resignation, or otherwise, ~~during the Recess of the Legislature of any State, the Executive thereof may make temporary Appointments until the next Meeting of the Legislature, which shall then fill such Vacancies.~~

3. No Person shall be a Senator who shall not have attained to the Age of thirty Years, and been nine Years a Citizen of the United States, and who shall not, when elected, be an Inhabitant of that State for which he shall be chosen.

4. The Vice President of the United States shall be President of the Senate, but shall have no Vote, unless they be equally divided.

5. The Senate shall chuse their other Officers, and also a President pro tempore, in the Absence of the Vice President, or when he shall exercise the Office of President of the United States.

6. The Senate shall have the sole Power to try all Impeachments. When sitting for that Purpose, they shall be on Oath or Affirmation. When the President of the United States is tried, the Chief Justice shall preside: And no Person shall be convicted without the Concurrence of two thirds of the Members present.

7. Judgment in Cases of Impeachment shall not extend further than to removal from Office, and disqualification to hold and enjoy any Office of honor, Trust or Profit under the United States: but the Party convicted shall nevertheless be liable and subject to Indictment, Trial, Judgment and Punishment, according to Law.

Section 4

1. The Times, Places and Manner of holding Elections for Senators and Representatives, shall be prescribed in each State by the Legislature thereof; but the Congress may at any time by Law make or alter such Regulations, except as to the Places of chusing Senators.

Enumeration refers to the census. The figure of 30,000 people represented by one representative is now irrelevant. Today, each member of the House roughly represents 500,000 people.
4. Vacancies Vacancies are filled through special elections called by the state's governor. Most of the state legislatures have granted their governors the ability to appoint a replacement instead of holding an election.
5. Officers of the House of Representatives The speaker of the House is the leader of the party that holds a majority of seats. He or she is elected by the members of the House. The speaker appoints the heads of the House committees. Impeachment means to bring charges against an official.
Section 3: The Senate
1. Number of Members and Terms of Office The Senate is made up of two senators from each state. Senators were originally elected by their state's legislators, but this has been changed by the Seventeenth Amendment. Today they are elected directly by the people of their state and serve a six-year term.
2. Staggered Elections; Filling Vacancies The authors of the Constitution wanted the senators to serve longer terms than the representatives in the House. They created a system of staggered elections, whereby one third of senators are elected every two years. The first senators were elected for two-, four-, or six-year terms, with subsequent elections for six-year terms. The terms of both senators from a particular state are arranged so that they do not terminate at the same time. Of the two senators from a state serving at the same time the one who was elected first (or if both were elected at the same time, the one elected for a full term) is referred to as the "senior" senator from that state. The other is referred to as the "junior" senator. The Seventeenth Amendment changed the method of filling vacancies in the Senate.
3. Qualifications of a Senator Senators must be at least thirty years old, United States citizens for at least nine years, and residents of the state they represent.
4. President of the Senate The vice president of the United States serves as president of the Senate. He or she only votes in the case of a tie. This is the vice president's only constitutional responsibility.
5. Other Officers of the Senate The Senate selects its officers, including a president pro tempore. When the vice president is absent, or if he or she has become president of the United States, the president pro tempore serves as the presiding officer.
6. Trial of Impeachments While the House impeaches, or bring charges against an official, the Senate tries the impeachments. When it tries an impeachment it convenes as a court. When the president of the United States is tried, the Chief Justice of the Supreme Court presides. A two thirds vote of the senators present at the impeachment trial is necessary to convict the official of the charges brought against him or her.
7. Penalty for Conviction An official found guilty by the Senate may only be removed from office and

prevented from holding other federal offices. The convicted official may be tried for the same offense in a regular court of law.

Section 4: Elections and Meetings

1. Holding Elections Congress has authority over the elections of its members. In 1845, Congress established the first Tuesday after the first Monday in November as the day for selecting presidential electors (those who vote in the electoral college).

2. Meetings The Twentieth Amendment changed the date of the opening of the regular session of Congress to January 3.

Section 5: Rules and Procedures

1. Organization The minimum number of members who must be present in order for the House or Senate to hold a session is a quorum. For a regular House session, the quorum is 218 of the 435 members. In order to fulfill this constitutional responsibility, in the absence of a quorum, 15 members may initiate a call of the House to compel the attendance of absent members.

2. Rules Each house sets its own rules. Either can punish members for disorderly behavior and expel a member by a two-thirds vote.

3. Journal Both houses are required to keep Journal of their proceedings. Both the House and the Senate publish a *Journal*. Each lists all bills, resolutions, votes, and messages from the president. This is not the publication known as *The Congressional Record. The Congressional Record* is the official record of everything said on the floor and all roll call votes. It is published daily by the Government Printing Office.

4. Adjournment Neither house may adjourn for more than three days or move to another location without the approval the other house.

Section 6: Pay, Privileges, and Restrictions

1. Pay and Privileges Members of Congress are paid by the federal government instead of the state they represent. The current salary for members of Congress is $145,100. A small number of leadership positions, like Speaker of the House, receive a somewhat higher salary. This clause has been changed by the Twenty-seventh Amendment.

Members cannot be sued or prosecuted for anything they say in Congress. They cannot be arrested while Congress is in session except for treason or serious crimes.

2. Restrictions Members of Congress cannot use their authority or pass laws to benefit them personally. They also cannot hold another position in the federal government while they are in office.

Section 7: Method of Passing Laws

1. Revenue Bills All bills for raising revenue, or money coming into the government, must originate in the House of Representatives. The Senate may propose or agree with amendments. Taxes are the main form of raising revenue. By tradition, general appropriation bills, or bills determining how money should be spent, also originate in the House of Representatives.

2. How a Bill Becomes Law A bill may only become a law by passing both the House and the Senate and then be signed by the president. If Congress is in

2. The Congress shall assemble at least once in every Year, ~~and such Meeting shall be on the first Monday in December, unless they shall by Law appoint a different Day.~~

Section 5

1. Each House shall be the Judge of the Elections, Returns and Qualifications of its own Members, and a Majority of each shall constitute a Quorum to do Business; but a smaller Number may adjourn from day to day, and may be authorized to compel the Attendance of absent Members, in such Manner, and under such Penalties as each House may provide.

2. Each House may determine the Rules of its Proceedings, punish its Members for disorderly Behaviour, and, with the Concurrence of two thirds, expel a Member.

3. Each House shall keep a Journal of its Proceedings, and from time to time publish the same, excepting such Parts as may in their Judgment require Secrecy; and the Yeas and Nays of the Members of either House on any question shall, at the Desire of one fifth of those Present, be entered on the Journal.

4. Neither House, during the Session of Congress, shall, without the Consent of the other, adjourn for more than three days, nor to any other Place than that in which the two Houses shall be sitting.

Section 6

1. The Senators and Representatives shall receive a Compensation for their Services, to be ascertained by Law, and paid out of the Treasury of the United States. They shall in all Cases, except Treason, Felony and Breach of the Peace, be privileged from Arrest during their Attendance at the Session of their respective Houses, and in going to and returning from the same; and for any Speech or Debate in either House, they shall not be questioned in anyother Place.

2. No Senator or Representative shall, during the Time for which he was elected, be appointed to any civil Office under the Authority of the United States, which shall have been created, or the Emoluments whereof shall have been encreased during such time; and no Person holding any Office under the United States, shall be a Member of either House during his Continuance in Office.

Section 7

1. All Bills for raising Revenue shall originate in the House of Representatives; but the Senate may propose or concur with Amendments as on other Bills.

2. Every Bill which shall have passed the House of Representatives and the Senate, shall, before it become a Law, be presented to the President of the United States: If he approve he shall sign it, but if not he shall return it, with his Objections to that House in which it shall have originated, who shall enter the Objections at large on their Journal, and proceed to reconsider it. If after such Reconsideration two thirds of that House shall agree to pass the Bill, it shall be sent, together with the Objections, to the other House, by which it shall likewise be reconsidered, and if approved by two thirds of that House, it shall become a Law. But in all such Cases the Votes of both Houses shall be determined by yeas and Nays, and the Names of the

Persons voting for and against the Bill shall be entered on the Journal of each House respectively. If any Bill shall not be returned by the President within ten Days (Sundays excepted) after it shall have been presented to him, the Same shall be a Law, in like Manner as if he had signed it, unless the Congress by their Adjournment prevent its Return, in which Case it shall not be a Law.

3. Every Order, Resolution, or Vote to which the Concurrence of the Senate and House of Representatives may be necessary (except on a question of Adjournment) shall be presented to the President of the United States; and before the Same shall take Effect, shall be approved by him, or being disapproved by him, shall be repassed by two thirds of the Senate and House of Representatives, according to the Rules and Limitations prescribed in the Case of a Bill.

Section 8

The Congress shall have Power

1. To lay and collect Taxes, Duties, Imposts and Excises, to pay the Debts and provide for the common Defence and general Welfare of the United States; but all Duties, Imposts and Excises shall be uniform throughout the United States;

2. To borrow Money on the credit of the United States;

3. To regulate Commerce with foreign Nations, and among the several States, and with the Indian Tribes;

4. To establish an uniform Rule of Naturalization, and uniform Laws on the subject of Bankruptcies throughout the United States;

5. To coin Money, regulate the Value thereof, and of foreign Coin, and fix the Standard of Weights and Measures;

6. To provide for the Punishment of counterfeiting the Securities and current Coin of the United States;

7. To establish Post Offices and post Roads;

8. To promote the Progress of Science and useful Arts, by securing for limited Times to Authors and Inventors the exclusive Right to their respective Writings and Discoveries;

9. To constitute Tribunals inferior to the supreme Court;

10. To define and punish Piracies and Felonies committed on the high Seas, and Offences against the Law of Nations;

11. To declare War, grant Letters of Marque and Reprisal, and make Rules concerning Captures on Land and Water;

12. To raise and support Armies, but no Appropriation of Money to that Use shall be for a longer Term than two Years;

13. To provide and maintain a Navy;

14. To make Rules for the Government and Regulation of the land and naval Forces;

15. To provide for calling forth the Militia to execute the Laws of the Union, suppress Insurrections and repel Invasions;

16. To provide for organizing, arming, and disciplining, the Militia, and for governing such Part of them as may be employed in the Service of the United States, reserving to the States respectively, the Appointment of the Officers, and the Authority of training the Militia according to the discipline prescribed by Congress;

17. To exercise exclusive Legislation in all Cases whatsoever, over such District (not exceeding ten Miles square) as may, by Cession of

session and the president does not sign the legislation within ten days, it becomes law without his signature. Within the ten days, the president may reject the legislation. This is called a veto. A veto returns the bill to the house which originated it. The president must include a message containing the reasons for the veto. The House and Senate then may schedule a vote to override the veto, or make the law over the president's disapproval. To override a veto, a two-thirds vote of those present in each house is necessary. If the vote fails to achieve two thirds in the first chamber, the second never receives the legislation. If a two-thirds vote is achieved in both bodies, the bill becomes law without the signature of the president. If Congress adjourns within ten days of submitting legislation to the president for his or her signature, and the president does not sign it or return it to Congress with objections, the legislation does not become law. This is known as a "pocket veto."

3. Presidential Approval or Veto A bill is a draft of a proposed law. A resolution is the legislature's opinion on an issue.

Section 8: Powers Delegated to Congress

1. Tax, Pay Debts; Provide for the National Defense Congress may raise and spend revenue. Federal taxes must be the same throughout the nation. Congress may do this to provide for the defense and welfare of the United States.

2. Borrowing The federal government may issue bonds to raise funds, which is borrowing on credit.

3. Commerce Congress may regulate national and international commerce, or business.

4. Naturalization and Bankruptcy Congress may set immigration policy, including naturalization, or how an immigrant becomes a citizen, and bankruptcy rules.

5. Currency Congress has the power to create national money, or currency.

6. Counterfeiting Congress protects the currency by preventing or punishing counterfeiters, or those who use illegal copies of money.

7. Postal System The Post Office was a cabinet level department. In 1970, the United States Postal Service replaced the Post Office Department.

8. Patents and Copyrights Congress may pass laws to protect patents of inventions and intellectual property rights, also called copyrights.

9. Court System Congress has the power to create a system of lower courts.

10. Piracy Congress has the right to control and protect citizens and ships when they are out of the country.

11. Declare War Congress has the power to make a declaration of war. However, troops may be sent into combat by the president without a formal declaration.

12. Army Congress may raise and support an Army.

13. Navy Congress may establish a navy.

14. Armed Forces Rules Congress may regulate the armed forces and establish procedures for military discipline.

15. Militia Congress may provide for a militia, now called the National Guard, to be organized by the states.

16. National Guard Congress may pass legislation governing the National Guard.

17. District of Columbia Congress has the right to exercise control over the District of Columbia and other federal property.

18. The "Elastic Clause" This clause gives Congress the right to make any law "necessary and proper" to carry out its powers.

Section 9: Powers Denied to the Federal Government

1. Slavery This is the compromise where slavery was to be prohibited no earlier than 1808.

2. Habeas Corpus Habeas Corpus is a Latin term meaning "you may have the body." In legal terms, it means that when an order of habeas corpus is issued by a judge, a law official must bring a prisoner to court and show why the prisoner must continue to be held. Habeas corpus allows the jailed person to be released
to the control of his or her lawyer before his or her trial. This can only be suspended during wartime.

3. Bills of Attainder and Ex Post Facto Congress may not pass a bill of attainder, a bill that punishes a person without a jury trial. The ex post facto clause means that a person cannot be prosecuted for a crime committed before the law prohibitting it is made.

4. Direct Taxes Congress could not directly tax individuals. This clause has been changed by the Sixteenth Amendment, which allowed an income tax.

5. State Exports Congress may not tax goods that move from one state to another.

6. Uniformity of Treatment Congress may not pass laws that favor one region over another in the regulation of trade.

7. Appropriation No money from the treasury may be spent without the consent of Congress.

8. Title of Nobility No title of nobility will be granted by the United States.

Section 10: Powers Denied to the States

1. Limitations Some powers granted or denied to the federal government are granted or denied to states. States cannot conduct foreign affairs, carry on a war, or control interstate and foreign commerce. This prevents overlapping authority of the federal and state laws. States also cannot pass bills of attainder and ex post facto laws.

2. Export and Import Taxes States may not tax imports and exports because that could interfere with Congress's power to regulate interstate and foreign commerce.

3. Duties, Armed Forces, War States cannot maintain their own army or navy, nor can they wage war. Additionally, states cannot make treaties with other nations or collect duties, or fees, from foreign ships.

Article II: The Executive Branch

particular States, and the Acceptance of Congress, become the Seat of the Government of the United States, and to exercise like Authority over all Places purchased by the Consent of the Legislature of the State in which the Same shall be, for the Erection of Forts, Magazines, Arsenals, dock-Yards, and other needful Buildings;—And

18. To make all Laws which shall be necessary and proper for carrying into Execution the foregoing Powers, and all other Powers vested by this Constitution in the Government of the United States, or in any Department or Officer thereof.

Section 9

1. ~~The Migration or Importation of such Persons as any of the States now existing shall think proper to admit, shall not be prohibited by the Congress prior to the Year one thousand eight hundred and eight, but a Tax or duty may be imposed on such Importation, not exceeding ten dollars for each Person.~~

2. The Privilege of the Writ of Habeas Corpus shall not be suspended, unless when in Cases of Rebellion or Invasion the public Safety may require it.

3. No Bill of Attainder or ex post facto Law shall be passed.

4. No Capitation, or other direct, Tax shall be laid, unless in Proportion to the Census or enumeration herein before directed to be taken.

5. No Tax or Duty shall be laid on Articles exported from any State.

6. No Preference shall be given by any Regulation of Commerce or Revenue to the Ports of one State over those of another; nor shall Vessels bound to, or from, one State, be obliged to enter, clear, or pay Duties in another.

7. No Money shall be drawn from the Treasury, but in Consequence of Appropriations made by Law; and a regular Statement and Account of the Receipts and Expenditures of all public Money shall be published from time to time.

8. No Title of Nobility shall be granted by the United States: And no Person holding any Office of Profit or Trust under them, shall, without the Consent of the Congress, accept of any present, Emolument, Office, or Title, of any kind whatever, from any King, Prince, or foreign State.

Section 10

1. No State shall enter into any Treaty, Alliance, or Confederation; grant Letters of Marque and Reprisal; coin Money; emit Bills of Credit; make any Thing but gold and silver Coin a Tender in Payment of Debts; pass any Bill of Attainder, ex post facto Law, or Law impairing the Obligation of Contracts, or grant any Title of Nobility.

2. No State shall, without the Consent of the Congress, lay any Imposts or Duties on Imports or Exports, except what may be absolutely necessary for executing it's inspection Laws: and the net Produce of all Duties and Imposts, laid by any State on Imports or Exports, shall be for the Use of the Treasury of the United States; and all such Laws shall be subject to the Revision and Controul of the Congress.

3. No State shall, without the Consent of Congress, lay any Duty of Tonnage, keep Troops, or Ships of War in time of Peace, enter into any Agreement or Compact with another State, or with a foreign

Power, or engage in War, unless actually invaded, or in such imminent Danger as will not admit of delay.

Article II

Section 1

1. The executive Power shall be vested in a President of the United States of America. He shall hold his Office during the Term of four Years, and, together with the Vice President, chosen for the same Term, be elected, as follows:

2. Each State shall appoint, in such Manner as the Legislature thereof may direct, a Number of Electors, equal to the whole Number of Senators and Representatives to which the State may be entitled in the Congress: but no Senator or Representative, or Person holding an Office of Trust or Profit under the United States, shall be appointed an Elector.

3. ~~The Electors shall meet in their respective States, and vote by Ballot for two Persons, of whom one at least shall not be an Inhabitant of the same State with themselves. And they shall make a List of all the Persons voted for, and of the Number of Votes for each; which List they shall sign and certify, and transmit sealed to the Seat of the Government of the United States, directed to the President of the Senate. The President of the Senate shall, in the Presence of the Senate and House of Representatives, open all the Certificates, and the Votes shall then be counted. The Person having the greatest Number of Votes shall be the President, if such Number be a Majority of the whole Number of Electors appointed; and if there be more than one who have such Majority, and have an equal Number of Votes, then the House of Representatives shall immediately chuse by Ballot one of them for President; and if no Person have a Majority, then from the five highest on the List the said House shall in like Manner chuse the President. But in chusing the President, the Votes shall be taken by States, the Representation from each State having one Vote; A quorum for this purpose shall consist of a Member or Members from two thirds of the States, and a Majority of all the States shall be necessary to a Choice. In every Case, after the Choice of the President, the Person having the greatest Number of Votes of the Electors shall be the Vice President. But if there should remain two or more who have equal Votes, the Senate shall chuse from them by Ballot the Vice President.~~

4. The Congress may determine the Time of chusing the Electors, and the Day on which they shall give their Votes; which Day shall be the same throughout the United States.

5. No Person except a natural born Citizen, or a Citizen of the United States, at the time of the Adoption of this Constitution, shall be - eligible to the Office of President; neither shall any Person be eligible to that Office who shall not have attained to the Age of thirty five Years, and been fourteen Years a Resident within the United States.

6. In Case of the Removal of the President from Office, or of his Death, Resignation, or Inability to discharge the Powers and Duties of the said Office, the Same shall devolve on the Vice President, and the Congress may by Law provide for the Case of Removal, Death, Resignation or Inability, both of the President and Vice President,

Section 1: President and Vice President

1. Power and Term Executive power is given to the president to enforce laws passed by Congress. The president and the vice president serve a term of four years. This clause has been changed by the Twenty-second Amendment.

2. Electoral System The electoral college system is a method of indirect popular election of the president. Federal office holders cannot serve as electors. Voters in each state vote for electors who are pledged to vote for a particular candidate. These electors, in turn, vote for the presidential candidate. Each state has a number of electors equal to the total number of their congressional delegation—the total of their senators and representatives.

3. Former Method of Election Under this original system, the House of Representatives elected Thomas Jefferson president in the election of 1800 when the electoral college resulted in a tie vote. This clause has been superseded by the Twelfth Amendment.

4. Time of Elections Congress determines the dates when the electors are chosen and when they vote. All electors must vote on the same day. Electors vote on the Monday after the second Wednesday in December.

5. Qualifications The president must be a citizen of the United States by birth, be at least thirty-five years old, and have been a resident of the United States for 14 years.

6. Filling Vacancies If the president is removed from office (impeached and convicted), dies, resigns, or is unable to function as president, the vice president becomes president. This clause has been changed by the Twenty-fifth Amendment, which deals with presidential disability. The Presidential Succession Act of 1947 mandates that if the president of the United States is incapacitated, dies, resigns, is for any reason unable to hold his or her office, or is removed from office, people in the following offices, in this order, will become president, provided they are qualified (as required by the Constitution): Vice President, Speaker of the House, President Pro Tempore of the Senate, Secretary of State, Secretary of the Treasury, Secretary of Defense, Attorney General, and the Secretaries for the following departments in order: Interior, Agriculture, Commerce, Labor, Health and Human Services, Housing and Urban Development, Transportation, Energy, Education, and Veterans Affairs.

7. Salary In 2001, the president's salary was raised to

706–709

$400,000, plus $50,000 for expenses. The president cannot receive any other income from federal or state governments while in office.

8. Oath of Office The oath of office is the promise a president makes to uphold the duties of the office and the Constitution. In a traditional inauguration ceremony, the president-elect places his or her hand on the Bible, raises his or her right hand, and takes the oath as directed by the chief justice.

Section 2: Powers of the President

1. Military, Cabinet, and Pardons The president serves as the commander-in-chief of the armed forces. He or she is the civilian in control of the military. He or she can authorize the use of troops overseas without declaring war. To declare war officially, though, he or she must get the approval of the Congress.

The president receives advice and assistance in executing the laws from what we now call the cabinet. The cabinet is made up of the head of each of the executive departments. Unlike the powers of the president, their responsibilities are not defined in the Constitution. This is the only reference to the cabinet in the Constitution.

The president may pardon, or excuse, people who have committed federal crimes except in cases of impeachment.

2. Treaties and Appointments The president is responsible for foreign policy. He or she may makes treaties with other nations; however, the Senate must approve any treaty before it becomes official. The president nominates officials, including Supreme Court justices and ambassadors, with the agreement of a majority of the Senate.

3. Filling Vacancies When the Senate is not in session, the president may fill vacancies by temporarily appointing officials.

Section 3: Duties of the President

The president presents information on the state of the union to Congress (this has become the annual State of the Union Address) and recommends legislation to Congress. The president cannot write bills. He or she can propose a bill, but a member of Congress must submit it for him or her. The president may call for special sessions of Congress. The president receives ambassadors of other nations and recognizes those lands as official countries.

Section 4: Impeachment of the President and Civil Officers

The president and other executive branch officeholders may be impeached for treason, bribery, and other high crimes and misdemeanors. If found guilty by the Senate he or she may be removed from office. Only Presidents Andrew Johnson and William J. Clinton have been impeached. Neither were found guilty.

Article III: The Judicial Branch

declaring what Officer shall then act as President, and such Officer shall act accordingly, until the Disability be removed, or a President shall be elected.

7. The President shall, at stated Times, receive for his Services, a Compensation, which shall neither be increased nor diminished during the Period for which he shall have been elected, and he shall not receive within that Period any other Emolument from the United States, or any of them.
8. Before he enter on the Execution of his Office, he shall take the following Oath or Affirmation:—"I do solemnly swear (or affirm) that I will faithfully execute the Office of President of the United States, and will to the best of my Ability, preserve, protect and defend the Constitution of the United States."

Section 2

1. The President shall be Commander in Chief of the Army and Navy of the United States, and of the Militia of the several States, when called into the actual Service of the United States; he may require the Opinion, in writing, of the principal Officer in each of the executive Departments, upon any Subject relating to the Duties of their respective Offices, and he shall have Power to grant Reprieves and Pardons for Offences against the United States, except in Cases of Impeachment.
2. He shall have Power, by and with the Advice and Consent of the Senate, to make Treaties, provided two thirds of the Senators present concur; and he shall nominate, and by and with the Advice and Consent of the Senate, shall appoint Ambassadors, other public Ministers and Consuls, Judges of the supreme Court, and all other Officers of the United States, whose Appointments are not herein otherwise provided for, and which shall be established by Law: but the Congress may by Law vest the Appointment of such inferior Officers, as they think proper, in the President alone, in the Courts of Law, or in the Heads of Departments.
3. The President shall have Power to fill up all Vacancies that may happen during the Recess of the Senate, by granting Commissions which shall expire at the End of their next Session.

Section 3

He shall from time to time give to the Congress Information of the State of the Union, and recommend to their Consideration such Measures as he shall judge necessary and expedient; he may, on extraordinary Occasions, convene both Houses, or either of them, and in Case of Disagreement between them, with Respect to the Time of Adjournment, he may adjourn them to such Time as he shall think proper; he shall receive Ambassadors and other public Ministers; he shall take Care that the Laws be faithfully executed, and shall Commission all the Officers of the United States.

Section 4

The President, Vice President and all civil Officers of the United States, shall be removed from Office on Impeachment for, and Conviction of, Treason, Bribery, or other high Crimes and Misdemeanors.

Article III

Section 1

The judicial Power of the United States shall be vested in one supreme Court, and in such inferior Courts as the Congress may from time to time ordain and establish. The Judges, both of the supreme and inferior Courts, shall hold their Offices during good Behaviour, and shall, at stated Times, receive for their Services a Compensation, which shall not be diminished during their Continuance in Office.

Section 2

1. The judicial Power shall extend to all Cases, in Law and Equity, arising under this Constitution, the Laws of the United States, and Treaties made, or which shall be made, under their Authority;—to all Cases affecting Ambassadors, other public Ministers and Consuls;—to all Cases of admiralty and maritime Jurisdiction;—to Controversies to which the United States shall be a Party;—to Controversies between two or more States; ~~between a State and Citizens of another State; between~~ Citizens of different States;—between Citizens of the same State claiming Lands under Grants of different States, and between a State, or the Citizens thereof, and foreign States, Citizens or Subjects.
2. In all Cases affecting Ambassadors, other public Ministers and Consuls, and those in which a State shall be Party, the supreme Court shall have original Jurisdiction. In all the other Cases before mentioned, the supreme Court shall have appellate Jurisdiction, both as to Law and Fact, with such Exceptions, and under such Regulations as the Congress shall make.
3. The Trial of all Crimes, except in Cases of Impeachment, shall be by Jury; and such Trial shall be held in the State where the said Crimes shall have been committed; but when not committed within any State, the Trial shall be at such Place or Places as the Congress may by Law have directed.

Section 3

1. Treason against the United States, shall consist only in levying War against them, or in adhering to their Enemies, giving them Aid and Comfort. No Person shall be convicted of Treason unless on the Testimony of two Witnesses to the same overt Act, or on Confession in open Court.
2. The Congress shall have Power to declare the Punishment of Treason, but no Attainder of Treason shall work Corruption of Blood, or Forfeiture except during the Life of the Person attainted.

Article IV

Section 1

Full Faith and Credit shall be given in each State to the public Acts, Records, and judicial Proceedings of every other State. And the Congress may by general Laws prescribe the Manner in which such Acts, Records and Proceedings shall be proved, and the Effect thereof.

Section 2

1. The Citizens of each State shall be entitled to all Privileges and

The judicial branch is the system of courts. Courts interpret the laws made by Congress.

Section 1: Federal Court System

This article establishes the judicial branch of government with the creation of the Supreme Court. This court is the highest court in the country. There are lower federal courts but they were not created by the Constitution. Congress established them using powers granted by the Constitution.

Section 2: Jurisdiction of Federal Courts

1. General Jurisdiction This clause describes the origin of the laws of the United States. Law and equity refers to the types of laws the colonies inherited from the British justice system. Law means common law, which is laws based on five centuries of judicial decisions in Great Britain. Equity refers to the special types of laws created in Britain for handling specific cases. Admiralty and maritime jurisdiction means laws applying to ships and shipping on oceans, lakes, rivers, and canals. This clause has been changed by the Eleventh Amendment.

Courts decide arguments about the meaning of laws and how laws are applied. Courts also determine whether laws violate the Constitution. The power is called judicial review. The power of judicial review provides checks and balances on the legislative and executive branches. Judicial review is not an explicit power given to the courts in the Constitution. It is an implied power. In an important early Supreme Court decision, *Marbury v. Madison* (1803), the courts' power of judicial review was determined.

2. Supreme Court Original jurisdiction means the right to try a case before any other court may hear it. Appellate jurisdiction means the right of a court to try cases appealed, or decisions that are protested, from lower courts.

The Supreme Court has authority over the federal courts but has only limited power over state courts. The Supreme Court has the final word on cases heard by lower federal courts (cases that are appealed to the Supreme Court). The Supreme Court writes procedures that federal courts must follow. All federal courts must abide by the Supreme Court's interpretation of laws passed by Congress, regulations issued by the executive branch, and the Constitution. The Supreme Court's interpretations of federal law and the Constitution also apply to the state courts, but the Court cannot interpret state law or issues arising under state constitutions, and it does not supervise state court operations.

3. Trials Persons accused of a crime have a right to a trial by jury, except in cases of impeachment. This right is expanded by the Fifth, Sixth, and Seventh Amendments.

Section 3: Treason

1. Treason Treason is the only crime specifically defined in the Constitution. Treason is to wage war against the United States or to give aid and comfort to its enemies. There must be at least two witnesses to the same act or a confession to convict someone of treason.

2. Punishment of Treason Punishment for treason cannot be extended to the children of a traitor.

Article IV: Relations Among States

Respect and unity among states is established.

Section 1: Official Acts and Records of States

Court decisions and official records of one state (such as birth certificates, wills, corporation charters) are respected in all the other states.

Section 2 Duties of States

1. Privileges Rights and protections for citizens must be equal in all states.

2. Extradition Governors of states have authority over returning a person charged with a crime to the state charging the person with the crime.

3. Fugitive Slaves This clause meant that a slave could not become a free person by escaping to a free state. The Thirteenth Amendment brought an end to slavery in 1865.

Section 3: New States and Territories

1. Admission of New States Congress may admit new states. This outlines the guidelines for applying for statehood.

2. Territories Congress has power over territories and other federal property.

Section 4: Guarantees to the States

The government must protect each state against invasion. The federal government may send troops into a state to maintain law and order.

Article V: Amendments: How to Change the Constitution is Established

Adaptability is one of the most important features of the Constitution. There are two methods of proposing amendments. A two-thirds majority in Congress may submit a proposed amendment to the states, or a national convention called by two thirds of the states' legislatures may propose an amendment. Three fourths of the states must approve, or ratify, an amendment before it may become law. No amendment has yet been proposed by a national convention called by the states.

Article VI: National Supremacy

Covers general provisions and "the law of the land."

1. Public Debts The new government will pay the debts of the colonies from the Revolutionary War and the government under the Articles of Confederation.

2. The Supreme Law Declares that the "supreme law of the land" is the Constitution. The Constitution and federal law have higher authority than state constitutions when they come into conflict.

3. Oaths of Office There are no religious qualifications for holding public office.

Article VII: Ratification

Immunities of Citizens in the several States.

2. A Person charged in any State with Treason, Felony, or other Crime, who shall flee from Justice, and be found in another State, shall on Demand of the executive Authority of the State from which he fled, be delivered up, to be removed to the State having Jurisdiction of the Crime.
3. ~~No Person held to Service or Labour in one State, under the Laws thereof, escaping into another, shall, in Consequence of any Law or Regulation therein, be discharged from such Service or Labour, but shall be delivered up on Claim of the Party to whom such Service or Labour may be due.~~

Section 3

1. New States may be admitted by the Congress into this Union; but no new State shall be formed or erected within the Jurisdiction of any other State; nor any State be formed by the Junction of two or more States, or Parts of States, without the Consent of the Legislatures of the States concerned as well as of the Congress.
2. The Congress shall have Power to dispose of and make all needful Rules and Regulations respecting the Territory or other Property belonging to the United States; and nothing in this Constitution shall be so construed as to Prejudice any Claims of the United States, or of any particular State.

Section 4

The United States shall guarantee to every State in this Union a Republican Form of Government, and shall protect each of them against Invasion; and on Application of the Legislature, or of the Executive (when the Legislature cannot be convened), against domestic Violence.

Article V

The Congress, whenever two thirds of both Houses shall deem it necessary, shall propose Amendments to this Constitution, or, on the Application of the Legislatures of two thirds of the several States, shall call a Convention for proposing Amendments, which, in either Case, shall be valid to all Intents and Purposes, as Part of this Constitution, when ratified by the Legislatures of three fourths of the several States, or by Conventions in three fourths thereof, as the one or the other Mode of Ratification may be proposed by the Congress; Provided that no Amendment which may be made prior to the Year One thousand eight hundred and eight shall in any Manner affect the first and fourth Clauses in the Ninth Section of the first Article; and that no State, without its Consent, shall be deprived of its equal Suffrage in the Senate.

Article VI

1. All Debts contracted and Engagements entered into, before the Adoption of this Constitution, shall be as valid against the United States under this Constitution, as under the Confederation.
2. This Constitution, and the Laws of the United States which shall be made in Pursuance thereof; and all Treaties made, or which shall be made, under the Authority of the United States, shall be the supreme Law of the Land; and the Judges in every State shall be bound

thereby, any Thing in the Constitution or Laws of any State to the Contrary notwithstanding.

3. The Senators and Representatives before mentioned, and the Members of the several State Legislatures, and all executive and judicial Officers, both of the United States and of the several States, shall be bound by Oath or Affirmation, to support this Constitution; but no religious Test shall ever be required as a Qualification to any Office or public Trust under the United States.

Article VII

The Ratification of the Conventions of nine States, shall be sufficient for the Establishment of this Constitution between the States so ratifying the Same.

Done in Convention by the Unanimous Consent of the States present the Seventeenth Day of September in the Year of our Lord one thousand seven hundred and Eighty seven and of the Independence of the United States of America the Twelfth. In witness whereof We have hereunto subscribed our Names,

George Washington
President and Deputy from Virginia

Delaware
George Read
Gunning Bedford, Jr.
John Dickinson
Richard Bassett
Jacob Broom

Maryland
James McHenry
Daniel of St. Thomas Jenifer
Daniel Carroll

Virginia
John Blair
James Madison, Jr.

North Carolina
William Blount
Richard Dobbs Spaight
Hugh Williamson

South Carolina
John Rutledge
Charles Cotesworth Pinckney
Charles Pinckney
Pierce Butler

Georgia
William Few
Abraham Baldwin

New Hampshire
John Langdon
Nicholas Gilman

Massachusetts
Nathaniel Gorham
Rufus King

Connecticut
William Samuel Johnson
Roger Sherman

New York
Alexander Hamilton

New Jersey
William Livingston
David Brearley
William Paterson
Jonathan Dayton

Pennsylvania
Benjamin Franklin
Thomas Mifflin
Robert Morris
George Clymer
Thomas FitzSimons
Jared Ingersoll
James Wilson
Gouverneur Morris

Attest: William Jackson, *Secretary*

How the proposed and signed Constitution is to be officially adopted by the states.

The Constitution only required ratification by nine of the thirteen states to come into effect.

Witnesses to the Constitution

Names of the delegates agreeing to the provisions of the Constitution.

Bill of Rights

At first, some states would not accept the Constitution. North Carolina was one of those states. After Congress passed the first ten amendments to the Constitution, called the Bill of Rights, North Carolina voted for the Constitution.

The Bill of Rights best expresses how the people's rights are protected. It keeps the government from taking away the freedom of individuals. The Bill of Rights limits the power of government by strengthening the rights of individuals. The majority rules in deciding issues of government through voting. But the Constitution makes sure that individual rights are not taken away.

Amendment 1: Freedom of Religion, Speech, Press, Assembly, and Petition

The government cannot tell someone how or how not to worship God. The government cannot stop people from saying or printing what they think. Anyone can criticize the government. A group can gather peacefully to debate what the government does. People can ask the government to correct wrongs.

Amendment 2: Right to Keep Arms

States have the right to form militias and citizens have the right to own guns.

Amendment 3: Quartering of Troops

The government cannot force citizens to house, or quarter, troops in their homes.

Amendment 4: Search and Seizure; Warrants

No soldier or police officer can enter a house or be housed on a person's property without his or her permission. If police do enter, they must have an order from a judge.

Amendment 5: Rights of Accused Persons

No one has to go to trial just because one person accuses another of a crime. A grand jury has to meet and decide if that person should be tried. No one tried and found not guilty can be tried again for the same crime. A person does not have to testify against himself or herself.

Amendment 6: Right to a Speedy Trial

A jury chosen from the people decides cases before a judge. Accused persons have the right to a speedy and fair trial, and they have the right to meet their accusers.

Amendment 7: Jury Trial in Civil Cases

Civil cases, meaning a case where a person sues another person, are entitled to jury trials when suing for more than $20. In practice, people do not go to federal courts unless a substantial sum of money is involved.

Amendment 8: Bail, Fines, Punishments

Guilty people must not be punished in a cruel way. Bail fines must not be excessive.

Amendment 9: Rights Not Listed are Retained

Amendment I

Congress shall make no law respecting an establishment of religion, or prohibiting the free exercise thereof; or abridging the freedom of speech, or of the press; or the right of the people peaceably to assemble, and to petition the Government for a redress of grievances.

Amendment II

A well regulated Militia, being necessary to the security of a free State, the right of the people to keep and bear Arms, shall not be infringed.

Amendment III

No Soldier shall, in time of peace be quartered in any house, without the consent of the Owner, nor in time of war, but in a manner to be prescribed by law.

Amendment IV

The right of the people to be secure in their persons, houses, papers, and effects, against unreasonable searches and seizures, shall not be violated, and no Warrants shall issue, but upon probable cause, supported by Oath or affirmation, and particularly describing the place to be searched, and the persons or things to be seized.

Amendment V

No person shall be held to answer for a capital, or otherwise infamous crime, unless on a presentment or indictment of a Grand Jury, except in cases arising in the land or naval forces, or in the Militia, when in actual service in time of War or public danger; nor shall any person be subject for the same offence to be twice put in jeopardy of life or limb; nor shall be compelled in any criminal case to be a witness against himself, nor be deprived of life, liberty, or property, without due process of law; nor shall private property be taken for public use, without just compensation.

Amendment VI

In all criminal prosecutions, the accused shall enjoy the right to a speedy and public trial, by an impartial jury of the State and district wherein the crime shall have been committed, which district shall have been previously ascertained by law, and to be informed of the nature and cause of the accusation; to be confronted with the witnesses against him; to have compulsory process for obtaining witnesses in his favor, and to have the Assistance of Counsel for his defence.

Amendment VII

In suits at common law, where the value in controversy shall exceed twenty dollars, the right of trial by jury shall be preserved, and no fact tried by a jury, shall be otherwise reexamined in any Court of the United States, than according to the rules of the common law.

Amendment VIII

Excessive bail shall not be required, nor excessive fines imposed, nor cruel and unusual punishments inflicted.

Amendment IX

The enumeration in the Constitution, of certain rights, shall not be construed to deny or disparage others retained by the people.

Amendment X

The powers not delegated to the United States by the Constitution, nor prohibited by it to the States, are reserved to the States respectively, or to the people.

Amendment XI

The Judicial power of the United States shall not be construed to extend to any suit in law or equity, commenced or prosecuted against one of the United States by Citizens of another State, or by Citizens or Subjects of any Foreign State.

Amendment XII

The Electors shall meet in their respective states and vote by ballot for President and Vice President, one of whom, at least, shall not be an inhabitant of the same state with themselves; they shall name in their ballots the person voted for as President, and in distinct ballots the person voted for as Vice President, and they shall make distinct lists of all persons voted for as President, and of all persons voted for as Vice President, and of the number of votes for each, which lists they shall sign and certify, and transmit sealed to the seat of the government of the United States, directed to the President of the Senate; —the President of the Senate shall, in the presence of the Senate and House of Representatives, open all the certificates and the votes shall then be counted; —The person having the greatest number of votes for President, shall be the President, if such number be a majority of the whole number of Electors appointed; and if no person have such majority, then from the persons having the highest numbers not exceeding three on the list of those voted for as President, the House of Representatives shall choose immediately, by ballot, the President. But in choosing the President, the votes shall be taken by states, the representation from each state having one vote; a quorum for this purpose shall consist of a member or members from two thirds of the states, and a majority of all the states shall be necessary to a choice. And if the House of Representatives shall not choose a President whenever the right of choice shall devolve upon them, before the fourth day of March next following, then the Vice President shall act as President, as in case of the death or other constitutional disability of the President. —* The person having the greatest number of votes as Vice President, shall be the Vice President, if such number be a majority of the whole number of Electors appointed, and if no person have a majority, then from the two highest numbers on the list, the Senate shall choose the Vice President; a quorum for the purpose shall consist of two thirds of the whole number of Senators, and a majority of the whole number shall be necessary to a choice. But no person constitutionally ineligible to the office of President shall be eligible to that of Vice President of the United States.

by the People

Rights not listed in the Constitution are kept by the people.

Amendment 10: Powers Not Listed are Reserved to the States and People

Any power not given to the national government nor to the states is held by the people.

Amendment 11: Suits Against States

Passed by Congress March 4, 1794. Ratified February 7, 1795. Article III, section 2, of the Constitution was modified by this amendment.

Places limits on judicial power. Lawsuits against a state must be tried in that state's courts.

Amendment 12: Election of President and Vice President

Passed by Congress December 9, 1803. Ratified June 15, 1804. Note: A portion of Article II, section 1 of the Constitution, was superseded by the Twelfth Amendment.

Changed the electoral college. Electors are to use separate ballots for president and vice president.

**Superceded by section 3 of the Twentieth Amendment.*

Amendment 13: Slavery Abolished

Passed by Congress January 31, 1865. Ratified December 6, 1865. Note: A portion of Article IV, section 2, of the Constitution was superseded by the Thirteenth Amendment.

Abolishes slavery. The Thirteenth, Fourteenth, and Fifteenth Amendments are sometimes called the "Reconstruction Amendments" because they followed the Civil War and were drafted to abolish slavery and prevent slavery under other names.

Amendment 14: Rights of Citizens

Passed by Congress June 13, 1866. Ratified July 9, 1868. Note: Article I, section 2, of the Constitution was modified by section 2 of the Fourteenth Amendment.

This amendment was designed to prevent state governments from violating the rights of former slaves after the Civil War. It has been used to extend almost all of the rights granted in the Bill of Rights to citizens and prevent state governments from denying those rights.

Section 1: Citizenship Defined

Declares that all persons born or naturalized in the United States are American citizens and citizens of their state of residence. This established the citizenship of former slaves. States cannot violate the rights of citizens, deprive any person of life, liberty, or property without due process of law, or deny any person the equal protection of the laws.

This has been used extensively by the Supreme Court to test the validity of state legislation based upon the due process and the equal protection clauses, which apply to all persons whether or not they are citizens of the United States.

Section 2: Representation in Congress

Representation in the House of Representatives must be made on the basis of the whole state population, excluding Native Americans not taxed. Reduction of a states Congressional representation is allowed if a state forbids male citizens over twenty-one years old the ability to vote.

Changed by section 1 of the Twenty-sixth Amendment.* **Section 3: Penalty for Rebellion

This excluded leaders of the Confederacy from holding state or federal offices unless Congress agreed to remove the ban by a two-thirds vote of each house. Most former Confederate leaders were allowed to return to public life by the end of Reconstruction.

Section 4: Public Debt

Confirms the public debt from the Civil War. However, the debt of the Confederacy was declared invalid. Former slave owners could not collect compensation for the loss of slaves.

Amendment XIII

Section 1

Neither slavery nor involuntary servitude, except as a punishment for crime whereof the party shall have been duly convicted, shall exist within the United States, or any place subject to their jurisdiction.

Section 2

Congress shall have power to enforce this article by appropriate legislation.

Amendment XIV

Section 1

All persons born or naturalized in the United States, and subject to the jurisdiction thereof, are citizens of the United States and of the State wherein they reside. No State shall make or enforce any law which shall abridge the privileges or immunities of citizens of the United States; nor shall any State deprive any person of life, liberty, or property, without due process of law; nor deny to any person within its jurisdiction the equal protection of the laws.

Section 2

Representatives shall be apportioned among the several States according to their respective numbers, counting the whole number of persons in each State, excluding Indians not taxed. But when the right to vote at any election for the choice of electors for President and VicePresident of the United States, Representatives in Congress, the Executive and Judicial officers of a State, or the members of the Legislature thereof, is denied to any of the male inhabitants of such State, being twenty one years of age,* and citizens of the United States, or in any way abridged, except for participation in rebellion, or other crime, the basis of representation therein shall be reduced in the proportion which the number of such male citizens shall bear to the whole number of male citizens twentyone years of age in such State.

Section 3

No person shall be a Senator or Representative in Congress, or elector of President and Vice President, or hold any office, civil or military, under the United States, or under any State, who, having previously taken an oath, as a member of Congress, or as an officer of the United States, or as a member of any State legislature, or as an executive or judicial officer of any State, to support the Constitution of the United States, shall have engaged in insurrection or rebellion against the same, or given aid or comfort to the enemies thereof. But Congress may by a vote of two thirds of each House, remove such disability.

Section 4

The validity of the public debt of the United States, authorized by law, including debts incurred for payment of pensions and bounties for services in suppressing insurrection or rebellion, shall not be questioned. But neither the United States nor any State shall assume or pay any debt or obligation incurred in aid of insurrection or rebellion against the United States, or any claim for the loss or emancipation of any slave; but all such debts, obligations and claims shall be held illegal and void.

Section 5

The Congress shall have the power to enforce, by appropriate legislation, the provisions of this article.

Amendment XV

Section 1

The right of citizens of the United States to vote shall not be denied or abridged by the United States or by any State on account of race, color, or previous condition of servitude—

Section 2

The Congress shall have the power to enforce this article by appropriate legislation.

Amendment XVI

The Congress shall have power to lay and collect taxes on incomes, from whatever source derived, without apportionment among the several States, and without regard to any census or enumeration.

Amendment XVII

Section 1

The Senate of the United States shall be composed of two Senators from each State, elected by the people thereof, for six years; and each Senator shall have one vote. The electors in each State shall have the qualifications requisite for electors of the most numerous branch of the State legislatures.

Section 2

When vacancies happen in the representation of any State in the Senate, the executive authority of such State shall issue writs of election to fill such vacancies: Provided, That the legislature of any State may empower the executive thereof to make temporary appointments until the people fill the vacancies by election as the legislature may direct.

Section 3

This amendment shall not be so construed as to affect the election or term of any Senator chosen before it becomes valid as part of the Constitution.

Amendment XVIII

Section 1

~~After one year from the ratification of this article the manufacture, sale, or transportation of intoxicating liquors within, the importation thereof into, or the exportation thereof from the United States and all territory subject to the jurisdiction thereof for beverage purposes is hereby prohibited.~~

Section 2

~~The Congress and the several States shall have concurrent power to enforce this article by appropriate legislation.~~

Section 3

~~This article shall be inoperative unless it shall have been ratified as an~~

Section 5: Enforcement

Congress may pass legislation to enforce the amendment. This is the basis upon which the Civil Rights Act of 1964 was passed.

Amendment 15: Right to Vote with No Racial Barriers

Passed by Congress February 26, 1869. Ratified February 3, 1870.

Section 1: African American Suffrage

The right of citizens to vote cannot be based on race, color, or previous condition of servitude (slavery). This did not give the right to vote to African American women. All women were still banned from voting in federal and most state elections.

Section 2: Enforcement

Congress may pass legislation to enforce this amendment. This amendment became the basis for the Voting Rights Act of 1965. **Amendment 16: Income Tax Authorized**

Passed by Congress July 2, 1909. Ratified February 3, 1913. Note: Article I, section 9, of the Constitution was modified by the Sixteenth Amendment.

The power to lay and collect taxes on incomes from whatever source.

Amendment 17: Election of Senators by Direct Popular Vote

Passed by Congress May 13, 1912. Ratified April 8, 1913. Note: Article I, section 3, of the Constitution was modified by the Seventeenth Amendment.

Prior to this amendment, senators were chosen by the state legislatures. This amendment changed the selection process to election by popular vote, giving citizens more control.

Amendment 18: National Prohibition of Intoxicating Liquors

Passed by Congress December 18, 1917. Ratified January 16, 1919. Repealed by the Twenty-first Amendment.

Prohibits manufacture, sale, or transportation of intoxicating liquors.

714–717

Amendment 19: Right to Vote for Women
Passed by Congress June 4, 1919. Ratified August 18, 1920.

Political action groups struggled for many years to extend the right to vote to women nationwide in both state and federal elections.

Amendment 20: "Lame Duck" Amendment
Passed by Congress March 2, 1932. Ratified January 23, 1933. Note: Article I, section 4, of the Constitution was modified by section 2 of this amendment. In addition, a portion of the Twelfth Amendment was superseded by section 3.

Section 1: New Term Dates
In the early years of our nation, without modern means of communication and transportation, a longer interval between the date of an election and the beginning of the term of office was necessary. It took time for the results of elections to be known and for public officials to make the sometimes long journey to Washington, D.C., from faraway states.

The session of Congress held immediately after an election still had the Representatives from the prior election. The terms for the newly-elected Representatives did not begin until 13 months after the election. Members who lost the election still served those 13 months until the new Representatives took office. This was a "Lame Duck" session.

"Lame Duck" is used to describe a president or any public officeholder who will not be returning when his or her current term ends. They may not be returning because they are not seeking reelection, or they were defeated in an intervening election, or their office is term-limited, as in the case of the president. The expression is also applied to a Congress which reconvenes after an election. A lame duck Congress continues in session with members known not to be returning still serving in it. The influence of the out-going officeholder is considered crippled, or "lamed," by the fact that he or she will soon be out of power.

To make the starting date of a new Congress and a new member's term coincide, this amendment changed the beginning of a member's term from March 4 to January 3. This amendment also shortens the time between the election of a new president and vice president and the inauguration.

Section 2: Meeting Time for Congress
Moves the date on which a new session of Congress began from the first Monday in December—13 months from the previous November elections—to January 3, just two months after the elections.

Section 3: Presidential Succession
If the president-elect dies before taking office, the vice president-elect becomes president.

Section 4: Filling Presidential Vacancies
If a presidential candidate dies while a presidential election is being decided in the House of Representatives, or a vice presidential candidate dies

~~amendment to the Constitution by the legislatures of the several States, as provided in the Constitution, within seven years from the date of the submission hereof to the States by the Congress.~~

Amendment XIX
The right of citizens of the United States to vote shall not be denied or abridged by the United States or by any State on account of sex.

Congress shall have power to enforce this article by appropriate legislation.

Amendment XX
Section 1
The terms of the President and the Vice President shall end at noon on the 20th day of January, and the terms of Senators and Representatives at noon on the 3d day of January, of the years in which such terms would have ended if this article had not been ratified; and the terms of their successors shall then begin.

Section 2
The Congress shall assemble at least once in every year, and such meeting shall begin at noon on the 3d day of January, unless they shall by law appoint a different day.

Section 3
If, at the time fixed for the beginning of the term of the President, the President elect shall have died, the Vice President elect shall become President. If a President shall not have been chosen before the time fixed for the beginning of his term, or if the President elect shall have failed to qualify, then the Vice President elect shall act as President until a President shall have qualified; and the Congress may by law provide for the case wherein neither a President elect nor a Vice President shall have qualified, declaring who shall then act as President, or the manner in which one who is to act shall be selected, and such person shall act accordingly until a President or Vice President shall have qualified.

Section 4
The Congress may by law provide for the case of the death of any of the persons from whom the House of Representatives may choose a President whenever the right of choice shall have devolved upon them, and for the case of the death of any of the persons from whom the Senate may choose a Vice President whenever the right of choice shall have devolved upon them.

Section 5
Sections 1 and 2 shall take effect on the 15th day of October following the ratification of this article.

Section 6
This article shall be inoperative unless it shall have been ratified as an amendment to the Constitution by the legislatures of three fourths of the

---

several States within seven years from the date of its submission.

Amendment XXI
Section 1
The eighteenth article of amendment to the Constitution of the United States is hereby repealed.

Section 2
The transportation or importation into any State, Territory, or Possession of the United States for delivery or use therein of intoxicating liquors, in violation of the laws thereof, is hereby prohibited.

Section 3
This article shall be inoperative unless it shall have been ratified as an amendment to the Constitution by conventions in the several States, as provided in the Constitution, within seven years from the date of the submission hereof to the States by the Congress.

Amendment XXII
Section 1
No person shall be elected to the office of the President more than twice, and no person who has held the office of President, or acted as President, for more than two years of a term to which some other person was elected President shall be elected to the office of President more than once. But this Article shall not apply to any person holding the office of President when this Article was proposed by Congress, and shall not prevent any person who may be holding the office of President, or acting as President, during the term within which this Article becomes operative from holding the office of President or acting as President during the remainder of such term.

Section 2
This article shall be inoperative unless it shall have been ratified as an amendment to the Constitution by the legislatures of three fourths of the several States within seven years from the date of its submission to the States by the Congress.

Amendment XXIII
Section 1
The District constituting the seat of Government of the United States shall appoint in such manner as Congress may direct:

A number of electors of President and Vice President equal to the whole number of Senators and Representatives in Congress to which the District would be entitled if it were a State, but in no event more than the least populous State; they shall be in addition to those appointed by the States, but they shall be considered, for the purposes of the election of President and Vice President, to be electors appointed by a State; and they shall meet in the District and perform such duties as provided by the twelfth article of amendment.

while a vice presidential election is being decided in the Senate, Congress may pass legislation to deal with the situation.

Section 5: Effective Dates
Sections 1 and 2 took effect in the 1934 Congressional elections and the 1936 presidential election.

Section 6: Time Limit for Ratification
The time period for ratification of this amendment by the states was limited to seven years.

Amendment 21: Repeal of National Prohibition
Passed by Congress February 20, 1933. Ratified December 5, 1933.

This amendment cancels the Eighteenth Amendment. This is an example of the adaptability of the Constitution to meet the changing needs of the citizens.

Amendment 22: Two-Term Limit for Presidents
Passed by Congress March 21, 1947. Ratified February 27, 1951.

Before 1951, the president could run for as many terms as he wanted. After serving two terms as president, George Washington chose not to run again. All other presidents followed his example until Franklin D. Roosevelt. Roosevelt successfully ran for office four times. In 1945, early in his fourth term, he died. Six years later, Congress passed this amendment limiting presidents to two terms. This amendment did not apply to President Truman, who held office at the time the amendment was ratified.

Amendment 23: Presidential Vote for District of Columbia
Passed by Congress June 16, 1960. Ratified March 29, 1961.

Enables residents of the District of Columbia to vote for president and vice President. This amendment gives Washington, D.C., three members in the electoral college. Residents of Washington, D.C., still do not have full representation in Congress.

Amendment 24: Poll Tax Banned in Federal Elections
Passed by Congress August 27, 1962. Ratified January 23, 1964.

States cannot require a poll tax for citizens to vote. People who have failed to pay any other taxes may still vote.

Amendment 25: Presidential Disability and Succession
Passed by Congress July 6, 1965. Ratified February 10, 1967. Note: Article II, section 1, of the Constitution was affected by the Twenty-fifth Amendment.

Covers presidential disability, vice presidential vacancies, and order of succession to the office of the president.

Section 1: Presidential Succession
If the president is removed from office, either by death, resignation, or as a result of impeachment, the vice president becomes the president. There had been some uncertainty until this amendment as to whether, upon a president's death, the vice president was actually the president or a vice president acting as president.

Section 2: Filling a Vacancy in the Vice Presidency
If the vice presidency is vacant, the president is to appoint a new vice president with the approval of the Congress. Until this amendment, there was no provision for dealing with a vacancy in the vice presidency. If a president died in office, the vice president then became president. The vice presidency was vacant for the rest of the term. Similarly, if a vice president died in office, the vacancy in the vice presidency existed through the president's term.

Section 3: Presidential Disability
If the president believes that he or she is unable to carry out the duties of the office, the president can send a written declaration to Congress informing them of the disability. The vice president becomes the acting president until the president is able to resume his or her duties. **Section 4**

If the president is unable to carry out the duties of the office, but is unable (as in the case of illness) or unwilling to inform Congress of his or her disability, the vice president and the majority of the president's cabinet can declare a president disabled. The vice president becomes acting president. If there is disagreement between the president and the vice president and the cabinet as to whether or not the president is disabled, then Congress must resolve the disagreement in 21 days. The term disability or inability is not defined in this amendment or in the Constitution, leaving the interpretation of

Section 2
The Congress shall have power to enforce this article by appropriate legislation.

Amendment XXIV
Section 1
The right of citizens of the United States to vote in any primary or other election for President or Vice President, for electors for President or Vice President, or for Senator or Representative in Congress, shall not be denied or abridged by the United States or any State by reason of failure to pay poll tax or other tax.

Section 2
The Congress shall have power to enforce this article by appropriate legislation.

Amendment XXV
Section 1
In case of the removal of the President from office or of his death or resignation, the Vice President shall become President.

Section 2
Whenever there is a vacancy in the office of the Vice President, the President shall nominate a Vice President who shall take office upon confirmation by a majority vote of both Houses of Congress.

Section 3
Whenever the President transmits to the President pro tempore of the Senate and the Speaker of the House of Representatives his written declaration that he is unable to discharge the powers and duties of his office, and until he transmits to them a written declaration to the contrary, such powers and duties shall be discharged by the Vice President as Acting President.

Section 4
Whenever the Vice President and a majority of either the principal officers of the executive departments or of such other body as Congress may by law provide, transmit to the President pro tempore of the Senate and the Speaker of the House of Representatives their written declaration that the President is unable to discharge the powers and duties of his office, the Vice President shall immediately assume the powers and duties of the office as Acting President.

Thereafter, when the President transmits to the President pro tempore of the Senate and the Speaker of the House of Representatives his written declaration that no inability exists, he shall resume the powers and duties of his office unless the Vice President and a majority of either the principal officers of the executive department or of such other body as Congress may by law provide, transmit within four days to the President pro tempore of the Senate and the Speaker of the House of Representatives their written declaration that the President is unable to discharge the

---

powers and duties of his office. Thereupon Congress shall decide the issue, assembling within forty eight hours for that purpose if not in session. If the Congress, within twenty one days after receipt of the latter written declaration, or, if Congress is not in session, within twenty one days after Congress is required to assemble, determines by two thirds vote of both Houses that the President is unable to discharge the powers and duties of his office, the Vice President shall continue to discharge the same as Acting President; otherwise, the President shall resume the powers and duties of his office.

Amendment XXVI
Section 1
The right of citizens of the United States, who are eighteen years of age or older, to vote shall not be denied or abridged by the United States or by any State on account of age.

Section 2
The Congress shall have power to enforce this article by appropriate legislation.

Amendment XXVII
No law, varying the compensation for the services of the Senators and Representatives, shall take effect, until an election of representatives shall have intervened.

presidential disability open to debate.

This amendment was used during the Nixon and Ford administrations. For the first time in our history two men who had not faced the voters in a national election became president and vice president. First, Vice President Spiro Agnew resigned on October 10, 1973. President Nixon nominated Representative Gerald R. Ford of Michigan to succeed him. Both Houses thereafter confirmed the nomination. Vice President Ford took the oath of office on December 6, 1973. Next, President Richard M. Nixon resigned his office August 9, 1974, and Vice President Ford immediately succeeded to the office and took the presidential oath of office at noon of the same day. Finally, President Ford nominated Nelson A. Rockefeller of New York to be vice president, which was confirmed by Congress. Mr. Rockefeller took the oath of office for the vice presidency on December 19, 1974.

Amendment 26: Voting Age Lowered to Eighteen Years
Passed by Congress March 23, 1971. Ratified July 1, 1971. Note: Section 2 of the Fourteenth Amendment was modified by section 1 of the Twenty-sixth Amendment.

Lowered the voting age to eighteen in all federal, state, and local elections. This amendment was the result of the public's belief that citizens who are serving in the military should have the right to vote.

Amendment 27: Congressional Pay
Originally proposed September 25, 1789. Ratified May 7, 1992.

Members of a session of Congress which has approved a pay raise may only receive the increase after the next election.

The Emancipation Proclamation

The Emancipation Proclamation was issued by President Abraham Lincoln in 1863 during the Civil War. It declared that the slaves in the Confederate states were free. This document later became the foundation of the Thirteenth Amendment to the Constitution

This document did not free all of the slaves. It protected slavery in the border states that did not join the Confederacy as well as areas of the South under Union control in Louisiana and Virginia.

However, the Emancipation Proclamation had other important effects. The Proclamation clarified for many Northerners the Union's cause and strengthened the war effort. It also freed approximately 500,000 African Americans who had escaped to free states. This allowed them to join–as about 200,000 of them did–the Union Army and Navy and fight their former owners.

JANUARY 1, 1863
BY THE PRESIDENT OF THE UNITED STATES OF AMERICA:

A PROCLAMATION.

Whereas, on the twenty second day of September, in the year of our Lord one thousand eight hundred and sixty two, a proclamation was issued by the President of the United States, containing, among other things, the following, to wit: "That on the first day of January, in the year of our Lord one thousand eight hundred and sixty three, all persons held as slaves within any State or designated part of a State, the people whereof shall then be in rebellion against the United States, shall be, thenceforward, and forever free; and the Executive Government of the United States, including the military and naval authority thereof, will recognize and maintain the freedom of such persons, and will do no act or acts to repress such persons, or any of them, in any efforts they may make for their actual freedom.

"That the Executive will, on the first day of January aforesaid, by proclamation, designate the States and parts of States, if any, in which the people thereof, respectively, shall then be in rebellion against the United States; and the fact that any State, or the people thereof, shall on that day be, in good faith, represented in the Congress of the United States by members chosen thereto at elections wherein a majority of the qualified voters of such State shall have participated, shall, in the absence of strong countervailing testimony, be deemed conclusive evidence that such State, and the people thereof, are not then in rebellion against the United States."

Now, therefore I, Abraham Lincoln, President of the United States, by virtue of the power in me vested as Commander in Chief, of the Army and Navy of the United States in time of actual armed rebellion against the authority and government of the United States, and as a fit and necessary war measure for suppressing said rebellion, do, on this first day of January, in the year of our Lord one thousand eight hundred and sixty three, and in accordance with my purpose so to do publicly proclaimed for the full period of one hundred days, from the day first above mentioned, order and designate as the States and parts of States wherein the people thereof respectively, are this day in rebellion against the United States, the following, to wit:

Arkansas, Texas, Louisiana, (except the Parishes of St. Bernard, Plaquemines, Jefferson, St. John, St. Charles, St. James Ascension, Assumption, Terrebonne, Lafourche, St. Mary, St. Martin, and Orleans, including the City of New Orleans) Mississippi, Alabama, Florida, Georgia, South Carolina, North Carolina, and Virginia, (except the forty eight counties designated as West Virginia, and also the counties of Berkley, Accomac, Northampton, Elizabeth City, York, Princess Ann, and Norfolk, including the cities of Norfolk and Portsmouth[]), and which excepted parts, are for the present, left precisely as if this proclamation were not issued.

And by virtue of the power, and for the purpose aforesaid, I do order and declare that all persons held as slaves within said designated States, and parts of States, are, and henceforward shall be free; and that the Executive government of the United States, including the military and naval authorities thereof, will recognize and maintain the freedom of said persons.

And I hereby enjoin upon the people so declared to be free to abstain from all violence, unless in necessary self defence; and I recommend to them that, in all cases when allowed, they labor faithfully for reasonable wages.

And I further declare and make known, that such persons of suitable condition, will be received into the armed service of the United States to garrison forts, positions, stations, and other places, and to man vessels of all sorts in said service.

And upon this act, sincerely believed to be an act of justice, warranted by the Constitution, upon military necessity, I invoke the considerate judgment of mankind, and the gracious favor of Almighty God.

In witness whereof, I have hereunto set my hand and caused the seal of the United States to be affixed.

Done at the City of Washington, this first day of January, in the year of our Lord one thousand eight hundred and sixty three, and of the Independence of the United States of America the eightyseventh.

By the President: ABRAHAM LINCOLN
WILLIAM H. SEWARD, Secretary of State.

George Washington
Term: 1789–1797
Party: Federalist[1]
Vice President: John Adams
State of Birth: Virginia
Birth Date: Feb 22, 1732
Death Date: Dec 14, 1799

John Adams
Term: 1797–1801
Party: Federalist
Vice President: Thomas Jefferson
State of Birth: Massachusetts
Birth Date: Oct 30, 1735
Death Date: July 4, 1826

Thomas Jefferson
Term: 1801–1809
Party: Demo-Republican
Vice President: Aaron Burr, George Clinton
State of Birth: Virginia
Birth Date: April 13, 1743
Death Date: July 4, 1826

James Madison
Term: 1809–1817
Party: Demo-Republican
Vice President: George Clinton, Elbridge Gerry
State of Birth: Virginia
Birth Date: March 16, 1751
Death Date: June 28, 1836

James Monroe
Term: 1817–1825
Party: Demo-Republican
Vice President: Daniel D. Tompkins
State of Birth: Virginia
Birth Date: April 28, 1758
Death Date: July 4, 1831

John Quincy Adams
Term: 1825–1829
Party: Demo-Republican
Vice President: John C. Calhoun
State of Birth: Massachusetts
Birth Date: July 11, 1767
Death Date: Feb 23, 1848

Andrew Jackson
Term: 1829–1837
Party: Democratic
Vice President: John C. Calhoun
State of Birth: South Carolina
Birth Date: March 15, 1767
Death Date: June 8, 1845

Martin Van Buren
Term: 1837–1841
Party: Democratic
Vice President: Richard M. Johnson
State of Birth: New York
Birth Date: Dec 5, 1782
Death Date: July 24, 1862

William Henry Harrison
Term: 1841*
Party: Whig
Vice President: John Tyler
State of Birth: Virginia
Birth Date: Feb 9, 1773
Death Date: April 4, 1841

John Tyler
Term: 1841–1845
Party: Whig
Vice President: None
State of Birth: Virginia
Birth Date: March 29, 1790
Death Date: Jan 18, 1862

James K. Polk
Term: 1845–1849
Party: Democratic
Vice President: George M. Dallas
State of Birth: North Carolina
Birth Date: Nov 2, 1795
Death Date: June 15, 1849

Zachary Taylor
Term: 1849–1850*
Party: Whig
Vice President: Millard Fillmore
State of Birth: Virginia
Birth Date: Nov 24, 1784
Death Date: July 9, 1850

Millard Fillmore
Term: 1850–1853
Party: Whig
Vice President: None
State of Birth: New York
Birth Date: Jan 7, 1800
Death Date: March 8, 1874

Franklin Pierce
Term: 1853–1857
Party: Democratic
Vice President: William King
State of Birth: New Hampshire
Birth Date: Novr 23, 1804
Death Date: Oct 8, 1869

James Buchanan
Term: 1857–1861
Party: Democratic
Vice President: John C. Breckinridge
State of Birth: Pennsylvania
Birth Date: April 23, 1791
Death Date: June 1, 1868

Abraham Lincoln
Term: 1861–1865**
Party: Republican[2]
Vice President: Hannibal Hamlin, Andrew Johnson
State of Birth: Kentucky
Birth Date: Feb 12, 1809
Death Date: April 15, 1865

Andrew Johnson
Term: 1865–1869
Party: Union[2]
Vice President: None
State of Birth: North Carolina
Birth Date: Dec 29, 1808
Death Date: July 31, 1875

Ulysses S. Grant
Term: 1869–1877
Party: Republican
Vice President: Schuyler Colfax
State of Birth: Ohio
Birth Date: April 27, 1822
Death Date: July 23, 1885

Rutherford B. Hayes
Term: 1877–1881
Party: Republican
Vice President: William Wheeler
State of Birth: Ohio
Birth Date: Oct 4, 1822
Death Date: Jan 17, 1893

James A. Garfield
Term: 1881**
Party: Republican
Vice President: Chester A. Arthur
State of Birth: Ohio
Birth Date: Nov 19, 1831
Death Date: Sept 19, 1881

Chester A. Arthur
Term: 1881–1885
Party: Republican
Vice President: None
State of Birth: Vermont
Birth Date: Oct 5, 1829
Death Date: Nov 18, 1886

Grover Cleveland
Term: 1885–1889[3]
Party: Democratic
Vice President: Thomas Hendricks
State of Birth: New Jersey
Birth Date: March 18, 1837
Death Date: June 24, 1908

Benjamin Harrison
Term: 1889–1893
Party: Republican
Vice President: Levi P. Morton
State of Birth: Ohio
Birth Date: Aug 20, 1833
Death Date: June 24, 1908

Grover Cleveland
Term: 1893–1897[3]
Party: Democratic
Vice President: Adlai E. Stevenson
State of Birth: New Jersey
Birth Date: March 18, 1837
Death Date: June 24, 1908

William McKinley
Term: 1897–1901**
Party: Republican
Vice President: Garret Hobart, Theodore Roosevelt
State of Birth: Ohio
Birth Date: Jan 29, 1843
Death Date: Sept 14, 1901

Theodore Roosevelt
Term: 1901–1909
Party: Republican
Vice President: Charles Fairbanks
State of Birth: New York
Birth Date: Oct 27, 1858
Death Date: Jan 6, 1919

William Howard Taft
Term: 1909–1913
Party: Republican
Vice President: James S. Sherman
State of Birth: Ohio
Birth Date: Sept 15, 1857
Death Date: March 8, 1930

Woodrow Wilson
Term: 1913–1921
Party: Democratic
Vice President: Thomas R. Marshall
State of Birth: Virginia
Birth Date: Dec 28, 1856
Death Date: Feb 3, 1924

Warren G. Harding
Term: 1921–1923*
Party: Republican
Vice President: Calvin Coolidge
State of Birth: Ohio
Birth Date: Nov 2, 1865
Death Date: Aug 2, 1923

Calvin Coolidge
Term: 1923–1929
Party: Republican
Vice President: Charles G. Dawes
State of Birth: Ohio
Birth Date: Nov 2, 1865
Death Date: Jan 5, 1933

Herbert Hoover
Term: 1929–1933
Party: Republican
Vice President: Charles Curtis
State of Birth: Iowa
Birth Date: Aug 10, 1874
Death Date: Oct 20, 1964

Franklin D. Roosevelt
Term: 1933–1945*
Party: Democratic
Vice President: John Nance Garner, Henry A. Wallace, Harry S Truman
State of Birth: New York
Birth Date: Jan 30, 1882
Death Date: April 12, 1945

Harry S. Truman
Term: 1945–1953
Party: Democratic
Vice President: Alben W. Barkley
State of Birth: Missouri
Birth Date: May 5, 1894
Death Date: Dec 26, 1977

Dwight Eisenhower
Term: 1953–1961
Party: Republican
Vice President: Richard M. Nixon
State of Birth: Texas
Birth Date: Oct 14, 1890
Death Date: March 28, 1969

John F. Kennedy
Term: 1961–1963**
Party: Democratic
Vice President: Lyndon B. Johnson
State of Birth: Massachusetts
Birth Date: May 29, 1917
Death Date: Nov 22, 1963

Lyndon B. Johnson
Term: 1963–1969
Party: Democratic
Vice President: Hubert H. Humphrey
State of Birth: Texas
Birth Date: Aug 27, 1908
Death Date: Jan 22, 1973

Richard M. Nixon
Term: 1969–1974[4]
Party: Republican
Vice President: Spiro T. Agnew, Gerald R. Ford
State of Birth: California
Birth Date: Jan 9, 1913
Death Date: April 22, 1994

Gerald R. Ford
Term: 1974–1977[5]
Party: Republican
Vice President: Nelson R. Rockefeller
State of Birth: Nebraska
Birth Date: July 14, 1913
Death Date: Dec 26, 2006

Jimmy Carter
Term: 1977–1981
Party: Democratic
Vice President: Walter F. Mondale
State of Birth: Georgia
Birth Date: Oct 1, 1924
Death Date:

Ronald Reagan
Term: 1981–1989
Party: Republican
Vice President: George H. W. Bush
State of Birth: Illinois
Birth Date: Feb 6, 1911
Death Date: June 5, 2004

George H. W. Bush
Term: 1989–1993
Party: Republican
Vice President: J. Danforth Quayle
State of Birth: Massachusetts
Birth Date: June 12, 1924
Death Date:

William J. Clinton
Term: 1993–2001
Party: Democratic
Vice President: Albert Gore, Jr.
State of Birth: Arkansas
Birth Date: Aug 19, 1946
Death Date:

George W. Bush
Term: 2001–
Party: Republican
Vice President: Richard Cheney
State of Birth: Connecticut
Birth Date: July 6, 1946
Death Date:

* Died in office
** Assassinated in office
[1] There were no parties in the first election. The parties formed during Washington's first term.
[2] The Republican National Convention of 1864 adopted the name Union Party and renominated Lincoln for president. The Union Party nominated Johnson, a Democrat, for vice president. Although frequently listed as a Republican vice president and president, Johnson returned to the Democratic Party when the Union Party broke apart after 1868.
[3] Second nonconsecutive term.
[4] Resigned August 9, 1974.
[5] Appointed Vice President in 1973 after Spiro Agnew's resignation; assumed presidency after Nixon's resignation.

A

Acapulco A port city on the Pacific Ocean and a famous tourist spot; in the 1500s an important harbor in the Spanish Empire.

Acadia The French colonial territory in northeastern North America that included parts of today's eastern Quebec, New Brunswick, Nova Scotia, and New England.

Africa The world's second largest continent. Western regions were the homelands of many ancestors of African Americans living today throughout the Americas.

Alaska A state of the United States located in northwestern North America. One of two states that does not touch the other 48.

Alberta A Canadian province located in the west central region. The province contains part of the rich Interior Plains and the Western Mountains.

Appalachian Mountains A mountain chain in eastern North America, reaching from Alabama in the United States into northeastern Canada.

Arctic Plains Canada's most northerly area, stretching almost to the North Pole. Most of the land is frozen nearly all year, so few things are able to grow during the short summer.

Aruba An island in the Caribbean Sea just off the Venezuelan coast (part of the Lesser Antilles) that is a territory of the Netherlands. Aruba's capital is Oranjestad.

Atlantic Ocean One of the world's largest bodies of water, separating North and South America from Europe and Africa.

Atlantic Coastal Plain A flat or sloping plain bordering the Atlantic Ocean and reaching from Maine into Florida.

B

Baffin Island Located northeast of the Canadian mainland. Sparsely inhabited, mostly by Native Americans known as Inuit.

Bahamas A group of islands off the southeastern coast of Florida. One of three island groups of Middle America.

Barbados A small nation occupying an island in the Lesser Antilles of the Caribbean Sea.

Bay of Campeche Southwestern section of the Gulf of Mexico, forming a wide shallow bay extending into southeastern Mexico.

Belize A small nation located on the northeastern coast of Central America in mainland Middle America.

Beringia A land bridge that once connected Asia and northwestern North America. Now covered by the waters of the Bering Strait.

Blue Ridge Mountains Part of the Appalachian Mountains that extend from West Virginia through North Carolina into Georgia.

Bonaire An island in the Caribbean Sea just off the Venezuelan coast (part of the Lesser Antilles) that is a territory of the Netherlands. Bonaire's capital is Kralendijk.

British Columbia Canada's most western province borders the Pacific Ocean.

C

Calgary Located on the western edge of the Interior Plains in southwestern Alberta. Calgary, now a cosmopolitan city, began as a frontier cattle town.

Canada The world's second largest nation, located in northern North America. Made up of ten provinces and two territories.

Canadian Shield A large forested plain extending south of the Arctic Plains and covering most of Canada. Soil that once covered the shield was pushed south by glaciers thousands of years ago, exposing an ancient, hard rock surface.

Canal Zone A 10-mile (16-km)-wide strip in Panama bordering the Panama Canal.

Cancún An island resort in southeastern Mexico off the northeast coast of the Yucatán Peninsula.

Caribbean Sea Part of the southern Atlantic Ocean between North and South America. Enclosed by the Lesser Antilles to the east and the Greater Antilles and Yucatán Peninsula to the west.

Caribbean Islands Located in the sea between North and South America, these lands are part of the Middle American region.

Central America Part of mainland Middle America, located south of Mexico on the land bridge connecting North and South America. Seven nations—Guatemala, Belize, Honduras, El Salvador, Nicaragua, Costa Rica, and Panama—are found there.

Central Lowlands The eastern part of a vast plains area that makes up much of the central part of the United States.

Central Volcanic Zone A major physical region of mainland Middle America that stretches from Guatemala southward to Panama. The zone has many active volcanoes that have caused damage to people and property.

Chesapeake Bay Located on the Atlantic coast, the bay has served as a rich fishing ground and has provided access to Baltimore.

Chiapas A state in southeastern Mexico, home of the modern Highland Maya.

Chichén Itzá A village in the Yucatán state of Mexico; once one of the principal centers of the Maya; extensive ruins, some still well preserved.

Chihuahua A northern state of Mexico; a rich silver-mining district.

Ciudad Juárez A border city in the northern Mexican state of Chihuahua, opposite El Paso, Texas.

Continental Divide An imaginary line twisting through the Rocky Mountains. The streams west of the divide flow toward the Pacific Ocean, and those to the east flow toward the Mississippi River and the Gulf of Mexico.

Costa Rica A nation located in Central America west of Panama, southwest of the Caribbean Sea, and east of the Pacific Ocean.

Cozumel An island off the northeast coast of Quintana Roo territory, in southeastern Mexico.

Cuba A nation occupying the largest island in the Caribbean Sea. One of four islands of the Greater Antilles.

Curaçao An island in the Caribbean Sea just off the Venezuelan coast (part of the Lesser Antilles) that is a territory of the Netherlands. Curaçao's capital is Willemstad.

D

Dominican Republic A nation that occupies two thirds of Hispaniola, a Caribbean Island.

Durango A state in northwestern central Mexico; industrial center known for its large mining operations.

E

El Salvador A nation in Central America on the Pacific Ocean.

England A once independent nation that is now linked with Wales, Scotland, and Northern Ireland to form the United Kingdom. Located on islands off the western coast of Europe. Homeland of

the founders of the 13 colonies from which the United States grew. London was for many years the seat of Canada's government.

Europe A small continent located on a peninsula of the Eurasian landmass. The homeland of people who conquered the Americas and settled there.

F

Fort St. George An English colonial settlement in North America founded in 1607 and lasting until 1608. It was located in the present-day town of Phippsburg, Maine near the mouth of the Kennebec River.

Four Corners An informal, but commonly used, name for the place where the states of Arizona, New Mexico, Utah, and Colorado meet.

France Western European nation that competed with England for control of North America. Ancestors of many of today's Canadians emigrated from this nation.

G

Grand Banks Shallow waters lying off the coast of Newfoundland. For centuries one of the world's richest fishing areas but now depleted by overfishing.

Grand Canyon Colorado River gorge in the northwestern corner of Arizona. (p. 324)

Great Lakes Five large lakes—Superior, Michigan, Huron, Erie, and Ontario—located along the border of the United States and Canada in central North America.

Greenland A large, barren island lying off the northeastern coast of North America and mostly within the Arctic Circle.

Great Lakes-St. Lawrence Lowlands The smallest of Canada's regions, but the center of about half of the nation's population. Located east of the Great Lakes and along the St. Lawrence River valley.

Great Plains The western part of a huge flat or rolling area that makes up a large section of central United States and Canada (see Interior Plains).

Greater Antilles A group of the largest islands in the Caribbean—Cuba, Jamaica, Hispaniola, and Puerto Rico.

Grenada An island nation in the Caribbean.

Guadalajara A densely settled city in the state of Jalisco, in western central Mexico; a rich agricultural and industrial area, and an important mining center.

Guanajuato For many centuries the wealthiest city in Mexico because of its silver and gold deposits; on the Mesa Central, north of Mexico City.

Guatemala A nation in Central America south of Mexico and north of the Pacific Ocean.

Gulf of Mexico East of Mexico and south of the United States, connected to the Atlantic Ocean and Caribbean Sea.

H

Haiti Shares the island of Hispaniola with the Dominican Republic.

Hawaiian Islands A large group of islands in the northern Pacific Ocean settled originally by Polynesian people. One of two states of the United States not connected to the other 48.

Hispaniola An island in the Caribbean divided between the Dominican Republic and Haiti. One of four islands of the Greater Antilles.

Honduras A nation in northern Central America on the Caribbean Sea.

Hudson Bay An inland sea in northern Canada.

I

Iberian Peninsula Located in southwestern Europe. A land area shared by Portugal and Spain, the first European countries to explore and settle in the Americas.

Imperial Valley A large agricultural area in southern California where fertile soil and a growing season that lasts nearly all year enable farmers to produce much of our nation's fruit and vegetables.

Interior Plains A vast, gently rolling agricultural region in central Canada connected to the Great Plains and Central Lowlands in the United States.

Iqualuit The capital and the largest city of Nunavut Territory, Canada. It is located on Frobisher Bay, on the southeastern part of Baffin Island.

Ireland A country in northwestern Europe occupying part of an island west of Great Britain. The homeland of many emigrants to the United States.

Isthmus of Tehuantepec Isthmus in southern Mexico, between the Bay of Campeche on the north and the Gulf of Tehuantepec on the south; 137 meters wide.

J

Jamaica An island nation in the Caribbean Sea. One of four islands of the Greater Antilles.

Jamestown Site of the first permanent English settlement in North America. Located on the coast of southeastern Virginia.

L

L'Anse aux Meadows The location where evidence of Norse settlement in North America was found. It is located on the island of Newfoundland, now part fo the Canadian province of Newfoundland and Labrador.

Labrador Located in the Canadian province of Newfoundland. Sparsely populated but contains some of Canada's best sources of wood, iron ore, and other minerals.

León A city in the central Mexican state of Guanajuato; known for its tanneries, flour mills, and leather and woolen goods.

Lesser Antilles A group of islands in the eastern Caribbean Sea.

M

Manitoba Canadian province midway between the east and western boundaries of the nation. Part of the Interior Plains region of Canada.

Matamoros A busy Mexican border town opposite Brownsville, Texas, near the Gulf of Mexico.

Mexico A nation south of the United States in mainland Middle America.

Mazatlán Famous resort and largest Mexican seaport on the Pacific coast.

Mesa Central The middle region of Mexico—the central part of the Mexican Plateau. Mexico City and Puebla are located here.

Mesa del Norte The northernmost section of the Mexican Plateau; lies between the Sierra Madre Oriental and the Sierra Madre Occidental.

Mexico City Capital and largest city in Mexico. Built on the site of the ancient Aztec capital, Tenochtitlán.

Mid-Atlantic A part of the Northeastern Region of the United States. Includes the states of Maryland, Delaware, New Jersey, Pennsylvania, and New York, as well as the District of Columbia, the site of the nation's capital city, Washington.

Midwest Region Includes states of Ohio,

Illinois, Indiana, Michigan, Wisconsin, Missouri, Iowa, Kansas, Minnesota, Nebraska, North Dakota, and South Dakota.

Mississippi River The longest river in the United States and North America, located in the central part of the nation. Flows from Minnesota south into the Gulf of Mexico.

Missouri River Flows from Montana to St. Louis, Missouri, where it joins the Mississippi River. Helped move people and freight westward, especially in the 1800s.

Monterrey The third-largest city in Mexico, near the border and Laredo, Texas; a center of international trade and manufacturing.

Montreal Canada's second largest city, located on the St. Lawrence River. The city serves as a transportation hub and financial center.

Mount McKinley Tallest mountain in North America, located in the Alaska Range. Native Americans call it Denali, which means "Great One."

N

New Brunswick Eastern Canadian province bordering the state of Maine. Part of the Appalachian Highlands region.

New England A part of the Northeast Region of the United States. Includes states of Maine, Vermont, New Hampshire, Massachusetts, Connecticut, and Rhode Island.

New France A colony established and held by France from 1609 to 1763. Occupied large areas in what are now Canada and the United States.

Newfoundland Easternmost Canadian province. Part of the Appalachian Highlands region.

New Orleans A city on the Mississippi River in Louisiana settled by France nearly 300 years ago. Has served as a major port for freight using the Mississippi River and the Gulf of Mexico.

New Spain Name often used to identify some of Spain's colonies. In the Western Hemisphere these were chiefly in North America and the Caribbean Sea.

New York City The largest city in the United States. A major port, commercial, and communications center located on the Mid-Atlantic coast.

Nicaragua A nation in Central America west of the Caribbean Sea and northeast of the Pacific Ocean.

North America The world's third largest continent, occupied by Canada and the United States. Geographers generally agree that the islands of the Caribbean, Mexico, and Central America are physically parts of North America. These latter countries, however, have their own cultural identity and are called Middle America.

Northern Hemisphere The half of the earth lying north of the Equator.

Northern Highlands A major physical region of mainland Middle America located in northern Mexico. Made up of two mountain ranges—the Sierra Madre Occidental and Sierra Madre Oriental—which flank a central plateau.

Northwest Territories Located in north central Canada. One of three territories in Canada.

Nova Scotia A small Canadian province bordered on the north by the Gulf of St. Lawrence and on the east by the Atlantic Ocean. Settled by Loyalists after the American Revolution.

Nuevo Laredo A town in the eastern Mexican state of Tamaulipas, on the Rio Grande, opposite Laredo, Texas.

Nunavut Territory A territory in northern Canada created for the Inuit, a Native American people.

O

Oaxaca A state in southeastern Mexico; conquered by the Spanish in 1521, was the home of Bento Juárez and Porfirio Díaz.

Ontario Canadian province in the east central part of the nation, lying north of the Great Lakes and south of Hudson Bay.

Ottawa Canada's capital city, located in the province of Ontario.

Ohio River A major river flowing from Pittsburgh southwestward to the Mississippi River. Continues to serve transportation needs of the United States.

P

Pacific Coast States A region of the United States that includes California, Oregon, and Washington.

Pacific Ocean A large body of water that stretches from the Arctic to Antarctica along the western boundaries of North and South America.

Panama A nation in Central America, connected to the continent of South America to the east. Borders the Caribbean Sea to the north and the Pacific Ocean to the South.

Panama Canal An important shipping lane built by the United States early in the 1900s. Links the Pacific Ocean with the Atlantic through the Caribbean Sea.

Pan-American Highway International highway system, extending from the United States-Canada border to Santiago, Chile; Mexico's primary road.

Pátzcuaro a town in the state of Michoacán, southwest Mexico; famous for its festivals.

Piedmont An area of rolling hills lying between the Atlantic Coastal Plain and Appalachian Mountains. Stretches from New Jersey to Alabama.

Plymouth Site of the landing of English colonists called Separatists or Pilgrims seeking religious freedom in 1620. In present-day Massachusetts.

Popocatépetl A volcano, sometimes active, in the Puebla state of southeastern central Mexico; stands almost 18,000 feet tall.

Portugal A nation on the Iberian Peninsula in south-western Europe. Explored, settled, and ruled Brazil as a colony.

Prince Edward Island Canada's smallest province on the eastern edge of the nation. Part of the Appalachian Highlands region.

Puebla A state in southeastern central Mexico; Puebla city is the fourth-largest in Mexico.

Puerto Rico An island commonwealth in the Caribbean Sea, transferred by Spain to the United States in 1898. One of four islands of the Greater Antilles.

Q

Quebec (city) A major Canadian city of French culture. Capital of the province of Quebec.

Quebec (province) The largest province and center of French culture in Canada. Located in eastern Canada.

R

Rio Grande Flows from Colorado southward into the Gulf of Mexico. The river marks the border between Texas and Mexico.

Rocky Mountains A chain of rugged

mountains in western North America. Stretches from Alaska through Canada and the United States into New Mexico.

Rocky Mountain States A region of the United States that includes Colorado, Wyoming, Montana, Idaho, Utah, and Nevada.

S

St. Lawrence River Flows from Lake Ontario and into the Gulf of St. Lawrence. Forms part of the boundary between the United States and Canada.

St. Lawrence Seaway A system of rivers, canals, and lakes that permits oceangoing ships to sail from the Atlantic Ocean to ports on the Great Lakes in central North America.

San Cristóbal de Las Casas A city in the southern Mexican state of Chiapas; today is a center of Highland Mayan culture.

San Francisco A major West Coast port and commercial center linking the United States with nations bordering the Pacific Ocean.

San Luis Potosí A state in central Mexico, northeast of León; a major industrial center, known especially for its silver mines.

San Miguel de Allende A town in the central Mexican state of Guanajuato; known for its large population of American citizens.

Saskatchewan A Canadian province in the central area of the nation. Landscape is occupied by vast Interior Plains.

Seattle Located in Washington in the Pacific Northwest. Serves as a major port linking the United States with the Pacific.

Siberia A vast northern area of Asia extending from the Ural Mountains to the Pacific Ocean. Native Americans, the first settlers in the Americas, crossed a land bridge from Siberia into modern-day Alaska.

Sierra Madre Occidental Range of mountains in Mexico running parallel to the Pacific Ocean coast and bordering the Mesa Central on the west; about 700 miles long.

Sierra Madre Oriental Range of mountains in Mexico running parallel to the Gulf of Mexico coast and bordering the Mesa Central on the east.

Sonora A state in northwestern Mexico on the coast of the Gulf of California; known for its silver mines.

Spain A nation on the Iberian Peninsula in south-western Europe. Explored, settled, conquered, and ruled (from the 1500s to the early 1800s) much of the Americas from the southern borders of the modern-day United States to the southern tip of South America.

Southwest States A region of the United States that includes Arizona, New Mexico, Oklahoma, and Texas.

Sun Belt An informal name for the region stretching from the southern states along the Atlantic coast through the Southwest into California. An area that has enjoyed rapid population and economic growth since the 1960s.

T

Taxco A town in the Mexican state of Guerrero known for the production of beautiful silver jewelry.

Tenochtitlán Capital of the ancient Aztec Empire. Located on the site of modern-day Mexico City.

Teotihuacán A town in the central state of México, 30 minutes northeast of Mexico City; site of famous Toltec ruins, including the Pyramid of the Sun, the Pyramid of the Moon, and of Quetzalcoatl.

Tijuana a town in Baja California Norte, in north-western Mexico; a popular tourist center and point of entry on the United States–Mexico border.

Toronto Capital and largest city of Ontario Province. Located in Canada's most heavily populated region.

Trinidad and Tobago A nation of the Lesser Antilles in the Caribbean Sea located north of South America. Composed of two islands.

U

United States of America A North American nation made up of 48 contiguous states, the District of Columbia, and Alaska and Hawaii.

Uxmal Ancient city in the state of Yucatán, southeast Mexico; capital of the later Mayan Empire.

V

Vancouver A major port city on Canada's southwestern coast. Provides important links between Canada and nations bordering the Pacific.

Vinland Part of North America settled by Leif Eiríksson and his Viking followers, about the year 1000.

W

Washington, D.C. The capital city of the United States, located near the Atlantic coast and on the borders of Virginia and Maryland.

Winnipeg A major midwestern Canadian city in southern Manitoba, near the United States border.

X

Xochimilco A lake in the Valley of Mexico, in central Mexico, only a few inches deep; site of the Floating Gardens of Aztec fame.

Y

Yucatán Peninsula A low, flat peninsula in southeast Mexico.

Yucatán Plain A major physical region of mainland Middle America of fertile flat land that extends south of the Yucatán Peninsula into Belize and Guatemala.

Yukon Territory Located in northwestern Canada along the Alaskan border. One of three territories in Canada.

Z

Zacatecas A state in central Mexico; known for its large mines and smelters.

GLOSSARY

This glossary will help you understand the Key Terms in this book and other important social studies terms.

A

abolish Do away with slavery.

abolitionists Those who favored doing away with slavery.

absolute location The unique spot on earth where a particular place is located, using coordinates of longitude and latitude.

absolute monarchs Hereditary rulers with life tenure whose powers are unlimited.

acid rain Sulfur and nitrogen released into the air by industries, killing vegetation.

adobe (ah·doh·bee) Native American house made of sun-dried mud and straw packed over wood.

affirmative action A policy or program to ensure equal opportunity in order to make up for past discrimination practices.

alliances Agreements between people or states to help one another.

Allied Powers France, Great Britain, Italy, and Russia, who were united in World War I against the Central Powers—Germany and Austria-Hungary.

allies Partners.

Allies Chiefly the United States, Great Britain, and the Soviet Union, who were united in World War II against the Axis Powers—Germany, Italy, and Japan.

amaranth A tall flowering plant with protein-rich seeds, grown by the Aztecs and used in their religious ceremonies.

amendments Changes to the Constitution.

Anaconda Plan The Union's strategy to divide the Confederacy and end the American Civil War, specifically by using blockades and controlling the Mississippi River.

Anansi Character in popular African folktales brought to the Caribbean.

Appalachian Mountains Eastern North America mountain range extending from Quebec to Alabama.

appeal A review of a lower court's ruling by a higher court.

archaeologists Scientists who study cultures of the past.

arid climate Excessively dry; having insufficient rainfall to support agriculture.

Arctic Attic Popular term referring to the vast spaces of Canada's Nunavut, Northwest, and Yukon Territories.

arms Weapons, including guns, bombs, or other devices.

Articles of Confederation (1781) First written Constitution of the United States, which emphasized the powers of the states.

asphalt Material used to pave roads.

assassinated Deliberately killed openly or secretly, often for political reasons.

assembly Group of elected representatives.

autocratic Kind of government in which one person has unlimited powers.

axis One of the horizontal or vertical lines that make up the grid of a line graph. Also, an imaginary line that runs from the North Pole and the South Pole.

Axis Powers Germany, Italy, and Japan, who were united in World War II against the Allies—chiefly the United States, Great Britain, and the Soviet Union.

Aztecs Native Americans that founded the Mexican empire conquered by Cortés in 1519.

B

barbecue Meat whole or split roasted over an open fire or a fire in a pit. The word is credited to the Taino language, from the Caribbean Island Native American tribe of the same name.

bauxite Mineral ore from which aluminum is refined. A large deposit has been found in Jamaica.

beavers Large, semiaquatic rodents at one time highly prized for their fur.

Beringia (beh·ren·gee·ah) Land bridge that connected Asia and the Western Hemisphere.

bilingual Ability to speak two languages with equal fluency.

Bill of Rights First ten amendments to the Constitution that guarantee the rights of the individual. Also, a document written by the English Parliament in 1689 that gave certain rights to the king's subjects.

Bleeding Kansas The name given the state of Kansas before the Civil War after violent debates between those who wanted Kansas to be a slave state and those who did not. Many people were killed

blockade A string of ships that blocks other ships from entering a harbor.

blues African American–derived songs usually describing loneliness or sadness.

board of county commissioners In the United States, the governing body of a county.

Boston Massacre Five colonists died when British soldiers fired into a crowd protesting British-imposed taxes.

Boston Tea Party Colonial protest where taxed tea was thrown into Boston harbor.

braceros Temporary laborers admitted legally into the United States to help with seasonal crop harvests.

brand A distinguishing mark made by burning with a hot iron—on cattle, for example—to identify ownership.

bribe Money or favor given or promised in order to influence the judgment or conduct of someone in a position of trust.

British Commonwealth of Nations An international group of nations that includes Great Britain and some of its former colonies.

British North America Act (1887) Created Canada's national government and gave Great Britain power to approve Canadian laws.

Brown v. Board of Education of Topeka, Kansas 1954 United States Supreme Court decision declaring school segregation unconstitutional.

bus boycott Organized nonviolent tactic used by African American citizens in Montgomery, Alabama, in 1955. They refused to ride the local buses until the segregated seating policy was changed.

C

cabinet Body of advisors of a head of state or a governor or a mayor.

cacao Beans used in making cocoa, chocolate, and cocoa butter.

Calgary Stampede July celebration in Calgary, Alberta, honoring the western heritage of Canada.

Calypso A type of music invented in the Caribbean. It is distinctive because the lyrics are emphasized rather than the instruments. Some consider it a distant

cousin of rap music.

campesinos Rural land dwellers in Middle America.

Canada Day July 1 legal holiday once called Dominion Day.

Canadian Pacific Railway (1885) Stretched from the Atlantic to the Pacific.

capital resources Goods produced and used to produce other goods and services.

cardinal directions The directions north, south, east, and west.

carnival Season or festival of merrymaking before Lent.

carpetbaggers Northerners who moved to the South during Reconstruction for economic or political gain.

cartographer A person who makes maps.

cash crop A product that can be sold for a profit.

caudillo A Spanish or Latin American dictator.

ceiba A tree sacred to the Maya; it has wide, above-ground roots, a huge trunk and branches stretching to 130 feet.

cenotes Limestone sinkholes that collect water runoff from storms.

Central Lowlands Flat and grassy rich farmland in the United States Midwest.

Central Pacific Railroad/Union Pacific Railroad Combined to create first railway across the West, from Nebraska to California.

Central Powers Germany and Austria-Hungary, who were united in World War I against the Allied Powers—France, Great Britain, Italy, and Russia.

Central Valley Valley of Sacramento and San Joaquin Rivers in California.

checks and balances The system in which the three branches of government in the United States limit the powers of one another to balance equally each branch.

Chol Native American language; one of three branches of Maya spoken in the Mexican state of Chiapas.

civil disobedience A strategy for causing social change by means of nonviolent resistence to unfair laws.

civil rights Constitutional guarantee that all citizens will receive equal rights.

Civil Rights Act The law passed by the U.S. Congress in 1964 that ended segregation.

climate Average weather—temperature, wind velocity, precipitation—at a place over time.

Coastal Plain Flat land that reaches from Maine to Florida, in a narrow strip along the Atlantic coast, then widens westward to Texas along the Gulf of Mexico.

Coastal Range Mountains extending along Pacific coast west of the Sierra Nevada and north through British Columbia to Alaska.

Cochineal A insect of the Andes whose brilliant red body was used to produce a dye by Native Americans and then the Europeans.

Cold War The name given to the dangerous rivalry between the United States and the Soviet Union from 1945 to the 1990s.

Columbian Exchange A process of exchanging needed, or wanted, items between the Spanish and the Native Americans; initiated in the sixteenth century. Included plants, animals, ideas, and technologies. Negative exchanges included diseases.

commerce The exchange or buying and selling of commodities on a large scale involving transportation from place to place.

Committees of Correspondence Groups of colonists formed in the 1770s to protest against taxes imposed by the British.

commodities Products of agriculture, such as eggs, grain, and cattle.

commonwealth An association of self-governing autonomous states more or less loosely associated in a common allegiance (as to the British crown).

communism Form of government in which the government alone decides how to use the resources of its country.

Communist Party The political party that was largely responsible for the leadership of the Russian Revolution in 1917, and that continued as the dominating force in the development of the Soviet Union. Even after the break-up of the Soviet Union in the 1990s, the Communist Party is still influential in Russia. Its programs are based upon the general principles set forth by Karl Marx and Friedrich Engles in the Communist Manifesto (1848).

competition The relationship between two or more businesses striving for the same customers.

compromise To reach an agreement to solve a problem that benefits both sides.

Compromise of 1850 Admitted California to the Union as a nonslave state. Utah and New Mexico entered with no decision on slavery.

concentration camps Where war and political prisoners, and refugees are confined.

concessions Favors given by a country to a foreign company to encourage it to do business with that country.

Confederate States of America, Confederacy The name of the independent government formed by the seceding Southern states. South Carolina was the first state to withdraw from the Union, in December 1860. The following year Mississippi, Florida, Alabama, Georgia, Louisiana, and Texas followed. North Carolina, Tennessee, Arkansas, and Virginia seceded shortly after the Battle of Fort Sumter, in April 1861.

confederation An association to further the common interests of its members.

Congress The legislative branch of the United States.

conquistador Those who conquer. The conquistadors were the leaders of the Spanish conquest of the Americas.

consent Agreement by the people.

conserve To protect from loss or harm; to preserve.

Constitution Document written in 1787 to create a strong national government for the United States that shares powers with the states, governs through three branches, and protects the rights of individuals through the Bill of Rights.

Constitutional Convention Meeting of 59 delegates in Philadelphia in May 1787 to debate whether to keep or revise the Articles of Confederation.

Constitution Act of 1982 Revised Constitution

Consumers A buyer of goods or services for personal use.on putting Canadians in charge of their government.

contiguous Being in contact with—touching along a boundary or at a point.

Continental Army The American army during the American Revolution.

continental climate Cold, snowy winters and summers either short and cool or long and hot.

Continental Divide North America's watershed, where waters flow west, north, or east.

continental drift The theory that the

continents slowly and constantly move within the earth. Compare plate tectonics.

continents The major land masses of earth: Africa, Antarctica, Asia, Australia, Europe, North America, and South America.

Convert To change someone's religious or political beliefs.

coral polyps Tiny sea animals, with limestone skeletons, that form coral.

Corn Belt Region of the Midwest where corn is a major crop.

counterfeit Anything made in imitation of something else with the intent to deceive.

countries Geographical areas that are independent political units. Countries have their own governments, laws, and populations.

county seat In the United States, the town where county government is located.

coureurs de bois (coo·ruhr·duh·bwah) French trappers who traded with Native Americans in Canada.

creole (kree·ol) People born in New Spain, today's Mexico, of Spanish parents.

Creole A dialect of French or Spanish.

crown corporations Companies owned and controlled by national and provincial governments in Canada.

cultural diversity Different ways of life practiced by different groups of people.

cultural mosaic The term used in Canada to describe how its different cultures remain unique while forming a whole society.

culture Ways of life and beliefs of a people.

D

Day of the Dead A fall holiday when Mexicans go into cemeteries to honor their dead ancestors.

D-Day Day set for launching a military operation. D-Day in Europe during World War II was June 6, 1944.

death rate The number of deaths per hundred or per thousand persons in a given group within a given time.

deciduous forests Trees that shed their leaves in autumn. Found in temperate climates.

Declaration of Independence July 4, 1776, document explaining why the American colonies should be separate from England.

de facto segregation The separation of races in fact but not supported by law.

Defeat To beat or win victory over, as in war.

deforestation The removal of forests. Deforestation has contributed to erosion and the loss of soil. See reforestation.

degree Unit of measurement indicating distance between lines of latitude and longitude. Also, a unit of temperature expressed in Fahrenheit (F) or Centigrade (C).

Delegates People selected or elected to represent the wishes of others at a meeting or convention. *See* REPRESENTATIVES.

deltas Triangular-shaped plains of sediment where rivers flow into large bodies of water.

demand The quantity of a good or service wanted at a specific price and time. See supply.

Democratic Based upon the principles of democracy or social equality, as in a "democratic government."

democracy System of government in which power is held and exercised by the people.

Democratic Party One of two major political parties in the United States.

density As regards to population, the average number of individuals per space unit (e. g., per square mile). Determined by amount of rainfall, farmland fertility, or availability of natural resources.

deported Legally sent back to one's own country, usually because of illegal entry.

depression (economic) A period of low general economic activity marked especially by rising levels of unemployment.

desalination The process of changing salty seawater into freshwater that can be used for drinking and irrigation, also called desalinization.

desert Very dry, barren land.

desert climate Less than 10 inches (25 cm) of rain a year.

Desert Storm The United States' military operation in 1991 to free Kuwait from the invading Iraqi forces.

desert vegetation Cactus and scrub bush grow here, but little else.

developed (country) One with a high level of industrialization and standard of living.

developing (country) Poor one trying to build an economy and a higher standard of living.

dictator Ruler with absolute power. An example was Adolf Hitler. See totalitarian.

Diplomats Persons, such as ambassadors, who have been appointed to represent a government in its relations with foreign governments.

Diversity Differing from one another. The United States is a land of diversity because many people live there.

distribution map Shows distribution of people, resources, climate, and vegetation.

District of Columbia Federal district that is the seat of the United States government.

Dominion Day Original name for the July 1 legal holiday in Canada celebrating self-governing status in 1867. Now called Canada Day.

Dred Scott v. Sanford 1857 Supreme Court case that ended compromises over slavery. The court said that Congress did not have the right to exclude slavery from the territories or the states.

Drought A shortage of rainfall.

dry climate Found within the temperate latitudes and near the tropical latitudes.

dry temperate grasslands Grasslands well suited for grazing.

due process Legal procedures outlined in the Constitution and amendments to protect an individual's rights.

Dust Bowl United States Southwest made barren by droughts and wind storms in the 1930s.

E

Earth Day April celebration in the United States observed to show concern for the environment.

earthquake A shaking or trembling of the earth that is volcanic or tectonic in origin.

Eastern Hemisphere The half of the earth east of the prime meridian.

ecology Study of the way plants and animals relate to one another and the environment.

ecosystem The complex of a community of organisms and its environment functioning as an ecological unit in nature.

ecotourism Ecological tourism. Entry fees to national preserves pay for the upkeep of the parks.

"El D.F." Mexican shorthand for the capital Mexico City.

El Niño An irregularly occurring flow of

unusually warm surface water along the western coast of South America that is accompanied by abnormally high rainfall in usually arid areas and that prevents upwelling of nutrient-rich cold deep water, causing a decline in the regional fish population. *See* la niña.

electoral college (United States) Delegates that officially elect the president and vice president.

electronic media Computers, radio, television, and movies.

elevation Height above sea level.

Ellis Island New York City port where most people from Europe entered America from 1892 to 1954.

Emancipation Proclamation President Abraham Lincoln's order on New Year's Day, 1863, freeing all slaves living in the Confederate states disloyal to the Union.

embargo A legal prohibition on commerce

emingrated/emigration Moving away from one's country to live elsewhere. See immigration.

environment All the surroundings of a place, such as land, water, weather, plants, and the changes people have made.

Environmental Protection Agency (EPA) Established by the United States government in 1970 to fight pollution.

Entrepreneur A person who starts his or her own business.

Equator Imaginary line circling the earth halfway between the North and South Poles, dividing the earth into two hemispheres.

Erie Canal First United States canal, from Albany, New York, to Buffalo, New York.

erosion Slow wearing away of soil and rocks by glaciers, running water, wind, or waves.

estuary A water passage where the tide meets a river current, especially an arm of the sea at the lower end of a river.

ethanol Ethyl alcohol, fuel made from sugar.

ethnic heritage One's ancestry.

ethnicity Refers to the quality or affiliation of people with the same cultural background, united by language, religion, or ancestry.

evergreen forests Trees with leaves that stay green year-round. Exist throughout the temperate latitudes.

executive (branch) Carries out laws passed by Congress. Headed by the president.

export To carry or send (as a commodity) to some other place (as another country). See import.

F

Faction A group of people who form a political group, such as a political party.

fall line Line marking the point where rivers descend from upland to lowland.

fault lines Breaks in the earth's crust.

federalism System of government where the national government and the states share power.

federal government The national government, which makes laws for the nation.

fiesta patronal (fee·ess·tah) Saint's day celebration in Spain and Middle and South America.

First Continental Congress Congress of colonial representatives that voted to stop all trade with England until the Intolerable Acts were repealed.

Five Themes of Geography Location, Place, Human-Environmental Interaction, Movement, and Region—the concepts used to describe a place on the earth.

forced migration The act of people involuntarily being moved from one country, place, or locality to another. The Trail of Tears is an example of this.

foreign affairs Relationships between nations.

foreign trade The buying and selling of goods between countries.

forest vegetation Exists in highland, temperate, and tropical climates.

fossil fuels Nonrenewable fuels, such as coal, oil, or natural gas, formed in the earth from plant or animal remains.

fossils Remains of plants or animals that lived long ago, preserved in rock.

Four Corners Where Arizona, New Mexico, Utah, and Colorado meet.

Fourteen Points President Woodrow Wilson's plans for peace, proposed ten months before the end of World War I. Terms called for fair treatment of Germany and redrawn boundaries, especially in Eastern Europe.

free enterprise The foundation of a capitalist economy, where private citizens, not government, make decisions to produce and market goods. This system in the United States operates with some government regulation to protect workers, customers, and the environment.

Freedmen's Bureau Organization created by President Lincoln and Congress that provided food, shelter, and medical care for freed slaves in the South. The bureau also helped needy whites, and ultimately provided medical care for more than a million people.

French and Indian War War fought in North America between the French and Native Americans and the British colonies, 1754–63.

futbol Throughout Latin America, the name of the game known here as soccer. It is the most popular sport in the world.

G

garifuna People of mixed African and Native American descent who live along the Atlantic coast of Central America, from Belize to Nicaragua.

gauge Distance between railroad tracks.

General Assembly Legislative branch of the government of North Carolina.

Geographical Information Systems (GIS) A computer system that records, stores, displays, and analyzes information about the features making up the earth's surface. GIS can generate two- or three-dimensional images of an area showing such features as hills, rivers, roads, and power lines.

Gettysburg Address President Abraham Lincoln's speech on November 19, 1863, dedicating the famous Pennsylvania battlefield cemetery of the Civil War.

glaciers Great sheets of ice moving slowly down a slope or valley.

Global Positioning System (GPS) Navigational aid that uses satellites to find absolute location.

global interdependence The theory that every country in the world is affected by what happens in other countries; much of the interdependence among nations is economic in nature, based on the production and trading of goods and services.

global warming The scientific theory that the earth is steadily getting hotter because the protective ozone layer is slowly but surely being eroded by man-made pollutants.

globalization The process of increasing the realtionships and interdependence of the world's markets and businesses.

"God Save the Queen" The anthem of Great Britain and Canada's national anthem until 1980.

gold rush A rush to newly discovered gold fields in pursuit of riches.

"Good Neighbor Policy" During Presidents Herbert Hoover's and Franklin Delano Roosevelt's administrations, a determination to cooperate with Latin American nations instead of using military power to bully them. This policy is generally considered to have been a success.

goods Something manufactured or produced for sale.

governor The highest executive in state government.

governor general Canada's official head of state. The queen of England's representative.

Grand Banks Shoal in the Atlantic Ocean southeast of Newfoundland. An area of historically rich fishing until recently.

Grand Canyon Colorado River gorge in the northwestern corner of Arizona. It is more than 1 mile (1.61 km) deep.

grasslands vegetation Exists in highland, temperate, and tropical climates.

Great Basin Low, dry region in the western United States between the Sierra Nevada and Wasatch Range.

Great Compromise An agreement during the Constitutional Convention (1787) in which delegates agreed that there would be two houses in the legislative branch of government. One house would have an equal number of representatives from each state. In the other house, representation would be based on population.

Great Depression The most devastating economic downturn in the nation's history. This depression began in October 1929 and raged throughout the 1930s.

Great Lakes Chain of five lakes—Superior, Michigan, Huron, Erie, and Ontario—in central North America.

Great Plains Plains west of the Central Lowlands in North America. Dry, with almost no trees.

grid A network of uniformly spaced horizontal and perpendicular lines (as for locating points on a map).

gross domestic product The total value of a country's goods and services produced in a given year.

Group of Eight (G-8) Organization of eight major industrial nations who meet periodically to discuss world economics and other issues. Established September 22, 1985. Members are Canada, France, Germany, Italy, Japan, Russia, the United Kingdom, and the United States.

guerrilla wars (guh·rill ·ah) Conflicts between groups of people who want change and dictators.

H

habitat The place or environment where a plant or animal naturally or normally lives and grows.

haciendas (ah·see·en·dahs) Large estates, usually in Spanish-speaking countries.

Harlem A famous Manhattan, New York City, community that was a center of African American culture in the early twentieth century.

harpoons Barbed spears or javelins used to hunt fish or whales.

Harvard College First college in the United States, founded in 1636.

haven A safe place.

hierarchy The classification of a group of people according to ability or to economic, social, or professional standing.

hieroglyphic Writing in picture symbols, not words.

high-tech industry Businesses that require specialized systems to make something.

highlands climate Determined by elevation—the higher a place is, the colder and windier.

Hispanic Latin Americans who speak Spanish or Portuguese. Those who have emigrated to the United States have come mainly from Middle America and South America.

Hispaniola (hiss·pan·nyo·lah) One of the four islands of the Greater Antilles in the Caribbean Sea. Site of the first permanent colony in the Americas (present-day Haiti and the Dominican Republic).

House of Burgesses Virginia's group of elected representatives.

House of Representatives One of two houses of the United States Congress.

hub The connection center of a transportation network. By 1860, Chicago had become a railroad hub for more than ten companies.

Hudson River School Art movement of the early nineteenth century in the United States characterized by landscape paintings of New York's Hudson Valley.

human characteristics of place Cultural and government elements of a place.

human-environmental interaction One of the Five Themes of Geography. Describes a place in terms of the environment's effect on humans who live there and how humans affect that environment.

human resources The workforce; also called human capital.

humid subtropical climate Cool, rainy summers and mild, rainy winters.

humid temperate grasslands Grasslands that grow on flat or rolling plains in fertile areas suitable for growing grain.

hunting and gathering Collection of food by killing game, catching fish, or eating edible wild plants.

hurricanes Tropical storms with winds of 74 miles (119 km) per hour or greater.

hydroelectric (high·drow·ee·leck·trik) The production of electricity by water power.

I

Ice Age A period of time that lasted for millions of years, when glaciers covered most of the earth.

ice hockey National sport of Canada.

igloos Inuit houses made of sod, wood, or stone when permanent or of blocks of snow or ice when temporary.

illiterates People who cannot read or write.

immigrants People who come to a country to take up permanent residence.

immigration The act of entering—and usually becoming established in—a country of which one is not a native for permanent residence. See emigration.

import To bring (as merchandise) into a place or country from another country. See export.

indentured servants English colonists to the Americas who agreed to work without pay in exchange for free passage across the Atlantic Ocean and room and board.

Independence Day The day the Declaration of Independence was adopted, July 4, 1776.

Indians Columbus's mistaken term for Native Americans he found in the

Caribbean. He thought he had landed in the Asian East Indies.

Indigo A deep blue dye made from xiquilite, a Central American plant.

Industrial Revolution Term for sweeping changes in the way goods were produced and the way people lived and worked. Began in England and spread throughout the world.

industrialized Any country with industries that produces goods its people need.

inequality Occurs when a few have more money or political power than others. Discrimination based on ancestry is a big factor.

infant mortality The number of infant deaths in a given time or place.

infrastructure The system of public works of a country, state, or region. Also, the resources—personnel, buildings, equipment—required for an activity.

Institutional Revolutionary Party (PRI) The political party that ruled Mexico from 1921 until 2000, when the National Action Party won the national election.

intermediate directions Directions between the cardinal directions—northeast, southeast, southwest, and northwest.

internal migration Moving from one place to another in the same country.

International Date Line Imaginary line, mainly along the 180°E longitude in the Pacific Ocean, that marks the boundary between one day and the next.

Internet Network of computer users and information.

Intolerable Acts American colonists' term for the laws passed by the British Parliament in response to the Boston Tea Party.

Inuit Native Americans who settled the far North of North America.

Iroquois Large Native American association of the Eastern Woodlands. Included the Cayuga, Mohawk, Oneida, Onondaga, Seneca, and Tuscarora people.

irrigation The watering of dry land by means of streams, canals, or pipes to grow crops.

isolationism A policy of national isolation by abstention from alliances and other international political and economic relations.

isthmus (Any narrow strip of land connecting large mainlands. Also called land bridges.

J

jai alai Court game similar to handball, popular in Cuba.

James Bay Project Hydroelectric power station in northern Quebec.

jazz Music derived from spirituals and blues.

Jim Crow laws Legal enforcement of discrimination against African Americans.

joint stock companies Special partnerships to raise monies for businesses.

judicial (branch) The United States Supreme Court and federal courts, which interpret laws passed by Congress.

Judiciary The branch of government that interprets the law; the court system.

Juries A group of citizens who listens to evidence given at civil and criminal trials and makes decisions as to the guilt or innocence of the accused person on trial.

K

Kansas-Nebraska Act (1854) Overturned the Missouri Compromise.

kayaks Inuit canoes.

Ku Klux Klan A post–Civil War secret society that supported white supremacy. These hate groups intimidated—and killed—African American men, women, and children.

L

land redistribution Division of large land holdings among the poorer citizens in an effort to relieve poverty.

landform A shape on the earth's surface, such as a plain, mountain, or valley.

landlocked Enclosed or nearly enclosed by land.

Landmarks Anything that easily recognizable, such as features of the landscape, monuments, buildings, or other structures.

"last best west" Phrase used in newspaper ads in 1885 urging people to come to Canada.

La Niña An irregularly occurring flow of unusually cold ocean temperatures in the eastern equatorial Pacific that is accompanied by wetter than normal conditions across the Pacific Northwest and dryer and warmer than normal conditions across much of the southern tier; winter temperatures are warmer than normal in the Southeast and cooler than normal in the Northwest. See el niño.

La Raza Cosmica (Cosmic Race) Complimentary term used by Mexicans to refer to the diversity of their population.

latitude Distance north or south of the Equator, expressed in degrees (°).

lava Molten rock under the earth's surface.

League of Nations President Woodrow Wilson's proposed international mediating body that offered provisions for the security of every country. His dream was turned down by the American public in the presidential election of 1920.

leeward Being in or facing the direction toward which the wind is blowing.

legislative (branch) Congress, which passes laws. There are two congressional houses, the Senate and the House of Representatives.

Legislature An elected or appointed body of people (representatives) with the responsibility and power to make laws for a province, state, or nation. See ASSEMBLY.

Lent The 40 days between Ash Wednesday and Easter. A time of penance and prayer.

Lexington and Concord Sites of the first battles of the American Revolution.

Lichen Plant-like growths of fungi and algae that are combined and form a crust-like growth on rocks or tree trunks.

life expectancy The average life span.

Line of Demarcation Drawn by Spain and Portugal dividing the Western Hemisphere. Spain kept lands west of the line, Portugal east of it.

literacy rate The degree to which a group of people can read and write.

literacy tests Used by some states to keep African Americans from voting by requiring people to read before being allowed to register to vote. The practice was outlawed by the Voting Rights Act passed in 1965. See also polls.

Livestock Farm animals, such as beef cattle, dairy cows, sheep, hogs,

chickens and turkeys.

location One of the Five Themes of Geography. Describes a place by its nearness to other places (relative location) or by its exact latitude and longitude (absolute location).

loess (less) Fertile, powdery, rockless soil found in North America, Europe, and Asia.

longitude Distance east or west of the prime meridian, expressed in degrees (°).

Lords Proprietors English owners of the colony of Carolina, present-day North Carolina and South Carolina.

loran Long-range navigation system used to find absolute location of a ship or airplane.

Lost Colony English colony attempted on Roanoke Island in modern-day North Carolina. All colonists disappeared before organizers returned. They had been delayed by England's sea battle with the Spanish Armada.

Louisiana Purchase In 1803, the United States acquired territory from France that would later become the states of Louisiana, Arkansas, Missouri, Minnesota, Iowa, Oklahoma, Kansas, Nebraska, North Dakota, South Dakota, Wyoming, Montana, and parts of Colorado.

Loyalists Colonists who sided with Great Britain in the American Revolution.

M

machetes Large, heavy knives used for cutting sugarcane and underbrush and as a weapon.

malnutrition Inadequate nutrition caused by poor diet.

Manifest Destiny The belief common in America in the 1800s that it was the fate of the United States to expand west to the Pacific Ocean; the phrase was coined in 1845 by journalist John L. O'Sullivan.

map key List of map symbols with explanation of what each symbol stands for.

map projection A way of representing a three-dimensional object on a two-dimensional surface.

Maple Leaf Canada's national flag.

maquiladora Mexican factory that assembles parts or raw materials from the United States into finished products; more than 1 million Mexicans work in the maquiladoras.

Mardi Gras Literally, Fat Tuesday, the last day of carnival celebration before Lent begins.

mariachi Mexican street band.

marimba A band of several people playing a xylophone at the same time.

Marine West Coast climate Cool, rainy summers and mild, rainy winters.

Marshall Plan United States aid to Europe after World War II.

mass production The making of goods in large quantities in factories, often using standard designs and assembly lines.

Massachusetts Fifty-fourth Most famous African American regiment of the Civil War.

Maya (migh·yah) Native Americans of Yucatán Peninsula in Mexico, Belize, and Guatemala.

Mayflower Compact (1620) Agreement among Pilgrims for a government of "just and equal laws" made aboard their ship, the Mayflower, before landing in Massachusetts.

mechanized farming Farming dependent on machinery to complete the work.

Mediterranean climate Hot, dry summers and mild, rainy winters.

megalopolis Thickly populated region encompassing more than one city.

mercantilism System of unequal trade established by England at the expense of the colonists.

mercenaries Soldiers who fight for money.

meridian Any line of longitude west or east of the prime meridian.

Mesa Central Middle region of Mexico—the central part of the Mexican Plateau. Mexico City and Puebla are located here.

Mesa del Norte Northernmost section of the Mexican Plateau. It lies between the Sierra Madre Oriental and the Sierra Madre Occidental.

mestizo (meh·stee·zoh) Person of mixed European and Native American ancestry. About half of the Mexican people are mestizo.

metropolitan Cities and the suburbs that surround them.

Mexican-American War (1846–48) Won by the United States. Under terms of the treaty, the United States acquired territory that would become Texas, California, Nevada, Utah, most of Arizona, and parts of New Mexico, Colorado, and Wyoming.

Mexican Revolution Initially, the uprising against Porfirio Diáz and his dictatorship; evolved into fighting between Mexicans with different ideas about Mexico's future.

mezcla Spanish for "mixture"; refers to the Mexican population.

Mid-Atlantic Eastern region of the United States: New York, New Jersey, Pennsylvania, Maryland, and the District of Columbia.

Mid-Atlantic Ridge Longest mountain chain in the world, 2.5 miles (4.03 km) underwater in the Atlantic Ocean.

Middle America Mexico, Central America, and the Caribbean Islands.

Middle Passage Long ocean voyage from Africa to America that brought slaves to the New World.

migrate To move from one region to another.

militia Army of citizens who come together during a crisis.

minerals Natural substances, such as iron, copper, or salt, obtained by digging.

minutemen American colonial citizen soldiers who would show up at a moment's notice when fighting broke out.

missions Self-contained villages built by missionaries to try to convert Native Americans to Christianity.

Missionaries People sent to another place to spread a religion.

Mississippi River Longest river in the United States, flows from north central Minnesota to the Gulf of Mexico.

Missouri Compromise (1820) Agreement in Congress admitting Missouri to the Union as a slave state and Maine as a nonslave state.

Mixtec Primary Native American language spoken in the Mexican state of Oaxaca.

Mojave Desert Desert of the Great Basin in the western United States.

monarchy Undivided rule or absolute sovereignty by a single person.

Monopoly Control by one business over the production or sale of a good or service.

monotheism Belief in one god.

Monroe Doctrine Policy begun by President James Monroe prohibiting European involvement in the affairs of the Western Hemisphere.

Mormons Members of the Church of Jesus Christ of Latter-day Saints.

mosaic Decoration made with small

pieces of variously colored material to form pictures or patterns. Canadiens compare their country to a mosaic.

movement One of the Five Themes of Geography. Describes a place by its movement of people, goods, and ideas.

mulattoes People of mixed European and African ancestry.

multinational Of or relating to more than two nationalities (a multinational society) or more than two nations (a multinational alliance); or having business divisions in more than two countries (a multinational corporation).

municipal Referring to local self-government of towns and cities.

mural A large picture painted directly on the walls and ceilings of buildings.

muskeg Wet and spongy flat lowland areas that are part of the Canadian Shield region of northern North America.

N

NAACP The National Association for the Advancement of Colored Persons, an organization that won a series of court cases that eventually overturned Plessy v. Ferguson.

NAFTA North American Free Trade Agreement between Canada, the United States, and Mexico.

Nahuatl Primary Native American language spoken in east central Mexico.

National Action Party Mexican political party that defeated the Institutional Revolutionary Party in 2000.

National Park System Created by the United States Congress in 1916. There are more than 384 acres in the system for recreation.

National Road Connected Maryland with territory north of the Ohio River. This improvement in transportation encouraged people to settle in the Midwest.

nationalized Ownership of industries taken over by the government.

Native Americans First people in the Western Hemisphere, not including the Inuit.

naturalized Those born in other countries who have been made citizens of the United States.

NATO An Alliance of nations, inlcuding the United States, Canada, and the United Kingdom, as well as other European nations. It was created to counter the Communist threat of the Soviet Union in Europe during the Cold War.

Navigation The process of plotting or directing the course of a vessel, usually a ship or airplane.

neighborhoods Communities moved into by immigrants to America that reminded them of home, where people spoke their language and shared their culture.

neutral Any country not engaged with any other country that is at war.

New Deal The legislative and administrative program of President Franklin D. Roosevelt designed to promote economic recovery and social reform during the 1930s.

New England Region in the northeastern United States: Connecticut, Maine, Massachusetts, Vermont, New Hampshire, and Rhode Island.

New France Possessions of France in North America before 1763.

New Laws of the Indies Spanish laws passed in the early 1500s banning the slavery of Native Americans.

nonrenewable resource Fuel, such as coal, gas, and natural gas, formed in the earth from plant or animal remains. See renewable resource.

NORAD The North American Aerospace Defense Command (NORAD). NORAD is a joint United States and Canadian organization charged with the missions of aerospace warning and aerospace control for North America. Aerospace warning includes the monitoring of man-made objects in space, and the detection and warning of attack against North America whether by aircraft, missiles, or space vehicles.

north arrow On most maps, a small arrow that points to the North Pole.

Northern Hemisphere The half of the earth north of the Equator.

Northwest Passage Rumored link between Atlantic and Pacific Oceans. It was never found.

nuclear weapon A device, such as a bomb or warhead, with great explosive power coming from the release of atomic energy.

Nunavut Newest territory of Canada created for the Inuit people. Also, Inuit word that means "our land."

O

obsidian Dark natural glass formed by cooling of molten lava.

"O Canada" Canada's national anthem.

oligarchy A government in which a small group exercises control, especially for corrupt and selfish purposes.

Oregon Trail The primary westward route across the country used by settlers of the Northwest in the 1840s and 1850s.

Otomi Primary Native American language spoken near Mexico City and in the Mexican states of Puebla and Veracruz.

overfishing When more fish are caught in a fishing ground than are hatched yearly.

override A bill becomes law without the president's signature; an override occurs when, after a president has vetoed a bill, Congress passes the bill with at least two-thirds of the votes in each house.

P

Pacific Rim Countries in or bordering on the Pacific Ocean.

Panama Canal Ship canal across the Isthmus of Panama built by the United States. Opened August 1914.

paracaidistas Rural Mexicans who move to Mexico City in huge numbers each year in search of a better life.

parallels Any lines of latitude north or south of the Equator.

pardon Forgiveness granted by the president to lawbreakers.

Parliament Supreme legislative body in Canada and Great Britain.

parliamentary government A system of government having the real executive power vested in a cabinet composed of members of the legislature who are individually and collectively responsible to the legislature.

party An organized political group.

patents Licenses giving inventors exclusive rights to make, use, or sell their inventions.

Patriots Colonists who wanted to be independent of England.

patron saint Special guardian of a person, place, or activity.

Petroleum A substance that occurs naturally formed from the remains of animals and plants that lived millions of years ago in a marine (water) environment. Over time, heat and pressure from layers of mud and rock helped the remains turn into crude oil . The word "petroleum" means "rock oil" or "oil from the earth." It also refers to crude oil and oil products in all forms. When distilled, it yields gasoline, kerosene, paraffin, and fuel oil, and other products which are used in fuels, lubricating oils, asphalt, and other products.

permafrost Permanently frozen soil below ground level, found in arctic regions.

physical map Shows landforms and elevation.

physical characteristics of place Natural features and landforms of a place.

Piedmont Rolling hills connecting the mountains and the Coastal Plain on the East Coast.

Pilgrims English religious group persecuted for not joining the Church of England. They founded Plymouth Colony.

place One of the Five Themes of Geography. Describes a spot on the earth by its physical (landforms and climate) and human (cultural and government) characteristics.

plank roads Made from wooden boards, built along stretches where heavy wagons traveled regularly. These roads were common in this country during the 1850s.

plantation (plan·tay·shun) Large farming estate where mainly one crop is grown.

plate tectonics Theory that the continents move around on large plates of rock. Compare continental drift.

Plateau A relatively flat highland.

plaza Public square in a city or town.

Plessy v. Ferguson 1896 United States Supreme Court decision making segregation legal.

political map Gives information about nations, states, provinces, counties, or cities.

polls The places where votes are cast or recorded. The Ku Klux Klan tried to keep African Americans away from the polls after the Civil War. See also literacy tests.

poll taxes Payments required of people who wanted to vote. The Voting Rights Act of 1965 made this illegal.

polytheism Belief in more than one god.

popular vote Vote by citizens. In the presidential election in the United States, citizens vote for members of the electoral college.

population distribution The statistical detailing of distinct populations within a certain area, state, or country, usually expressed in map or graph form.

population growth rate The percentage of population increase in a specific place over a specific period of time.

population profile Graph that shows the characteristics of a country's population.

Porfiriato The name for the long rule (1876–1911) in Mexico of the caudillo Porfirio Díaz, a mestizo hero in the fight against the French. He was toppled by the Mexican Revolution.

postindustrial Describes today's society. Technology that produces knowledge and information.

prejudices Negative opinions formed beforehand or without knowledge or examination of the facts; bias.

prairie Land that has deep fertile soil, tall coarse grasses, and few trees.

precedents Standards for others to follow.

precipitation A deposit on the earth of hail, mist, rain, sleet, or snow.

president Head of the executive branch.

presidential government A system of government, as in the United States, in which the president is constitutionally independent of the legislature.

primary industries Those industries that gather and sell natural resources—oil, natural gas, minerals, timber, and farm crops.

prime meridian Line of longitude (0°) from which longitude east and west is measured.

prime minister Chief executive of a parliamentary government.

print media Newspapers, books, and magazines.

provinces Political divisions of a country, as in Canada, similar to states in the United States.

Prosperity Economic growth and high employment rates; an economic boom.

public opinion The views of the people on a topic.

pueblo Dwelling of Native Americans in southwestern United States. Also the name used by the Spanish for the people who lived there.

Puritans English religious group persecuted for their faith. They founded Massachusetts bay Colony.

Q

quaternary economic activities Those activities responsible for collecting, processing, and manipulating information; for example, business management and data processing.

quetzal A bird sacred to the Maya; an endangered species that cannot live in captivity, and is thus a symbol for freedom.

quotas Laws limiting the number of immigrants.

R

racism The belief that one race is superior to another.

radar Navigation system that uses radio waves to detect and locate objects.

rain shadow effect Exists when mountain peaks block rain from the leeward side.

ratify To approve and sanction formally. A majority of a state's votes for an amendment, making it an article of their state constitution or the United States Constitution.

rebelled To have resisted, refused to support, or opposed with force a government or ruler.

Reconstruction President Lincoln's plan to reorganize and rebuild the defeated South after this country's Civil War.

recycling Discarding glass, paper, or metal for reuse.

redistribution of wealth The shifting wealth from a rich minority to a poor majority. Income redistribution has been the focus of some international development efforts.

reforestation The action of renewing forest cover by planting seeds or young trees. See deforestation.

reform To make changes that improves a government or organization.

refugee A person who flees to a foreign country or power to escape danger or persecution.

reggae Jamaican music with chants and a strong, steady beat that is popular throughout the Caribbean.

region One of the Five Themes of Geography. A region is a particular place on earth that contains many similar characteristics, such as landforms, climate, natural resources, language, and politics, among others.

relative location Approximate location found by using nearby references.

religion A personal set or institutionalized system of religious

attitudes, beliefs, and practices.

religious persecution Being treated unfairly because of one's religious beliefs.

Religious Toleration Act Colonial Maryland law giving religious freedom to most faiths.

renewable resource One that is capable of being replaced by natural ecological cycles or sound business practices. See nonrenewable resource.

repeal Revoke or undo a law through legislation.

representative democracy That system of government in which the many are represented by persons chosen from among them, usually by election. See republic.

Representatives People selected or elected to stand for and vote for the wishes of others at a meeting or convention. See DELEGATES.

republic Form of government in which people elect their leaders by voting. See representative democracy.

Republican Party One of two major political parties in the United States, formed in 1854 by opponents of slavery.

reservations Tracts of land set aside by the government beginning in 1871. Native Americans were relocated to these reservations, and some of their descendants continue to live there today.

resistance Opposing something that you disapprove of or disagree with.

retirement community Group of retired people living together within a larger society.

retreated Having withdrawn all troops to a new position in order to escape the enemy's forces or after a defeat.

revolution Overthrow of an existing political system and its replacement with another.

Ring of Fire A rim of volcanoes, from Japan to Alaska to Chile, encircling the Pacific Ocean.

ritual Ceremonies or traditions used in a place of worship or for special occasions.

rivalry Competition.

rock 'n' roll Music derived from jazz, rhythm and blues, country, and gospel.

Rocky Mountains Mountain range extending from northern Alaska to New Mexico. Also western region of the United States: Colorado, Wyoming, Montana, Idaho, Utah, and Nevada.

Rough Riders Members of the 1st U. S. Volunteer Cavalry regiment in the Spanish American War commanded by Theodore Roosevelt.

royal proclamation Orders publicly announced by the king or queen in a monarchy.

rural Open land usually used for agriculture.

S

sapodilla Central American tree that produces chicle, which is used to make chewing gum.

sanctions Measures taken by one or more nations to apply pressure on another nation to conform to international law or opinion. Such measures usually include restrictions on or withdrawal of trade, diplomatic ties, and membership in international organizations.

scalawags White Southerners who supported Reconstruction after the American Civil War, often for private gain.

scale Relative size as shown on a map, such as one inch = 100 miles (161 km).

scarcity Limited resources; when society does not have enough resources to produce enough to meet people's wants.

scientific farming Applying the findings of science to farming.

seasons The four quarters into which the year is divided: spring, summer, autumn, winter.

secede To withdraw from an organization. Southern states seceded from the Union in the early 1860s, setting off the Civil War.

Second Continental Congress (1775) Chose George Washington to head the Revolutionary War against the British.

secondary economic activities Those activities in which workers take raw materials and produce something as a finished product; for example, manufacturing.

secondary industries Those industries that make goods from primary products.

secular Not controlled by a religious body or concerned with religious or spiritual matters.

sediment Mud and soil particles small enough for river water to carry.

segregated Practicing the separation or isolation of a race, class, or ethnic group by discriminatory means, as in a segregated society.

Senate One of two houses of the United States Congress.

Separatists Those who wish Quebec to be separate from Canada.

separate but equal The idea, approved by the United States Supreme Court in Plessy v. Ferguson (1896), that the entrenched policies of segregation were legal, that segregation did not violate African American rights under the Constitution.

service industries Productive or profit-making enterprises that help people and businesses, such as restaurants, banks, and schools.

sharecropping Financial arrangement whereby former slaves and poor white farmers rented farmland and shared a portion of the harvest with the landowners. Sharecroppers, however, rarely made a profit, and the system prevented African Americans from getting out of poverty.

Sherman's March Union General William T. Sherman's devastating Civil War campaign from Atlanta to Savannah, Georgia, in 1864.

Silicon Valley California headquarters for computer companies.

slash-and-burn farming Clearing land for planting by cutting and burning vegetation.

slavery Owning people as property.

smelting Using furnaces to separate metal from mined ore.

Smithsonian Institution Collection of many famous museums in Washington, D.C.

smog Fog made heavier and darker by smoke and chemical fumes.

snowshoes Light oval frames strengthened by crosspieces and strung with thongs. Allows someone to walk on soft snow without sinking.

socialist One who advocates or practices socialism: a system or condition of society in which the means of production are owned and controlled by the state.

Social Security A U. S. government program established in 1935 to include old-age and survivor's insurance, contributions to state unemployment insurance, and old-age assistance. This was one of FDR's New Deal programs.

software The entire set of programs, procedures, and related documentation associated with a computer system.

Southeast Eastern region of the United States: Virginia, Tennessee, West

Virginia, Kentucky, North Carolina, South Carolina, Georgia, Florida, Alabama, Mississippi, Louisiana, and Arkansas.

Southern Hemisphere The half of the earth south of the Equator.

Sovereignty A country's power and ability to rule itself and manage its own affairs.

Spanish Armada Fleet of war ships that invaded England and was defeated, beginning Great Britain's domination of the Atlantic Ocean and eventually North America.

spawn Refers to fish laying eggs.

spirituals Emotional religious songs developed by African Americans.

St. Lawrence Seaway Waterway of locks, canals, and the St. Lawrence River that permits passage of deep-draft vessels between the Atlantic Ocean and the Great Lakes.

Stamp Act Passed by the British Parliament in 1765 imposing taxes on the colonists.

standard of living In economics, the measure of consumption and welfare of a country, community, class, or person. Individual standard-of-living expectations are heavily influenced by the income and consumption of other people in similar jobs.

Stanley Cup National Hockey League championship trophy.

state government Makes state laws. Shares power with the federal government.

steelpan Music from the Caribbean played by hammering on oil drum bottoms.

steppe Level and treeless areas in regions of extreme temperature range and loess soil.

steppe climate Not as dry as desert climates. Sometimes called semiarid regions.

stereotype Something conforming to a fixed or general pattern.

stock A share in business ownership.

storm surges Large waves created by hurricane winds that can cause enormous destruction and flooding.

strikes The stoppage of work by a number of workers with the purpose of reaching a certain end.

strip mine An efficient, though controversial, method of extracting coal by stripping soil from veins of coal. Environmentalists say that this method causes erosion.

subarctic climate Found in northern Canada and most of Alaska. Very cold but warm enough for trees to grow.

subjects People who are under the rule of another or others, such as a king or queen in a monarchy.

subregion A subdivision of a region; one of the primary divisions of a biogeographic region.

subsistence agriculture Farming or a system of farming that produces a minimum and often inadequate return to the farmer.

suburbs Communities on the edge of cities.

suburb Small community that is connected to a large city.

Sun Belt Warm states stretching from California to Florida.

supply The act or process of filling a want or need; the quantities of goods or services offered for sale at a particular time or at one price. See demand.

Supreme Court (United States) Highest judicial court in the land.

surplus More than of what is needed or required. See SCARCITY.

surrendered/surrender When soldiers give up fighting.

sustainable resource A resource harvested or used in such a way that it is not depleted or permanently damaged.

sweatshops A shop or factory in which workers are employed for long hours at low wages and under unhealthy conditions.

symbols Anything that stands for something else, such as a blue line standing for a highway on a map.

T

tariffs Taxes imposed by a government on imported goods.

taro Tropical plant grown for its edible tuber, similar to a potato.

tax A fee charged by a government on goods, services, or income.

telecommuter One who works at home via telephone and computer.

temperate Having a moderate climate.

temperate climate Characterized by a lack of extremes in temperature.

tenement houses Rundown apartment buildings.

tepee (tee·pee) Skin-covered tent once used by Native Americans of the Great Plains.

terraced fields Series of horizontal ridges made in a hillside to increase arable land, conserve moisture, and minimize erosion.

territories Political divisions in Canada with less power than provinces.

terrorism Generally thought to be the use, or threatened use, of violence, including killing or injuring people or taking hostages, to intimidate a government in order to achieve a goal, usually political. Terrorist acts take many forms and occur all over the world. They are not confined to one place, one religion, or one form.

terrorists Individuals or groups, some sponsored by governments, who systematically use violence in an attempt to make nations change their ways of doing things.

tertiary economic activities Those activities promoting, distributing, selling, or using what is made from raw materials; for example, education, finance, office work, and retailing.

textiles Machine-produced cloth.

theocracy A government that claims to rule with divine authority. Iran is an example.

Thirteenth Amendment The legislative change to the Constitution in 1865 that abolished slavery in the United States.

Three-Fifths Compromise An agreement reached by delegates to the Constitutional Convention in which enslaved African Americans would be counted as three fifths of an individual for purposes of population.

Tidewater The area along the coast where waters rise and fall each day from ocean tides.

tiendas Mexican shops.

Tierra Caliente Or Hot Land. Central American elevation zone that extends from sea level up to about 2,500 feet. Temperatures are hot, and the main crops are bananas, sugarcane, and rice.

Tierra Fria Or Cold Land. Central American elevation zone that extends from about 6,000 feet to 12,000 feet above sea level. Main activities here are growing potatoes and grains, and grazing livestock.

Tierra Helada Or Icy Land. Central American elevation zone above 12,000 feet.

Tierra Templada Or Temperate Land. Central American elevation zone that extends from about 2,500 feet to 6,000 feet. Most people in this region live in

this zone, where temperatures are mild. Major crops are coffee, corn, wheat, and vegetables.

time zone A geographical region within which the same standard time is used.

toleration Allowing people to follow their own beliefs, especially religious.

toll A fee charged for the use of roads or bridges.

Toltecs The people that dominated central and southern Mexico prior to the Aztecs.

topographic Of, relating to, or concerned with topography.

topography The art or practice of graphic delineation in detail usually on maps or charts of natural and man-made features of a place or region, especially in a way to show their relative positions and elevations.

tornado A violent destructive swirling wind accompanied by a funnel-shaped cloud that progresses in a narrow path over the land.

totalitarian Of or relating to a political regime based on subordination of the individual to the state and strict control of all aspects of the life and productive capacity of the nation, especially by force. See dictator.

trade Dealings between persons, groups, or countries; the business of buying and selling or bartering commodities.

trade deficit When one country buys more goods from other countries than it sells.

trade surplus When one country sells more goods to other countries than it buys.

trade winds Those that blow almost constantly toward the Equator from the northeast.

trading partners Countries that trade closely with each other.

Trail of Tears Forced migration of Cherokee Native Americans from the Southeast to Indian Territory in 1830.

transcontinental railroad The first rail system that connected the east and west coasts of America. The Union Pacific Railroad, laying track westward from Omaha, Nebraska, met the Central Pacific Railroad, laying track eastward from Sacramento, California, on May 10, 1869, at Promontory, Utah.

transnational Extending or going beyond national boundaries. Transnational corporations are those that do business with other countries.

Treaty of Paris 1763 treaty. France ceded most of its North American empire to England.

Treaty of Paris 1783 treaty between the United States of American and Great Britain. Ended the American Revolutionary War.

tribal governments A governing body of a tribe, community, village, or group of Native Americans or Alaska Natives.

tributaries Rivers or brooks feeding larger rivers or brooks or lakes.

Tropic of Cancer Latitude 23.5°N that marks the northern boundary of the Tropics.

Tropic of Capricorn Latitude 23.5°S that marks the southern boundary of the Tropics.

tropical grasslands Grasslands that grow in lowland areas of the Tropics.

tropical rain forests Marked by lofty broad-leafed evergreens forming a continuous canopy.

tropical rain forest climate Annual rainfall of at least 100 inches (254 cm). Alternates between hot and rainy seasons.

tropical savanna climate Alternates between rainy and dry seasons.

Tropics The region lying between the Tropic of Cancer (23.5°N) and the Tropic of Capricorn (23.5°S), where temperatures remain hot all year.

truck farms Farms that produce vegetables for the market.

trust territories Territories supervised by other nations. Guam and American Samoa are territories of the United States.

Tsotsil Native American language; one of three branches of Maya spoken in the Mexican state of Chiapas.

tsunamis (soo·nah·meez) Huge destructive ocean waves caused by earthquakes and volcanic eruptions.

tundra Vast, treeless plain in the northern parts of North America, Asia, and Europe.

tundra vegetation Includes lichens, mosses, algae, and—briefly in the short summers—wild flowers.

tundra climate Arctic or subarctic with a layer of permafrost below ground.

Tzeltal Native American language; one of three branches of Maya spoken in the Mexican state of Chiapas.

U

umiaks Open Inuit boat made of a wooden frame covered with animal hide.

Underground Railroad Escape system by which fugitive slaves were secretly helped to reach the North or Canada.

union A group of workers who are organized for the purpose of gaining better wages, hours, and other benefits.

Union The northern states that fought to preserve the United States during the Civil War.

Union Jack United Kingdom flag.

United Nations An international organization established in October 1945 whose purpose was, and is, to maintain international peace and security.

United States Constitution In 1787, the Articles of Confederation were dropped in favor of this document, which emphasized a stronger national government and the rights of the individual.

urban Of, relating to, characteristic of, or constituting a city.

urbanization Process by which the proportion of a population living in or around towns and cities increases through migration as the agricultural population decreases. A relatively recent phenomenon, dating back only about 150 years to the beginning of the Industrial Revolution.

V

vegetation Plant life.

veto To reject a bill passed by Congress.

vice president Second in command to the president; also serves as president of the Senate.

Virgin of Guadalupe The patron saint of Mexico.

volcano A vent in the crust of the earth from which usually molten or hot rock and steam come forth.

voluntary migration To move from one country, place, or locality to another as an act of free will. See forced migration.

W

War Hawks Congressmen who urged President James Madison to wage war against Great Britain prior to the War of 1812.

War of 1812 War between the United States and Great Britain in 1812.

Warsaw Pact A Cold War Alliance between the Societ Uion and Central and Eastern European Communist nations.

Washington, D.C. The capital of the United States.

water pollution The contamination of waters, especially with man-made waste.

watershed A region or area bounded peripherally by a divide and draining ultimately to a particular watercourse or body of water.

wattle and daub A construction method for some Native American homes. Wattle is poles interwined with twigs, reeds, or branches, used for walls and roofs. Daub is the mud or clay or other substance that is smeared over the wattle to create a solid surface.

weather State of the atmosphere with respect to heat or cold, wetness or dryness, calm or storm, clearness or cloudiness.

Western Hemisphere The half of the earth west of the prime meridian.

wigwams Native American huts in North America having a framework of poles overlaid with tree bark or animal hides.

Wilderness Road Opened up over the Appalachian Mountains into Kentucky by Daniel Boone.

windward Being in or facing the direction from which the wind is blowing.

World Bank An autonomous agency that has a functional relationship with the United nations. Provides loans and technical assistance for economic development projects in developing member countries; encourages co-financing for projects from other public and private sources.

World War I War fought in Europe between the Central Powers and the Allied Powers, 1914–1918.

World War II War fought in Europe, North Africa, Asia, and the Pacific Ocean between the Allies and the Axis, 1939–1945

Y

Yucatec Maya Primary Native American language spoken in the Yucatán Peninsula.

Z

Zapatista National Liberation Army Anti-NAFTA protesters, mainly Mayan farmers from Chiapas, who are concerned with issues of self-government and the survival of Native American cultural identity.

Zapotec Primary Native American language spoken in the Mexican state of Oaxaca.

zero growth No increase in population in a specific area over a given time.

CREDITS

Acknowledgements

52, Excerpt from *Five Letters: 1519–1526* by Hernándo Cortés, translated by J. Bayard Morris, Copyright 8 (196C). Reprinted by permission of W.W. Norton & Company; 199–200, Excerpt from *The Promised Land* by Mary Antin, Copyright 8 1912. Reprinted by permission of Houghton Mifflin Company. All rights reserved; 201, Excerpt from *The Jungle* by Upton Sinclair, Copyright 8 1971. Reprinted by permission of R. Bentley; 300, Excerpt from *Wooden Ship*, Copyright 8 1978 by Jan Adkins. Reprinted by permission of Houghton Mifflin Company. All rights reserved; 320, Excerpt from *The Treeless Plains*, Copyright 8 1967 by Glen Rounds. Reprinted by permission of Holiday House; 387, Taken from *A Prairie Boy's Summer*, Copyright 8 1975 by William Kurelek, published by Tundra Books; 493, Excerpt from *The Brief and Summary Relation of the Lords of New Spain* by Alonso de Zorita, translated and edited by Benjamin Keen, page 213, Copyright 8 1963. Used by permission of Rutgers University press.

Index
Infodex, Raleigh, North Carolina

Maps
Mapping Specialists Limited

Photographs
AP.....................AP/Wide World Photos
BC.....................Bettmann/Corbis
DJ.....................Dan Johns
GSPA..............Gibbs Smith, Publisher Archives
GCNY.............The Granger Collection, New York
IM.....................Jim Akchedak
JIC....................© 2007 Jupiter Images Corporation
LOC..................Library of Congress Prints and Photographs Division
NCC.................North Carolina Collection
NCSU...............North Carolina State University
NCT.................North Carolina Division of Travel and Tourism
NGS.................National Geographic Image Collection
NW...................North Wind Picture Archives
PAM.................Provincial Archives of Manitoba
SS.....................Image Copyright of Artist, 2007 used under license from Shutterstock, Inc.

Prelims: ii (t) Kansas State Historical Society, Topeka, (b) Detail, Oklahoma Arts Council/John Jernigan; 90 "Christopher Columbus," by Sebastiano del Piombo, Metropolitan Museum of Art; iii (t) NW, (m) Layne Kennedy/Corbis, (b) State Historical Society of South Dakota; iv (t) BC (b) LOC; v (t) SS/R, (m) SS/Ronnie Howard, (b) E. C. Stangler/Photophile, (br) Bishop Museum, Honolulu; vi (t) Hulton-Deutsch Collection/Corbis(bl) SS/July Flower, (br) SS/Sergey r; vii (t) The Grand Tenochtitlan (1945), by Diego Rivera, National Palace, Mexico City, Robert Frerck/Odyssey, (br) The Newark Museum/Art Resource, (mr) Demetrio Carrasco/JAI/Corbis, viii (t) SS/Christophe Testi/CreativeShot, (b) Frans Lemmens/The Image Bank/Getty Images x Rusdy Faris/Corbis.

Chapter One: 2 (t) AP/Bob Jordan, (b) SS/Michael Shake; 3 (t) AP/Bob Jordan, (b) AP/Ric Feld, (br) SS/Thomas E. Fawls; 4 (t) AP/Jars Sailors; 4-5 Jocelyn Augustino/FEMA; 5 (t) Buddy Mays/Corbis, (m) Phil Schermeister/Corbis, (b) AP/Eric Gay; 6 (t) Annie Griffiths Belt/Corbis, (b) Folly Mooney/Corbis, (m) AP/Rs; Vasquez, (b) Tim Thompson/Corbis, (br) Little Rock Convention & Visitors Bureau; 8 (t) AP/Carrizo Ouoro; 9 (t) AP/Richard Cummins, (m) AP/Beth Keiser, (m) Kevin Fleming/Corbis; 10 (t) Vian Photos, (inset) JA/NCSU, (m) Dallas & John Heaton/Corbis, (br) Jon Hicks/Corbis; 11 (t) David Muench/Corbis, (inset) NCMH, (b) AP/Don Heupel; 11 (t) Craig Aurness/Corbis, (m) Richard T. Nowitz/Corbis, (b) BC, (inset) AP/Joel Andrews; 11-12 James P. Blair/Corbis, 12 (m) James P. Blair/Corbis, (inset) Buddy Mays/Corbis; 15 (t) Phil Schermeister/Corbis, (b) SS/priam_68; 16 Orange County Economic Development Commission.

Chapter Two: 18–19 NASA; 20 (inset) AP/NASA, (b) AP/Peter Fredin; 22 NH/NCSU; 25 AP/Daniel Miller; 26 (t) BC; 26–27 (t) BC, (t) NOAA, Gift of Mr and Mrs. Maurice R. Smith; 27 (t) William Hubbell/Woodlin Camp, (t) Courtesy of Interograph Corporation, 31 (inset) GSPA

Chapter Three: 34 (t) SS/Natalia Bratslavsky, (b) SS/Frank Boellmann; 36 Gary Braasch/Corbis; 37 NASA; 38-39 NGS; 40 (t) SS/Vesn Bogaerts; 41 NASA; 42 (m) Carl Pellegrini Photography, (b) Annie Griffiths Belt/Corbis; 44 SS/Christophe Testi; 46 SS/Hege Nijeron; 47 DJ/NCSU; 48 SS/Christa DeRidder; 50 Neal Hutcheson/NCSU; 52 Scott T. Smith/Corbis; 57 SS/Robert O. Brown Photography; 53 (inset) LOC; 55 (s, b) William Russ/NCT; 57 NASA.

Chapter Four: 58–59 Tom Morrison/South America Pictures; 60–61 G. Dagli-Orti (Paris); 62 Gary Rasmussen; 64 SS/Marcn Regalia; 66 DJ/NCSU; 67 Gary Rasmussen; 68 (t) M, JIC, (remaining) Kansas State Historical Society, Topeka; 69 BC; 70 (t) 218 US Church Archives; 72 SS/SGC; 73 (inset) JIC, (b) Arizona Historical Society; 75 Courtesy Cahokia: City of the Sun; 76 GSPA; 77 Geoffrey Clements/Corbis; 78 GSPA; 80-81 North Carolina Museum of History; 82 Gary Rasmussen; 83 GSPA; 83 NCT.

Chapter Five: 88–89 Oklahoma Arts Council/John Jernigan; 90 "Christopher Columbus," by Sebastiano del Piombo, Metropolitan Museum of Art; 91 NW; 92 (d) Organization of American States Photo Library, (bl) SS/Piotr Sikora; 92-93 & 93 (tr) Rare Book Collection, UNC-Chapel Hill Library; 93 (r) NGS; Helgason; 94 (t) JIC, (t inset) Archivo Iconografico/Corbis, 95 (t) Oklahoma Arts Council/John Jernigan; 95 NW; 96 The Institute of Texas Cultures; 97 GCNY; 98 GSPA; 98-99 Peter Richard Cummins; 100 Nik Wheeler/Corbis 101 LOC; 102 (t) GCNY, (b) Peter Harheldt/Arnett/s/Corbis, 103 Robert E. Gesseler, A.W.S., W.H.S. Courtesy of PNC Bank, Delaware; 107 (t) Gary Rasmussen, (b) JIC; 108 (t) BC, (b) LOC; 109 (t) Jerry Cotten/NCC, (r) Maryland Historical Society; 110 Archive Photos; 111 BC; 112 GCNY; 113 New Hampshire Historical Society; 116 (bl) "William Penn," by Francis Place/Historical Society of Pennsylvania, 117 (inset) Reprinted by permission; 119 (t) AP/Chuck Burton, (m) AP, (b) AP/Ross Taylor; 121 Pilgrim Hall Museum, Plymouth, Massachusetts.

Chapter Six: 122-123 Yale University Art Gallery; 124-125 PoodlesRock/Corbis; 127 Richard T. Nowitz/Corbis; 128 (m) Pilgrim Society/Pilgrim Hall Museum, (b) LOC; 128 (b) Photography Collection, Miriam and Ira D. Wallach Division of Art, Prints and Photographs, The New York Public Library, Astor, Lenox and Tilden Foundations; (br) LOC; 130 BC; 132 GSPA; 133 Archives Iconografico/Corbis; 134 (t) GSPA, (inset) Courtesy of the Massachusetts Historical Society; BC; 135 National Archives; 136 (inset) Courtesy of the Massachusetts Historical Society; BC; 137 BC; 138 (b, br) LOC; 139 LOC; 142 NW; 143 LOC; 144 NW; 145 Amon Carter Museum, Fort Worth, Texas; 146 (t) LOC, (inset) NARA; 149 LOC.

Chapter Seven: 150-151 United States Capitol Historical Society; 153 (t) National Archives and Records Administration, (b) BC; 154 Monticello/Thomas Jefferson Foundation; 155 BC; 156 Independence National Historical Park; 158 Archive Iconografico/Corbis, 159 (tl) Archive Iconografico/Corbis; 160 BC; 161 "A View of New Orleans taken from the Plantation of Marigny," (1803), by Boquete de Woiseri, also known as "The American Eagle Over New Orleans," Chicago Historical Society 1932.0018; 162 (m) NGS; 163 Painting "Lewis and Clark: The Departure from St. Charles. May 21, 1804" by Gary R. Lucy, Courtesy of the Gary R. Lucy Gallery, Inc., Washington, MO – www.garylucy.com; 163 (t) Missouri Historical Society, (b) State Historical Society of South Dakota, (br) Rare Book Collection, UNC-Chapel Hill Library; 164 BC; 165 LOC; 167 "The Trail of Tears," by Robert Lindneux, Woolaroc Museum, Bartlesville, Okla.; 169 BC; 170 (t) California State Library, Sacramento, (inset) Science Museum/P. T. Andrew; 171 Layne Kennedy/Corbis.

Chapter Eight: 174-175 National Park Service; 176 BC; 177 LOC; 178 BC; 179 Manuscripts, Archives and Rare Books Division, Schomburg Center for Research in Black Culture, The New York Public Library, Astor, Lenox and Tilden Foundations; 180 Sophia Smith Collection, Smith College; 181 Kansas State Historical Society, painting by John Steuart Curry; 182 LOC; 183 Fort Sumter National Monument; 184 (bl) Museum of the Confederacy, (br) Corbis; 185 (t, mr) BC, (ml) Southern Historical Collection, UNC-Chapel Hill Library; 186-187 LOC; 188 LOC; 190 BC; 191 LOC; 192 (bl) JA/NCSU, Courtesy of the Nashville Depot, (br) BC; 193 BC; 194 LOC; 195 (t) SS/Jodi Hutchison, (tr) State Archives; 196 Granger; 199 Granger.

Chapter Nine: 200-201 Utah State Historical Society; 202 (t) David Muench/Corbis, (b) Kentucky Historical Society; 203 (t) GCNY, (b) NCC; 204 (t) GSPA; 205 LOC; 207 (tl) Gary Rasmussen, (br) BC; 208-209 Albany Institute of History & Art; 210 BC; 211 Rare Book Collection of N. C.; 210 Archive of N. C.; 212 (b) Corbis, (inset) Bob Brown/Progressive Image/Corbis; 213 SS/Joy Brown; 214 (inset) indians, (b) indians; 215 BC; 216 (inset) Corbis, (inset) Karen Tweedy-Holmes/Corbis, (br) Little Rock Convention & Visitors Bureau; 217 (b) Andrew J. Russell Collection, Oakland Museum of California; (br) Underwood & Underwood/Corbis, (br) BC; 221 (t) BC, (inset) LOC; 222-223 LOC; 227 (t) Nebraska State Historical Society Photograph, (b) BC; 221 (t) BC, (inset) LOC; 222-223 LOC; 227 (t) Nebraska State Historical Society Photograph, (b) BC; Museum of Nebraska History Collections.

Chapter Ten: 228-229 LOC; 232 BC; 233 Corbis; 234 SS/Tráfim Heuze; 236-237 LOC; 238 (ml) LOC, (b) Ellis Island Immigration Museum; 239 Ellis Island Immigration Museum; 240 BC; 241 (t) LOC; 244-245 BC; 246 (bl) Underwood & Underwood/Corbis; 242 Corbis; 243 Archives of N. C.; 244 (inset) BC; 246 (inset) Argus Photos/Corbis, (b) Keith Dannemiller/Corbis; 247 SS/Richard Thornton; 248 Ed Funkhouser, Anna and Marco Roland; 249 LOC; 251 Shannon Stapleton/Reuters/Corbis.

Chapter Eleven: 254 (b) GSPA; 254 BC; 255 (t) BC, (b) GCNY; 256 LOC; 257 (t) LOC, (b) Corbis; 259 (t) LOC, (b) National Portrait Gallery, Smithsonian Institution/Art Resource; 260-261 BC; 262 (t) LOC, (b) Oscar White/Corbis, (br) Paul L. Fair/Corbis, (m) BC; 266 Underwood & Underwood/Corbis; 267 BC; 268 SS/University of Kentucky, (b) Corbis; 269 LOC; 270-271 LOC; 272 AP; 273 (t) BC, (b) Hulton-Deutsch/Corbis; 274 Corbis; 275 National Archives; 276 Fort Bragg Historical Office; 277 LOC; 278 (t) LOC, (bl) GSPA; 279 Rare Book Collection, UNC-Chapel Hill Library; 277 LOC; 280 Japanese American National Museum; 281 AP

Chapter Twelve: 286-287 BC; 288 NASA; 289 LOC; 291 BC; 292 NARA; 293 BC; 294 (t) BC, (r) AP; 295 REUTERS/Pool/Beth Kaiser; 297 AP; 298 Courtesy of Alex M. Rivera; 299 UPI/BC; 300-301 LOC; 302 BC; 303 SS/Laurence Gough; 304 (t) BC, (b) Courtesy Sophia Smith Collection; 305 BC; State Archives of N.C.; 305 (tr) LOC, (b) UPI/Bettmann Newsphoto/Corbis, (inset) JA/North Carolina State University, (b) SS/Ramona Heim; 306 SS/Roman/Jock Demitry; 308 AP/John Hayes; 308 (tr) SS/Johnny Lye, (inset) Courtesy of the Nokia Corporation; 310 LOC; 311 AP